HANDBOOK OF PHILOSOPHY OF EDUCATION

The *Handbook of Philosophy of Education* is a comprehensive guide to the most important questions about education that are being addressed by philosophers today. Authored by an international team of distinguished philosophers, its thirty-five chapters address fundamental, timely, and controversial questions about educational aims, justice, policy, and practices.

Part I (Fundamental Questions) addresses the aims of education, authority to educate, the roles of values and evidence in guiding educational choices, and fundamental questions about human cognition, learning, well-being, and identity. Part II (Virtues of Mind and Character) is concerned with the educational formation of personal attributes that are often seen as essential to flourishing individuals and societies. This section includes chapters on the cultivation of intellectual and character virtues, the nature and formation of expertise, Stoic virtues, and intellectual vices. Part III (Education and Justice) addresses fundamental and emerging issues of educational justice, from equal educational opportunity, racial domination, and linguistic justice in education, to educational problems of mass migration, global educational justice, the education of working children around the world, and the costs of higher education and upward mobility. Part IV (Educational Practices) addresses controversial aspects of contemporary education – pedagogical, curricular, and managerial practices – that deserve careful examination. These include controversies surrounding free speech and instruction in controversial issues; anti-racist, sustainability, and sex education; and the unfulfilled promises and demoralizing impact of high-stakes accountability schemes.

The format and jargon-free writing in this volume ensure that topics are interesting and accessible, helping facilitate the work of advanced students and professionals in Education.

Randall Curren is Professor of Philosophy and Professor of Education at the University of Rochester, USA.

HANDBOOK OF PHILOSOPHY OF EDUCATION

Edited by Randall Curren

NEW YORK AND LONDON

Cover image: Christ Church Meadow, Oxford – R. Curren

First published 2023
by Routledge
605 Third Avenue, New York, NY 10158

and by Routledge
4 Park Square, Milton Park, Abingdon, Oxon, OX14 4RN

Routledge is an imprint of the Taylor & Francis Group, an informa business

Library of Congress Cataloguing-in-Publication Data
Names: Curren, Randall R., editor.
Title: Handbook of philosophy of education / edited by Randall Curren.
Other titles: Philosophy of education
Description: New York, NY : Routledge, 2023. | Includes bibliographical references and index.
Identifiers: LCCN 2022012822 (print) | LCCN 2022012823 (ebook) | ISBN 9781032000053 (Hardback) | ISBN 9781032000039 (Paperback) | ISBN 9781003172246 (eBook)
Subjects: LCSH: Education--Philosophy. | Education--Forecasting.
Classification: LCC LB14.7 .H3637 (print) | LCC LB14.7 (ebook) | DDC 370.1--dc23/eng/20220707
LC record available at https://lccn.loc.gov/2022012822
LC ebook record available at https://lccn.loc.gov/2022012823

ISBN: 978-1-032-00005-3 (hbk)
ISBN: 978-1-032-00003-9 (pbk)
ISBN: 978-1-003-17224-6 (ebk)

DOI: 10.4324/9781003172246

Typeset in Bembo
by MPS Limited, Dehradun

CONTENTS

ACKNOWLEDGEMENTS

This *Handbook* would not have existed without the encouragement and assistance of many people, beginning with the Routledge Editor for Philosophy of Education Matthew Friberg, who recruited me to fill the void created by the advanced age of my 2003 Blackwell *Companion to the Philosophy of Education* and Harvey Siegel's 2009 *Oxford Handbook of Philosophy of Education*. Such volumes may remain landmarks in the development of their respective subfields of philosophy for many years, but over time they become less representative of the current state of inquiry and less helpful to advancing it. Matt approached me on March 5th, 2020, as I was preparing my department's Pandemic Scenario Continuity of Business Plan, and his enthusiasm for the project as it began to take shape in August of that year persuaded me that academic life in the Age of COVID would be more than endless rounds of administrative and instructional emergencies. He and the Editorial Assistant for this volume, Jessica Cooke, have been unfailingly supportive through every phase of its development and production. I am very grateful to them both.

My expectation that the opportunity to work with dozens of the world's most talented philosophers of education would make the orchestration of this volume a rewarding experience was confirmed throughout its development. I owe the contributors my warmest thanks not just for the excellence of their chapters, collaborative spirit, and friendship, but for all they have done to advance a field that has truly flourished in the twenty years since my work on the *Companion*. For their formative advice and suggestions regarding the plan for this volume I owe thanks to Meira Levinson, Philip Cook, Gina Schouten, Larry Blum, and Danielle Zwarthoed. Finally, and with apologies to anyone whose assistance I may be overlooking, I owe my Philosophy and Education Librarian, Eileen Daly-Boas, an autographed copy of this *Handbook* and my profuse thanks for her wonderfully resourceful work in answering a multitude of bibliographic inquiries.

CONTRIBUTORS

Danielle Allen is James Bryant Conant University Professor at Harvard University. A political philosopher and public policy expert focused on democracy innovation, public health and health equity, justice reform, education, and political economy, she has chaired numerous commission processes and led development of influential policy roadmaps. She also directs the Democratic Knowledge Project, a K–16 civic education provider. Her books include *Our Declaration: A Reading of the Declaration of Independence in Defense of Equality*, *Cuz: An American Tragedy*, and *Talking to Strangers: Anxieties of Citizenship since Brown v. Board of Education.*

Ariel C. Armony is Vice Provost for Global Affairs, Director of the University Center for International Studies, and Professor in the Graduate School of Public and International Affairs at the University of Pittsburgh. Prior to his current role, he led the University of Miami's Institute for Advanced Study of the Americas. He has been a Fulbright scholar, Rockefeller Foundation scholar, and residential fellow at the Woodrow Wilson International Center for Scholars. He has published on democratization and civil society, transnational repression, the globalization of cities, and the relationship between China and Latin America.

David Bakhurst is George Whalley Distinguished University Professor at Queen's University at Kingston. He is the author of *Consciousness and Revolution in Soviet Philosophy* (Cambridge, 1991) and *The Formation of Reason* (Wiley-Blackwell, 2011), and co-editor of *The Social Self* (Sage, 1995), *Jerome Bruner: Language, Culture, Self* (Sage, 2001), and *Education and Conversation: Exploring Oakeshott's Legacy* (Bloomsbury, 2016). His philosophical interests include metaphysics, epistemology, ethics, and Russian philosophy and psychology. He is a Fellow of the Royal Society of Canada.

Heather Battaly is Professor of Philosophy at the University of Connecticut. She specializes in epistemology, ethics, and virtue theory. She is the author of *Virtue* (Polity, 2015), co-editor of *Vice Epistemology* (Routledge, 2020), and editor of *The Routledge Handbook of Virtue Epistemology* (2018) and of *Virtue and Vice, Moral and Epistemic* (Blackwell, 2010). She has published widely on the topics of intellectual virtue and intellectual vice. Her current projects focus on humility, closed-mindedness, and vice epistemology.

Sigal Ben-Porath is Professor of Education, Philosophy, and Political Science at the University of Pennsylvania. She received her doctorate in political philosophy from Tel-Aviv University in 2000, after which she joined Princeton University's Center for Human Values as a post-doctoral fellow. She chaired Penn's Committee on Open Expression 2015–2019. Her books include *Free Speech on Campus* (Penn Press, 2017), *Making Up Our Mind: What School Choice is Really About* (with Michael Johanek, University of Chicago Press, 2019), and the forthcoming *Campus Wars and the Struggle for Democracy.*

Lauren Bialystok is Associate Professor in the Department of Social Justice Education at the Ontario Institute for Studies in Education at the University of Toronto. She received her PhD in Philosophy (also at the University of Toronto) and specializes in ethics, identity, and education. She has conducted empirical and theoretical research on sex education since 2015 and is co-author (with Lisa Andersen) of *Touchy Subject: The History and Philosophy of Sex Education* (University of Chicago Press, 2022).

Lawrence Blum is (Emeritus) Distinguished Professor of Liberal Arts and Education, and Professor of Philosophy, at the University of Massachusetts Boston. He is the author of *"I'm Not a Racist, But": The Moral Quandary of Race* (Cornell, 2002), *High Schools, Race, and America's Future* (Harvard Education Press, 2012) and *Integrations: The Struggle for Racial Equality and Civic Renewal in Public Education* (with Zoë Burkholder, University of Chicago Press, 2021).

Nico Brando is Derby Fellow at the University of Liverpool and a former Newton International Fellow of the British Academy at the Centre for Children's Rights, Queen's University Belfast. His work in moral and political philosophy and practical ethics is focused on issues pertaining to children. He has published in leading education, philosophy, and political science journals. He is also the editor of the book *Philosophy and Child Poverty* (Springer, 2019).

Harry Brighouse is Mildred Fish Harnack Professor of Philosophy, Carol Dickson Bascom Professor of the Humanities, Affiliate Professor of Education Policy Studies, and Director of the Center for Ethics and Education at the University of Wisconsin-Madison. He is co-author of *Family Values: The Ethics of Parent-Child Relationships* (Princeton, 2014) and *Educational Goods: Values, Evidence and Decision-Making* (Chicago, 2018), and co-editor of *The Aims of Higher Education: Problems of Morality and Justice* (Chicago, 2015). He wrote *On Education* (Routledge, 2005) on his own.

Nancy Cartwright FBA FAcSS is Professor of Philosophy at Durham University and Distinguished Professor at the University of California San Diego, having worked previously at Stanford University and the London School of Economics. She is a methodologist/philosopher of the natural and human sciences, focusing on the social and economic sciences, with special attention to evidence, objectivity, and how to put scientific knowledge to work. Her latest books are *Nature, the Artful Modeler* and *Improving Child Safety: Deliberation, Judgement and Empirical Research* with Eileen Munro, Jeremy Hardie, and Eleonora Montuschi.

Ann E. Cudd is Provost and Senior Vice Chancellor and Professor of Philosophy at the University of Pittsburgh. Prior to her current role she served as the Dean of the College and Graduate School at Boston University, and before that as Vice Provost and Dean of Undergraduate Studies and University Distinguished Professor of Philosophy at the University of Kansas. A founding member of the Society for Analytical Feminism, her work focuses on oppression, capitalism, and the role of higher education in addressing inequality and promoting democratic engagement.

Julian Culp is Assistant Professor of Philosophy and Fellow of the Center for Critical Democracy Studies at The American University of Paris. He is the author of *Global Justice and Development* (Palgrave, 2014), *Democratic Education in a Globalized World* (Routledge, 2019), and numerous articles in such journals as *Theory and Research in Education*, *Third World Quarterly*, and the *European*

Journal of Political Theory. He is also co-editor of *Education and Migration* (Routledge, 2020) and the book series *Philosophy of Education – Debates and Constellations* (mentis Verlag).

Randall Curren is Professor of Philosophy and Professor of Education (secondary) at the University of Rochester and held a concurrent membership at the Institute for Advanced Study in Princeton (2012–2013) and professorships at the Royal Institute of Philosophy (London) and the Jubilee Centre for Character and Virtues at the University of Birmingham (UK) (2013–2015). His recent works include *Living Well Now and in the Future* (with Ellen Metzger, MIT Press, 2017; Beijing Normal UP, 2021, in Chinese) and *Patriotic Education in a Global Age* (with Charles Dorn, University of Chicago Press, 2018).

Johannes Drerup is Professor of Philosophy of Education and Educational Theory at TU Dortmund, Germany and Guest Professor at the Free University of Amsterdam, the Netherlands. His research interests lie in the areas of philosophy of education, philosophy of childhood, and political and moral philosophy. He is author of *Kontroverse Themen im Unterricht* (Reclam, 2021) and coeditor of the forthcoming *Cambridge Handbook of Democratic Education* (with Julian Culp and Douglas Yacek, Cambridge University Press).

Catherine Z. Elgin is Professor of the Philosophy of Education at Harvard Graduate School of Education. She is an epistemologist whose research spans the philosophy of science, the philosophy of art, and the philosophy of education. She is the author of *True Enough, Considered Judgment, Between the Absolute and the Arbitrary, With Reference to Reference*, and co-author with Nelson Goodman of *Reconceptions in Philosophy and Other Arts and Sciences.*

Matt Ferkany is Associate Professor of Philosophy at Michigan State University. His work brings ideas in environmental ethics, virtue theory, philosophy of education, and philosophy of science to ethical problems in science and environmental education. It has been supported by the Spencer Foundation and published in numerous journals.

Tammy Harel Ben Shahar is Senior Lecturer at the University of Haifa Faculty of Law. Her research focuses on the philosophical and legal aspects of educational justice and distributive justice more generally. She is the recipient of several grants and awards, including the German-Israel Foundation grant and the Israel Science Foundation grant. In addition to teaching and research she is the Academic Director of the Haifa University Legal Clinics.

Kathryn E. Joyce is a postdoctoral research associate in Values and Public Policy at the Princeton University Center for Human Values and the Education Research Section in the School of Public and International Affairs. She received her doctorate in philosophy from the University of California, San Diego in 2020. She specializes in political philosophy and philosophy of education, focusing on normative, methodological, and epistemological issues associated with the evidence-based approach to education policy and practice.

David Kidd is a principal investigator at the Harvard Graduate School of Education's Project Zero and the Chief Assessment Scientist for the Democratic Knowledge Project. He received a PhD in Social Psychology from the New School for Social Research in 2015, and currently works on new approaches to evaluation and assessment in the humanities, including in ethics and civic education.

Philip Kitcher is John Dewey Professor of Philosophy Emeritus at Columbia University. His most recent books are *Moral Progress* and *The Main Enterprise of the World: Rethinking Education.* He is a fellow of the American Academy of Arts and Sciences and of the British Academy, a member of the American Philosophical Society, and an Honorary Fellow of Christ's College, Cambridge.

Ben Kotzee is Reader in Philosophy of Education at the University of Birmingham and Deputy Director of the Midlands Graduate School ESRC Doctoral Training Partnership. He researches questions in applied epistemology and applied ethics, with a particular focus on professions and professional development. He is editor of *Education and the Growth of Knowledge: Perspectives from the Social Sciences and Virtue Epistemology* (Wiley-Blackwell, 2013) and editor-in-chief of the journal *Theory and Research in Education.*

Kristján Kristjánsson is Professor of Character Education and Virtue Ethics in the Jubilee Centre for Character and Virtues at the University of Birmingham, UK. His interests lie in research on character and virtues at the intersection between moral philosophy, moral psychology, and moral education. He has published six books on those issues, including *Aristotelian Character Education* (Routledge, 2015), which won the British Society for Educational Studies Prize as the Best Education Book of the year. He is the editor of *Journal of Moral Education.*

Anthony Simon Laden is is Professor of Philosophy at the University of Illinois at Chicago and Associate Director of the Center for Ethics and Education at the University of Wisconsin-Madison. He is the author of *Reasoning: A Social Picture* (Oxford, 2012) and numerous articles on reasoning together, the politics of identity, and the philosophy of John Rawls. He is currently working on a book with the tentative tile, *How Democracy Doesn't End.*

Meira Levinson is Juliana W. and William Foss Thompson Professor of Education and Society at Harvard Graduate School of Education. She is currently working to start a global field of educational ethics, modeled partially after bioethics, that is philosophically rigorous, disciplinarily and experientially inclusive, and both relevant to and informed by educational policy and practice. Her work in this area includes *Dilemmas of Educational Ethics* and *Democratic Discord in Schools* (both co-edited with Jacob Fay), *No Citizen Left Behind*, and JusticeinSchools.org.

Colin M. Macleod is Professor of Philosophy and Law at the University of Victoria. His research focuses on issues in contemporary moral, political and legal theory with a special focus on egalitarian justice; children, families, and justice; and democratic ethics. He is the author of *Liberalism, Justice, and Markets* (OUP, 1998), co-editor with David Archard of *The Moral and Political Status of Children* (OUP, 2002), and co-author with Ben Justice of *Have a Little Faith: Religion, Democracy and the American Public School* (University of Chicago Press, 2016).

Christopher Martin is Associate Professor of Philosophy and Education at the University of British Columbia. His current research focuses on issues relating to the nature and role of educational institutions in liberal societies. His most recent book is *The Right to Higher Education: A Political Theory* (Oxford University Press, 2022).

Jennifer M. Morton is the Penn Presidential Compact Associate Professor of Philosophy at the University of Pennsylvania and a Senior Fellow at the Center for Ethics and Education at the University of Wisconsin-Madison. Her research is focused on how agents reason and act under conditions of adversity and how educational institutions shape our agency. She is the author of *Moving Up Without Losing Your Way* (Princeton University Press, 2019), which won the Frederic W. Ness Award from the Association of American Colleges and Universities.

Duncan Pritchard is UC Distinguished Professor of Philosophy and Director of the *Center for Knowledge, Technology and Society* at the University of California, Irvine. His monographs include *Epistemic Luck* (OUP, 2005), *The Nature and Value of Knowledge* (co-authored, OUP, 2010), *Epistemological Disjunctivism* (OUP, 2012), and *Epistemic Angst: Radical Skepticism and the Groundlessness of Our Believing* (Princeton University Press, 2015). His most recent book is *Scepticism: A Very Short Introduction* (OUP, 2019).

Doris A. Santoro is Professor of Education at Bowdoin College. A philosopher of education who conducts empirical research on teachers' moral and ethical concerns, she is author of *Demoralized: Why Teachers Leave the Profession They Love and How They Can Stay* and articles in the *American Journal of Education, Educational Theory, Studies in Philosophy and Education,* and *Teachers College Record.* She is co-editor of *Principled Resistance: How Teachers Resolve Ethical Dilemmas* and a Senior Associate Editor for the *American Journal of Education.*

Gina Schouten is Professor of Philosophy at Harvard University. Her research focuses on matters of justice and political legitimacy. She has written about educational justice and gender justice, and about whether political liberalism can constitute an adequate theory of legitimacy. Her 2019 book, *Liberalism, Neutrality, and the Gendered Division of Labor,* argues that the state may legitimately enact social policy aimed at promoting a gender-equal sharing of domestic and unpaid caregiving work, even consistent with the constraints of liberal neutrality.

Nancy Sherman is University Professor and Professor of Philosophy at Georgetown University and was the inaugural Distinguished Chair in Ethics at the U.S. Naval Academy. A *New York Times* Notable Author, her most recent book is *Stoic Wisdom: Ancient Lessons for Modern Resilience* (2021). Her other books include *Afterwar, Stoic Warriors, Making a Necessity of Virtue, and The Fabric of Character.* She has written for the *New York Times, Washington Post,* and *Los Angeles Times* and contributes frequently to many other media outlets in the U.S. and elsewhere.

Adam Swift is Professor of Political Theory in the Department of Political Science at University College, London. He is co-author of *Family Values: The Ethics of Parent-Child Relationships* (Princeton University Press, 2014) and *Educational Goods: Values, Evidence and Decision-Making* (University of Chicago Press, 2018). He wrote *How Not to Be A Hypocrite: School Choice for the Morally Perplexed Parent* (Routledge, 2003) and *Political Philosophy: A Beginners' Guide for Students and Politicians* (Polity, 4th ed 2019) on his own.

Yael (Yuli) Tamir is the President of Beit Berl College and an adjunct professor at the Blavatnik School of Government, Oxford University. She served as Israel's Minister of Immigration (1999-2001), Minister of Education (2006-2009), and Deputy Speaker of the Knesset, and was Professor at Tel-Aviv University and a scholar-in-residence at Princeton, Harvard, the European University in Florence, the Central European University in Budapest, NYU, and Penn. A recipient of many academic awards, her publications in moral, political, and educational philosophy, feminism, and human rights include *Why Nationalism* (Princeton, 2019).

Winston C. Thompson is Associate Professor in the Department of Educational Studies and Associate Professor in the Department of Philosophy (by courtesy) at The Ohio State University. A former Fellow-in-Residence at the Edmond J. Safra Center for Ethics at Harvard University, Thompson's scholarship explores ethical and political dimensions of educational policy and practice, including issues of race and other identity categories.

Bryan R. Warnick is Professor of Philosophy of Education in the Department of Educational Studies at Ohio State University. He is co-author of *Spare the Rod: Punishment and the Moral Community of Schools* (University of Chicago Press, 2021), *Understanding Student Rights in Schools* (TC Press, 2012), and *Imitation and Education: A Philosophical Inquiry into Learning by Example* (SUNY Press, 2008). His interests include educational ethics, school shootings and security, school discipline, and the educational significance of economic systems.

Paul Watts is a Lecturer in the Jubilee Centre for Character and Virtues at the University of Birmingham, UK, where he teaches on the MA Character Education program. His research interests include the practical application of character education, teacher education, and how teachers use and value stories as a vehicle for character education. He is co-author of *Understanding Character Education: Approaches, Applications and Issues* (Open University Press, 2021).

Dustin Webster is PhD student at the University of Pennsylvania Graduate School of Education. He has a professional background in a variety of roles in K–12 education, including working in the after-school context, teaching English abroad, and most recently teaching 5th grade. His interests include character and virtue education, educational ethics, economic mobility and education, and philosophy in K–12 schools.

Daniel M. Weinstock is Katharine A. Pearson Chair in Civil Society and Public Policy in the Faculty of Law and of Arts, Professor in the Department of Philosophy and in the Institute for Health and Social Policy, and Associate Dean for Research in the Faculty of Law, at McGill University. His research has spanned a wide range of topics in moral and political philosophy, from the just management of ethnocultural and religious diversity in modern liberal democracies, to state policy with respect to children, families, and educational institutions.

Quentin Wheeler-Bell is Associate Professor of Philosophy of Education in the Department of Educational Leadership & Policy Studies at Indiana University. His research interests include critical theory, critical pedagogy, democratic theory, and policy issues such as school choice, integration, and urban poverty. His work has appeared in *Educational Policy*, *Educational Theory*, *Philosophical Inquiry in Education*, *Critical Education*, *Journal of Curriculum Studies*, and other leading publications.

Danielle Zwarthoed earned a PhD in Philosophy (Paris Est, 2013), taught Economic and Social Ethics for a few years at the Hoover Chair (Université catholique de Louvain, Belgium), and then decided to switch discipline and teach History in high school in the region of Paris. Her philosophical research appears in journals such as *Theory and Research in Education*, the *Journal of Applied Philosophy*, and *Ethical Theory and Moral Practice*. She is the co-editor of *Education and Migration* (Routledge, 2020).

INTRODUCTION

Randall Curren

When I last edited a volume of this kind twenty years ago, I wrote that the philosophy of education had enjoyed a notable resurgence, "fueled in part by developments in related branches of practical philosophy" (Curren 2003: 1). Education being the dauntingly complex human endeavor that it is, I hastened to add that there are several sub-fields of philosophy besides ethics and political philosophy that have informed work in philosophy of education. I also noted that there had been growing interest in the history of philosophy of education, and that philosophers of education were bringing their methods and perspectives to bear on public and theoretical debates about education and philosophical aspects of teaching and curricula. Notable features of the landscape were Critical Thinking (CT) and Philosophy for Children (P4C) movements that spanned philosophy and education. Another notable feature was a rough division of labor in which philosophy of education was still often framed as a foundational aspect of teacher education in schools of education – and was thus focused on K-12 education – while philosophers employed in philosophy departments were at greater liberty to address issues in higher education. Collectively, these patterns and developments justified a volume with sections on historical and contemporary movements, teaching and learning, the politics and ethics of schooling, and higher education.

Philosophy of education has flourished through the intervening years in ways that require a different structure and focus, if one is to accurately represent the current state of inquiry and provide what is most helpful to advancing it. It has grown impressively stronger as a field of practical philosophy, overlapping with ethics, social and political philosophy, feminist philosophy and philosophy of race, the philosophy of childhood and children, moral psychology, and epistemology. New journals, research centers, organizations, and funding have nurtured growing collegial engagement and collaboration between education-focused researchers in philosophy departments, departments and schools of education, history, psychology, sociology, political science, law, and other fields. New lines of inquiry have addressed diverse aspects of educational justice; human flourishing; intellectual, moral, and civic virtues; pathologies of public discourse and threats to democracy; environmental and sustainability education; and other important topics.

The state of the world for which rising generations must be prepared is less benign than it was twenty years ago, and any field of study with a stake in humanity's future must find ways to respond to the challenges we all face: the imperiled state of work, democracy, civic life, public knowledge, public health, countless species, a stable climate, and eight other earth systems on which we all depend.[1] These challenges are overwhelmingly global in scope, and it is only as one global community that we can address them effectively. Philosophy of education is growing more global in its

DOI: 10.4324/9781003172246-1

perspective, and it increasingly embraces the value of philosophical work being empirically well-informed and collaborative in its engagement with other disciplines, as it seeks to engage the educational problems of our time meaningfully. To recognize this is not to deny the value of historical scholarship in philosophy of education and the lessons it can offer. I take these lessons to begin with the ancient propositions that education – not law or technology – is the fundamental means by which a civilization can be preserved, that it can only succeed as a collective enterprise, and that it is only through institutions that honor and cultivate norms of respect for reason and evidence that we can enjoy the benefits of a society in which we reason together, face our problems squarely, and manage to solve the problems that matter most.

This *Handbook* is shaped by these lessons and developments in the field. It is forward-looking in featuring emerging issues that will be important in the years ahead, while also addressing fundamental perennial questions. These perennial questions of educational aims, authority, responsibilities, content, and conduct frame and infuse the entire volume. Part I (Fundamental Questions) addresses the nature and aims of education, authority to educate, the roles of values and evidence in guiding educational choices, and fundamental questions about human cognition, learning, well-being, and identity. Part II (Virtues of Mind and Character) is concerned with the educational formation of valuable attributes – virtues – that have been extensively investigated and defended in recent years as essential to flourishing individuals and societies. This section includes chapters on the cultivation of intellectual and character virtues, the nature and formation of expertise, Stoic virtues, and intellectual vices. Part III (Education and Justice) addresses fundamental and emerging issues of educational justice, from equal educational opportunity, racial domination, and linguistic justice in education, to educational problems of mass migration, global educational justice, the education of working children around the world, and the costs of higher education and upward mobility. Part IV (Educational Practices) addresses controversial aspects of contemporary education – pedagogical, curricular, and managerial practices – that deserve careful examination. These include controversies surrounding free speech and instruction in controversial issues; anti-racist, sustainability, and sex education; and the unfulfilled promises and demoralizing impact of high-stakes accountability schemes.

Part I: Fundamental Questions

The chapters of Part I address fundamental questions about education, how these questions can be meaningfully addressed, and how decisions about educational policies and practices should be made: What aims are most important in education? On what grounds should some aim or aims be given priority over others? What is most important to achieving such educational aims as facilitating students' success in meeting life's challenges, democratic citizenship, and living well, or the development of their powers of reason, knowledge, and understanding? What are the respective roles of values and evidence in educational decision-making? Which values and what kinds of evidence? Who should make decisions about children's education? What considerations are relevant to deciding who should make these decisions? How are all these questions related to matters of justice? What would a comprehensive theory of educational justice look like?

Philip Kitcher's opening chapter identifies some crucial limitations of the currently ascendent conception of what is prudent and sensible in education. What is ascendent the world over is education in Science, Technology, Engineering, and Mathematics (STEM subjects) aiming at individual and national economic competitiveness and growth. Kitcher argues that such education is not a sensible way to prepare young people for the world they will inhabit, since it not only ignores the most important difficulties they will face but makes things worse by accelerating the disappearance of rewarding work and the destabilization of Earth's climate, which is already driving large-scale human migration, contributing to public health crises, and making the planet less habitable. His defense of an alternative – education for global democratic problem-solving – rests on the premise that education should prepare young people, individually and collectively, to address and solve the problems they will face, and should mitigate, not exacerbate, those problems.

Kitcher is not alone in arguing that today's global problems call for global democratic solidarity, and this implies some understanding of ourselves as members of an inclusive global public with the potential to engage in democratic cooperation.[2] Danielle Allen and David Kidd's chapter addresses underlying questions of civic identity formation and inclusivity, with reference to the endangered state of democracy in the United States. Drawing on sociocultural theories of learning and development, they argue that it is important for schools to support students' integration of the dispositions, knowledge, and skills central to a democratic civic role with their other identities, such as race, gender, or religion. Their approach is focused on helping students bring their distinctive identities into civic life in ways that are effective, equitable, and self-protecting.

My own chapter addresses the nature of well-being, happiness, and flourishing and their roles in education. It addresses the ethical significance of students' well-being and the relationships between students' needs, well-being, and academic success, drawing on important findings in Basic Psychological Needs Theory. It proposes a role for basic needs in educational justice and addresses the basis of claims about the aims of education, while defending flourishing as the paramount aim of education and identifying the cultivation of capabilities, understanding, and virtues as the primary developmental sub-aims. It concludes by redefining the ideal of a *just school community* and insisting that justice in enabling everyone to live well applies both now and with respect to future generations. Educational justice and equality of opportunity would be, in this sense, not simply present-regarding (*synchronic*), but intergenerational (*diachronic*) (Curren & Metzger 2017; Curren 2018).

The chapters by David Bakhurst and Catherine Elgin continue and deepen the discussion of developmental aims of education by addressing the role of an adequate philosophy of psychology in cultivating students' rational powers, and the disciplinary and pedagogical foundations of understanding and epistemic autonomy. Bakhurst rejects a conception of the mind as a self-contained, self-sufficient subjective world of thoughts and experiences, in favor of one that sees our rational capacities as present in and expressed by our embodied engagement with the world. He explains how the latter grounds a view of education as the cultivation of powers of reason through initiation into traditions of thought and action, and he concludes that a variety of epistemic aims of education – the imparting of knowledge, development of reason and powers of mind, and facilitation of autonomous epistemic agency – are inseparable. Elgin's disciplinary and pedagogical perspective on these aspects of education leads her to similar conclusions: Students' epistemic agency is an important aim of education that is evident in a great deal of K-12 educational practice. It is grounded in subject matter disciplines that can enable students to see, think about, and understand aspects of the world in new ways, if they embrace the resources of these disciplines as their own. Their education should enable them to grasp and reflectively endorse disciplinary standards of judgment, understanding why practitioners in the different disciplines favor their criteria of reason or evidence, and understanding how those criteria can be challenged responsibly.

Chapters 6, by Harry Brighouse and Adam Swift, and 7, by Kathryn Joyce and Nancy Cartwright, take us from these general questions about the aims of education and fundamental aspects of achieving them, to the basis of specific decisions regarding educational policy and practice that are made in specific circumstances by specific people. Rejecting the influential idea that educational decision-making should be "data-driven," Brighouse and Swift point out that sound decision-making requires knowing what one has reason to value, knowing what options are available, and having evidence concerning the likely effects of choosing those options. It must therefore be "value-led and data-informed." The chapter presents a step-by-step model for how to engage in such decision-making and illustrates this model with reference to school financing, charter schools, and proficiency grouping in classrooms. In doing this, Brighouse and Swift provide a suggested set of values: (1) educational aims consisting of capacities conducive to the flourishing of students and those with whom they interact, (2) equality, adequacy and concern for the worse off, and (3) other values such as goods of childhood, parental rights, and democratic ideals. Joyce's and Cartwright's chapter focuses on predictions about how prospective policies are likely to play out in specific settings. Although evidence from randomized controlled trials (RCTs) is widely viewed as the gold-standard, they argue that it is neither sufficient nor necessary to ground education policies; the kinds of information needed can only be obtained through a mix of research methods, theory, and local sources. Like Brighouse and Swift, they reject a "value-free" conception of evidence-based decision-making.

Brighouse and Swift's second chapter turns from the *basis* of specific decisions regarding educational policy and practice, to the question of *who* should make the decisions about children's education. Relying on the same values enumerated in their chapter on educational decision-making, they argue that consequentialist considerations weigh in favor of placing educational decisions in the hands of whoever's decision, in the specific context, is most likely to yield the outcomes most consistent with the relevant values. Judgments may differ regarding the relative weightings of values and assessments of the evidence, and these differing judgments may favor different assignments of decisional authority. Other non-consequentialist considerations, such as parents' rights and children's rights, could also lead to different assignments of decisional authority. While their analysis should be helpful in many instances, it offers no solution to contentious disagreements about educational authority, let alone who has the authority to decide who gets to decide matters concerning children's education.[3]

Meira Levinson rounds out our consideration of fundamental questions by asking what a comprehensive theory of educational justice would look like. She notes that some steps have been taken beyond simply importing theories of distributive justice directly into philosophy of education, but she rightly observes that no comprehensive theory of educational justice has been proposed. The method she uses to reach some preliminary criteria for what would constitute an adequately comprehensive theory is a detailed case analysis. Based on this initial case analysis of an ethically complex decision a teacher must make on the spur of the moment, she concludes that such a theory would, among other things: (a) recognize that children are not fully rational and do not reliably comply with schools' expectations; (b) coherently integrate corrective and distributional aspects of justice; (c) define boundaries for the social construction of difference; and (d) be informed by a more comprehensive collection of case studies.

Part II: Virtues of Mind and Character

Virtue studies has been a burgeoning arena of interdisciplinary research focused on epistemic, moral, civic, and other virtues, and it has substantially enriched philosophical work on the epistemic, moral, and civic aims of education. The emergence of virtue ethics as an influential approach to normative ethical theory in the 1980s (Slote & Besser-Jones 2015), and subsequent emergence of virtue epistemology as an approach to defining the nature of knowledge (Battaly 2019), have played formative roles in these developments, though virtue-focused work on the epistemic, moral, and civic aims of education is not inherently beholden to orthodox forms of virtue ethics or virtue epistemology. The fundamental merit of a virtue-focused perspective for philosophy of education is that it concerns the nature, formation, and functioning of desirable human attributes that educators might do well to cultivate. A merit of the interdisciplinary character of virtue studies is that it has made it possible to not only develop philosophical accounts of the relevant virtues but also psychological models and measures that can inform educational practice.

Duncan Pritchard and Heather Battaly open this section with chapters on intellectual character education. Pritchard argues that the overarching epistemic goal of education is the development of virtuous intellectual character, contrasting it with the goal of students becoming critical thinkers. A goal of teaching for virtuous intellectual character would be for students to value truth as an intellectual good, and Pritchard considers the objection that this would make such teaching an objectionable form of indoctrination. He responds, in part, that teaching students to value truth can scarcely be a violation of their intellectual autonomy, because valuing truth is foundational to acquiring intellectual autonomy. Battaly explains the current standard approach to education for virtuous intellectual character, involving such things as exposure to exemplars of intellectual virtues and practice in emulating them. She then pivots from virtue epistemology to vice epistemology, which addresses the character, origins, and remediation of intellectual vices, such as closed-mindedness, intellectual arrogance, and epistemic injustice. She argues that the standard approach isn't likely to help students in whom intellectual vices are already well-established, and that if tendencies toward intellectual vices are widespread, then systemic changes in education and the structures that engender intellectual vices will be required. The standard approach would play a less central role than its proponents, including Battaly, have assumed.

The acquisition of expertise is a prominent aspect of technical, professional, and higher education, but there are two broad views of its nature, which Ben Kotzee dubs the "cognitive" and "skills-based" accounts. His chapter examines these approaches in detail and concludes that neither of them offers guidance for the educational development of expertise. He argues that the educational formation of expertise should be understood in the context of occupational preparation, and that the development of trustworthiness should be a central aspect of it.

Virtues of resilience, "grit," and gratitude have gone mainstream in recent years, capturing the imagination of a public hungry for self-help nostrums and government officials seeking remedies for the desperation of young people "lost in transition" from high school to life, as pathways of opportunity have disappeared (Paterson et al. 2014: Smith et al. 2011). Nancy Sherman brings to this scene – and the suffering associated with persistent racism, a pandemic, threats to democracy, and a planet on fire – an authoritative and well-practiced command of Stoic lessons for handling worst-case scenarios. How can we face our vulnerability to misfortune and injustice, mitigate our fear, and help those we mentor and teach do the same? Stoic resilience is as much an art of social connection as an art of managing one's own responses to aspects of the world beyond one's control, and a central aim of Sherman's chapter is to explain how these different aspects of it are compatible. Paul Watts and Kristján Kristjánsson close out Part II with a chapter on character education, which they identify as any form of holistic moral education that is focused on the development of enduring virtues of character, aims to promote human flourishing, and is founded on a general theory of virtue. Their chapter distinguishes some leading perspectives on character education and it addresses some controversies pertaining to these perspectives, the main approaches to developing character, and methods of evaluating the success of character-education programs. It concludes with a discussion of the potentially positive outcomes for students and schools.

Part III: Education and Justice

There was a time when education in schools, colleges, and universities occupied fewer years and hours of people's lives, the lines between work and education were less clear, and the completion of high school and higher degrees made less difference to labor market and life outcomes. In 1945, only half of US residents had any formal education beyond elementary school, there were only a few million students enrolled in secondary schools versus about 450 million today, and only 5 percent of adults completed baccalaureate degrees versus about 30 percent today (Baker 2011: 10–11). Meanwhile, across the globe, college enrollments grew from about 1 percent of college-age youth in 1900 to 20 percent in 2000, and the rising tide of college graduates enabled universities to create a growing multitude of postgraduate programs (Sachs 2015: 243–254; Baker 2014; Collins 1979). In the United States today, college graduates comprise half of the populations of several major cities (Baker 2014), a baccalaureate degree is all but essential to a middle-class existence (Duncan & Murnane 2011), and those without college degrees are experiencing declining life expectancy, owing to deaths of despair by suicide, drug overdose, and alcohol (Case & Deaton 2020). The only thing more costly than obtaining a college degree is failing to obtain one, proving once again that invention is the mother of necessity.

In this context, the irresistible point of departure for Part III is the ideal of equal educational opportunity. It has meant many things, and Gina Schouten devotes her chapter to what it *should* mean. She argues that educational justice is foundational to social justice and that we should regard education as *just* when it equalizes students' prospects for living good lives. Equalization of this kind is presently unattainable, but she argues we can and should make progress toward it by using education to improve the life prospects of those who are badly off, assigning moral weight to students' interests in proportion to how bad their prospects for living well are. Schouten's focus on distributional justice regarding educational contributions to students' prospects of living well connects it in significant ways to my own chapter and Brighouse and Swift's chapters. Colin Macleod's chapter on non-preparatory dimensions of educational justice also intersects with these chapters, but on the theme of students' present well-being – the goodness of children's lives as children. The resources and opportunities available to children in schools plays a significant role in their access to important goods of childhood, and Macleod argues that fair access to these goods is an important dimension of educational justice.

The quality of children's lives and their future opportunities are both at stake in Nico Brando's chapter on child work and education, which is the first of four that offer global perspectives on aspects of educational justice. In affluent countries today, it is taken for granted that children belong in school preparing for adulthood, not going to work, yet almost one-fifth of the world's school-aged children do not go to school, often because they are at work. Brando examines the conceptual and ethical issues at stake, using examples from around the world. What are "education" and "work" and how are they related? What are the arguments for banning children from working and making schooling compulsory, and what are the costs of this compulsion-and-ban approach? Brando documents ways in which the difficult circumstances of many children's lives make the compulsion-and-ban approach both ineffective and ethically problematic, and he concludes that the needed reforms include accommodations to improve working children's access to education.

There are meanwhile over 80 million people in the world today – one percent of humanity – who have been forcibly displaced from their homes, including 30 million who have fled their countries and are seeking asylum or awaiting resettlement by the United Nations Human Rights Agency (UNHCR).[4] Most of these refugees languish for years in "temporary" refugee camps or work in the underground economies of cities in the Global South, and over 40 percent of them are children with limited to nonexistent educational opportunities (Parekh 2020). Many other international migrants who are seeking a better life beyond their home countries would not qualify as refugees, because their reasons for migrating are economic and often rooted in climate change, but their situations also raise questions of educational justice that demand the attention of philosophers. Danielle Zwarthoed focuses on three specific issues: (1) the relevance of citizenship education for children who will not get citizenship in their country of residence; (2) equality of opportunity for students whose families lack the linguistic and cultural capital important to opportunities in the country of arrival; and (3) fair distribution of educational costs and benefits, in a world in which people do not always work and pay taxes in the country that paid for their education.

Linguistic and global justice in education are topics addressed more broadly by Daniel Weinstock and Julian Culp. Weinstock is concerned specifically with bilingual education and its relationship to linguistic justice. He begins with the presumption that there are very strong reasons for children to be educated bilingually, when it is feasible, and asks whether there are specific contexts in which this presumption is overridden. He considers the case of asymmetrical bilingualism, or contexts in which the two languages in which bilingual systems educate children differ in their capacity to attract speakers, and "nation-building" arguments for unilingual education to establish a single language across an entire territory. He concludes that in some contexts there are valid moral reasons favoring unilingual education, even if bilingual education is feasible, but that in many contexts the arguments made for unilingual education are not sound. Turning to global educational justice, Culp points out that work on educational justice has generally retained a domestic focus, even as political philosophers have developed and debated theories of global justice. He argues that philosophers of education cannot safely assume that the views they hold regarding aspects of educational justice will be immune to revision when considerations of global justice are factored in. His chapter aims to take the field in an important new direction by presenting a democratic conception of global educational justice.

Education has been reshaped in countries across the world by neoliberalism, a globally influential policy orientation that advocates the introduction of market mechanisms in all aspects of social life. Lawrence Blum identifies some central features of neoliberal doctrine and argues that neoliberal principles of competition, consumerism, and choice cannot serve as foundations of a sound and equitable public education system. Focusing on charter schools as an important manifestation of neoliberalism in education, he details limitations of the evidence that charter advocates rely on in asserting that charter schools are superior to traditional public schools, and he examines the role of charter management organizations and private foundation funding in limiting innovation and competition within the charter sector. While a segment of this 'marketized' sector sees itself as advancing racial justice in education, Blum argues that this is limited by its narrow *human capital* approach to education, the inequality it creates by serving a relatively advantaged segment of disadvantaged students, its failure to acknowledge the impact of poverty on educational outcomes, and its devaluing of students' family cultures.

Racial justice is front and center in Quentin Wheeler-Bell's chapter, which addresses the nature of racial domination and presents a critical approach to addressing racial domination in and through education. Along the way it presents and critiques three influential conceptions of what is essential to racial justice in and through education: *multicultural education*, *equal educational opportunity*, and *integrating* schools. The chapter explains how a critical approach to racial justice in education is grounded in a critique of racial domination and is focused on democratic empowerment, equipping students through conversations and inquiry with morally reflective understanding of structures of power and how to deepen democracy.

Part III closes with three chapters on higher education and justice, by Jennifer Morton, Christopher Martin, and Ariel Armony and Ann Cudd. Morton notes that many proponents of equal opportunity have come to regard universities as institutions that can and should reduce existing inequalities by admitting more low-income students and enabling them to climb the economic ladder. This would make upward mobility a central mission of higher education today, much as upward mobility was seen as a central mission of universal secondary education by leaders of public-school movements and labor unions in the late nineteenth and early twentieth centuries (Peterson 1985). Morton calls for a reevaluation of mobility as an ideal, detailing its costs to those who experience it, to the society, and to institutions of higher education themselves. She argues that equal opportunity in higher education should be focused on ensuring that the educational goods inherent to its mission – knowledge, personal transformation, and value acquisition – are available to all who wish to pursue them. The costs of higher education are an important aspect of availability, and Martin addresses the question of who should bear those costs. Approaching this as a problem of distributive fairness, he argues that the aims of higher education make a great deal of difference to what is fair. The aims he considers are upward mobility and personal autonomy. He undertakes an investigation of the conditions in which it could be reasonable to treat higher education as a universal right, provided at public expense, and arrives at the conclusion that this would require an educational aim that would make higher education a genuinely universal benefit to all the members of the society. Personal autonomy could be one such aim, he argues.

Armony and Cudd offer further reflections on equality and access in higher education, but they do so in the context of a more systematic assessment of higher education's shortcomings. They focus on three basic tensions that colleges and universities need to address: (a) between embracing competition and elite education versus emphasizing more equality and access; (b) between fostering open debate and providing safe spaces for minorities; and (c) between universities as ivory towers and universities as institutions devoted to the common good. Their examination of these tensions yields some proposals for redefining higher education in a post-pandemic world.

Part IV: Educational Practices

Justice and the formative and further aims of education remain important in Part IV, but the focus shifts to specific and controversial aspects of pedagogical, curricular, and managerial practices. The first three chapters pertain to free speech, discussion of controversial subject matter in schools, and the allegation that controversial subject matter is often presented in colleges and universities is ways that indoctrinate students. There are rich connections between these chapters and those by Bakhurst, Elgin, Pritchard, Battaly, and Wheeler-Bell, as well as the three that follow in Part IV.

Sigal Ben-Porath and Dustin Webster devote the opening chapter to a fuller examination of the controversy surrounding free and inclusive speech in education addressed by Armony and Cudd, and they do so with reference to both schools and universities. They examine the legal history of speech restrictions in schools, emphasizing the role of free inquiry and academic freedom. In higher education, they argue that there are justified boundaries to open expression associated with respect for evidentiary practices and enabling every member of an academic community to participate in the development and dissemination of knowledge. Like all rights, the right to free speech has boundaries and context matters. Focusing on schools and the controversy over teaching controversial subject matter, Johannes Drerup affirms the civic educational value of students debating controversial issues. There is public controversy, and a variety of philosophical theories, regarding which issues should count as controversial. Should the reality of human-caused climate change be treated as controversial in schools because many people are unaware of, or unmoved by, the existence of overwhelming scientific consensus on this subject? Clearly not, but such debates are now highly polarized politically and teachers are being subjected to criticism that may inhibit the kind of education that could foster a more constructive civic culture. Drerup critiques two of the most influential criteria for what would make a topic too controversial to teach and proposes an alternative.

Anthony Laden's chapter is similar in reflecting the highly polarized civic climate in which education in many countries now operates, but his focus is the allegation that higher education in the United States is awash in left-wing indoctrination. He surveys the standard responses to this allegation but draws on work in social epistemology to argue that the allegation is not fundamentally about teachers changing their students' beliefs in illegitimate ways. He argues that the underlying source of anxiety about the changes observed in students is that they arise from the fact that the *epistemic networks* into which college students are initiated are also *trust networks* that have a social dimension. Initiating students into the most reliable epistemic networks that humanity has created is a fundamental aspect of the education described by Bakhurst, Elgin, and others, but students who were not already enculturated into the epistemic world of higher education before they began college can be transformed by that enculturation in ways that may alienate them from their home communities. Laden concludes with suggestions for how teachers can mitigate the potential for such alienation.

The next three chapters concern some of the most controversial topics taught – and not taught – in schools today: climate, sex, and racism. There are strong arguments for teaching all of these topics, but none of them is easy to teach well and they are all contested ground in culture wars waged on the battlefield of education policy. In the case of climate change, there was an inflection point around 2010, when it became clear to environmental educators that their task was more complicated than overcoming information deficits. The limitations of science cognition and communication became hot topics, but the political polarization of climate beliefs and massive funding of climate misinformation present challenges related to those addressed by Battaly and Laden. It is in this context that Matt Ferkany examines a widely discussed diagnosis of the causes of climate contrarianism and its implications for climate, science, and sustainability education. An important question at stake is whether science teachers should deprioritize science knowledge and understanding and focus more on enabling students to distinguish reliable science from disinformation. Ferkany argues that resistance to consensus climate science has many causes, including confusion about the relationship between values and scientific information. Teaching sustainability ethics and socio-scientific reasoning might help, but curricula and sensible standards for this are nearly non-existent. Ferkany concludes that implementing such standards and curricula should come first before we conclude that science knowledge and understanding should be deprioritized.

Lauren Bialystok confronts a paradoxical aspect of the controversy surrounding sex education: parental anxieties are fixated on the idea that teachers might teach sex in ways that increase their children's likelihood of having sex, yet sex is *never* taught in schools. 'Sex education' may not even be an intelligible concept, since unlike every other school subject it literally involves no teaching of the thing – the art – itself. Children learn sex outside of schools, so Bialystok's question is how to combine sex and education in the context of 21st-century Western schooling. Where and how do young people learn about sex? What do we want from school-based sex education? What we teach in schools is *para-* and *meta-sex education*, and Bialystok argues that this re-conceptualization can help us see the limitations of our political discourse and design better curricula.

Winston Thompson's chapter is thematically linked to Drerup's, regarding what can be taught as noncontroversial, Allen and Kidd's, regarding identify formation, and Wheeler-Bell's, regarding education that is antiracist or promotes racial justice. It is methodically analytical in addressing different conceptions of race, the complexity of racial identity formation as a pedagogical goal, whether and how different approaches to teaching race might be mutually compatible, and arguments for and against what is popularly known as antiracist education. Its civic-minded hope is that further thoughtful analyses of race may contribute to more productive deliberations about the teaching of race in the future.

The remaining chapters all pertain to managerial practices in education and their impact on teachers and students, understanding the term "managerial" to include disciplinary and administrative practices both within schools and pertaining to the management of schools more broadly. Disciplinary practices and ability grouping are common features of schools, addressed by Bryan Warnick and Tammy Harel Ben Shahar. Warnick's chapter argues that there are very strong arguments against punishment in schools, but punishment can still be justified as a way to initiate needed conversations. While punishment inherently involves moral disapproval, which can be appropriate, Warnick argues that specific forms of punishment (such as corporal punishment and expulsions) and racial disparities in who is and is not punished for the same offenses, may send unacceptable "secondary" messages. He concludes that restorative justice is a promising approach to school punishment because it coheres with educational ideals of reason, cooperation, personal responsibility, and mutual understanding. Grouping students of similar perceived ability into different classes, tracks, or schools is another very common practice, and Harel Ben Shahar argues that the concept of ability it relies upon is ambiguous. She examines both of the possible conceptions of 'ability' involved and concludes that neither can justify the forms of ability grouping that are widely used.

High stakes testing and its corrupting and demoralizing impact on schools, students, and teachers has been a matter of widespread concern, and Yuli Tamir addresses it from the perspective of a former Minister of Education. The Programme for International Student Assessment (PISA) of the Organization for Economic Co-operation and Development (OECD) has promoted a cycle of global testing in math, science, and reading and rankings of educational systems, claiming that better educational outcomes in these subjects will reliably yield economic growth. Tamir addresses the damaging effects of PISA accountability and argues that the claim on which it is premised is false. While PISA results reflect the social and economic background of the children tested, she concludes that increasing a country's level of education often has no effect on economic growth. PISA fosters the illusion that education can be improved and poverty alleviated without major social change to close social and economic gaps and make societies more just and inclusive. PISA accountability has meanwhile had a corrupting effect on education, dictating the essence of educational practice, impoverishing classrooms, increasing the already high level of stress in schools, and making educators the scapegoats for society's failures. Doris Santoro's research has documented the impacts of such pressures on teachers, arguing that what is typically referred to as 'burnout' or job dissatisfaction is often the more ethically troubling phenomenon of demoralization, in which the conditions of teachers' work thwart their access to the inherent moral rewards of their work. Her chapter presents an analysis of forms of this phenomenon involving racialized failures to recognize and validate teachers as having legitimate moral perspectives, judgments, and aspirations that animate their work. Santoro's chapter and my own agree in regarding the intrinsic satisfactions of teachers' moral aspirations as important both to their own professional well-being and to their students' well-being and academic progress.

Notes

1 The reference to eight other earth systems relies on a nine-factor "planetary boundaries" model of sustainable human burdens on earth systems. For an overview and links to current findings on specific boundaries that humanity has crossed and is at risk of crossing, see the website of the Stockholm Resilience Centre: https://www.stockholmresilience.org/research/planetary-boundaries.html. At the time of this writing, there is growing evidence that four of these boundaries have been crossed, putting planetary systems on which we depend at risk. See Persson et al. (2022).

2 See, e.g., Curren & Metzger (2017): ch. 6; Curren & Dorn (2018): ch. 6.

3 These contentious disagreements have been shaped in the United States in recent years by assertions of an unlimited and exclusive right of parents to control their children's education, and they notably included (for some years) a debate over homeschooling. Public educational authority in the United States. has been weakened by a series of high court decisions beginning with *Wisconsin v. Yoder, et al.* 406 U.S. 205 (1972), and by a widespread collapse of regulatory oversight of homeschooling. It is meanwhile not a coincidence that the United States is presently the only country in the world that has not ratified the United Nations Convention on the Rights of the Child (https://www.ohchr.org/en/professionalinterest/pages/crc.aspx). On the legal context, see Blokhuis et al. (2021); Blokhuis & Curren (2021). On the history and philosophical issues, see Dwyer & Peters (2019). On current efforts to advance children's rights, see http://www.responsiblehomeschooling.org; https://childrenfirstcanada.org/.

4 See https://www.unhcr.org/ph/figures-at-a-glance

References

Baker, D. P. (2011) "Forward and Backward, Horizontal and Vertical: Transformation of Educational Credentialing in the Schooled Society," *Research in Social Stratification and Mobility* 29(1): 5–29.

Baker, D. P. (2014) *The Schooled Society: The Educational Transformation of Global Culture*. Stanford, CA: Stanford University Press.

Battaly, H. (ed.) (2019) *The Routledge Handbook of Virtue Epistemology*. New York: Routledge.

Blokhuis, J. C. & Curren, R. (2021) "The Judicialization of American Education," in *Oxford Research Encyclopedia of Education*. Oxford: Oxford University Press, https://doi.org/10.1093/acrefore/9780190264093.013.1602

Blokhuis, J. C., Feldman, J., Imber, M. & van Geel, T. (2021) *Education Law*, 6e. New York: Routledge.

Case, A. & Deaton, A. (2020) *Deaths of Despair and the Future of Capitalism*. Princeton: Princeton University Press.
Collins, R. (1979) *The Credential Society: An Historical Sociology of Education and Stratification*. New York: Academic Press.
Curren, R. (2003) *A Companion to the Philosophy of Education*. Oxford: Blackwell Publishing.
Curren, R. (2018) "Living Well Now: What Does It Take?" National Public Radio *13.7 Cosmos and Culture* blog, https://www.npr.org/sections/13.7/2018/01/21/562805068/living-well-now-what-does-it-take
Curren, R. & Dorn, C. (2018) *Patriotic Education in a Global Age*. Chicago: University of Chicago Press.
Curren, R. & Metzger, E. (2017) *Living Well Now and in the Future: Why Sustainability Matters*. Cambridge, MA: MIT Press.
Duncan, G. J. & Murnane, R. J. (eds.) (2011) *Whither Opportunity: Rising Inequality, Schools, and Children's Life Chances*. New York: Russell Sage Foundation.
Dwyer, J. G. & Peters, S. F. (2019) *Homeschooling: The History and Philosophy of a Controversial Practice*. Chicago: The University of Chicago Press.
Parekh, S. (2020) *No Refuge: Ethics and the Global Refugee Crisis*. Oxford: Oxford University Press.
Paterson, C., Tyler, C. & Lexmond, J. (2014) *Character and Resilience Manifesto: The All-party Parliamentary Group on Social Mobility*, http://www.centreforum.org/assets/pubs/character-and-resilience.pdf
Persson, L., Carney Almroth, B. M., Collins, C. D., Cornell, S., et al. (2022) "Outside the Safe Operating Space of the Planetary Boundary for Novel Entities," *Environmental Science & Technology* 56: 1510–1521, https://pubs.acs.org/doi/pdf/10.1021/acs.est.1c04158
Peterson, P. (1985) *The Politics of School Reform 1870–1940*. Chicago: University of Chicago Press.
Sachs, J. D. (2015) *The Age of Sustainable Development*. New York: Columbia University Press.
Slote, M. & Besser-Jones, L. (eds.) (2015) *The Routledge Companion to Virtue* Ethics. London: Routledge.
Smith, C., Christoffersen, K., Davidson, H. & Snell Herzog, P. (2011) *Lost in Transition: The Dark Side of Emerging Adulthood*. Oxford: Oxford University Press.

PART I

Fundamental Questions

1

EDUCATION FOR A CHALLENGING WORLD

Philip Kitcher

The Wrong Problems

In many nations around the globe, contemporary educators understand that the young people they teach will face significant challenges. Reasonably, they identify their task as one of preparing their students for the difficulties they will encounter. Unfortunately, they focus on the wrong problems. The curricula they design and the styles of education they envisage are badly suited to the serious perils of the future.

Ever since Margaret Thatcher decided that learning is another commodity to be traded in a minimally regulated market, since Seoul National University carried out an ambitious building program in which numerous large buildings devoted to applied sciences and engineering dwarf the single structure devoted to the humanities and social sciences, and since the most enlightened American president of the past half century declared that students need more Science, Technology, Engineering, and Mathematics, large segments of liberal education have been hacked away, in the interests of training a workforce capable of competing in the global economy. Music, visual art, foreign languages, literature, philosophy, anthropology, and even history are declared irrelevant. They must make way for cutting-edge sciences (especially molecular biology and computer science), and for subjects relevant to the marketplace (finance, business studies.) Adieu Monet, Ade Beethoven, Farewell Shakespeare – hello fashion studies and video game design.

Many of the most eloquent writers on education, from Rousseau, Mill, and DuBois to Martha Nussbaum and Harry Brighouse, deplore this educational trend (Nussbaum 1997, 2010; Brighouse 2006). They regard the subjugation of education to alleged economic constraints as neglecting two of the most important educational goals: the development of the person, and the shaping of the citizen. I sympathize, and, elsewhere, I have joined the supporting chorus (Kitcher 2021). My complaint in what follows, however, will not take the standard form of demonstrating that Thatcherite training is a recipe for stunted development. Instead, I shall argue for attending to challenges that are all too frequently overlooked in educational contexts. If "relevance" is the watchword for the trend to which I have pointed, it would be a good idea to take a careful look at the full range of difficulties the young people of today will have to face. The blinkered and myopic idea that they must be shaped to compete in a global economy exhibiting unfettered capitalism, should be replaced by a more serious account of *all* the challenges the coming decades will bring.

Indeed, as we shall discover, the partial vision of Thatcherite reformers subverts the most significant aims of "relevant" education. The problem is not simply that the envisaged goals *neglect*

DOI: 10.4324/9781003172246-3

preparation for important challenges. The problem is that achieving those goals would make the hardest problems our descendants will face more intractable than they otherwise would be. If you are bent on relevance, concerned to arm the young for the most taxing struggles to come, you would be ill-advised to pursue the kinds of education the Thatcherites favor.

To see this, we need to understand the threats to which a "relevant" education – one focused on subjects with technological and commercial promise – would be a reasonable response, to consider the vulnerabilities caused by that response, and to recognize the dangers created for our descendants.

Global Competition

In the early 1990s, when I was asked by the Library of Congress to prepare a report on the ethical and social implications of the Human Genome Project, I was surprised by the conception of that venture then prevalent in Washington. I was not so naïve as to believe that members of Congress (and their staff, the people with whom I had most contact) were thrilled by the thought of "reading the Book of Life" or "deciphering the Code of Codes." I did expect, however, that their support for the HGP centered on the prospect of cures for hereditary diseases, many of them devastating. I was mistaken. Again and again, I heard the same enthusiastic prediction. "Our leading role in biotechnology will keep us ahead of the Japanese." (Then, as now, East Asia was the home of perceived threat to American business, although the exact location was different.)

Nor does contemporary enthusiasm for STEM, and similar initiatives, express Darwin's thought that "there is grandeur in this view of life" and that all children deserve to gain appreciation of the splendid vision. The point of requiring chemistry and encouraging business majors is to generate winners in an international competition, people who will make the next breakthroughs to advance technology or find new techniques for selling. The bottom line of education is ... the bottom line.

Nobody thinks, of course, that more than a tiny fraction of those who are taught the "relevant" subjects will be the pioneers who maintain the economic strength of the nation. The net must be cast wide in order to catch all of the sparsely distributed big fish. A somewhat larger, but still small, percentage of the young will be able to participate as helpers, serving as technical elaborators of the Next Big Idea. The vast majority will make no use of whatever has been dinned into them in their classes in science or commerce. They will have to find a different niche in the labor market.

It is, oddly, a debased version of a Nietzschean vision. The "free spirits" are the captains of industry, no longer dancing on the mountaintops, but commanding the world from their gilded mansions. The "herd," however, are as faceless and as unnoticed as they always have been.

Except, of course, that communications technology has transformed their predicament. Even in the age of the telegraph or of the telephone, labor economists could assume that successful new ventures might yield a "liberal reward of labor," providing decent pay and working conditions for the brilliant entrepreneur's fellow citizens. Today, production can be outsourced, carried on in parts of the world where workers are sufficiently desperate to accept subsistence wages and to toil for long hours in cramped spaces. Coupled to increasing possibilities of automation, the trend is already transforming human labor. The remaining jobs for the many students whose prowess in the "relevant" subjects falls below the top level will be those resisting exportation and automation – primarily positions involving human contact.

Perhaps such positions might require a different set of skills, refined by a different style of education? Whether or not that is so, the emphasis on finding all the (scarce) Business Leaders of the Future tells against deviating from the plan. Although some service jobs are intrinsically satisfying – most teachers are not "in it for the money," and receptionists, nurses, flight attendants and gardeners all find satisfaction in what they do (Autor & Kitcher 2018) – the stereotype of service work regards it as second-rate, menial, "unproductive labor." Under the pressures of no-holds-barred capitalism, many nations are erasing any line dividing service workers from servants. What servants need from education is not any refinement of empathy or of social skills. They simply have to know their place.

I have sketched (broadly and somewhat crudely) the contours of a world in which educational policy is obsessed with the demand to identify and train the people who can become contenders in a ruthless global economy. Any world like that is likely to exhibit some familiar features.

1. Large and increasing economic inequality, among nations and within nations.
2. A sense that what is important in life is amassing material possessions, either for their own intrinsic value or for enjoying the power to display one's wealth.
3. Declining concern for public goods, especially those that benefit the poor.
4. Growing discontent among many segments of the population, as people see themselves as having been deprived of the opportunities available to earlier generations, as being "left behind."
5. The withering of many forms of community, and the breakdown of social solidarity.

My list is ordered, with the aspects of contemporary life most closely connected with the current version of capitalism at the beginning, and the links becoming less direct as it proceeds. In principle, it might be possible to avoid the later pathologies in democratic societies where the citizens were able to identify where their interests lie. In practice, nations that advertise themselves as democracies have often commodified the transmission of information (so that many of their citizens are profoundly misinformed) and the education provided for the young does not equip them to reflect critically on their predicament. The result is one of the great ironies of "democracy" as it exists today. In the act through which they are supposed to express their political freedom, voters frequently select candidates and policies diametrically opposed to their central goals and desires.

A discussion of the educational trend of the past four decades should ask two questions: If the policy of emphasizing subjects with technological and commercial relevance is pursued, how can societies avoid the features on my list? Is a world with those features one that we want for our children and grandchildren? Contemporary economists have provided excellent analyses of the problems with unfettered capitalism, thereby showing how difficult it is to answer the first question positively (Atkinson 2015; Case & Deaton 2020; Deaton 2013; Stiglitz 2002, 2012, 2019). Many of the most distinguished recent contributions to the philosophy of education have argued for visions of human life and of human societies supporting a negative answer to the second (Brighouse 2006; Delbanco 2012; Nussbaum 2010). I shall add a further complaint. A world with the socioeconomic features I have listed is disastrously ill-prepared to meet challenges any rational, well-informed person should expect – challenges to our species that are as severe as any it has faced in recorded history.

The Real Problems

Falling into poverty is a bad thing. So, if technological innovation and business acumen are viewed as defenses against that outcome, it is no wonder they are prized. Yet human material well-being can be affected by factors quite independent of the character of economic life. Environmental catastrophes have a way of subverting production, even when the social conditions have been honed to ideal efficiency. At this stage of the twenty-first century, nobody should be surprised at the "news" of increasing rates of environmental catastrophe in the coming decades.

Two kinds of coming catastrophes are evident. At a time when all nations are grappling with a pandemic, the long-neglected message issued by Laurie Garrett in the 1990s (Garrett 1994) can no longer be ignored. More generally, the predicted (even the presently achieved) elevation of the Earth's mean temperature above pre-industrial levels will bring increasing rates of dangerous heatwaves, prolonged droughts, raging wildfires, monsoons and storms causing destructive floods, human migration on an unprecedented scale – and vastly expanded opportunities for the evolution of disease vectors and for existing infectious agents to jump from non-human organisms to our own species. Thus, the two types of catastrophe are not completely independent. Some future plagues will occur without any contribution from global heating (as COVID-19 apparently did); others will be side effects of changes in ecological relations.

Until relatively recently, future environmental threats have often been characterized in terms of single changes: the average sea-level in a particular location will rise by such-and-such an amount. While predictions of this form are useful for certain kinds of planning – they can be used, for example, in decision-making about whether a particular area should be resettled – concentrating on them underestimates the severity of the challenges future decades (and centuries) will bring. Often, what matters isn't an average, but the tail of a distribution. Regions vulnerable to rapidly spreading wildfires will be less affected by the mean value of the local temperature than by the frequency of days in which extremely high temperatures occur. Yet, even thinking in terms of isolated episodes sells the danger short. Our focus should be on the probabilities of cascades of effects (Wallace-Wells 2019).

Thus, in considering infectious disease, the intensity of the challenge is not determined by the course of the initial outbreak. As has become very clear, much depends on whether the first wave of infections can be confined, on whether the infectious agent can mutate fast enough to evade existing treatments and methods of prevention, on whether the course of its evolution attenuates the damaging effects or augments them. Nor can the harmful consequences be measured simply in terms of mortality rates, even if they are supplemented by considering long-term effects on survivors. Efforts to respond to epidemics or pandemics often interfere with patterns of behavior, disrupting work and radically lowering productivity, disturbing the education of the young, preventing the elderly and the sick from receiving the care they need, and so forth. Indirect consequences of a plague can shape the destiny of a nation (or a region) and even the career of a religion (McNeill 1976; Stark 1996).

These points are amplified in the case of climate change. The climate agreement reached in Paris in 2015 imposed minimal obligations on the signatories. Since then, very few nations are on course to reach (or approximate) the targets set. Unless far more stringent programs for reducing emissions are introduced, and far greater compliance shown, it is virtually certain that areas of the world, currently inhabited by a billion people, will become uninhabitable by mid-century. The immediate consequence will be displacement of a very large number of people. They will not be driving serenely to more hospitable destinations. With very high probability, they will have limited supplies of food and fresh water, their chances of practicing the most elementary forms of hygiene will be very low, and they will attempt to travel through areas occupied by other groups (with whom there is often a history of tensions) who are themselves struggling. Human migration at levels orders of magnitude less than what we can expect has already caused enormous human suffering and generated political conflicts. How will nations – both desperate nomads and their intended hosts – cope when the numbers of the homeless mount into the tens, or even hundreds, of millions?

On every continent, an overheated planet will witness cascades of disruptive effects. This month's wildfires succeed last month's floods; the latest wave of migrants spread disease; battles over water sources escalate into full-scale warfare. It is no exaggeration to suppose that, by later in this century, every nation will have to devote a significant portion of its resources to mopping up after recurrent disasters. Pride in the ability to outmuscle others in the global marketplace will have to be tempered by recognition of the repeated shocks to the national economy.

Perhaps, instead of concentrating on building up the muscles of the most talented few, it might be worth considering how education might help *all* those whom these predictable cascades will challenge to come to terms with their perilous world?

Doubts about Democracy

From ancient times to the present, many commentators have agreed that democracy is messy, and some have concluded that it is dangerous. Whether the trouble is supposed to lie in the native unintelligence of the masses, or whether it is the product of their ignorance, the expected result is the same. Democracies will fail to identify threats in time to avert them, or even to manage them. Eventually, the populace will yearn for a wise and capable leader who can preserve whatever they have been able to retain. A strongman answers the call. Whether this improves the situation is, as Winston Churchill famously reminded the world, somewhat dubious.

With respect to the challenges posed by infectious disease and by the recurrent catastrophes of a humanly-overheated world, the reasons to distrust democracy are abundantly clear. Several of the most distinguished commentators on the slow and often-interrupted efforts to limit global heating despair of the prospects of any democratic society coming close to doing what is necessary. "We know how to steer the world to a bearable future," they tell us, "but our politicians lack the will to lead a reluctant electorate. If it were only seen as a purely administrative matter, all would be well. Each nation would delegate absolute authority to a manager, who would organize the transition to a sustainable world."[1] Perhaps in line with Plato's *Republic*, the envisaged managers are assumed to have been shown the Form of the Good. Sadly, however, the autocrats available in the contemporary world – and there is no longer a small sample of them – don't exhibit either the wisdom or the incorruptibility that Plato required of Guardians.

A century ago, a thoughtful American, surveying the many ill-conceived policies favored by the electorate of his nation, argued that contemporary societies were simply too complex to leave the choice of leaders to the masses. Walter Lippmann exposed the myth of the "omnicompetent citizen," a character sufficiently intelligent and well-informed, and equipped with enough free time to work through the major issues of the day, and to arrive at well-grounded opinions reflecting that individual's personal interests and values (Lippmann 1925/2017). Since approximations to that imaginary voter do not exist, he concluded, government should be left to experts.

Lippmann's recommendation will hardly do for the contemporary world. The lack of consensus on expertise is a commonplace of our times, and, in badly polarized nations, any anointed leader, allegedly qualified to steer the ship of state, would strike a significant portion of the populace as introducing a new form of tyranny. Indeed, in most of the nations primarily responsible for the emissions driving the planet to its overheated condition, instituting a climate czar with the power to make the needed changes would arouse the violent opposition of a majority of citizens. In many instances, a *large* majority.

So, what is to be done?

Deepening Democracy

Lippmann's analysis of his times sparked one of the most sophisticated public debates in the history of the United States (and, perhaps, of any nation.) America's premier philosopher, John Dewey, took up the cudgels on behalf of democracy. The remedy, he suggested, was not to abandon democracy, but to deepen it.

Dewey is most famous for a book he published roughly a decade before his exchange with Lippmann. *Democracy and Education* is one of the classics of the philosophy of education, although I believe its deep message has not been fully appreciated. The conjunction of the title is easily read as pointing to something Dewey firmly believed: one goal of education is to produce young people ready to participate in democratic life. All too often, however, those who claim to follow Dewey take a further step. They interpret preparation for citizenship in a narrow way, as emphasizing the role of "civic education" in the curriculum. (Dewey frequently rails vehemently against the idea that "teaching the civics" is central to education.) The importance of the title's juxtaposition lies elsewhere – in an insightful conception of democracy.

The surface of democratic life displays the elections and the voting often regarded as sufficient for democracy to take hold. Deeper analysts of democracy would point to the constitutional protections, to the freedoms assured to citizens, and to the role of free exchange of ideas in helping voters align their electoral choices with their interests. Dewey, however, takes a further step: democracy, he contends, "is more than a form of government; it is primarily a mode of associated living, of conjoint communicated experience" (Dewey 1916/1975: 93). The title of his seminal book was chosen to express a striking and apparently bizarre claim. Democracy *is* Education.

Instead of starting with the organization of a nation-state, Dewey recognizes democracy as existing at many scales. Families, small towns, boards for housing developments, sports teams, orchestras, and large numbers of other groups joined in some common venture can proceed democratically – or they can be administered by some individual (or body of individuals) whose decisions are always law. When we attend to the smaller scales (as in my list of examples), the tendency to emphasize voting diminishes. More important are processes in which opinions are expressed, negotiations conducted, and minds changed. Autocratic families still exist (unfortunately), but, in many parts of the world, most people would be horrified by a return to the convention that the "head" of the family has absolute authority. Moreover, a family in which decisions were taken by assembling the members, presenting the options, and proceeding immediately to a vote would appear only slightly less perverse. In family councils, we expect people to present their points of view, we anticipate that others will listen, that there will be attempts to see the situation through one another's eyes, and that the eventual outcome will be one that each member can live with. If, after lengthy discussion, the process ends with one party discontented, that is a matter for regret.

Like Tocqueville before him, Dewey saw this kind of democracy as important not only for families but at larger scales as well. New England Town meetings were almost certainly not ideal versions of democratic exchange, but both theorists viewed them as exemplifying an important element in democracy: the need for *mutual learning* and decisions framed on the basis of *mutual engagement*. The democratic citizen is committed to living and working with others. At the core of democracy is a felt solidarity with one's fellows. Because of that solidarity, coming to appreciate their perspectives isn't simply discovering what *they* want, how *they* view things. Rather it is a process through which those who listen improve their own initial inclinations, coming to recognize what *they themselves* most fundamentally desire. Democratic exchange aims at the construction of a "conjoint experience," one in which the individual selves unite to form a "we."

So far, I have attempted to make vivid the guiding idea behind Dewey's provocative thesis. Let me now try to elaborate it more precisely. A *decision situation* arises when some group of people faces alternatives for going on, and the group is divided with respect to which option should be preferred. The *scale* of the decision situation is determined by the size of the set of *stakeholders*, the people whose lives will be affected by the selection of one of the options. Direct participation is possible when the scale is relatively small, when all the stakeholders can come together and exchange their perspectives on the situation. When that is not possible, democratic exchange must be carried on by representatives. Representation is fine-grained when each difference among perspectives that the stakeholders would acknowledge receives its own representative; it is coarse-grained when the perspectives are so numerous that some of them must be lumped together. When that occurs, the ranges of variation covered by the representatives should be approximately equal.

A group counts as a democracy when it is committed to resolving decision situations through democratic exchange. When a decision situation arises, the option chosen is determined by a deliberation meeting three conditions:

> *Inclusion*. Every stakeholder's perspective is represented. Only the perspectives of stakeholders are represented. The representation is at the finest grain feasible in the situation.
> *Information*. Participants only appeal to statements that are well-supported by the available evidence.

> *Engagement.* Each participant attempts to make others vividly aware of the perspectives that participant represents. Those who listen attempt to enter in to the perspectives of the others. Each participant seeks an outcome all can tolerate.

Although much could be said about these conditions, I shall restrict myself to the most essential clarifications. These affect the *Information* and *Engagement* conditions.

Many attempts at deliberation break down because those involved are allowed to make assertions, with which others disagree, without any evidence for the controversial statements. The *Information* condition disallows this. Speakers are not allowed to be dogmatic – there are no "conversation-stoppers." Yet, as I have already noted, disagreement can extend to what counts as evidence for a claim. When that occurs, participants in democratic exchange must work together to probe the inferences and premises advanced by rival parties. They have to expose fallacious reasoning, and to work together to determine reliable canons of investigation. Here, too, mutual engagement is important. All too often in today's discussions, people cling to a position because they fear the consequences of relinquishing it. "If *that* becomes widely accepted, the impact on my life will be severe", they – reasonably – claim. Philosophers have frequently supposed that, when complex issues, involving both facts and values, are at stake, the appropriate procedure is to settle the facts first, and then approach issues of value on the basis of a shared conception of the facts. This is an impoverished picture. In any joint deliberation in which people have to undertake inquiry together, one commitment must be in place from the start: nobody is to be left vulnerable in light of the final decision. Whatever becomes widely accepted, there will be protections for the lives of those who might be adversely affected. Why would anyone agree to joint deliberation with people who refused to offer such guarantees?

Mutual engagement requires a willingness to see the world from the viewpoint of each of those who have a stake in the issue. On the basis of those vicarious experiences, deliberators must actively seek a way of satisfying at least some of the central aspirations of each perspective. It may be achieved through compromise as typically understood: the option chosen takes the views with which participants enter the discussion and stitches together parts from each. Deliberators should also appreciate the possibility of a different approach. Through the process in which ideas are exchanged, they should seek new ways of conceptualizing the situation from which their deliberation has sprung, endeavoring to find a hitherto unoccupied viewpoint that will accommodate the wishes of all, as they have evolved in the course of the sequence of mutual identifications. The emergent consensus may be viewed, by each participant, as inferior to the preference voiced at the beginning of the proceedings. What counts is that all find it acceptable.

If no solution of this form can be found, mutually engaged discussions can try for a weaker form of agreement. The latest debate about what is to be done belongs to a long sequence. History matters. Deliberators can attend to the ways in which past decisions have affected various groups, and, when they cannot identify an outcome acceptable to all, they can try for a record of decision-making with which each of the parties can live. Solidarity can be preserved by ensuring that no segment of society feels permanently marginalized.

All three of the conditions are *ideals* – and thus may be dismissed as utopian. "How," a skeptic may ask, "could actual societies ever engage in conversations meeting these standards, or even approximating them?" The question misunderstands the usefulness of ideals, as pragmatists often conceive them. To be sure, there are ideals people sometimes reasonably aim to realize. There are, however, many others – including inconsistent sets of ideals – that prove valuable in diagnosing the shortcomings of a present situation, and thus marking a direction in which a group of people (or a whole society) might make progress. Besides *progress to* (teleological progress) there is also *progress from* (pragmatic progress), achieved by recognizing some features of the current predicament as problematic, and, wholly or partly, amending it (Kitcher 2017). So, the three conditions point to the ills of actual conversations about important and difficult questions. Those conversations often fail to include the perspectives of all those who have a stake in the issue. They are frequently full of falsehoods, inaccuracies, and unsupported claims, sometimes dominated by blunt dogmatism. Above all, they rarely exhibit efforts at sensitive listening, serious attempts to understand what worries those who disagree with us, to enter into their approach to the world, and to feel its impacts through their skins. As pragmatists concede, perfection along any of these three dimensions is humanly impossible. The concession doesn't doom efforts to make deliberations *more* inclusive, *better* informed, and *more deeply* engaged than they currently are.

A progressive Deweyan democracy is a society that, besides exhibiting the machinery of free elections and the standard constitutional protections, institutionalizes processes of deliberation on major issues of policy and aims to make those discussions more inclusive, more informed, and more mutually engaged than they have previously been.

Revisiting the Doubts

The outlined account of "Deweyan democracy" offers my reading of Dewey's own response to Lippmann's abstract doubts.[2] Their debate focused on a general question. How can a democratic society, one with many policy issues to decide, and containing divergent views on a significant fraction of those issues, arrive at policies representing the "will of the people"? No specific question occupied Dewey and Lippmann. Hence, presenting a recipe for a more deeply democratic society, one that might emerge given world enough and time, was sufficient to address Lippmann's central complaint.

Our situation is different. The environmental threats are *urgent*, and they take very specific forms. Deepening democracy might be a good thing to do. But is it relevant to the challenges I have hailed as the principal problems for our descendants?

With respect both to infectious disease and to global heating, future generations will be aided by whatever we can do to mitigate the coming dangers and by whatever is done to help them adapt to the harsher circumstances in which they will live. At present, as climate scientists have tirelessly pointed out, the world is doing far too little on either score. Could a commitment to Deweyan democracy improve the situation?

Diagnosis first. Let's ask what currently inhibits climate action of the required intensity. The trouble stems from a four-sided dilemma (or, more pedantically, a quadrilemma).[3] The following desirable outcomes are difficult to achieve together:

1 A relatively benign future human environment
2 Not worsening the lives of those who already live precariously
3 Not preventing the economic development for which poorer nations yearn
4 Preserving the main achievements (social and cultural) of the human past.

Different constituencies within the human population emphasize the value of these outcomes more or less heavily. Many young people, concerned about the world they will inherit, urge rapid action to limit emissions of greenhouse gases. Those who have not yet chosen their socioeconomic trajectories – and who do not have a stake in the continued possibility of particular types of work – are less afraid of potential disruptions. The poor, including those who live in affluent societies, are alarmed when they consider the sweeping changes to energy production, worrying that their already precarious lives will become even more difficult. Developing nations regard the principal emitters of the past (and of the present – *plus ça change*) as having wantonly created an environmental mess, while demanding that developing countries pay the price by limiting their own economic development. Finally, many people, from many cultures and social strata, are concerned that valuable achievements will be sacrificed, either in efforts to limit global heating, or as a result of the catastrophes to come.

Without a proposal for balancing these goals, one that all the diverse constituencies can live with, efforts to mitigate climate change are doomed to failure. The pattern of past negotiations among nations, as they have determined the "emissions reduction targets" at which each should aim, exemplifies the problem. Giving priority to their competitive position in the cutthroat global economy, each nation is anxious not to emerge from the transition to a sustainable environment and find themselves disadvantaged. Thus, any commitments to reforming their generation of energy are inevitably too little and too late. Further, as the Paris agreement teaches us, the inadequate commitments are unlikely to be kept.

Within countries, political leaders are compelled to appease electors whose sense of their own vulnerability inclines them to resist the radical changes climate activists (rightly) recommend as necessary to avert a harsh future environment. Contemporary global capitalism has eroded the forms of support on offer in the heyday of welfare states, and simultaneously, greatly increased the proportion of the populace whose lives are precarious. In consequence, the foolish and dangerous practice of subsidizing traditional energy sources continues, even as the use of fossil fuels becomes more expensive than a switch to renewable forms of energy.

Once the structure of the problem is exposed, the answer seems evident. What the world needs is a way of reconciling conflicting demands, one a diverse human population will accept as an acceptable way to go on. Or, more exactly, an ongoing process of negotiating the balance – as new occurrences affect the chances of satisfying the four different aspirations, and as new information clarifies the future trajectories of those chances – in which the interests of all will be represented, and in which there will be a genuine effort not to sacrifice any constituency.

In short, the road to successful mitigation of global heating lies through Deweyan democracy – on an international scale.

Skepticism Renewed

Traveling that road, however, would require more time than we have. At least, so skeptics think. Moreover, when we reflect on the periodic meetings among national leaders, and the disappointments they regularly generate, it seems there are grounds for skepticism. No magic wand exists to transform the character of the discussions, turning the participants into the deliberators Deweyan democracy celebrates. The first two conditions on the conversation do not seem particularly troublesome. Many (but not all) of the discussions are inclusive, and, for the most part, participants are well-informed. True, there's a pronounced tendency to base premises on ideology – in this instance, economic dogma. Progress might begin by suspending the faith and considering alternatives to rapacious hyper-competitiveness.

The root of the problem is the third condition. Mutual engagement is virtually non-existent. National leaders listen to their peers with a simple goal in mind: How can their comprehension of the perspectives of others be used to arrive at an outcome advancing their own ends? To resolve the quadrilemma, more than that is required. Instrumental listening must give way to something more empathetic, an openness that no longer treats the other participants as mere means.

So, skeptics draw the sorry conclusion. Place the same people in the same situation as often as you like. They will always fall dismally short of their loveable – but fictitious – Deweyan counterparts. *Perhaps* an advance might be made if education were reoriented, aimed toward instilling the virtues so conspicuously lacking in our non-Deweyan exchanges. But, even if educators came up, today, with a good plan for doing that, it would take at least a generation. And that much time isn't available.

Although it's a powerful case, the argument isn't decisive. Education, as Dewey often reminded his readers, isn't finished when the learner leaves school. An old dog sometimes learns new tricks. If my diagnosis of the failures of climate activism were to be widely accepted, the participants in future deliberations might take serious steps toward emulating the Deweyan discussants. Moreover, as the effects of past insouciance about global heating become ever more apparent – in the parade of floods and wildfires and heatwaves and droughts – national leaders may be encouraged to seek a diagnosis. The hold of economic ideology may die hard, attentive and other-directed listening may be far from perfect. Nevertheless, adults are often able to amend their conduct when they are told about the conventions governing a particular social interaction. Amateur clowns do not tell jokes at funerals.

Some directed efforts at fostering engaged conversation are encouraging. At a range of levels, people have been able to work together to achieve greater harmony. James Fishkin and his co-workers have attained some successes with respect to a variety of groups on a variety of issues (Fishkin 2010); more relevant to the present discussion is the French citizens' convention on climate change, insightfully analyzed by Hélène Landemore (Landemore ms.).

Finally, even if advances are slow, climate science recognizes the costs, *at any stage*, of failing to reform our ways of generating energy. If the process only begins a generation from now, the world our great-grandchildren inhabit will be very bad. But, if it doesn't begin then, it will be even worse. It's never too late to mitigate.

Really Relevant Education

Mitigation is only half the story. The world's children must be taught the skills required for adaptation to a world in which environmental challenges recur. What they will primarily need is an ability to work together, to combine their forces and resources to blunt the damage inflicted here, there, and everywhere. Given the likely perils of the future, the strategy of seeking entrepreneurs who will deliver the Next Technological Gizmo for the Next Popular Fad will be the subject of morose sick jokes.

I have elsewhere suggested a program of education conducive to the solidarity Deweyan democracy demands (Kitcher 2021). It starts early, with exercises in joint planning in which all pre-school children engage. As they grow, the exercises become ever more complex and more challenging. The instilling of skills in including others, critically evaluating evidence, and, above all, in serious and empathetic listening is accompanied and fostered by an interactive course of study, in the humanities and social sciences, aimed at cultivating self-understanding and appreciating the lives – and the aspirations – of a diverse human population. Nor is this to be confined to the early years. Preparing and extending solidarity takes a lifetime.

There's an obvious challenge to the points I have been making. "Technology has the power to liberate us from the quadrilemma. Geoengineering will dissolve the problem." Yet we should ask some questions. Would the chances of success be increased by a neo-Thatcherite program, discarding the emphasis on "market skills," and even replacing the quest for nifty devices to boost national productivity with a search for people who could solve a very specific problem? Would that work better than investing in a cooperative effort to bring together leading scientists, established as well as newly minted, with interest in the problem, and a diverse array of backgrounds?

Affirmative answers are, I think, mere speculations. Even optimists, though, should worry about a third question. Would a technological breakthrough be sufficient? For to *implement* the conjectural advance, different factions within countries (as well as the nations of the world) will have to work together. Here, the recent course of the COVID pandemic points a clear moral. The breakthrough, in this instance, was easy and predictable. Thanks to a well-established body of science – molecular biology and virology were ready for application[4] – vaccines have been produced with astounding speed. We have been given the Holy Grail. Nevertheless, infection surges on, as the cup is withheld, or spilled, or simply refused. Without serious attention to the goal of educating citizens – ideally, citizens of the world – the power of any technology to do good will always be needlessly limited.

The generations who come after us will almost certainly be challenged by the physical environment negligent ancestors have bequeathed to them. They will need to recognize what is worth conserving, and what can be dispensed with. To the extent that they acquire that discriminatory ability, they will almost certainly wonder why their careless forebears placed so much emphasis on meaningless toys, and lost sight of so many things that matter. If they exercise the virtues that I hope they have learned, sadness will temper their justifiable anger.

Traditional liberal education is an important part of Really Relevant Education because, when it is developed sensitively, with attention to each individual child, it can induce an understanding of what is worth pursuing. As the people who will come after us struggle to decide what must be given up and what retained, they will benefit from abilities to reflect on what matters most to them. Because their conclusions will probably vary, they too will have to negotiate an acceptable balance. Despite the shocks they repeatedly experience, if they are able to carry out those negotiations – if they are able to make progress as Deweyan democrats – their lives may even go better than ours.

Since 1789, the banner words of the French Revolutionaries have been reduced to a pair. "Liberty" and "Equality" feature centrally in our socio-political discussions. "Fraternity" – or, better, its more general cousin, "Solidarity" – has dropped out of the picture.[5] It's a genuine loss. For solidarity is crucial to the best development we can achieve of liberty and equality.

Really Relevant Education would make it central once again. In doing so, it would expose the educational trend of the past forty years for the grotesque parody it is.[6]

(Related Chapters: 2, 3, 20, 21, 25, 27, 29, 34.)

Notes

1 Sophisticated elaborations of this line of thought were offered by the economist, Jeffrey Sachs, and the philosopher, Dale Jamieson, at a workshop at Columbia University in December 2018.

2 The response tries to make more exact the notion of solidarity underlying Dewey's appeal for "the great Community" (Dewey 1927/1984).

3 This diagnosis of the difficulties of climate action is elaborated and defended in Kitcher and Keller (2017).

4 One of the odd quirks of history is the continuity between the 20th century pandemic and its 21st century counterpart. Molecular biology began in 1944 with the identification of DNA as the genetic material, a discovery made by Oswald Avery and two colleagues. As John Barry's illuminating historical study makes clear, Avery was a leading figure in the attempts (ultimately unsuccessful) to find a medical solution to "the Spanish flu" (Barry 2004). His decades of dedicated work later launched a discipline that has paid off handsomely in our own times.

5 Although some philosophers interested in education have tried to reintroduce it. See Callan (1997); Curren and Elenbaas (2020).

6 Many thanks to Randy Curren for his characteristically astute advice on an earlier draft.

References

Atkinson, A. (2015) *Inequality*. Cambridge MA: Harvard University Press.

Autor, D. & Kitcher, P. (2018) "As You Like It: Work, Life, and Satisfaction," in S. Rangan (ed.) *Capitalism Beyond Mutuality*. New York: Oxford University Press, 139–160.

Barry, J. M. (2004) *The Great Influenza*. New York: Viking Penguin.

Brighouse, H. (2006) *On Education*. London: Routledge.

Callan, E. (1997) *Creating Citizens*. New York: Oxford University Press.

Case, A. & Deaton, A. (2020) *Deaths of Despair and the Future of Capitalism*. Princeton: Princeton University Press.

Curren, R. & Elenbaas, L. (2020) "Civic Friendship," Insight Paper, JCCV, University of Birmingham, https://www.jubileecentre.ac.uk/userfiles/jubileecentre/pdf/insight-series/RC_LE_CivicFriendship.pdf

Deaton, A. (2013) *The Great Escape*. Princeton: Princeton University Press.

Delbanco, A. (2012) *College: What It Is, Was, and Should Be*. Princeton: Princeton University Press.

Dewey, J. (1916/1975) *Democracy and Education*. Carbondale IL: Southern Illinois University Press.

Dewey, J. (1927/1984) *The Public and its Problems*. Carbondale IL: Southern Illinois University Press.
Fishkin, J. (2010) *When the People Speak: Deliberative Democracy and Public Consultation*. Oxford: Oxford University Press.
Garrett, L. (1994) *The Coming Plague*. New York: Farrar, Straus and Giroux.
Kitcher, P. (2017) "Social Progress," *Social Philosophy and Policy* 34(2): 46–65.
Kitcher, P. (2021) *The Main Enterprise of the World: Rethinking Education*. New York: Oxford University Press.
Kitcher, P. & Keller, E. F. (2017) *The Seasons Alter: How to Save Our Planet in Six Acts*. New York: W. W. Norton.
Landemore, H. (ms.) "Can Citizens Make the Law? Evidence from the French Citizens' Convention for Climate (2019-21)," unpublished.
Lippmann, W. (1925/2017) *The Phantom Public*. New York: Routledge.
McNeill, W. (1976) *Plagues and Peoples*. Garden City NY: Anchor Books.
Nussbaum, M. (1997) *Cultivating Humanity*. Princeton: Princeton University Press.
Nussbaum, M. (2010) *Not for Profit: Why Democracy Needs the Humanities*. Princeton: Princeton University Press.
Stark, R. (1996) *The Rise of Christianity*. Princeton: Princeton University Press.
Stiglitz, J. (2002) *Globalization and its Discontents*. New York: W.W. Norton.
Stiglitz, J. (2012) *The Price of Inequality: How Today's Divided Society Endangers our Future*. New York: Norton.
Stiglitz, J. (2019) *People, Power, and Profits: Progressive Capitalism for an Age of Discontent*. London: Allen Lane.
Wallace-Wells, D. (2019) *The Uninhabitable Earth*. New York: Penguin Random House.

2

CIVIC LEARNING FOR THE 21ST CENTURY: DISENTANGLING THE "THIN" AND "THICK" ELEMENTS OF CIVIC IDENTITY TO SUPPORT CIVIC EDUCATION

Danielle Allen and David Kidd

Alongside efforts to expand and invigorate civic education in the United States, researchers, educators, and advocates in disciplines from psychology to education to political science have worked to clarify how to best prepare young people for sustained, ethical, and effective civic participation that is supportive of democracy. The goal has been to lay a theoretical foundation for renewed investment in civic education. The challenge has been to integrate research on youth development from psychology with analysis from political science of the kinds of participation needed in healthy constitutional democracies. A potential pitfall has been that any answer to the question of how best to prepare young people for their roles in a democracy might implicitly translate the priorities of one or another partisan ideology into an educational framework.

In this chapter, we propose a framework for defining "deeper civic learning" that reaches beyond ideology to core elements of civic participation that are needed to keep any constitutional democracy alive. We will argue that deeper civic learning involves the development of a civic identity that can support the integration of personal identity elements, shared (or group) identity elements, knowledge-based understanding, and skills-based creativity in the successful performance of a civic role. First, we define Deeper Civic Learning, drawing on the framework of Mehta and Fine (2019). Then, we characterize the civic role that shapes the objectives of civic education, and we take up the concept of civic identity that anchors the performance of a civic role. Finally, we review the different components of identity development that must converge in the successful development of a civic identity. We leave for another occasion the question of how disciplinary knowledge and skills-based creativity are integrated into civic identity.

Deeper Civic Learning

Despite inevitable points of disagreement or ambiguity, there appears to be widespread agreement that civic education must constitute more than transferring knowledge of democratic institutions and practices from teacher to learner. Advances in learning science show that deep learning consists of more than knowledge transfer in nearly any domain (Mehta & Fine 2019). Additionally, decades of research on civic development and engagement more specifically show that knowledge may be necessary, but

DOI: 10.4324/9781003172246-4

that it is not sufficient to sustain authentic civic participation (Levine & Kawashima-Ginsberg 2017). Truly effective civic education prepares and encourages learners to take active roles as contributors within a domain, granting access to new communities of practice and identities (Lave & Wenger 1991), even as they integrate knowledge-based understanding into that role performance.

As Mehta and Fine (2019, 2015) argue, deeper learning involves a triad of identity, mastery, and creativity. Their research, based on close study of teaching and learning in three distinct types of schools, shows that learning is most effective and engaging when rigorous engagement with disciplinary content (i.e., mastery) is clearly connected to issues that matter to students and their communities (i.e., identity) and opportunities to put their knowledge and skills to use in the production of original work (i.e., creativity). In this view, which builds on sociocultural theories of learning (Lave & Wenger 1991), learning is a process of becoming a member of a community of practice. Students acquire a new set of skills and knowledge they can deploy in a new role that is valued and embedded within their broader personal sense of self or identity.

But if deeper learning depends on the performance role that students will adopt to integrate their motivation, understanding, and skills, which role defines the sphere of civic education?

The Civic Role and Civic Identity

Constitutional democracies invite citizens and residents into many roles: voter, elected official, public servant, community leader, activist, journalist, juror, and soldier, among others (Allen 2016). To understand the civic role that should anchor civic education in a democracy, however, we need to identify the role that serves as the foundation for all of these. We turn now to a definition of democracy and to identification of the core elements of a civic role in a democracy.

For our definition of democracy, we adopt that offered in the American Academy of Arts and Science (AAAS) report, *Our Common Purpose*:

> In the twenty-first century, democracy refers to a political system in which legislative and chief executive decision-makers are elected by majority or plurality rule by eligible voters, with a presumption that the franchise approaches universal adult suffrage among legal citizens and that mechanisms are in place to protect ideological, religious, ethnic, and other demographic minorities. … In traditions of American political thought, all these terms capture forms of rights-based representative government in which 1) elected government leadership is constrained by constitutionalism, the rule of law, the separation of powers, the free expression of the people, and the legal protection and moral affirmation of the rights of individuals; and 2) groups and parties that are not part of electoral majorities cannot easily be disenfranchised or suffer loss of rights. We do not naively claim that more democracy simply in the form of more participation will solve our problems. We seek instead to achieve healthy connections between robust participation and political institutions worthy of participation.
>
> *(AAAS 2020: 2–3)*

All students should enter adulthood with the knowledge and practice-honed skills they need for effective civic engagement in a constitutional democracy defined as above. They should come to understand themselves as *members of a self-governing community committed to shared decision-making.*[1] This is the core definition of the civic role in a constitutional democracy.

Fulfilling this role requires knowledge about the political institutions in which one fulfills that role, skills at carrying out the many functions necessary for the operations of constitutional democracy, and adherence to the norms necessary to maintain those twinned practices of self-government and shared decision-making. With regard to the necessary norms, political scientists Steven Levitsky and Daniel Ziblatt (2018) identify mutual toleration and institutional forbearance as normative guardrails for the survival of democracy. We argue that, additionally, three core civic attitudes and dispositions – efficacy, equitability, and self-protection – are necessary to support the twinned practices of self-government and shared decision-making. In fact, these dispositions are closely related to the guardrail norms and support them.[2] As we discuss later, equitability on our definition sustains the norms of mutual toleration and institutional forbearance. Importantly, these norms and dispositions offer a "thin," not "thick," picture of what is necessary for a civic role in a constitutional democracy. Taken together, they by no means define the whole of what a person "ought" to do or what a "good life" consists of. They are only a "thin" layer of such a picture, leaving much for any individual to fill out to achieve a "thick" picture or comprehensive view about their definition of a good life.[3]

To put this in the terms of political philosophy, we identify those developmental elements that are necessary for people to make decisions together, including in conditions of diversity and disagreement, as definitional of the civic role, and we remain agnostic about the particular conceptions of a good life that any developing civic participant might integrate into their identity, provided that that conception of human goods does not undermine the norms needed for shared decision-making in a community of free and equal self-governing citizens. As Ronald Dworkin puts it:

> People who take personal responsibility for deciding what kind of life is valuable for them can nevertheless accept that issues of justice – about how the different and sometimes competing interests of all citizens should be accommodated – must be decided collectively, so that one decision is taken as authoritative for all. There is nothing in that proposition that challenges individual responsibility to decide what life to live given the resources and opportunities that such collective decisions leave to him ... A genuine political community must ... be a community of independent moral agents. It must not dictate what its citizens think about matters of political or moral or ethical judgment, but must, on the contrary, provide circumstances that encourage them to arrive at beliefs on these matters through their own reflective and finally individual conviction.
>
> *(Dworkin 1996: 26)*

This approach is also articulated by the philosopher John Rawls (1971) in *A Theory of Justice* as defining the parameters of a political system in terms of definitions of "right," and the need for protections of the basic rights that support the operations of self-government among free and equal citizens, rather than in terms of "the good," or a comprehensive view about all aspects of human morality.

To exercise their civic role and to form a complete civic identity, however, people have to do work to integrate the "thin identity" elements of their civic role with the other elements of their identity, both personal and group identities, that contribute to their comprehensive picture about how to live and their thick conception of their own identity. Dworkin uses the example of a member of an orchestra as an analogy to a political community. Just as our political institutions make decisions that bind us all, an orchestra conductor may decide how the orchestra will interpret a particular piece and that decision must be "binding on all" (1996: 25) the members of the orchestra. In this context, Dworkin writes,

> No musician sacrifices anything essential to his control over his own life, and hence to his self-respect, in accepting that someone else has that responsibility, but it would plainly be otherwise if the conductor tried to dictate not only how a violinist should play under his direction, but what standards of taste the violinist should try to cultivate. No one who accepted responsibility to decide questions of musical judgment for himself could regard himself as a partner in a joint venture that proposed to decide them for him.
>
> *(Dworkin 1996: 25–26)*

Just as a member of an orchestra has to integrate the role identity of orchestra member with the personal and group identities that shape the musician's musical judgment, so too in civic life we have to integrate our civic role with the personal and group identities that shape our values and commitments. Along with acquiring civic habits and skills, the development of a civic identity therefore requires clarifying moral and ethical commitments.

The work of integrating our personal and group identities with our civic role is necessary for the achievement of psychological integrity. It does also, however, fulfill another function. While we may have a "thin" conception of identity with regard to our civic role, our motivation to participate as a member of the civic community will inevitably flow from our "thick" identities connected to our personal and other group identities. The "thin" elements of identity connected to our civic role help us know *how* to participate in civic life, but they cannot in themselves provide an answer to the question of *why* we should participate in civic life. For that, we need to rely on our fuller conception of the goods we seek. That is, an understanding of personal and shared values gives direction to individual engagement. This self-understanding of our thicker identities also provides a foundation for articulating civic aspirations that help to orient and motivate collective action, a critical task in a diverse democracy (Finnemore & Jurkovich 2020).

With this background in mind, we can now define "civic identity." Civic identity consists of the integration of an individual's understanding of their role as a member in a community of shared decision-making with their personal and group-based identities and values as well as with the disciplinary knowledge and skills-based creativity needed for the performance of any specific instance of a civic role. In other words, civic identity integrates individualized and shared identity elements and manifests in uptake of a civic role that supports civic participation. Though the importance of values, attitudes, and dispositions to civic development is widely accepted in the field (e.g., Levine & Kawashima-Ginsberg 2017), there has been less consensus regarding exactly what they are and how they relate to civic identity. We seek to address this confusion by highlighting the need for civic participants to integrate "thin" identity elements with "thick" identity elements. The result of focusing on this work of integration in civic identity is a secondary recognition that the content defining civic identity will vary from person to person, depending on what elements of personal and group identity they bring to integrate into the performance of their civic roles, alongside the thin identity elements flowing from the civic role itself. This necessary variation in the content of civic identity from person to person perhaps helps explain why it has been so hard for researchers to pin down its exact content. All that can be pinned down *a priori* are the thin elements of civic identity attached to the civic role, defined as being *a member of a self-governing community committed to shared decision-making.*

With an account of civic identity in hand, we can now turn to developmental questions. Given the definition of civic identity we have set out above, how do young people come to develop their civic identity? Informing much recent work on active civic learning, Youniss et al. (1997) described a civic development trajectory in which young people become introduced to the practices of adult civic engagement, coming to form civic identities that sustain participation over time. With the thin conception of the civic role in a constitutional democracy in hand, and an initial idea of the work of integration necessary to form a civic identity, we can build on Youniss et al. to clarify the developmental trajectory that supports civic learning. To be useful in guiding civic education, an account of the developmental trajectory undergirding the emergence of a civic identity must provide a framework for distinguishing between personal, group-based, or ideological aspects of civic identity and those that should be held in common by virtue of flowing from the underlying, shared civic role. In other words, it is necessary to tease apart what elements of civic identity should be promoted in all civic education as elements of the civic role, and which should be determined by individuals and their most immediate communities. It is also necessary to consider how a civic education can effectively support the integration of personal, group-based, and ideological elements of civic identity *that learners choose for themselves* with those shared aspects of civic identity *that flow from the civic role*. Deeper learning in the context of civic education, or "deeper civic learning," consists of the activation of a civic identity to achieve two kinds of integration – integration of the individual and shared elements of identity; and integration of identity, disciplinary knowledge, and skills in the performance of a civic role. The theoretical foundation for civic education therefore depends on understanding these two projects of integration. In the remainder of this chapter, we focus on the first, reserving the second type of integration for another occasion.

Civic Identity Development

Adolescence as a Period of Exploration

Most civic education in the United States, when it happens at all, is focused in students' late middle school and high school years, a period even casual observers can describe as one of rapid growth and, often, difficulty. Decades of psychological research tend to confirm this observation, at least in the United States and similar cultural environments. Dominant in developmental psychology, Eriksonian, or neo-Eriksonian, models of identity and its development are especially helpful to understanding civic identity, and adolescent development, more broadly (e.g., Damon 2008; Youniss et al. 1997).

Erikson's (1950) theory of identity development, based in the psychoanalytic tradition, posits that individuals encounter crises or turning points as they age, with adolescents grappling with role confusion as they encounter new opportunities for autonomy equipped with rapidly developing social and cognitive capacities. Although subsequent researchers have largely concurred that adolescence is a key period of identity development, it is increasingly accepted that the process may continue well beyond young adulthood (Côté & Levine 2002). Regardless of their age, individuals are thought to formulate their identities by choosing among available identities, especially vocational and ideological identities, and synthesizing these into a coherent sense of self (Kroger & Marcia 2011). That is, they need to figure out *who they are*.

The process through which people move beyond role or identity confusion is generally understood as entailing a phase of *exploration*, a period in which individuals learn about and experiment with different roles and identities, followed by *commitment*, the point at which an individual makes an informed and authentic decision regarding their identity (Marcia 1966). Depending on the completion of these two phases, an individual can be roughly categorized within four identity statuses (Kroger & Marcia 2011): Identity diffusion (no exploration or commitment), foreclosure (no exploration, commitment to externally assigned identity), moratorium (exploration but no commitment), and achievement (exploration followed by commitment). Adolescence is most often associated with identity exploration, with young people sometimes appearing or feeling unmoored but excited as they navigate the moratorium stage prior to making commitments and reaching the stage of identity achievement.

The process of integrating chosen identities into a global sense of self depends on personal and social factors (Côté & Levine 2002). Individuals need to find ways of reconciling the demands of new identities with their personality characteristics, experiences, and goals. In educational contexts, for example, students may more readily adopt discipline-specific identities (e.g., scientist) when they can link aspects of their personal identity (e.g., curiosity) to the new identity (Kaplan & Flum 2012; Brickhouse et al. 2000). The adoption and integration of new identities also depends on the ways in which the individual's community affirms or contests the attainment of new identities (Côté & Levine 2002). Traditional gender stereotypes, for example, may increase the likelihood that others affirm a boy's adoption of an engineer identity. Moreover, while a boy might find it easy to integrate their gender identity with their engineer identity, a girl may experience difficulty achieving coherence insofar as her gender identity is seen as conflicting with her engineer identity (Godwin et al. 2016). In these cases, social factors suggest the compatibility or incompatibility of different social identities, rendering the task of achieving internal coherence of identities within a sense of self more or less difficult.

Connecting Eriksonian Models of Identity Development with Sociocultural Approaches

Research motivated by sociocultural, situationist, and social psychological theories helps ground the personal factors (e.g., attachment style; Kroger & Marcia 2011) and processes (e.g., exploration; Marcia 1966) focal in the Eriksonian tradition in a social context (Vignoles et al. 2011). Sociocultural or situationist models of identity development highlight the role of engaging with others and with a cultural tool kit (e.g., technologies, practices) in shaping identity. Participating in communities of practice allows an individual to begin mastering the knowledge, skills, values, and norms that, once acquired, form the basis of an individual's role-specific identity (Lave & Wenger 1991; Penuel & Wertsch 1995; Wenger 2010). Identity development, in this view, occurs through performing that identity in a way that is perceived as authentic by the self and by others.

Hand and Gresalfi (2015) describe identity development as a joint accomplishment, reflecting both the opportunities afforded to individuals and how individuals engage with those opportunities. In this view, individuals' differences in personality, values, and experiences may dispose them to take more or less advantage of various opportunities for participation within or across domains. Similarly, the range of opportunities for participation in activities may affect the extent to which engagement supports identity development. For example, a student's interest in the outdoors may increase their likelihood of developing a scientist identity if their science classes allow them to pursue that interest by studying ecological issues. In addition, their study of ecology in science classes should encourage active participation in scientific practices, allowing the student to see themself and be seen by others as a practicing ecologist. This sociocultural approach resonates with research showing that learners are motivated by opportunities to satisfy basic psychological needs (Ryan & Deci 2017) of autonomy, competence, and relatedness (e.g., Liu et al. 2009; Makkonen et al. 2021). When activities are structured and presented in ways that provide clear opportunities for meaningful role adoption, self-expression, and collaboration, individuals are more likely to become deeply identified with the roles.

The sociocultural and situationist accounts of identity development draw attention to how individuals' identity is situated in a specific community and set of practices, norms, and tools. This approach explicitly recognizes that identities are, to some extent, linked to particular domains, such as science, but that they must also be connected to one's personal identity or global sense of self, including social identities. The affordances and constraints of that community present or limit opportunities for identity development (Hand & Gresalfi 2015). In this way, the sociocultural perspective helps clarify the tasks of educators interested in cultivating identity by focusing attention on creating learning environments and activities that accultrate learners into a disciplinary community of practice. For example, identity development can be supported by promoting understanding of the domain, helping learners identify and take on important roles, and providing opportunities for students to draw on their lived experiences (Godwin et al. 2016) and exercise agency in ways congruent with their personal identities (Brickhouse et al. 2000; Nasir & Hand 2008).

Authentic Activation of Civic Identity

With this sociocultural understanding of identity development in hand, we can more clearly understand the task of helping young people "thicken" their civic roles. Many people see American identity as largely overlapping with a White racial identity (Devos & Sadler 2019; Schildkraut 2014; Martinez-Fuentes et al. 2020; Molina et al. 2015; Phinney et al. 1997), and this identity "thickens" the civic role by linking it to a particular set of cultural traditions, values, and goals (Brewer 2009; Hart et al. 2011; Martinez-Fuentes et al. 2020; Pehrson et al. 2009). Yet, it is not necessary that civic identity is construed in terms of a purportedly shared national identity, and how individuals "thicken" their civic identities may differ depending on their personal and social identities. That is, the civic role can be "thickened" in diverse ways without compromising its "thin" foundation, and capitalizing on this potential is important to authentic civic development.

Research on civic development brings more clarity to how youth link their civic identities to their other social identities, including but not limited to their national identity. Findings from detailed studies of civic purpose focused on members of minority groups provide a clear example: Civic purpose, often driven by shared democratic values, was further given direction and strength by concerns for the needs and interests of groups of people with whom young people identified, ranging from families or particular communities, to racial and national groups (Malin et al. 2015; see also Kirshner 2009). Other research has similarly found evidence of a positive relation between racial/ethnic identity development and civic efficacy among minority youth (Bañales et al. 2020; Hipolito-Delgado & Zion 2017). The link between racial/ethnic identity and civic identity, however, does not appear to entail a diminished sense of commitment to the nation as a whole, with minority youth endorsing patriotic statements to the same extent as White youth while expressing relatively greater concern for securing rights for minorities and improving race relations (Flanagan et al. 2009). Rather than tying their civic role identities primarily to a superordinate American identity narrowly defined to align with the thick identities of a subset of the population, young people, especially members of minority groups, may be most motivated to take civic action when they can "thicken" their civic identities with the values and aspirations of other social identities. This also opens up the possibility of evolving definitions of an American identity over time.

A Sociocultural Understanding of Civic Identity

Viewed through the lens of sociocultural theories of identity development, civic identity development can be seen as the consolidation of civic knowledge, civic skills, and civic attitudes and dispositions into a social role identity. This is most likely to happen when individuals are given opportunities for authentic engagement in the civic domain, and when they are able to integrate the identity elements connected to their civic role with other important identities, including personal, social, and other role identities (Flanagan et al. 2011; Levine & Kawashima-Ginsberg 2015). Accordingly, promoting positive civic identity development requires attention to both encouragement of authentic participation in civic roles themselves and strategies for helping individuals connect the identity elements connected to their civic role with knowledge, skills, values and aspirations associated with other identities.

The Relationship Between Ethnic and Racial Identity Formation, Hard Histories, and Civic Identity

Many sources of personal identity and group identity are relevant to the work of integrating the various features of identity into a civic identity, anchored in the civic role. These sources can include personality, religion, and cultural worldview. They can also include demographic or elective dimensions of identity: gender and sexuality, race and ethnicity, language community, profession, and so on. In the context of the U.S., ethnic and racial identity formation requires special attention because the prominence of race and ethnicity in American history and political life ensures that fulfillment of the civic role will require interacting with these conceptual categories. Civic participants need to understand their own relationships to ethnic and racial categories in order to have a firm ground for their own choice-making and participation. How they perform their civic role will impact the operations of race and ethnicity in our society and in so doing will interact with those aspects of a learner's identity that are connected to race and ethnicity. In order for those interactions to support healthy growth of agency and self-understanding, learners need to find ways to bring to the surface those aspects of their racial and ethnic identity that are impacted by participation in the civic role, and they need to be able to achieve alignment.

Students often begin to engage with their civic roles by processing the news, and the news inevitably brings in questions of race and racism. As Adrienne Stang puts it:

> Beginning in middle school, and often sooner, students come to the classroom with questions about what they are seeing. Many of them arrive with powerful emotions. They may be angry, scared, shocked or simply curious. Some may express feelings of shame or guilt; others may respond with denial. To understand the violence that they see on social media, they need to explore the history of race and racism. Part of this investigation requires that they learn about civic agents like [John] Lewis, who fought against institutional racism.
>
> *(Stang forthcoming)*

Learners need an opportunity to develop understanding about their own racial and ethnic identity, about what it means to them in their own meaning-making, about how the meanings of ethnic and racial identities have changed over time. Importantly, students from different racial and ethnic backgrounds typically experience very different developmental trajectories (see Figure 2.1). As Beverly Tatum (2017) has argued, drawing on Janet Helms's (1990) work on racial identity development, the trajectories are necessarily different because students of color often wake up to the presence of race in our world because they experience a racist encounter. Anger, confusion, and alienation can result. In contrast, white students' do not themselves experience racism but do come to recognize its existence and the privilege of whiteness. Feelings of guilt and shame can result. Both students can also encounter racism, or discover privilege, by studying history. Teachers have the job of co-processing these moments of discovery with adolescent learners in ways that can help those learners re-integrate their psyches, and achieve a healthy connection with others of all races. The goal is for learners from both categories to internalize a positive identity self-conception, able and willing to work productively in multiracial environments.

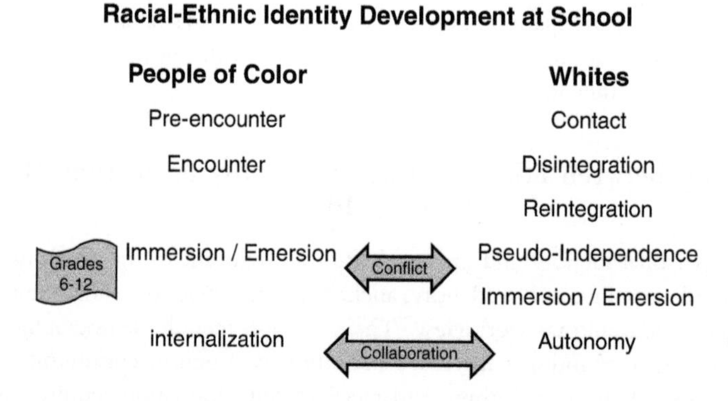

Figure 2.1 Racial-ethnic identity development trajectories for People of Color and Whites, as described by Helms (1990) and Tatum (1997).

In addition, issues of ethnic and racial identity interact with potential civic roles. Consider the different reactions to a Bill of Rights activity in a suburban classroom with a predominantly white population and an urban population with primarily students of color. The students in the first classroom gravitated in their interest to the First Amendment, and the themes of free expression. The students in the second classroom gravitated in their interest to the Fourth Amendment, and its treatment of rights in relation to search and seizure. In the context of the U.S., where the operations of our legal system unfold very differently for urban and suburban communities, communities of color and white communities, the salient features of our institutions will differ for different communities (Lerman & Weaver 2014). The civic role of the students in the urban classroom includes the experience of being over-policed. The civic role of the students in the suburban classroom does not include that experience. Students need to understand why they see and experience civic roles as they do, and part of the answer to that question lies in demographic features of identity. This example also underscores how much variation there will be for students, not only in what aspects of thick identity they bring to the formation of their civic identity, but also in which aspects of the civic role are most salient to them, as they consider forming their own civic identity and performing a civic role. The point of contact between ethnic and racial identities and understandings of potential civic roles is particularly fraught for young learners, and this demands of teachers that they bring great intentionality and care to their support of identity exploration and formation.

Integrating elements of racial and ethnic identity with identity elements connected to the civic role is of paramount importance. The need to achieve this integration further underscores how the journey to an authentic, integrated civic identity will be different for different students. Understanding that the developmental trajectory is itself diverse is fundamentally important for being able to support all learners in their civic development.

Core Attitudes and Dispositions of Civic Identity: Efficacy, Equitability, and Self-Protection

Personal development, the impacts of socio-cultural context, and the impacts of racial and ethnic identity in particular ensure that every learner will have a different path toward the development of a civic identity and that that identity will differ from learner to learner. Nonetheless, it is also important to identify the elements of identity connected to the civic role that all learners should be seeking to integrate with other aspects of their identity.

Shared Identity Elements Connected to Civic Role

We focus on three civic attitudes and dispositions: civic efficacy, equitability, and self-protection. Scholarship on civic development has, of course, considered a much wider array of attitudes and dispositions, including civic duty (Zaff et al. 2010), critical consciousness (Diemer et al. 2017), civic purpose (Malin et al. 2015), and nationalism (Hart et al. 2011), to name a few. These factors are clearly linked to how individuals understand themselves in relation to their communities, and there is good evidence that variation in each accounts for differences in civic behavior. In these ways, they contribute to individuals' civic identities.

Our goal, however, is to identify only the "thin" identity elements connected to the civic role as things that might be taught to everyone. The dispositional sets that scholars have historically focused on have often been broader. This reflects the fact that scholars often focus on painting a single, homogenized picture of civic identity that should be cultivated for all students, and they often implicitly import thicker conceptions into that picture. Yet the broad goals of civic education should be negotiated so that they do not inherently favor or discourage different political orientations, insofar as those political orientations are not fundamentally anti-democratic (e.g., totalitarian, theocratic). The attitudes and dispositions universally fostered by civic education should be as relevant and meaningful to a democratic socialist as they are to a libertarian, to an activist concerned with LGBTQ+ rights as to one seeking to ensure hunters' access to firearms.

Achieving ideological neutrality in the conceptualization of core civic attitudes and dispositions does not require that educators avoid controversial topics in the classroom or dissuade students from exploring different political philosophies. Instead, it requires that we focus on identifying as necessary only the limited set of dispositions actually needed to enable learners to function effectively as *members of a self-governing community committed to shared decision-making.* Attitudes and dispositions for efficacy, equitability, and self-protection are critical to navigating the diverse values and goals in increasingly complex democracies (Allen 2015). They are critical to helping people learn how to navigate conversations on critical issues. And they can be best developed through practicing difficult discussions and engaging thoughtfully with different perspectives. The point is to help young people feel competent to participate in civic life and do so with integrity and without seeking to dominate or exclude others. With this in mind, we define and argue for civic efficacy, equitability, and self-protection as the core dispositional elements of civic identity.

Civic Efficacy

Civic efficacy refers to a sense of being able to participate in civic life effectively, and it is therefore a direct indicator of the extent to which an individual feels they have agency within the civic community. Beyond navigating the institutions and processes of official government, efficacy in a democracy requires that one have the confidence and ability necessary to engage with others and persuade them to join a collective effort (Allen 2004). This view of civic efficacy is similar to that underlying a number of large-scale studies of civics education, including a state-wide study in California (Kahne 2005), and the 2009 International Civic and Citizenship Education Study (ICCS; Schulz et al. 2010). From a sociocultural learning theory perspective, feelings of efficacy, or the capacity for taking action within a domain, both reflect and motivate sustained participation (Takahashi 2011), and there is substantial evidence of a reciprocal relationship of civic efficacy and civic participation (Bandura 1993; Cohen & Chaffee 2013; Gastil & Xenos 2010; Schulz et al. 2010).

Researchers have also distinguished this form of efficacy from belief in the responsiveness and effectiveness of the government, or external efficacy. Compared to external efficacy, internal efficacy is more strongly related to civic participation (Gastil & Xenos 2010), and, in some cases, high levels of internal efficacy paired with relatively low levels of external efficacy may be most likely to prompt action, particularly among members of historically marginalized groups (Kahne & Westheimer 2006).

Equitability

Concern for equality is a core value of democratic societies, and its development has received substantial attention from researchers interested in civic education. Theoretical and operational definitions of equality vary in important ways. They range from conventional concerns for basic fairness in the distribution of opportunities and services (e.g., trust in the American promise; Flanagan et al. 2007) to critical identification and confrontation of systemic injustices (e.g., justice-oriented citizenship; Westheimer & Kahne 2004). In the context of civic education, definitions of equitability need to be compatible with different political beliefs and goals. One way of achieving this is to think of equitability in terms of how civic actors can manage competing interests as they work towards a more equitable democracy.

Creating an inclusive democratic society capable of maximizing the benefits of diversity and confronting injustices will require new or augmented modes of civic behavior (Allen 2016). To address these challenges, Allen (2004) argues that members of democratic communities should seek to engage in political friendship. In democracies, people will inevitably find themselves on the winning and losing sides of different debates and deliberations. Rather than see the failure to achieve consistent consensus as a flaw, Allen (2004) argues that it should be accepted and dealt with openly. This requires acknowledging the sacrifices of others and helping ensure that their sacrifices will be reciprocated.

The long-term reciprocity described by Allen (2004) is probably familiar to anyone who has developed and maintained friendships, which are often typified by the pursuit of rough parity in what members of the relationship give to and take from each other (Fiske & Haslam 1996; Rai & Fiske 2011). The challenge is not to educate people so that they understand or value reciprocity – they already do – but to help them apply their capacities for friendship to the civic sphere. This means learning to share power when making decisions and to distribute benefits and burdens according to agreed upon standards of fairness. How power is shared, whether through joint decision-making or turn-taking, and how benefits and burdens are allocated, whether to establish equality of opportunity or outcome, will remain important questions to resolve, but political friendship provides a framework for equitably resolving these questions.

It is important to clarify that we do not propose that achieving political friendship is an easy task: Over the course of the history of the U.S. the sacrifices of entire groups have been systematically ignored or devalued just as benefits flowing from those sacrifices have accrued to dominant members of society. Accordingly, for political friendship to provide a basis for equitability, we must be clear-eyed about our difficult histories and their persistent impacts. This is true for both beneficiaries and victims of historical or current inequities, but the burdens and challenges of this work will vary for these groups.

Self-Protection

Increasingly, and especially among young people, civic engagement is pursued online, and recent work examining youth online civic engagement has highlighted the need to develop motivation for responsible and self-protecting participation that accounts for risks including misinformation and harassment (Allen & Light 2015; Choi et al. 2017; James et al. 2010; Kahne & Bowyer 2017; Kim & Choi 2018; Levine & Kawashima-Ginsberg 2017). Online forums for discourse can quickly become toxic (Jones et al. 2013), and seemingly private behavior or speech can easily become part of a lasting and very public digital record (Shresthova 2016). Discourse surrounding civic issues online often includes misinformation, which can lead to diminished trust and increase the likelihood of radicalization (Hodgin & Kahne 2018), and sharing it can threaten one's credibility.

These threats to young civic actors are not unique to online environments, of course, and the ethical commitments that attenuate them are equally relevant offline. Respectful online behavior is associated with lower likelihood of perpetrating or becoming the victim of online harassment (Jones & Mitchell 2016), and reflecting on one's own biases and the quality of the information one consumes online can reduce vulnerability to fake news and propaganda (Hodgi & Kahne 2018; Vraga et al. 2015). Self-protective commitments to interpersonal respect and intellectual integrity, though especially vital in the online environment, help set ethical guidelines relevant to all civic engagement.

Conclusion

Educating for an inclusive, just, and resilient American democracy in an increasingly diverse and complex society requires that we disentangle a "thin" civic role from the "thick" identities that give it direction and authenticity. In this chapter, we link political philosophy and psychology to clarify the developmental tasks of emerging civic actors and to do so in ways that attenuate the risk of ideological bias in civic education. This account highlights the importance of helping young people understand the "thick" identities they and others bring with them into civic life, while emphasizing the need to connect those "thick" identities to a "thin" concept of the civic role that represents the knowledge, skills, and attitudes and dispositions needed to sustain constitutional democracy and a community of self-governing equals engaged in shared decision-making. Focusing on the attitudes and dispositions central to the civic role, we describe how efficacy, equitability, and self-protection support sustained, ethical, and productive civic engagement without tilting the scales in favor of conservative or liberal conceptions of an ideal democratic society.

Civic knowledge and skills, too, are important, and they should be clearly defined in future work that attends to how they can best support the authentic integration of "thick" identities with the "thin" civic role for young people. Grounding this work in a commitment to helping learners become efficacious, equitable, and self-protecting civic actors directs attention to what knowledge and skills young people will need to operate their democracy effectively and ethically. Educators, in this view, need to be equipped to support students as they develop their "thin" civic role identities, and educators must be accorded the flexibility needed to accommodate and respond productively to the "thick" identities their students bring into the classroom. Students should graduate with a clear grasp of key civic knowledge, skills, and, especially, attitudes and dispositions that ensure they pursue their civic goals in ways that are effective, equitable, and self-protecting. At the same time, their motives, aspirations, and strategies in civic life should authentically reflect their own identities and values. This will strengthen the bonds of reciprocal trust needed to realize the benefits of diverse experiences and values that constitute one of democracy's greatest promises.

(Related Chapters: 1, 3, 14, 21, 22, 26, 27, 31.)

Notes

1 The definition of this role is expansively treated as a concept of moral membership in the community of a constitutional democracy in Ronald Dworkin, "The Moral Reading and the Majoritarian Premise": "A political community cannot count anyone as a moral member unless it gives that person a part in any collective decision, a stake in it, and independence from it" (Dworkin 2017: 24). See *Law's Empire* (Dworkin 1986), and "Equality, Democracy, and Constitution: We the People in Court," (Dworkin 1990).

2 These three dispositions align with the three conditions of moral membership in the community of a constitutional democracy outlined by Ronald Dworkin (2017). See note 1.

3 The original contrast between "thick" and "thin" normative views derives from the work of Clifford Geertz (1973) to develop a methodology for the "thick" description of culture. This analytical vocabulary was then extended to moral and political philosophy by Geertz' colleague at the Institute for Advanced Study, Michael Walzer (1994), in his book *Thick and Thin: Moral Argument at Home and Abroad.*

References

Allen, D. (2004) *Talking to Strangers: Anxieties of Citizenship since Brown v. Board of Education*. Chicago: University of Chicago Press.

Allen, D. (2015) "Reconceptualizing Public Spheres: The Flow Dynamics Model," in D. Allen & J. S. Light (eds.) *From Voice to Influence: Understanding Citizenship in a Digital Age*. Chicago: The University of Chicago Press, 178–207.

Allen, D. (2016) *Education and Equality*. Chicago: University of Chicago Press.

Allen, D., & Light, J. S. (2015) "Introduction," in D. Allen & J. S. Light (eds.) *From Voice to Influence: Understanding Citizenship in a Digital Age*. Chicago: The University of Chicago Press, 1–15.

Bañales, J., Hoffman, A. J., Rivas-Drake, D., & Jagers, R. J. (2020) "The Development of Ethnic-Racial Identity Process and Its Relation to Civic Beliefs among Latinx and Black American Adolescents," *Journal of Youth and Adolescence* 49: 2495–2508.

Bandura, A. (1993) "Perceived Self-Efficacy in Cognitive Development and Functioning," *Educational Psychologist* 28(2): 117–148.

Brewer, M. B. (2009) "Social Identity and Citizenship in a Pluralistic Society," in E. Borgida, C. M. Federico, & J. L. Sullivan (eds.) *The Political Psychology of Democratic Citizenship*. Oxford: Oxford University Press, 153–175.

Brickhouse, N. W., Lowery, P., & Schultz, K. (2000) "What Kind of a Girl Does Science? The Construction of School Science Identities," *Journal of Research in Science Teaching* 37(5): 441–458.

Choi, M., Glassman, M., & Cristol, D. (2017) "What It Means to Be a Citizen in the Internet Age: Development of a Reliable and Valid Digital Citizenship Scale," *Computers & Education* 107: 100–112.
Cohen, A. K., & Chaffee, B. W. (2013) "The Relationship between Adolescents' Civic Knowledge, Civic Attitude, and Civic Behavior and Their Self-Reported Future Likelihood of Voting," *Education, Citizenship and Social Justice* 8(1): 43–57.
Côté, J. E., & Levine, C. G. (2002) *Identity Formation, Agency, and Culture: A Social Psychological Synthesis*. Mahwah, NJ: Lawrence Erlbaum Associates Publishers.
Damon, W. (2008) *The Path to Purpose: Helping Our Children Find Their Calling in Life*. New York: Free Press.
Devos, T., & Sadler, M. (2019) "Context Diversity Predicts the Extent to Which the American Identity is Implicitly Associated with Asian Americans and European Americans," *Asian American Journal of Psychology* 10(2): 182–193.
Diemer, M. A., Rapa, L. J., Park, C. J., & Perry, J. C. (2017) "Development and Validation of the Critical Consciousness Scale," *Youth & Society* 49(4): 461–483.
Dworkin, R. (1986) *Law's Empire*. Cambridge, MA: Harvard University Press.
Dworkin, R. (1990) "Equality, Democracy, and Constitution: We the People in Court," *Alberta* Law *Review* 28(2): 324–346.
Dworkin, R. (1996) Freedom's Law*: The Moral Reading of the American Constitution*. Cambridge, MA: Harvard University Press.
Dworkin, R. (2017) "The Moral Reading and the Majoritarian Premise," in *Deliberative Democracy and Human Rights*. New Haven, CT: Yale University Press, 81–115.
Erikson, E. H. (1950) *Childhood and Society*. New York: Norton
Finnemore, M., & Jurkovich, M. (2020) "The Politics of Aspiration," *International Studies Quarterly* 64(4): 759–769.
Fiske, A. P., & Haslam, N. (1996) "Social Cognition Is Thinking about Relationships," *Current Directions in Psychological Science* 5(5): 143–148.
Flanagan, C., Levine, P., & Settersten, R. (2009) *Civic Engagement and the Changing Transition to Adulthood*. Medford, MA: Center for Information and Research on Civic Learning and Engagement.
Flanagan, C., Martínez, M. L., & Cumsille, P. (2011) "Civil Societies as Cultural and Developmental Contexts for Civic Identity Formation," in L. A. Jensen (ed.), *Bridging Cultural and Developmental Approaches to Psychology: New Syntheses in Theory, Research and Policy*. Oxford: Oxford University Press, 113–137.
Flanagan, C., Syvertsen, A., & Stout, M. (2007) *Civic Measurement Models: Tapping Adolescents' Civic Engagement*. Medford, MA: The Center for Information and Research on Civic Learning and Engagement.
Gastil, J., & Xenos, M. (2010) "Of Attitudes and Engagement: Clarifying the Reciprocal Relationship between Civic Attitudes and Political Participation," *Journal of Communication* 60(2): 318–343.
Geertz, C. (1973) *The Interpretation of Cultures*. New York: Basic books.
Godwin, A., Potvin, G., Hazari, Z., & Lock, R. (2016) "Identity, Critical Agency, and Engineering: An Affective Model for Predicting Engineering as a Career Choice," *Journal of Engineering Education* 105(2): 312–340.
Hand, V., & Gresalfi, M. (2015) "The Joint Accomplishment of Identity," *Educational Psychologist* 50(3): 190–203.
Hart, D., Richardson, C., & Wilkenfeld, B. (2011) "Civic Identity," in S. J. Schwartz, K. Luyckx, & V. Vignoles (eds.) *Handbook of Identity Theory and Research*. New York: Springer, 771–787.
Helms, J. (1990) *Black and White Racial Identity Theory, Research, and Practice*. Westport, CT: Greenwood Press.
Hipolito-Delgado, C. P., & Zion, S. (2017) "Igniting the Fire within Marginalized Youth: The Role of Critical Civic Inquiry in Fostering Ethnic Identity and Civic Self-Efficacy," *Urban Education* 52(6): 699–717.
Hodgin, E., & Kahne, J. (2018) "Misinformation in the Information Age: What Teachers Can Do to Support Students," *Social Education* 82(4): 208–212.
James, C., Davis, K., Flores, A., Francis, J. M., Pettingill, L., Rundle, M., & Gardner, H. (2010) "Young People, Ethics, and the New Digital Media," *Contemporary Readings in Law and Social Justice* 2(2): 215–284.
Jones, L. M., & Mitchell, K. J. (2016) "Defining and Measuring Youth Digital Citizenship," *New Media & Society* 18(9): 2063–2079.
Jones, L. M., Mitchell, K. J., & Finkelhor, D. (2013) "Online Harassment in Context: Trends from Three Youth Internet Safety Surveys (2000, 2005, 2010)," *Psychology of Violence* 3(1): 53–69.
Kahne, J. (2005) *California Survey of Civic Education Survey Items*. Oakland, CA: Civic Engagement Research Group at Mills College (CERG).
Kahne, J., & Bowyer, B. (2017) "Educating for Democracy in a Partisan Age: Confronting the Challenges of Motivated Reasoning and Misinformation," *American Educational Research Journal* 54(1): 3–34.

Kahne, J., & Westheimer, J. (2006) "The Limits of Political Efficacy: Educating Citizens for a Democratic Society," *PS: Political Science & Politics* 39(2): 289–296.

Kaplan, A., & Flum, H. (2012) "Identity Formation in Educational Settings: A Critical Focus for Education in the 21st Century," *Contemporary Educational Psychology* 37(3): 171–175.

Kim, M., & Choi, D. (2018) "Development of Youth Digital Citizenship Scale and Implication for Educational Setting," *Journal of Educational Technology & Society* 21(1): 155–171.

Kirshner, B. (2009) "'Power in Numbers': Youth Organizing as a Context for Exploring Civic Identity," *Journal of Research on Adolescence* 19(3): 414–440.

Kroger, J., & Marcia, J. E. (2011) "The Identity Statuses: Origins, Meanings, and Interpretations," In S. J. Schwartz, K. Luyckx, & V. L. Vignoles (eds.) *Handbook of Identity Theory and Research*. New York: Springer, 31–53.

Lave, J., & Wenger, E. (1991) *Situated Learning: Legitimate Peripheral Participation*. Cambridge: Cambridge University Press.

Lerman, A., & Weaver, V. (2014) *Arresting Citizenship: The Democratic Consequences of* American *Crime Control*. Chicago: The University of Chicago Press.

Levine, P. & Kawashima-Ginsberg, K. (2015) *Civic Education and Deeper Learning*. Boston: Jobs for the Future.

Levine, P., & Kawashima-Ginsberg, K. (2017) *The Republic Is (Still) at Risk—and Civics Is Part of the Solution*. Medford, MA: Jonathan M. Tisch College of Civic Life.

Levitsky, S., & Ziblatt, D. (2018) *How Democracies Die*. New York: Broadway Books.

Liu, W. C., Wang, J. C. K., Tan, O. S., Koh, C., & Ee, J. (2009) "A Self-Determination Approach to Understanding Students' Motivation in Project Work," *Learning and Individual Differences* 19(1): 139–145.

Makkonen, T., Tirri, K., & Lavonen, J. (2021) "Engagement in Learning Physics through Project-Based Learning: A Case Study of Gifted Finnish Upper-Secondary-Level Students," *Journal of Advanced Academics* 32(4): 501–532.

Malin, H., Ballard, P. J., & Damon, W. (2015) "Civic Purpose: An Integrated Construct for Understanding Civic Development in Adolescence," *Human Development* 58(2): 103–130.

Marcia, J. E. (1966) "Development and Validation of Ego-Identity Status," *Journal of Personality and Social Psychology* 3(5): 551–558.

Martinez-Fuentes, S., Umaña-Taylor, A. J., Jager, J., Seaton, E. K., & Sladek, M. R. (2020) "An Examination of Ethnic-Racial Identity and US American Identity among Black, Latino, and White Adolescents," *Identity* 20(3): 208–223.

Mehta, J., & Fine, S. (2015) *The Why, What, Where, and How of Deeper Learning in American Secondary Schools*. Boston: Jobs for the Future.

Mehta, J., & Fine, S. (2019) *In Search of Deeper Learning*. Cambridge, MA: Harvard University Press.

Molina, L. E., Phillips, N. L., & Sidanius, J. (2015) "National and Ethnic Identity in the Face of Discrimination: Ethnic Minority and Majority Perspectives," *Cultural Diversity and Ethnic Minority Psychology* 21(2): 225–236.

Nasir, N. I. S., & Hand, V. (2008) "From the Court to the Classroom: Opportunities for Engagement, Learning, and Identity in Basketball and Classroom Mathematics," *The Journal of the Learning Sciences* 17(2): 143–179.

Pehrson, S., Vignoles, V. L., & Brown, R. (2009) "National Identification and Anti-Immigrant Prejudice: Individual and Contextual Effects of National Definitions," *Social Psychology Quarterly* 72(1): 24–38.

Penuel, W. R., & Wertsch, J. V. (1995) "Vygotsky and Identity Formation: A Sociocultural Approach," *Educational Psychologist* 30(2): 83–92.

Phinney, J. S., Cantu, C. L., & Kurtz, D. A. (1997) "Ethnic and American Identity as Predictors of Self-Esteem among African American, Latino, and White adolescents," *Journal of Youth and Adolescence* 26(2): 165–185.

Rai, T. S., & Fiske, A. P. (2011) "Moral Psychology Is Relationship Regulation: Moral Motives for Unity, Hierarchy, Equality, and Proportionality," *Psychological Review* 118(1): 57–75.

Rawls, J. (1971) *A Theory of Justice*. Cambridge, MA: Harvard University Press.

Ryan, R. M., & Deci, E. L. (2017) *Self-Determination Theory: Basic Psychological Needs in Motivation, Development, and Wellness*. New York: Guilford Press.

Schildkraut, D. J. (2014) "Boundaries of American Identity: Evolving Understandings of 'Us'," *Annual Review of Political Science* 17: 441–460.

Schulz, W., Ainley, J., Fraillon, J., Kerr, D., & Losito, B. (2010) *ICCS 2009 International Report: Civic Knowledge, Attitudes, and Engagement among Lower Secondary School Students in 38 Countries*. Amsterdam: International Association for the Evaluation of Educational Achievement (IEA).

Shresthova, S. (2016) "Between Storytelling and Surveillance: The Precarious Public of American Muslim Youth," in H. Jenkins, S. Shresthova, L. Gamber-Thompson, et al. (eds.) *By Any Media Necessary: The New Youth Activism*. New York: New York University Press, 149–185.

Stang, A. (forthcoming) "Co-Processing Narratives of Enslavement and Abolition," in *Teaching the Hard Histories of Racism: A Guide for K-12 Educators.*

Takahashi, S. (2011) "Co-constructing Efficacy: A 'Communities of Practice' Perspective on Teachers' Efficacy Beliefs," *Teaching and Teacher Education* 27(4): 732–741.

Tatum, B. (2017) *Why Are All the Black Kids Sitting Together in the Cafeteria?: And Other Conversations about Race.* New York: Basic Books.

Vignoles, V. L., Schwartz, S. J., & Luyckx, K. (2011) "Introduction: Toward an Integrative View of Identity," in S. J. Schwartz, K. Luyckx, V. L. Vignoles (eds.) *Handbook of Identity Theory and Research.* New York: Springer, 1–27.

Vraga, E. K., Tully, M., Kotcher, J. E., Smithson, A. B., & Broeckelman-Post, M. (2015) "A Multi-Dimensional Approach to Measuring News Media Literacy," *Journal of Media Literacy Education* 7(3): 41–53.

Walzer, M. (1994) *Thick and Thin: Moral Argument at Home and Abroad.* Notre Dame, IN: University of Notre Dame Press.

Wenger, E. (2010) "Communities of Practice and Social Learning Systems: The Career of a Concept," in C. Blackmore (ed.) *Social Learning Systems and Communities of Practice.* New York: Springer, 179–198.

Westheimer, J., & Kahne, J. (2004) "What Kind of Citizen? The Politics of Educating for Democracy," *American Educational Research Journal* 41(2): 237–269.

Youniss, J., McLellan, J. A., & Yates, M. (1997) "What We Know about Engendering Civic Identity," *American Behavioral Scientist* 40(5): 620–631.

Zaff, J., Boyd, M., Li, Y., Lerner, J. V., & Lerner, R. M. (2010) "Active and Engaged Citizenship: Multi-Group and Longitudinal Factorial Analysis of an Integrated Construct of Civic Engagement," *Journal of Youth and Adolescence* 39(7): 736–750.

3

ENABLING EVERYONE TO LIVE WELL

Randall Curren

Well-being in education has become an important focus of multidisciplinary research and reform efforts in recent years. This has been stimulated by the dramatic growth of interdisciplinary research on well-being, and by growing awareness of the limitations of education for economic competitiveness and damaging effects of associated pressures on students and teachers. Philosophers, psychologists, and others have brought a variety of perspectives to bear on the ethical and educational significance of students' and teachers' well-being and on living well or flourishing as an aim of education. Arguments have been made for the inherent and instrumental value of enhancing students' well-being, and an accumulating body of research suggests that schools that meet the needs crucial to student and teacher well-being are more likely to engender and sustain meaningful learning. Many educators have long accepted that unmet student needs can be an obstacle to learning and they have accepted some responsibility to address those needs. State education authorities have for their part begun to acknowledge the importance of student well-being, but they continue to resist the proposition that teacher well-being matters both inherently and as a foundation of student learning.

The ethical questions at stake cannot be adequately addressed without more specificity about the nature of the needs and aspects of well-being involved and how they should figure into an account of educational responsibilities or justice. What roles, if any, should well-being and needs play in a theory of justice, in defining a just system of education, or in conceptualizing a just school community? There are also important questions to address concerning the status of living well or flourishing as an aim, or as the *overarching* aim, of education. What is the basis of claims about the aims of education? What is flourishing and what is its role in the scheme of educational aims? How can education promote flourishing? These are the questions addressed in the sections that follow.

Well-Being, Happiness, and Flourishing

Well-being pertains to the quality of lives and the ways in which the lives of individuals of various species can go well or badly for them and be made better and worse by things good and bad for them.[1] Plants can exhibit well-being in this broad sense, as the conditions in which they live do, or do not, harm them and do, or do not, provide what is good for them. They can be said to thrive or flourish to the extent that they have what they need to sustain healthy growth and functioning characteristic of their species. Sentient creatures can similarly thrive or flourish, or not, but are distinctive in consciously experiencing some aspects of how well their lives are going. Pain is often a

DOI: 10.4324/9781003172246-5

sign of actual or prospective harm to an organism and its life prospects, both objective and subjective, for instance. Creatures that can think, form bonds and plans, and coordinate their actions in mutually agreeable ways can not only experience their lives as pleasant and painful, but also in such ways as more or less frustrating or satisfying, happy or unhappy, successful or unsuccessful, good or bad. Thought, language, and position in a social world add nuance and moral elements to the objective dimension of how well a life is going, nuance to its subjective dimension, and the possibility of self-assessments of life satisfaction that are more or less aligned with or transcend these objective and subjective dimensions of well-being.

These objective, subjective, and self-assessment aspects of well-being are all present in the lives of human beings, and this has given rise to a variety of philosophical and psychological conceptions and measures of well-being – objective, subjective, and hybrid conceptions of well-being, including conceptions of happiness and flourishing (*eudaimonia*, living well), and measures of subjective, somatic, mental health, and flourishing or eudaimonic well-being (Lee, Kubzansky & Vanderweele 2021; Vitterosø 2016a; David et al. 2013; Waterman 2013; Kahneman et al. 1999). Leading philosophical theories of happiness have regarded it in various ways – as a positive emotional state, as satisfaction with one's life, or as pleasure (Haybron 2013) – and psychologists have often used a self-report questionnaire that combines assessments of life satisfaction and balance of positive and negative affect (SWB or Subjective Well-Being; Diener 1984; Diener et al. 1985), or a related combination of scales, as a measure of happiness. This "state of mind" conception of happiness is often contrasted with a more comprehensive conception of happiness as a "life that goes well for the person leading it" (Vitterosø 2016b: 3; cf. Kraut 1979). The latter equates happiness with well-being in all its aspects, and in doing so deviates from ordinary usage. In wishing our friends health and happiness, for instance, we typically think of good health as foundational to happiness, not as part of it, though we would readily agree that these are two aspects of personal well-being. In the interest of clarity, I will speak of *happiness* exclusively in the ordinary "state of mind" sense, and use the term *flourishing* to signify a comprehensive, all-inclusive, or *eudaimonic* conception of well-being.[2]

The principal source of this second conception of happiness is the classical Greek term *eudaimonia*, as used by Aristotle, and the fact that it has often, though not altogether convincingly, been translated as "happiness." The announced topic of Aristotle's *Nicomachean Ethics* is living well (*eu zên*) or – what is presented as synonymous – *eudaimonia*, the highest end to which all human beings aspire (Barnes 1984: 1730 [*NE* I.1–2 1095a15–20]). What do people aspire to? Do they "just want to be happy"? I am convinced that Aristotle accurately perceived that what human beings aspire to is living well or flourishing in a sense that implies a life both happy and admirable (*kalon*). The kind of life that he identifies as what is in fact the best in this two-fold sense – the singularly happiest and most admirable life of which human beings are capable – is one that makes theoretical contemplation (*theoria*) in conformity with theoretical wisdom (*sophia*) its highest aim (Kraut 1989; Reeve 2012; Curren 2019). This conception of the naturally best life for human beings is the basis of his claim that "there are branches of learning and education which we must study merely with a view to leisure spent in intellectual activity, and these are to be valued for their own sake" (Barnes 1984: 2122 [*Pol.* VIII.3 1338a8–12]), though there is more to his theory of education than this implies (Curren 2000, 2013b). The narrowness and empirical implausibility of this specific conception of flourishing disqualifies it as a basis for contemporary social and educational policy and practice, but the underlying idea that fulfilling one's potential well is the key to happiness and a good life has many adherents.

The broadly Aristotelian conception of human flourishing that has been immensely influential in the philosophy and psychology of well-being, and in philosophy of education, is typically taken to be a comprehensive conception of well-being encompassing healthy or optimal growth and functioning, implying fulfillment of potential (implicitly or explicitly 'positive' or optimal in its qualities) and happiness in a sense that includes both pleasure and satisfaction (Ryan et al. 2013).[3] A central aspect of this understanding of flourishing, and one that has been the focus of considerable research, is the "Aristotelian Hypothesis" that fulfilling our potential well – which is to say, in activities that exhibit goodness or virtues – is foundational to happiness. Suffice it to say, for now, that there is substantial empirical support for this hypothesis (Curren 2019, 2013a; Ryan & Deci 2017; Curren & Metzger 2017: 80–84; Besser-Jones 2014). It does not follow that all activities that a person can engage in admirably are also pleasant and satisfying for her – there is no singularly best activity for all human beings. There is thus some tendency among researchers and educators to think of flourishing in terms of an *individual's* potential, which roughly translates as the fulfillments of their human potentialities that would be best *for them* (in the two-fold sense or in light of a comprehensive conception of well-being).[4] A recent definition of flourishing in philosophy of education that reflects this broadly Aristotelian conception of human flourishing defines it as "optimal continuing development of human beings' potentials," notably in relationships and "activities that are meaningful, i.e. aligned with both their own values and humanistic values, in a way that is satisfying to them" (De Ruyter, Oades and Waghid, 2020).[5]

Research on flourishing has involved combinations of measurement instruments, including SWB and measures of stress (e.g., cortisol levels), mental health, and quality of task engagement (e.g., energy, persistence, and "flow" [Csikszentmihalyi 1990]), while various self-report instruments have been proposed as comprehensive measures of "optimal human functioning" (PWB or Psychological Well-Being; Ryff 2016: 95; Ryff & Keyes 1995) or flourishing (e.g., the PERMA-Profiler measure [Butler & Kern 2015]; see also Lee, Kubzansky & VanderWeele 2021). Kennon Sheldon has rightly observed that insofar as the latter are comprehensive measures of well-being or flourishing, they are not strictly measures of *psychological* well-being, and in doing well-being research what we often need is distinct measures of different aspects of well-being, so we can better understand how the latter are related to one another (Sheldon 2016, 2018). We want to understand such things as the impact of life goal orientations (e.g., image, wealth, and status-seeking *versus* personal growth, relationship, or service oriented) on happiness. Living well is largely a matter of the activities in which one engages, so measures of flourishing and attempts to promote it would properly focus on *eudaimonic activities* – activities that fulfill our potential in ways that are at the same time both good and personally satisfying (Curren 2019, 2020b; Sheldon 2018; Charles 2015).

The Ethical Significance of Students' Present Well-Being

With this understanding of well-being, happiness, and flourishing in mind, we can now address their significance in the sphere of education. Several aspects of students' well-being matter ethically. Perhaps most obviously, the unhappiness, stress, and loss of childhood pleasures that many students experience in high-stakes, poorly funded, and often punitive learning environments diminish their present happiness and often their physical and mental health. Health, happiness, and these pleasures or *goods* of childhood – such as carefree play – have ethical significance that should weigh heavily in decisions that affect the lives of children (Macleod 2018; Bagattini & Macleod 2015; Brennan 2014). This ethical significance must be given due consideration in assessing the consequences of educational decisions made from the highest levels of policy to the most granular ones made at countless points in the day of a classroom.

Such weighing of children's well-being in assessing the likely consequences of educational decisions is not enough to fulfill educators' responsibilities to their students, however. Even if we add that ongoing sacrifice of an individual child's present well-being could only be justified on the grounds that it would advance that very child's future well-being, there is more to consider than aggregate consequences.[6] While the impact of acts and policies on increments of well-being always matter ethically, we must ask whether there are also specific duties or rights at stake, principles of justice regarding access to goods that are essential to well-being, or specific needs that must be met as a matter of justice. A partial, legalistic answer is that, at least in common law jurisdictions such as the U.S., the state has responsibilities to safeguard and promote the well-being and developmental interests of all children, and these responsibilities are given effect in standards of custodial care for institutions. With regard to schools, these typically include provisions pertaining to safety, adequacy of instruction, and meals. Yet, from an ethical standpoint – the standpoint of justice – it is an open question how a government's "duty of protection to consult the welfare, comfort and interests of [each] child in regulating its custody during the period of its minority" should be spelled out as specific requirements of justice (*In re Gould*, 174 Mich. 6663 (1913)).

Resolving this question is beyond the scope of this chapter, but there are at least three general approaches that could be considered. The first, developed by John Rawls (Rawls 1971), identifies a set of *primary goods*, conceptualized as "social conditions and all-purpose means that are generally necessary" to pursuing a good life (Rawls 2001: 57). These are mostly conceived with adults in mind, and this limits their value for understanding what a society owes children with respect to their present well-being, as opposed to their future adult powers, rights, and opportunities. Rawls counts *institutional bases of self-respect* as a primary good (58), and this clearly imposes a duty on educational institutions to treat all children as equals, however different they may be with respect to race, ethnicity, or other differences.[7] The significance of this for children's happiness and overall well-being can hardly be exaggerated, but the direct significance of other primary goods, such as *freedom of movement and choice of occupation*, would be limited to preparatory or future-regarding aspects of schooling.

The Capabilities Approach (CA) as developed by Martha Nussbaum has wider direct significance for children's well-being in educational contexts, because it identifies *central capabilities* to function in ways that are for the most part essential to being and living well across the lifespan, such as having good health, bodily integrity, pleasurable experiences, and using one's imagination in "experiencing and producing works and events of one's own choice" (Nussbaum 2011: 33; cf. 2003). Education would properly focus on nurturing *internal capabilities* – the developmental aspects of *combined capabilities* (or simply *capabilities*), the substantive freedoms to function in ways essential to living well in the social, political, and economic circumstances of one's life (Nussbaum 2011: 20–21). Schools could scarcely succeed in this developmental task without allowing and encouraging children to actually function in these ways (23), so a CA perspective on educational justice with respect to children's development would warrant an ongoing – not just future – empowerment of children that would be favorable to their present well-being. As institutions that are not just responsible for the development of internal capabilities but play a significant role in determining children's *combined capabilities* or what they can actually be and do *in the institutional circumstances of their lives*, schools would also have duties of justice that are not subordinate to their preparatory function. Nussbaum presents her version of the CA as a human rights approach by making a case for regarding capabilities to function in ways sufficient for a minimally decent life of dignity as human rights. Affirming these as human rights across the lifespan would have the effect of specifying fundamental custodial duties with respect to foundational aspects of children's present well-being, as well as their future well-being. One of those duties, undoubtedly beneficial to students' well-being, would be to provide them with opportunities to use their imagination in "experiencing and producing works and events of [their] own choice" (Nussbaum 2011: 33).

A third approach would identify rights pertaining to the satisfaction of *basic needs* related to the fulfillment of human potentials important to living well. Variations on such a view might be little different from Nussbaum's version of the CA, but (in Curren 2022) I have identified starting points for one that is distinctive in focusing on needs that play a central role in the psychological research that is arguably most helpful to addressing the relationships between children's well-being and their academic progress. These psychological needs can arguably function as a comprehensive set of basic needs, much as *physical health* and *autonomy* are intended to do in the influential needs-based approach of Len Doyal and Ian Gough (Doyal & Gough 1991). As in their approach and the one developed by Gillian Brock (Brock 2009), the needs in question are foundational to human agency, and thereby success in participating in society and pursuing goals. Addressing students' needs has been a significant aspect of educators' understanding of their responsibilities (as noted above), but the language of needs has played a remarkably small role in theories of justice (Brock & Miller 2019) and work in the ethics of education. We can begin to rectify this by recognizing that creating conditions in schools that are *need-supportive* or favorable to the satisfaction of the psychological needs in question might be conducive to students' present well-being, conducive to students' academic success, and ethically compulsory on a needs-focused theory of educational justice.

Well-Being, Needs, and Learning

Turning to the relationships between children's well-being and their academic progress, there is a robust body of evidence establishing the causal significance of positive emotions for physical health and longevity (Conway et al. 2013; Fredrickson 2013). Institutional arrangements that induce a preponderance of negative emotions in students are likely to result in additional harm to their health and life outcomes. Furthermore, we have decades of widely replicated research: (1) indicating that student learning and conduct are strongly influenced by satisfactions and frustrations of basic psychological needs that are predictive of happiness and unhappiness: and (2) identifying specific ways in which learning environments and teacher behaviors can be more or less *need-supportive* or favorable to the satisfaction of these needs (Ryan & Deci 2017: 351–381). This shows that student well-being and academic success are interrelated in ways that make a focus on what students need doubly important. It also identifies specific forms of need-support that make a difference to both well-being and learning.

To be specific, Basic Psychological Needs Theory (BPNT) posits the existence of three universal psychological needs defined as *nutrients that are essential for growth, integrity, and well-being* (Ryan & Deci 2017: 10–12, 80–101). Frustration of these needs leads to observable and serious psychological and somatic harms related to impairment of growth, integrity, thriving, and fulfillment of potential. From a philosophical perspective, these needs constitute "Aristotelian necessities" (Foot 2001: 15) for living well or flourishing, while felt aspects of need frustration and satisfaction constitute natural signs of things good and bad for human beings (Curren 2013a, 2019).[8] The needs are for *autonomy* (self-directedness congruent with personal values and sense of self), *relatedness* (a supportive social climate and affirming relationships), and *competence* (experiencing oneself as capable); and the related potentialities can be broadly categorized as *intellectual* or *agentive* (the potential for rational self-determination), *social*, and *productive* (the potential to create and do things) (Ryan et al. 2013; Curren 2013a, 2022). A central, cross-culturally replicated finding is that the satisfaction of all three of these basic psychological needs through fulfillment of related potentials is essential to and predictive of well-being, measured in a variety of ways (Chirkov et al. 2011; Ryan et al. 2008; Ryan & Deci, 2001, 2017). Related research on the relationships between Nussbaum's central capabilities and well-being, and between perceived access to Rawls's primary goods and well-being, have shown that these relationships are mediated by satisfaction of the three basic psychological needs (DeHaan et al. 2016; Bradshaw et al. forthcoming).[9]

BPNT is a key explanatory component of Self-Determination Theory (SDT), which has grown from an influential series of studies on intrinsic and extrinsic motivation five decades ago to a systematic theory of motivation, development, and well-being, built on decades of widely replicated research (Ryan & Deci 2017). Important to understanding the relationships between student well-being and learning is the fact that basic psychological needs play key roles not only in well-being but in learning, through the regulation of motivation and uptake and integration of values and goals. Satisfaction of children's relational, competence, and autonomy needs grounds their acceptance of new goals and values as their own, and autonomous motivation (acting from values and goals that one identifies as one's own) is the only kind of motivation that is consistently positively associated with academic achievement (Taylor et al. 2014). Attempts to motivate learning through controlling pressure (e.g., high-stakes exams or shaming) tend to displace autonomous motivation (including intrinsic or curiosity and interest-based motivation), and yield less meaningful learning. Absence of intrinsic motivation is bad for learning and for students (Gottfried et al. 2008).

What studies find is that extrinsic goal framing of the reasons students should engage in learning (e.g., to do well on tests) is counterproductive (Vansteenkiste et al. 2009). Lack of need-support predicts amotivation, low academic performance, low academic self-esteem, behavioral problems, and intention to drop out of school (Legault et al. 2006), whereas support for students' autonomy, relatedness, and competence needs tends to sustain students' autonomous motivation to learn (Jang et al. 2010) and has value in reducing violence and promoting friendliness and caring among students (Assor, Kaplan, Feinberg & Tal 2009; Kaplan & Assor 2012). Satisfaction of these needs is also foundational to character development generally (Curren 2017; Curren & Ryan 2020). Putting controlling pressure on teachers is similarly counterproductive. It tends to undermine the quality of teaching by triggering controlling behaviors toward students, frustrating the latter's needs for autonomy and positive connection, and preempting autonomous motivation to learn (Ryan & Brown 2005; Pelletier & Sharp 2009). All three of teachers' basic psychological needs may be frustrated in the process, as they are compelled to act in ways they often experience as failures to serve their students' interests (see Santoro 2018).

With regard to what is and is not need-supportive, a distinctive contribution of SDT has been to identify eight specific teacher behaviors that are autonomy supportive: "listening to students, making time for students' independent work, giving students an opportunity to talk, acknowledging signs of improvement and mastery, encouraging students' effort, offering progress-enabling hints when students [seem] stuck, being responsive to students' comments and questions, and acknowledging students' experiences and perspectives" (Ryan & Deci 2017: 367; see Reeve & Jang 2006; Reeve et al. 1999). Need-support with respect to competence pertains to optimizing the degree, pace, and variety of challenge through the structuring of learning tasks and guidance, so that students can experience progress in meeting challenges. The need for positive relatedness is as much a need to affirm others' value as it is a need to receive such affirmation, and its satisfaction and frustration are a function of the qualities not only of ongoing relationships, but also transitory social interactions and the wider social world one inhabits. Relational need-support in schools must therefore encompass teacher-student relationships ("Does my teacher like me?"), peer relationships ("Can I make friends in my school?"), and the social tenor of the school generally ("Is there tension and conflict? Are people treated unfairly? Are the people in this school kind and caring?")

In sum, the lessons of well-established research findings for promoting students' present well-being are that: (1) students' positive emotions are important to their health, longevity, and other well-being outcomes; (2) students' present well-being and educational progress are substantially co-regulated by how need-supportive their learning environments are; (3) there are identifiable educational reforms that could make educational environments and teaching more need-supportive, and thereby better for students – more favorable to their present well-being, learning, and progress in living well. The cumulative lessons of this section and the preceding one are that (a) students' present well-being matters because it is ethically important in its own right; (b) it is important as an object of educators' custodial responsibilities that can be specified as matters of fundamental justice; and (c) it is instrumentally important to and deeply *entangled with* students' learning. Some sacrifice of near-term well-being may be unavoidable in preparing children for the future, but such trade-offs are not as empirically or ethically as simple as they may seem. It is time to ask what role students' future well-being or flourishing should play in our understanding of educational aims.

Why Flourishing? Justifying Educational Aims

Ideas about the nature and aims of education are often interrelated, as they are in assertions about *real* or *true* education. Much as Aristotle did, we may conceive of a true, proper, or just institution as one that serves or fulfills a function that defines its nature. One might say, as Martha Nussbaum has, that "Resistance to female education is increased when its proponents push for *real* education, by which I mean an overall empowerment of the woman" (Nussbaum 2003: 340, italics added). In this instance, as in Aristotle, real or proper education is determined not by how existing institutions *do* function but by a background theory of how they *should* function – in this case, to empower, create internal capabilities, or promote the development of attributes conducive to living well (Nussbaum 2003, 2011).

In seeking to justify claims about the aims of education, is there any alternative to relying on a background theory of justice? I shall argue there is not. The social scientific and conceptual alternatives do not work. They more or less assume that it is in the nature of education to have inherent purposes or aims that can be revealed through social science or the analysis of concepts that track reality.

An approach that was quite influential in sociology of education assumed that what determines an institution's true nature or defining function is its role in an existing social system. This is illustrated by the neo-Marxist educational sociology of the 1970s, which held that the failure of public schooling in the U.S. to create economic and social equality was not an accident but a product of its success in serving its actual function, which was to preserve forms of inequality required by a capitalist economy (Bowles & Gintis 1977). The underlying *functionalist* doctrine was that economic relationships are "primary" or determine the functions of other institutions, and those other "secondary" institutions – including educational institutions – have no independent power to shape any other institution (Baker 2014). The conservative spin on this doctrine is that the function of education is *of course* to serve the interests of the economy, and that it often fails or is inefficient by this measure. Functionalist models of educational systems have been largely supplanted by *credentialist* (e.g., Collins 1979) and *neo-institutionalist* (e.g., Baker 2014) alternatives, which view the development of educational systems as a product of the interests of the individuals involved, notably students' and families' interest in obtaining credentials that confer competitive advantage. These non-functionalist alternatives do not posit the existence of an inherent institutional function. Even if they did, it would not tell us what the function or purpose of educational systems *should* be. The ethical relevance of explanatory models of how educational systems function is simply to inform our understanding of what is possible and how what is desirable and possible is best achieved.[10]

The ideas about educational aims offered by other social sciences are no more apt for defining or prioritizing educational purposes. An anthropological approach might be to regard educational institutions as ones that initiate the young into the practices and norms of a culture and community, while historical approaches might trace and contrast the varied ways in which different approaches to education have prepared differently situated students in different ways for different kinds of lives and social roles. The understanding of education these disciplines provide could be immensely helpful in ensuring we take less for granted about what is inevitable and desirable in education, but it would not dictate what we aspire to as a society or in our own educational endeavors. These are the questions fundamentally at stake: *What* should we aspire to achieve through education, collectively and individually? *How* do we succeed in this aspiration?

A different approach, predicated on conceptual analysis, reached its zenith shortly before neo-Marxist functionalist approaches did in the 1970s (Curren et al. 2003). Most influential in advancing this approach was R. S. (Richard) Peters, whose examination of the terms *education*, *training*, and *conditioning* led him to hold that education "involves essentially processes which intentionally transmit what is valuable in an intelligible and voluntary manner and which create in the learner a desire to achieve it," the processes being initiation into forms of knowledge through which powers of mind are enhanced (Peters 2007 [1965]: 63; see Curren 2020c).[11] If we supposed that all this is really built into our word *education* and its counterparts in other languages and eras, what would it show? Would it tell us that transmitting forms of knowledge and enhancing powers of mind are the only aims consistent with the nature of education? What normative or ethical weight would it have? The answer to this question is that its normative weight would be merely linguistic. In itself, it would neither justify education so conceived nor disqualify alternatives to it. If we have good ethical reasons to prioritize initiating students into human practices that could be arenas of *eudaimonic activity* for them, and those practices include ones that do not qualify as forms of knowledge, all that Peters' exercise in conceptual analysis could show is that our justified initiation of students into such non-epistemic practices could not properly be called *educating*, and the benefits would not qualify as aspects of an *education*. We should then, in deference to proper English usage, be required to call the initiation into human practices we are ethically justified in providing something else. We could invent a new word for it. Or another way to reform our linguistic practices would simply be to carry on with the word "education" and agree that the better schools we're operating will count as educational institutions.

A Constructivist Alternative

Having eliminated some variations on the theme that educational institutions have inherent or *natural* aims, revealed by science or by distinctions of language that reveal the nature of things, I propose a *constructivist* alternative – an approach that sets aside questions about *true* aims (or *truths* about educational aims) and focuses on what aims and ordering of aims we *have reason* to accept as authoritative in educational policy and practice. Aims of education are from this perspective "constructions of reason."

The constructivist arguments of Kant and Rawls present us with thought experiments in which we adopt an impartial perspective on what we would choose to impose on ourselves collectively as rules of morality (Kant) or constitutional principles (Rawls), imaging that we know general truths about human beings and nothing specific about ourselves.[12] In Rawls's "Original Position" version of this, the general truths we can know include matters of scientific consensus (Rawls 1971, 2001). Adopting this methodology, we could ask not only what the principles regulating society's major institutions should be, but also how their functions or aims should be defined. I have argued that our general answer would be that the point of living in a society and having institutions would be to enable us to live well or flourish – from an impartial perspective, all of us, to the extent that is possible – and that we would recognize the need for institutions that enable individuals to develop the attributes that are conducive to living well (Curren 2013a, b; Curren & Metzger 2017: 72–86). It is reasonable to call these formative institutions educational, and it is not inconsistent with the ideal of free and equal citizenship in a pluralistic society (or Rawls's ground rules for what can be considered behind the "veil of ignorance") to rely on central findings in SDT in arguing that the basic categories of attributes in question are capabilities, understanding, and virtues.[13] This is the basic outline of a constructivist argument for identifying flourishing or living well as the general aim of education and identifying the development of these forms of personal attributes as sub-aims. Given what is known about the foundational role of basic psychological needs and need-support in human development, well-being, and rewarding fulfillment of potential – i.e., flourishing – one could continue by working out the details of a need-focused account of educational justice.[14]

How Can Education Promote Flourishing?

If the foregoing is correct, then an essential aspect of just societies is that they provide all children with educational institutions whose fundamental task is to prepare them to live well. Living well involves ongoing fulfillment of each of three basic forms of human potential – agentive, social, and productive – and enabling students to fulfill this potential involves the cultivation of associated capabilities, understanding, and virtues. Cultivating these attributes depends, in turn, on schools supporting the satisfaction of students' basic psychological needs for autonomy, relatedness, and competence. Essential to the success of this enterprise is that students have *pathways of opportunity* within and beyond their schools and experience themselves as making progress along those pathways in living well (Curren 2020b, forthcoming). Without this, schools can neither justly expect nor reliably obtain students' willing cooperation in the school's mission (Curren 2020a).

People are, of course, different in their strengths, inclinations, tastes, and backgrounds, and consequently different also in what they become good at and find personally rewarding. In order to experience the progress in their lives that is important to their present happiness and life prospects, they will need many and varied opportunities to discover what kinds of activities and pursuits can be eudaimonic *for them*. In simple terms, they need opportunities to discover what they can be good at and like doing. From the perspective of what makes for a meaningful life, this also involves opportunities to expand their horizons of value – opportunities for them to encounter and value the goods at stake in a vast and evolving world of human practices they might find meaningful. Experiencing competence, positive connection to others, and self-determination in devoting oneself to things that have value independent of oneself is what eudaimonic activities consist of, and having such experiences is what children most need in order to experience progress in their lives.

In order to provide the opportunities that students need to find their way in living well, schools must consequently set aside the notion that their mission is simply to equip students with "knowledge and skills" that are instrumentally useful to them outperforming each other and "getting ahead" in a quest for wealth and status. Since having materialistic values is demonstrably bad for people – leading to lower-quality personal relationships, lower personal well-being, and more health problems (Kasser, 2016; Ryan & Deci 2017) – educational leaders should systematically examine the values that permeate schools, define school missions that are not just about students getting ahead, reframe the value of education in less instrumental terms (see Brighouse 2005, 2008; Curren 2020b; de Ruyter 2007), and "teach happiness." That is, they should provide direct instruction in the science and philosophy of wellbeing and related skills of self-care – knowledge of what is actually conducive to happiness, reflectiveness about what it would mean to live a good life oneself, and self-regulative capacities (Morris 2015; Seligman et al. 2009; Waters 2011).

Educational systems must also recognize that while students' progress in living well involves strands of development and activities that will never be the basis of paid employment, a eudaimonically just society will involve fair terms of cooperation in enabling everyone to live well, to the extent this is possible. This necessarily involves educating students in ways that equip them to contribute to others being able to live well. It won't always, or even the majority of the time, involve paid employment, but often it will, and students' experience of progress in their lives will depend in part on seeing a financially viable path forward.

School leaders should define value-focused school missions with an eye to creating cooperative school communities that are *eudaimonic* – conducive to flourishing – and *just* in the opportunities they provide, their disciplinary practices, and their general treatment of students. The ideal of *just school communities* is an important one from the perspective of value acquisition, disciplinary policies, and the social life of schools – things that matter a great deal to the present well-being and life prospects of students, particularly those who struggle to meet academic and behavioral expectations. Elaborating this ideal from the standpoint of psychologically-informed eudaimonic justice is helpful to understanding how damaging exclusionary punishments of children are, and why and how schools should be more focused on nurturing students' capacities of rational self-governance (Curren 2020a). Self-regulation and judgment are foundational to students fulfilling their agentive potential and living well, and they are built on more than disciplinary knowledge that usefully informs students' understanding of the world (Curren 2014). Schools must structure learning in ways that promote ethical reflection and allow students to develop and exercise their own judgment, while acquiring the understanding essential to making their way in the world. Providing opportunities for students to use and develop their own judgment does not require giving students direct democratic control of schools, as Lawrence Kohlberg's original model of just school communities envisioned (Power 1988), but it should involve "enlisting students in taking responsibility for the school's success in ways that rely on their own developing judgment and satisfy their need for (bounded) autonomy" (Curren 2020a: 128).

Seriousness about students' well-being and future flourishing would require more focus on the qualities of student engagement in activities of learning, and less on the acquisition of knowledge and skills *per se*.[15] The structuring of activities should provide choice, supporting students' need for self-determination. It should optimize the level of difficulty to sustain growth while enabling students to experience themselves as competent most of the time. It should enable students to relate to others – teachers and peers – in ways that enable them to satisfy their need for positive connection. A eudaimonically just school community would nurture a *partnership in learning* involving shared authority and responsibility for the community's success in its mission to enable everyone in it to live well. No such partnership and mission can succeed unless teachers' own needs and judgment are respected. This involves hiring teachers who are prepared to promote the flourishing of all students and giving them the space and support to experience the inherent rewards of excelling in this.[16]

Conclusion

For generations, parents have made sacrifices in order to give their children a better future – a future in which they are successful and respected members of their communities, enjoying some security in the rewards this entails. They have needed to believe in a world of opportunity in which we can all live well for generations to come, if we all contribute to society in ways that sustain opportunities for others to live well. Today, as the ways we live have an impact on planetary systems that threaten to permanently diminish opportunities to live well in the future (Curren & Metzger 2017, 2019), it may seem ludicrous to suggest we should refocus education on enabling everyone to live well. How many people will have any serious prospect of flourishing? Shouldn't we be preparing students for generation upon generation of sacrifices, just to stabilize the systems and institutions we have too long taken for granted? A concluding answer to this perfectly reasonable challenge is that focusing on what is actually essential to living well, instead of economic growth, is profoundly important. More people could be happier with less – living better, more flourishing lives, with less damaging impact – if we focused on what we actually need.

(Related Chapters: 1, 2, 4, 5, 6, 8, 10, 13, 14, 15, 16, 32, 34, 35.)

Notes

1 Valerie Tiberius emphasizes that well-being is a prudential concept, not an inherently moral one, in holding that "well-being in the broadest sense is what we have when our lives are going well for us, when we are living lives that are not necessarily morally good, but good *for us*" (Tiberius 2006: 493). This does not rule out the possibility – which many of us concerned with well-being believe to be actually the case – that moral qualities matter to our well-being, prudentially, in such a way that it is *good for us* and essential to our well-being that we possess and enact virtues in the activities of our lives. See, e.g., Foot 2001.

2 It is worth noting that this comprehensive or eudaimonic conception of well-being is sometimes seen as entailing a kind of completeness, such that a flourishing life is "lacking in nothing that would make it richer or better" (Nussbaum 2008: s90). The alternative I am recommending is more in line with Nussbaum's Capability Approach (CA) to justice in the promotion of human functioning consistent with living well (Nussbaum 2003, 2011), in taking all aspects of well-being to be ethically significant while understanding *flourishing* or living well as a threshold concept. On this view, individuals can be described as living well or flourishing if they are doing well in all relevant respects, even if they suffer misfortunes that diminish their happiness or lack things that might make their lives better.

3 See Vitterosø 2016b for a table of 41 descriptions of eudaimonia, where the elements of what I describe as typical appear repeatedly.

4 This is sometimes discussed in terms of a *true* or *authentic* self (e.g., Schlegel et al. 2013), but what is ethically and educationally important is respect for self-determination and providing sufficiently diverse opportunities for children to discover what they can be good at and find rewarding – what kinds of activities can be eudaimonic *for them*. This can be described quite accurately as involving a process of self-discovery, without invoking the concept of a true self. On the ethics of supporting children in this process of self-discovery essential to flourishing, see Curren 2020b.

5 Kristján Kristjánsson's definition of flourishing notably omits any reference to pleasure, satisfaction, or happiness, in taking flourishing to be "the (relatively) unencumbered, freely chosen and developmentally progressive activity of a meaningful (subjectively purposeful and objectively valuable) life that actualises satisfactorily an individual human being's natural capacities in areas of species-specific existential tasks at which human beings (as rational, social, moral and emotional agents) can most successfully excel" (Kristjánsson 2020: 1, 10). It is in this respect not a comprehensive conception of well-being and is less apt as an aim of education or concern of justice. For further work on the conceptualization of flourishing in philosophy of education, see de Ruyter 2004, 2007, 2015; de Ruyter & Wolbert 2020; Wolbert et al. 2015, 2018; Kristjánsson 2016. Harry Brighouse has argued that education should "aim to improve children's prospects for leading flourishing lives" (Brighouse 2008: 60), while declining to step into controversies surrounding the concept of flourishing. His approach relies on Richard Layard's (2005) "Big Seven" list of predictors of happiness as a proxy for antecedents of flourishing (Brighouse 2006, 2008: Brighouse et al. 2018), on the assumption that we have good evidence regarding what is conducive to happiness but "no direct evidence concerning what makes people flourish" (Brighouse 2008: 62). The use he makes of Layard's list (financial situation, family relationships, work, community and friends, health, personal freedom, and personal values; Layard 2005) nevertheless reveals an implicit understanding of flourishing as involving fulfillment of basic forms of human potential (e.g., social and creative) and values compatible with fulfilling those forms of potential well. The research in Self-Determination Theory (SDT) that is addressed later in this chapter does bear directly on what enables people to flourish, and Brighouse relies on it indirectly (regarding values or life goal orientations) through his references to a decade of SDT research summarized by SDT researcher Tim Kasser (Kasser 2002).

6 I am sidestepping some obvious complications here, such as the fact that teachers must frequently make decisions that balance the interests of some students against those of other students and must do so on the fly as situations in their classrooms unfold. The reference to *ongoing* sacrifice of an individual child's present well-being is meant to acknowledge this reality, while noting that ethically conscientious teachers would aim for equity over the long run, so that no student's near-term or long-term well-being was being sacrificed to that of others' near-term or long-term well-being. Another complication pertains to discipline and punishment in educational contexts, and whether punishment that sacrifices a child's near-term or long-term well-being to that of other children could be justified. My position is that justifiable disciplinary policies would not have this effect; they would benefit the child disciplined as well as the school community generally (Curren 2020a).

7 On the related theme of self-esteem in education, see Ferkany (2008).

8 Following Foot (2001: 15), I use the term "Aristotelian necessities" to refer to necessities that must be fulfilled in order for a member of a species "to be as they should be, and to do that which they should do" in order to live well or flourish.

9 It would be similarly predictable that the antecedents of happiness that Brighouse has relied on as a proxy for antecedents of flourishing (Brighouse 2006, 2008; Brighouse et al. 2018) are related to happiness and flourishing (as defined in this chapter) in ways that are mediated by the satisfaction of these same psychological needs and fulfillment of related forms of potential.

10 Regarding what is possible, it is significant that neo-institutionalism is not wed to the view that educational systems are merely "secondary" institutions that have no independent power to shape society. David Baker argues that his fellow sociologists have been so fixated on the Industrial Revolution that they have failed to recognize we are in the midst of a global Educational Revolution that has radically transformed the world, including the nature of work (Baker 2014). Grasping this could be helpful to enacting meaningful educational reform in the service of human flourishing. See Curren (2017) and (forthcoming).

11 In using an example of conceptual analysis from Peters' work I do not intend to be offering a critique of other arguments he made in defense of his conception of education as initiation into forms of knowledge. It would take us too far afield to examine those other arguments in order to supplement the argument I am making that what is required to justify claims about educational aims is *ethical* arguments. All I have the space for here is to eliminate two influential alternatives to ethical arguments.

12 See also Scanlon (1998), whose moral constructivism I briefly address in Curren & Ryan (2020).
13 If the approach these arguments yield is "perfectionistic," it is a form of perfectionism consistent with liberal neutrality regarding a diversity of reasonable conceptions of the good. I argue in Curren (2022) that it is not "perfectionistic" in the anti-pluralistic sense in which this charge has been made by "hedonic" psychologists against SDT's eudaimonism.
14 Careful readers will grasp that on the resulting conception of the aims of education, schools that effectively advance these aims are good for children because they provide things that human children need, because they share a specific life form. The goodness of good schools will be, in an obvious sense, *natural*. This is correct, but it does not entail any requirement of morality or justice that schools provide what children need. Constructivism provides a bridge from what is good and bad to what is right and wrong, required as a matter of justice and forbidden.
15 It is an open question whether proper regard for students' well-being requires *systemic* rethinking of curricula. See White (2011) for an argument that schools should abandon a curriculum of traditional school subjects in the interest of students' well-being. A contrasting view is that a general education in some forms of disciplinary knowledge may be essential to acquiring the good judgment, grounded in understanding of the world, that is foundational to adult flourishing (Curren 2014).
16 I am grateful to Gina Schouten, Jason Blokhuis, Matt Ferkany, and Tony Laden for providing some very helpful editorial suggestions and comments on the penultimate draft of this chapter.

References

Assor, A., Kaplan, H., Feinberg, O., & Tal, K. (2009) "Combining Vision with Voice: A Learning and Implementation Structure Promoting Teachers' Internalization of Practices based on Self-Determination Theory." *Theory and Research in Education* 7(2): 234–243.

Bagattini, A. & Macleod, Ca. (eds.) (2015) *The Nature of Children's Well-being: Theory and Practice*. Dordrecht: Springer.

Baker, D. P. (2014) *The Schooled Society: The Educational Transformation of Global Culture*. Stanford, CA: Stanford University Press.

Barnes, J. (1984) *The Complete Works of Aristotle*, vol. 2. Princeton: Princeton University Press.

Besser-Jones, L. (2014) *Eudaimonic Ethics: The Philosophy and Psychology of Living Well*. New York: Routledge.

Bowles, S. & Gintis, H. (1977) *Schooling in Capitalist America: Educational Reform and The Contradictions of Economic Life*. New York: Basic Books.

Bradshaw, E., DeHaan, C., Parker, P., Curren, R., Duineveld, J., Di Domenico, S., & Ryan, R. (forthcoming) "The Perceived Conditions for Living Well: Positive Perceptions of Primary Goods linked with Basic Psychological Needs and Wellness," *Journal of Positive Psychology*, 10.1080/17439760.2021.1991446https://psyarxiv.com/c8sj4/.

Brennan, S. (2014) "The Goods of Childhood and Children's Rights," in F. Baylis & C. Mcleod (eds.) *Family-Making: Contemporary Ethical Challenges*. Oxford: Oxford University Press, 29–45.

Brighouse, H. (2005) "Channel One, the Anti-Commercial Principle, and the Discontinuous Ethos," *Educational Policy* 19(3): 528–549.

Brighouse, H. (2006) *On Education*. London: Routledge.

Brighouse, H. (2008) "Education for a Flourishing Life," *Yearbook of the National Society for the Study of Education* 107(1): 58–71.

Brighouse, H., Ladd, H. F., Loeb, S., & Swift, A. (2018) *Educational Goods: Values, Evidence, and Decision-making*. Chicago: University of Chicago Press.

Brock, G. (2009) *Global Justice: A Cosmopolitan Account*. Oxford: Oxford University Press.

Brock, G. & Miller, D. (2019) "Needs in Moral and Political Philosophy," in E. N. Zalta (ed.) *The Stanford Encyclopedia of Philosophy* (Summer 2019 Edition), https://plato.stanford.edu/archives/sum2019/entries/needs/.

Butler, J. & Kern, M. L. (2015) "The PERMA-Profiler: A Brief Multidimensional Measure of Flourishing," available from http://www.peggykern.org/questionnaires.html

Charles, D. (2015) "Aristotle on Practical and Theoretical Knowledge," in D. Henry and K. M. Nielsen (eds.) *Bridging the Gap Between Aristotle's Science and Ethics*. Cambridge: Cambridge University Press, 71–93.

Chirkov, V. I., Ryan, R. M., & Sheldon, K. M. (eds.) (2011) *Human Autonomy in Cross-cultural Context: Perspectives on the Psychology of Agency, Freedom, and Well-being*. Dordrecht: Springer.

Collins, R. (1979) *The Credential Society: An Historical Sociology of Education and Stratification*. New York: Academic Press.

Conway, A. M., Tugade, M. M., Catalino, L. I., & Fredrickson, B. L. (2013) "The Broaden-And-Build Theory of Positive Emotions: Form, Function, and Mechanisms," in S. A. David, I. Boniwell I., & A. C. Ayers (eds.) *The Oxford Handbook of Happiness*. Oxford: Oxford University Press, 17–34.

Csikszentmihalyi, M. (1990) *Flow: The Psychology of Optimal Experience*. New York: Harper and Row.

Curren, R. (2000) *Aristotle on the Necessity of Public Education*. Lanham, MD: Rowman & Littlefield.

Curren, R. (2013a) "Aristotelian Necessities," *The Good Society* 22(2): 247–263.

Curren, R. (2013b) "A Neo-Aristotelian Account of Education, Justice, and the Human Good," *Theory and Research in Education* 11(3): 232–250.

Curren, R. (2014) "Judgment and the Aims of Education," *Social Philosophy and Policy* 31(1): 36–59.

Curren, R. (2017) *Why Character Education?* London: Wiley-Blackwell, *Impact Series*, http://onlinelibrary.wiley.com/doi/10.1111/imp.2017.2017.issue-24/issuetoc.

Curren, R. (2019) "Wisdom and the Origins of Moral Knowledge," in E. Grimi (ed.) *Virtue Ethics: Retrospect and Prospect*. Dordrecht: Springer, 67–80.

Curren, R. (2020a) "Punishment and Motivation in a Just School Community," *Theory and Research in Education* 18(1): 117–133.

Curren, R. (2020b) "Transformative Valuing," *Educational Theory* 70(5): 581–601.

Curren, R. (2020c) "Peters Redux: The Motivational Power of Inherently Valuable Learning," *Journal of Philosophy of Education* 54(3): 731–743.

Curren, R. (2022) "Social Issues: A Self-Determination Theory Perspective," in R. Ryan (ed.) *Handbook of Self-Determination Theory*. Oxford: Oxford University Press.

Curren, R. (forthcoming) "Children of the Broken Heartlands: Rural Isolation and the Geography of Opportunity," *Social Theory and Practice*.

Curren, R. & Metzger, E. (2017) *Living Well Now and in The Future: Why Sustainability Matters*. Cambridge, MA: MIT Press.

Curren, R. & Metzger, E. (2019) "Education in the Anthropocene: A Pragmatic Approach," *On Education. Journal for Research and Debate* 4, https://www.oneducation.net/no-04_april-2019/education-in-the-anthropocene-a-pragmatic-approach/

Curren, R., Robertson, E., & Hager, H. (2003) "The Analytical Movement," in R. Curren (ed.), *A Companion to The Philosophy of Education*. Oxford: Blackwell, 176–191.

Curren, R. & Ryan, R. M. (2020) "Moral Self-Determination: The Nature, Existence, and Formation of Moral Motivation," *Journal of Moral Education* 49(3): 295–315.

David, S. A., Boniwell, I., & Ayers, A. C. (eds.) (2013) *The Oxford Handbook of Happiness*. Oxford: Oxford University Press.

DeHaan, C. R., Hirai, T., & Ryan, R. M. (2016) "Nussbaum's Capabilities and Self-Determination Theory's Basic Psychological Needs: Relating Some Fundamentals of Human Wellness," *Journal of Happiness Studies* 17(5): 2037–2049.

de Ruyter, D. J. (2004) "Pottering in the Garden? On Human Flourishing and Education," *British Journal of Educational Studies* 52(4): 377–389.

de Ruyter, D. J. (2007) "Ideals, Education, and Happy Flourishing." *Educational Theory* 57(1): 23–35.

de Ruyter, D. J. (2015) "Well-being in Education," in J. Suissa, C. Winstanley, & R. Marples (eds.) *Education, Philosophy and Well-being: New Perspectives on the Work of John White*. London: Routledge, 84–98.

de Ruyter, D. J., Oades, L. and Waghid, Y. (2020) *Meaning(s) of Human Flourishing and Education*. A research brief by the International Science and Evidence Based Education Assessment. An Initiative by UNESCO MGIEP. Downloadable at: https://mgiep.unesco.org/iseea

de Ruyter, D. J., & Wolbert, L. (2020) "Human Flourishing as an Aim of Education," in *Oxford Research Encyclopedia of Education* (Oxford University Press, 2020), DOI: 10.1093/acrefore/9780190264093.013.1418

Diener, E. (1984) "Subjective Well-Being," *Psychological Bulletin* 95: 542–575.

Diener, E., Emmons, R. A., Larsen, R. J., & Griffin, S. (1985) "The Satisfaction with Life Scale," *Journal of Personality Assessment* 49: 71–75.

Doyal, L. & Gough, I. (1991) *A Theory of Human Need*. Houndsmills: Macmillan.

Ferkany, M. (2008) "The Educational Importance of Self-Esteem," *Journal of Philosophy of Education* 42(1): 119–132.

Foot, P. (2001) *Natural Goodness*. Oxford: Clarendon Press.

Fredrickson, B. L. (2013) "Positive Emotions Broaden and Build," *Advances in Experimental Social Psychology* 47: 1–53.

Gottfried, A. E., Gottfried, A. W., Morris, P. E., & Cook, C. R. (2008) "Low Academic Intrinsic Motivation as a Risk Factor for Adverse Educational Outcomes: A Longitudinal Study from Early Childhood Through Early Adulthood," in C. Hudley & A. E. Gottfried (eds.) *Academic Culture and the Culture of School in Childhood and Adolescence*. Oxford: Oxford University Press, 36–69.

Haybron, D. M. (2013) "The Nature and Significance of Happiness," in S. A. David, I. Boniwell, & A. C. Ayers (eds.) *The Oxford Handbook of Happiness*. Oxford: Oxford University Press, 303–314.

In re Gould, 174 Mich. 663 (1913).

Jang, H., Reeve, J., & Deci, E. L. (2010) "Engaging Students in Learning Activities: It Is Not Autonomy Support or Structure, but Autonomy Support and Structure," *Journal of Educational Psychology* 102(3): 588–600.

Kahneman, D., Diener, E., & Schwarz, N. (eds.) (1999) *Well-being: The Foundations of Hedonic Psychology*. New York: Russell Sage Foundation.

Kaplan, H., & Assor, A. (2012) "Enhancing Autonomy-supportive I-thou Dialogue in Schools: Conceptualization and Socio-emotional Effects of an Intervention Program," *Social Psychology of Education* 15: 251–269.

Kasser, T. (2002) *The High Price of Materialism*. Cambridge, MA: MIT Press.

Kasser, T. (2016) "Materialistic Values and Goals," *Annual Review of Psychology* 67: 9.1–9.26.

Kraut, R. (1979) "Two Conceptions of Happiness," *The Philosophical Review* 88(2): 167–197.

Kraut, R. (1989) *Aristotle on the Human Good*. Princeton: Princeton University Press.

Kristjánsson, K. (2016) "Recent Work on Flourishing as the Aim of Education: A Critical Review," *British Journal of Educational Studies* 65(1): 87–107.

Kristjánsson, K. (2019) *Flourishing as The Aim of Education: A Neo-Aristotelian View*. London: Routledge.

Layard, R. (2005) *Happiness*. London: Penguin.

Lee, M. T., Kubansky, L. D., and VanderWeele, T. J. (eds.) *Measuring Well-Being: Interdisciplinary Perspectives from the Social Sciences and the Humanities*. New York: Oxford University Press.

Legault, L., Green-Demers, I., & Pelletier, L. (2006) "Why do High School Students Lack Motivation in the Classroom? Toward an Understanding of Academic Amotivation and the Role of Social Support," *Journal of Educational Psychology* 98(30): 567–582.

Macleod, Co. (2018) "Just Schools and Good Childhoods: Non-preparatory Dimensions of Educational Justice," *Journal of Applied Philosophy* 35: 76–89.

Morris, I. (2015) *Teaching Happiness and Well-being in Schools. 2nd ed.* London: Bloomsbury.

Nussbaum, M. (2003) "Women's Education: A Global Challenge," *Signs: Journal of Women in Culture and Society* 29(2): 325–355.

Nussbaum, M. (2008) "Who Is the Happy Warrior? Philosophy Poses Questions to Psychology," *The Journal of Legal Studies* 37: s81–s113.

Nussbaum, M. (2011) *Creating Capabilities: The Human Development Approach*. Cambridge, MA: Harvard University Press.

Pelletier, L. & Sharp, E. (2009) "Administrative Pressures and Teachers' Interpersonal Behavior," *Theory and Research in Education* 7(2): 174–183.

Peters, R. S. (2007) "Education as Initiation," in R. Curren (ed.) *Philosophy of Education: An Anthology*. Oxford: Blackwell Publishing, 55–67. Originally published in R. D. Archambault (ed.) (1965) *Philosophical Analysis and Education*. New York: Humanities Press, 87–111.

Power, C. (1988) "The Just Community Approach to Moral Education," *Journal of Moral Education* 17(3): 195–208.

Rawls, J. (1971) *A Theory of Justice*. Cambridge, MA: Harvard University Press.

Rawls, J. (2001) *Justice as Fairness: A Restatement*. Cambridge, MA: Harvard University Press.

Reeve, C. D. C. (2012) *Action, Contemplation, and Happiness: An Essay on Aristotle*. Cambridge, MA: Harvard University Press.

Reeve, J., Bolt, E., & Cai, Y. (1999) "Autonomy-supportive Teachers: How They Teach and Motivate Students," *Journal of Educational Psychology* 91(3): 537–548.

Reeve, J. & Jang, H. (2006) "What Teachers Do and Say to Support Students' Autonomy During a Learning Activity," *Journal of Educational Psychology* 98(1): 209–218.

Ryan, R. M. & Brown, K. W. (2005) "Legislating Competence: The Motivational Impact of High Stakes Testing as an Educational Reform," in A. J. Elliot & C. S. Dweck (eds.) *Handbook of Competence*. New York: Guilford Press, 354–374.

Ryan, R. M., Curren, R., & Deci, E. L. (2013) "What Humans Need: Flourishing in Aristotelian Philosophy and Self-Determination Theory," in A. S. Waterman (ed.) *The Best Within Us: Positive Psychology Perspectives on Eudaimonia*. Washington, D.C: American Psychological Association, 57–75.

Ryan, R. M. & Deci, E. L. (2001) "On Happiness and Human Potentials: A Review of Research on Hedonic and Eudaimonic Well-Being," in S. Fiske (ed.). *Annual Review of Psychology*. Palo Alto, CA: Annual Reviews Inc., 52: 141–166.

Ryan, R. M. & Deci, E. L. (2017) *Self-Determination Theory: Basic Psychological Needs in Motivation, Development, and Wellness*. New York: Guilford Press.

Ryan, R. M., Huta, V., & Deci, E. L. (2008) "Living Well: A Self-Determination Theory Perspective on Eudaimonia," *Journal of Happiness Studies* 9: 139–170.

Ryan, R. M. & Weinstein, N. (2009) "Undermining Quality Teaching and Learning: A Self-Determination Theory Perspective on High-Stakes Testing," *Theory and Research in Education* 7(2): 224–233.

Ryff, C. D. (2016) "Beautiful Ideas and the Scientific Enterprise: Sources of Intellectual Vitality in Research on Eudaimonic Well-Being," in J. Vitterosø (ed.) *Handbook of Eudaimonic Well-being*. Dordrecht: Springer, 95–107.

Ryff, C. D., & Keyes, C. L. M. (1995) "The Structure of Psychological Well-being Revisited," *Journal of Personality & Social Psychology* 69: 719–727.

Santoro, D. A. (2018) *Demoralized: Why Teachers Leave the Profession They Love and How They Can Stay*. Cambridge, MA: Harvard Education Press.

Scanlon, T. M. (1998) *What We Owe Each Other*. Cambridge, Mass.: Belknap Press.

Schlegel, R. J., Hirsch, K. A., & Smith, C. M. (2013) "The Importance of Who You Really Are: The Role of the True Self in Eudaimonia," in A. S. Waterman (ed.) *The Best Within Us: Positive Psychology Perspectives on Eudaimonia*. Washington, D.C: American Psychological Association, 207–225.

Seligman, M. E. P., Ernst, R. M., Gillham, J., Reivich, K., and Linkins, M. (2009) "Positive Education: Positive Psychology and Classroom Interventions," *Oxford Review of Education* 35(3): 293–311.

Sheldon, K. M. (2016) "Putting Eudaimonia in Its Place: On the Predictor, Not the Outcome, Side of the Equation," in J. Vitterosø (ed.) *Handbook of Eudaimonic Well-being*. Dordrecht: Springer, 531–541.

Sheldon, K. M. (2018) "Understanding the Good Life: Eudaimonic Living Involves Well-Doing, Not Well-Being," in J. P. Forgas & R. F. Baumeister (eds.) *The Social Psychology of Living Well*. New York: Routledge, 116–136.

Taylor, G., Jungert, T., Mageau, G. A., Schattke, K., Dedic, H., Rosenfield, S., et al. (2014) "A Self-Determination Theory Approach to Predicting School Achievement over Time: The Unique Role of Intrinsic Motivation," *Contemporary Educational Psychology* 39(4): 342–358.

Tiberius, V. (2006) "Well-Being: Psychological Research for Philosophers," *Philosophy Compass* 1(5): 493–505.

Vansteenkiste, M., Soenens, B., Verstuyf, J., & Lens, W. (2009) "'What is the Usefulness of Your Schoolwork?' The Differential Effects of Intrinsic and Extrinsic Goal Framing on Optimal Learning," *Theory and Research in Education* 7(2): 155–163.

Vitterosø, J. (ed.) (2016a) *Handbook of Eudaimonic Well-being*. Dordrecht: Springer

Vitterosø, J. (2016b) "The Most Important Idea in the World: An Introduction," in J. Vitterosø (ed.) *Handbook of Eudaimonic Well-being*. Dordrecht: Springer, 1–24.

Waterman, A. S. (ed.) (2013) *The Best Within Us: Positive Psychology Perspectives on Eudaimonia*. Washington, D.C: American Psychological Association.

Waters, L. (2011) "A Review of School-Based Positive Psychology Interventions," *The Australian Educational and Developmental Psychologist* 28(2): 75–90.

White, J. (2011) *Exploring Well-being in Schools: A Guide to Making Children's Lives More Fulfilling*. London: Routledge.

Wolbert, L. S., de Ruyter, D. J., & Schinkel, A. (2015) "Formal Criteria for the Concept of Human Flourishing: The First Step in Defending flourishing as an Ideal Aim of Education," *Ethics and Education* 10(1): 118–129.

Wolbert, L. S., de Ruyter, D. J., & Schinkel, A. (2018) "What Kind of a Theory Should Theory on Education for Human Flourishing Be?" *British Journal of Educational Studies* 67(1): 25–39.

4
MIND, REASON, AND KNOWLEDGE

David Bakhurst

In her 1958 article, "Modern Moral Philosophy," Elizabeth Anscombe argued that moral philosophy stood in urgent need of a viable philosophy of psychology (Anscombe 1958). By this she did not mean that ethicists should heed the empirical findings of psychologists. Rather, Anscombe meant that doing moral philosophy was impossible without an adequate philosophy of human thought and action that could elucidate such themes as agency and intention, practical reasoning and practical knowledge, against the background of human life and language. My view is that philosophy of education is equally dependent on a philosophy of psychology, as Anscombe understood that term. Not that I think that philosophy of education is as dire as Anscombe took the moral philosophy of her day to be. On the contrary, philosophy of education is in many ways a vibrant discipline. But, any attempt to illuminate education must be informed by conceptions of mind, reason, and knowledge, and this is true whether we are discussing general issues about the nature and ends of education or highly specific matters of pedagogical method or curriculum development. This chapter aims to reveal how this is so, and to sketch the outlines of a philosophical psychology that offers a framework that can enhance philosophy of education.

Preliminaries

Let us begin with some preliminary thoughts about the three concepts under scrutiny: mind, reason, and knowledge. A creature with a *mind* is able to do certain things: it is aware of, and can represent, its environment, and it can respond to that environment in action. The cat hears a sound behind the baseboard, understands that a mouse is scampering in a certain direction, and, wanting to catch the mouse, positions itself accordingly. As such, a creature exhibits intelligence to the degree to which it can identify and determine solutions to problems its environment presents: in this case, identifying and predicting the movement of a mouse in order to catch it. Intelligence, of course, is not a single trait. In our example, it involves skills of spatial cognition, object quantification and classification, appreciation of causal relations, and calculative behavior that might be described as *reasoning*. The cat's behavior certainly evinces *knowledge* – of the layout of the environment, of the position of its prey, of how best to catch it.

A human mind is capable of perceptual awareness mediated by concepts that enable us to articulate thoughts in conceptual form. We see the table – i.e., we bring the experience under the concept *table*, thereby seeing the table *as* an object of a certain kind. Moreover, we see the table *as needing a wipe* or *as being elegant*, and we can express these ways of seeing in words just as we can

DOI: 10.4324/9781003172246-6

think "Won't it be wonderful when we're all around that table again!" By such thoughts, we represent how things are, might be or could have been; we evaluate and imagine, express needs, wants, hopes, and intentions, which we can realize in action (e.g., by wiping the table, setting it, and so on). It is important that human perceptual awareness, thought and action are self-conscious. We are not just aware of the table, but aware that we are aware. In thinking, we know what we think and when we act intentionally there is a description of what we are doing that we know to be true (of course, this does not preclude the possibility of unconscious mental states, any more than it precludes the possibility of unintentional action of which the agent is unaware).

A being that has all this has the power of *reason*. The word "reason" has a variety of meanings, exemplified in the sentence, "A being with reason reasons about reasons." In its first occurrence, "reason" is, as Hume might have put it, the mind's capacity to determine how things are, what is true and what is false. To this we might add, with Kant, that reason's mandate is also to unify our conception of the world, and to understand the principles of its unification, so that it represents a coherent whole of mutually supporting beliefs providing, so far as possible, a complete explanation of how things are. In its second occurrence, to "reason" means to deliberate (e.g., to think, question, argue, infer, conclude, hypothesize, evaluate, etc.) about what to believe or to do. And in its third occurrence, a "reason" is a consideration that favors thinking such-and-such or doing so-and-so. Many animals act for reasons, but only human beings think and act *in light of* a self-conscious appreciation of reasons and engage in what Robert Brandom calls "the game of giving and asking for reasons" (Brandom 2000). Human beings are expected to justify themselves by appeal to their reasons for thinking and acting as they do. We are rational agents, and the rationality of our thoughts and deeds is a measure of the soundness of the strategies by which we determine what we have reason to think or do. A being that exercises reason well has *knowledge* of what to think and do. Human knowledge requires not just that an agent has true beliefs; we have knowledge only if we are able to offer grounds that justify our thoughts and actions. So the power of reason is at once the capacity for knowledge.

The nature of mind, reason, and knowledge has been debated since the dawn of philosophy. However, I would expect most philosophers to agree, albeit cautiously, with these preliminary remarks, though some will complain about what is left out, and controversy is certain to begin as soon as we try to explain and develop the ideas. But before we go further, let us pause to take in the intimate relation between these concepts and questions of education. First, among the aims of education are the following: to equip students with knowledge and understanding, both theoretical (knowledge of fact) and practical (knowledge of what to do and when and how to do it), and to cultivate in them the means to acquire knowledge and understanding, in the forms of skills of inquiry and critical thinking, practical abilities, and good habits of mind (virtues, intellectual and moral), so that they may exercise good judgment, make good choices, and excel in their lives. Our concepts of mind, reason, and knowledge influence how we understand all this. Second, those concepts are equally at play, explicitly or implicitly, in our conceptions of how to assess and evaluate students. Third, they also influence our views of the nature of teaching and learning, of what it is to offer and receive knowledge, to think independently, to have a mind of one's own. Fourth, they inform our understanding of learning disabilities, of the intellectual, emotional and developmental challenges that many students face. And fifth, they bear on fundamental curricular distinctions, such as the familiar dichotomy between intellectual and applied pursuits.

It is because the concepts of mind, reason, and knowledge enter so deeply into such foundational matters that philosophy of education is beholden to philosophy of psychology in Anscombe's sense of the term. Of course, we cannot pretend to develop a definitive theory of mind, reason, and knowledge that will settle these matters once and for all. The concepts will remain essentially contestable. But we can aspire to bring to consciousness the conceptions that inform our thinking and interrogate them critically, so that we can appreciate their limitations and ensure that they enrich and enable, rather than thwart or ensnare, the theory and practice of education.

A Familiar Picture

Let us first examine a familiar picture of the mind associated with 17th and 18th century philosophy, especially the work of Descartes and the British empiricists. Very few philosophers would openly embrace this conception today, though many of its tenets continue to influence both theoretical and popular conceptions of mind, reason and knowledge.

According to this picture, my mind is akin to a private theatre of ideas which are disclosed immediately only to me, the being, or self, whose mind it is. I have immediate access only to the contents of my own mind, of which I am directly conscious; my awareness of things beyond my mind is indirect, mediated by mental representations. Moreover, my mental states are immediately given to me alone, others know what I think and feel only by inference from my behavior. The mind is thus akin to a self-contained subjective world with a single inhabitant. The contents of this world are states (perceptions, beliefs, imaginings, ideas) that purport to represent how things are beyond its boundaries, as well as states (emotions, wants, hopes, intentions) that respond to things as they are represented to be, with a view, perhaps, to changing them through action.

On this view, reason is understood primarily as a capacity to operate on mental states. Theoretical reason is concerned to deploy principles of inference to establish the cogency of our thoughts. Its end is knowledge, which thinkers possess when they hold appropriately grounded beliefs that accurately represent how things are. Practical reason, in contrast, is concerned with the determination of action. For some, such as Descartes, Locke, and Rousseau, we can establish substantive truths about how we should live by the exercise of our "natural reason." Hume, in contrast, vehemently denied that reason can determine the proper ends of action. For him, the purposes with which we act are fixed entirely by our desires and reason's role is exclusively instrumental, limited to determining the means by which our ends may be realised.

The familiar picture raises familiar puzzles. The first is ontological. Descartes, of course, famously argued that mind is a substance utterly different in kind from matter. Thoughts are not, nor could they be, material because they lack the essential property of material entities, namely, "extension": they are not in space as material things necessarily are. While some of Descartes's contemporaries, such as Hobbes, argued that minds are material and aspired to give mechanical explanations of psychological phenomena, it was not until the mid- to late-20th century that philosophers began seriously to attempt to show systematically that mental states are physical phenomena, either by aspiring to identify them with brain states or by arguing that they, while not strictly identical with brain states, were nonetheless instantiated in the brain or realised by brain functioning. Yet such physicalist accounts often preserved the idea of the mind as a private theatre of representations (Dennett [1991: 107] speaks of "Cartesian materialism") and encountered enormous difficulties explaining the subjective phenomenology (or "felt quality") and the intentionality (or "aboutness") of mental phenomena. The intractability of these difficulties led some thinkers to embrace "eliminitivism" about the mental, the view that our familiar forms of psychological description and explanation were a "folk theory" of mind that was ultimately destined to be supplanted by rigorous neuroscientific approaches to psychological explanation (see, e.g., Churchland 2013). But eliminitivism, by rejecting the very conceptual apparatus in terms of which we understand our mental lives, thereby denied itself the means to identify the phenomena that philosophy and psychology seek to understand, namely, our mental lives as we live them (Bruner 1990; Bakhurst 2005). So an antimony remained: neither dualism nor physicalism and no obvious third way.

The familiar picture also invites a host of epistemological problems. If a mind is acquainted with the world only via the mediation of ideas, how can it ever determine that the world is as its ideas represent it to be? The problem is graphically illustrated by Descartes's famous evil genius hypothesis, reborn in the 20th century as the brain-in-a-vat thought experiment. Descartes, of course, posed his sceptical problem in order to refute it, but alas the problem proved more enduring than his solution. And the problem pertains, of course, not just to knowledge of external objects, but also of other minds, knowledge of which, on this picture, is doubly indirect. As one can never "enter" another mind; another person's perceptions, thoughts and feelings are not possible objects of one's experience and can only be inferred from the other's behavior. But such inferences are obviously fragile, and so nothing, apart from its pre-philosophical implausibility, can definitively exclude the possibility of solipsism.

Let us now explore how aspects of the familiar picture can influence our thinking about education. On such a view, what it is for a thinker to know, understand, learn, etc. is cast in terms of transactions within the thinker's mind: knowledge demands justified belief and that is provided by the apprehension of appropriate relations between mental states. Understanding is, or involves, a lucid apprehension of concepts, ideas, thoughts. Reasoning is inference, movement from one thought to another. These ideas are naturally allied to what we might call "epistemic individualism," a stance that combines two theses, one descriptive and one normative. The descriptive thesis holds that individual minds are equipped with the wherewithal to acquire knowledge through the exercise of powers of reason with which they are naturally endowed. These powers enable them to deploy concepts – which they possess either innately or acquire from experience – to fashion a conception of the world. The rational capacities employed in developing a scientific conception are merely an extension of those employed in creating our familiar everyday conception of reality. Correspondingly, the normative thesis maintains that each individual is responsible for keeping their own epistemic house in order. No-one should believe anything simply on the say so of another: one can be in good standing, epistemically speaking, only in so far one can produce appropriate reasons for one's beliefs, and a reason is appropriate only if one can say why it has the epistemic force it does. In this sense, individual minds have both the power, and the obligation, to be self-sufficient.

Such a position is graphically illustrated by Descartes's philosophy, but it has been widely influential and no more so than in education. It is present in the familiar idea that intelligence is a "natural gift," as well as the view that education is essentially a process of scaffolding the maturation of children's natural abilities to learn for themselves, a view found in many traditional conceptions of learning as well as in progressive "child-centred" approaches that emphasize individual invention and discovery. The view therefore sets significant constraints on the extent to which we can think of education as *forming* our powers of reason. In addition, its conception of epistemic independence influences our understanding of successful learning and, correspondingly, of appropriate assessment: the test of students' abilities is what they can do independently and that defines for us what we mean by someone's "own work." To master some subject-matter is to be able to articulate what is true and why, and someone can be said really to *know* only if they can do this unaided.

The familiar picture also brings with it a sharp distinction between intellectual activity and bodily movement. The mind is the domain of intelligence, and the intelligence of thinkers is measured by the quality of their reasoning and judgement. Some judgements issue in intentions or acts of will, but as these occur inside the mind, they are at best the causes of our bodily actions that take place in the external world. It thus becomes difficult to see intelligence as *immanent* in bodily movement, to understand our mindedness as present in what we do. Accordingly, the picture provides a rationale for the distinction between intellectual and applied subjects, mental and manual labour, a distinction that has traditionally borne considerable significance in the construction of curricula and in the privileging of propositional knowledge-that over bodily know-how.

The picture of individual minds as self-contained and self-sufficient makes it hard to see teaching as a process in which minds can meet or be truly open to another. Rather, teaching involves conveying, imparting, or transmitting knowledge, as well as inspiring in others the motivation to learn, though in harmony with the epistemic individualism noted above, the teacher can impart only the shell of knowledge: the student must make it her own. The picture, especially in its dualist versions, might be invoked to plead the importance of mystery and spirituality in education, just as its physicalist renditions will be prone to entertain ideas about the educational significance of neuroscience. Finally, the picture suggests a certain conception of the ends of education: education primarily aspires to create the conditions in which the powers of mind with which we are naturally endowed can develop and flourish, so that individuals can fruitfully exercise their reasoning skills in the acquisition of knowledge.

Transcending The Familiar Picture

The familiar picture, for all its dominance in the early-modern period and the Enlightenment, and its subsequent influence up to the present, has long been contested by thinkers – such as Hegel, Marx, Nietzsche, Vygotsky, Dewey, Heidegger, Ryle, Wittgenstein, and McDowell – whose work bears on education in significant ways. The reader will no doubt expect me to maintain that it is fundamentally flawed and its influence on education desultory. And so I will, but with two important qualifications. First, the position I have outlined is a composite of various ideas that naturally consort together, but of course it is possible to embrace some components and not others (indeed, one can interpret some in ways that explicitly rule out others). Now many philosophers will question the value of such a sketch. They are interested in what one *must* believe, not in what people do or might believe, so they would see little point in making a straw man out of views that can be so easily contested and disavowed in whole or part. But since my brief is to explore how philosophical conceptions influence our ideas of education, it helps to step back and reflect on some of the most general conceptions that have informed how we think of mind, reason, and knowledge, particularly since we may not always be aware of their power over us. Second, while I reject the familiar picture, it is important to recognize that its elements would not have endured were there not some truth, even some deep truth, in them. So it is not that I intend simply to erase this picture and replace it with another. Rather, I want to suggest that there are more fruitful ways to do justice to the phenomena the familiar picture tries to capture, while incorporating them into a more satisfying view of the life of the mind better fit to illuminate and inspire educational theory and practice.

First, we must resist the image of the mind as a place occupied by entities directly available only to the self whose mind it is. It is curious that a conception of the mind associated with Descartes – who resolutely denied that mental phenomena are in space – is so quick to deploy spatial metaphors. Let us instead think of a creature's mental powers as informing and enabling its life-activity in ways we may hope to explain and illuminate. Instead of speaking of a creature's mind, as if it were some place within it, let us think of the creature as *minded*, that is, possessing powers of sentience and sapience, the exercise of which enable it to live a certain kind of life. This is not to deny the reality of our "inner lives"; the point is rather to recognize that events in consciousness are events in the life of an embodied being; and the unity and integrity of consciousness cannot be understood without recognizing that conscious life is lived in the world (see McDowell 1996: lecture 5). My inner life is thus an aspect of my being-in-the-world and not something that merely runs in parallel with my life as a bodily being.

In harmony with this, it is important to countenance just how much of the life of the mind is lived in public space. It is simply not true that it is impossible for others to be directly acquainted with our thoughts and feelings. Knowledge of other minds is not always the outcome of inference, for the minds of others can be immediately manifest to us. The most obvious way this is so is that we can literally speak our minds. I can say what I think and you, understanding me, thereby know what I think. It is not that when I say what I think, my words are merely the external manifestation of some hidden process. Rather, my thoughts are present in my words. Of course, I can, deliberately or unintentionally, say the opposite of what I think, or express my thoughts poorly. I may lie, dissemble, or pretend. But it does not follow that, when I speak sincerely and intelligibly, you are aware of anything less than my state of mind. Similarly, my emotions, wants or intentions may be present in my actions or my demeanor: my grief, dismay, anxiety, or anger may be there in my expression or my behavior. And once again, just because I can feign such emotions, attitudes and feelings does not mean that they are not to be beheld when I am not feigning. This view of the "visibility" of the mental is an important corrective, allowing us to transcend the idea that our knowledge of other minds is always speculative, akin to a theoretical construction, and countenance the idea of a genuine meeting of minds – a sharing of mental states and attitudes where two minded beings can be as one. This is a more favourable context in which to understand the idea of joint, shared, and collective intentionality and grasp the various senses in which we can share commitments, ends, actions and activities, as well as illuminating the second-personal (I–thou) relations that are critical to the interaction of teacher and learner, to the summons to learn and to the yearning to be taught.

Second, it is vital to work with an expansive construal of our rational powers. As we observed above, it is central to human life that we act not just *for* but *in light of* reasons. We apprehend those reasons *as* reasons, make them the object of critical evaluation, and offer them up to others (and to ourselves) to justify our beliefs and our behavior. We can weigh reasons against one another, deliberate, and make up our minds about what to think or do, and we can articulate our self-conscious appreciation of what the balance of reasons favours. However, it is a mistake to construe responsiveness to reasons entirely in terms of overt reasoning or deliberation. Of course, we sometimes work out what to think or do in just that way: we arrive at a judgement in a process akin to formulating an argument, which we can rehearse to justify our thoughts and actions. It is important to note, however, that even then deliberation is not always *prior* to the expression of thought. We sometimes "think on our feet" in public space. Consider a teacher spontaneously responding in a class: here she works out what to say in the course of saying it. And sometimes our spontaneous responsiveness to reasons takes the form of embodied action, issuing not from deliberative judgements, but from an intuitive apprehension of what the situation calls for. Think here of a jazz musician improvising with others: her playing is not the outcome of overt practical reasoning, but it is nonetheless responsive to reasons "in the flow." Her grounds for playing as she does may be reconstructed after the fact (though this need not involve a verbal articulation of practical reasoning – it could take the form of a demonstration). Similarly with the soccer player who effortlessly reads the game and knows how to find space and perfectly weight passes: this is the activity of a being that is responsive to the normative profile of her circumstances, who knows she ought to move *here* or strike the ball *just so* in response to the reasons before her in the moment. Thus, not all responsiveness to reasons is "in the head." Our mindedness can reside in how we comport ourselves in the world and, as in our examples, in harmony with the mindedness of others, for among the things the musician and the footballer respond to is the rational responsiveness of others (fellow musicians, teammates, and opponents).

If we embrace an expansive conception of reason and see our mindedness as a dimension of our embodied life-activity, played out in a social world, then we can recognize that there is nothing other-worldly or super-natural about our rational powers. In this way, our position "naturalizes" the mental. At the same time, however, it gives no comfort to the kind of physicalism that would reduce mental life to brain functioning. As John McDowell (1996) has argued, following Wilfrid Sellars (and ultimately Kant), the modes of discourse that render our mental lives intelligible portray us as acting rationally through the apprehension of reasons. This style of explanation is very different from natural-scientific forms of explanation that subsume events under causal laws, and there is no prospect of reducing the former to the latter. It is one thing to explain something by "placing it in the space of reasons" another to represent it as an expression of natural law. But this does not entail an ontological cleavage between mind and body. Rather, there is but one thing, the life-activity of human beings, which is open to more than one mode of explanation. If we see our deeds as issuing from our self-conscious responsiveness to reasons, then we represent ourselves as rational, intelligent, free beings; if we see our behavior, or what happens to us, as merely the result of causal forces, then we represent ourselves as material beings subject to natural forces. These two ways of seeing are two perspectives on the same thing, but only the first discloses our rational nature. On such a view, mental states and properties should be seen as states and properties of *persons* – that is of a certain kind of natural being – and not as states and properties of some part of a person (e.g., of the brain). It is persons who think and feel and not their brains (though of course much must be going on in their brains for this to be possible).

Lessons for Education

Transcending the familiar picture has many implications for the ways we should think about education. For example, the personalist view just articulated stands as a corrective to scientistic programs of "brain-based learning", which speak as if it is brains which do the learning rather than students (see Bakhurst 2008). Of course, human beings are animals and it is good for our educational practices to be informed by what we know about the conditions in which animals like us flourish and learn – that students are rested and adequately fed, that unreasonable demands are not placed on their powers of attention and concentration, that we do not assume that all students learn in the same way, that learning disabilities are understood and accommodated, and so on – familiar facts that we might look to empirical psychology to illuminate further. But we should see ourselves as educating people, not brains, and should be wary of speculation, sometimes allied to brain-based approaches, about enhancing students' powers of knowledge by pharmaceutical and technological means.

In my view, such enhancement would not be an educational act at all, for education is, as Michael Oakeshott (1991) famously put it, initiation into the conversation of humanity, and that necessarily involves a sustained and protracted process of formation, or *Bilding*, requiring engagement with multiple disciplinary voices and practices as they are encountered in texts, in culture and social activity, and in the person of one's teachers. Such a conception, sometimes called "liberal education," sees education as a relation between a developing person and culture. It is thus profoundly at odds with the idea of "natural reason" and attendant conceptions of epistemic individualism, for the process of initiation is seen as one in which students inherit a conception of the world, together with the concepts and traditions of thought that enable them to articulate and reflect upon it (see Curren 2014). For Oakeshott (2001) – and for such like-minded (though otherwise diverse) thinkers as Vygotsky (1986), Bruner (1997), Peters (2007), and Ilyenkov (2009), children's rational powers are not simply given parts of their nature so that each child can find the world anew for itself. We become rational beings as our personhood is formed through our initiation into culture, and so to educate is not merely to scaffold the autonomous development of individual learners; it is the process in which rational agents come to be, in which they acquire the "second nature" that fits them for a distinctively human form of life.

If equipped with a suitably expansive conception of mind, reason, and knowledge, such a conception can serve to correct some of the traditional stereotypes of liberal education as bookish and overly intellectual. If we take seriously the idea that we are embodied minds – denying not just that we are "ghosts in the machine" but also that our minds are physical entities within us, like daleks in their "pepperpots" – then we can recognize that our mindedness is the form of our life-activity, to put it in an Aristotelian idiom. Our intelligence does not reside only in mental operations conducted behind the scenes of action; intelligence can be present, not just in words, but in bodily movement, in the immediacy of our responsiveness to reasons in action, the expression of habits or virtues, and the exercise of physical skill.

This adjustment in our thinking should make us wary of embracing a rigid distinction between theoretical and practical knowledge: recognizing the embodied mind speaks against sharp distinctions between intellectual and applied pursuits; mental and manual labor; academic and vocational subjects – dichotomies that have influenced curricular thinking since formal schooling began.

Indeed, we need to rethink the tired distinction between dispassionate reason, purely cognitive in its orientation, and "appetitive" states such as emotion, feeling, attitude, passion, and mood. On the view I propose – which has pecedents in Plato's view of education as the training of desire, as well as in Aristotle – appetitive states can enter into and inform our responsiveness to reasons, helping us discern where reasons lie by directing our attention to normatively significant features of situations. Moreover, such states can also constitute a rational response: our joy can be rationally motivated by our appreciation of reasons to celebrate; our despair warranted by the dismalness of our situation. Thus, if education is the formation of reason, we must seek to educate not just our powers of deliberation and reasoning, but habits, passions, and emotions.

Attunement to such matters is reflected in recent interest in virtue epistemology (see, e.g., Baehr 2011). While it has long been argued that the development of critical thinking is an important educational end, it is becoming widely recognized that critical thinking is typically too narrowly defined in terms of reasoning, conceived as the articulation and evaluation of arguments, at the expense of the cultivation of epistemic virtues, such as curiosity, scepticism, intellectual humility, and creativity, qualities that enhance our ability to discern epistemic relevance, appreciate evidence, and weigh reasons for belief.

Similar lessons apply, I believe, to moral education. Too often, moral education is understood as instruction in how to behave, in moral principles and their application to particular cases. But such an understanding omits something more fundamental. What, we must ask, is a moral reason? In my view, moral reasons are features of situations that have a distinctive normative significance, which we identify with the terms "moral" or "ethical." So, *that they are going hungry* is a reason to feed them; *that he is embarrassed* is a reason to stop teasing him; *that it is fair* is a reason to pay equally for equal work (see Dancy 1993). But to appreciate such reasons for what they are is to understand not just their general character, but how and in what way they present as morally relevant in particular cases and what consequences this has for how we should act. This requires appropriate concepts, sensibilities, emotions, and routes of feeling. The moral learner must therefore be enabled to discern moral salience, and this is as much, if not more, a matter of cultivating virtues and moral motivation, as it is of training in styles of moral reasoning. It requires an education *in what matters*, and this is a task of education *as a whole* and not something that can be parcelled into a discrete subject called "moral education" (Bakhurst 2020).

It might seem that my emphasis on mind as embodied and enacted slights the inner, self-conscious character of our mental lives so celebrated in Cartesian, empiricist, and Kantian approaches, and hence the view I recommend suffers from flaws similar to those that beset behaviorism. But this is not so. The point is to understand how our mental powers inform the life-activity of beings like us (and here "inform" is meant to have an Aristotelian resonance). So the intention is not to deny or explain away "the inner," but to see the life of the mind as a dimension of the life of a certain kind of animal. We need to hear the phrase "rational animal" as referring to something in whom the rational and the animal are a unity, rather than two independently intelligible components somehow yoked together (Bakhurst 2011: ch.3). As I observed above, the life of rational animals is self-conscious life. This is because judgement is essentially self-conscious: when I judge that things are thus and so, either by apprehending them in perception or by reasoning to a conclusion about how the facts lie, I know that I so judge. This self-consciousness is the source of the special relation that a person has to their own mental states. This relation should not be understood on the model of perception, as it so often is on the familiar picture (where only I can look into my mind and see what is there). It derives rather from our agency: I know what I think because I make up my mind what to think in acts of judgement that are necessarily self-conscious (see Moran 2001). Something similar is true of intentional action. As Anscombe (1958) showed, when I act intentionally there is a description of my act under which I know what I am doing, and I know this not because I *observe* what I am doing, but because my self-consciousness determines what it is I am doing intentionally. I cannot be intentionally starting my car unless I know that that is what I am doing. Of course, in doing this, there may be many things I am doing unintentionally (e.g., annoying my neighbours, startling the cat) and these I may or may not know I am doing. But, self-consciousness necessarily enters into intentional action.

These considerations about the self-conscious character of judgement and intentional action may appear esoteric philosophical theses. But, they are actually of critical significance in the philosophy of education. This is because they suggest that our powers of reason can be brought to actuality through education, for no human being is born knowing what it is thinking or doing (Rödl 2020). The form of our self-consciousness requires the exercise of conceptual powers that are acquired only in a process of formation or *Bildung* – education in the broadest sense. So Anscombian reflections on self-consciousness, when properly developed, strongly favour the idea of education as initiation, where education is understood, not as a merely contingent modification of the human condition, but as central to the very possibility of our form of animal life. Kant remarked that it was a scandal that philosophy had still not yet dispelled the spectre of scepticism about our knowledge of the external world (Kant 1998: 121 [Bxxxix]), but in my view the real scandal of philosophy is that such scant attention has been paid to the place of education in human life, as if our powers of mind, reason, and knowledge could be understood in abstraction from the processes of their actualization.

Conclusion: Knowledge, Reason and The Ends of Education

But let us conclude by reflecting for a moment on Kant's scandal. Has philosophy succeeded in dispelling the spectre of scepticism so that we may speak with confidence of education as imparting nothing less than knowledge? I think so, for the view I have propounded leaves scant room for philosophical scepticism. For Anscombe, the kind of self-knowledge definitive of intentional action is no self-contained phenomenon of introspective awareness, for in acting intentionally I know what I am doing – not merely what I take myself to be doing or what I am trying to do – and this presupposes knowledge of the world beyond the mind. So if intentional thought and action is possible at all, we must have knowledge of the external world. Indeed, the very idea of an *external* world should be dropped, resting as it does on the contrast, central to the familiar picture, between the external domain of material objects and the "inner" world of the mind. But the more we see our mindedness as embodied and enacted, the easier it becomes to recognize that rational beings are of the world, not set apart from it.

For those who seek a less transcendental and more direct refutation of sceptical anxieties, I believe there is promise in the "disjunctivist" approaches of McDowell (1998), Rödl (2007), Pritchard (2012) and Kern (2017), but as these views do not lend themselves to summary treatment, I will not elaborate (but see Bakhurst 2018 for detailed discussion). Instead, I will simply point to recent developments in epistemology that are important for the philosophy of education. The past three decades have seen increasing recognition of the significance of knowledge as a *social* phenomenon.

In the 1990s, the heyday of postmodernism, it became fashionable to argue that true and real were "social constructions," fashioned by our discursive practices and modes of conceptualisation and meaning-making. Accordingly, claims to objective knowledge were viewed as suspect – at best they were ungrounded, at worst a vehicle of intellectual authoritarianism. While the ensuing "culture wars" had some salutary effects – e.g. by challenging entrenched historical narratives, welcoming voices and perspectives that had long been marginalized, and bringing into view the social context of the production of scientific knowledge – the simple-minded relativism that became the hallmark of the postmodern condition had a generally desultory influence on educational theory (see Phillips 1995; Hacking 1999; Bakhurst 2011: ch. 2). The late 1990s, however, saw the beginnings of a very different approach to the social dimensions of knowledge with the emergence of the discipline of social epistemology, the advocates of which typically saw no irrevocable conflict between the sociality of knowledge and its objectivity. Alvin Goldman, in his pathbreaking *Knowledge in a Social World* (1999), was quick to see the bearing of this new approach to questions of education, and the ensuing three decades have seen the production of much work on testimony (knowledge acquired from the word of others), collective epistemic agents, disagreement, misinformation, and epistemic injustice, all of which has significant educational applications (see Goldman & O'Connor 2021). While it is fair to say that dialogue between social epistemologists and philosophers of education remains in its infancy (though see Kotzee 2014; Bakhurst 2020), the prospects for fruitful engagement are bright.

Many social epistemologists hold that the philosophical study of knowledge should be informed by psychology. How does this relate to the claim with which I began this essay, namely that the philosophy of education needs to be complemented by a philosophy of psychology, as Anscombe understood that term? For Anscombe, as we saw, the philosophy of psychology does not mean the philosophical appropriation of the empirical findings of psychologists. It is rather the philosophical exploration of concepts central to understanding thought and action. Not that this exploration is an entirely *a priori* exercise, as Anscombe's method, inspired by Wittgenstein, is to understand those concepts in the context of the role that they, and the phenomena they disclose to us, play in our lives. But this is a very different approach from that taken by much scientific psychology, which tends to take a "sideways-on" stance on human behavior, rather than explicating it, as the philosopher must, from within.

For all that, however, psychology is a very diverse field and, I believe, there is much within it that can illuminate philosophical studies of education. Earlier, I followed McDowell by distinguishing two irreducible styles of explanation we can bring to events in human lives. We can view human beings as rational agents and explain their doings by placing them "in the space of reasons," or we can view human beings as material things and explain the happenings in which they are involved by appeal to natural law. The distinction speaks against forms of reductionism that seek to explain mind, reason, and knowledge exclusively by natural-scientific means. At the same time, however (and as I have stressed throughout this chapter), human beings are part of the order of nature, and so a sound approach will not parcel our lives into two streams of events, the rational and the causal, but seek to embrace the unity of the rational and the animal in our lives. If we focus, not on particular events, but on stretches of human activity, we find the interplay of causal and rational forces, so that some aspects of the activity will be explicable by rational means, others causally, and still others that will require both modes of intelligibility in consort (see Bakhurst 2011: ch. 6). There are styles of psychology – exemplified, for instance, by Vygotsky, Bruner and Tomasello (see, e.g., his 2014, 2019) – that appreciate this well. They offer theories of human development that are genuinely scientific in method and aspiration, yet eschew reductionism, and deploy modes of explanation fit for the elucidation of rational life, in all its depth and complexity. Psychology of such a kind has much to teach us and can rightly inform a philosophy of psychology to enhance philosophy of education.

Let me finish, then, by asking what light the themes of this essay might cast on the vexed question of education's ends. To answer this, we should discriminate two voices in which the question might be asked. If one poses it in pedagogical voice – if one treats it as a question about what teaching should aspire to achieve – then the answer must surely enumerate a considerable number of diverse ends: to impart knowledge; to encourage independence of mind and autonomous decision-making; to build confidence; to inspire and motivate; to develop critical thinking; to cultivate intellectual virtues and other good habits; to awaken moral and aesthetic skills and sensibilities; to promote health and well-being; to prepare students for further education or equip them to enter the job market; and on and on. I do not see how to organize these ends into a hierarchy or the desirability of doing so.

If one poses the question in philosophical voice, the question takes a different form. Now we are looking for something that will enable us to express the unity that inheres in the concept of education, which will, of course, be a unity in diversity. In this regard, there are various candidates, including: the imparting, sharing, and expansion of knowledge; the formation of reason; the awakening and development of powers of mind; autonomy, conceived as the power to determine for oneself what to think or do. I think, however, that if we heed the position I have sought to develop here, there is no real need to choose between these options, for, once unpacked and developed, they all amount to the same thing. Education is the medium by which a certain kind of life comes to be: the life of reason, life with knowledge, life that is minded in the way that human life is minded. This, we can say, is thinking life, so long as we understand thinking, not as a specific activity (one among a number of "psychological functions"), but as a mode of being that finds expression not just in silent soliloquy, but also in word and deed. This is the very fabric of our lives, a fabric woven by education.

(Related Chapters: 5, 10, 11, 12, 26, 27, 28, 29, 33.)

References

Anscombe, G. E. M. (1958) "Modern Moral Philosophy," *Philosophy*, 33(124): 1–19.
Anscombe, G. E. M. (2000) *Intention*. 2nd edition, revised. Cambridge, MA: Harvard University Press.
Baehr, J. (2011) *The Inquiring Mind: On Intellectual Virtues and Virtue Epistemology*. Oxford: Oxford University Press.
Bakhurst, D. (2005) "Strong Culturalism," in D. Johnson and C. Erneling (eds.) *The Mind as a Scientific Object: Between Brain and Culture*. New York: Oxford University Press, 413–431.
Bakhurst, D. (2008) "Minds, Brains and Education," *Journal of Philosophy of Education* 42(3–4): 415–432.
Bakhurst, D. (2011) *The Formation of Reason*. Oxford: Wiley-Blackwell.
Bakhurst, D. (2018) "Trouble with Knowledge," *Philosophy* 93(3): 433–453.
Bakhurst, D. (ed.) (2020) *Teaching and Learning: Epistemic, Metaphysical and Ethical Dimensions*, *Journal of Philosophy of Education* (Special Issue), 54(2).
Brandom, R. (2000) *Articulating Reasons*. Cambridge, MA: MIT Press.
Bruner, J. (1990) *Acts of Meaning*. Cambridge, MA: Harvard University Press.
Bruner, J. (1997) *The Culture of Education*. Cambridge, MA: Harvard University Press.
Churchland, P. (2013) *Matter and Consciousness*. 3rd edition (first edition 1984). Cambridge, MA: MIT Press.
Curren, R. (2014) "Judgement and the Aims of Education," *Social Philosophy and Policy* 31(1): 36–59.
Dancy, J. (1993) *Moral Reasons*. Oxford: Blackwell.
Dennett, D. (1991) *Consciousness Explained*. New York: Little, Brown and Company.
Goldman, A. (1999) *Knowledge in a Social World*. Oxford: Clarendon Press.
Goldman, A. and O'Connor, C. (2021) "Social Epistemology," in E. N. Zalta (ed.) *Stanford Encyclopedia of Philosophy*. https://plato.stanford.edu/archives/spr2021/entries/epistemology-social/. Accessed 26 July, 2021.
Hacking, I. (1999) *The Social Construction of What?* Cambridge, MA: Harvard University Press.
Ilyenkov, E. V. (2009) *The Ideal in Human Activity*. Pacifica, CA: Marxist Internet Archive.
Kant, I. (1998) *Critique of Pure Reason*. Translated and edited by P. Guyer and A. W. Wood. Cambridge: Cambridge University Press.
Kern, A. (2017) *Sources of Knowledge: On the Concept of a Rational Capacity for Knowledge*. Cambridge, MA: Harvard University Press.
Kotzee, B. (ed.) (2014) *Education and the Growth of Knowledge*. Oxford: Wiley-Blackwell.
McDowell, J. (1996) *Mind and World*. 2nd edition with a new introduction by the author. Cambridge, MA: Harvard University Press.
McDowell, J. (1998) "Knowledge and the Internal," in his *Meaning, Knowledge, and Reality*. Cambridge, MA: Harvard University Press, 395–413.
McDowell, J. (2011) *Perception as a Capacity for Knowledge*. Milwaukee, WI: Marquette University Press.
Moran, R. (2001) *Authority and Estrangement*. Princeton, NJ: Princeton University Press.
Oakeshott, M. (1991) "The Voice of Poetry in the Conversation of Mankind," in his *Rationalism in Politics and Other Essays*. New and Expanded Edition. Indianapolis: Liberty Fund, 488–541.
Oakeshott, M. (2001) *The Voice of Liberal Learning*. Indianapolis: Liberty Fund.
Peters, R. S. (2007) "Education as Initiation," in R. Curren (ed.) *Philosophy of Education: An Anthology*. Oxford: Blackwell, 192–205.

Phillips, D. C. (1995) "The Good, the Bad and the Ugly: The Many Faces of Constructivism," *Educational Researcher* 24(7): 5–12.
Pritchard, D. (2012) *Epistemological Disjunctivism*. Oxford: Oxford University Press.
Rödl, S. (2007) *Self-Consciousness*. Cambridge, MA: Harvard University Press.
Rödl, S. (2020) "Teaching, Freedom and the Human Individual," *Journal of Philosophy of Education* 54(2): 290–304.
Tomasello, M. (2014) *A Natural History of Human Thinking*. Cambridge, MA: Harvard University Press.
Tomasello, M. (2019) *Becoming Human: A Theory of Ontogeny*. Cambridge, MA: Harvard University Press.
Vygotsky, L. S. (1986) *Thought and Language*. Revised edition, A. Kozulin (ed.). Cambridge, MA: MIT Press.

5

UNDERSTANDING AS AN EDUCATIONAL OBJECTIVE

Catherine Z. Elgin

Explain, describe, illustrate, show your work – such instructions frame homework assignments, problem sets, term paper instructions, exams. Students are expected to display their grasp of the topics the assignments concern. To succeed, it is typically not enough for students to parrot back the information they have been given or routinely apply rules they have been taught. They are supposed to draw on what they've been taught and demonstrate that they can do something academically appropriate with it. If such demands are properly keyed to the courses of study – if, that is, they actually provide insight into what students have learned – they afford evidence that objectual understanding – that is, understanding of a topic or subject matter – is a fundamental educational goal. Educators organize programs, courses, lesson plans, and individual assignments with the goal of enhancing the understanding of the subjects they teach. Then they assess student work by judging the extent to which it manifests enhanced understanding. The aim of achieving and leveraging understanding frames the delineation of disciplines as well as curricular and pedagogical decisions about how and what to teach, how and what to assess. My aim in this paper is to explain and justify education's emphasis on enhancing understanding.

Following Kvanvig (2003), let us distinguish between propositional understanding and objectual understanding. The difference is captured in the grammar of attributions. If a sentence has the form, "*S* understands that *p*" or "*S* understands why *p*," the understanding in question is propositional. It pertains to a particular matter of fact that can be expressed in a proposition. If the direct object is a noun denoting a topic, a subject matter, or a body of information – "*S* understands φ" – the understanding is objectual. In what follows, I will use the term "understanding" without a modifier to refer to objectual understanding. My thesis is that a major goal of education is and should be increasing and deepening objectual understanding. The scope of such understanding can be narrow or wide – understanding chemistry or covalent bonds, basketball or the Lakers' defensive strategy, the French Revolution or the storming of the Bastille. The topic may be a priori or a posteriori, normative or descriptive, factual or fictional. One might understand the extinction of the dinosaurs, the obligations of citizens, the importance of Cantor's theorem, the dangers en route to Mordor. Regardless of these differences, such understanding is holistic. It concerns systematic links across a range of phenomena, not a discrete, isolated matter of fact. Although it typically embeds some understandings-why and understandings-that, the objectual understanding of a topic is not exhausted by or reducible to propositional understanding.

DOI: 10.4324/9781003172246-7

Understanding a Topic

From the earliest grades, students study history, a discipline that seems thoroughly grounded in facts. We might suppose that the goal is for them to come to know important historical facts – for example, when the Battle of Hastings took place or who invented the steam engine. Standard instructional practice belies this. History teachers are not satisfied with the performance of students who merely know what happened. To see why they are not, it pays to follow Morton White and distinguish between a chronicle and a historical narrative (White 1965). A chronicle is a record of facts about the past; a historical narrative establishes connections among them. The distinction is conceptual, not chronological. Although a chronicle provides data for a historical narrative, we should not imagine that its chronicle is complete before a history is written. A chronicle and the associated history each influence the development of the other. As a history emerges, a historian realizes that the chronicle needs additional facts. Still, the distinction is epistemologically useful in that it enables us to isolate different elements in our understanding of the past.

A chronicle is just a list of facts. It makes no connections. The position of an entry on the list is arbitrary. No order is even implicit. So, for example, a chronicle of facts about Julius Caesar available to fifth-graders might include:

Died: 44 BCE
Roman general
Born: 100 BCE
Killed on the Ides of March
Kidnapped by pirates
First Roman emperor
Crossed the Rubicon
Fought in the Gallic Wars
Married three times
Marched with his army on Rome.

If the instructional objective were simply that the students know these facts, the teacher could just require them to memorize the chronicle. Successful students could then reel off the facts by rote. But the history teacher's objective is different. She wants the students to begin to understand Caesar's rise and fall, the ways it related to earlier events and set the stage for later ones, the ways it impacted the history of the Roman Empire and of the West. That requires a history, not just a chronicle. The students should learn to appreciate how the facts listed in the chronicle relate to one another as well as to further matters that do not appear on the list.

A history organizes the facts listed in the chronicle, relating them to one another. It establishes a temporal order, causal relations, dependencies; it makes logical connections, draws distinctions, provides explanations. It uses words like "because," "in order to," "after" and "therefore," which are not to be found in the chronicle. The historical narrative omits and augments. For example, an elementary school history of Caesar's rise and fall might omit mention of his multiple marriages on the ground that they don't seem to matter to the understanding it seeks to provide. It might augment "crossed the Rubicon" to emphasize that Caesar crossed from the north to the south because he was heading for Rome. It might contend that his intention to lead his army to Rome explains his crossing the Rubicon. It might take his crossing the Rubicon as evidence that Caesar was ambitious. It might go on to suggest that his ambition led to his assassination. The history then weaves the facts of the chronicle into a narrative that makes sense of the episode it deals with.

Although the narrative seems simple, it is epistemically complex. To convert a chronicle into a history requires criteria of relevance, evidence, and importance. Decisions about ordering, augmentation, and omission go beyond the facts that the chronicle supplies. Taxonomy and vocabulary may be crucial. Does the available evidence support the contention that Caesar was ambitious? Does it support the contention that he crossed the Rubicon out of ambition? Answers to such questions depend on the criteria of acceptability in play. They determine whether the chronicle supplies the sort of evidence required to attribute character traits and motives. Through the historical narrative, the students begin to glean insight into such matters.

The students are given the narrative, not just the chronicle. They may experience it as a seamless whole, telling the story of Caesar's rise and fall. It might seem that all the epistemological work is done by the writer of the text; the students are oblivious to it. But the seemingly seamless narrative admits of a sort of epistemological factor analysis – a factor analysis that figures in what they are expected to do with the narrative. They need to take it apart. They may be asked to distinguish between the brute facts which would appear in the chronicle and the interpretive elements which would figure in the explanations of those facts. For example, they may be expected to recognize that the sorts of considerations that could reasonably be adduced to argue that Caesar was ambitious are different from the sorts of considerations that could reasonably be adduced to argue that he fought in the Gallic Wars. They may be expected to distinguish between important and unimportant facts. Does it matter that he was kidnapped by pirates, or is that just an odd bit of trivia? In preparing to write an essay, they may be advised to start by making a chronicle of the facts they want to include, then to go on to write an account that connects those facts.

In describing a chronicle, I said nothing about what qualifies a statement of fact for inclusion. Even though a chronicle is just a list, it is not an arbitrary list. It is a list of facts about a particular episode, event or era. We wouldn't find "Platypuses are monotremes" or "The Red Sox won the 2004 World Series" in the chronicle we have been discussing. They have nothing to do with Caesar. Nor would we find "Caesar disliked beans," since even if it is true, there is no evidence for it. Evidently, statements of fact qualify for inclusion in a particular chronicle by being recognized as satisfying disciplinary demands for accuracy, relevance, and justification. The discipline of history underwrites the statement that Caesar was killed on the Ides of March. It certifies that the statement satisfies its standards. Disciplinary norms thus figure in establishing criteria for inclusion in a chronicle. Omissions matter. If the chronicle is constructed in a way that omits important material, or the narrative excludes or elides it, the history is flawed. So the student who begins work on her essay by writing a chronicle should recognize that the facts that she lists should be ones that historians would deem relevant, accurate, and sufficiently well established. To satisfy that requirement, she needs at least an implicit grasp of the discipline's criteria.

The narratives, both those the students read and those they write, may disclose gaps and incongruities. Questions arise, grounded in the connections that have been forged. If Caesar was a general, fighting a land war in Gaul, how did he even encounter pirates, much less get kidnapped by them? How did his participation in the Gallic wars bear on what happened when he moved on Rome? As her understanding of history grows, the student should be able to identify significant gaps, incongruities, and biases in the emerging account, and begin to recognize or develop strategies for resolving them. Minimally, she should appreciate that the gaps, incongruities, and biases show how and where her current understanding is limited. For this she needs to take a critical stance. Even a fifth-grader's understanding of Caesar's rise and fall involves considerably more than knowledge of discrete facts. To make sense of the episode requires respecting the relevant epistemic standards, norms, and criteria. It involves making the sorts of connections that satisfy the grade-appropriate standards of the discipline and eschewing those that do not.

There is nothing special about history here. A similar schema applies to the emergence of understanding in other disciplines. Although White applies his conception of a chronicle exclusively to the discipline of history, we can think of scientific understanding starting with a chronicle of scientific facts – perhaps facts about covalent bonds. The chronicle might consist of a list of covalent compounds:

Oxygen – O_2
Chlorine – Cl_2
Water – H_2O
etc.

It might include statements like

Covalent compounds share two or more electrons.

The scientific chronicle would not include the statement that the compounds are covalent *because* they share two or more electrons. It would not say how they come to share electrons or why it matters that they do. Explanatory connections go beyond the material expressly presented in the corresponding chronicle. A scientific account, like a historical narrative, systematizes and organizes the material in its chronicle to establish logical, spatiotemporal, and explanatory connections. Unlike most historical narratives, however, a scientific account includes models that serve as mediators (see Morgan & Morrison 1999), linking individual matters of fact with overarching scientific laws. We understand the facts by, in effect, filtering them through the mesh that a model provides. The models are not themselves statements of *fact*, however, for they are known not to be true. I characterize them as felicitous falsehoods (Elgin 2017). Others take them to be approximations (see Khalifa 2017; Grimm 2016). Either way, an understanding that represents covalent bonds as Lewis structures, or one that appeals to $pV = nRT$ to explain the relation between temperature and pressure in a gas, does not restrict itself to literal truths. The permissibility of such deviations derives from the science's conception of the sort of understanding it seeks to provide. That conception underwrites the conviction that the deviations from truth are, in the context where the models function, not difference-makers (see Strevens 2008). A student incorporating such models and laws in her understanding of the phenomena ought not, of course, take them to be true. Rather she needs to appreciate both that they are not strictly true and that their divergence from truth does not discredit them.

To go from a scientific chronicle to a systematic understanding involves establishing relations that underwrite explanations, observations, demonstrations, and experiments. As in the move from a chronicle to a history, some elements of the scientific chronicle may be set aside on the grounds that they are mere curiosities or outliers that the science need not accommodate, or on the grounds that they fall within the province of a different discipline. Factors that were not listed in the chronicle may be introduced. These might include as yet undetected matters of fact, such as further covalent compounds, distinctions between types of covalent bonds, intermediate steps that need to be filled in, as well as new or refined models and idealizations. They are justified to the extent that they strengthen the network.

The emerging account must satisfy relevant criteria of evidence and relevance. It must exclude considerations that are deemed scientifically impermissible. Although it may be reasonable for the historian to adduce Caesar's ambition to explain his crossing the Rubicon, it would be impermissible (except perhaps metaphorically) for the scientist to adduce the atom's ambition to complete its electron shell to explain a covalent bond. Like the student of history, the student of a science must be sensitive to the gaps and incongruities in her nascent understanding. She should recognize questions it leaves open, and should have some idea how scientifically to approach them. She needs to understand the relevant scientific methods, what they deliver, and why and to what extent their results are creditable. Here too, understanding goes beyond knowledge of established facts. The successful chemistry student must do more than memorize the chronicle. She needs to grasp the connections the science finds among the items listed in the chronicle. She also needs to appreciate why the science takes these connections to hold, to be explanatory, and to be significant. Only with an appreciation of the relevant methods, norms, and standards does the student understand the subject matter.

This way of putting things may sound intellectually too sophisticated to characterize K-12 student learning. But it is, I suggest, what students achieve when they come to understand a topic. That understanding dawns slowly. There is no suggestion that young students are self-consciously aware of the norms, standards and criteria implicit in their substantive grasp of a subject matter. But even young students are regularly asked to explain, to give examples, to extrapolate to further cases, to draw inferences that go beyond the explicit content of the instruction they have been given. To do so non-accidentally, they need to be at least implicitly aware of the epistemic norms, standards, and criteria that govern the discipline. Over time, I suggest, if they continue in the discipline, what was implicit becomes explicit. They learn how to think like a historian or a chemist or a geographer. As they internalize and endorse the epistemic norms and standards, those norms and standards provide a basis for critical assessment of the ways the discipline approaches its subject. Although this may not be explicit, they come to understand not just the subject, but the nature of their understanding of the subject.

What does this achieve? *An* understanding of a topic is a network of acceptable epistemic commitments in reflective equilibrium – that is, a network whose elements are reasonable in light of one another and the network as a whole is at least as reasonable as any available alternative when judged against one's antecedent commitments about the subject. Such a network of commitments must be grounded in fact, be duly responsive to evidence, and enable non-trivial relevant inferences and perhaps actions to foster one's cognitive ends (Elgin 1996, 2017). These conditions need to be spelled out.

To say that an understanding must be grounded in fact is not to say that it must consist only or even mainly of true statements of fact. Contemporary science consists largely of idealizations and models that are known to be literally false. Many earlier theories were only approximately true. Such science nevertheless constitutes an understanding of the phenomena because the ways that and the extent to which the models diverge from the facts make no difference to the understanding they figure in. For example, at the level where the model is apt, the factors that the ideal gas law, $pV = nRT$, ignores are trivial. So, setting them aside, as real but unworthy of consideration, fosters the understanding of gas dynamics.

Divergences from truth are also common in early education. A young student's initiation into botany is apt to involve an extremely simplified explanation of photosynthesis. The complexities of the topic and the methods for investigating it are beyond his reach. But even if such a highly simplified explanation qualifies as grounded in fact, it might seem that the requirement that the network of commitments be at least as good as any available alternative precludes attributing any genuine understanding to the child. There are a vast number of better, albeit more complicated, alternatives on offer. What this objection shows is that the requirement is indexed to an audience. The network of commitments about photosynthesis gleaned by the second-graders constitutes an understanding insofar as, given their level of cognitive development, it is at least as good as any alternative available to them. It would be both unreasonable and fruitless to bombard them with the information that botanists regularly draw on. A good second-grade lesson would provide the students a basic grasp of the process, which gives them something to build on. It is true enough. The schematic understanding he achieves provides a springboard for further learning. It puts young students in a position to take the next steps. Understanding comes in degrees. So, a second-grader can display some understanding of photosynthesis; a fifth-grader, a greater understanding, a graduate student in botany a far greater understanding.

An epistemic network must answer to evidence. This requires that there be evidence, identifiable and certifiable as such. Networks for which there is no evidence, and networks which make predictions which are not borne out by evidence afford no understanding. Astrology, for example, does not constitute an epistemic network. Even if astrological commitments are mutually supportive, astrologists make causal predictions about the influence of celestial arrangements on terrestrial events which are not borne out. Either they are trivial, or they are too vague to be tested, or they are falsified upon testing. The evidence requirement does more than discredit pseudo-science. It underwrites the idea that students should recognize not just what an account claims, but also what evidence supports it. They should be poised to reject accounts that are not backed by evidence. They should be able to answer the question, "How do we know that?"

Beyond the Information Given

Students should be able to go beyond the information given. Trivial inferences count for little. They simply articulate what was obvious anyway. But students should be able to solve further problems, extrapolate to new cases, draw effective analogies, generate plausible hypotheses on the basis of what they have learned. This is the educational dimension of the requirement that the network enable non-trivial inferences and actions. Its importance is not exhausted by what it shows about current mastery. A network in reflective equilibrium should provide leverage for further inquiry. It should equip students to build on what they currently understand. In demonstrating their mastery, the students discover that they can do more with the material than what they have been explicitly taught. This puts them in a position to see not just that, but also how, the subject is open-ended. There is more to be discovered.

The growth of understanding is flexible, fallible, and dynamic. A network's equilibrium may be upset by new findings – findings that its methods enabled it to uncover. This is an asset, not a liability. It enables us to remove previously accepted errors, ill-advised strategies, unreliable methods. Whether or not the current equilibrium is flawed, it is open to further elaboration and expansion. So, the acceptability of a given network of commitments is not expected to be permanent. New questions, techniques, and standards are apt to call it into question. In light of new considerations, it is susceptible to reevaluation. That being so, there is benefit in students' revisiting material they previously studied. More is involved than learning a few further facts. When the students who studied Caesar in fifth grade learn more about the history of Rome, they may conclude that Caesar's multiple marriages, which they had dismissed as merely personal, actually played a role in forging important political alliances. They then have reason to integrate Caesar's marriages into their emerging understanding of the period. That gives them an incentive to query other considerations that they had set aside. Because the networks of epistemic commitments that constitute understandings of a topic do not purport to provide the last word, they are springboards for the advancement of understanding. The recognition that current understanding is limited and may be flawed makes sense of how investigators proceed at the cutting edge of inquiry. It also makes sense of what goes on in education. There is then a continuum from the earliest education up to and beyond the cutting edge of inquiry.

A good exam asks students to manifest their disciplinary understanding of the material being studied. A high school chemistry student taking an exam on covalent bonding will cast her answers in the language of chemistry: molecules, atoms and electrons, as well as Lewis structures, orbitals and bonds. That terminology marks the distinctions that are deemed to be important to chemistry's understanding of its domain. In properly using that terminology, she shows a recognition of how the science frames its topics. Although she will make some literal statements of fact – e.g., "H_2O is a covalent compound" – her answers are apt to involve statements and diagrams that describe the phenomena via models and idealizations that are not literally true. In her reliance on models and diagrams, she is no different from professional chemists. To be sure, theirs are more sophisticated. But both the student and the professional understand covalent bonds in terms of models that diverge from the phenomena. For her answer to be duly responsive to evidence, she must draw on, and frame it in terms of, the sorts of considerations that chemistry counts as evidence. It will not do to simply assert that she has it on good authority that H_2O is a covalent compound, even though it is, and the authority she relies on is epistemically responsible. Her answer should, at least implicitly, reflect that she recognizes evidence is relevant and why. She should make it clear that it is reasonable to reflectively endorse her conclusion given evidence of this kind. Her understanding of covalent bonds should enable her to draw non-trivial inferences about the subject. She thus needs to be sensitive to the kinds of inferences that are acceptable in high school chemistry, and which of these are relevant to the question. She needs to be aware of what considerations and modes of argument she can draw on to back her claim. She should recognize what factors she cannot afford to omit. The student is expected to be and display that she is attuned to the methods, standards, resources, and orientations of the discipline. It is not enough to give a list of known facts about covalent bonds. Depending on the question, she may be asked to go further – not only to draw non-trivial inferences, but perhaps to speculate about what would be the case if the bond were weaker.

Reflective Endorsement

An understanding of a topic is a network of commitments in reflective equilibrium. *To* understand a topic is to accept such a network – that is, to be willing and able to use it in non-trivial inferences and actions when one's ends are cognitive (see Elgin 2017). A willing but clueless chemistry student has no grasp of covalent bonds. An unwilling but clued-in chemistry student is loath to reason and act on what the network of commitment provides. The ability requirement involves competence. For Mariah to understand the phenomenon, she must be able to reason appropriately about, and engage in appropriate actions regarding, covalent bonds. This might involve inferences, analogies, extrapolations. It might involve designing and executing experiments or contriving idealized models. It would also involve knowing the limits within which her reasoning and actions are appropriate. If she is able, she can do such things. The willingness requirement is a matter of reflective endorsement. In being willing to accept the network, Mariah adopts it as her own. She acknowledges that it provides resources to promote her cognitive ends with respect to a branch of chemistry.

Epistemic acceptance is a higher-order stance; it involves more than merely appreciating what the network is committed to. Jennifer Lackey's creationist teacher vignette shows this. Stella, Lackey says, is a young earth creationist. For religious reasons, she flatly rejects the theory of evolution. Nevertheless, she teaches it to her biology students (see Lackey 2008). She is adept at working within the theory's network of commitments. She can show how and why it supports the claim that *Homo sapiens* evolved from *Homo erectus*. She readily works out the implications of the theory. But she does not reflectively endorse the theory or its implications. She considers them wildly incorrect. She recognizes both that and why the theory of evolution is the consensus opinion in biology. But she does not understand the origin of species in terms of it; for when her ends are cognitive, as opposed to merely pedagogical, she is unwilling to use it. She refuses to stand behind it. Her students take the further step. Convinced by her teaching, they hold that the theory of evolution accounts for the diversity of life on earth. They reflectively endorse the theory. They are willing and able to draw on the resources it supplies to provide reasons for biological claims.[1] Unlike their teacher they understand the origin of species.

To reflectively endorse a network of commitments is to undertake an epistemic responsibility. The agent must consider herself willing and able to supply reasons in defense of the network and the inferences and actions it licenses. She has thus to recognize the relevant reasons and their strength. Again, this may sound epistemically too ambitious. But it amounts to her being in a position to give a cogent answer to questions like "Why should we think *that*?" If a fourth-grader gives a grade-level appropriate answer to such a question, she discharges her epistemic responsibility. Recall that a network that provides an understanding equips those who reflectively endorse it with the capacity to make *non-trivial* inferences. Such inferences are neither easy nor obvious. So, a student who understands a subject both needs to and is equipped to use her own judgment about the subject.

Although what she has been taught supplies resources, she has to go further – to manipulate the commitments to answer new questions, formulate and solve new problems, perhaps set new epistemic ends.

A worry arises. Inasmuch as the networks a student endorses are largely the fruits of her education, might her pretensions to epistemic autonomy be spurious? If she considers *e* to be evidence for *p* only because this is what chemistry counts as evidence, or she considers *s* to be a reason for *q* only because that is what history counts as a reason, she seems to be a victim of indoctrination. Her opinions are not her own. That she stands behind the disciplinary mandates shows only that the indoctrination was effective. But education is not indoctrination. It involves the development of both critical thinking skills and the propensity to deploy them (see Siegel 1988). If the student both appreciates that this is what chemistry counts as evidence, and she is convinced that chemistry gives her good reason to count it as evidence, the situation is different. For then she reflectively endorses the standards by which chemistry judges such things.

Students should learn both why practitioners in the different disciplines favor their criteria of reason or evidence, and how those criteria can responsibly be challenged. This is not so difficult as it might seem. Even young students have the ability to recognize when a consideration they are inclined to credit does not fit comfortably with what they have been taught. When a student who has been taught that every event has a cause learns that radioactive decay involves the random emission of particles, she recognizes that the new information does not fit what she has learned. Even if she is in no position to resolve the tension, the recognition itself gives her a stance for thinking critically about what she has learned. When a student who has been taught that justice is blind learns that a disproportionate number of African Americans are convicted of crimes, she has reason to question what she has been taught. This is not to suggest that she always will or always should abandon what she has been taught. But the tension she finds is evidence that all is not epistemically well. If the student has been deprived of cognitive resources for looking further, or has been disincentivized from looking further, she is a victim of indoctrination. If she recognizes the mismatch, has an incentive to look further, and has some idea about how to look further, she is capable of functioning as an epistemically autonomous agent. If she is motivated to look for mismatches and investigate what they reveal, her education has served her well.

Equilibrium can be destabilized by new insights, new information, new methods, new perspectives. So rather than treating what they have learned so far as fixed and final, students need to learn when and how to revise their views. Rarely, if ever, are there clear-cut decision procedures for making such revisions. In learning to think critically students develop the skills and propensity to consider what is to be said for and what is to be said against accepting (or continuing to accept) a commitment *c*; what are the epistemic and non-epistemic risks that accompany accepting *c*, rejecting *c*, suspending (that is, neither accepting nor rejecting) *c*; what plausible alternatives there are to *c* and what is to be said for and against each of them. In acquiring these skills and propensities, they learn to use their own judgment. To use one's own judgment is not a matter of deciding on the basis of a whim or a personal preference. It is a matter of weighing alternatives when the answer is not clear (and sometimes when grounds on which to weigh are themselves matters of controversy). Since whatever an epistemic agent chooses is what she reflectively endorses, she recognizes that she is expected to be able to defend her choice, to provide reasons (even if not conclusive reasons), to stand behind her choice and her reasons for making that choice.

Conclusion

I have argued that familiar pedagogical and assessment practices presuppose that a central goal of education is to promote objectual understanding. I have drawn my examples from K-12 classes to emphasize that the goal runs through the fabric of education; it is not restricted to the ivory tower. I highlighted the capacities students develop to extend and critique what they are explicitly taught. These capacities are integral to epistemic autonomy.

Still, one might wonder *why* promoting such autonomy should be a goal of disciplinary instruction. If the topic is the structure of covalent bonds or the rise of the Roman Empire, why isn't it preferable to simply convey the currently best grade-level-accessible information about the topic and grade students on the basis of their ability to reproduce that information? It is overwhelmingly likely that current experts know more about the topic than students can glean from their clumsy, awkwardly designed science projects or their sketchy, less than well- documented term papers. This would make sense *if* our goal were to bring it about that the students have the best currently available information about the topic they are studying. When that is the goal, deferring to experts, and insuring that students grasp expert opinion is justifiable. So, for example, it might be a good strategy in sex-ed classes on avoiding sexually transmitted diseases. But history and science (as well as other academic disciplines) are different. Insisting that high school chemistry students know the current (duly simplified) consensus on covalent bonds, merely because it is the best scientists can now do, seems unwarranted. It invites the challenge, "Why do we have to learn *that*?" The challenge is reasonable, not only because few of them aspire to be chemists, but also because scientific understanding is dynamic. The consensus is apt to change. So, if we want to say that students should master the current (duly simplified) consensus, the reason must be more than its status. It must be because the mastery they acquire through learning about what is now understood about covalent bonds will equip them with something valuable – something that will endure when they have forgotten that chlorine is a covalent compound, and when the consensus evolves.

They learn how to see and think about a range of phenomena from the orientation that a particular discipline provides. That orientation supplies standards of evidence and argument, modes of representation, techniques, models, and measuring devices. It shows how to access the phenomena from a particular point of view, and it shows why such access is both valuable and open to legitimate challenge. To gain these benefits, however, the students need to adopt the orientation. They need to learn to operate within its parameters, to satisfy its standards of rigor, to assess their outputs by its requirements. That is, they need to function as epistemic agents, not mere spectators.

The account I have sketched may seem remote from everyday teaching and learning. It credits even the youngest students with perhaps surprising levels of epistemological sophistication. But when we reflect on the assignments teachers give and on the capacity of students to complete those assignments successfully, we recognize that even young students are adept at identifying evidence, drawing inferences, making analogies, formulating and defending arguments bearing on the topics they study. Teachers are apt to focus on day-to-day learning objectives; policy makers, on year-to-year objectives. But insofar as these objectives are justified, their rationale lies in their broadening and deepening the resources students possess for thinking well. Subject matters ground education. They put students in touch with the world. And they equip students with resources for thinking broadly and deeply about the world. "All which schools can do or need to do for pupils, insofar as their minds are concerned..., is develop their ability to think" (Dewey 1916: 152).

(Related Chapters: 1, 3, 4, 10, 11, 12, 26, 27, 28, 29.)

Note

1 Scholars can understand theories that they do not reflectively endorse. So, Stella's stance vis à vis the theory of evolution might be like a classicist's stance toward ancient Greek religion. Each takes a body of commitments as the object to be understood. Each understands what the theory is committed to. But neither understands the phenomena the theories purport to concern via the theories in question. See Malfatti 2019.

References

Dewey, J. (1916) *Democracy and Education*. New York: The Free Press.
Elgin, C. (2017) *True Enough*. Cambridge MA: MIT Press.
Elgin, C. (1996) *Considered Judgment*. Princeton: Princeton University Press.
Grimm, S. (2016) "Understanding and Transparency," in S. Grimm, C. Baumberger & S. Ammon (eds.) *Explaining Understanding: New Essays in Epistemology and Philosophy of Science*. New York: Routledge, 212–229.
Khalifa, K. (2017) *Understanding, Explanation, and Scientific Knowledge*. Cambridge UK: Cambridge University Press.
Kvanvig, J. (2003) *The Value of Knowledge and the Pursuit of Understanding*. Cambridge: Cambridge University Press.
Lackey, J. (2008) *Learning from Words*. Oxford: Oxford University Press.
Malfatti, F. (2019) "Can Testimony Generate Understanding?" *Social Epistemology* 33(6): 477–490.
Morgan, M. and Morrison, M. (eds.) (1999) *Models as Mediators*. Cambridge, UK: Cambridge University Press.
Siegel, H. (1988) *Educating Reason: Rationality, Critical Thinking and Education*. New York: Routledge.
Strevens, M. (2008) *Depth: An Account of Scientific Explanation*. Cambridge, MA: Harvard University Press.
White, M. (1965) *Foundations of Historical Knowledge*. New York: Harper & Row.

6

VALUES AND EVIDENCE IN EDUCATIONAL DECISION-MAKING

Harry Brighouse and Adam Swift

Some Cases

Imagine a Governor of a State that has suddenly seen an upturn in revenues. She can increase State funding of k-12 education by 20%. The legislature has decided to spend half the extra money on an across-the-board increase in per-student funding but is divided on whether to target the other half to students with disabilities or students in poverty.

Now imagine a School Board member with the deciding vote on whether to authorize a new "no-excuses" charter school being proposed for a low-income neighborhood in the district. The organization proposing the school has a track record of success running similar schools in nearby districts.

Imagine, finally, a middle school Principal. Her District leadership, her teachers, and the parents of the students all trust her. She can choose whether to group the students in Mathematics and English Language Arts classes according to how proficient they are, or to put them in comprehensive, mixed-proficiency classes.

Value-Led and Data-Informed

In order to decide what to do, in each case, the agent needs the best data about the probable effects of the different options. If she's lucky, similar options have been tried, and monitored, in similar circumstances elsewhere. If she's *really* lucky, randomized controlled trials have been done, and she has colleagues who are skilled in understanding and applying the knowledge such trials produce. However good the data she can get access to, though, it will not tell her what to do. Data are like a map. If the map is sufficiently detailed, and if the user is sufficiently skilled at reading it, and knows where she is, it will help her work out *how to get where she wants to go*. But the map cannot tell her *where she should go*. The same applies to data. If they are sufficiently good, and the user is sufficiently skilled at interpreting them, and has a good enough understanding of the status quo, they are invaluable in helping decide what choice to make, given some desired set of outcomes. But they are silent on what outcomes to seek.

To use a map effectively you need to know roughly where you are, and roughly where you want to go. In fact, you need to know where you are and where you want to go even to know which map or maps will be useful to you. Similarly, in educational decision-making (and policy decisions more generally), you need to know what you have reason to value in order to use the data effectively and even in order to know what data are relevant. A simple slogan for educational decision-making would be "value-led, and data-informed."

DOI: 10.4324/9781003172246-8

Unlike "data-driven decision-making," this slogan makes sense. But it does not denigrate the importance of data. Consider the map analogy one more time. Imagine that someone wants to get to Los Angeles but has (literally) no idea where in the world she currently is. It's helpful that she knows where she wants to go, but she's never going to get there. Without learning more, her choice about what move to take next is more likely to lead her away from Los Angeles than towards it. Or suppose she does know where she is, but she has no map; not even something scribbled on a napkin, no road signs, and no celestial information. In that case she is completely helpless. If she finds something scribbled on a napkin, and believes it to be reliable, she can make some non-random move. But, still, she'd prefer a Rand-McNally road map. And if her ultimate aim is to find a particular street in MacArthur Park she'd want something more detailed. Values guide decisions, but data are indispensable, and, other things equal, better (relevant) data lead to better decisions.

No amount of evidence however reliable or detailed, will tell our Governor, School Board member, and Principal what they should do. In order to know what to do, they need to know what they have reason to value. They also need evidence about the likely effects of various feasible options. How can they most fruitfully think about the values and evidence together?

A Model

We'll offer a basic model of how values and evidence should be combined to make policy, which can be summarized in the following schema (Brighouse et al. 2018). The initial headings may suggest that the procedure is a linear sequence – do (1) before moving onto (2), and so on – but our fuller description of them will make clear that in practice they interact. Think of them as distinct elements in the process rather than a sequence to be followed:

1. Identify the main values in play,
2. Identify the key decisions relevant to those values,
3. Assess the options in light of the values,
4. Establish what is the best policy overall in the circumstances.

Identify the Main Values in Play

The agents in question start by identifying the main values in play. These must include not only the values immediately pertinent to the area of decision-making under scrutiny but also those relating to other areas where policy changes may have collateral effects. Education does not only happen in schools, and what does happen in schools is influenced by many other factors such as housing, healthcare and levels of poverty (Duncan & Murnane 2011). While the work of establishing the values is philosophical, views about collateral effects must be informed by social science. Although social-scientific evidence cannot tell anyone what values they have reason to care about, exactly which of the values we have reason to care about are, or are not, in play in the context of any particular policy decision is in part an empirical matter. So even at this stage of the procedure both values and evidence are relevant.

It is common for education scholars to talk about "social justice" or "equity"; sometimes they will refer to the "common good" or "democracy." But these terms are usually used rather loosely. Careful analysis of the more specific, distinct, values subsumed under such labels can help us understand better which considerations are at stake in any attempt to identify one option as better or worse than another.

Our Governor, Principal, and School Board member will all want a finer-grained specification than "social justice" or "equity." Should they place higher value on equalizing educational resources, or on prioritizing benefit to the less advantaged students, or perhaps, on equalizing educational *outcomes*?

In the Governor's case, taking into account how well each is currently addressed in the funding system she has inherited, which disadvantage is more morally urgent: poverty or disability? They will all want to know the likely effects of the plausible choices they might make on the distribution of educational resources and outcomes, but perhaps there will be collateral effects on other things that matter: might the daily lived experience of being in school be impacted, independently of whatever effects the decisions have on achievement? And, if so, how much should she care about that, relative to the distributive effects? Given the possibility that charter schools might benefit some disadvantaged students at a cost to others (suggested by some evidence she'll encounter in stage 3), the School Board member might want help thinking about that kind of trade-off. She will also want to know which educational outcomes she has reason to care about, so that she can assess whether the dimensions on which some proposed school might benefit students (test scores, graduation rates) are good proxies for those. Like the others, the Principal, attending to the evidence (see stage 3) which distinguishes effects on productivity (overall levels of achievement) and on equality (distribution of achievement between groups) may want to know what to value in terms of distribution.

Some people are reluctant to think seriously about values because they are skeptical about the possibility of objectivity or rigor. Others may avoid this part of the process because it can quickly seem so complicated that it is just not worth the effort. The list of values may look too long, the differences between them too subtle or trivial. Philosophers have a tendency to introduce ever-finer distinctions, to increase complexity to a level that can be hard to map on to the issues that confront policymakers. But it does not have to be like that. Brighouse et al. identify a clear and manageable list of the values most relevant to the assessment of education policy (Brighouse et al. 2018: 19–43).

The list contains three categories of value. The first articulates the direct aims of education: the capacities that, when developed, conduce to the flourishing of the individuals who are being educated and those with whom they will interact. These include the capacities to be economically effective, to make autonomous judgments about how they should live their lives, to form and maintain meaningful and fulfilling personal relationships, to be able to engage competently and fairly in collective decision-making, to treat others as their equals, and to be personally fulfilled (White 1995, 2011).

The second category of value concerns distributions. It would be convenient if the same policies tended to produce the maximum amount of all these different good things for everybody. In practice we have to make trade-offs. Different people will be affected in different ways, so we also have to think about how opportunities for well-being, and the educational goods that contribute to them, are distributed. Different distributive values – equality, adequacy, and concern for the worse off – may conflict (Brighouse & Swift 2014; Jencks 1988; Satz 2007; Schouten 2012).

Finally, other values, not directly concerned with the production or distribution of educational goods, also need to be taken into account. These include considerations such as the goods intrinsic to childhood, parents' rights to make choices about their children's education, and respect for local autonomy, or for democratic processes more generally. These considerations can be conceived in different ways. Some, such as childhood goods, may be thought of as other – non-educational – values that policy makers should care about producing and distributing well. Others, such as parents' rights and respect for democratic processes, may more naturally be framed in non-consequentialist terms and understood as standing independent of the promotion and distribution of good outcomes altogether (compare Brighouse et al. 2018: 27–28 and Clayton et al. 2021: 831–836).

The list attempts systematically to set out the aims of education and the various values that are most relevant to the assessment of education policy. But it is only a proposal: your own careful philosophical reflection might incline you to revise it. The guiding idea is that decision-makers needn't start from square one every time they're confronted with a trade-off. They can reliably turn to a toolkit of relevant value considerations.

We have deliberately used the phrase "have [or has] reason to value" rather than simply "value." This is because responsible agents, especially when their decisions will affect other people, do not simply decide on the basis of their unreflective prejudices or "gut" feelings. They are bound to deliberate, carefully, about what actually matters: what they have *reason* to value, not simply what they *happen* to value. Further, in order to make an all things considered judgement it is not enough merely to identify the values at stake, it is necessary also to *weigh* them. Given multiple values and a non-ideal world, trade-offs are inevitable. Identifying the values helps us see what is at stake – what we are choosing between. But to come down in favor of a particular option we need more than that. We need judgments about the relative importance (or value) of the different values at stake. We need to weigh the different normative considerations against each other and come to an overall judgment.

How do we go about establishing what the right normative considerations are – what we have reason to value? Moral and political philosophers frequently invoke the process of reflective equilibrium. The ideas behind reflective equilibrium are that we can get closer to knowing what can be justified regarding matters of value by giving particular scrutiny to judgments that we know are especially likely to be flawed, and that through the right kind of reason-giving and reason-taking we can learn from one another's insights. We look at principles we take ourselves to be committed to, and our judgements about particular cases. Then we try to identify contradictions. When we find contradictions, we know we have a falsehood – we have not achieved reflective equilibrium – but we don't know what the falsehood is. We do, however, know that some of our principles and judgments align well with our self-interest, and that we possess the all-too-human tendency to be biased in our own favor. We may identify some judgments and principles that align well with received opinion and which we have reason to suppose that we have not considered carefully. We may also notice that some of our judgments are not very stable. And we can identify judgments and principles that morally decent, thoughtful people disagree with us about. Judgements and principles that meet any or all of those conditions are always suspect, and we start by subjecting them to scrutiny, ideally in reasoned and reasoning dialogue with people who have different experiences, backgrounds, and views from our own. We do this, as best we can, until we have a coherent set of beliefs, with our general principles matching our judgments about particular cases. The process doesn't guarantee truth, any more than the scientific method guarantees the truth of scientific claims. But it is what we have at our disposal, and there is good reason to think that it will generally improve our beliefs (Daniels 1979; Knight 2017; Rawls 2001).

Identify the Key Decisions Relevant to Those Values

In (1), we used the deliberately loose phrase "in play" because the process of identifying values involves a variety of different elements. At its most abstract, the task is to set out the range of different values relevant to education, and, more narrowly, those that are most pertinent to the kind of decision presented. But (2) requires something more specific. We need a sense of which values in particular our policy proposals should *be directed* towards. Are we concerned about low educational standards overall, about the low achievement of those at the bottom, or about the gap between them and those at the top? Are we worried that schools are focusing on the wrong things, or are we concerned that parents do not have enough (or have too much) influence over their children's schooling? We should, of course, try to keep all values in mind, so that we are sensitive to the full range of trade-offs between them. But in practice our analysis is likely to be prompted by a sense that one or two things in particular are the ones that really matter, or are the ones where action is most urgent. Perhaps that sense will be rather vague initially, but we have to start with some feeling that things should be better, and a sense of where action is particularly needed.

Suppose you start from a concern about the standard of basic numeracy and literacy among the lowest achievers. The worry will almost certainly have something to do with the way numeracy and literacy skills relate to people's opportunities for well-being as adults, and their capacity to contribute to the flourishing of others. It will probably also reflect a concern with the way those skills are distributed across the population (and the consequent distribution of flourishing), though whether that distributive concern has anything to do with equality may be more doubtful. Whatever you judge to be really troubling, the next task is to identify some key decisions that look as if they are most relevant to the realization of the relevant values. What are the different ways that you might plausibly address whatever now seems to be the problem?

That will depend in part on who you are. We simplified things in our opening examples by specifying exactly what options are on the table. In real life, decision-makers are usually not so lucky – a range of options may be available, some options might not be obvious, and other options, though easy to discern, might not obviously be genuinely available. It might be, for example, that resistance from parents, or teachers, or principals, or even voters, will prevent them from happening. The method we're suggesting is supposed to help decision-makers at all levels, from those devising national-level policies that will affect every school in the country to those in charge of individual schools, or even classrooms. They might be trying to improve the numeracy and literacy skills of the lowest-achieving children in their school or in their class. Or they might be thinking about more systemic attempts to raise standards at the bottom by changing the way children are allocated to different schools, or by reforming the way schools are financed. What decisions are plausibly relevant to the values clearly depends on what exactly they are trying to achieve and what decision-making options are actually available.

Every decision-maker, whether in education or elsewhere, and however close to or distant from the impact of the decision, identifies a space for action, either implicitly or explicitly. The procedure calls for explicitness: figure out what range of actions one really has available to one and choose from within that set. The aim at this stage is to identify decisions about actions that are plausible in two senses. The actions should be plausible in that they could actually be put into practice and, if put into practice, they would contribute to the values identified in (1). It is not going to be sensible to spend time (at step (3), which involves assessing the likely effects of the different options), on proposals that from the start look very unlikely either to achieve the desired goals, or to have any realistic chance of being carried out. We need to know what is feasible. Identifying the feasible set requires careful, evidence-based, description of existing states of affairs: to judge where we can realistically hope to get to from here we need to know precisely where we are. We also need predictions – with probabilities and timescales – about the likely effects of any things we might do to change the situation. All this requires an adequate understanding of the relevant social mechanisms and causal processes. Some goals may be feasible in the long run but completely unrealistic here and now, while choices that we make now may well change what is feasible in the longer term. Like the evaluative task, these judgments are extremely difficult. We have to be realistic about what kind of evidence can be expected. Sometimes we will have to make and act on judgments about what to do when the evidence can give us nothing more than a best guess about what will happen if we do it.

Even if they may be feasible in the longer-term, we cannot directly access our preferred states of affairs, so we have to pay attention to the dynamics that our actions are likely to set in motion. This creates still more uncertainty. Perhaps, for example, the use of lotteries in the admission of children to oversubscribed schools could, in the long run, produce more integrated schools, since proximity to the school (and hence property prices) would play a smaller role in the allocation process. However, the immediate effect of any move to introduce lotteries in some circumstances might be to drive more affluent parents out of the public school system altogether and into even more segregated and socially divisive private schools. If so, we could not avoid hard judgments about how much to aim for when, how to balance more likely short-term gain against lower probability long-term gain, how to weigh small but more robust progress against bigger but more easily reversed progress, and so on. These uncertainties create plenty of room for disagreement about what should be *done*, in terms of policy, even between those who would *evaluate* concrete outcomes in the same way.

Political constraints affect what is feasible. These include not only the electoral considerations confronting democratically elected politicians competing for votes, but also less obvious ways in which decision-makers have to keep an eye on how their decisions will be received by others (Gilabert & Lawford-Smith 2012). So, consider our school Principal, trying to decide whether to implement achievement grouping. One group of teachers is specifically opposed to achievement grouping. They will go along with it, because they trust her, but she knows they will not be happy with it. She will then find herself balancing the cost of that unpopularity, in terms of how it restricts her options when it comes to subsequent decisions, against whatever benefit might be produced by achievement grouping.

Judgments about feasibility are probabilistic. Perhaps, for example, early intervention policies aimed at children whose parents are not giving them experiences they need for healthy development will be experienced by those parents as a form of cultural imperialism, an attempt to impose white middle class norms (Pitzer 2014; Woodson & Love 2019). If so, that might lead to non-cooperation and backlash that leaves the children no better off and resources wasted. Perhaps some variants of those policies have a better chance of achieving the desired outcomes than others, and are more respectful of parents' preferences, but those policies are also more expensive so are less likely to gain the requisite political backing to make them realistic options. Is it feasible to improve children's early development by achieving a political consensus willing to support expenditure on policies that are less likely to alienate parents? The decision-maker may have to make a probabilistic judgment, and one derived from a host of other probabilistic judgments nested within it.

We would warn against erring too much on the side of caution in determining what the plausible actions are. One should be willing to consider innovative or radical actions that may differ from those on the current policy agenda. It is not until (3) that we get into the business of carefully assessing how likely it is that any given proposal would in fact achieve the desired goals, and at what cost in terms of other values. At this stage, the aim is simply to begin to focus our thinking, and to make the task in (3) manageable, by identifying a practicable set of proposals to work with. The question here is: what actions would be worth investigating seriously as an attempt to achieve the values identified in (1)?

Often some of the key decisions are obvious candidates, simply because they are already on the policy agenda. This means that much of what happens at (3) is the evaluation of already-existing proposals.

Assess the Options in Light of the Values and Evidence

The third step is to judge, as best one can, in the light of the best available evidence, what the effects will be of the decisions identified in stage (2) with respect to the values identified in stage (1). The short list of proposals was adopted at (2) because they seemed most relevant to the values identified in (1). Now one has to consider which decision will in fact produce the desired results. Perhaps, though initially attractive, more thorough investigation suggests that one decision will not actually help at all, or it will help only with respect to some values with costs to others, or it will produce only negative consequences. Now we are exploring the question of what outcomes are actually feasible in the circumstances that we face.

We have already made clear that decision-making should not be – indeed cannot be – data-driven. It must be value-driven: talk of "what works" makes no sense unless one has a value-informed goal in mind. But decision-making must be data-*informed*: indeed, if it is not data-informed, the values cannot guide it effectively, because every decision is a shot in the dark.

Think of our Governor. Suppose she has reason to care about reducing inequalities of outcomes that affect both low-income students and students with disabilities. She also has reason to care about their daily lived experience. So, she will want to know something about the likely effects of the specific amount of extra spending she is considering in relation to both. What is the evidence concerning the effects of additional spending on the outcomes and lived experience of low-income children compared with the effects on students with disabilities (Berry & Reback 2006; Jackson et al. 2016; Krueger 1999; Ladd 2012; Ladd & Fiske 2011; Verstegen 2011)? Are mechanisms in place to ensure that additional funds will actually be spent on the students for whom it is intended and, if not, does she have evidence that it will be spent in those ways?

Now consider our School Board member. She will want to know the likely effects of the new school on the outcomes for students in that school. Most studies of charter schools, whether in low-income areas or elsewhere, focus on standardized test results in reading and mathematics. But she will want evidence about the effects on a much wider range of learning outcomes than just those, especially if the effects on test scores are not large (Booker et al. 2007; Booker et al. 2008; Booker et al. 2008; Booker et al. 2011). And she will not want to restrict her attention to the effects on those students who attend the school. She is responsible to all the students in the district, and she will judge gains at the new school differently if they are at the expense of other schools in the district. Perhaps, for example, those drawn into the new school will not constitute a representative sample of the students in the district.

Consider, finally, our Principal, deciding whether to implement proficiency grouping in mathematics and reading lessons. She will want to consult the wealth of evidence on the effects of tracking on a range of the variables she has reason to value. These might include: the distribution of learning in reading and math; the absolute level of learning in reading and math; the daily lived experience of the students (is one of the decisions more likely than the other, for example, to prompt bullying, or feelings of worthlessness?); the social learning (positive or negative) that occurs when students are in classrooms with much higher, or much lower, achieving students. She will immediately notice that researchers have unearthed evidence relevant to some of these values but not to others and that, even among those they have focused on, the studies do not all point in one direction (Gamoran 2009; Huang 2009). The data will underdetermine her decision, even if she knows what she has reason to value. She can, if she has the time, or the support from staff in the school or district, delve further, and try to learn what studies bear on circumstances relevantly like hers.

This point – that the decision-makers should delve into what studies bear *on circumstances like theirs* – applies in any case. Even if the research had all pointed in one direction, and it related to all the values the Principal had reason to care about, *still* she would do well to delve further, if she has reason to believe her circumstances differ from those which have been studied. The evidence is often not decisive and always requires careful interpretation. Let's consider proficiency grouping. One influential finding, that gains to higher achieving students are offset by losses to low achieving students, came from a study of the UK at a time when lower achieving groups were routinely assigned bigger student:teacher ratios than higher achieving groups (Kerckhoff 1986). If our Principal has the freedom to create smaller student:teacher ratios for the lower achieving students, she might think the study has little bearing on her circumstances. The evidence suggests that, when proficiency grouping occurs, higher achieving students encounter more challenging curricula, and more discussion-based instructional techniques, than lower achieving students (Gamoran 2009: 8). That would be a very good reason for the leader of a large District, who has very limited influence over what happens in the classroom, to be wary of tracking. But a *principal* might have a critical mass of experienced high-quality teachers who are skilled at discussion-based instructional techniques, will follow a rigorous curriculum, and are happy to teach the lower achieving students. She controls the assignment of teachers to classes, so proficiency grouping might have very different effects in her school than in most that are studied. Finally, some research suggests that whereas proficiency grouping of all students for all subjects throughout the school day reduces the achievement of lower achievers relative to mixed-ability grouping, regrouping students according to proficiency in specific subject areas can improve their achievement (Connor et al. 2007; Slavin 1987). A principal might reject proficiency grouping if her only option is all-subject groupings but embrace it if she has the freedom to group students differently for different subjects.

Consider, now, the gold standard of evidence in the social sciences: the randomized controlled trial (RCT). RCT's test interventions by choosing a population and randomly selecting some for the intervention while using the others as a control. With large enough populations RCT's can reliably pick up an average effect. But effect sizes vary within the affected population, and, of course, even if the effects are positive for most, they are likely to be negative for some. Suppose an RCT evaluating a math curriculum in 40 sites finds that it has a significant positive effect on average, but that for 8 of the sites there is no effect, and for 8 more the effect is negative. Knowing that the average effect is positive is not a good enough reason to adopt it in your site. You need to know whether your site is relevantly like the sites in which it had a positive effect, or relevantly like those where the effect was absent or negative. The RCT does not tell you that information. It doesn't even tell you which similarities are relevant (Cartwright & Hardie 2012).

Even with the best available information about the present and the past, good decisions about the future rely on careful judgment. When considering a curricular package, it is useful to consult the What Works Clearinghouse, a US government database which collects evidence about the effectiveness of different programs, to help identify programs that have been successful. But the merits of a particular curriculum may well depend on the local context and may change as new programs and goals are developed. A judicious decision-maker will also consider the needs of her students and how those needs compare with those of the participants in the study. She will consider whether more promising approaches have been developed, even if untested, that might work better given her goals and contexts., and the likely response of her particular students to those approaches. As Kathryn Joyce and Nancy Cartwright explain:

> because context does significantly affect effectiveness, it will seldom be possible to replicate results by moving a program as implemented in study sites to new settings. If the program is to work in a context it will have to be fitted to that context, and this seldom involves just tinkering around the edges or implementing it well. Rather, it requires getting all the right features in place that will allow the program to work here and guarding against features that can derail it here. So the work is harder than one might expect: If the program is to be effective, a context-local program plan must be built.
>
> *(Joyce & Cartwright 2020: 1048)*

To make things more difficult, the most wide-ranging questions – designing systems for school finance or governance, choosing certification requirements, or setting up charter school laws – are often those least directly informed by empirical research. No randomized experiments have tested (or in many cases could test) the efficacy of these types of policies, and even correlational, quasi-experimental studies are rare and often unfeasible. Instead, decision-makers tend to draw on data that are peripherally related to the decision in question, anecdotal information, and their own intuitions about important mechanisms to consider. In choosing certification requirements, for example, decision-makers may draw on information about whether teachers who have taken more math courses in college are more effective at increasing student learning. While relevant, this information must be carefully assessed: even if teachers who have taken more math *are* more effective, mandating additional courses in a certification system may fuel unintended consequences. For example, poor-quality, low-cost coursework options might spring up if teachers seek certification but are not actually interested in their own improvement. Alternatively, the observed relationship between math classes and effectiveness may be driven by more effective teachers choosing to take more math, rather than the causal effect of math classes on effectiveness. In practice, then, all judgments about the evidence, like judgements about feasibility, are multi-faceted and, inevitably, probabilistic.

This stage requires the decision-maker to take many different factors into account. Judgments are required, for example, about what agents are actually capable of in the circumstances, and about whether incentives are well calibrated to induce those actors to act as the policy requires. Policy reforms that look great on paper can flop because they overestimate what classroom teachers, or school principals, are actually competent to deliver. They can misunderstand the incentive structures faced by those teachers and principals, or how those incentive structures interact with the motivation they bring to their work. Or they can simply fail to provide the resources (funding, training) that would be needed for the reform to achieve its desired effects.

Despite the multiplicity of relevant considerations, we can describe the judgments at this stage as being essentially of two kinds: first, judging the quality of the available research; second, judging what the best research about what works in other situations tells you about what will work in your situation.

From our description, this stage might sound impossibly challenging. The evidence might seem like a map of the wrong place, or at best one with lots of crucial details left out. Decision-makers can, and do, manage the challenges by relying on authoritative sources. Most countries have a modest infrastructure that presents research for the consumption of decision-makers. This includes professional journals such as the *Times Education Supplement* in the U.K., and *Education Week*, *Phi Delta Kappan*, and *Educational Leadership* in the U.S.A., consultants and providers of professional development, and, of course, Schools of Education that prepare pre-service teachers and administrators. But decision-makers cannot rely on those authorities *entirely*: authorities do not speak with one voice and some do not act in good faith. The decision-maker has to develop the judgment to be able to discern which purported authorities are worth listening to.

Establish What Is the Best Policy Overall in the Circumstances

The last step is to identify the policy that brings the greatest expected return in terms of the values identified at the first stage. This involves comparing the various actions identified (in step 1), in terms of their probable effects (assessed in step 3), to see which is likely to yield the best overall outcome available in the circumstances. We can think of this, in terms familiar from decision theory, as working out which of the actions available to us in our circumstances yields the greatest expected utility – with "utility" here understood as a weighted index or combination of the values. As we have said, there are several such values, and these need to be balanced or weighed against each other to evaluate overall outcomes. We also need to factor in the various probabilities of achieving those outcomes.

Working out which is the best policy, all things considered, is thus a complex enterprise. One proposal might have a very good chance of bringing about modest improvements with respect to values that are only moderately weighty, while another is less likely to achieve aims that, if achieved, would be hugely valuable. A third might be very likely substantially to improve the situation with respect to one value while risking making it worse with respect to others. And the counterfactuals can be hard to know. Consider now our School Board member, deciding whether to authorize a new, no-excuses, charter school. She can get evidence on the effects of no-excuses charter schools elsewhere on the children who persist in those schools. But the most rigorous evidence concerns only such things as test scores, graduation rates, and college matriculation rates. Especially if graduation rates and college matriculation rates are low and differences small, she might care more about effects that are not rigorously measured, like students' mental health and long-term employment outcomes, because those tell her somewhat more than small differences in graduation rates about the values she has reason to care about. And, even for the evidence she has, she doesn't know for sure whether it applies in her case partly because it's just one school, and partly because the full effects of the new school will depend on what happens in other schools within its ecosystem as a result of its being founded. There is very little evidence about the effects of no-excuses charter schools on the schools which surround them, and those effects presumably vary depending on what those schools are actually like. She can't just assume that the schools surrounding the no-excuses schools that have been studied are relevantly like the schools in her district. We cannot predict the overall return to any decision with anything close to certainty. We can, however, try to assess which decision has the best expected outcome in the light of the available evidence.

Conclusion

Although it may sound complicated, we consider the 4-step approach that we have outlined above to be a codification of the way in which people *already* go about the business of making decisions about education. It's a systematic, explicitly analytical, presentation of the elements that are almost inevitably involved in the making of a considered decision. It's commonsense that the aim is to improve things, to make them better (or at least avoid making them worse), and it's obvious that decision-makers face trade-offs between different ways in which things could be better (or worse), as well as having to assess what is actually likely to happen as a result of any particular decision. Whatever decision is made will in effect reflect judgments of the kind we have set out. Our goal has been mainly to bring those judgments to consciousness – to break them down into their different elements, and to show how those elements can be combined – so that decision-makers can think, and act, with greater clarity and precision.[1]

(Related Chapters: 3, 7, 8, 9, 15, 16, 21, 33.)

Note

1 We are grateful to Helen F. Ladd and Susanna Loeb for the collaboration on which this chapter draws, and to our editor, Randall Curren for several improving suggestions.

References

Anderson, E. (2007) "Fair Opportunity in Education: A Democratic Equality Perspective," *Ethics* 117(4): 595–622.

Berry, C. J., & Reback, R. (2006) "Tinkering Toward Accolades: School Gaming under a Performance Accountability System," in T. J. Gronberg & D. W. Jansen (eds.) *Improving School Accountability*, vol. 14. Bingley, UK: Emerald Group Publishing Limited, 1–34.

Booker, K., Gilpatric, S. M., Gronberg, T., & Jansen, D. (2007) "The Impact of Charter School Attendance on Student Performance," *Journal of Public Economics* 91(5–6): 849–876.

Booker, K., Gilpatric, S. M., Gronberg, T., & Jansen, D. (2008) "The Effect of Charter Schools on Traditional Public School Students in Texas: Are Children Who Stay Behind Left Behind?" *Journal of Urban Economics* 64(1): 123–145.

Booker, K., Sass, T., Gill, B., & Zimmer, R. (2008) "Going Beyond Test Scores: Evaluating Charter School Impact on Educational Attainment in Chicago and Florida," in *Mathematica Policy Research Reports* (0c525c84b96141a4925b9d3bea923729; Mathematica Policy Research Reports). Princeton: Mathematica Policy Research.

Booker, K., Sass, T., Gill, B., & Zimmer, R. (2011) "The Effects of Charter High Schools on Educational Attainment," *Journal of Labor Economics* 29(2): 377–415.

Brighouse, H., Ladd, H. F., Loeb, S., & Swift, A. (2018) *Educational Goods: Values, Evidence, and Decision-Making*. Chicago: University of Chicago Press.

Brighouse, H., & Swift, A. (2014) "The Place of Educational Equality in Educational Justice," in. K. Meyer (ed.) *Education, Justice, and the Human Good*. London: Routledge, 14–33.

Cartwright, N., & Hardie, J. (2012) *Evidence-Based Policy: A Practical Guide to Doing It Better* (1st edition). Oxford: Oxford University Press.

Clayton, M., Mason, A., Swift, A., & Wareham, R. (2021) "The Political Morality of School Composition: The Case of Religious Selection," *British Journal of Political Science* 51: 827–844.
Connor, C. M., Morrison, F. J., Fishman, B. J., Schatschneider, C., & Underwood, P. (2007) "The Early Years: Algorithm-guided Individualized Reading Instruction," *Science* 315(5811): 464–465.
Daniels, N. (1979) "Wide Reflective Equilibrium and Theory Acceptance in Ethics," *The Journal of Philosophy* 76(5): 256–282.
Duncan, G. J., & Murnane, R. J. (2011) *Whither Opportunity? Rising Inequality, Schools, and Children's Life Chances*. New York: Russell Sage Foundation.
Gamoran, A. (2009) "Tracking and Inequality: New Directions for Research and Practice," WCER Working Paper No. 2009–6, in *Wisconsin Center for Education Research (NJ1)*. Madison, WI: Wisconsin Center for Education Research.
Gilabert, P., & Lawford-Smith, H. (2012) "Political Feasibility: A Conceptual Exploration," *Political Studies* 60(4): 809–825.
Huang, M.-H. (2009) "Classroom Homogeneity and the Distribution of Student Math Performance: A Country-level Fixed-effects Analysis," *Social Science Research* 38(4): 781–791.
Jackson, C. K., Johnson, R. C., & Persico, C. (2016) "The Effects of School Spending on Educational and Economic Outcomes: Evidence from School Finance Reforms," *The Quarterly Journal of Economics* 131(1): 157–218.
Jencks, C. (1988) "Whom Must We Treat Equally for Educational Opportunity to be Equal?" *Ethics* 98(3): 518–533.
Joyce, K. E., & Cartwright, N. (2020) "Bridging the Gap Between Research and Practice: Predicting What Will Work Locally," *American Educational Research Journal* 57(3): 1045–1082.
Kerckhoff, A. C. (1986) "Effects of Ability Grouping in British Secondary Schools," *American Sociological Review* 51(6): 842–858.
Knight, C. (2017) "Reflective Equilibrium," in A. Blau (ed.) *Methods in Analytical Political Theory*. Cambridge: Cambridge University Press, 44–64.
Krueger, A. B. (1999) "Experimental Estimates of Education Production Functions," *The Quarterly Journal of Economics* 114(2): 497–532.
Ladd, H. F. (2012) "Education and Poverty: Confronting the Evidence," *Journal of Policy Analysis and Management* 31(2): 203–227.
Ladd, H. F., & Fiske, E. B. (2011) "Weighted Student Funding in the Netherlands: A Model for the U.S.?" *Journal of Policy Analysis and Management* 30(3): 470–498.
Pitzer, H. (2014) *Deficit Discourse, Urban Teachers' Work and the Blame Game* [Syracuse University]. Ann Arbor, MI: ProQuest Dissertations Publishing.
Rawls, J. (2001) *Justice as Fairness: A Restatement*. Cambridge, MA: Harvard University Press.
Satz, D. (2007) "Equality, Adequacy, and Education for Citizenship," *Ethics* 117(4): 623–648.
Schouten, G. (2012) "Fair Educational Opportunity and the Distribution of Natural Ability: Toward a Prioritarian Principle of Educational Justice," *Journal of Philosophy of Education* 46(3): 472–491.
Slavin, R. E. (1987) "Ability Grouping and Student Achievement in Elementary Schools: A Best-Evidence Synthesis," *Review of Educational Research* 57(3): 293–336.
Verstegen, D. A. (2011) "Public Education Finance Systems in the United States and Funding Policies for Populations with Special Educational Needs," *Education Policy Analysis Archives/Archivos Analíticos de Políticas Educativas* 19: 1–30.
White, J. (1995) *Education and Personal Well-being in a Secular Universe*. London: University of London, Institute of Education.
White, J. (2011) *Exploring Well-Being in Schools: A Guide to Making Children's Lives more Fulfilling*. London: Routledge.
Woodson, A. N., & Love, B. L. (2019) "Outstanding: Centering Black Kids' Enoughness in Civic Education Research," *Multicultural Perspectives* 21(2): 91–96.

7

HOW SHOULD EVIDENCE INFORM EDUCATION POLICY?

Kathryn E. Joyce and Nancy Cartwright

As in other areas of social policy, there's been a significant shift toward evidence-based decision-making in education. The evidence-based education (EBE) movement aims to improve policy outcomes by basing decisions on reliable evidence regarding the relative effectiveness of policy options. This chapter explores the evidence relevant to decisions about education policy. We start with a broad outline of policy arguments. From there, we home in on the evidence needed to support descriptive premises, focusing on the sort of predictions central to EBE.

Evidence-based Policy Decisions

Decision-makers at every level, from federal policymakers to practitioners, must decide how best to achieve their goals. Broadly speaking, their decisions are "evidence-based" when they are supported by the best available information about the options under consideration. To capture this idea, we suggest thinking of evidence-based decisions as the conclusions of sound arguments. Sound arguments are made up of relevant, trustworthy premises that jointly imply – or warrant – the conclusion. Each premise counts as evidence for the conclusion because it speaks to the truth of the conclusion.[1]

What Kind of Premises Are Relevant to Policy Arguments?

Conclusions of policy arguments – policy decisions – are normative, meaning they are claims about what should be done. Both normative and non-normative premises are relevant to these conclusions.[2] Normative premises make action-guiding claims that reflect values. Examples include claims that identify appropriate policy aims, specify their relative importance, or provide moral criteria for evaluating expected costs and benefits. While normative premises are indispensable, good policy arguments also require descriptive premises, including causal predictions about the likely effects of policy options and claims assessing the feasibility of implementing them in the target setting. Consider the following example of a policy argument:

1. Our current priority is to increase graduation rates in our school district. *(normative claim)*
2. Strategies likely to increase graduation rates involve either lowering graduation standards or improving learning opportunities to help more students meet graduation standards. *(descriptive claim)*

DOI: 10.4324/9781003172246-9

3 Given the value of achieving the rich set of educational outcomes currently required for graduation, our strategy should involve improving learning opportunities but not lowering graduation standards. *(normative claim)*
4 Policy A, as we would implement it in our district, is likely to significantly improve students' opportunities to learn. *(descriptive claim)*
5 Policy A is likely to improve learning opportunities more than alternative options. *(descriptive claim)*
6 Implementing Policy A in our district is feasible. *(descriptive claim)*
Therefore,
7 We should adopt Policy A. *(normative conclusion/policy decision).*

The first premise states a policy aim for decision-makers at the district-level and indicates that it's the most important. The second identifies strategies that are likely to contribute to the policy aim. The third asserts a value-based constraint on policy strategies. The fourth is a causal prediction about the likely effects of implementing Policy A in the district and the fifth is a prediction about the comparative effects of available policies. The sixth premise is, of course, a feasibility assessment. Assuming they are trustworthy, each premise provides evidence that, taken together, warrants the normative conclusion.

What Makes These Premises Trustworthy?

Premises are trustworthy when the best available evidence provides a good reason for thinking they are true. Each premise in a policy argument should itself be the conclusion of a sound argument.

The information that can serve as evidence corresponds to the type of claim the premise contains. Normative claims are supported by interpretations of the values in play, their relative importance, and what's required to realize them in practice.[3] Interpretations are usually informed by a broader system of values that take into account what society is trying to achieve through education, benefits for students, educational entitlements, the effects of education on life prospects, and other consequences for society and individuals (Brighouse et al. 2018).

In keeping with the evidence-based policy approach, this chapter focuses on evidence for descriptive premises. Policy arguments can include a wide range of descriptive claims, but they require predictions and feasibility assessments. Often, they are informed or motived by evaluations of current policies both in the present setting and elsewhere. The subsequent sections of this chapter discuss the evidence that can make these premises trustworthy.

Before turning to descriptive premises, we want to say something to discourage two common misconceptions about EBE that focusing on them seems to invite. The first is that causal claims generated by experimental research are supposed to dictate policy decisions. The second is that EBE excludes value-based considerations from the decision-making process.

It's fair to say that the EBE movement has been primarily concerned with procuring evidence of effectiveness to support predictions. Many have taken this to indicate that, according to EBE, causal claims alone are sufficient to warrant evidence-based policy decisions (e.g., Biesta 2007; Smeyers 2007; Smeyers & Smith 2014). This impression seems to be reinforced by rhetoric on the part of some EBE advocates, especially the "what works" framing, and the fact that randomized controlled trials (RCTs) are treated as the gold-standard when it comes to evidence for policymaking (Slavin 2008). As critics rightly point out, however, decisions about education policy must be informed by values (e.g., Biesta 2007, 2010). But this is in no way incompatible with using the best evidence available to inform the decision, along with the other relevant considerations, such as the distribution of expected costs (including opportunity costs), resources, possible side effects (both positive and negative), and local factors (norms, duties, regulations).

Thus, our presentation eschews the narrow, "value-free" conception of evidence-based decision-making. Values play an essential role by supporting the normative premises, which, to reiterate, are necessary for any argument with a normative conclusion – including education policy arguments.

So, we agree that causal claims are insufficient for policy conclusions, but we maintain that trustworthy predictions about the likely effects of policy options are indispensable to good policy arguments. However, we do not think evidence from RCTs should be treated as the gold-standard for predictions because, as we argue below, RCT results cannot independently justify them. As we consider what evidence *can* justify predictions, however, we must keep in mind that predictions are premises in broader policy arguments.

Evidence for Policy Predictions

Policy predictions are *ex ante* causal claims about what will happen if an intervention (e.g., policy, practice, program) is used in a particular target setting (e.g., classroom, school, district, state). Supporting them requires information about the target setting and causal factors – which we call "support factors" but are also called "moderators" – that affect whether and to what extent the intervention affects the outcome (supposing it can affect it at all).

Causes are generally teams of factors that work together. Interventions are comprised of one or more causal factors. When they *cause* or *produce* effects, that typically means the intervention *contributes* to the effect with the help of *support factors*. Although it plays a necessary causal role, the intervention itself is insufficient for the observed effect because the other team members – support factors – must do their part for the effect to occur.[4]

For example, reducing class sizes has improved learning outcomes in many settings with the help of support factors: there must be adequate space to accommodate more classes, access to enough qualified teachers to cover all the classes, and the resources needed to support them – to name just a few (Bohrnstedt & Stecher 2002). Without these and any other necessary support factors, reducing class sizes won't improve learning outcomes. But, with the requisite support factors, reducing class sizes is sufficient for a positive contribution to improving learning outcomes.

There are a few further things to notice about support factors. Some interventions can be supported by different sets of factors any one of which is sufficient for the effect so long as one complete set is in place. There may be some factors that are part of every set. In the case of reducing class sizes, for instance, any complete set of support factors will include having enough qualified teachers. Additionally, some support factors are likely to be required for any intervention to produce its intended effect. For example, we can assume that regular attendance and rapport between teachers and students are necessary support factors for most educational interventions. Finally, interventions that, with their support factors, are sufficient for an effect are often unnecessary because there are other ways of producing that effect.

Predictions about an intervention must include a premise identifying the requisite support factors and a premise indicating that they will be present in the target while the intervention is in use. If there's evidence that they won't be, that's enough to predict that the intervention won't work in the target. If they will be, we have established one premise and can move on to the next, which concerns available causal pathways in the target setting.

An intervention, along with its support factors, can only positively contribute to outcomes in the target if the local context affords a causal pathway for it to do so (Cartwright & Hardie 2012). That means the intervention's causal process can operate start to finish without interruption and nothing will undermine its contribution. Causal pathways are influenced by many contextual factors within educational settings and the broader social environment. Given the complexity of educational contexts, assessments will always be inexact, but there are some key things to consider.

When assessing the availability or possibility of securing a causal pathway, it's important to think about how other causal processes operating in the target might influence the intervention's causal process. Consider a few examples. If a school has recently introduced several new policies and programs, teachers might have trouble orienting themselves to the intervention under consideration or seeing how it's supposed to fit in with the other new additions. Students might also struggle to keep track of it, given the other changes. The extent to which the intervention aligns with state standards, other goals, or the broader curriculum could influence uptake. Or it could be that attachment to the program being replaced creates resistance on the part of students, parents, or teachers. Finally, scheduling adjustments could disrupt or derail interventions that require frequently and consistently practicing skills in the classroom.

Even if the setting allows the causal process to unfold without disruption, some contextual factors might undermine the intervention's contribution. These include things like school dynamics or practices that affect motivation and resources that determine learning readiness. We can certainly expect students' background knowledge and proficiencies to influence effects. Computer-based programs require computer literacy, for example. Interventions that are too basic or redundant are unlikely to positively contribute to outcomes. The same is true of reducing class sizes. Imagine a setting where class sizes are small enough for students to get plenty of attention from teachers. In that case, there may be no pathway through which reducing class sizes could improve outcomes – not because support factors are absent or the intervention cannot be implemented, but because class size is already positively affecting outcomes, not detracting from them.

Analyzing the problems candidate interventions are meant to address may reveal insight about these issues or other factors that bear on causal pathways. Presumably, those making predictions will be planning to replace or supplement an unsatisfactory program or policy. If there's to be a causal pathway for the intervention under consideration, whatever is derailing or undermining the current intervention must not have the same effect on the replacement or supplement. But a factor that derails one causal process may not derail another. Similarly, features of the setting that detract from the effects of one intervention may boost (or at least be irrelevant to) the effects of another. For example, if students' circumstances make it difficult for them to do homework, there might be a causal pathway available for an intervention that doesn't rely on homework.

A supplemental intervention may address impediments and thereby improve the performance of other interventions. For instance, creating afterschool homework clubs might address factors outside of school that interfere with homework. Likewise, introducing incentives, presenting the value of homework differently, or modifying existing incentives to guard against preemption of autonomous motivation, could address problems related to low motivation (Vansteenkiste et al. 2009; Reeve et al. 1999). In cases where contextual factors that impede outcomes cannot be addressed, interventions may be able to reduce their influence. Free or reduced cost breakfast and lunch programs are a familiar example of interventions that are intended to reduce the negative effects of food instability or malnourishment.

Assuming they are trustworthy, premises ensuring the presence of support factors and a causal pathway justify predicting that the intervention will work in the target. Importantly, warranted predictions are still uncertain. Instead of "it will work," predictions should be stated as "it will *probably* work." Warranted predictions indicate that there's good justification for expecting the intervention to positively contribute to desired outcomes. Further information can sometimes help us judge the size or significance of the contribution, but these are generally rough estimates.

What kind of evidence is needed to support these premises? As our description of them suggests, local knowledge and judgment play crucial roles – both in determining whether support factors will be in place and in assessing causal pathways. Decision-makers might have some of this knowledge themselves, but they will likely have to consult teachers, staff, administrators, and other stakeholders who are familiar with the setting and have a good sense of what it will (or could) be like when the intervention is in use. However, they also require evidence from education theory and research.

Education theorists and researchers can produce evidence for these predictions by identifying support factors and contextual factors relevant to causal pathways that hold fairly generally. As we mentioned, some of these might be the same across interventions (e.g., regular attendance, trust/rapport). Although some broadly applicable factors are a matter of common sense, others are identified and explained by theory and empirical analyses. For example, "learning readiness" is now widely recognized thanks to a variety of research from educational psychologists, sociologists, cognitive scientists, and learning theorists (e.g., Booth & Crouter 2008). Ethnographies, case studies, and other qualitative studies continue to enhance our understanding of it. All of this provides useful information about a particular aspect of causal pathways.

Even when causal factors are relevant to education practice across settings and interventions, we often need more specific information about how and when they might matter to assess their potential impact on particular interventions in particular settings. This is true of broad demographic characteristics like race, gender, and socioeconomic status (Joyce 2019, Joyce & Cartwright 2018).

Beyond broadly applicable causal factors, predictions require evidence about the support factors that are specific to the intervention under consideration and contextual factors relevant to the pathways in the particular target setting. Identifying them requires information about how the intervention is supposed to work, which comes from theories of change and research that outlines the intervention's causal process or mechanism (see Cartwright 2020; Cartwright et al. 2020).

Instead of relying on evidence from these kinds of sources, the EBE movement aims to support predictions with evidence from RCTs, which are thought to produce better evidence for causal claims. However, RCTs don't provide information about support factors or causal pathways. So how are they supposed to support predictions?

The Standard EBE Strategy for Supporting Predictions

Like other policy areas, EBE relies on RCTs to produce evidence of general effectiveness that can then be used to support predictions (Eisenhart & Towne 2003; Maxwell 2004; Mosteller & Boruch 2002). As one prominent advocate describes it, EBE is supposed to "support use of specific programs evaluated in comparison to control groups and found to be effective and replicable" (Slavin 2020: 22). Interventions are "effective" when they work across a wide range of educational settings and so can be expected to work in particular settings of interest to decision-makers (unless they are highly atypical); they are "replicable" when they can be expected to produce the same effects that they have produced in RCTs in new settings. Essentially, the goal is to *establish* predictions that are ready to serve as premises in policy arguments. That way, decision-makers can simply choose "with confidence" from an array of "proven, replicable programs that are ready for them to use" (Slavin 2020: 22, 25).

At least when it comes to education, however, this strategy is unrealistic. RCTs cannot supply, or even support, all the premises needed for arguments that warrant policy predictions. Indeed, RCTs do not provide *any* evidence for predictions unless there are premises linking study settings to target settings. After briefly discussing what we learn from RCTs, we explain why that information cannot independently support predictions as intended by the EBE movement. Then, we consider what premises are needed if information from RCTs is to play a role in supporting predictions.

As we shall see, predictions can be "based" on evidence from RCTs in that the other premises in the argument support an inference from RCT-backed causal claims about study settings (i.e., "the intervention worked there") to a prediction about the target (i.e., "the intervention will work here"). However, as our previous discussion indicates, warranted predictions need not rely on evidence from RCTs. Either way, predictions require information about *how* the intervention operates, which comes from the sources discussed above.

Education RCTs

RCTs are used to evaluate the impact of interventions because, when internally valid, they justify ascribing observed effects to the intervention (see Morrison 2021). We call this result a *causal ascription*.

The basic idea is simple. RCTs attempt to create groups that are identical except that one receives the intervention being tested (treatment group) and the other (control group) does not. Participants are randomly assigned to treatment and control groups because random assignment is supposed to help balance known and unknown causal factors between groups. If the groups are similar enough to balance in terms of factors that could affect the outcomes, then differences in outcomes can be ascribed to the intervention. In medicine and some areas of social policy, the control group might receive a placebo or nothing at all. By contrast, in education, the control group usually continues to receive whatever programs are currently being used in those districts, schools, or classrooms. For example, in a study testing a new program that teaches students to read using phonograms, the control group will use a different reading program that doesn't use phonograms. Thus, it's sometimes referred to as the "comparison" group.

Since this section focuses on how trustworthy RCT results can inform predictions about other settings, we'll take internal validity for granted going forward. But we want to emphasize that we do so only for the sake of argument. We realize that RCTs aren't always internally valid, especially in education (Morrison 2021; Simpson 2017). One general problem is that random assignment can't be expected to succeed in producing balance in any single run of a study (Deaton & Cartwright 2018). In a study with a small sample, balance is unlikely. Expecting that half of the students who would do better anyway end up assigned to the intervention and half to the control when an experiment is conducted once is like assuming that if you flip a fair coin 100 times it will come up heads on 50 of the flips and tails on the rest. The larger the sample, the more likely random assignment will create a distribution with some desired level of balance in a single run, but actual balance is still unlikely.

Another problem is that, even when random assignment does create groups that are balanced enough, it doesn't ensure that groups will stay balanced over the course of the study. They may become imbalanced due to changes in the distribution of causal factors that occur during the study. Some differences could arise due to the study itself. When possible, researchers use masking or blinding so participants don't know whether they are in the treatment or control group. This is meant to protect balance by discouraging changes in attitudes (e.g., feeling discouraged or hopeful) or behaviors (e.g., putting in more or less effort) that could affect outcomes. However, masking is seldom possible within education RCTs. So, education researchers have little control over post-assignment changes, even those associated with the study itself. Other differences can arise because those who receive the intervention go to different classrooms or have different teachers or meet at different times, which exposes them to causal factors that matter but that those in the control group don't experience.

Using RCT Results to Support Policy Predictions

Clearly, causal ascriptions, even if true, cannot directly support predictions: facts about what *did* happen in some setting(s) don't indicate what *will* – *or* is likely to – happen elsewhere. But trustworthy causal ascriptions can play a role in arguments that warrant predictions. We'll outline and evaluate three kinds of predictions informed by causal ascriptions from RCTs. Each option represents a strategy for getting from a premise stating that an intervention "worked somewhere" to the conclusion that it "will (probably) work here," i.e., in a particular target setting. We start with what we take to be the most promising of these strategies. However, the standard EBE approach tries to avoid this option in favor of the other two, which rely more heavily on RCTs. We argue that these RCT-centered alternatives are ultimately less promising because they rely on assumptions that are often unmet in education and cannot consistently provide useful guidance for decision-makers.

Strategy 1: Comparing Causal Pathways and Support Factors

The fact that an intervention worked in a study shows that it *can* work for some subjects under some circumstances – those present in the study setting(s). Getting from "it can work under some circumstances" to "it will work here" requires additional premises identifying the circumstances under which the intervention can work and indicating that those circumstances will be present in the target setting while the intervention is in use. If so, then we're justified in predicting that the intervention will also work there.

As the discussion above suggests, the relevant circumstances include the set of support factors that worked with the intervention to produce the effect and other features of the context that provided a causal pathway for the intervention. Since the intervention contributed to an effect in the study setting, we know that a sufficient set of support factors were present there and derailers absent so that a causal pathway was available. The key is to identify the causal pathway. The next step is to identify what support factors would be required and what derailers prevented in order for a similar pathway to be available in the target setting. The final step is to determine whether that set of support factors will be present and those derailers absent or guarded against in the target. This kind of prediction has the following structure:

1 The intervention produced positive effects somewhere.
2 The intervention can produce positive effects via the causal pathway it followed there.
3 P is the causal pathway it followed there.
4 The support factors that would enable P in the target are S and the possible derailers for P in the target are D.
5 S will be present along with the intervention in the target and D will be absent or guarded against.
Therefore,
6 The intervention will produce positive effects in the target.

Causal ascriptions from RCTs can support the first premise, which implies the second premise. RCTs don't provide any evidence for the third premise, however, which takes much more investigation of what happened in the study. The fourth premise requires both detailed information about the target setting and some theoretical understanding of what could make P possible and what could make it very unlikely. Similarly, the fifth premise requires detailed information about the target setting.

Does the fact that the first and second premise are supported by evidence from RCTs strengthen the prediction? An argument is only as strong as its weakest premise. The only way using evidence from RCT results could strengthen the argument is by making the premises they support more trustworthy than they would be otherwise. Since other research methods can support causal ascriptions, this depends on the internal validity of the RCT in question and the other research available.[5] As previously mentioned, requirements for internal validity cannot always be satisfied in educational settings. Regardless, the argument still relies on a great deal of evidence from other sources to support the remaining premises. Using RCTs certainly doesn't make those premises any more trustworthy.

Strategy 2: Assessing External Validity

A more common EBE strategy involves identifying types of settings where effects that occurred in RCTs are supposed to be replicable. The idea is to assess external validity to determine whether the RCT results extend to another setting – namely, the target. This kind of prediction has the following structure:

1 An intervention produced positive effects in an RCT (or multiple, combined RCTs).
2 An identical intervention will produce the same effects in target settings that are sufficiently similar to the study setting(s).

3 The target is sufficiently similar to the study setting(s).
Therefore,
4 The intervention will produce the positive effects in the target that it produced in the study setting(s).

This argument is valid, but here too, the premises cannot be supported solely by evidence from RCTs. The first premise, of course, reports RCT results. The second premise reflects the principle of representation, which must be satisfied for results to be externally valid: if the study site is genuinely *representative* of the target, then what's true of the study site is true of the target. In this case, a study site represents a target when they are sufficiently similar in terms of characteristics that affect the effectiveness of the intervention in question. So, they must be sufficiently similar in terms of support factors and causal pathways. If they are, then the effects of the intervention can be replicated in the target – assuming it's implemented with *fidelity*. Implementing the intervention with fidelity in the target means using the exact version that was used in the study in exactly the same way. This "fidelity" assumption is important since representation only licenses extending facts about the study sample to other (represented) sites. The fact being extended in the prediction (observed effects) pertain to a specific intervention, not variations of it.

For example, suppose the average effect of a reading program for a study population of fourth graders is a six-point improvement on a reading comprehension test. If the study population represents fourth graders in a target site in terms of all causal factors relevant to the reading program, then the average effect of the program for fourth graders in the target is also six points on that reading comprehension test. As it's commonly described in EBE materials (e.g., What Works Clearinghouse 2017), the average fourth grader in the target who receives the intervention will improve their score on the test by six points. It's important to keep in mind, though, that RCT results are *comparative* – they indicate how the intervention in the treatment group performed, on average, compared to the intervention in the control group. So, decision-makers could only expect similar effects if they are replacing an intervention that's similar in quality to what the control group received.

Like the previous strategy, supporting the remaining premises – in this case premise 3 – requires information about both the study setting and that of the target. Decision-makers must gather evidence about their target site to support the claim that the settings are sufficiently similar. Instead of studying the causal pathway to identify the relevant factors for it to carry through in the target, researchers generally list broad demographic characteristics that they think should ensure sufficient similarities to allow the same causal pathway. Then, decision-makers are encouraged to rely on evidence from studies conducted in settings similar to their target site in terms of those characteristics. However, researchers usually offer little evidence, if any, to show that those characteristics are most relevant such that their presence is a good enough indicator of the causal pathway (Joyce 2019). Thus, using them to assess representation leads to unwarranted predictions.

The inference this strategy draws is similar to the one drawn in the previous strategy and the premises are just as hard – perhaps harder – to support. Satisfying the representation and fidelity requirements needed to establish that results are replicable is a tall order – even more so when researchers identify more descriptors in an attempt to capture those that matter instead of identifying the causal pathway. Matching more characteristics makes establishing representation more demanding without making the prediction more trustworthy. Additionally, researchers may be unable to accurately describe the exact version of the intervention used in the study, especially when the intervention isn't discrete and self-contained. Even with an accurate description, though, it may be challenging to use it with high-fidelity in a new setting (Lingenfelter 2016).

An additional disadvantage of this strategy is that it provides little to no guidance in cases where the target isn't sufficiently similar to any RCT-tested policy options. Decision-makers might adjust their target settings so they are sufficiently similar, but this could be a mistake if those changes end up negatively affecting the intervention or other processes in the school. Moreover, decision-makers aren't concerned about producing the *same* results, they want to produce the best results possible in their setting. Since that's the case, focusing on replication may be a bad idea.

Strategy 3: Determining "What Works" in General

The dominant EBE strategy is to support inferences from RCT results to predictions by generating evidence that speaks to the general effectiveness of tested interventions, i.e., how they generally perform across settings of interest. These claims are typically expressed as claims about "what works." It's common to say that an intervention works, or is effective, if it has produced positive effects, on average, across multiple study sites (e.g., Connolly et al. 2017; Slavin 2020; What Works Clearinghouse 2017). That's supposed to show that it can work under the conditions found in many different places. The idea is that if an intervention is known to be generally effective across educational settings, then it can be expected to work in a new educational setting. That doesn't mean it *always* works – just that it works reliably enough to justify predictions about new cases. The form of this prediction is deceptively simple:

1 The intervention works in most educational settings.
  Therefore,
2 It will work in the target setting.

Supporting predictions by establishing general effectiveness claims is common in domains like medicine where interventions often have stable causal capacities. For example, acetaminophen has a stable causal capacity to reduce fevers: it reliably does so across a broad, diverse range of individuals and circumstances. The fact that it's generally effective in this sense justifies the expectation that it will reduce fevers in new cases.

Likewise, general effectiveness claims about educational interventions that hold true over a range of settings would justify predictions about settings within that range – the argument above captures this inference. However, this strategy assumes that educational interventions, like acetaminophen, have stable causal capacities across a wide range of educational settings. In EBE, the intended range seems to be quite broad since decision-makers across the U.S. are encouraged to use this strategy.[6] This assumption is dubious in education, as is the idea that RCTs can provide sufficient evidence for general effectiveness claims (Joyce & Cartwright 2019; Kvernbekk 2016; Maxwell 2004; Morrison 2021).

Not all "causes" are stable – social interventions and other causes operating in social domains often are *not* stable, or if they do have a stable capacity, the range of stability is narrow and subject to change as contexts shift and evolve (Cartwright & Hardie 2012). To say that an intervention has a stable causal capacity across a range of settings is to say that the requisite support factors will be present and an appropriate causal pathway will be available in all of them. This is the case for acetaminophen across human beings because it reduces fevers through a biological causal pathway that's available across the vast majority of normally functioning human bodies despite expected differences (e.g., age, height, blood type, resting heart rate, geographical location). It seems unlikely that this will be true of educational interventions across most settings of interest to decision-makers despite their different attributes (e.g., other causal processes operating there, resources, teachers' skills, students' expectations).[7]

Even if *some* educational interventions (amenable to testing in RCTs) do have stable causal capacities across a range that's broad enough to justify predictions on the intended scale, there's little reason to think this will usually be the case. Indeed, few, if any have been identified. Research findings that are generally applicable in education typically concern things like learning processes, adolescent cognitive development, and correlations between social factors and academic outcomes rather than the effectiveness of discrete interventions (Lingenfelter 2016; Walters et al. 2009). For that reason, this may be a poor strategy for supporting predictions about education policies.

Aside from that worry about interventions, RCTs provide insufficient evidence for general effectiveness claims. Identifying stable causal capacities and the range of stability takes more information than we can get from a series of RCTs alone.

Conducting multiple RCTs in different places and combining results is meant to create a larger, more diverse sample that will represent a broad range of educational settings. Since the samples being combined are not randomly selected, we can't expect a larger sample to provide a sufficient balance of known and unknown causal factors. While it's true that larger samples comprised of participants from different settings are likely to represent more settings than single studies, the combined sample may not be representative enough to support predictions across settings of interest.

In a recent evaluation of 11 large-scale RCTs, Stuart et al. (2017) identifies several similarities between study sites that differentiate them from the broader set of targets. If RCTs are conducted in similar populations or settings, combining their results won't yield a more representative sample. For example, they find that RCTs tend to be conducted near universities with qualified education researchers. Suppose such universities are usually located in large cities. The sample we would get from combining these RCT results wouldn't be more representative of the broader population along dimensions related to location and proximity to resources associated with the presence of universities. That means they wouldn't support predictions about how the tested intervention would perform in rural settings—unless of course we know that those factors are irrelevant to its performance and so need not be represented.

Education settings aren't similar enough to assume that conducting and combining multiple large RCTs will yield a representative sample. Especially since, again, the support factors and pathways can vary widely by intervention. Unless we can be sure that we have a representative sample – representative of the target, not the general population – predictions require assessing representation by making the sort of comparisons described above; as we saw, that requires identifying causally relevant factors.

Additionally, RCTs report the *average* effect for the treatment group. If the impact of an intervention varied significantly across RCT sites, knowing the average effect for the combined sample won't be useful for making predictions about a particular target. Decision-makers would need information about how the intervention performed in different sites and why effects varied – which RCTs don't provide.

A similar problem arises for all these strategies because RCTs report the average treatment effect but not the distribution of effects across participants. A higher average in the treatment group indicates that at least some *unidentified* individuals in that group improved. But, when considering interventions, decision-makers are often interested in how their effects are likely to be distributed across students in the target – not just the average. Some policy goals involve directing benefits toward particular individuals or groups – like low-performing students or students at risk of attrition, for instance. They may sometimes be able to adopt interventions designed to help only the intended students (e.g., individual tutoring for students who are behind), but often interventions will be delivered to an entire class, school, or district. So, decision-makers need information that's helpful for estimating the distribution of benefits and burdens across students.

The upshot is that RCTs, alone or combined, cannot independently support policy predictions. Predictions that draw inferences from RCTs require information about causal pathways from other sources, including theory, (non-experimental) research, and local knowledge. Since that's the case, using evidence from RCTs doesn't necessarily strengthen predictions. Moreover, even supported inferences from RCTs can fail to provide useful guidance for decision-makers who want to produce the best – as opposed to the same – outcomes in their target and care about how those outcomes are distributed.

Evidence for Feasibility Assessments and Implementation Planning

Much of the information that's relevant to predictions is relevant to feasibility assessments and implementation planning. Research investigating causal pathways and processes can thus provide some of the evidence needed to support them, but implementation science is also useful and both assessing feasibility and implementation planning rely heavily on local knowledge and judgment.

Assessing the feasibility of adopting an intervention means deciding whether it's possible to successfully implement it within parameters set by the target and evaluating the expected costs and benefits of doing so. Once decision-makers have information about an intervention's causal pathway, they must determine whether those conditions can realistically be met and maintained in the target site. This isn't simply a matter of manipulating variables. In addition to securing resources, it may require training, buy-in, and coordination among educators. For decision-makers relying on RCT-centered predictions, the task is to assess the feasibility of implementing the intervention with fidelity.

Implementation planning involves deciding how to use the intervention in the target. While decision-makers clearly need a sense of how interventions would be implemented to assess feasibility, working out the finer details may occur after policy decisions have been made. Decision-makers who won't be directly involved in the implementation (e.g., members of the school board or parent/teacher association) may not participate in planning at this later stage. Still, education research can provide useful information about how the intervention works and what factors can support or derail it. Additionally, implementation science offers insights about how practitioners can build the capacity to successfully plan and implement new interventions in general (e.g., Blasé et al. 2015; Fixsen et al. 2015). Improvement science studies how outcomes of particular interventions vary across contexts in an attempt to identify factors that support or detract from the success of the implementation or the performance of the intervention (e.g., Bryk 2015; Lewis 2015).

Planning to implement an RCT-backed intervention with fidelity may be relatively straightforward if detailed instructions are available. However, practitioners must still decide how the intervention will fit within the broader curriculum and make practical arrangements. Aiming for fidelity without understanding the causal process limits options because instructions will provide little guidance for adapting the intervention in ways that align it with other programs, capitalize on teachers' abilities, improve students' outcomes, or improve experiences for the practitioners and students involved. By contrast, information about how the intervention operates and its causal pathway can help practitioners adjust implementation without undermining the performance of the intervention.

While implementation planning that doesn't rely (solely) on fidelity may sometimes be more complicated, it might also be more effective. Research on the implementation of RCT-backed programs like *Success for All* indicate that, while not planned, adjustments are almost always made because practitioners find them necessary (Datnow & Castellano 2000; Lingenfelter 2016; Peurach 2011). Thus, information about causal processes and pathways could also be useful for fidelity-oriented implementation planning by supporting evidence-based decisions about how best to adjust programs when problems arise.

Conclusion

We've explained how evidence from a variety of sources can (and should) be used to support education policy decisions. We defined evidence-based claims – including policy decisions – as the conclusions of arguments made up of relevant, trustworthy premises that, taken together, warrant them. Although policy arguments yield normative conclusions, we focus on the evidence needed to support their descriptive premises, homing in on predictions about how candidate interventions are likely to perform in specific targets. The EBE movement favors predictions supported by RCTs, but we argued that RCTs are an unnecessary and insufficient source of evidence. Like descriptive premises regarding feasibility and implementation, trustworthy predictions require evidence from a mix of research methods, theories, and local sources – including practitioners on the ground who are familiar with the context and who will participant in implementing chosen policies.

(Related Chapters: 6, 8, 9, 21, 34.)

Notes

1 For more on the argument theory of evidence, see Cartwright and Hardie (2012).
2 Hume famously claims that normative conclusions about what "ought" to be done don't follow solely from descriptive claims that state facts about what "is" – arguments with normative conclusions must include at least one normative premise.
3 See the chapter on values and evidence in educational decision-making by Brighouse and Swift in this volume and Schouten and Brighouse (2015) for discussion of value-based normative claims relevant to policy arguments.
4 Mackie (1965) calls these INUS conditions: A set of factors that are each *I*nsufficient but *N*ecessary for producing an effect; the set of factors itself is *U*nnecessary but *S*ufficient for the effect. For discussion related to education, see Cartwright and Hardie (2012) and Kvernbekk (2016).
5 Random assignment is only advantageous when study groups must be balanced in terms of *unknown* factors. If the factors are known, researchers can manually create balanced groups.
6 Advocates generally agree that this is the ideal we should aim for but admit that many more RCTs are needed to get there. However, our criticisms of this strategy pertain to the assumptions on which it relies, not the current evidence-base.
7 Unless they operate through a causal pathway that's typically available across all normally functioning human beings like acetaminophen does. This may be true of some interventions that address basic psychological needs, for example.

References

Biesta, G. (2007) "Why 'What Works' Won't Work: Evidence-based Practice and the Democratic Deficit in Educational Research," *Educational Theory* 57(1): 1–22.
Biesta, G. J. J. (2010) "Why 'What Works' Still Won't Work: From Evidence-Based Education to Value-Based Education," *Studies in Philosophy and Education* 29(5): 491–503.
Bohrnstedt, G. W., & Stecher, B. M. (2002) *What We Have Learned about Class Size Reduction in California* (No. ED471331). Sacramento, CA: California Department of Education.
Booth, A., & Crouter, A. C. (eds.) (2008) *Disparities in School Readiness: How Families Contribute to Transitions into School*. Mahwah, NJ: Lawrence Erlbaum.
Brighouse, H., Ladd, H. F., Loeb, S., & Swift, A. (2018) *Educational Goods: Values, Evidence, and Decision-Making*. Chicago: University of Chicago Press.
Blasé, K. A., Fixsen, D., Sims, B. J., & Ward, C. S. (2015) *Implementation Science: Changing Hearts, Minds, Behavior, and Systems to Improve Educational Outcomes*. Oakland, CA: The Wing Institute.
Bryk, A. S. (2015) 2014 "AERA Distinguished Lecture: Accelerating How We Learn to Improve," *Educational Researcher* 44(9): 467–477.
Cartwright, N. (2020) *Using Middle-Level Theory to Improve Programme and Evaluation Design* (CEDIL Methods Brief). London: Centre of Excellence for Development Impact and Learning.
Cartwright, N., Charlton, L., Juden, M., Munslow, T., & Williams, R. B. (2020) *Making Predictions of Programme Success More Reliable* [CEDIL Methods Working Paper]. London: Centre of Excellence for Development Impact and Learning.
Cartwright, N., & Hardie, J. (2012) *Evidence-based Policy: A Practical Guide to Doing it Better*. Oxford: Oxford University Press.

Connolly, P., Biggart, A., Miller, S., O'Hare, L., & Thurston, A. (2017) *Using Randomised Controlled Trials in Education* (1st edition). London: SAGE Publications.

Datnow, A., & Castellano, M. (2000) "Teachers' Responses to Success for All: How Beliefs, Experiences, and Adaptations Shape Implementation," *American Educational Research Journal* 37(3): 775–799.

Deaton, A., & Cartwright, N. (2018) "Understanding and Misunderstanding Randomized Controlled Trials," *Social Science & Medicine* 210: 2–21.

Eisenhart, M., & Towne, L. (2003) "Contestation and Change in National Policy on 'Scientifically Based' Education Research," *Educational Researcher* 32(7): 31–38.

Fixsen, D., Blase, K., Metz, A., & Van Dyke, M. (2015) "Implementation Science," in J. Wright (ed.) *International Encyclopedia of the Social & Behavioral Sciences* (2nd ed., Vol. 11). Amsterdam: Elsevier, 695–702.

Hume, D. (2009) *A Treatise of Human Nature* (D. F. Norton, ed.). Oxford: Oxford University Press.

Joyce, K. E. (2019) "The Key Role of Representativeness in Evidence-based Education," *Educational Research and Evaluation* 25(1–2): 43–62.

Joyce, K. E., & Cartwright, N. (2018) "Meeting our Standards for Educational Justice: Doing Our Best with the Evidence," *Theory and Research in Education* 16(1): 3–22.

Joyce, K. E., & Cartwright, N. (2019) "Bridging the Gap Between Research and Practice: Predicting What Will Work Locally," *American Educational Research Journal* 57(3): 1045–1082.

Kvernbekk, T. (2016) *Evidence-based Practice in Education: Functions of Evidence and Causal Presuppositions.* London: Routledge, Taylor & Francis Group.

Lewis, C. (2015) "What Is Improvement Science? Do We Need It in Education?" *Educational Researcher* 44(1): 54–61.

Lingenfelter, P. E. (2016) *Proof, Policy, and Practice: Understanding the Role of Evidence in Improving Education* (First edition). Sterling, VA: Stylus Publishing, LLC.

Mackie, J. L. (1965) "Causes and Conditions," *American Philosophical Quarterly* 2(4): 245–264.

Maxwell, J. A. (2004) "Causal Explanation, Qualitative Research, and Scientific Inquiry in Education," *Educational Researcher* 33(2): 3–11.

Morrison, K. (2021) *Taming Randomized Controlled Trials in Education: Exploring Key Claims, Issues and Debates.* London: Routledge, Taylor & Francis Group.

Mosteller, F., & Boruch, R. F. (eds.) (2002) *Evidence Matters: Randomized Trials in Education Research.* Washington, D.C.: Brookings Institution Press.

Peurach, D. J. (2011) *Seeing Complexity in Public Education: Problems, Possibilities, and Success for All.* Oxford: Oxford University Press.

Reeve, J., Bolt, E., & Cai, Y. (1999) "Autonomy-supportive Teachers: How They Teach and Motivate Students," *Journal of Educational Psychology* 91(3): 537–548.

Schouten, G., & Brighouse, H. (2015) "The Relationship between Philosophy and Evidence in Education," *Theory and Research in Education* 13(1): 5–22.

Simpson, A. (2017) "The Misdirection of Public Policy: Comparing and Combining Standardised Effect Sizes," *Journal of Education Policy* 32(4): 450–466.

Slavin, R. E. (2008) "Evidence-Based Reform in Education: What Will it Take?" *European Educational Research Journal* 7(1): 124–128.

Slavin, R. E. (2020) "How Evidence-based Reform will Transform Research and Practice in Education," *Educational Psychologist* 55(1): 21–31.

Smeyers, P. (2007) "The Relevance of Irrelevant Research; The Irrelevance of Relevant Research," in P. Smeyers & M. Depaepe (eds.) *Educational Research: Why 'What Works' Doesn't Work.* Dordrecht: Springer Netherlands, 95–108.

Smeyers, P., & Smith, R. (2014) *Understanding Education and Educational Research.* Cambridge: Cambridge University Press.

Stuart, E. A., Bell, S. H., Ebnesajjad, C., Olsen, R. B., & Orr, L. L. (2017) "Characteristics of School Districts That Participate in Rigorous National Educational Evaluations," *Journal of Research on Educational Effectiveness* 10(1): 168–206.

Vansteenkiste, M., Soenens, B., Verstuyf, J. and Lens, W. (2009) "What is The Usefulness of Your Schoolwork? The Differential Effects of Intrinsic and Extrinsic Goal Framing on Optimal Learning," *Theory and Research in Education* 7(2): 155–163.

Walters, P. B., Lareau, A., & Ranis, S. H. (eds.) (2009) *Education Research on Trial: Policy Reform and the Call for Scientific Rigor* (1st ed). London: Routledge.

What Works Clearinghouse (2017) *Standards Handbook 4.0.* https://ies.ed.gov/ncee/wwc/Docs/referenceresources/wwc_standards_handbook_v4.pdf

8

WHO SHOULD MAKE DECISIONS ABOUT CHILDREN'S EDUCATION?

Harry Brighouse and Adam Swift

Human children arrive in the world profoundly vulnerable and profoundly dependent. They are small, easily damaged, incapable of feeding themselves, poorly placed to recognize danger, and utterly powerless in its face. Without adults to shelter, nourish, and protect them, they would die.

They are also incapable of preparing themselves to become the kind of adult who can fend for themselves in society, let alone contribute to it. Shelter, nutrition, and protection are not enough. They need to be raised and educated. Somebody needs to make decisions about how.

The focus of this chapter will be on formal education: that is, the intentional production of knowledge, skills, attitudes, and dispositions that influence the ability of children to flourish and contribute to the flourishing of others over the life course. The question is: who should make decisions about children's education?

For adults, the default decision-makers are adults themselves. Governments may invest in inducing the development of skill sets seen as economically or socially valuable, thus creating incentives to which they expect adults to respond. But in a free society with flexible labor markets the expectation is that, as long as educational providers are regulated well enough to protect clients from fraud or exploitation, adults themselves will generally make the best decisions about their own educational pathways. And, as those most affected by the outcomes, they have the right to decide for themselves, even if they choose badly.

We don't think the same about children. Of course, children do, inevitably, make educational decisions all the time. Within the limits of their own agency (limits which, usually, expand over time, though in a complicated and uneven manner) they decide whether to pay attention to what is being said to them, whether to do as they are told, how to interact with their peers and with adults, and myriad other matters (Archard 2014). That they make these decisions is part of the learning process itself. But unlike (most) adults they lack the basic education – the basic knowledge, skills, dispositions, and attitudes – needed to choose well, and we do not consider them genuinely responsible for the choices they make. So at least two kinds of decisions about their education really must be made by some adult or adults: first, what they should learn, second, how resources devoted to supporting their learning should be distributed among them.

We're going to focus on the question of who should make these decisions. But in our view answers to that question are connected to the answers to the questions of what should be learned and how learning should be distributed. So, we're going to start by sketching answers to those questions, and then see what those might mean for the question of who should decide.

DOI: 10.4324/9781003172246-10

What Should Children Learn?

We propose, but do not argue for, a rather abstract account of what students should learn. We think it is correct, but we outline it here not so much to persuade you of that as to help you get a fix on the discussion of our main topic: who should decide? If you prefer a subtly – or unsubtly – different account of what children should learn, our invitation, when you reach sections 3 and 4, is to think about how – or whether – your different view about what children should learn affects your judgment about our discussions in those sections.

Our account of what children should learn rests on the idea that it is very important they enter adulthood as people who are well-equipped to flourish and to contribute to the flourishing of others. It does not depend on a detailed, specific, conception of human flourishing: people flourish in a vast array of different ways. But we can discern six broad capacities each of which must be developed well in order for someone to flourish and contribute to the flourishing of others in the kinds of society under consideration. We call these capacities, taken together, *educational goods*: the knowledge, skills, attitudes, and dispositions needed to flourish and contribute to the flourishing of others (Brighouse et al. 2018).[1]

Capacity for Economic Productivity

In market economies, unless an individual has extremely wealthy parents or some other source of guaranteed income, flourishing depends on his or her ability to participate effectively in the economy. Some people will not need to work for an income to meet their needs, but we cannot identify most of them in advance, so a sensible policy will equip all children to participate in the economy. Even those with independent sources of income usually benefit from the kinds of capability that labor markets reward. Developing individuals' economic productivity – for example through enhancing their cognitive skills – is also in the interest of the broader society: the increased economic capability of the educated person increases the aggregate stock of human capital that society can harness to the benefit of all.

Capacity for Personal Autonomy

Children benefit from the ability to make and act on well-informed and well-thought-out judgments about how to live their lives. For human beings to flourish, they need to find a way of life that is suited to their particular personalities and desires. Some people may flourish within the constraints laid down by the religious strictures of their parents, but others may be stunted by those same requirements. Knowledge of other religious views, and non-religious views, supports flourishing by providing the opportunity for the individual to choose alternatives, or aspects of them. Even with knowledge of the alternatives, the self-knowledge, habits of mind, and strength of character to make the appropriate alternative choice are also required. The same logic applies to choice of occupation. Some children find themselves under very heavy parental pressure to pursue a particular occupational path. The non-autonomous person will follow the path chosen by her parent because of lack of knowledge of alternatives, or of self-knowledge, or of emotional independence. The autonomous person, by contrast, will have sufficient knowledge of the relevant considerations and sufficient fortitude to make the parental pressure a small influence on her choice. Whether, ultimately, she chooses for or against should depend on her own, independent, judgment of the fit between the occupation and her interests (Feinberg 2007).

Capacity for Democratic Competence

Democracy works well when citizens have the ability to use their political institutions to press their own interests, to engage in reasoned political deliberation, and to give due weight to the legitimate interests of others. Educating a child to have the knowledge, skills, attitudes and dispositions that enable and incline her to become an effective and morally decent participant in social life and political processes benefits both her and her fellow citizens. The knowledge and skills needed for democratic competence are various and depend on context. A basic understanding of the history of a society's political institutions is usually valuable, as is the ability and disposition to bring reason and evidence to bear on claims and arguments made by others. Institutions vary considerably in the informational demands they place on citizens, and in the deliberative resources they provide. The US electoral system, for example with its numerous levels of government and frequent elections, places high demands, especially in those states where candidates for most elections may not register their party affiliation on the ballot paper. Political advertising gives citizens very limited help in their deliberations. Democratic systems with less numerous and frequent elections and more controls over political advertising may make it easier for citizens to participate in an informed and meaningful way. Many policy issues are hard for citizens to evaluate because they lack a good understanding of the way the institutions work, and of the possible side effects of any proposed reform. Producing the capacity for democratic competence is non-trivial (Callan 1997; Gutmann 1999; Macedo 2003).

Capacity to Treat Others as Moral Equals

Equal respect for the basic dignity of persons underlies the idea that everybody has the same fundamental human rights, regardless of their sex, race, religion or nationality, and grounds norms against discrimination in hiring, promotion, and government provision. Treating others as equals does not require that we care about strangers as much as we do about our family members, or ourselves. Nor does it rule out judgments that people are unequal with respect to attributes like strength, intelligence, or virtue. It means simply that we regard all people as fundamentally equal in moral status. That attitude and the accompanying dispositions are important for flourishing. Racism, for example, does not have to be legally enforced in order to be damaging. Even without legal discrimination, black Americans continue to be disadvantaged, due not only to the continuing material effects of legal discrimination but also to their treatment by others who, often unconsciously, assume superiority. The experience of slights grounded in assumptions of racial superiority – as with gender, sexuality, or physical or mental abilities – undermines the self-respect and self-confidence of the slighted, making it harder for them to flourish. The impact is worse if the slighted themselves share the attitude that they are inferior, or, while not sharing it, are nonetheless disposed to accept the slights as their due. Developing and, crucially, *exercising* the capacity to treat other people as moral equals is important, also, for properly balancing the pursuit of one's own flourishing with the obligation to contribute to the flourishing of others.

Capacity for Healthy Personal Relationships

Recent empirical literature confirms the commonsense view that successful personal relationships tend to be part of a happy life. The same is probably true of a flourishing life. For most of us, flourishing requires a variety of relationships, including some that are lasting and intimate. People derive meaning from their relationships with their spouses, their parents and children, their close friends, and even from looser ties with acquaintances in their neighborhoods and at work. Successful personal relationships require certain attributes – emotional openness, kindness, a willingness to take risks with one's feelings, trust – that do not develop automatically but are in large part responses to one's environment. We can hope that families will provide an environment in which a child will develop these qualities but not all will do so, and, even if they do, these lessons can be supplemented and reinforced by other institutions, including schools.

Capacity for Personal Fulfillment

Healthy personal relationships are important for flourishing, but so too are complex and satisfying labor, and projects that engage one's physical, aesthetic, intellectual and spiritual faculties. People find fulfilment and satisfaction in music, literature, and the arts; in games and sports; mathematics and science; in religious practice. These and other activities enable them to exercise and develop their talents and meet complex challenges. A great deal of paid work is dreary or carried out in the context of stressful status hierarchies, and people in such jobs have limited opportunities to flourish at work. School is a place in which children's horizons can be broadened: they can be exposed to – and can develop enthusiasms for and competence in – activities that they would never have encountered through familial and communal networks, and which, sometimes, suit them better than any they would have encountered in those ways (White 2011).

How Should Resources Supporting Learning be Distributed Among Children?

As in the previous section, we will offer a rather abstract account, this time of how resources should be distributed, without much argument. Again, if you disagree with the answer offered in this section, we invite you to consider what your disagreement here means for the discussion in the rest of the chapter.

Educators often refer to distributive values by talking about "equity" in education. But exactly what they mean by equity is often not clear. The California Department of Education, for example, in one document defines equity, variously, as the "*aim of ensuring that all students benefit equally*" from schooling, and as requiring that schools produce "*comparably high academic achievement and other positive outcomes for all students on all achievement indicators.*" But, given that students have different levels of investment outside of the school, these definitions conflict: achieving the first would reflect out-of-school inequalities, whereas achieving the second would require counteracting them (Levinson et al. n.d.).

We offer three different distributive goals, each of which we think is valuable, but the relative urgency of which may depend on the circumstances. Some educational choices may be expected to bring gains with respect to all three, sometimes achieving one distributive aim might involve tradeoffs with the others (Schouten 2012). We frame them in terms of the distribution of *educational goods*, as characterized above, but obviously the production of educational goods requires the deployment of resources supporting learning: having established what distribution of educational goods we should be aiming for, decision-makers have to judge what distribution of learning resources will produce that outcome (Jencks 1988; Gutmann 1999; Brighouse et al. 2018).

Adequacy

Advocates of adequacy agree that everyone should meet some threshold level of educational goods, though they differ in how they define that threshold. Some set it as being able to command a living wage in the economy in adulthood (Tooley 2009); others as educational goods sufficient to ground a just rule of law (Curren 2000: 192–201); others as sufficient education to be able to participate as equals in civic and political affairs (Anderson 2007). The appeal of this approach is obvious: a just society would provide everyone with the developmental resources needed to reach the specified threshold. Adequacy, however, provides no insights into what would be a fair distribution for those above the threshold, and, in practice, specifying such a threshold is difficult and can seem arbitrary.

Equality

No child is responsible for their social background, or even for their level of natural talent, so allowing either to affect educational outcomes results in some being disadvantaged due to factors beyond their control. And because educational success plays a substantial role in labor market success, and labor market outcomes are highly unequal, inequality of educational goods has substantial consequences in terms of people's unequal prospects in life. That seems unjust. However, achieving *full* equality of educational goods would require measures that seem unacceptable. For differences in natural ability not to affect educational outcomes, those with high levels would have to be neglected, or even disabled, to the ultimate detriment of all: we would have to level down outcomes in order to make them equal. Similarly, given what we know about the intergenerational transmission of advantage, considerable interference in family life would be needed to prevent social class from influencing educational outcomes. Still, despite the constraints set by other weighty values, equal educational outcomes are, *pro tanto*, desirable (Brighouse & Swift 2014a; Ben-Shahar 2015).

Benefitting the Less Advantaged

The third distributive value avoids the leveling down problem without requiring that we identify an adequacy threshold. The idea is simple: inequalities in educational goods are valuable if they work to improve the prospects for flourishing of those who are worse off. This allows for investment in those with high levels of natural talent if there's a reasonable expectation that the resulting increase in productivity can be channeled to those who have the strongest claim to the extra benefits. Such benefits need not themselves take the form of educational goods. For example, the opportunities for flourishing of the cognitively impaired might be improved more by distributing educational goods in a manner conducive to technological, medical or social development than by distributing them so as to increase their possession of educational goods themselves.

We've articulated answers to the questions of what children should learn and how learning resources should be distributed among them, in sufficiently abstract terms to allow for a good deal of disagreement about exactly how they should be operationalized. Assume these are the correct answers. Who should have the power to make the relevant decisions?

A Consequentialist Framework

Suppose that we were considering how to allocate decision-making power within an organization that had certain reasonably well specified aims, and in which there were no pre-existing constitutional constraints on the answer. A natural rule would be simply to allocate power in the way that was calculated to reach the right decisions, and to implement them effectively.

We'll explore shortly what this allocation might look like in practice. But before doing so, we should note that the two considerations we have laid out – concerning what children should learn and how resources should be distributed – are not the only consequences that matter. The quality and distribution of children's education are surely important. But so are other policy priorities, like public health, transportation, efficient capital markets, and national security. Delivering on some of those priorities (like public health) may be entirely congruent with educational priorities, but trade-offs are sometimes unavoidable, and children's education, while always a high priority, should not trump everything else. Even within education policy, the quality and distribution of education are not the only outcomes of concern. The well-being of teachers matters, and not only because it is instrumental for high quality learning. Free societies place considerable value on free choice of occupation and freedom of movement, so conscripting teaching labor, or severely restricting the operation of labor and housing markets, would be unacceptable even if they would optimally serve the two fundamental goals we've articulated.

Even focusing narrowly on the interests of children themselves, education is not all we should be concerned with. Childhood is not just *preparation* for a life; it is, itself, *part of* a life. How well people's childhoods go – the quality of their daily lived experience, both in their family and in whatever educational settings they attend – matters in itself, not only because it affects what happens later. Some philosophers refer to this aspect of child wellbeing as "childhood goods." Some goods – like carefreeness, innocence of certain evils, and apparently pointless play – may only be attainable, or may be more abundantly attainable, in childhood. Others – such as laughter, happiness, friendship, freedom from bullying – may be equally or sometimes more readily attainable, in adulthood, but their value in childhood is not tied to their developmental value (Brennan 2014; Gheaus 2015). Children have an interest in all the goods we have mentioned, and other childhood goods, whether or not they benefit them educationally, and even, to some extent, if they, *conflict with* their purely developmental interests.

When we ask, then, which decision-makers would make the best decisions, the relevant consequences to factor into the judgment are not only the production and distribution of educational goods, as discussed in the previous two sections, but also the production and distribution of non-educational goods, as outlined in the previous two paragraphs. So, which decision-maker or decision-makers would be most likely to produce the best outcomes?

Imagine, first, placing all the decision-making power in the hands of parents. Parents normally have a wealth of knowledge about their children, and generally care a great deal about their wellbeing (including, but not restricted to, their educational outcomes). So, they can normally be relied on to put considerable weight on their children's interests. Advocates of strong claims about parents' rights to make decisions concerning their children's education typically appeal to this kind of consideration. There will, sadly, be exceptions to these generalizations, so parents' decisions cannot be regarded as entirely sacrosanct and immune from public scrutiny. But the thought is that, as a matter of policy, parents will tend to make better decisions because they are better informed about their own children, and more strongly motivated to do the best for them, than any alternative decision-maker.

The suggestion is not, of course, that parents should do all the educating themselves. In modern complex societies, families typically lack the capacity to give their children everything they need even for participation in the economy. Teaching mathematics beyond basic numeracy, and reading beyond basic literacy, are really difficult, requiring skills that most parents lack and that it would be, at best, inefficient for them to acquire. Even if parents had sole decision-making power, they would have to rely on third parties – teachers, and schools – to provide educational services. That solves the problem of their incompetence to educate but brings another problem to the surface. To make good decisions, parents have to be able to monitor the quality of the education their children are receiving. This is extremely difficult even for well-educated parents with time, leisure, and understanding of how institutions work. Education is a complex process, and education within schools is particularly so. Children's development is hard to monitor because it happens unevenly over time, and information about what is actually happening within schools and classrooms is in any case hard to access. Even principals and teachers have limited knowledge about what is happening in schools. So, the information problem parents face in ensuring the quality of education is very challenging.

One problem with the suggestion, then, is that parents' motivation to promote their children's interests, and up-close knowledge of their individual abilities and personalities, may not be enough. This would be so even if we were concerned only with parents' ability to make good educational decisions for their own children.

A second problem is that parents' decisions may fail to give proper weight to the interests of others. Taking into account the interests of affected third parties, parents may underinvest, over-invest, or mis-invest, in their children's education. They may, for example, focus on the capacity to participate in the economy to the detriment of the capacity for democratic competence and the capacity to treat others as equals. Some parents willfully, others negligently, raise their children to be racist or sexist, or homophobic; others willfully or negligently inculcate doctrinal commitments that present undue barriers to taking seriously the interests of others when they are advanced in democratic debate. Giving parents full decision-making power puts others at risk of wrongful harms inflicted by the mis-educated, and it undermines the ability of the mis-educated children themselves to contribute to the flourishing of others.

Now, put those values aside, and think just about the labor market. Parents, left to their own devices, are unlikely to be motivated to advance the distributive goals we identified in the previous section. Their concern is typically to promote the interests of their own children. Even if they were motivated by those distributive goals, they are not well placed to coordinate investment in children's education in such a way as to produce, for example, fair competition in the labor market. Affluent parents can invest heavily in their children's competitive advantage, while low-income parents cannot. Without government intervention to ensure that gaps in preparation do not track gaps in parental labor market success, opportunities would be extremely unequal. The general point is that giving complete decision-making power over resource allocation to parents puts distributive goals in jeopardy (Hill 2017).

A third problem is that parents may misidentify their children's interests or fail to strike the right balance between various educational goods even as those concern their own children's prospects for flourishing. A big risk of this kind is a failure adequately to promote children's development of the capacity for autonomy. Unconstrained, parents might overreach in their shaping of their children's values. There is widespread consensus that parents are permitted, and perhaps indeed required, to inculcate *some* values in their children, such as honesty and treating others as moral equals. But philosophers disagree about the extent to which, and ways in which, it is legitimate for parents deliberately to influence their children's religious and ethical commitments more generally (Macleod 1997; Clayton 2006; Brighouse & Swift 2014b; Swift 2020). That parents shape their children's values in ways that reflect their own is probably an inevitable side effect of the many intimate interactions that are essential components of a successful parent-child relationship. But children have an interest in becoming adults who can make and act on their own independent judgments about how to live their lives, and that places a limit on what parents may legitimately do to shape their values. With sole decision-making power, some parents will – some willfully, some negligently – go beyond what is legitimate. Some, such as those convinced of the truth of their own religious views, will do so in the belief that they are thereby benefitting their children. And other parents, who are inclined to foster their children's autonomy, may find it easier to strike the right balance if other forces, such as schools, are recognized as legitimate counterweights.

If vesting all decision-making power in parents has the problems we've identified, should we look for an alternative agent? The most natural alternative (and the only one we are going to consider) is the state. As far back as Plato, philosophers have recognized that government might have some proper role in decision-making about children's education. Why not vest all decision-making power in the state?

Remember that we are currently considering a purely consequentialist framework. In the next section we will consider the possibility that parents have some sort of right to decision-making power that limits the state's role, but here we are focusing on consequences concerning what children learn, how that learning is distributed, and other public policy outcomes. Unlike parents, the state is accountable to third parties, has a remit to be concerned impartially with the outcomes of all students, and is concerned with ensuring proper levels of investment in the development of all children within its jurisdiction. It is better placed than parents to gather reliable information about what happens in schools and – because it has information about many schools and can make comparisons over time – much better placed to make sense of that information in context. Some of the problems with parents as decision-makers need not arise.

Just because states can do a better job than parents can does not mean that they will. One of the fears we expressed about parents is that they might willfully or negligently raise their children to be racist, sexist, or homophobic. If the state has a clear commitment to combat racism, sexism, or homophobia, and the competence to see that commitment through, then it will not be a problem if the state has all the decision-making authority. Yet that is by no means always the case. Our guess is that the great majority of schools in the liberal democratic world today have institutional commitments to combat those ills. But we doubt that the same was true of schools when we were children. And we were raised in the U.K.: most public schools in many parts of the U.S. were thoroughly committed to reproducing the racist and sexist attitudes that prevailed in society well into the 1970s, and they reproduced and reflected the homophobic attitudes that prevailed without needing any kind of commitment to doing so. Further, the highly racially segregated character of schooling throughout the U.S. from the late 1920s was a direct consequence of government activity which aimed at, and succeeded in, racially segregating neighborhoods, thus undermining the ability of schools to foster democratic competence and the capacity to treat others as equals even if they wanted to do that (Rothstein 2017).

Even liberal democratic states do not always pursue, let alone achieve, the educational goals we have prescribed. If we look at states outside the liberal democratic world, things are worse still. Many authoritarian, totalitarian, and ethnonationalist states use schooling to foster a passive, obedient, and intolerant population, deliberately and systematically frustrating the achievement of the goals we have prescribed.

Similarly, whereas school funding arrangements in some parts of the world reflect states' commitment to mitigating the effects of social class background on educational outcomes, this is not true everywhere. Because of its federal structure and heavy reliance on local funding, the U.S. is a fascinating case study. Most school funding comes from the local level, and local expenditure is highly unequal: affluent students residing in property-rich districts receive far more than low-income students in property-poor districts. So, government at the local level reproduces background inequalities. Financial support at the level of individual states constitutes a smaller fraction of school funding, and this is, mostly, distributed *very* roughly equally between districts on a per-pupil basis. So, state-level government does not attempt to reproduce, but does a little to mitigate, background inequalities. The federal government, which provides about 10% of total spending on public k-12 education, targets the lion's share of its funding to low-income students and students with disabilities. So, the federal state is deeply committed to mitigating the effects of background inequalities.[2] Currently the state considered as a whole (including local, state-level, and federal authorities together) probably pursues the distributive outcomes better than parents left to themselves would. But it is far from unified in its efforts, and those efforts combined fall far short of what would be required for the distributive goals we have described. And, again, non-liberal and non-democratic states, which are accountable only to certain factions of society, often spend money accordingly, maintaining and sometimes worsening inequality (Amini & Commander 2012; Yang et.al. 2014).

Parents can't be relied upon to achieve the ends we have prescribed. Nor can states. The consequentialist approach will not assume that either parents or states should have all decision-making power, but it will seek to divide that power between them in whatever way is most likely to result in the desired outcomes. The exact allocation of that power – which agents should get to decide exactly what – is a matter of dispute among reasonable people. Many, including commentators who are otherwise skeptical about state power, think that the state should play some significant role in funding education and determining how funds should be allocated. Some think the state should have considerable say over the curriculum, especially insofar as it has effects that go beyond the good of the individual child. Few believe that parents should have no discretion about what school their child attends, and the quite ambitious distributive goals we have described allow for parental choice as long as the state plays an appropriate role in allocating funds and regulating the quality of schools (Brighouse 2000). But, as we emphasized, states vary considerably both in their will to achieve desirable outcomes, and their capacity to do so. The appropriate distribution of decision-making power might be quite different in different contexts depending on the aims and capacities of the state in question.

Non-Consequentialist Considerations

Not everyone believes that only consequences matter. We suggested, that left to themselves, parents might exert undue influence in shaping their children's values, but the view that parents have the right to raise their children in ways that tend to reproduce their own ethical and religious commitments is certainly widespread. Some justify that right by appealing to its allegedly beneficial consequences, but others adopt a more deontological approach. Here the thought is that parents are entitled to exert extensive control over their children's upbringing – just as they are entitled to exert extensive control over their own lives – whether or not that is conducive to good outcomes. Some philosophers endorse that view. Think of Charles Fried's claim that the right to "form one's child's values, one's child's life plan" is grounded in the "basic right not to be interfered with in doing these things for oneself" (Fried 1978). William Galston, similarly, says that "the ability of parents to raise their children in a manner consistent with their deepest commitments is an essential element of expressive liberty" (Galston 1991). Article 26 of the UN Declaration of Human Rights recognizes that children have a right to education but subjugates it to parents' "prior right to choose the kind of education that shall be given to their children" (UN General Assembly 1948). The International Covenant on Economic, Social and Cultural Rights asserts that parents have the liberty to "ensure the religious and moral education of their children in conformity with their own convictions" (UN General Assembly 1966). The underlying assumption here is not that it will be better for children's education if their parents get to shape their children's values. *Maybe* it will. But the thought that parents have a *right* to do that is that parents should be permitted to do it even where it will not.

The exact content of this purported parental right, even if one concedes it exists, is, like the content of other rights, a matter of debate. Should it include total control over the child's environment? In practice, liberal states tend to grant parents *de jure* rights that they can use to induct their children into their own religious and ethical outlooks, and to try to make sure that those children reach adulthood seeing the world in similar ways. Parents have exclusive rights to determine what materials are read to their children, and are available for the children to read, at home; to talk to them and determine who else can talk to them at home; to take them to church (or forbid them to attend church), to concerts, to sporting events; to determine what food goes on their plate, what music they listen to, and what television they watch. Not only may parents raise their children, at home, as members of particular faith or cultural communities but they can also, if they have the resources, ensure that their children attend schools that will reinforce the message. Perhaps allowing parents to do all of these things is enough to respect parental rights, so that there is nothing wrong with the state imposing considerable regulation on what happens to the child in formal educational settings and requiring that they attend those settings. If so, then we might think of those rights as constraints on the consequentialist framework rather than as alternatives to it: parents should have whatever decision-making power is needed to ensure that their rights are protected, and the remaining decision-making powers should be distributed according to the consequentialist framework. Or perhaps – and we think Fried's comment implies this – states may not even require school attendance, and must cede complete control to parents, so there is no room at all for the consequentialist framework to operate.

Claims about parents' rights are the most common way for non-consequentalist considerations to come into accounts of who should make decisions about children's education, but they are not the only way. Some insist that children themselves have rights that make it impermissible for anybody – parents or the state – to treat them in certain ways, even if treating them in those ways would be good for them (Clayton et al. 2021). We listed the capacity for autonomy as among the educational goods that would be taken into account by a decision-maker concerned to make good decisions, and we appealed to the way in which having and exercising that capacity contributes to flourishing. But one might regard the development of their capacity for autonomy as something to which children are entitled whether or not its development will benefit them: perhaps what really matters is that they are able to make and act on their own judgments about how to live, not that they judge well or wisely. Another version of child-focused non-consequentialism appeals not to the importance of children's developing the capacity for autonomy as an "end-state" to be achieved, but rather to their moral "independence." On that view, children's rights are violated whenever anybody – parent or state – intentionally directs them towards controversial views that they might reasonably reject, for example by enrolling them into a particular religion. That would be wrong, on this view, even if the children in question also developed the capacity for autonomy (Clayton 2012).

In practice, it probably doesn't make much difference whether the capacity for autonomy is valued on consequentialist or non-consequentialist grounds. Either way, decision-making power should be allocated in whatever way makes it likely that children develop that capacity. The view that decision-makers must respect children's moral independence, and refrain from any attempt to transmit their own particular religious or ethical views, sets a harder constraint but the overall picture remains the same, and indeed the same as it did in the case of parents' rights. Decision-making should be distributed in whatever way is best suited to protecting children's rights; any remaining powers could be distributed in accordance with the consequentialist framework.

Conclusion

Our answer to the question, "Who should make decisions about children's education?" is: "it depends." It depends partly on normative or philosophical judgments. If, for example, some non-consequentialist value crowds out all others then the answer is simple. Suppose that parents have an absolute right to make every decision about education regardless of how well those decisions serve their children or anybody else: then, simply, parents should make all those decisions. Or suppose that it doesn't matter whether children develop the capacity for autonomy, or that it's not important how educational goods are distributed. In those cases, too, it might be appropriate to give parents more control over their children's education than our analysis would suggest. And it depends partly on empirical judgments. To the extent that consequentialist considerations should play a role in deciding the allocation of decision-making power such issues as the capacity, and will, of the particular state in a specific time and place, and indeed the capacities and wills of families, will inform the answer. As our discussion implies, a full and direct answer would require a careful weighing of the different considerations at stake *in specific circumstances*. In the foregoing discussion we have provided normative resources needed to approach the issue.

We have not even tried to answer a different, and some might think more important, question: who should make decisions about who should make decisions about children's education? The resources we have provided are intended both to guide those making decisions and to help identify who should make them. But even those who endorse our approach may, and surely will, disagree about how to balance different educational goods, or about the relative importance of distributive values, or about the proper content of parents' or children's rights. They will probably disagree also in their empirical judgments about the likely effects of different decisions that might be made, and about who, in practice, is likely to make better or worse decisions. Others may reject our approach altogether. Disagreement is rife. Who, then, should have the power to decide who should make decisions about children's education? The question of who has the sovereignty or authority to decide who gets to decide matters concerning children's education – a version of the "jurisdictional boundary problem" (Laborde 2017) – is so hard that we have not even broached it.

(Related Chapters: 3, 6, 7, 9, 15, 16, 21, 27, 30, 34.)

Notes

1 For discussion of how these categories figure in real-world choices about curricular standards, see Brighouse and Mullane (2018).

2 For more detail see Brighouse et. al. 2018: ch. 5.

References

Amini, C. & Commander, S. (2012) "Educational Scores: How Does Russia Fare?" *Journal of Comparative Economics* 40(3): 508–527.

Anderson, E. (2007) "Fair Opportunity in Education: A Democratic Equality Perspective," *Ethics* 117(4): 595–622.

Archard, D. (2014) *Children: Rights and Childhood* (3rd ed.). Routledge.

Ben-Shahar, T. (2015) "Equality in Education – Why We Must Go All the Way," *Ethical Theory and Moral Practice* 19(1): 83–100.

Brennan, S. J. (2014) "The Goods of Childhood, Children's Rights, and the Role of Parents as Advocates and Interpreters," in F. Bayliss &C. MacLoed (eds.) *Family-Making: Contemporary Ethical Challenges*. Oxford: Oxford University Press, 35–52.

Brighouse, H. (2000) *School Choice and Social Justice*. Oxford: Oxford University Press.

Brighouse, H., Ladd, H. F., Loeb, S., & Swift, A. (2018) *Educational Goods: Values, Evidence, and Decision-Making*. Chicago: University of Chicago Press.

Brighouse, H. & Mullane, K. (2018) "Aims and Purposes of a State Schooling System: The Case of California," *Getting Down to Facts II*. Policy Analysis for California Education.

Brighouse, H., & Swift, A. (2014a) "The Place of Educational Equality in Educational Justice," in K. Meyer (ed.) *Education, Justice and the Human Good*. London: Routledge, 14–33.

Brighouse, H., & Swift, A. (2014b) *Family Values: The Ethics of Parent-Child Relationships*. Princeton: Princeton University Press.

Callan, E. (1997) *Creating Citizens: Political Education and Liberal Democracy*. Oxford: Oxford University Press.

Clayton, M. (2006) *Justice and Legitimacy in Upbringing*. Oxford: Oxford University Press.

Clayton, M. (2012) "The Case Against the Comprehensive Enrolment of Children," *The Journal of Political Philosophy* 20(3): 353–364.

Clayton, M., Mason, A., Swift, A. & Wareham, R. (2021) "The Political Morality of School Composition: The Case of Religious Selection," *British Journal of Political Science* 51(2): 827–844.

Curren, R. (2000) *Aristotle on the Necessity of Public Education*. Lanham, MD: Rowman and Littlefield.

Feinberg, J. (2007) "The Child's Right to an Open Future," in *Freedom and Fulfillment: Philosophical Essays*. Princeton: Princeton University Press, 76–97.

Fried, C. (1978) *Right and Wrong*. Cambridge, MA: Harvard University Press.

Galston, W. A. (1991) *Liberal Purposes: Goods, Virtues, and Diversity in the Liberal State*. Cambridge: Cambridge University Press.

Gheaus, A. (2015) "The 'Intrinsic Goods of Childhood' and the Just Society," in A. Gattini & C. Macleod (eds.) *The Nature of Children's Well-Being*. Dordrecht: Springer, 35–52.

Gutmann, A. (1999) *Democratic Education*. Princeton: Princeton University Press.

Hill, H. C. (2017) "The Coleman Report, 50 Years On: What Do We Know about the Role of Schools in Academic Inequality?" *The ANNALS of the American Academy of Political and Social Science* 674(1): 9–26.

Jencks, C. (1988) "Whom Must We Treat Equally for Educational Opportunity to be Equal?" *Ethics* 98(3): 518–533.

Laborde, C. (2017) *Liberalism's Religion*. Cambridge, MA: Harvard University Press.

Levinson, M., Geron, T., & Brighouse, H. (n.d.) *Conceptions of Educational Equity*. (ms on file with authors).

Macedo, S. (2003) *Diversity and Distrust: Civic Education in a Multicultural Democracy*. Cambridge, MA: Harvard University Press.

Macleod, C. M. (1997) "Conceptions of Parental Autonomy," *Politics and Society* 25(1): 117–140.

Rothstein, R. (2017) *The Color of Law: A Forgotten History of How Our Government Segregated America*. New York: Liveright.

Schouten, G. (2012) "Fair Educational Opportunity and the Distribution of Natural Ability: Toward a Prioritarian Principle of Educational Justice," *Journal of Philosophy of Education* 46(3): 472–491.

Swift, A. (2020) "Parents' Rights, Children's Religion: A Familial Relationship Goods Approach," *Journal of Practical Ethics* 8(2): 30–65.

Tooley, J. (2009) *Education without the State*. London: Institute of Economic Affairs.

UN General Assembly (1948) *Universal Declaration of Human Rights*, 10 December 1948, 217 A (III), Article 7, available at: http://www.refworld.org/docid/3ae6b3712c.html [accessed 16October2013].

UN General Assembly (1966) *International Covenant on Economic, Social and Cultural Rights*, 16 December 1966, United Nations, Treaty Series, vol. 993: 3.

White, J. (2011) *Exploring Well-Being in Schools A Guide to Making Children's Lives More Fulfilling*. London: Routledge.

Yang, J., Huang, X., & Liu, X. (2014) "An Analysis of Education Inequality in China," *International Journal of Educational Development* 37: 2–10

9
THEORIZING EDUCATIONAL JUSTICE

Meira Levinson

There are hundreds, perhaps thousands, of good articles and books about justice and education. Philosophers have done robust work on topics including school choice, the aims of education, the content of the curriculum, school financing, special education and inclusion, parents' vs. states' vs. children's rights, creating just classrooms and schools, school discipline, and dozens of other salient issues. I am struck, however, by the fact that virtually no contemporary theorist has proposed a comprehensive theory of educational justice itself.

Michael Merry gestures toward doing so in *Educational Justice*, but he focuses primarily on issues of inclusion, exclusion, and choice rather than developing a truly comprehensive theory of educational justice; furthermore, he explicitly rejects systematic theory-building about educational justice in light of the importance of always attending to empirical particulars (Merry 2020). By contrast, Harry Brighouse et al. argue in *Educational Goods* that one can (and should) integrate a broadly applicable normative theory with empirical data in making educational policy decisions, and they propose a theory of educational goods plus additional non-education-specific values as an approach to doing so (Brighouse et al. 2017). But like Merry, Brighouse et al. frame their work as a proposed "method for assessing and evaluating policy options" (Brighouse et al. 2017: 1), rather than as a substantive general theory. Winston Thompson has gone the furthest in arguing for "a uniquely educational genre of justice" (Thompson 2016: 3), building on Robbie McClintock's theory of formative justice. In contrast to both Merry and Brighouse et al., Thompson argues (following McClintock) that educational justice should be theorized not as a subgenre of political justice but instead on its own terms, as a theory of children's just development of potentialities (Thompson 2016; Cherry 2017). He points out that many of the classic questions that philosophers ask about educational justice, from the aims of education to distribution of educational resources to allocation of legitimate authority over children's learning, can be formulated in terms of educationally-specific questions about the finite opportunities that children have to develop their manifold potentialities. I am excited to see how Thompson's project unfolds over time, as I think it has immense potential of its own, but I also have some concerns about developing a theory of educational justice primarily from the top down and on the basis of a single abstract concept such as formative justice.

My purpose in this chapter, therefore, is to offer some initial reflections about the project of theorizing educational justice on its own terms from the bottom-up: *why* we should do so, *how* we might go about it, and if we were to do so, *what* we would be theorizing about. For reasons of space and coherence, I will treat "education" as referring to formal, school-based teaching and learning; I will also concentrate solely on children. I take it as given that schools' aims, practices, and policies

DOI: 10.4324/9781003172246-11

with regard to children are an appropriate central focus of educational justice, and hence that starting with children in schools is a reasonable place to begin, even if not to end.

I start by presenting a case that I trust readers will intuitively recognize as a paradigmatic dilemma of educational justice: whether and how to accommodate one child's special needs in a mainstream class setting. In so doing, I start neither from an analytic concept nor from a hypothesized original position, but instead from phenomenological experience. This is in part because I want to start with an educational relationship that is not already grounded in – and potentially limited by – prior political concepts or assumptions. I also think that phenomenological approaches may be warranted by the intrinsically "non-ideal" features of theorizing about education; if nothing else, it is helpful to confront head-on what it means to theorize about children and not just presumptively free and equal adults. At the same time, I have intentionally chosen a case that is relatively idealized, with few hints of external social injustice infecting the internal decisions that have to be made within the school.

The rest of the chapter draws out elements of this dilemma in order to establish some key characteristics of any coherent theory of educational justice. Insofar as extant ideal theories of justice rest on fundamental principles about agents and institutions that I show are nonsensical in the educational context, I conclude that questions of educational justice cannot be resolved solely by applying more general theories of justice about and for adults. Rather, educational justice requires an original normative theory that will also likely incorporate "non-ideal" methods and principles.

Rocky Choices: One Dilemma of Educational Justice[1]

Rivers Elementary School is a public primary school in a wealthy school district in the United States. It has a reputation for outstanding academics, a nurturing school culture, and ready responsiveness to parents' concerns. Kate, the eight-year-old daughter of an art historian and a doctor, has proved to be one of Rivers' more challenging students. Her first few years were "delightful," in the words of her first-grade teacher. During the summer before second grade and into that fall, however, Kate became increasingly oppositional for reasons that no one could identify. By the spring of second grade, she was regularly disrupting class by shrieking and banging her desk, causing other children to cry or even cower in fear. After being diagnosed with "nonspecific opposition-defiance disorder," she received an Individualized Education Plan (IEP) that included a part-time aide and other accommodations intended to help her remain in a mainstream setting. Her parents also agreed that during her outbursts, she would be removed to the "Think Room," which is a form of solitary confinement used to help children contain themselves. Although the Think Room is controversial within the district – many teachers and parents see it as developmentally inappropriate and punitive – both Kate and her parents were grateful to have a place that she could go when school became overwhelming.

Kate's third grade teacher, Ms. Brown, was a twenty-two-year veteran with certifications in general education, special education, and science. Ms. Brown had a soft spot for "tough kids," and asked to have Kate assigned to her class; Kate's parents were thrilled, and Mr. Thomason, the school principal, readily agreed. Knowing that Kate's classmates got upset about her behavior, Ms. Brown led conversations with the students about inclusive communities that honor many kinds of difference. The children excitedly identified their many differences and discussed how classroom norms and procedures enable everyone to "be their best selves." At the same time, many children privately expressed concern about Kate's continued disruptions. They knew that Ms. Brown was not open to accusations that "Kate messes everything up," but they did complain to their parents and each other when an exciting learning activity came to an abrupt end during one of Kate's mini-explosions. Some children also seemed so concerned about setting Kate off that they concentrated more on mollifying her than on the subject of the lesson.

In light of these concerns, a group of parents met with Principal Thomason to discuss Kate's participation in class. These parents expressed concern about classroom safety and culture. They also questioned the academic rigor of a class that was sporadically disrupted. In response, Mr. Thomason expressed support for Ms. Brown, and emphasized that all children are entitled by law to the least-restrictive appropriate educational setting. At the same time, Mr. Thomason reassured the parents that "it is of paramount importance that every child feel safe and secure in class, ready and able to learn." At the end of the meeting, one of the lead parents – the only father in the group – thanked Mr. Thomason for his concern and said he hoped he wouldn't have to "take it to the next level" in response to continued disruptions.

Mr. Thomason met with Ms. Brown the next day. She was frustrated that the parents had not contacted her directly and said that the parents' own concerns were feeding their children's worries. "It's not the kids who are scared of Kate; it's the parents," Ms. Brown explained. "They say stuff to their kids over dinner, about how Kate shouldn't be there or is disrupting other kids' learning, and then the children come in the next day with complaints that they never had and blow things all out of proportion."

In response, Mr. Thomason emphasized that he was responsible for all children and their families. "If you see Kate starting to get upset, I want you to ring for help so an adult can escort Kate to the Think Room," Mr. Thomason instructed. "Remove Kate from the classroom *before* she explodes. That way, Kate can feel some success that she hasn't disrupted another day of learning, and her classmates can feel confident Kate won't be allowed to get out of hand. We can't afford to let this escalate. No need to get the superintendent involved." Mr. Thomason was firm; although Ms. Brown tried to protest, he made it clear their meeting was over.

The following Monday, Kate came in late, looking agitated. Her parents told Ms. Brown she had had a rough morning but was eager to get to school to learn about rocks – a favorite subject. Students were working in small groups to classify rocks by their sedimentary, metamorphic, or igneous characteristics. Ms. Brown assigned Kate to work with two boys, Philip and Frank. Both boys were welcoming, although Philip, who identified as a "future world-famous inventor," had occasionally gotten upset about Kate's disruptions in the past. It was his father who had threatened Mr. Thomason with "taking it to the next level." Frank was a soft-spoken, reserved child. A struggling reader, he often seemed to disengage from classroom activities if they seemed too challenging. Ms. Brown worried about his self-confidence, reminding him frequently that he was a great thinker and observer, even if "your brain needs extra help matching letters to sounds."

Initially, the group work went smoothly. Frank took on the role of holding each rock up for examination. All three children expressed their opinion about its classification; finding that they were unanimous, Philip recorded the group's decisions on a worksheet. About ten minutes in, however, the two boys began to squabble over the designation of a rock. Philip insisted it was igneous; Frank was sure it was metamorphic. Kate did not take a position in the debate. Instead, she squirmed and moved away, as if trying to shield herself from the conflict. She then returned to the table, but again seemed undone by the boys' vehement disagreement. The boys weren't misbehaving – to the contrary, they were passionately involved in the science task at hand – but their argument continued unabated.

Ms. Brown was across the room, helping a group that was struggling with the classification exercise; they kept trying to organize the rocks by shape and size. Noting Kate's increasing distress, however, Ms. Brown crossed the classroom and quietly asked Kate if she would like to switch groups. Kate refused, seeming hurt. She did not want to walk away from the important work she had already done sorting rocks! Ms. Brown then turned to Philip and Frank. "Why don't you present your debate to Kate, and let her be the judge?" But Kate nervously shook her head, feeling pressure at being in the spotlight. Frank, uncharacteristically, also scowled. He was on the verge of convincing Philip he was right, he felt; this wasn't the time to start over!

Ms. Brown could tell that Kate was close to breaking down. She had little time to decide what to do. Should she pursue her tactic of having the boys present their argument to Kate for adjudication, potentially agitating Kate to the point of no return, leaving the other group to founder, and risking censure from her principal? Should she send Kate preemptively to the Think Room, causing her to miss the lesson for which she had worked so hard to get to school? Should she move one of the boys out of the group, effectively punishing them for doing their work, and undercutting Frank's newfound academic engagement and self-assertion? Should she shift to whole class instruction, scrapping the current lesson plan and perhaps diminishing all children's active engagement in learning? What was the right course of action?

Theorizing Educational Justice: Necessary Presuppositions and Features

There are a number of struggles and dilemmas built into the case above: curricular, pedagogical, political, social, administrative, and ethical (among others). Some of these are certainly dilemmas of justice: of who is owed what and why. What are Kate, Frank, Philip, and the other children in the class each owed, and how should potential conflicts in satisfying those obligations be resolved? Furthermore, who is responsible for making such determinations, for setting the conditions under which justice might be done, and for actually enacting just decisions? Are these the same or different agents? Ms. Brown clearly has duties of justice, and presumably Mr. Thomason does, too, as head of school. How about the parents? The children in the class? The US government has taken a stand in declaring that Kate has the right to a "free and appropriate public education" – a right that it notably does *not* attribute to students without diagnosed special needs; is this claim a defensible one, and is the federal government the right entity to make it? Some (but not all) of these dilemmas of justice are bound up in questions about sameness and difference: what does it mean to treat like as like in this case? Which differences matter, how, and why? Of what relevance are Kate's mental illness, Frank's dyslexia, Philip's confidence, or the other group's confusion over principles of classification?

I raise these questions not to answer them, but to highlight how the case embodies some paradigmatic dilemmas of justice in general, and of educational justice in particular. I also wish to note that this is arguably an "ideal" case, in that it occurs in a well-resourced school and district with highly trained school personnel, involved parents, and no evident history of domination, oppression, or other forms of institutionalized social injustice more broadly speaking. It is the kind of case that would arise even in a "well-ordered society" (Rawls 1971). The question I want to address is how we might go about theorizing educational justice in a way that would help us address a case such as Kate's. Most specifically, what features of the educational context or subjects would any theory of educational justice have to take as given in order to reason meaningfully about the kinds of dilemmas that arise in this case?

Children Are Appropriately Non-compliant, Sometimes Because They're Also Unreasonable and/or Irrational

Let's begin with Kate herself. Kate poses a challenge in large part because she is defiant and disruptive. She does not allow the class to get on with its work. In some ways, Kate is an outlier in this regard. But on the other hand, misbehavior and disruption of others' projects are normal, even developmentally healthy, features of childhood. We would be very worried about a toddler or adolescent, for example, who never acted out, tested limits, or tried to substitute his or her independent judgment in place of adults' advice/directions. This is true in matters of justice and morality as much as in anything else. Children snatch things from one another, refuse to share, attack others physically and emotionally, renege on promises, manipulate parents and siblings, lie, coerce, and wantonly interfere with others' projects – often all in a day's work. In theorizing educational justice, therefore, one must assume that the primary subjects of such justice – children – will at least sometimes be non-compliant and fail to fulfill their obligations to others.

Such normatively condemnatory terms as "attack, snatch, renege, and coerce," may feel like the wrong way to characterize children's actions, since young children, at least, are not morally responsible for their non-compliance. But this illuminates another essential presupposition of any plausible theory of educational justice: namely, that children have not yet learned to reason properly about moral obligations to others nor fully to regulate their actions even when they know what morality demands. That's one important responsibility of adults, to help children develop moral cognition, emotion, and self-regulation (Dahl 2019; Malti et al. 2021). It's also important to note that children may be unreasonable or even irrational about non-moral actions – not only as Kate is when she is in the throes of her mental illness, but also as Frank arguably is when he withdraws from lessons that are specifically designed to help him learn essential reading skills, or as Philip and Frank both are when they push their argument to the stage that is likely to trigger an outburst from Kate. It would be much easier for Ms. Brown to fulfill her duties of educational justice (whatever those turn out to be) if Kate could recognize the boys' argument as a part of learning, if Frank would reliably engage with equal vigor in future lessons were he to be shut down now, if Philip would recognize that his own behavior was partly to blame when he tells his father over dinner that Kate exploded during science class (leading his father, say, to contact the superintendent), and even if the other group could figure out that classifying rocks by their origins has nothing to do with classifying them by size. But such complaints also miss the point. Sure, Ms. Brown would have an easier time enacting justice if her charges were consistently compliant, reasonable, and rational. But then she wouldn't actually be dealing with *children*, who are the primary subjects of any theory of educational justice. Again, therefore, any theory of educational justice must take account of the fact that its primary subjects – children – are sometimes non-compliant and unreasonable, and similarly that methods for fostering compliance and reason are themselves an essential object of theorizing about educational justice.

Corrective and Distributive Justice Need to Be Theorized Simultaneously

Because both compliance and reason (including reasonable emotions) are *products* of educational justice, rather than being stipulated presuppositions as they are, say, in Rawlsian ideal theory, any exercise in theorizing educational justice must simultaneously address both corrective and distributive concerns. In other words, the theory must address the just correction of children's behavior, and also the just distribution of educational goods. Neither can be set aside for a future date.

We would consider it outrageous if the fact that a child was obstreperous at age five, for example, was offered as a moral justification for his failing in school at age 13, let alone his inability to qualify for living-wage work or a place in college at age 18. One can easily give a *causal* account of this child's trajectory: getting in trouble initially leads him to develop a self-concept as a "bad kid"; he fulfills his expectations by misbehaving and being punished further; these punishments cause him to miss lessons and get behind; he eventually disengages from school altogether since he feels like a failure at every stage. This is a depressingly common occurrence. But we would presumably disavow any theory of educational justice that claimed this child's poor life outcomes were *just deserts* for his behavior as a five-year-old. So, a theory of educational justice has in some way to disavow responsibility in at least some of its subjects, while also giving an account of why, when, and how the transition from blamelessness to blameworthiness, from childish innocence to adult responsibility, is both effected and administered.

Furthermore, distributive and corrective justice are not only each part of any theory of educational justice, but they are also intimately intertwined. This is true for two reasons. First, a theory of educational justice has to clarify which elements of children's development are subjects for distributive versus corrective justice – or if both simultaneously, how the two should be understood in relation to one another. When Ms. Brown works with Kate to help her control her behavior, for example, is she helping Kate acquire key social and emotional skills – and hence distributing educational goods – or is she teaching Kate how to comply with others' appropriate expectations – and hence administering corrective action? Is such a distinction even meaningful? A plausible theory of educational justice could potentially characterize all exercises in corrective justice in distributive terms, insofar as the aim of correction is to help children develop social, emotional, and intellectual capacities (other-orientation, perspective-taking abilities, self-control, capacity to delay gratification, etc.) that are essential for shared social life. A competing and equally plausible theory of educational justice, however, could define corrective justice as that which fosters children's development as moral agents – as people who can properly be held morally responsible and be evaluated as deserving (or non-deserving) – while defining distributive justice as that which, say, enables children's acquisition of essential primary goods. This maintains conceptual distance between the two. I take no position here on the proper definition of or relationship between distribution and correction in a theory of educational justice; my point is simply to show that any theory of educational justice will need to attend to such questions.

Second, distributive and corrective justice are also intertwined on an empirical level, insofar as how teachers deal with a disruptive child has both corrective and distributive consequences for all concerned (see Curren 2000 for a thoughtful exegesis of this relationship). A child like Kate who is removed from the classroom in response to (the threat of) an outburst, for example, is not only experiencing (let's say) corrective justice, but is simultaneously being denied access to educational goods. She can no longer learn about rock classification, nor about working effectively in groups, by directly observing rocks' characteristics and discussing their features with Philip and Frank. She is also potentially being prevented from developing the skills and dispositions that will help her remain in class more consistently, which negatively impinges on her social, emotional, and academic development. If Ms. Brown leaves Kate in the classroom until she explodes, however, then this impinges on all the other students' access to academic educational goods. At the very least, they will stop classifying rocks for the time it takes Ms. Brown to call for someone to remove Kate; they will also likely be distracted for a few minutes afterward. It may also affect their emotional and social well-being, making it further challenging the next time Kate is in the classroom for some children to concentrate on learning rather than on mollifying her. If Ms. Brown alternatively reassigns Philip to a different group or shifts to whole-class instruction about rocks in hopes of preventing Kate from exploding, then this also has distributive consequences for other students in the class. So, for both conceptual and empirical reasons, a theory of educational justice must attend to both distributive and corrective considerations and theorize appropriate relationships between them.

Educational Justice Even in a "Well-ordered School" Is Neither Stable nor Closed

Now let's say that Ms. Brown rightly believes that the most educationally just course of action would be to shift to whole class instruction and invite Philip and Frank to present their arguments to the whole class. The class would benefit from Philip and Frank's modeling of scientific reason-giving; Frank would receive academic affirmation (he's right that the rock is metamorphic); the group that is confused about classification principles may learn better from their peers why size is irrelevant; and Kate would have an opportunity to collect herself emotionally so she could then reengage academically. But Ms. Brown also knows that students are likely to misinterpret her decision to switch up the lesson. For instance, she fears that Kate, Frank, and Philip will all perceive that Kate's contributions to the group aren't valuable and conclude that academic engagement matters more than inclusion of diverse learners, even though neither of those is actually true nor are reasons that Ms. Brown would shift the lesson plan.

Ms. Brown is now in a bind. What may *be* most educationally just from an adult perspective may not be *perceived* by the students as most just, and it may even teach students lessons about educational justice that are antithetical to what she actually wants them to learn. As a result, Ms. Brown may conclude that it is better to take a different approach – say, to pull Philip and Frank aside and explain to them that their vehement argument is excluding Kate, thus teaching them important lessons about inclusion and social-emotional awareness even as the scientific lessons are lost – because it will (somewhat paradoxically) teach students better lessons about justice despite otherwise being the less just action.

Rather than a stable system providing an exemplar that all are moved to embrace and maintain, therefore, the most just educational institutions will be dynamic systems that intentionally accommodate instability and change. Educators may have an end state in mind that they want their students eventually (as adults) to achieve and maintain, but their actions in the here-and-now may look quite different from, and even at the extremes be antithetical to, that end state because of where their students are developmentally. In this respect, educational justice is both *being* and *becoming*, bootstrapping itself from the imperfect present to the more perfectly imagined future. Any plausible theory of educational justice must take this dynamism into account and treat it as a core feature of the theory, rather than as an exception to the norm.

A second reason that even the most idealized theory of educational justice must disavow both stability and closure is because children enter and exit school every day from institutions – namely, families – that are themselves not necessarily internally ordered by justice, and that also externally interact with schools in unequal and sometimes destabilizing ways. This is not to say that considerations of justice are irrelevant to family life.[2] But it is to say that justice is not the highest good *within* families; love and care should trump, as might a number of other values.

There will also always be significant differences *between* families that, even if they do not result from injustice, threaten the stable realization of educational justice. Children from a linguistically minority family who do not speak the language of school instruction will be at least temporarily disadvantaged when they start school, for example, and they may continue to be disadvantaged if their parents and teachers remain unable to communicate with one another. There may also be cultural mismatches in expectations about, say, what it means for a parent to support a child's learning. A child whose parents are undergoing a nasty divorce may come to school distracted and angry. A quiet child may get somewhat lost in the shuffle of a large, emotive family with lots of siblings. Examples also obviously fall on the positive side of the ledger; a child whose parents are authors may enter school with a strong identity as a capable writer, while a family with lots of children at the same school may benefit from institutional knowledge about how the place runs and what is essential for success. Note that none of these differences necessarily reflects any broader social injustices or even any disagreements between families about the value of school success – but they still have a profound influence on children's preparation for and potential for success in school.

Once such further differences do enter the picture – disagreements over the value of higher education, say, or over a child's obligations to concentrate on school versus church versus domestic chores or paid work – then educationally-relevant inequalities become even further exacerbated, and any pretense to the school's being able to function as a closed and stable system (even under idealized circumstances) becomes impossible to hold onto.[3]

I suggested above that educational justice is dynamic, always moving children from the compromised "now" toward a more perfect "what might be." Now we see that schools are also daily effecting a second kind of dynamic shift, from the disorderly, unregulated education that families are providing their children outside the school day to the orderly, regulated education being provided within the school walls. The school's porosity means that it cannot treat its own educational provision as a self-contained, closed system. Rather, it must constantly mediate between what it expects of and for children and what children's parents and guardians expect of and for them. Any theory of educational justice must offer an account of the school's responsibilities, if any, to address such differences.

Educational Justice Is Recursive and Plastic, as Are "Natural" and "Socially Constructed" Differences

One reason these non-school-based inequalities matter in the context of educational justice is that they both shape and are shaped by what happens in schools. Ideal theories of justice about adults tend to talk about "natural endowments," treating individuals' capacities essentially as fixed, and then debating the extent to which such endowments should influence life-chances in a variety of ways. Meritocratic theorists may embrace the association between endowments and life success, while luck egalitarians, say, may try to mitigate the effects of such endowments on the grounds that they constitute "brute luck." From an educational perspective, however, this approach is nonsensical. The whole point of education is that it is an inherently *developmental* enterprise: education enables people to master and apply new knowledge, ideas, skills, habits, dispositions, etc., that they did not previously have.[4] Any theory of educational justice, therefore, must treat children's capacities as plastic; that's what makes it a theory about *education*. Furthermore, as we consider what is owed to children, we must recognize that children's capabilities are themselves developed or retarded by the provision of education itself. Hence, educational justice is also recursive: what happens at one point in time may profoundly influence a child's ability to benefit from educational resources at a later point in time.

This recursivity and plasticity are central to what makes theorizing educational justice so challenging, because it means that difference is both an input and an output: it is both an independent and a dependent variable. Students come in with differences, and these differences will shape not only what they potentially need from schools, but also how they will make use of or respond to what schools do for/with/to them. Consider Frank and Philip, for example. Philip is a strong reader and confident learner. He sees himself as embracing intellectual challenges; his aspiration, after all, is to be a world-famous inventor. By contrast, Frank is a struggling reader who feels self-conscious about his dyslexia. He disengages from learning activities when he suspects they will be too hard for him. Frank is not only starting further behind, therefore, but he also will likely need much more support simply to move the same amount, let alone to catch up with Philip. Helping Frank learn and succeed in third grade may well be much more resource-intensive than helping Philip learn and succeed in third grade. On the other hand, these differences aren't fixed. Once Frank does learn how to compensate for his dyslexia, for example, his newfound confidence plus his native intellectual skills may kick in and enable him to catch up to or even surpass Philip academically. If Frank gets intensive literacy support in third grade, therefore, he could be an academic high-flyer for the rest of his school career. These services may come at a cost to Philip, however, as his opportunities to develop his talents are restricted by Ms. Brown's inattention. Frank and Philip may end up with equal outcomes – but at a cost to equality of opportunity, which is usually thought to trump equality of outcomes in contemporary theories of social justice.

Part of the task of any theory of educational justice is thus to set boundaries around the social construction of difference: around incoming difference, outgoing difference, and differences required to mediate children's pathways between the two. At Rivers Elementary, for example, there is disagreement about whether Kate's incoming differences are socially acceptable. Should a classroom be expected to accommodate a child who frequently disrupts academic learning and makes other students fearful? Ms. Brown clearly believes yes; Philip's father is far more skeptical. Students' capabilities leaving school are also significantly constructed by their educational experiences. How much heterogeneity versus homogeneity should be produced and/or tolerated by a just educational system?

These are tough questions that go far beyond debates about adequacy versus equality or the "achievement gap." They touch on fundamental questions about human identity (Curren 2020; Howard 2015). Some disability activists and theorists, for example, argue that the deployment of intense therapies such as those used to "cure" kids of autism is in fact a means to deny their identities and to impose an unjustified hegemonic normative conception of neurotypical development (Rosqvist et al. 2020). "What you see as pathology, I see as me," they in effect are saying. At what point does a just educational system have to take such claims seriously and back off its transformative vision? Education always begins as at least in part a paternalistic exercise: we believe we can see for children possibilities for both being and becoming that they cannot see for themselves. We can see Frank's future as a strong reader. We can see a future for Kate as a master of her inner life and outward behavior. When and where does such exercise of paternalistic judgment end? These, too, are questions that any theory of educational justice must address.

Educational Justice Must Address Justice Across (and Within) a Lifespan

The dynamic and recursive natures of educational justice are reminders of the importance of *time* in distributing educational goods. As a developmental theory, educational justice must contend with children's time-bound transition from developmentally appropriate but still non-ideal states of irrationality and unreasonableness to more ideal states. As a theory that recognizes recursion, educational justice must take account of the fact that a person's access to educational goods at time T1 will change both their need for and even their capacity to make use of educational goods at time T2. Any theory of educational justice must also contend with temporality in a third way: namely, by addressing how to distribute bads and goods across a person's lifespan.

When a child asks, "Why do I have to go to school?", we usually offer a future-oriented answer, about how their own lives will go better as a result. We recognize that even the most joyful school often subjects children to experiences and expectations that they would avoid if they could: taking tests, sitting quietly without squirming, working with people they don't like, studying subjects that bore them. This seems relatively unproblematic, as a number of theories provide fairly compelling accounts of why it is okay to force children to engage in activities that they would not freely choose, but that their adult selves will be glad they were forced to do. "You'll thank me for it later" does have at least some moral weight – which is one reason that Philip, Frank, and Kate all find themselves in a classroom together with Mrs. Brown.

At the same time, there must be some limit to the hardships that it is okay to impose on children in the present for the sake of their future adult lives – and what that limit is seems to be rarely specified in theory or in practice. Consider the "Think Room," which some parents consider so inappropriately punitive that they have threatened litigation to shut it down. One objection to the Think Room might be that children (perhaps excluding Kate) don't actually benefit from being sent there. In this case, Rivers Elementary should presumably find a different way of removing children from the classroom who are disruptive or need to calm down. But another objection might be that even if it does have some benefit – say, children hate feeling isolated, so they control their behavior in class to avoid being sent to the Think Room – the present-day pain of being sent there is too great to be justified by the long-term benefit. I believe that any theory of educational justice needs to address this kind of question: when, why, and how the goods of childhood balance against the goods of adulthood, and more generally how to distribute goods across a lifespan.

Educational Justice Must Address Both the Aims and the Practices of Education

In grappling with these questions about the social construction of difference and the present- versus future-orientation of schools, a theory of educational justice must therefore address both the aims and the practices of education. A classroom that prepared all children equally to work compliantly and efficiently on the factory floor, for example, would not be just simply because it treated students equally. But at the same time, a theory of educational justice can't be confined to the aims of education, nor can the aims of education help us derive everything we need to know about educational justice.

When there are a number of children in a classroom with a variety of academic needs, and a teacher has to judge how to address them, then her knowing that the ultimate aim of education is to foster students' capacities for autonomy, say, is likely insufficient for guiding her lesson planning. Furthermore, depending on the circumstances in which she is teaching, the teacher may rightly judge that she is unable to achieve that aim altogether. What we might think of as the "technology" of education – pedagogies, setting, resources, context – therefore partially determines what aims are possible. But likewise, the aims also partially shape which technologies are developed and deployed.

Theorizing educational justice thus needs to take place on multiple levels. In part, a theory of educational justice should address questions that arise *in* the classroom, school, and district – for example, questions about what principles and practices should guide a teacher like Ms. Brown when she is trying to meet diverse students' needs, or how a school district should allocate places at high-quality schools. But theories of educational justice also need to address questions *about* these spaces – questions such as what range of students should be in the classroom in the first place, what aims schools should strive to achieve, and whose voices and preferences should be attended to, in what ways, in answering these first two questions. For instance, what role if any should the parents at Rivers Elementary have in shaping school policies and practices around inclusive classrooms or the existence of the Think Room?

Furthermore, educational justice needs to be theorized in part in the intersection between these spaces *in* and *about* schools, since judgments about justice at one level has implications for what questions arise, and what answers are delivered, at the other level. There is value in integrating micro, meso, and macro perspectives in the process of theorizing about educational justice – if there is some way to do so without ending up with a bloated or incoherent theory. Finally, these different levels of analysis may be useful only if they are informed by the kinds of pragmatic perspectives and understandings that arise in practice, and not just in theory. Although theorizing educational justice is an inherently philosophical activity, it should be informed by concrete understandings of pedagogy, child development, organizational perspectives on schools and districts, political analyses, and so forth. Otherwise, I fear that we will end up asking the wrong philosophical questions, and reaching the wrong answers, because we misunderstand the landscape of possible actions in any particular situation. In thinking about Ms. Brown's decisions regarding Kate, Philip, and Frank, for instance, it is essential that we recognize that her choices include not just corrective or administrative moves (such as removing Kate from the class) but also a wide variety of pedagogical moves, such as shifting to whole-class instruction, making Kate the judge of the boys' debate, or changing a student's group.

Some Final Thoughts about Epistemology, Methodology, and Completeness

These considerations are obviously not exhaustive. They arise solely from one case; other cases may raise utterly new issues that a theory of educational justice would need to address. There are important questions about the epistemology and methodology of constructing a theory of educational justice from the ground up that also require attention: case selection, case analysis, saturation (meaning that one is no longer encountering new questions or identifying new theoretical features), connecting ideal and non-ideal theory and principles, and so forth.

Theorizing educational justice is also an explicitly multidimensional exercise. It demands that one address issues specific to *education*, such as indoctrination, human capital development, teaching and learning, and education as a primary good or resource. It demands that one address issues specific to *children*, such as development, children's interests in the present versus their interests as future adults, and family membership. Educational justice will also benefit from being theorized with respect to *schools as institutions*, including discipline, control, classroom dynamics (Geron 2021), and curriculum provision. And, of course, there are considerations of *justice* itself, regarding the aims, criteria, procedures, goods or resources or opportunities, and so forth. In evaluating the aims of education, for instance, a theory of educational justice will need to address how and to what extent these aims should be responsive to broader theories of justice.

This is simply a beginning, therefore, not an end. But I hope it is a constructive starting point for theorizing educational justice from the ground up.

(Related Chapters: 3, 6, 8, 14, 15, 16, 32, 33.)

Notes

1 I have slightly adapted this case from Levinson and Ben-Porath (2016). I am grateful to both Sigal Ben-Porath and to Harvard Education Press for permission to reuse the case here. I have also received incredibly helpful feedback on previous versions of this chapter from colleagues at the following universities and meetings: CIDE Mexico, Hebrew University, Haifa, Warwick, Edinburgh, Oxford, Institute of Education UCL, Université de Montréal, Harvard, Tel Aviv, American Philosophical Association Central Division, and Society for Applied Philosophy. I am particularly grateful to Adam Swift and Randall Curren for their insights about this chapter and the larger project.

2 For convincing arguments as to why justice is *an* important value both within and among families, see Brighouse and Swift (2014); Okin (1991).

3 This is not even to mention parents' direct interactions with the school in trying to claim educational benefits for their children, and potentially denying them to others. I do not address the parents' meeting with Mr. Thomason due to space constraints, but it obviously raises important questions about parent partiality and educational justice.

4 For a developmentally-attuned account of corrective justice in an educational context, see Curren (2013).

References

Brighouse, H., Ladd, H. F., Loeb, S., & Swift, A. (2017) *Educational Goods: Values, Evidence, and Decision-Making*. Chicago: University of Chicago Press.

Brighouse, H., & Swift, A. (2014) *Family Values: The Ethics of Parent-Child Relationships*. Princeton: Princeton University Press.

Cherry, M. (2017, Dec. 8) *Winston Thompson on Educational Justice* (No. 30). https://www.podbean.com/site/EpisodeDownload/PB7E8FDFQCI8C

Curren, R. (2000) *Aristotle on the Necessity of Public Education*. Lanham, MD: Rowman & Littlefield Publishers.

Curren, R. (2013) "A Neo-Aristotelian Account of Education, Justice, and the Human Good," *Theory and Research in Education* 11(3): 231–249.

Curren, R. (2020) "Transformative Valuing," *Educational Theory* 70(5): 581–601.

Dahl, A. (2019) "Chapter One – The Science of Early Moral Development: On Defining, Constructing, and Studying Morality from Birth," in J. B. Benson (ed.) *Advances in Child Development and Behavior, Vol. 56*. Atlanta, GA: JAI, 1–35.

Geron, T. (2021) *Opening the Black Box of Teacher Ethical Decision-Making: Three Papers in Educational Ethics*. Unpublished Dissertation Proposal. Cambridge, MA: Harvard Graduate School of Education.

Howard, D. S. (2015) "Transforming Others: On the Limits of 'You'll Be Glad I Did It' Reasoning," *Res Philosophica* 92(2): 341–370.

Levinson, M., & Ben-Porath, S. (2016) "Rocky Choices: Scientific Inquiry, Discipline, and Mental Illness at Rivers Elementary," in M. Levinson & J. Fay (eds.) *Dilemmas of Educational Ethics: Cases and Commentaries*. Cambridge, MA: Harvard Education Press, 39–43.

Malti, T., Galarneau, E., & Peplak, J. (2021) "Moral Development in Adolescence," *Journal of Research on Adolescence* 31(4): 1097–1113.

Merry, M. S. (2020) *Educational Justice: Liberal Ideals, Persistent Inequality, and the Constructive Uses of Critique*. London: Palgrave Macmillan.

Okin, S. M. (1991) *Justice, Gender, and the Family*. New York: Basic Books.

Rawls, J. (1971) *A Theory of Justice*. Cambridge, MA: Belknap Press of Harvard University Press.

Rosqvist, H. B., Chown, N., & Stenning, A. (eds.) (2020) *Neurodiversity Studies: A New Critical Paradigm, Vol, I*. London: Routledge.

Thompson, W. C. (2016) "Rethinking Discussions of Justice in Educational Research: Formative Justice, Educational Liberalism, and Beyond," *Teachers College Record* 118(10): 1–16.

PART II

Virtues of Mind and Character

10
CULTIVATING INTELLECTUAL VIRTUES

Duncan Pritchard

Introductory Remarks

Our interest is in the educational importance of cultivating intellectual character, where this is understood in the specific sense of cultivating *virtuous* intellectual character, and thus the intellectual virtues that comprise virtuous intellectual character. To this end, we will begin by exploring the epistemic goals of education and outlining why the cultivation of intellectual character is a plausible candidate to be the overarching epistemic goal of education. We will also be examining why the development of intellectual character should be concerned with cultivating the intellectual virtues specifically, as opposed to developing other elements of a subject's integrated cognitive skills and abilities, such as her critical thinking capacities. Finally, we will consider some of the practical and theoretical issues involved in incorporating the intellectual virtues into one's pedagogical practices.

The Overarching Epistemic Goal of Education

Education serves many purposes, not all of them obviously epistemic. For example, it clearly serves social, political, and practical purposes. Nonetheless, a fundamental goal of education is clearly epistemic, in that it is hard to understand what an educational practice might be that didn't cultivate the subject's epistemic capacities, such as by helping that subject to acquire new knowledge or develop new cognitive skills. Indeed, a putatively educational practice that by design didn't have any positive epistemic outcomes for the learners – which was merely indoctrination of falsehoods, for example – would not be regarded as a genuine educational practice at all, even if the proponents of this educational program insisted on labelling it in this fashion (Robertson 2009; Pritchard 2013; Baehr 2016).

Relatedly, many of the non-epistemic goals of education only make sense if they are combined with epistemic goals. Think, for example, of the idea that education has an important role to play in a democratic society of helping to produce informed citizens (Gutmann 1987; Galston 1989; Ravitch 2001; Ben-Porath 2006; Crittenden & Levine 2018; Curren & Dorn 2018). This would clearly be a social and political goal of education. And yet it also has a core element that is manifestly epistemic. One cannot create politically informed citizens unless one informs them, and that involves giving them the knowledge and skills needed to navigate the relevant political terrain.

But what is the epistemic goal of education? One might antecedently think that it simply involves ensuring that students have useful knowledge and cognitive skills. The problem with this way of

DOI: 10.4324/9781003172246-13

thinking about the epistemic goals of education, however, is that it is compatible with practices that seem antithetical to the educational enterprise. In particular, these epistemic states and skills could be instilled within students via rote learning. Indeed, this might be the most effective way of instilling them. And yet, these days at least, we would not consider such a pedagogical approach as having much in the way of educational merit. For one thing, while in one sense students might be learning facts and skills via this method, there isn't much by way of teaching taking place – in fact, the teacher seems rather superfluous to this process (a security guard might be just as effective). For another, the epistemic states and skills that the students are acquiring are epistemically quite impoverished. For example, students who have mastered arithmetical tables via rote learning may not gain any real understanding of mathematical concepts, and as a result it is unlikely that they will be able to use what they have learned to extend their knowledge and skills further by themselves.

This issue has taken on a new dimension in the technological age that we live in, whereby much of our most commonplace knowledge and skills is becoming increasingly off-loaded to technology. If education is just about ensuring that students can reliably reproduce facts or perform certain activities, and both can in many cases be done equally well (indeed, usually much better) via the use of technology, then it seems that in the future educators won't have much to do. For many educational tasks we could dispense with the educators and simply upgrade the technology. Conversely, if we believe that no amount of technological off-loading of this kind can mitigate the need for education, then that suggests that there is more to the epistemic goals of education than simply instilling facts and skills into students.[1]

The foregoing suggests that the overarching epistemic goal of education is not merely the development of epistemic states, like true belief or knowledge, and cognitive skills, but rather the cultivation of good intellectual character. Intellectual character refers to the subject's integrated set of cognitive skills and abilities, which collectively represents the intellectual aspect of that agent's character. Good intellectual character is thus the integrated set of the subject's cognitive skills which reflect well on the intellectual aspect of the subject's character.

To see why good intellectual character might be important from an educational point of view, think again about our rote learners. Although they are acquiring new cognitive skills, they are not developing their intellectual character. Instead, this skill development is entirely piecemeal and passive. We want our students to be active learners rather than passive recipients of information and skills, and that means developing the kinds of skills that are representative of a good intellectual character. Compare, for example, how the rote teaching of arithmetic might contrast with a pedagogical approach that aims instead to help students to understand what it is that they are learning. In the latter case, the curiosity of the students will be stimulated, as will their intellectual autonomy as they employ their understanding to expand what they have learned in new directions. The students are doing more than passively mastering a particular cognitive skill, but rather acquiring it actively, through their own endeavors to understand (under the guidance of the educator), and in the process they are cultivating good intellectual character traits. This ensures that the cognitive skill they are learning is integrated within their wider set of cognitive skills, so that it can lead to the self-directed development of new knowledge and skills. What the educator is doing is using the teaching of this specific cognitive task to foster the wider goal of enhancing the student's good intellectual character.

One important advantage of thinking of the overarching epistemic goal of education as being the cultivation of good intellectual character is that it can capture the sense in which education promotes epistemic autonomy. Educators undoubtedly want their students to know specific facts and to be able to master specific cognitive skills. One cannot learn chemistry, for example, without knowing key facts about the periodic table. But the ultimate goal of education is not merely the imparting of epistemic states and skills, but rather the development of the kind of higher-level cognitive skills that enable students to think for themselves and, crucially, learned for themselves. It is not enough for the budding chemist to merely regurgitate what they have learnt (e.g., by appealing to the authority of the teacher, or what is written in the textbook), but they must also be able to understand it, and that means being able to explain why it is true, to be able to articulate and defend their knowledge. That requires the higher-level cognitive skills that are part of a good intellectual character, such as the ability to marshal reasons in support of one's beliefs and in the process critically reflect on the evidential basis for those beliefs.

The importance of these intellectual character traits becomes particularly evident once one turns from fairly uncontentious matters of fact – of a kind that would be taught in a school chemistry class, for example – to more controversial subjects where the facts are open to question. Consider the teaching of history, for example. For a subject matter like this it is crucial that students learn how to think critically about the information presented to them and are not merely passive recipients of it. A student who merely regurgitates historical facts, for example, has only the most minimal grasp of the subject matter of history, especially when compared with a student who has a rich and nuanced appreciation of the subject, one that informs, and is informed by, their experience of the contemporary world.

Good Intellectual Character

So what constitutes a good intellectual character? Thus far we have charactered this notion largely in terms of certain core critical thinking skills, such as a responsiveness to evidence, a willingness to critically evaluate evidence and reasons, an ability to articulate a rational defense of a viewpoint, and so on. These are all clearly general features of a good intellectual character, and not merely cognitive skills exclusively concerned with a particular cognitive task. In particular, these are all high-order cognitive skills, in the sense that they play a managerial role in one's overall cognitive economy by governing one's intellectual activities in general as opposed to being devoted to specific cognitive tasks (like, for example, arithmetic). Moreover, they are essentially active cognitive skills too, in that they involve an active intellectual engagement with the subject matter, as opposed to being the kind of cognitive skill that can be acquired and manifested entirely passively.

One conception of a good intellectual character that could be in play when it comes to the overarching epistemic goal of education could thus be the development of a kind of critical rationality. On this proposal, education is devoted to cultivating good intellectual character in the specific sense of *critically rational intellectual character*. Such a thesis has some prominent defenders in the literature.[2] I want to argue instead, however, for a more demanding conception of good intellectual character that specifically concerns the intellectual virtues. On this alternative model, the good intellectual character that is the overarching epistemic goal of education is to be understood as *virtuous intellectual character*.[3] As we will see, there is a great deal of overlap between these two conceptions of the overarching epistemic goal of education. In particular, a virtuous intellectual character entails a critically rational intellectual character, but not *vice versa*. It will thus be important for our purposes to spell out why the former is a more demanding conception of good intellectual character, and what practical implications this has for educational practice.

A subject's virtuous intellectual character is the integrated set of her cognitive skills and abilities, including, crucially, the distinctive cognitive skills that meet the specific conditions to qualify as intellectual virtues. The intellectual virtues are admirable intellectual character traits, such as curiosity, intellectual humility, intellectual tenacity, conscientiousness, and intellectual courage. On the standard construal of these character traits, they have several distinguishing features.[4]

Intellectual virtues involve a distinctive kind of motivational state, in that to manifest an intellectual virtue is for one's virtuous activity to be grounded in a fundamental valuing of, and thus desire for, the truth (such that one is concerned with forming accurate beliefs, avoiding error, and so forth) (Pritchard 2021b). This is what sets the intellectual virtues apart from other virtues, such as moral virtues (e.g., the virtue of compassion), as the latter involve a different, non-intellectual, motivational state. One important consequence of this feature of the intellectual virtues is that one cannot manifest them in a purely strategic fashion. There might, for example, be a practical utility in presenting oneself as intellectually humble, but if it is this motivation that grounds one's apparently intellectually humble behavior, then this isn't the manifestation of a genuine intellectual virtue.

Intellectual virtues are not innate cognitive abilities, but rather must be acquired, ideally through the emulation of virtuous subjects that the agent is in direct contact with. Moreover, intellectual virtues are unlike some other cognitive skills (such as riding a bike) in that even once acquired they can still be lost – one must keep cultivating one's intellectual virtues in order to retain them, as without cultivation one can find oneself drifting towards one of the corresponding intellectual vices associated with that intellectual virtue. The process of acquisition requires reflective engagement on the part of the subject – one cannot acquire an intellectual virtue in an entirely passive fashion. Mastering an intellectual virtue requires practice, a process known as habituation. The goal is to make the manifestation of intellectual virtue automatic, such that it becomes second-nature (which means that although reflection is required to acquire the intellectual virtues, once mastered there need be no reflection involved in their manifestation). The difficulty of mastering an intellectual virtue lies in navigating between the two corresponding intellectual vices, the intellectual vice of excess and the intellectual vice of deficiency. For example, the intellectual virtue of curiosity lies between the corresponding intellectual vice of excess involved in being overly curious, such as when one is motivated to pursue pointless or irrelevant inquiries, and the corresponding intellectual vice of deficiency, as when one is simply lacking in curiosity.

A further feature of the intellectual virtues that is important for our current concerns is that they are held to be – in common with the virtues more generally, such as the moral virtues – highly valuable character traits, both in instrumental and non-instrumental (final) terms. Their instrumental value should be clear, as these are desirable character traits that are desirable in part because they are so practically useful. Think, for example, of the practical drawbacks of being a dogmatic individual who is resistant to new or unwelcome evidence. The practical value of an intellectual virtue like intellectual humility thus lies in how it helps agents to avoid such practical drawbacks (in this case by being open to new and unwelcome evidence).

The intellectual virtues are held to not only be instrumentally valuable, however, but also finally valuable. They are constituent parts of what it is to live a good life of human flourishing, what the ancient Greeks referred to as *eudaimonia*. One can see the plausibility of this proposal: even if one removes all the practical advantages of the intellectual virtues, one would still prefer to be an intellectually virtuous subject than to not be.[5]

With the intellectual virtues so construed, it should be clear that possessing the integrated set of these character traits, and thus having a virtuous intellectual character, entails having a critically rational intellectual character. The intellectually virtuous subject would be conscientious in her assessment of the evidence that she has for her opinions, would have the intellectual humility to non-dogmatically weigh-up new evidence that comes her way, would be curious about alternative opinions, would have the intellectual courage to consider unpopular viewpoints that are nonetheless suggested by the evidence, and so on. Interestingly, however, while virtuous intellectual character entails critically rational intellectual character, the converse is not the case.

There are two main (and closely related) differences between critical rational capacities and intellectual virtues. First, there is the crucial difference that critical rational capacities don't demand the motivational component that is essential for the intellectual virtues. In particular, one can have the cognitive skills associated with a critically rational intellectual character without those skills being motivated by any fundamental valuing of, and thus desire for, the truth. On the contrary, one could consistently manifest those skills in a purely strategic fashion. The expertise of a leading lawyer, for example, could involve a purely strategic employment of critically rational cognitive skills, in that the lawyer has no particular concern for the truth but only, say, for winning cases. As we have seen, however, the intellectual virtues are not like this, in that one cannot manifest an intellectual virtue without one's virtuous behavior being grounded in a desire for the intellectual good of truth.

This relates to a second fundamental difference between critical rational capacities and intellectual virtues. While both are quite general cognitive skills, in that they can be employed across a range of subject matter (as opposed to being tied to a particular cognitive task), the intellectual virtues are nonetheless much richer in content than critical rational capacities. What I mean by this is that they are essentially tied to who one is as a person, where that includes such important features of one's personhood as one's fundamental values. This is the sense in which developing a student's intellectual virtues is thereby helping them to develop as a person, as opposed to merely training that student to master certain cognitive skills, including cognitive skills of a quite general kind (such as critical rational capacities).

With these contrasts between virtuous intellectual character and critically rational intellectual character in mind, consider a subject who has developed critical rational capacities and where these capacities are in addition grounded in the motivational state that is associated with the intellectual virtues (after all, while one can manifest the critical rational capacities without this motivational state, the former doesn't preclude the latter). Notice, however, that in such a case it is hard to see why the subject wouldn't eventually end up displaying the intellectual virtues. The subject's rational behavior would be rooted in their fundamental values, and so would be naturally described in terms of character traits like being curious, being intellectually conscientious, and so forth, rather than merely in terms of certain general cognitive capacities. This point reinforces the idea that despite the close overlaps between critically rational intellectual character and virtuous intellectual character, it is virtuous intellectual character that is the more demanding notion. It also reminds us of the fundamental importance of educating for virtuous intellectual character rather than just critically rational intellectual character, since where they come apart it is the former that is more desirable from an educational point of view. While we certainly do want students to develop their critical rationality, we want them to do so while also recognizing the importance of the truth, and not merely in a strategic fashion. This means that we want the development of critical rationality to be part of a wider enhancement of their intellectual personhood, and that entails the cultivation of a virtuous intellectual character.[6]

Objections

A number of objections have been raised to the idea that we should be educating for virtuous intellectual character. Some of these concerns are really objections to the nature of intellectual virtues, as opposed to being specific to the idea of putting the intellectual virtues into the heart of the educational enterprise. For example, there have been empirical challenges to the very idea that character traits like virtues explain behavior in the manner alleged, as opposed to that behavior being more attributable to purely 'situational' factors. While this literature has mostly focused on the moral virtues in this regard, it has been argued that one can extend this objection to the intellectual virtues specifically. If that's right – and note that the 'situationist' critique of virtue theory is highly contentious, so this is a big 'if' – then obviously that would be a devastating blow to any educational proposal that essentially appealed to the intellectual virtues.[7]

Of the objections that specifically concern putting the intellectual virtues at the heart of education, rather than intellectual virtue theory more generally, we can distinguish between broadly practical and theoretical concerns. On the former front, for example, there are empirical issues regarding how one goes about measuring the educational development of virtue, and intellectual virtue in particular (Curren & Kotzee 2014; Kotzee 2015; Carter et al. 2019). Moreover, there are practical (as well as theoretical) problems posed by the role of exemplars involved in the acquisition of the intellectual virtues in educational settings, particularly in terms of the difficulty of ensuring that students are appropriately related to such exemplars, given that one cannot realistically expect educators to be, on the whole, intellectual paradigms.[8] In what remains of this chapter, however, I want to focus on a largely theoretical challenge to casting educational practices in terms of the cultivation of virtuous intellectual character.

The theoretical objection I want to consider is the concern that making the cultivation of virtuous intellectual character central to education involves a kind of problematic indoctrination of students. One can see the general contours of the argument by comparing educating for virtuous intellectual character with educating for critically rational character. In the latter case, one can acquire the relevant skills without thereby adopting any axiological commitments regarding their final (as opposed to merely instrumental) value. Accordingly, it is consistent with this approach that the student goes on to apply the critical spirit to critical rationality itself, and so is skeptical about its ultimate value. In contrast, to master the intellectual virtues is precisely to internalize the relevant motivational component, which means in turn to recognize, and thereby value accordingly, the finally valuable intellectual good of truth. Educating for virtuous intellectual character thus brings with it fundamental axiological commitments that other approaches to the epistemic goal of education don't incorporate (Siegel 2016).

Note that this feature of educating for virtuous intellectual character is not an unfortunate consequence of the proposal but right at its very heart. As we saw above, it is built into the very idea of virtuous intellectual character that it has this axiological feature. If that's right, then this is not an objection that can be avoided by refining the position, as if one takes this element of the view away, then what remains would not qualify as a *bona fide* version of the original proposal.

On closer inspection, however, it is far from clear why the proponent of educating for virtuous intellectual character should be so concerned by this objection. Sure, this approach involves instilling in students a fundamental respect for the truth, and thus for such things as accuracy, evidence, avoiding falsehood, and so on. But is that really so contentious? It is not as if this involves demanding of students that they endorse the specific values of a particular culture (such as Christian values, say), much less that it would instill values that are controversial. Certainly, some people have no respect for the truth, but this is widely regarded as a failing on their part, and it would be odd for an educational practice to be faulted for helping students to avoid such a failing.

Moreover, given the fundamental role of epistemic goals in educational practices that we noted above, it would be an unduly narrow conception of the goals of education that didn't include a concern for the truth. Consider, for example, the idea that education serves the civic function of creating informed citizens that we outlined earlier. Could such a social and political goal really be achieved via education without also instilling in students a respect and concern for the truth? Can we even make sense of the idea of students being motivated by such civic concerns and yet at the same time being indifferent to the truth and all that involves (such as being unconcerned about the accuracy in their beliefs in this regard)? That strikes me as implausible.

Note too that the idea that students shouldn't be encouraged as part of an educational practice to care about the truth, but must decide about something like this entirely independently, seems to itself presuppose an important axiological claim. That is, it seems to presuppose that intellectual autonomy is an overarching value that governs the educational enterprise. But why would that value be any less contentious in this regard than the value of truth? Moreover, it is hard to see how students are meant to manifest intellectual autonomy without also acquiring a desire for the truth. Being intellectually autonomous entails being able to make up one's own mind about what to believe (and thus what to value), but in order to competently do that one needs to know the facts that are relevant to making this decision, and that surely requires one to care about the truth. The crux of the matter is that it seems that a desire for the truth is a foundational value in this regard, in that it is a value that needs to be in place in order for more specific values, like the value of intellectual autonomy, to function. This would also explain why educating for virtuous intellectual character involves both instilling a desire for the truth and also giving students the skills to be genuinely intellectually autonomous. Properly understood, the latter isn't in conflict with the former; instead, its proper manifestation presupposes the former.

A final point I want to make about this line of objection is that it may get run together with a slightly different kind of criticism associated with educating for virtuous intellectual character. This is that any conception of education that has the virtues (and thus the intellectual virtues) at its heart is thereby incorporating a particular European-centric cultural framework, and hence is implicitly espousing hegemonic ideas about its cultural superiority. I think this objection is misplaced since it conflates the general structure of the proposal with a particular way of applying that proposal. We may primarily get our conception of the virtues, and thus the intellectual virtues, from Ancient Greece, but it would be a mistake to think that the ideas at issue are tied to this particular cultural tradition. Indeed, this is simply factually incorrect, in that one finds broadly virtue-theoretic proposals, including ones with a specific focus on the intellectual virtues, in several other cultural traditions.[9] More generally, there is nothing particularly European-centric about placing an important premium on the value of the truth, as lots of different cultural traditions incorporate the very same concern.

It follows that while one might elect to educate for the intellectual virtues by embedding them within a certain cultural tradition that one wishes to eulogize, this is in no way essential to the guiding idea in play. Furthermore, educating for the intellectual virtues would be antithetical to any such exercise in cultural hegemony anyway, as one would be giving students the intellectual skills to identify the problematic nature of what is being proposed. Virtuous intellectual character is not a friendly bedfellow of propaganda. The upshot is that allowing the intellectual virtues a fundamental role in one's educational practices is entirely compatible with an educational approach that has no truck with the idea of the inherent superiority of a particular cultural tradition.[10]

Concluding Remarks

We have argued that there is an overarching epistemic goal to education, and that this is the development of good intellectual character. Moreover, we have seen that the specific sense of good intellectual character that is relevant in this regard is virtuous intellectual character, and thus involves the cultivation of the intellectual virtues.[11]

(Related Chapters: 4, 11, 12, 13, 14, 25, 26, 27, 28, 29.)

Notes

1 This issue has recently been explored in an acute form in terms of the relevance of *extended cognition* to education, whereby technology becomes a part of a subject's cognitive processes, and hence enables them to directly gain knowledge and skills that would have otherwise taken considerable training. See, for example, Pritchard (2014a, 2016, 2018), Heersmink & Knight (2018), Kotzee (2018), and Pritchard et al. (2021). For further discussion of the epistemological implications of cognitive augmentation in general, see Carter & Pritchard (2019).

2 The foremost contemporary defender of this thesis is Siegel (1988, 1997, 2003, 2016, 2017). See also Scheffler (1973), who offers an influential precursor to this contemporary proposal (and which Siegel has described as an important influence on his thinking in this regard).

3 For some recent defenses of this general account of the overarching epistemic goal of education, see Pritchard (2013, 2016, 2018, 2020), Baehr (2015, 2021), and Croce & Pritchard (2022). For discussion, see also Hyslop-Margison (2003), Battaly (2006), MacAllister (2012), Sockett (2012), Watson (2018), Byerly (2019), and the essays collected in Baehr (2016). There is also a wider literature exploring the virtues in general and education, usually with a specific focus on the moral rather than intellectual virtues. See, for example, Carr (2014) and Kristjánsson (2015).

4 The standard account of the intellectual virtues is broadly Aristotelian. See Zagzebski (1996) for a highly influential neo-Aristotelian account of the intellectual virtues. See also Roberts & Wood (2007), Worley (2009), and Baehr (2011). For a useful recent survey of the literature on the intellectual virtues, see Battaly (2014).

5 Classically, this point is often expressed in terms of how the intellectually virtuous subject has wisdom, at least in the sense of practical wisdom (*phronesis*), if not also in terms of theoretical wisdom (*sophia*). Whatever circumstances one faces in life, it is better to confront them with wisdom than without. See, for example, Whitcomb (2010), Baehr (2012), and Curren (2014).

6 For further discussion of the educational debate between proponents of virtuous intellectual character and proponents of critically rational intellectual character, see Siegel (2017), Hyslop-Margison (2003), Huber & Kuncel (2016), Baehr (2019), and Carter et al. (2019).

7 Harman (1999; 2000) and Doris (2002) offer influential presentations of the situationist critique of virtue theory. For an important response, see Jayawickreme et al (2014). For a key defence of the application of this situationist critique to the specifically intellectual virtues, see Alfano (2012). For some responses to the latter, including with the epistemology of education specifically in mind, see Pritchard (2014b), Baehr (2017), and Carter & Pritchard (2017).

8 Much of this discussion mirrors more general issues about the role of exemplars in virtue-based educational theory, though recently there has been some specific discussions of the intellectual virtues in this regard. On the former front, see Zagzebski (2010; 2017), Croce & Vaccarezza (2017), Croce (2019, 2020), Korsgaard (2019), Kristjánsson (2020). On the latter front, see Porter (2016), Tanesini (2016), Alfano & Sullivan (2019), van Dongen (2017), and Croce & Pritchard (2022).

9 See, for example, Ryan & Mi (2018), which discusses the relationship between the intellectual virtues and Confucian thought.

10 Consider, for example, the 'Anteater Virtues' project that I run at the University of California, Irvine, and which is devoted precisely to bringing the cultivation of virtuous intellectual character into heart of the curriculum. The project is explicitly not cast in European-centric terms, however, as a range of disciplinary perspective and cultural traditions are represented. For an evaluation of the effectiveness of this pedagogical intervention, see Orona & Pritchard (2021). Another example of an educational initiative concerned with the development of virtuous intellectual character without in the process focusing on European-centric cultural ideas is the prison education project described in Pritchard (2019, 2021a).

11 I am grateful to Randy Curren for detailed feedback on a previous version of this chapter, and to Harvey Siegel for helpful discussions of the topics covered.

References

Alfano, M. (2012) "Extending the Situationist Challenge to Responsibilist Virtue Epistemology," *Philosophical Quarterly* 62: 223–249.

Alfano, M., & Sullivan, E. (2019) "Negative Epistemic Exemplars," in S. Goguen & B. Sherman (eds.) *Overcoming Epistemic Injustice: Social and Psychological Perspectives*. Lanham, MD: Rowman & Littlefield, 17–32.

Baehr, J. (2011) *The Inquiring Mind: On Intellectual Virtues and Virtue Epistemology*. Oxford: Oxford University Press.

Baehr, J. (2012) "Two Types of Wisdom," *Acta Analytica* 27: 81–97.

Baehr, J. (2015) *Cultivating Good Minds: A Philosophical & Practical Guide to Educating for Intellectual Virtues* (available at: https://intellectualvirtues.org/why-should-we-educate-for-intellectual-virtues-2-2/).

Baehr, J. (ed.) (2016) *Intellectual Virtues and Education: Essays in Applied Virtue Epistemology*. London: Routledge.

Baehr, J. (2017) "The Situationist Challenge to Educating for Intellectual Virtues," in M. Alfano & A. Fairweather (eds.) *Epistemic Situationism*. Oxford: Oxford University Press, 192–215.

Baehr, J. (2019) "Intellectual Virtues, Critical Thinking, and the Aims of Education," in P. Graham, M. Fricker, D. Henderson, N. Pedersen & J. Wyatt (eds.) *Routledge Handbook of Social Epistemology*. London: Routledge, 447–457.

Baehr, J. (2021) *Deep in Thought: A Practical Guide to Teaching for Intellectual Virtues*. Cambridge, MA: Harvard Education Press.

Battaly, H. (2006) "Teaching Intellectual Virtues: Applying Virtue Epistemology in the Classroom," *Teaching Philosophy* 29: 191–222.

Battaly, H. (2014) "Intellectual Virtues," in S. van Hooft (ed.) *Handbook of Virtue Ethics*. London: Acumen, 177–187.

Ben-Porath, S. R. (2006) *Citizenship Under Fire: Democratic Education in Times of Conflict*. Princeton, NJ: Princeton University Press.
Byerly, T. R. (2019) "Teaching for Intellectual Virtue in Logic and Critical Thinking Classes: Why and How," *Teaching Philosophy* (Online First: 10.5840/teachphil201911599).
Carr, D. (2014) *Educating the Virtues: An Essay on the Philosophical Psychology of Moral Development and Education*. London: Routledge.
Carter, J. A., Kotzee, B., & Siegel, H. (2019) "Educating for Intellectual Virtue: A Critique from Action Guidance," *Episteme* (Online First: 10.1017/epi.2019.10).
Carter, J. A., & Pritchard, D. H. (2017) "Epistemic Situationism, Epistemic Dependence, and the Epistemology of Education," in M. Alfano & A. Fairweather (eds.) *Epistemic Situationism*. Oxford: Oxford University Press, 168–191.
Carter, J. A., & Pritchard, D. H. (2019) "The Epistemology of Cognitive Enhancement," *Journal of Medicine & Philosophy* 44: 220–242.
Crittenden, J., & Levine, P. (2018) "Civic Education," E. Zalta (ed.) *Stanford Encyclopedia of Philosophy*. https://plato.stanford.edu/entries/civic-education/
Croce, M. (2019) "Exemplarism in Moral Education: Problems with Applicability and Indoctrination," *Journal of Moral Education* 48: 291–302.
Croce, M. (2020) "Moral Exemplars in Education: A Liberal Account," *Ethics & Education* 15: 186–199.
Croce, M., & Pritchard, D. H. (2022) "Education as the Social Cultivation of Intellectual Virtue," in M. Alfano, C. Klein & J. de Ridder (eds.) *Social Virtue Epistemology*. London: Routledge, 583–601.
Croce, M., & Vaccarezza, M. S. (2017) "Educating through Exemplars: Alternative Paths to Virtue," *Theory and Research in Education* 15: 5–19.
Curren, R. (2014) "Judgment and the Aims of Education," *Social Philosophy & Policy* 31: 36–59.
Curren, R., & Dorn, C. (2018) *Patriotic Education in a Global Age*. Chicago: University of Chicago Press.
Curren, R., & Kotzee, B. (2014) "Can Virtue be Measured?" *Theory and Research in Education* 12: 266–282.
Doris, J. (2002) *Lack of Character: Personality and Moral Behavior*. Cambridge: Cambridge University Press.
Galston, W. (1989) "Civic Education in the Liberal State," in N. Rosenblum (ed.) *Liberalism and the Moral Life*. Cambridge, MA: Harvard University Press, 89–102.
Gutmann, A. (1987) *Democratic Education*. Princeton, NJ: Princeton University Press.
Harman, G. (1999) "Moral Philosophy Meets Social Psychology: Virtue Ethics and the Fundamental Attribution Error," *Proceedings of the Aristotelian Society* 119: 316–331.
Harman, G. (2000) "The Nonexistence of Character Traits," *Proceedings of the Aristotelian Society* 100: 223–226.
Heersmink, R., & Knight, S. (2018) "Distributed Learning: Educating and Assessing Extended Minds," *Philosophical Psychology* 31: 969–990.
Huber, C. R., & Kuncel, N. R. (2016) "Does College Teach Critical Thinking? A Meta-Analysis," *Review of Educational Research* 86: 431–468.
Hyslop-Margison, E. (2003) "The Failure of Critical Thinking: Considering Virtue Epistemology as a Pedagogical Alternative," *Philosophy of Education Society Yearbook* 2003: 319–326.
Jayawickreme, E., Meindl, P., Helzer, E. G., Furr, M., & Fleeson, W. (2014) "Virtuous States and Virtuous Traits: How the Empirical Evidence Regarding the Existence of Broad Traits Saves Virtue Ethics from the Situationist Critique," *Theory and Research in Education* 12: 283–308.
Korsgaard, M. T. (2019) "Exploring the Role of Exemplarity in Education: Two Dimensions of The Teacher's Task," *Ethics & Education* 14: 271–284.
Kotzee, B. (2015) "Problems of Assessment in Educating for Intellectual Virtue," in J. Baehr (ed.) *Intellectual Virtues and Education: Essays in Applied Virtue Epistemology*. London: Routledge, 142–160.
Kotzee, B. (2018) "Cyborgs, Knowledge and Credit for Learning," in J. A. Carter, A. Clark, J. Kallestrup, S. O. Palermos, & D. H. Pritchard (eds.) *Extended Epistemology*. Oxford: Oxford University Press, 221–238.
Kristjánsson, K. (2015) *Aristotelian Character Education*. London: Routledge.
Kristjánsson, K. (2020) "Aristotelian Character Friendship as a 'Method' of Moral Education," *Studies in Philosophy and Education* 39: 349–364.
MacAllister, J. (2012) "Virtue Epistemology and the Philosophy of Education," *Journal of Philosophy of Education* 46: 251–270.
Orona, G. A., & Pritchard, D. H. (2021) "Inculcating Curiosity: Pilot Results of an Online Module to Enhance Undergraduate Intellectual Virtue," *Assessment & Evaluation in Higher Education* (Online First, DOI: 10.1080/02602938.2021.1919988).
Porter, S. L. (2016) "A Therapeutic Approach to Intellectual Virtue Formation in the Classroom," in J. Baehr (ed.) *Intellectual Virtues and Education: Essays in Applied Virtue Epistemology*. London: Routledge, 221–239.

Pritchard, D. H. (2013) "Epistemic Virtue and the Epistemology of Education," *Journal of Philosophy of Education* 47: 236–247.
Pritchard, D. H. (2014a) "Virtue Epistemology, Extended Cognition, and the Epistemology of Education," *Universitas: Monthly Review of Philosophy and Culture* 478: 47–66.
Pritchard, D. H. (2014b) "Re-evaluating the Epistemic Situationist Challenge to Virtue Epistemology," in A. Fairweather & O. Flanagan (eds.) *Naturalizing Epistemic Virtue*. Cambridge University Press, 143–154.
Pritchard, D. H. (2016) "Intellectual Virtue, Extended Cognition, and the Epistemology of Education," in J. Baehr (ed.) *Intellectual Virtues and Education: Essays in Applied Virtue Epistemology*. London: Routledge, 113–127.
Pritchard, D. H. (2018) "Neuromedia and the Epistemology of Education," *Metaphilosophy* 49, 328–349.
Pritchard, D. H. (2019) "Philosophy in Prisons: Intellectual Virtue and the Community of Philosophical Inquiry," *Teaching Philosophy* 42(3): 247–263.
Pritchard, D. H. (2020) "Educating for Intellectual Humility and Conviction," *Journal of Philosophy of Education* 54: 398–409.
Pritchard, D. H. (2021a) "Philosophy in Prison and the Cultivation of Intellectual Character,"*Journal of Prison Education and Reentry* 7: 130–143.
Pritchard, D. H. (2021b) "Veritic Desire," *Humana Mente: Journal of Philosophical Studies* 14:1–21.
Pritchard, D. H., English, A., & Ravenscroft, J. (2021) "Extended Cognition, Assistive Technology and Education," *Synthese* 3–4: 8355–8377.
Ravitch, D. (2001) "Education and Democracy," in D. Ravitch & J. P. Viteritti (eds.) *Making Good Citizens*. New Haven, CT: Yale University Press, 15–29.
Roberts, R. C., & Wood, W. J. (2007) *Intellectual Virtues: An Essay in Regulative Epistemology*. Oxford: Oxford University Press.
Robertson, E. (2009) "The Epistemic Aims of Education," in H. Siegel (ed.) *Oxford Handbook of Philosophy of Education*. Oxford: Oxford University Press, 11–34.
Ryan, S., & Mi, C. (2018) "The Contribution of Confucius to Virtue Epistemology," in S. Stich, M. Mizumoto & Eric McCready (eds.) *Epistemology for the Rest of the World*. Oxford: Oxford University Press, 65–76.
Scheffler, I. (1973) *Reason and Teaching*. Indianapolis, IN: Hackett.
Siegel, H. (1988) *Educating Reason: Rationality, Critical Thinking, and Education*. New York: Routledge.
Siegel, H. (1997) *Rationality Redeemed? Further Dialogues on an Educational Ideal*. New York: Routledge.
Siegel, H. (2003) "Cultivating Reason," in R. Curren (ed.) *A Companion to the Philosophy of Education*. Oxford: Blackwell, 305–331.
Siegel, H. (2016) "Critical Thinking and the Intellectual Virtues," in J. Baehr (ed.) *Intellectual Virtues and Education: Essays in Applied Virtue Epistemology*. New York: Routledge, 95–112.
Siegel, H. (2017) *Education's Epistemology: Rationality, Diversity, and Critical Thinking*. Oxford: Oxford University Press.
Sockett, H. (2012) *Knowledge and Virtue in Teaching and Learning: The Primacy of Dispositions*. London: Routledge.
Tanesini, A. (2016) "Teaching Virtue: Changing Attitudes," *Logos & Episteme* 7: 503–527.
van Dongen, J. (2017) "The Epistemic Virtues of the Virtuous Theorist: On Albert Einstein and His Autobiography," in J. van Dongen & H. Paul (eds.) *Epistemic Virtues in the Sciences and the Humanities*. Dordrecht, Holland: Springer, 63–77.
Watson, L. (2018) "Educating for Good Questioning: A Tool for Intellectual Virtues Education," *Acta Analytica* 33: 353–370.
Whitcomb, D. (2010) "Wisdom," in S. Bernecker & D. H. Pritchard (eds.) *Routledge Companion to Epistemology*. London: Routledge, 95–105.
Worley, P. (2009) "The Virtues of Thinking: An Aristotelian Approach to Teaching Thinking," *Discourse: Learning and Teaching in Philosophical and Religious Studies* 9: 143–150.
Zagzebski, L. (1996) *Virtues of the Mind: An Inquiry into the Nature of Virtue and the Ethical Foundations of Knowledge*. Cambridge: Cambridge University Press.
Zagzebski, L. (2010) "Exemplarist Virtue Theory," *Metaphilosophy* 41: 41–57.
Zagzebski, L. (2017) *Exemplarist Moral Theory*. Oxford: Oxford University Press.

11

INTELLECTUAL CHARACTER EDUCATION: SOME LESSONS FROM VICE EPISTEMOLOGY

Heather Battaly

As an applied branch of virtue epistemology, the field of intellectual character education has focused on two main topics. It has argued that facilitating intellectual virtue is a goal of education, perhaps even its primary goal, and it has offered practical guidance for educators who are interested in facilitating intellectual virtues in their classrooms.[1] This chapter explores that practical guidance – i.e., the "standard approach" to facilitating intellectual virtues in classrooms (Porter 2016: 222). Section 1 explains the key features of the standard approach, as well as some "standard" objections and replies. Section 2 brings recent work on intellectual vices and vice epistemology to bear on the standard approach.[2]

Whereas virtue epistemology examines the structure, etiology, and acquisition of qualities that make us good thinkers, such as open-mindedness, intellectual humility, intellectual courage, and epistemic justice, vice epistemology examines the structure, etiology, and amelioration of qualities that make us bad thinkers, such as closed-mindedness, intellectual arrogance, intellectual timidity, and epistemic injustice. This chapter uses insights from vice epistemology to draw two lessons for intellectual character education. The first is that some students are already on their way to developing intellectual vices (for which they are not blameworthy) and aren't likely to be helped by the standard approach. To help these students make progress toward intellectual virtue, the standard approach would at least need to be combined with classroom strategies for ameliorating intellectual vices. The second is that tendencies toward intellectual vices may be prevalent among our students (and ourselves) and caused by systemic factors – intellectual vice may be the rule rather than the exception. Accordingly, any progress made in the classroom, by combining the standard approach with ameliorative strategies, is likely to be ephemeral if systemic changes aren't made.

Where does this leave the standard approach? That is an open question worthy of further exploration. The conclusion suggests that priority be given to systemic changes and ameliorative strategies, and that the standard approach be reserved for later use.[3] In short, vice epistemology shows us that the role of the standard approach is not as central as many of us (myself included) might have thought.

The Standard Approach and Standard Objections

Intellectual virtues are qualities that make us good thinkers. One way to be a good thinker is to have qualities that reliably produce "epistemic goods" – true beliefs, knowledge, and understanding. On the "reliabilist" analysis of intellectual virtue, *any* stable quality of ours that reliably produces

DOI: 10.4324/9781003172246-14

epistemic goods will count as an intellectual virtue. Thus, 20/20 vision will be an intellectual virtue, as will acquired skills in critical thinking (according to many standard approaches[4]), and acquired character traits such as open-mindedness (provided they are reliable – i.e., consistently produce epistemic goods).[5] Another way to be a good thinker is to have praiseworthy character traits that express a commitment to epistemic goods and a motivation to pursue them. On this "responsibilist" analysis, intellectual virtues must be acquired character traits (rather than hard-wired capacities or skills) that involve valuing and caring about epistemic goods.[6] They are also usually reliable.[7] Responsibilists count traits such as open-mindedness, intellectual humility, and epistemic justice as intellectual virtues, and take the structure of intellectual virtues to be analogous to the structure of Aristotelian moral virtues (*NE* II). Accordingly, they think that intellectual virtues require acquired dispositions of appropriate behavior, motivation, affect, and perception. To illustrate, we might understand the virtue of intellectual humility as a disposition to be appropriately attentive to, and appropriately own, one's intellectual limitations (e.g., lack of knowledge, cognitive mistakes, deficits in cognitive skills) because one is motivated by epistemic goods (Whitcomb et al. 2017). Here, we see a disposition of perception in appropriate attentiveness to one's intellectual limitations, a disposition of behavior and affect in appropriate owning of one's limitations, and a disposition of appropriate motivation, viz. for epistemic goods. Owning will (at least) involve behaviors, such as admitting one's lack of knowledge about a topic, and affective responses, such as feeling dismay about one's lack of knowledge.[8] Below, I focus on responsibilist intellectual virtues, or at least intellectual virtues that involve acquired dispositions of appropriate behavior, motivation, affect, and perception.[9] On the assumption that it is valuable to help our students make progress in acquiring such intellectual virtues, what can we do in our classrooms to help?

A The Standard Approach

The standard approach to intellectual character education advises a combination of: (1) formal instruction about the intellectual virtues; (2) exposure to exemplars of virtue; (3) practice in *identifying* actions that exemplars would perform and in *identifying* motivations and emotions that exemplars would have; (4) practice in *performing* actions that exemplars would perform and in *having* motivations and emotions they would have; (5) practice in recognizing situations in which the virtue in question is relevant; and (6) reflection on one's development. The standard approach thus echoes Aristotle's idea that we develop virtues through the repeated practice of appropriate actions: "For the things we have to learn before we can do, we learn by doing, e.g., men become builders by building and lyre-players by playing the lyre; so too we become just by doing just acts, temperate by doing temperate acts, brave by doing brave acts" (Aristotle 1984: 1743 [*NE* II.1103a31–1103b1]). In other words, we develop stable patterns of appropriate action, motivation, emotion, and perception via repeated practice under the guidance of exemplars.

Accordingly, advocates of the standard approach have suggested several in-class activities and assignments that provide students with opportunities to practice appropriate actions, motivations, emotions, and perceptions.[10] For instance, they recommend in-class group activities (e.g., discussions about the ethics of vaccine distribution) that give students opportunities to perform appropriate actions, e.g., to consider alternative ideas and perspectives (to do what open-minded people would do), to admit their ignorance about a topic (to do what intellectually humble people would do), to defend a belief or claim (to do what intellectually courageous people would do), and so forth. These activities typically ask students to try to perform actions that, e.g., open-minded (or intellectually humble, etc.) people would perform, and subsequently ask them to evaluate whether they succeeded, what their motivations and emotions were, and whether they were motivated by epistemic goods or by the fact that they were assigned a group activity (6 above). These activities are transparent – they inform students that they will encounter opportunities to practice doing what, e.g., open-minded (or intellectually humble, etc.)

people would do. Thus, they don't help students learn to recognize and notice such opportunities for themselves. Accordingly, advocates of the standard approach recommend additional assignments that give students the opportunity to practice sizing up situations for themselves and recognizing occasions to, e.g., consider alternative ideas, admit their ignorance about a topic, defend a belief, and so forth (5 above). Such assignments might ask students to monitor classroom discussions, throughout the course, for situations to perform open-minded (etc.) actions, or even to look for such situations outside of the classroom, in (e.g.,) their evaluations of the media, or in their conversations about a range of topics (e.g., political, social, scientific) on-line, at work, or with friends or family.

Importantly, the standard approach takes virtues such as open-mindedness, intellectual humility, etc. to lie in an Aristotelian mean between "vices" of excess and "vices" of deficiency. To illustrate, it takes the virtue of intellectual humility to lie in something like a mean between "vices" of excess, such as servility, and "vices" of deficiency, such as arrogance. Whereas a virtuously humble person is appropriately attentive to and appropriately owns their intellectual limitations, a servile person is overly attentive to and *over*-owns their limitations. They are humble to a fault – their limitations may constantly come to mind, they may obsess about them, care too much about them, and feel defeated and overwhelmed by them (Whitcomb et al. 2020). In contrast, an arrogant person will be insufficiently attentive to and *under*-own their limitations – they won't be humble enough. They may be oblivious to their limitations or in denial about them, or they may not care about changing them, or may feel outraged whenever someone points them out. The key point for present purposes is that "hitting the mean" in one's actions, as virtuous people do, requires avoiding "vices" of deficiency and "vices" of excess.

The standard approach recognizes that it will be difficult for students to practice performing actions, such as intellectually humble or open-minded ones, that "hit the mean," unless they first know what target they are supposed to hit and what "vices" they are supposed to avoid. In short, it will be difficult for students to *become* more virtuous unless they know how to accurately *identify* virtuous actions and discriminate them from actions that aren't virtuous. Accordingly, advocates of the standard approach recommend formal instruction about the intellectual virtues and vices, and exposure to exemplars of virtue, as methods for explaining what the virtues (of intellectual humility, or open-mindedness, etc.) are, what they aren't, and what virtuous actions and motivations look like in a range of different situations (1 and 2 above). They note that exemplars can be especially useful in helping students home in on virtuous actions. To illustrate, though exemplars of (e.g.,) intellectual humility won't constantly attend to, or own, every cognitive limitation they have, there will be many situations in which they attend to and own some of their cognitive limitations. Repeated exposure to exemplars of intellectual humility might thus help students learn which limitations it is appropriate to attend to and own in which situations, and in which ways, and why. Formal instruction might likewise help students understand why it is valuable to care about truth and knowledge, and how desires to (e.g.,) look smart, win debates, and get good grades can compete with motivations for epistemic goods. To help students further improve their skills in *identifying* virtuous actions, motivations, and emotions, the standard approach also advises practice (3 above). It recommends classroom activities that use a range of examples[11] of intellectual actions and motivations – some virtuous, others not – to give students practice in figuring out which intellectual actions and motivations are virtuous, which aren't, and why.

B Standard Objections

Along with the standard approach come standard objections to it. Here, I briefly consider four. First, one might worry that the standard approach is unjustly "imposing" its views about what is virtuous on students. By way of reply, this would only be a concern if we seriously doubted the value of truth, knowledge, and understanding. Advocates of the standard approach think that intellectual virtues help us gain an *appreciation* for the value of truth, knowledge, and understanding (Curren 2019), in addition to helping us gain more of these *goods* themselves (Battaly 2016). In short: as long as true beliefs, knowledge, and understanding *are* valuable, this objection lacks force.

The second objection is that by encouraging students to imitate the behavior of exemplars, the standard approach is training students to clone behavior without understanding it, to act by rote rather than acquire intellectual virtue. In response, while the standard approach does endorse (Aristotelian) "habituation," it points out that this process is hardly one of mindless copying and repetition (Sherman 1989). Exemplars will *explain* their actions, motivations, and perceptions – they will explain why they perform some actions and not others, why some features of a context are especially salient, and why caring about truth matters – in an effort to help learners eventually become self-sufficient. For their part, learners won't mindlessly parrot what exemplars do either; instead, they will try to understand the salient features of the exemplar's actions and context, and apply them to their own contexts. Nor will learners mechanically repeat the very same action again and again, regardless of context (Curren 2019: 478). Rather, they will try to get increasingly closer to the context-sensitive actions of exemplars, by noting the degree to which their previous attempts to do so succeeded or failed (Battaly 2015: 152). In sum, borrowing from Jason Baehr, "educating for intellectual character growth requires educating for deep understanding" (2016b: 128).

Relatedly, third, one might worry that for the standard approach to succeed, educators would themselves need to be exemplars of intellectual virtue. Advocates of the standard approach have provided two avenues of reply. First, they have argued that educators themselves need not be exemplars of intellectual virtue, since they can find exemplars elsewhere. Educators can find examples of intellectually virtuous exemplars in popular fiction and film, and in a wide range of professional fields, including (e.g.,) research science, medicine, and journalism. Second, advocates of the standard approach have argued that while consistent dispositions of virtuous action and motivation are needed in role models, perfection isn't needed. They thus make it easier for educators to count as role models in the first place. To put this differently, the standard approach has relaxed Aristotle's requirements on virtue possession in two key ways. (A) Whereas Aristotle thought that virtuous people wouldn't have competing motivations and wouldn't struggle to perform virtuous actions, the standard approach allows virtuous people to be *enkratic*. Along these lines, Michel Croce (2020) has expanded the set of virtuous role models beyond "saints," who have all of the virtues, to include "heroes," who only have one virtue, and *enkratic* people, who have to overcome competing motivations in order to perform virtuous actions.[12] (B) The standard approach requires consistency, but not perfection, for virtue-possession; it requires us to be "good enough" (Swanton 2003: 24), even if we aren't intellectual saints. In short, it has moved toward a "threshold" view that allows for degrees of virtue-possession, once one has met (and exceeded) a threshold of consistency that is required for basic virtue-possession. It likewise allows room for growth in virtue and for getting closer to perfecting one's dispositions of virtuous action and motivation.

Fourth, one might object that even if the standard approach is successful at helping students perform intellectually virtuous actions, it might fail to facilitate intellectually virtuous motivations. Responsibilist virtues involve autonomous valuing of epistemic goods – being motivated by the intrinsic value of epistemic goods. They require caring about truth, knowledge, and understanding for their own sakes, and not (merely) for the sake of extrinsic rewards. But, students might do what intellectually virtuous people do, not because they care about truth for its own sake, but because they want to get good grades (and high-paying jobs). Educational psychologists Edward Deci and Richard Ryan have argued that using external rewards or admonishments, like grades and deadlines, to facilitate student behavior succeeds in eliciting the targeted behavior, but may do so at a price. These methods don't help students develop intrinsic motivations to engage in the targeted behavior, and can even undermine intrinsic motivations they might already have.[13] If correct, their studies show that emphasizing assignments and grades will neither facilitate, nor sustain, autonomous valuing of epistemic goods. In reply to this worry, Deci and Ryan argue that educators can facilitate intrinsic motivations by supporting the autonomy of students and acknowledging their skills. Accordingly, their Self-Determination Theory (SDT) emphasizes methods such as: "creating time for students' independent work, giving students an opportunity to talk . . . . encouraging students' effort, offering progress-enabling hints when students seemed stuck, being responsive to students' comments and questions, and acknowledging students' experiences and perspectives" (Ryan & Deci 2009: 184). Randall Curren (2019) likewise contends that facilitating intrinsic motivations requires supporting students' autonomy and self-determination. He thus encourages learning tasks that "provide students with manageable challenges that build their capabilities and confidence while allowing them to experience themselves as competent . . ." (2019: 476). He points out that if challenges are too difficult, students will get discouraged and won't identify with the value of truth or adopt it as a value of their own. Curren helpfully explains SDT's distinction between motivations that are "controlled" as opposed to autonomous. In his words, motivations that are "externally induced by a superior's direct orders, threat of punishment, or offer of a reward" are "controlled" (2019: 477).[14] Whereas, to have autonomous motivations for epistemic goods, students must identify with the value of truth (etc.) and autonomously adopt that value as their own. To be clear, none of these scholars advocates abandoning grades. Rather, they advise emphasizing pedagogical methods that support students' autonomy, in addition to, and over and above, methods that support motivations for extrinsic rewards such as grades. Curren adds that facilitating intrinsic motivations, and intellectual virtues more generally, will also require educational systems that intrinsically value epistemic goods (over and above testing). As we will see below, vice epistemology raises a similar point.

Lessons from Vice Epistemology

Vice epistemology examines the structure, etiology, and amelioration of qualities that make us bad thinkers, such as intellectual arrogance, intellectual servility, closed-mindedness, and epistemic injustice.[15] Vice epistemologists largely agree that we need not be blameworthy for coming to possess intellectual vices, since we might have unwittingly acquired them from our environments; at least, we need not be blameworthy in the traditional sense of the term, which would require having had control over their acquisition.[16] This section uses etiological insights from vice epistemology to draw two lessons about the standard approach. First, if intellectual vices can be caused by localized factors, such as neglectful or abusive relationships, then we should expect some of our students to have already begun to develop them (Porter 2016: 231). These students have *not* been "primed" to develop intellectual virtues (Porter 2016: 226). Nor do they enter our classrooms in a "neutral" state; i.e., without any tendencies either toward virtues *or* toward vices. Rather they arrive with some tendencies toward intellectual vices already in place. Part II.A. argues that on its own, the standard approach isn't likely to help students who have already begun to develop intellectual vices make progress toward intellectual virtues. To help, it would at least need to be combined with classroom strategies for ameliorating intellectual vices. Second, if intellectual vices can be caused by systematic factors, as suggested in Part II.B., then we should expect tendencies toward vices to be widespread among our students (and ourselves). We should expect them to be the rule rather than the localized exception. Accordingly, any progress we might make in the classroom, by combining the standard approach with ameliorative strategies, is likely to be undone unless systemic changes are also made. In short, using classroom strategies to ameliorate tendencies toward vice is one thing, eradicating systemic (and other external) causes of vice is another.[17]

The Need for Ameliorative Strategies

One of the insights of vice epistemology is that intellectual vices can be unwittingly acquired and can begin to develop in childhood and adolescence, when we have little control over our developmental trajectories and before we are even aware of the ways that dispositions develop.[18] If this is correct, and if localized conditions in the lives of individual students can contribute to the development of intellectual vices, then we can expect at least some of our students to have begun to develop them. To illustrate, consider students who arrive in our classrooms with tendencies to over-own their intellectual limitations and under-own their intellectual strengths.[19] These students may tend to, e.g., doubt, lack confidence in, or underestimate their intellectual skills, achievements, and knowledge, and tend to emphasize, be preoccupied with, or overestimate their intellectual deficits, mistakes, and ignorance. They may even (incorrectly) judge themselves to be intellectually inferior to their peers, thinking they have little to contribute to the classroom. In the words of Steve Porter, some students have already developed a "distorted, internalized representation" of themselves as incompetent and ignorant; they may believe they are "dumb," or will never learn, or will always be behind (2016: 226). In short, some of our students have already begun to develop intellectual servility. Alessandra Tanesini (2021: Ch. 9) argues that while some students arrive in our classrooms with tendencies toward servility, others arrive with tendencies toward intellectual arrogance.[20] These students are prone to over-own their intellectual strengths and under-own their intellectual limitations.[21] They may tend to, e.g., focus on, emphasize, and overestimate their skills, achievements, and knowledge, while ignoring, denying, or underestimating their deficits, mistakes, and ignorance. They may even (incorrectly) judge themselves to be superior to their peers – to be "the smartest student in the class" – thinking classroom discussions should center on them.

There are good reasons for thinking that localized factors can contribute to the development of intellectual servility and arrogance in individual students. In this vein, Porter argues that the low self-esteem caused by caregiver neglect can contribute to servility (2016: 31). Somewhat ironically, the low self-esteem caused by caregiver neglect may also contribute to arrogance; arrogant students may be over-compensating for low implicit self-esteem (Tanesini 2021: 103).[22] But, whether or not *neglectful relationships* ultimately prove to be causes of servility and arrogance, and leaving the actual identification of such localized causes to interdisciplinary empirical studies, the key point is this. As long as localized conditions *are* among the causes of intellectual vices, we can expect at least some students to arrive in our classrooms having already begun to develop them.

Will the standard approach help students who have already begun to develop vices? The answer is likely to depend on the *degree* of vice they have developed. While the standard approach may help students with relatively low degrees of a vice, who aren't far from developing virtues, it is less likely to help students who have already developed higher degrees of a vice. Below I explain why, using the vices of servility and arrogance, and the virtues of intellectual humility and intellectual pride, as illustrations.

The Problem of Failing to Recognize and Emulate Exemplars. First, students who have already developed higher degrees of a vice, such as servility or arrogance, may not recognize or emulate exemplars of virtue. Why not? Students with higher degrees of intellectual servility are likely to view themselves as intellectually inferior and unable to improve (Porter 2016: 226). Tanesini argues that they are also likely to lack "the motivation to improve," and to instead be motivated to be accepted by others, which can incentivize further servility (2021: 196). Given their motivations for acceptance, these students may mistakenly think that virtuously humble and proud people are arrogant – that they *over*-own their strengths and *under*-own their limitations. They may instead admire people like themselves, who in fact tend to under-own strengths and over-own limitations – who are in fact servile. In other words, these students may identify the wrong people as exemplars of virtue. Moreover, even when they identify the right people as exemplars of virtue, they still won't be likely to emulate them. Students who think they are intellectually inferior and unable to improve will be likely to view the actions and motivations of exemplars of humility and pride as so far ahead that they are entirely out of reach (Tanesini 2021: 199). They are even likely to view the actions and motivations of the *enkratic* exemplars endorsed by Croce (2020) as out of reach. If anything, these students are likely to re-affirm their view of themselves as inferior and recede into despondency. Analogous problems arise for students who have developed higher degrees of arrogance. They may mistakenly think that exemplars of humility and pride are intellectually servile – that they *under*-own strengths and *over*-own limitations – and may instead admire people like themselves, who are in fact arrogant. Further, even when they do correctly identify exemplars, they will be more likely to undermine them than to emulate them, due to motivations of envy, perceived threat, and ego defense (Tanesini 2021: 200).

The Problem of Practicing Vicious Acts. Suppose, for the moment, that we could solve the problem above; i.e., suppose we restricted our view to students, with higher degrees of a vice, who somehow managed to both correctly identify exemplars and to try to make progress toward them. The second problem is that these students may still end up practicing actions that are vicious, instead of virtuous, thus further cementing the vice in question. Recall that the standard approach provides opportunities for practicing virtuous actions, such as appropriate owning. But, as Tanesini (2021: 197) observes, every opportunity the standard approach provides to practice appropriately owning strengths and limitations will simultaneously be an opportunity to practice under- or over-owning them.[23] This is because the standard approach recommends in-class activities and assignments in which students decide what to do. Arguably, students who are motivated enough to try to make progress toward virtuous humility and pride, but who are still generally prone to servility or arrogance, would end up practicing *under*-owning and *over*-owning more often than they would end up practicing appropriate owning. Ironically, these activities of the standard approach might serve to reinforce and exacerbate the developing vices of these students.

The Error Problem.[24] Suppose, for the moment, that we could also solve the second problem. The third problem for the standard approach is that it will sometimes be right for students with higher degrees of a vice to perform actions that exemplars would *not* perform. The standard approach, with its emphasis on emulating actions that exemplars *do* perform, fails to grasp the importance of these cases. As Ben Kotzee et al. put the point: "In our intellectual conduct, non-virtuous people sometimes should perform actions that virtuous people would not perform, exactly because they are not (yet) virtuous" (2019: 14). Indeed, they may *need* to perform actions a virtuous person would not perform, in order to avoid acting in ways that are straightforwardly vicious.[25] To explain, let's begin with Robert Johnson's (2003) example of a chronic liar who has decided to reform his character. In order to avoid performing vicious acts of lying, the liar keeps track of his lies and their bad effects, and his progress in becoming more honest, and reminds himself of these things whenever he is tempted to lie. Though an exemplar of honesty wouldn't (need to) do any of these actions, they are the right actions for the chronic liar to perform – else he'll end up doing something much worse (lying). Note that neither Aristotelian exemplars nor Croce's (2020) *enkratic* exemplars would need to do these actions: *enkratic* exemplars wouldn't need to keep track of any lies since they wouldn't lie.[26] An analogous point applies to students with higher degrees of servility or arrogance who are trying to make progress toward virtue. They may need to do things that exemplars of virtuous humility and pride wouldn't do, in order to avoid acting in ways that are servile or arrogant. To illustrate, a student with a high degree of arrogance may need to give a curt response to a peer's well-reasoned objection, in order to avoid ignoring the peer altogether, even though this isn't what a humble exemplar would do – assume that, in this case, the exemplar (Aristotelian or *enkratic*) would consider whether her own view was mistaken.[27] In the illuminating words of Liezl van Zyl:

> Attempting to emulate the virtuous is not the only, or even the best way to improve one's character. We may first have to do things that are not characteristic of the fully virtuous, such as asking for advice, or taking steps needed to overcome one's fears or lack of confidence ... Those of us who are severely lacking in (some) virtue(s) will first have to focus our efforts, not on trying to act like the virtuous, but on trying *not* to act in ways that are characteristic of the vicious.
>
> *(van Zyl 2011: 87)*

On van Zyl's view, those of us who are developing virtues should focus on avoiding vicious actions, even if this means doing things an exemplar wouldn't do.

The upshot of these problems is that on its own, the standard approach isn't likely to help students who have already developed a relatively high degree of a vice, such as servility or arrogance, make progress toward virtue. To help these students, we would at least need to combine the standard approach with strategies for ameliorating intellectual vices.

What might such ameliorative strategies include? This is an open question that warrants further exploration. Here, I make a start on some suggestions.[28] We saw above that the motivations and self-representations of students who are prone to servility and arrogance (respectively) can prevent them from recognizing and emulating exemplars of intellectual virtue, and from practicing virtuous actions. Arguably, (1) ameliorative strategies would need to include methods for weakening these motivations and self-assessments, and more broadly, for weakening motivations and self-assessments that exemplars of intellectual virtue would not have. For instance, in the cases of servility and arrogance (respectively), ameliorative strategies would need to include techniques for weakening (e.g.,) motivations to be accepted by others, and motivations to defend the ego from perceived threats, which stand in the way of intrinsic motivations for epistemic goods (and for learning and intellectual improvement more generally). They would likewise need to include techniques for reducing mis-representations of the self as intellectually inferior or superior (respectively). Along these lines, Tanesini has proposed techniques that involve increasing the self-esteem of students through self-affirmation, while Porter has suggested a kind of "intellectual therapy," which uses student-teacher relationships to repair motivations and self-representations.

We also saw above that even the actions and motivations of *enkratic* exemplars will be out of reach for students with higher degrees of servility and arrogance (respectively), and that these students will sometimes need to perform actions that (even) *enkratic* exemplars would not perform. Arguably, (2) ameliorative strategies would need to expand the range of role models even farther, beyond Croce's (2020) *enkratics*. They would need to include role models whose motivations and actions are within reach of students with higher degrees of servility and arrogance. Whereas *enkratic* exemplars fall just short of perfect Aristotelian virtue, we can expect ameliorative strategies to include role models who are *far* from perfect and are even servile and arrogant (respectively) themselves, albeit less servile and arrogant than the students for whom they serve as models. These role models would share some of the same behaviors and motivations with the students for whom they serve as models, but crucially, they would also have made progress in reducing their servility and arrogance – progress which students would be encouraged to emulate.[29] We can likewise expect these role models to perform actions that Aristotelian and *enkratic* exemplars wouldn't perform – e.g., to give curt responses to peers, in order to avoid arrogantly dismissing them. Students would also be encouraged to emulate behaviors like these, which would help them avoid acting in ways that are straightforwardly vicious.

Finally, and contra van Zyl (2011), it is worth considering whether ameliorative strategies would also need to encourage these students to emulate some vicious actions, specifically actions of the *opposing* vice. To use Aristotelian language, it is worth considering whether students with higher degrees of a vice might need to "drag [them]selves away to the contrary extreme" in order to "get into the intermediate state" (Aristotle 1984: 1751 [*NE* II.9.1109b5]). That is, whether students with higher degrees of servility might need to emulate some actions that are arrogant in order to reduce their servility, and whether students with higher degrees of arrogance might need to emulate some actions that are servile in order to reduce their arrogance.

In sum, the first lesson of vice epistemology is that some students arrive in our classes having already developed higher degrees of intellectual vices. On its own, the standard approach isn't likely to help these students make progress toward intellectual virtues. We would first need to use strategies for ameliorating their vices, reserving the standard approach for later use. The second lesson of vice epistemology, addressed below, is that even if ameliorative strategies were to succeed in reducing intellectual vices, and even if the standard approach was then to succeed in helping students make further progress toward virtue, these effects would be short-lived.

The Need for Systemic Change

Using classroom strategies to ameliorate tendencies toward intellectual vice is one thing, eradicating external causes of intellectual vice is another.[30] Even if combining ameliorative strategies with the standard approach helped students make progress toward virtues in the classroom, any such progress would be ephemeral if the underlying causes of vice weren't also removed. In the poignant words of Ian Kidd, we would be "playing a febrile from of ameliorative whack-a-mole" (2020: 80). We would be treating the symptoms of vice without treating the cause. Accordingly, if caregiver neglect is a localized causal contributor to the development of intellectual vices, then we should expect continuing relationships of neglect to erode some or all of progress made in the classroom.

The problem multiplies when we take the second lesson of vice epistemology into account, *viz.* systemic factors, such as widespread epistemic injustice, can contribute to the development of intellectual vices. Along these lines, Miranda Fricker (2007) and José Medina (2013) have argued that systemic epistemic injustice can contribute to the development of a range of intellectual vices, including servility and arrogance. To explain, on Fricker's view, testimonial injustice occurs when identity prejudices, such as racism and sexism, cause hearers to assign deflated levels of credibility to some speakers and excessive levels of credibility to others. Fricker argues that when identity prejudices are systemic, speakers whose credibility and competence is repeatedly and persistently denied can "lose confidence in [their] general intellectual abilities to such an extent that [they are] genuinely hindered in [their] educational or ... intellectual development" (Fricker 2007: 47). They are even at risk for developing the intellectual vices of cowardice and servility (2007: 49–50). On the other end of the spectrum, speakers such as the "puffed up fellow," whose credibility and competence are repeatedly and persistently assumed, are at risk for developing the intellectual vices of arrogance, closed-mindedness, and dogmatism (2007: 20). Medina likewise argues that persons who are marginalized along multiple axes of their social identities, and are systematically subjected to credibility deficits and dismissals, are at risk for doubting their abilities, lacking confidence in themselves, and for acquiring "an extreme form of ... humility" (2013: 41). Whereas, persons who are privileged along multiple axes of their social identities, and are systematically assigned credibility excesses and intellectual authority, are at risk for arrogance – for thinking themselves superior, and being dismissive. Roughly, Medina's view is that systemic testimonial injustice is likely to lead to servility in members of marginalized groups, and to arrogance in members of privileged groups, though he is careful to note that these are rough generalizations that allow for exceptions and for localized causes of servility and arrogance (2013: 40). If Fricker and Medina are correct in thinking that epistemic injustice is endemic, then we should expect tendencies toward intellectual vices to be prevalent among our students (and ourselves). We should expect most students to arrive in our classrooms having already developed tendencies toward intellectual vices.

Making matters even worse, there are additional systemic factors that can contribute to the development of epistemic vices. Following Kidd, several scholars have pointed out that educational systems themselves can "corrupt" students, by cementing and stabilizing their tendencies toward intellectual vices.[31] In this vein, Lani Watson (2020) and Casey Johnson (2020) have argued that educational systems which emphasize test-taking, such as No Child Left Behind, not only impede the development of intellectual virtues like humility,[32] but incentive vicious behaviors, such as arrogantly pretending to know answers, or in cases of servility, doubling-down on beliefs in one's inferiority.

There are two key upshots of the second lesson. First, if tendencies toward intellectual vices are widespread amongst our students, then the relevance of the standard approach recedes even further. Second, ameliorative strategies won't produce lasting effects, and systemic changes are required. We will need to make systemic changes, in education and in power structures more broadly, in order to help students make lasting progress in reducing intellectual vices and gaining intellectual virtues. We will need to treat the systemic causes of intellectual vice in order to escape the game of "ameliorative whack-a-mole."

Open Questions

Vice epistemology tells us that most students arrive in our classrooms having already developed tendencies toward intellectual vices. If this is correct, then what should we do to help students make progress toward intellectual virtues? That is an open question. The analysis presented in this chapter suggests that systemic changes must be made, if any progress toward virtues is to be lasting. Accordingly, we should at least advocate for systemic changes that will remove the causes of intellectual vice. Of course, systemic change takes time. While we are working toward it, should we also develop classroom strategies for ameliorating intellectual vices? Progress in reducing vices might be useful, even if ephemeral – it is worth exploring whether ephemeral relief is better than no relief at all. Should we also employ the standard approach? Does it still have a role to play? That, too, is an open question. As mentioned above, the standard approach might help students who have developed lower degrees of a vice, or students who have somehow avoided developing vices. The standard approach is also likely to be useful in later stages of development, particularly after ameliorative strategies have been employed and systemic changes have been made. For these reasons, I'm not inclined to eliminate it. Though I am inclined to admit that if the insights of vice epistemology are correct, the role of the standard approach is not as central as many of us (myself included) had previously thought.[33]

(Related Chapters: 4, 5, 10, 12, 26, 27, 28, 29.)

Notes

1 See, for instance, Baehr 2013, 2016a, 2016b, 2021; Battaly 2006, 2015, 2016a; Byerly 2019, Curren 2019; King 2021. See also information about the Intellectual Virtues Academy middle-school and high-school in Long Beach, CA: https://www.ivalongbeach.org/ and https://www.academylongbeach.org/
2 See, for instance, Kidd et al. 2020.
3 See also Battaly forthcoming.
4 For an alternative approach to critical thinking, see Paul and Elder (2014).
5 On reliabilist intellectual virtue, see for instance Sosa 2007 and Greco 2010.
6 On responsibilist intellectual virtue, see for instance Baehr 2011, Montmarquet 1993, Zagzebski 1996.
7 Baehr 2011 argues that intellectual virtues do not conceptually *require* the reliable production of epistemic goods, whereas Zagzebski 1996 argues that they do.
8 Owning won't involve "taking responsibility" for one's intellectual limitations since one need not be responsible for coming to have them.
9 I endorse pluralism about intellectual virtues (and vices); see Battaly 2015 and 2019a.
10 See, e.g., Baehr 2021; Battaly 2006, 2015, 2016; Ritchhart 2002; Ritchhart et al. 2011; Roberts 2016.
11 These examples often feature the intellectual actions and motivations of, e.g., scientists and journalists, as well as characters in fiction and film. See, for instance, Battaly 2006, 2015, 2016.
12 See also Zagzebski 2017.
13 See Deci et al. 2001; see also Curren 2019: 477.
14 See also Curren & Ryan 2020.
15 See, e.g., Battaly 2020; Cassam 2019; Fricker 2007; Kidd et al. 2020; Kidd 2020; Medina 2013; Tanesini 2021.

16 Explorations of alternative accounts of blameworthiness are underway in vice epistemology. See, e.g., Battaly 2019b; Cassam 2019: Ch. 6; Fricker 2016; Tanesini 2021: Ch. 8.
17 The arguments in this section are based on Battaly forthcoming.
18 Relatedly, see Sher 2006: 12.
19 On the virtues of pride and humility, see Whitcomb et al. 2017; Battaly 2021 and forthcoming.
20 See also Tanesini 2016.
21 Tanesini's accounts of intellectual humility, arrogance, and servility are in the same family as the "limitations-owning" account of Whitcomb et al., but the details differ.
22 Tanesini argues that arrogance can be a defensive response to low implicit self-esteem; arrogant people can display high explicit self-esteem as an over-compensation for low implicit self-esteem.
23 Within the classroom, we can expect this to be correlated with practice that isn't adequately guided.
24 This is van Zyl's term (2011: 82); see also Kotzee et al. (2019: 13).
25 Vicious actions are a sub-set of actions a virtuous person would not perform. This means that one can perform acts a virtuous person wouldn't perform (e.g. because they don't need to), without performing vicious acts.
26 Though they would still struggle against the temptation to lie, *enkratics* (unlike *akratics*) succeed in overcoming that temptation and tell the truth.
27 This example is adapted from Kotzee et al. 2019: 14.
28 See also Battaly forthcoming.
29 Students with higher degrees of vice initially need role models like these. As they make progress, they can graduate incrementally to role models with lower degrees of vice and higher degrees of virtue.
30 The arguments in this section are based on Battaly forthcoming.
31 See Kidd 2018, 2020; and Monypenny 2021 on hostile classrooms.
32 See also Curren 2019: 478, for the argument that systems emphasizing high-stakes testing undermine intrinsic motivation.
33 Thanks to Randall Curren for comments and discussion.

References

Aristotle (1984) Nicomachean Ethics, in J. Barnes (ed.), *The Complete Works of Aristotle, Vol. 2*. Princeton, NJ: Princeton University Press.
Baehr, J. (2011) *The Inquiring Mind*. Oxford: Oxford University Press.
Baehr, J. (2013) "Educating for Intellectual Virtues: From Theory to Practice," *Journal of the Philosophy of Education* 47: 248–262.
Baehr, J. (ed.) (2016a) *Intellectual Virtues in Education: Essays in Applied Virtue Epistemology*. New York: Routledge.
Baehr, J. (ed.) (2016b) "Is Intellectual Character Growth a Realistic Educational Aim?" *Journal of Moral Education* 45(2): 117–131.
Baehr, J. (2021) *Deep in Thought: A Practical Guide to Teaching for Intellectual Virtues*. Cambridge MA: Harvard Education Press.
Battaly, H. (2006) "Teaching Intellectual Virtues: Applying Virtue Epistemology in the Classroom," *Teaching Philosophy* 29(3): 191–222.
Battaly, H. (2015) *Virtue*. Cambridge: Polity Press.
Battaly, H. (2016) "Responsibilist Virtues in Reliabilist Classrooms," in J. Baehr (ed.) *Intellectual Virtues in Education*. New York: Routledge, 163–183.
Battaly, H. (2019a) "A Third Kind of Intellectual Virtue: Personalism," in H. Battaly (ed.) *The Routledge Handbook of Virtue Epistemology*. New York: Routledge, 115–126.
Battaly, H. (2019b) "Vice Epistemology has a Responsibility Problem," *Philosophical Issues* 29(1): 24–36.
Battaly, H. (2020) "Closed-mindedness as an Intellectual Vice," in C. Kelp and J. Greco (eds.) *Virtue Theoretic Epistemology*. New York: Cambridge University Press, 15–41.
Battaly, H. (2021) "Countering Servility through Pride and Humility," *Midwest Studies in Philosophy* XLV.
Battaly, H. (forthcoming) "Educating for Intellectual Pride and Ameliorating Servility in Contexts of Epistemic Injustice," *Educational Philosophy and Theory*.
Byerly, T. R. (2019) "Teaching for Intellectual Virtue in Logic and Critical Thinking Classes: Why and How," *Teaching Philosophy* 42(1): 1–27.
Cassam, Q. (2019) *Vices of the Mind*. Oxford: Oxford University Press.
Croce, M. (2020) "Moral Exemplars in Education: A Liberal Account," *Ethics and Education* 15(2): 186–199.

Curren, R. (2019) "Virtue Epistemology and Education," in H. Battaly (ed.) *The Routledge Handbook of Virtue Epistemology*. New York: Routledge, 470–482.
Curren, R. & Ryan, R. M. (2020) "Moral Self-determination: The Nature, Existence, and Formation of Moral Motivation," *Journal of Moral Education* 49(3): 295–315.
Deci, E. L., Koestner, R., & Ryan, R. M. (2001) "Extrinsic Rewards and Intrinsic Motivation in Education: Reconsidered Once Again," *Review of Educational Research* 71: 1–27.
Fricker, M. (2007) *Epistemic Injustice*. Oxford: Oxford University Press.
Fricker, M. (2016) "Fault and No-fault Responsibility for Implicit Prejudice," in M. Brady and M. Fricker (eds.) *The Epistemic Life of Groups*. Oxford: Oxford University Press, 33–50.
Greco, J. (2010) *Achieving Knowledge*. New York: Cambridge University Press.
Johnson, C. (2020) "Teaching to the Test: How Schools Discourage Phronesis," in I. J. Kidd, H. Battaly, & Q. Cassam (eds.) *Vice Epistemology*. London: Routledge, 225–238.
Johnson, R. (2003) "Virtue and Right," *Ethics* 113: 810–834.
Kidd, I. J. (2018) "Epistemic Corruption and Education," *Episteme* 16(2): 220–235.
Kidd, I. J. (2020) "Epistemic Corruption and Social Oppression," in In I. J. Kidd, H. Battaly, & Q. Cassam (eds.) *Vice Epistemology*. New York: Routledge, 69–85.
Kidd, I. J., Battaly, H., & Cassam, Q. (eds.) (2020) *Vice Epistemology*. London: Routledge.
King, N. L. (2021) *The Excellent Mind*. New York: Oxford University Press.
Kotzee, B., Carter, J. A., & Siegel, H. (2019) "Educating for Intellectual Virtue: A Critique from Action Guidance," *Episteme*: 1–23. doi:10.1017/epi.2019.10
Medina, J. (2013) *The Epistemology of Resistance*. Oxford: Oxford University Press.
Monypenny, A. (2021) "Between Vulnerability and Resilience: A Contextualist Picture of Protective Epistemic Character Traits," *Journal of Philosophy of Education* 55(2): 358–370.
Montmarquet, J. A. (1993) *Epistemic Virtue and Doxastic Responsibility*. Lanham, MD: Rowman & Littlefield.
Paul, R. & Elder, L. (2014) *Critical Thinking: Tools for Taking Charge of Your Professional and Personal Life*, 2nd ed. Lanham, MD: Rowman & Littlefield.
Porter, S. L. (2016) "A Therapeutic Approach to Intellectual Virtue Formation in the Classroom," in J. Baehr (ed.) *Intellectual Virtues in Education*. New York: Routledge, 221–239.
Ritchhart, R. (2002) *Intellectual Character*. San Francisco: Jossey-Bass.
Ritchhart, R., Church, M., & Morrison, K (2011) *Making Thinking Visible*. San Francisco: Jossey-Bass.
Roberts, R. C. (2016) "Learning Intellectual Humility," in J. Baehr (ed.) *Intellectual Virtues in Education*. New York: Routledge, 184–201.
Ryan, R. M. & Deci, E. L. (2009) "Promoting Self-determined School Engagement: Motivation, Learning, and Well-being," in K. R. Wentzel & A. Wigfield (eds.) *Handbook of Motivation at School*. New York: Routledge, 171–195.
Sher, G. (2006) *In Praise of Blame*. New York: Oxford University Press.
Sherman, N. (1989) *The Fabric of Character: Aristotle's Theory of Virtue*. Oxford: Clarendon Press.
Sosa, E. (2007) *A Virtue Epistemology*. New York: Oxford University Press.
Swanton, C. (2003) *Virtue Ethics*. New York: Oxford University Press.
Tanesini, A. (2016) "Teaching Virtue: Changing Attitudes," *Logos and Episteme* VII(4): 503–527.
Tanesini, A. (2021) *The Mismeasure of the Self: A Study in Vice Epistemology*. Oxford: Oxford University Press.
van Zyl, L. (2011) "Right Action and the Non-Virtuous Agent," *Journal of Applied Philosophy* 28(1): 80–92.
Watson, L. (2020) "Knowledge is Power: Barriers to Intellectual Humility in the Classroom," in M. Alfano, M. Lynch, & A. Tanesini (eds.) *The Routledge Handbook of the Philosophy of Humility*. New York: Routledge, 439–450.
Whitcomb, D., Battaly, H., Baehr, J., & Howard-Snyder, D. (2017) "Intellectual Humility: Owning Our Limitations," *Philosophy and Phenomenological Research* XCIV(3): 509–539.
Whitcomb, D., Battaly, H., Baehr, J., & Howard-Snyder, D. (2020) "The Puzzle of Humility and Disparity," in M. Alfano, M. Lynch, & A. Tanesini (eds.) *The Routledge Handbook of the Philosophy of Humility*. New York: Routledge, 72–83.
Zagzebski, L. (1996) *Virtues of the Mind*. Cambridge: Cambridge University Press.
Zagzebski, L. (2017) *Exemplarist Moral Theory*. New York: Oxford University Press.

12

THE FORMATION OF EXPERTISE

Ben Kotzee

Introduction

In the philosophy of education, the topic of expertise is usually associated with thinking about vocational or professional education. However, the concept of expertise is important far beyond thinking about educating students for a career. One natural way to describe what the educator does in providing a subject-based education is to inculcate expertise in that subject; this makes the concept influential not only in vocational, but in general education. Moreover, the concept has a bearing on a range of educational debates: Is exceptional performance predicted by an inherited cognitive capacity like "intelligence" or is it mostly learned (the "nature/nurture debate")? Are there limits to the skills that some children can learn and how should this influence educational opportunities (the debate regarding "ability and disability")? Is ability general or specific (the "generality/specificity" debate)? Should schools principally aim to transmit knowledge or practical competencies (the "content or skills" debate)? As Ellen Fridland and Carlotta Pavese put it:

> ... questions of skill and expertise are important not only for our particular, theoretical understanding of these specific notions but, more broadly, for our understanding of intelligence, cognition, and practical knowledge, full stop.
>
> *(Fridland & Pavese 2021: 1–2)*

In 20th century philosophy, it was Gilbert Ryle who most influenced the debate on skill and expertise. Ryle was responsible for drawing the distinction between knowing that something is the case and knowing how to do something, and he held that knowing that something is the case is best understood not as representing something to oneself, but as being able to *do* something – that is *think* (Ryle 1945). According to the Cartesian picture of thinking, which Ryle calls "intellectualism," skilled action is based on a prior representation in one's mind of (a) how the world is and (b) how one seeks to change it through action. Ryle thought that this cannot be right. Representing is itself an action and if one always needed to represent the world before one could act, then any representation would have to be preceded by another representation. This is Ryle's famous "regress"' argument against intellectualism (Ryle 1949: 19).

Stanley and Williamson (2001) provide the most prominent counter-blast against Ryle. They hold that knowing how should really be understood as a form of knowing that. Stanley and Williamson note that constructions containing the word "know" often come in "wh" form, for instance "know whether," "know who," "know why," etc. Stanley and Williamson emphasise that

DOI: 10.4324/9781003172246-15

all the other wh-constructions can be parsed in terms of knowing that something is the case, and they suggest that know how constructions can be parsed like that too: someone who knows how to do *x*, knows the way *w* that is the way to do *x*. This is Stanley and Williamson's "intellectualist" alternative to Ryle. According to Stanley and Williamson, knowing how to do something is simply knowing the way to do that thing. In contemporary epistemology, the debate regarding the nature of know how has become all but synonymous with the question of whether we should understand know how in intellectualist or anti-intellectualist terms.[1]

While theories of "expertise" and of "know how" overlap, there are also distinct differences: theorists of know how seek to analyse the nature of know how, while theorists of expertise also work to understand the social role that expertise plays in our knowledge economy. Moreover, theorists of expertise are often as interested in the question of how to foster expertise as in the question of what exactly it is. While there is great cross-fertilisation between study of the two concepts, study of "know how" is largely a technical matter within epistemology, while larger questions of "expertise" are studied across a wide range of fields including philosophy of science, psychology, sociology, politics and education.

In what follows I discuss two broad views that have taken shape regarding the nature of expertise in philosophy. I dub them the "cognitive" and "skills-based" accounts of expertise.[2]

Cognitive Accounts of Expertise

Cognitive accounts view expertise as consisting in cognitive contact with the world (in a sense to be unpacked below). Cognitive accounts see accurate intellectual insight as valuable in itself: for instance, it is valuable in itself to understand that saltpetre can be an oxidant. However, cognitivists also see intellectual insight as the key ingredient that enables successful practical action: for instance, the insight that adding saltpetre to sulfur and carbon creates an explosive mixture was the intellectual key to the invention, manufacture, and use of gunpowder, with all its various civil and military applications. On the cognitive view, the expert is the person who – more than the novice – has intellectual insight into how the world works and how objects can be manipulated for practical benefit. This intellectual insight enables the expert to undertake practical tasks on behalf of the novice, or enables them to inform the novice on how to undertake those tasks themselves.

In social epistemology, John Hardwig (1985) first stresses that most people stand in a relation of epistemic dependence to experts for much of their ordinary knowledge. While printing, universal education, and (today) the world-wide web have provided people with impressive stores of knowledge regarding science, history, geography, etc, most people did not discover that knowledge independently; their knowledge relies on expert testimony. Hardwig holds that deferring to expert testimony is justified and that the expert/novice relationship is foundational to science. As a system for dividing intellectual labor, science relies on the idea that experts should *specialise* in order to advance their own fields, but it also relies on the idea that lay people will *trust* experts' findings in those fields. Otherwise expert knowledge will not spread to benefit the whole community. Like Hardwig, Alvin Goldman (1999) views expertise in light of the knowledge or information that the expert is able to share with the lay person. He defines being an expert as follows:

> S is an expert in domain D if and only if S has the capacity to help others (especially laypersons) solve a variety of problems in D or execute an assortment of tasks in D which the latter would not be able to solve or execute on their own.
>
> *(Goldman 2018: 4)*

Goldman has a truth-based account of what it means to be an expert – the expert is the one who believes more truths about an area or question. For Goldman, only the believing the *truth* matters. He holds that, no matter how one came by the truth or how shaky one's ground for believing that truth is, ultimately it is the grasp of a truth about how the world works that enables successful practical action in it. This position is called "veritism" (Goldman 1999: 3). Others who advance broadly truth-based accounts of expertise are David Coady (2012: 28) and James Hikins and Richard Cherwitz (2011).

Other authors propose not a truth-based account, but a knowledge-based account of expertise. On the knowledge-based account, the expert is not the one who holds more true beliefs than the non-expert, but the one with more knowledge. Like truth-based accounts, knowledge-based accounts are also informational; however, the advantage of the knowledge-based account of expertise over the truth-based account is that it rules out a form of epistemic luck. A novice may stumble on a true belief by accident, but, on the knowledge account, the novice is not yet an expert (with regard to the subject matter of that belief). A person needs to have good evidence or justification for beliefs in the domain if they are to be an expert. Authors who propose a knowledge account of expertise include Elizabeth Fricker (2006) Sanford Goldberg (2009) and Stephen Turner (2001).

A third possible cognitive account is the understanding account. Catherine Elgin (2004, 2006) suggests that the highest epistemic good is not knowledge, but understanding; moreover, she holds that understanding involves a form of knowledge-how (2017: ch. 3). Oliver Scholz applies this kind of thinking to expertise and pushes the matter further. He holds that the expert is not the one who believes more truths or has more knowledge in an area, but the one who *understands* that area better (Scholz 2009: 193). Scholz holds that what distinguishes the expert is understanding their field in depth. Whereas any lay person can come to know some isolated facts about a domain, the expert will have thousands of closely connected opinions about the domain. Importantly, not all of the experts' detailed beliefs will be true. Because the expert is one who *investigates* their domain, they will inevitably ask complicated questions and (sometimes) come to the wrong answer about them; this means that the expert may even have *more* false beliefs (amongst plentiful correct beliefs) in their belief set than a well-read novice (who may only have a few beliefs about the domain, but those mostly correct). For Scholz, what makes an expert is not the ratio of true to false beliefs, but the effort to go deeper in their domain and to connect new discoveries with one another in an overall explanatory picture (even at the risk of believing some falsehoods).

Jamie Watson (2021: 57–59) outlines a number of advantages of the cognitive account of expertise:

i The cognitive account is simple, because it explains expertise in terms of epistemic authority. Epistemic authority (meaning simply: having more true belief/knowledge/understanding about a certain matter than another person) is a ubiquitous and easily understandable epistemic phenomenon and the 'expert' is simply the person with epistemic authority.
ii The cognitive account provides a simple explanation for why we defer to experts: the expert can be relied on to know and/or understand the truth and is a source of epistemic help and advice.
iii The cognitive account is objective. Because it is an objective matter whether a belief is true, or whether someone has knowledge or understanding, it is clear who is the expert regarding some matter and who not.
iv The cognitive account is realistic, because it explains expertise as a feature of the real world. According to the cognitive account, the world works in a certain way and the expert discovers how. The expert can then use this knowledge of how the world works to achieve practical goals in the world for themselves or for others.

However, a number of criticisms of the cognitive account are also regularly made:

i The cognitive account overestimates the importance of true belief/knowledge/understanding about *how* a practical task can be achieved theoretically speaking and underestimates the bodily practice, or dexterity or (even) physical strength that might be required to achieve that task.

ii The cognitive account is overoptimistic in its trust in experts. Often, accurate cognitive contact with the world does not automatically translate into good expert advice; for instance, we can think of cases in which those with epistemic standing do not have the communicative skill or the patience to convey their knowledge sympathetically to novices. Moreover, one can also think of cases in which those with epistemic authority systematically withhold information from novices or might even cheat novices from a position of epistemic advantage. Critics hold that, next to epistemic advantage, an element of trustworthiness is also needed if the expert's advice is to be worth following.

iii Purely cognitive accounts cannot account for the relativity that inevitably accompanies judgements of who is expert. Who should be regarded as expert is relative to the time of judgement; for instance, Galileo was clearly an expert astronomer during his lifetime, but today we would count him as, at best, a self-taught eccentric. Expertise is also relative to the place of judgement; for instance, someone who speaks and writes fluent Japanese and lives in England would be classed as an expert on Japanese, but in Japan, those skills are mundane.

iv Above, we saw that the objectivity and realism that are features of the cognitive account are regarded as a strength. However, by the same token, the cognitive account makes it hard to settle the question of who is an expert. As we saw, the cognitive account equates expertise with more true beliefs, or more knowledge or understanding. This means that the question of who is the expert regarding a certain matter cannot be solved separately from the question of what is true. However, often the truth of the matter is exactly what is in dispute; for instance, in science, it is not uncommon for two different scientific camps to hold opposite views and both to insist that their view is true. For this reason, the account gives laypeople (who are, by hypothesis, not able to say what is true or not) no help or advice on how to identify the experts that they are to trust.[3]

Skills-Based Accounts

The best-known objection to the cognitive account of expertise is the first objection discussed above: that theoretical or "book" knowledge regarding how something is to be done does not translate into the practical ability to do that thing. Michael Polanyi is a famous proponent of the idea that knowledge is not explicit but is tacit. A chemist by training, Polanyi held that even within that most intellectual of settings, the laboratory, science advances through intuition, feeling, and hands-on experience of solving problems rather than by formulating encompassing hypotheses and testing them, once and for all, in perfectly conceptualised experiments. Much scientific knowledge is "tacit," (Polanyi 1958, 1966). Michael Oakeshott held similarly that political principles cannot be formulated rationally, and one must learn about politics through experience. According to Oakeshott:

> Theoretical knowledge can be learned from a book; it can be learned from a correspondence course … . It can be learned by heart, repeated by rote and applied mechanically …
>
> *(Oakeshott 1962: 8)*

However,

> … practical knowledge can neither be taught nor learned, but only imparted and acquired. It exists only in practice and is acquired only by apprenticeship to a master …
>
> *(Oakeshott 1962: 9–10)*

Polanyi and Oakeshott both advance the idea that there exists a kind of knowledge that one cannot grasp and communicate linguistically; rather than being captured intellectually and expressed in language, this kind of knowledge can only be shown in masterful practical action. According to the skills-based account, the cognitive or "head" side of expertise (true belief/knowledge/understanding) is either not essential to expertise or is, at worst, actively damaging to expertise. Instead, expertise consists in masterful practical action "with the hand" (that need not be accompanied by thinking). Christopher Winch (2010a) calls this the "fluency" account of expertise and Montero (2016) has dubbed it the "just do it" account of expertise.

The skills-based account has strong roots in Eastern philosophy (Garfield & Priest 2020: 29–39). In recent years, however, one set of literatures has proven particularly influential in crystalizing its claims: Hubert Dreyfus and Stuart Dreyfus's book *Mind Over Machine* (1986) and reactions to it. Dreyfus and Dreyfus consider the possibility of artificial intelligence and argue that computers will never be able to think. They base their argument on the uniqueness of human expertise. Human expertise, such as the fine physical skill involved in doing karate, playing the violin, or painting a masterwork, is the result of long practice and is embodied in the arms, legs, and fingers of human experts as much as in their thoughts or brains. Through their studies of novices and experts in fields like flying, chess, driving, and second language learning, Dreyfus and Dreyfus concluded that while novices cling tightly to rules for guiding their actions, as they become more expert people begin to pay less conscious attention to rules. They begin to act more intuitively and automatically and (even) become free to improvise. Dreyfus and Dreyfus suggest that this process happens in five stages: the performance of the novice is characterised by rigid adherence to taught rules or plans, but the novice gradually sheds this reliance on explicit rules when she progresses through the stages of "advanced beginner," "competent," and "proficient" until she reaches the stage of being expert. At that point she no longer relies on rules, guidelines, or maxims for how she performs, but acts from an intuitive grasp of situations based on deep tacit understanding (Dreyfus & Dreyfus 1986: 19–36).

According to Evan Selinger and Robert Crease, Dreyfus and Dreyfus's account of expertise consists of three claims: (1) the expert perceives the most important features of the context intuitively, (2) the expert can act in the context fluently, without having to pause for thought, and (3) the expert's subjective experience of their action has been transformed – the expert experiences their actions as being smooth, fluid, and essentially thought-less (Selinger & Crease 2006: 213–245).

As Selinger and Crease explain, the Dreyfus account has the following advantages:

i It does capture, in a phenomenological sense, what it feels like to be an expert. Expert action often appears effortless; in particular, novices who struggle to perform an action often admire the seeming effortlessness with which experts perform difficult actions.

ii Furthermore, the account explains a phenomenon that is familiar to all of us: that "overthinking"' or general overattentiveness to our performance can ruin a performance that we are well capable of making. (In sport, this is called "choking" or "the yips.")

However, the following criticisms are also often made against the Dreyfus and Dreyfus account.

i The Dreyfus account contains no helpful educational advice for fostering expertise. While it is possible, on the Dreyfus account, to instruct a novice how to become competent – by following the rules for the action – it is not possible to *teach* the proficient performer to become expert. The expert, on the Dreyfus account becomes expert themselves, through repeated doing; after all, there is no "rule" for "how to leave the rules behind." While the Dreyfus account encourages the aspiring expert to "let thought go" and "just do," it can offer no concrete advice on how *exactly* to improve, and, as we know, it is unfortunately common for people to "just do" things over and over, without ever getting better.

ii The Dreyfus account renders expertise subjective and makes it impossible for non-experts to measure or evaluate the degree of the expert's expertise. Recall that, on the Dreyfus view, expertise is embodied and is not capable of being codified in language. This emphasis on embodiment means that the expert, who contains their expertise in their body, cannot communicate it to another. As Steven Fuller puts it, phenomenology that stresses the "craft-like" character of expertise makes one think " … an act of professional judgement [is] tantamount to a magic trick … " (Fuller 2006: 148)

iii The subjectivity of expertise (point ii) also makes the authority of the expert hard to justify. Because the expert's level of expertise is only clear to *them* and not to non-experts, the expert cannot explain to the lay person why they should be trusted. Naturally, this raises the question of whether the expert really is expert – or whether they merely pretend to be expert.

iv The Dreyfus account has no place for expertise in rule-bounded activities. Much professional and skilled work is rule-bound. A prime example is the law: lawyers work with laws (rules) and their expertise consists in helping clients follow those rules. Likewise, we could say that the work of, for instance, police officers, air traffic controllers, and (even) sports umpires consists in ensuring that rules are followed. When it comes to forms of expertise like these, it would clearly be wrong to suggest that expertise amounts to "overcoming" rules or acting above and beyond the rules.

v Automaticity is not sufficient for expertise. From our own experiences, we know that there are many things that we can do automatically and without thinking about it, for instance, driving to work or making a cup of tea. However, it would be odd to say that, because we do these things automatically, we are "experts" at them (Selinger & Crease 2006: 213–245).

The Concept of Expertise in the Philosophy of Education

In the field of education broadly, those who write about expertise often approach the topic based on a prior research interest in practical vocational preparation rather than discipline-based or theoretical education. Many of those who write about expertise in education are already committed, either by their research focus, or by a prior theoretical position, to the skills or practice-based conception of expertise. In the philosophy of education, major contributions to thinking about expertise include books by Winch (2010a), Simpson and Beckett (2018), and Mark Addis and Christopher Winch (2019). On the whole, the discussion in the philosophy of education is more balanced, even though proponents of the skills-based view are still dominant voices in the field.

For instance, the papers collected together in Simpson and Beckett (2018) are avowedly "anti-cognitivist." Simpson and Beckett hold that the cognitivist program dominates in philosophy, cognitive science, and psychology.[4] They draw attention, however, to the countervailing line of thought that was influential in the 20th century, especially in phenomenology and in the (later) Wittgenstein (Simpson & Beckett 2014: 564). In his remarks on tool-use, for instance, Heidegger explains how we perceive objects in the world as instruments for achieving tasks (or raw materials to work on); objects become salient to us in their practical guise. Moreover, as Dreyfus and Dreyfus do fifty years later, Heidegger points out that working with these tools is largely automatic and that we perceive our tools as extensions of our own bodies (Heidegger 1962: 98). These ideas on tools and technology were later re-absorbed into analytic philosophy as the idea that the mind is "extended" and includes not only our brains, but also our bodies and, even, tools (Clark 2004, 2010).

Not only does the extended mind thesis put pressure on cognitivism about expertise, a number of authors also hold that the idea of the social or *distributed* mind challenges the idea that expertise is a cognitive grasp of techniques for performing actions. Paul Hager, for instance, stresses that occupational work is usually done in groups and that we quite naturally speak not of an individual person who can achieve some task, but of teams, companies, or economic systems as having developed or being able to provide a service or product (Hager 2014). This means, among other things, (1) that much practical knowledge is not held in the head of individuals, but is distributed around the group, (2) that much of this group knowledge is encoded in interaction between experienced members of teams and is therefore tacit, and (3) that expert knowledge is not known once and for all, but consists in constant team-based adaptation and change over time (Hager 2014).

Richard Menary and Michael Kirchhoff take ideas from both the extended mind tradition and the distributed cognition tradition to show that expertise is not "all in the head" but depends on immersion in cultural practices with technology (2014: 611-14). In earlier work, Menary (2007, 2010) notes the familiar point that pen and paper are cognitive tools, while in later work he stresses that these tools depend on cultures for their effectiveness (Menary 2013). For instance (my own example), when an engineer draws a complicated design (probably rubbing out and re-drawing multiple times) their thought is not in their head, but on the page. Moreover, the engineer's paper workings contain standard symbols, for instance the American Society for Mechanical Engineers' standard symbols for engineering drawing. The existence of the standardised engineering symbology saves the engineer the trouble of inventing symbols himself and makes his workings readable by other engineers using the same system; it therefore makes *available* a mode of thinking to him that was not available (a) without paper and (b) to him alone. Using the example of mathematics, Menary and Kirchhoff stress that even seemingly very intellectual expert knowledge and skill is not in the head, but can only be actualised through using culturally agreed modes of expression in physical form, such as on paper (Menary and Kerchoff 2014: 614–619).

Contra Simpson and Beckett, Michael Luntley warns against some of the excesses of the skills-based view in the philosophy of education. Luntley holds that the skills-based view dominates in the field of professional education. He notes how many writers in the education literature start with the relatively modest claim that there is *some* difference between knowledge that and knowledge how, but immediately take this to the strong conclusion that knowledge how must be understood in Dreyfusian terms (Luntley 2009: 356–359). First, Luntley deflates some of the phenomenological claims themselves: expertise does not in most cases consist in completely intuitive sensing and action that is devoid of thought. Compare (my own example) how the expert carpenter does not *intuit* how big a room is, *intuit* what size and shape furniture to install and then *automatically act* to create that furniture. The expert carpenter measures obsessively, draws multiple plans, costs them precisely, makes components to fit in the workshop, and often also needs to make new plans to fit together pre-made furniture components *in situ* during installation. It may appear an intuitive matter, but anyone who has done carpentry or seen a carpenter at work knows how much *thought* goes into successful furniture installation.

More than correcting Dreyfus and Dreyfus's phenomenology, however, Luntley also questions whether we should change our picture of the nature of practical knowledge or rationality based on the phenomenology of expert action. Luntley surveys the dispute between Dreyfus (2005, 2007) and McDowell (2007) on whether expert perception is qualitatively different from novice perception.[5] The dispute turns on whether expert perception is conceptual or not: for McDowell, perception is always conceptual in the sense that, in perception, we can notice particular objects or features, classify them, and then reason about them (either theoretically or practically). Dreyfus, on the other hand, argues that expert thinking about the practical world is *non*-conceptual: the expert does not think in terms of pre-existing categories but acts intuitively in the moment using actions that are wholly suited to that moment. Concepts are judgements of similarity ("this one is like these other ones") and for Dreyfus the height of acting expertly in a particular situation is that both the situation and the expert action are like no other (hence, non-conceptual).

Luntley takes McDowell's side in this dispute. He concedes that, phenomenologically speaking, expert perception appears different from novice perception. However, he holds that this is not because expert perception is non-conceptual, but because it is "activity-dependent" (2009: 359–364). Luntley stresses that activity itself (what activity one engages in and how) opens up new ways for the novice to perceive situations. For instance, the baker may demonstrate to her apprentice, while engaged in a round of baking, how to tell (through sight, smell, and touch) whether a loaf of bread is cooked. The fact that we have no word for how cooked bread looks, sounds, or smells, does not mean that we cannot bring to mind *that* look, sound, or smell. Luntley holds that, in the end, the perception that the expert engages is not mysteriously different from ordinary perception; the expert just knows what to look or listen out for.

Whereas Luntley offers an intellectualist and Simpson and Beckett an anti-intellectualist perspective on expertise, Winch offers an integrative picture. Winch's interest is more in practical expertise, and, indeed, the thrust of his work is to vindicate Ryle's conception of expertise in the educational context. Despite his overall anti-intellectualism, however, Winch retains considerable intellectualist sympathies. He holds that subject knowledge or expertise is often inextricably linked to practical expertise. Indeed, in his picture of vocational education, Winch gives an essential role to subject-based theoretical education ("underpinning knowledge") as part of an overall programme of vocational preparation (Winch 2010a: 98–116).

Winch reviews the intellectualism/anti-intellectualism debate that has sprung up in the wake of Stanley and Williamson's criticism of Ryle and he holds that the implications of Ryle's work for education have not adequately been spelled out. First, and most obviously, the nature of knowledge how will have implications for pedagogy and curriculum in vocational education. If it is true (as the intellectualists say) that knowledge how can adequately be captured in the form of propositional sentences describing ways or procedures to perform successful practical action, then vocational education can be conducted in a largely communicative or informative mode. However, if knowledge how cannot be captured adequately or completely in propositions, the "remainder" of knowledge how will have to be codified in curricula and taught in a different format. Drawing on Ryle's remarks regarding the "gradability" of knowledge how (Kremer 2021), Winch holds that the main thing that is *not* captured in propositional form is the fact that knowledge how admits of degrees. One either knows *that* something is the case or not, but knowledge *how* can be manifested in actions of varying levels of proficiency, from inexpert to fully expert. The *degree* to which one knows how to do something is described by what Winch calls "intelligence epithets." When we describe how someone does something, we use words like "hesitatingly" or "smoothly," "amateurishly" or "artfully." However, when we say that someone knows that something is the case, we do not qualify this with a description of *how well* they know it ... they just know it. Winch holds that intelligence epithets are a crucial part of the vocational educator's toolbox, but that an intellectualist conceptual scheme does not leave adequate space for them (Winch 2010a: ch. 2; Winch 2010b).

In order to furnish the right conceptual scheme for vocational education, Winch distinguishes between the "subject"[6] and the "occupational" sense of the word "expertise" (Winch 2010a: 2). Winch holds that Stanley and Williamson's intellectualist view of expertise is tied up with the subject view of expertise and may well make sense for that view; however, he argues that another conceptual scheme is needed to make sense of the occupational sense of expertise. For Winch, an occupation is a: "... practice of a traditionally established mode of economic activity, with its own internal identity and standards of excellence" (Winch 2010a: 15). He holds that the performance of many occupations (although not all) requires mastery of a specific body of occupational knowledge; however, above and beyond that, there is more that goes into having the knowledge to work in an occupation. Most real skilled work involves not only the application of one technique over and over again, but involves applying a wide range of skills in a number of different situations. Moreover, most real work involves working independently and in teams not only to perform actions, but to plan, coordinate, and evaluate what actions are to be performed in the first instance.[7] Winch holds that, in the occupational sense, expertise is not the execution of tasks in the most efficient way (in Stanley and Williamson's sense of "knowing the way to do something"), but more like the management of projects. He writes that what is important about working in an occupation

> ... is not the practice of a bundle of skills but the way in which they are integrated into a form of agency ... In Germany such occupational action capacity or *berufliche Handlungsfähigkeit* of, for instance, a carpenter, is not merely the set of skills that he possesses but the ability to practice in real-life conditions in such a way as to earn his living as a carpenter, to gain the respect of colleagues, apprentices and customers and to satisfy the criteria of excellence that are internal to carpentry.
>
> *(Winch 2010b: 560)*

Winch draws our attention to the fact that the expert is not just someone who has mastered the relevant techniques, but is an *agent* who plays a role or performs a function in the real world economy. What our conceptual scheme needs to capture is not just the techniques that the expert has mastered to perform specific actions, but the overall capacity of the agent to play an economic role.

Educating For Expertise

Authors like Winch, Simpson and Beckett, and Luntley have noted that the standard accounts of expertise do not provide much advice on how to *foster* the kind of expertise that is useful, occupationally speaking. This is the case not only for a cognitive account like that offered by Goldman, or by Stanley and Williamson, that equates expertise with knowing a technique. Oddly, it is also true of the Dreyfus account that is so influential in education. Simplifying considerably, one may hold that Goldman's account is an externalist one and Dreyfus and Dreyfus's account internalist. Goldman, after all, holds that expertise amounts to believing truths (and believing more truths than falsehoods). This makes his account objective or externalist. Whether one is an expert or not is settled by whether what one believes is largely true; and whether one's beliefs about empirical matters *are* true is not visible from the first-person point of view, but is only visible from the position of God (or from the position of the end of inquiry). Equally, one may say that Dreyfus and Dreyfus, have a rather subjective or internalist view of expertise. Like all phenomenologists, Dreyfus and Dreyfus are interested in the experience of becoming and being expert. In their account, they stress that expert knowledge is bodily knowledge, rather than mental knowledge – in itself, this point is neither objective nor subjective. However, Dreyfus and Dreyfus also hold that, to the expert him/herself, that bodily knowledge is experientially available and that the feeling of fluency in action and direct contact, through tools, with raw materials, is an essential aspect of expertise (see above). For Dreyfus and Dreyfus, it is the experts themselves who can best tell whether they are expert or not.

In itself, this observation (that Goldman's stance is external and Dreyfus and Dreyfus's internal) does not settle anything about what is the best philosophy of expertise; that question must be settled in its own terms. However, to the educator who is attempting to develop expertise amongst her students, each of these two accounts bequeaths a different problem. When we know what is the truth about some scientific matter and when we know how grasp of that truth translates to a practical technique to solve a practical problem, then it is obvious that the teacher should teach both that truth and that technique to foster expertise amongst her students. However, when the truth itself is in question, it is not helpful to say "teach the truth." Goldman's objective or truth-based account of expertise seems too externalist to be helpful in that case – what the educator needs instead is some immediately accessible guidance regarding what is most likely true or is most likely the best technique. On the other hand, whatever guidance the educator offers cannot be *too* subjective. When a student struggles to pick up some kind of skill, it is not helpful for the teacher to say, "just keep practicing until it feels to you as if you have become expert." What both student and teacher need in that case is a more objective standard for when performance counts as expert. What the practical educator (and their student) needs is an indication of whether expertise is developing in the right direction that is objective enough to be worthwhile, but subjective enough to provide educative guidance.

Winch counsels us, when studying expertise, to pay attention not only to individual skills, but to the productive work that experts do and to the occupations that they practise. Hardwig (1985) and Goldman also make clear that the reason *why* we have experts is to make possible the division of labor. So let us turn our eye away from devising a philosophical account of "expertise" to the question of how educators can promote the formation of experts as agents in a socio-economic system.

The reason for dividing labor between agents is that we are all cognitively and physically limited: one person usually cannot perform all the economic tasks needed for survival and, even if they could (*à la* Robinson Crusoe) survive in the wild all on their own, they could do still better by dividing work through sharing and specialising. Quast (2018a) notes, however, that the division of economic labor does not just depend on two or more people specialising in different techniques of production, it also depends on interpersonal trust. In the division of labor, the client must trust the expert enough to allow her to perform the relevant task for him; if the client does not allow the expert to "get on with the job," there is no division of labor. Moreover, the expert has to be worthy of the client's trust; if the client can perform a task for himself more easily (all things considered) than the "expert" could, then there would be no point in contracting the expert to do it.[8] As a result, systems to make salient how trustworthy an expert is and also how much the client in turn trusts the expert have developed. The trustworthiness of the expert is shown in something like a history of excellent expert work that has been acknowledged by other clients (which is why experts often exhibit their best work and collect accolades from past clients) and trustingness is shown in the discretion a client allows the expert (which is why the most expert experts are allowed to work independent of oversight). As Quast holds, our society has developed "reputational systems" that

> keep various forms of cooperation ongoing by identifying and assessing relevant authorities. The better the given rating, the more trustworthy the recognized authority, the more unrestrained the trust which is placed in it which, in turn, is accompanied by greater responsibility.
>
> *(Quast 2018a: 18)*

On this picture, the expert has to be able to do a better job than the client (this is an objective matter and may be a matter of better knowledge of technique than the client), but the client also has to know when to contract an expert and which expert to ask to do the job (this is a reputational matter). Goldman, one might say, focuses only on the objective or "supply side" of expertise and does not give much attention to the fact that the client will not contract the expert if they do not have some reputational reason to trust the expert (thereby overlooking the more subjective "demand side" in the division of labor). As Quast puts it, the expert needs, in addition to primary competence, also a ...

> secondary explanatory competence, the function of which is to establish and retain mutual trust between experts and clients ... [and] in order to establish and sustain mutual trust, experts also need to be appropriately virtuous, that is, must be disposed to properly estimate and communicate the scope and limitations of their competences and be willing to give an account of their performances when appropriate ...
>
> *(Quast 2018b: 407)*

These secondary competences are explored far less often in the literature on expertise and provide fertile terrain for the philosophy of education to investigate.

While pointing out the importance of secondary competences, Quast does not explain how they can be fostered through education. Luckily, authorities ancient and contemporary have advice in this regard. Plato, for instance, stresses that, next to being the master of a technique, the expert must also be able to "provide an account" (a *logos*) of their expertise, that is, be able to explain it. In a famous passage in the *Laws,* Plato contrasts a doctor of slaves with the free doctor who treats freemen. The doctor of slaves has learned his trade by experience (*empeiria*) and can give no *logos* for the treatments he administers; by contrast, the free doctor has a *logos* and communicates it to his patients. Gregory Vlastos holds that the free doctor acts like a teacher to their patients and does not give "... autocratic orders, but educates his patients into health" (Vlastos 1941: 289). In a voluntary division of labor, the expert who can "educate" rather than "order" will clearly be the expert who most wins a client's trust, so a *logos,* in Plato's sense, does seem to be an important expert competence. Aristotle expresses many of the same sentiments. It is well known that Aristotle regards a *logos* or right account to be a crucial part of moral virtue (Moss 2014). Aristotle holds that the same is true of technical virtue or *techne*; indeed, according to the definition he offers *techne* is "a state of capacity to make, involving a true course of reasoning (*logos*)" (Barnes 1984: 1800 [*NE* VI.4 1140a10]). Just as with the example of the more and less expert doctor, Aristotle also holds that a master craftsman (*technites*) is more expert than an artisan (*cheirotechnes*); being able to provide a *logos* of their craft they are able to teach their *techne* to apprentices or other learners.

In Ryle's work, we also saw a connection between being expert and either having undergone a certain course of education or training oneself and being able to educate others (in turn). Ryle does not hold that one must be *taught* something in order to have a certain skill; he holds it to be very admirable that we can sometimes teach ourselves to do something (and, indeed, technical progress is only possible on the basis that people can teach themselves to do entirely new things). However, Ryle holds that there is a logical connection between expertise and learning. Recall how Ryle stresses that "intelligence epithets" make sense to describe the performance of know how; judgements about how well a person does something, graded from inexpertly to expertly, are an integral part of know how (but not of knowledge that). For Ryle, it is the learnability of know how that underlies our uses of intelligence epithets when we speak about know how. As Michael Kremer puts it:

> ... the difference between learning-how and learning-that *explains* the facts about gradability. Knowledge-how must come in degrees, because learning-how brings *improvement* in knowledge-how.
>
> *(Kremer 2021)*

Moreover, as Winch explains, the improvement in question is "normative" (2010a); it is clearly *better* to act *more expertly* (and less amateurishly), making it part of the very concept of expertise that the expert strives to learn and to perform better.[9] This does not mean that it is not possible for the expert to do bad work on occasion; but it means that, conceptually, the expert is not only the one who performs well, but is aware that it is possible to perform even better and strives to perform better. This ever-present "room for improvement" is visible in the gradable language we use regarding expert performance, but it also makes sense in the context of the division of expert labor. If an expert is not always *trying* to do better work, they are not genuinely trying to make the division of labor work more efficiently – it is part and parcel of the idea of dividing labor that all role players must strive (at least in principle) to work ever more efficiently. Interestingly, the fact that striving to improve one's performance is part of being an expert leads Ryle to sounding a distinctly intellectualist note in his account of expertise: if the expert is going to be capable of evaluating their own performance and making improvements to it, the expert must "know what they are doing, in what circumstances, how well or poorly it is going, and so on ..." (Johansen 2021: 99–112). Because the expert monitors their own performance and tries to improve it, the expert's expertise is definitely not "mindless" as some have formulated the accusation against Ryle. This is also why Ryle, just like Plato and Aristotle, makes room for explanation of expertise to be part and parcel of expertise. As Ryle puts it:

> It is always possible in principle, if not in practice, to explain why he [a knower-how] tends to succeed, that is, to state the reasons for his actions. It is tautology to say that there is a method in his cleverness.
>
> *(Ryle 1945: 228)*

The relevance of education to expertise is not only that the education enables experts to acquire the primary and secondary competences necessary to be an expert, expertise is essentially an ability that is amenable to conscious improvement. Being an expert is, conceptually, the end result of a process of learning – a process that never truly ends. What expertise is, and how it is acquired and improved, must therefore always be considered in tandem.

(Related Chapters: 4, 5, 10, 11, 14, 28, 29.)

Notes

1 For overviews, see Bengson and Moffett (2011), Stanley (2011), and Montero (2016).
2 An excellent overview is Watson, (2021). Detailed discussions are collected in Fridland and Pavese (2021).
3 For a detailed discussion, see Watson (2021: 59–82).
4 They add to this list the philosophy of education – a conclusion that I doubt. See Winch (2010a).
5 See Schear (2013) for extensive discussion.
6 In the sense of "school subject": history, geography, mathematics, science, etc.
7 Sometimes, *not doing anything* can be work: compare the doctor who decides not to treat a complaint, the journalist who decides not to publish a story, or the police officer who decides not to make an arrest.
8 This is but one element of what is called the 'principal/agent' problem. For discussion, see Goodwin (2010).
9 Luntley (2009) makes the same point.

References

Addis, M. & Winch, C. (eds.) (2019) *Education and Expertise*. Oxford: Wiley. Previously published as: Addis, M. and Winch, C. (eds.) (2017) *Special Issue: Education and Expertise*, *Journal of Philosophy of Education* 51(3): 555–688.

Barnes, J. (ed.) (1984) *The Complete Works of Aristotle, Vol 2*. Princeton: Princeton University Press.

Bengson, J. & Moffett, M. (2011) *Knowing How: Essays on Knowledge, Mind and Action*. Oxford: Oxford University Press.

Clark, A. (2003) *Natural Born Cyborgs*. Oxford: Oxford University Press.

Clark, A. (2010) *Supersizing the Mind: Embodiment, Action and Cognitive Extension*. Oxford: Oxford University Press.

Coady, D. (2012) *What to Believe Now*. Oxford: Wiley-Blackwell.

Csikzentmihalyi, M. (1990) *Flow: The Psychology of Optimal Experience*. New York: Harper and Row.

Dreyfus, H. & Dreyfus, S. (1986) *Mind Over Machine*. London: Simon and Schuster.

Dreyfus, H. (2005) "Overcoming the Myth of the Mental," *Proceedings and Addresses of the American Philosophical Association* 7(2): 47–65.

Dreyfus, H. (2007) "The Return of the Myth of the Mental," *Inquiry* 50(4): 352–365.

Elgin, C. (2004) "True Enough," *Philosophical Issues* 14: 113–121.

Elgin, C. (2006) "From Knowledge to Understanding," in S. Hetherington (ed.) *Epistemology Futures*. Oxford: Clarendon, 199–215.

Fricker, E. (2006) "Testimony and Epistemic Authority," in J. Lackey & E. Sosa (eds.) *Epistemology of Testimony*. Oxford: Oxford University Press, 225–250.

Fridland, E. & Pavese, C. (eds.) (2021) "Introduction to the Routledge Handbook of Skill and Expertise," in *The Routledge Handbook of Skill and Expertise*. London: Routledge, 1–26.

Fuller, S. (2006) "The Constitutively Social Character of Expertise," in E. Selinger & R. Crease (eds.) *The Philosophy of Expertise*. New York: Columbia University Press, 342–357.
Garfield, J. & Priest, G. (2021) "Skill and Virtuousity in Buddhist and Daoist Philosophy," in E. Fridland & C. Pavese (eds.) *The Routledge Handbook of Skill and Expertise*. London: Routledge, 29–39.
Goldberg, S. (2009) "Experts, Semantic and Epistemic," *Nous* 43(4): 581–598.
Goldman, A. (1999) *Knowledge in a Social World*," Oxford: Oxford University Press.
Goldman, A. (2018) "Expertise," *Topoi* 37(1): 3–10.
Goodwin, J. (2010) "Trusts in Experts as a Principal-Agent Problem," in C. Reed & W. Tindale (eds.) *Dialectics, Dialogue and Argumentation: An Examination of Douglas Walton's Theories of Reasoning and Argument*. London: College Publications, 133–143.
Hager, P. (2014) "Practice and Group Learning," *Educational Philosophy and Theory* 46(6): 584–599.
Hardwig, J. (1985) "Epistemic Dependence," *Journal of Philosophy* 82(7): 335–349.
Heidegger, M. (Trans: Macquarrie, J. & Robinson, E.) (1962) *Being and Time*. London: Blackwell.
Hikins, J. & Cherwitz, R. (2011) "Dimensions of Expertise: Why 'Reality' and 'Truth' Matter and How We might Find Them," *Social Epistemology* 25(3): 291–308.
Johansen, T. (2021) "Techne in Aristotle's Taxonomy of Knowledge," in E. Fridland & C. Pavese (eds.) *The Routledge Handbook of Skill and Expertise*. London: Routledge, 76–87.
Kremer, M. (2021) "Gilbert Ryle on Skill as Knowledge-How," in E. Fridland & C. Pavese (eds.) *The Routledge Handbook of Skill and Expertise*. London: Routledge, 100–112.
Luntley, M. (2009) "Understanding Expertise," *Journal of Applied Philosophy* 26(4): 356–370.
McDowell, J. (2007) "What Myth?" *Inquiry* 50(4): 338–351.
Menary, R. (2007) *Cognitive Integration: Mind and Cognition Unbounded*. Basingstoke:Palgrave Macmillan.
Menary, R. (2010) "Cognitive Integration and the Extended Mind," in R. Menary (ed.) *The Extended Mind*. London: MIT Press, 227–244.
Menary R. (2013) "Cognitive Integration, Enculturated Cognition and the Socially Extended Mind," *Cognitive Systems Research* (25–26): 26–34.
Menary, R. & Kirchhoff, M. (2014) "Cognitive Transformations and Extended Expertise," *Educational Philosophy and Theory* 46(6): 610–623.
Montero, B. (2016) *Thought in Action: Expertise and the Conscious Mind*. Oxford: Oxford University Press.
Moss, J. (2014) "Virtue and Phronesis in Aristotle's Ethics," *Phronesis* 59(3): 181–230.
Oakeshott, M. (1962) *Rationalism in Politics and Other Essays*. London: Methuen.
Polanyi, M. (1958) *Personal Knowledge: Towards a Post-critical Philosophy*. Chicago: University of Chicago Press.
Polanyi, M. (1966) *The Tacit Dimension*. London: Routledge.
Quast, C. (2018a) "Expertise: A Practical Explication," *Topoi* 37(1): 11–27.
Quast, C. (2018b) "Towards a Balanced Account of Expertise," *Social Epistemology* 32(6): 397–419.
Ryle, G. (1945) "Knowing How and Knowing That," *Proceedings of the Aristotelian Society* 46(1945-6): 1–16.
Ryle, G. (1949) *The Concept of Mind*. Chicago: University of Chicago Press.
Schear, J. (2013) *Mind, Reason and Being-in-the-World: The McDowell-Dreyfus Debate*. London: Routledge.
Scholz, O. (2009) "Experts: What They are and How We Recognize Them – a Discussion of Alvin Goldman's Views," *Grazer Philosophische Studien* 79(1): 187–205.
Selinger, E. & Crease, R. (eds.) (2006) *The Philosophy of Expertise*. New York: Columbia University Press.
Simpson, D. & Beckett, D. (2014) "Introduction," *Special Issue: Expertise, Pedagogy and Practice, Educational Philosophy and Theory* 46(6): 563–568.
Simpson, D. & Beckett, D. (eds.) (2018) *Expertise, Pedagogy and Practice*. London: Routledge.
Stanley, J. (2011) *Know How*. Oxford: Oxford University Press.
Stanley, J. & Williamson, T. (2001) "Knowing How," *Journal of Philosophy* 98(8): 411–444.
Turner, S. (2001) "What is the Problem with Experts?" *Social Studies of Science* 31(1): 123–149.
Vlastos, G. (1941) "Slavery in Plato's Thought," *Philosophical Review* 50(3): 289–304.
Watson, J. C. (2021) *Expertise: A Philosophical Introduction*. London: Bloomsbury.
Winch, C. (2010a) *Dimensions of Expertise*. London: Bloomsbury.
Winch, C. (2010b) "Vocational Education, Knowing How and Intelligence Concepts," *Journal of Philosophy of Education* 44(4): 551–567.

13

STOIC LESSONS FOR AN UNCERTAIN FUTURE*

Nancy Sherman

The Stoics teach us to be prepared for worst-case scenarios: pre-rehearse what they call "the bads" in life, dwell in the future, imagine what might happen so that we can better face the slings and arrows of fortune. They also teach us to be vigilant about interpretations and bias: control begins by monitoring attention to the impressions to which we give assent. In addition, they counsel "mental reservation," a kind of hedging of bets, so that we can become more adaptive in the face of changing information. These are basic Stoic techniques for mitigating fear and cushioning against vulnerability in uncertain times. Silicon Valley dubs them Stoic lifehacks, workarounds for what the Stoics would call "the art of living."

But what is often missed in the modern Stoicism conversation is the idea that we are socially interdependent, and resilience depends not just on individual will, but on social support. We are "woven together" by a "common bond," with "scarcely one thing foreign to another," the Stoic Roman Emperor, Marcus Aurelius writes, telegraphing an earlier ancient Greek Stoic image, from Stoicism's founder Zeno, of a cosmic city (Aurelius 2011: Bk. 7.9). Our preparedness to face the present and future depends on our own will and the will of others in coordinated, well-informed, and cooperative efforts. As we face increasing anxiety and uncertainty in today's teaching environment, exacerbated by a pandemic, catastrophic climate change, persistent racism, and more, what are ancient Stoics' lessons for modern resilience? Are Stoic methods of strengthening our will at odds with the Stoic sense of social connection? I argue that they are not, but the story requires an immersion in Stoic terms and concepts.

External Goods become Indifferents

Marcus's image of our social connectedness is powerful. Jotting notes to himself during the Germanic campaigns, he paints a visceral picture. The detritus of the battlefield is on his mind: Picture a hand and head lying apart from the rest of the body. This is what a person makes of himself when he cuts himself off from the world. We can't be "at home in the world," a Stoic catchphrase, if our good is reduced to self-interest or our resilience is reduced to self-reliance.

* This essay is adapted from my book *Stoic Wisdom: Ancient Lessons for Modern Resilience* (Sherman 2021) with permission of Oxford University Press © 2021 Nancy Sherman.

DOI: 10.4324/9781003172246-16

Still, it is hard to square the Stoic idea of social connectedness with their view that our vulnerability rests in things precisely outside our own virtue. One way the Stoics try to make the case is by arguing that external goods, good friends and family, enlightened political institutions and communities, social esteem and respect – all these are not themselves part of happiness. They grant common sense and say these are things that, in general, we are naturally attracted to as human beings. They are "preferred." Their opposites are things that, in general, we naturally avoid. They are "dispreferred." But they insist that their presence or absence cannot make or break happiness. They are not *real* goods, as Aristotle had insisted. Rather, they are "indifferents" – for they do not make a difference to happiness positively or negatively. For all that, they still play a substantive role in our lives. Indeed, virtue involves wisely selecting or rejecting them. Wise selection or rejection requires learning a new skill set of affective and behavioral attitudes that can help us navigate how we engage with those externals, including our attachments to others.

The view is challenging, no less in ancient times than now. But one thing crucial to remember is that the term "indifferents" (*adiaphora*) does not mean "indifference." We are by birth and breeding neither indifferent to these goods or bads nor should we harden ourselves to become so. Still, learning to live in a Stoic way requires fundamental recalibration of values. In particular, we need to learn behaviorally and not just intellectually that preferring or dispreferring indifferents involves going for them or avoiding them in a way that isn't filled with restless yearning or panicky aversion. So not only do the Stoics have a different valuation system for what other ancients more broadly thought of as real goods or their opposites. In addition, they carve out a distinctive kind of approach and avoidance behavior toward them that is meant to inculcate calm – we go for externals without sticky, acquisitive attitudes; we reject others without fearful avoidance or anxious dread. Learning how to cultivate those new attitudes is part of Stoic training. And the striving critical to stabilizing that new value scheme is itself a Stoic way of life. So, while the Stoic sage may be too exalted a model – the human turned divine – the sage arrived where she is through strategies for minimizing the deleterious impact of what is truly outside our control. And these are strategies, the Stoics teach, for all of us to adopt. They are what is involved in aspiration and moral progress.

Assent to Impressions

Tempering vulnerability begins by drawing a line between our psychological faculties and what lies outside. Epictetus famously opens the *Encheiridion* this way: "Some things in the world are up to us, while others are not. Up to us are our faculties of judgment, motivation, desire, and aversion – in short, everything that is our own doing. Not up to us are our body and property, our reputations, and our official positions – in short, everything that is not our own doing" (Epictetus 2018: Ch. 1). Many of us would protest right off the bat at where the line is drawn. Even if we can't fully avoid disease, penury, ignominy, loss of work or safe homeland, some of us can do some things some of the time to protect our health, material means, the communities we live and raise our children in, the quality of our relationships, and so on. Epictetus grants that. But at some point, he argues, our armor and efforts, even that of the most privileged and secure among us, will be no match for natural or human-made misfortune. That is Epictetus's core claim: We are all hostages of fortune in some way or other.

Fine. We can grant him that. But we still might object that there is no hard line between controlling what is outside and what is inside. For after all, what's inside is vulnerable, too. Our capacity for judgment might be impaired by traumatic brain injuries or an aging brain or other disabilities, our cravings not in line with what we want to want, our fears pathological phobias rooted in psychological syndromes we wish we didn't have. Equally, there are epistemic biases. What we see may be tainted by implicit bias and what we judge to be the case may be less "our doing" than the product of privileged standpoints and access. This is, of course, a modern view of the psyche and of knowledge. The Stoic view, by contrast, is radically volitional. In significant ways, not often recognized by interpreters, they expand what is within our control. Indeed, the Stoics will go on to argue that we can turn our gaze not only outward but inward so that we can monitor patterns of attention and cognitive bias.

The locus of control on the Stoic view is our assent to impressions, or how things seem to us from the sensory input from outside and from within. Assent is the mechanism by which we tacitly say "yea" or "nay" to that input. It is the volitional moment in judgment, motivation, desire, or aversion. So, we may assent to a perceived insult as an evil, a bad thing that is distressing, or to disease as a perceived threat to be feared, or to wealth as a perceived good to be desired and acquired, or to a relationship as something we can't imagine living without. Each of these is an evaluative judgment – an acceptance that what appears is a good or bad. In the case of evaluative judgments that are emotions, such as anger or fear, or desire, or pleasure or distress, the evaluations are "umphy"; they engage us affectively and impel us (through "impulses" or *hormai)* to action. They are motivational. *Hormê* is the cognate of our word "hormone," and like that organic substance, it stimulates action. But it does so through the mediation of the mind.

Seneca explains it this way: "Anger is undoubtedly set in motion by an impression received of a wrong. But does it follow immediately on the impression and break out without any involvement of the mind? Or is some assent by the mind required for it to be set in motion? Our view is that it undertakes nothing on its own, but only with the mind's approval" (Seneca 1995: Bk. 2.3–4). Emotion is, thus, a kind of voluntary action (Seneca 1995: Bk. 2.4). Through assent we implicitly frame and grasp the world propositionally and act on the resulting opinions or judgments. Emotions involve agency.

Epictetus insists that with agency comes responsibility: "It is not things themselves that trouble people, but their opinions about things … So, whenever we are frustrated, or troubled, or pained, let us never hold anyone responsible except ourselves, meaning our own opinions" (Epictetus 2018: Ch. 5). The idea is intuitive. We are inveterate interpreters at the most basic level of perception, seeing a penny, to take a simple example, as having three-dimensional depth when we really only see its flat two-dimensional face. We always see and assess from what philosophers call an "epistemic standpoint."[1]

But as we said, we are not always free spontaneously to choose those standpoints. How we see may be others' impositions, sometimes invisible – "hidden persuaders," whether through the work of those with power and authority or social media influencing our opinions. How we see or interpret situations can also be the result of systemic and profound forms of domination. So, a teenage girl's crippling sense of shame as a rape victim may be someone else's opinion that she has internalized. The work of patriarchy and shaming runs deep. Similarly, a young altar boy's fear of a pedophilic priest's continued assaults may get muted by the priest's sacred robes and his avuncular role at the Sunday family table. The inner world can be a socialized construct. And it isn't always an enlightened place for freedom or peace. Yet it may be a retreat when external forces give few other options. The young boy finds safety in his mind, even if through psychological dissociation. Epictetus, himself once enslaved, finds inner freedom when outer freedom isn't possible. Subordinated, pressured, or in captivity, we push our will to the limit.

We can push the limit out fairly far, but again, we may be constrained by access to input, blinders we don't even know we wear, intense pressure from authorities, as well as sheer fatigue or fear of adverse consequences. Assent to impression, or its opposite, suspension of assent, itself has limits in giving us freedom.

Still, the Stoic approach to mental discipline always involves trying to strengthen effortful will and slow down impulsive thinking that can cloud our judgment.

What are other Stoic techniques for being proactive in the face of an uncertain future?

Pre-rehearsal of Bads

One of the better-known Stoic mental exercises for training for uncertainty is pre-rehearsing future evils or bads. The idea is this: Try to anticipate the traps that lie ahead. Don't be caught off guard. The exercise goes back to the early Greeks. Cicero approvingly quotes a fragment from Euripides:

> I learned this from a wise man: over time
> I pondered in my heart the miseries
> to come: a death untimely, or the sad
> escape of exile, or some other weight
> of ill, rehearsing, so that if by chance
> some one of them should happen, I'd not be
> unready, not torn suddenly with pain.
> *(Cicero 2002: Bk. 3.29)*

Euripides, he says, in turn, takes a lesson from the pre-Socratic Anaxagoras who legend has it said when his son died, "I knew my child was mortal." The Stoics turn the teaching into a pre-meditation exercise: Regularly rehearse potential future evils to mitigate the shock of accident and tragedy (Cicero 2002: Bk. 3.30).

I don't think I have ever uttered Anaxagoras's remark in an undergraduate class on Stoic ethics without my students being horrified at the message. They roll their eyes in disbelief. It's cold and callous, they say. They can't believe I'm expecting them to take Stoicism seriously, if that's what it teaches. It's as if I told them then and there that their parents don't love them or were willing to abandon them any moment. It takes a lot of back-pedaling to make the Stoic message appealing. I typically do. And I begin with the fact that the Stoics, and especially Epictetus, went in for shock and awe. He clearly succeeded. Still, the gist of the message, I suggest, is quite humane: we shouldn't run from the fact of our mortality. (Kiss your child good-bye in the morning as if it might be the last time.) To stop running from the fact of our mortality takes work. It takes daily pre-rehearsal and a willingness to actually think about potential losses. The Stoics claim that if we do, we can mute some of the "freshness" of a sudden loss. The Greek term here for "fresh" is telling. *Prosphatos* connotes not nearness in time, but "rawness," as in freshly slaughtered meat (Cicero 2002: Bk. 3.52).[2] We need advance exposure if we are to weaken the visceral assault of close-up losses. The technique, presumably, involves more than just an incantation of words: "I always knew my child was mortal." "Dwelling in advance" (Cicero 2002: 222) may take immersion in imagination,[3] but also some teasing and love, both tokens of attachment.

When my mother, Beatrice Sherman, was in her mid-nineties and in a nursing home, I often thought about how we would talk about death. She was healthy, but I knew the end would soon come and I knew her well – that she wanted to avoid talking about death at all costs. She wasn't a talker at the best of times. When I asked her about a book (she read three or four novels a week) I was lucky if I got out of her, "It was fine." That was her standard response: "Fine." Life was fine. She wasn't a complainer. But she was into denial of death. And so at some point, I decided we would have to make a joke of it. I would ask every so often as we talked about how much she liked the Hebrew Home and her caregivers and friends. "Remind me, Mom. We didn't sign up for the immortality plan, did we?" "Because if we did, it's going to be really expensive!" She would smile gently. She was very beautiful. And she chuckled a bit. Of course, she never said the words: "I always knew I was mortal." But she thought the idea. She couldn't talk about death. It just wasn't her style. But I think our little repeated pre-rehearsal, our joke and my teasing about the immortality plan, made her last days easier for both of us. We shared our mortality, and we shared not dreading death, together. Pre-rehearsing mortality didn't diminish our attachment. It helped us practice our shared loss.

My mother died just three days after we danced together, she in her wheelchair, and I swirling her around with other "couples" on the "dance floor" at the nursing home. She had been coughing a lot the week before, and we both knew that the end might be near. The antibiotics weren't working. The nurses were monitoring her closely. We spent the last day together, in her room, facing death together. Our little whimsical joke about the immortality plan was preparation, she for leaving this world and me for saying good-bye and that it was going to be on my mom's terms: "fine."

Pre-rehearsal, as I've intimated, is a form of pre-exposure, a desensitization ahead of time. If events don't occur, then we take it as a gain (Cicero 2002: Bk. 3.58). In the case of death, the question is only when. Through pre-rehearsal, we don't deny attachment. We frame it by accepting loss.

There are contemporary, clinical parallels to the notion of pre-rehearsal. Some may be more familiar with exposure techniques that work on desensitization after the fact. Clinicians have for some time successfully used evidence-based prolonged exposure (PE) therapy after the fact, to reduce posttraumatic stress disorder (PTSD). PE is a form of cognitive behavioral therapy (CBT, itself with roots in Stoicism),[4] during which patients confront (*in vivo* or through imagination) situations or events that are reminders of traumatic situations, though now experienced in safe settings. Through repeated approach, rather than avoidance, the fear response is deconditioned rather than reinforced. Take the case of military service members exposed to the constant threat of improvised explosive devices. Survival depends on quickly responding to those threats. But the fear response can become overreactive. Hypervigilance is adaptive in a war zone, but not always after war, at home when thunderclaps are heard as gunfire, fresh bumps on a pavement read as newly planted bomb sites, a black plastic bag on a lawn a hiding place for an explosive. Re-exposure to stressors by talking about them, seeing them in virtual settings, revisiting and processing memories in a relationship where there is trust and safety becomes a way of deconditioning both the avoidance response and hyperreaction. The "neutral" garbage bag on a lawn or new bump on the neighborhood road over time loses its associated negative valence (Hendriks et al. 2018).

In more recent studies, researchers have begun to investigate pre-treatment exposure. "Attention bias" (or to cast the idea in Stoic terms, our assent to impressions) is modulated by balancing focus between threat and neutral stimuli. The idea is to learn to shift attention, so that we develop perceptual and cognitive resources for focusing not just on threat, but on neutral situations. Research suggests that advance training of this sort in shifting focus between threat and unthreatening stimuli reduces anxious hypervigilance characteristic of PTSD (Badura-Brack et al. 2015; Lazarov et al. 2019; Ilan Wald et al. 2013). In a related research experiment, Israeli Defense Force combat soldiers in units likely to face potentially traumatic events were exposed to "attention bias modification training" sessions (Wald et al. 2016: 2633). Through computer programs, they were trained to attend to threat "in an attempt to enhance cognitive processing of potentially traumatic events." The idea is to make the response to stress cues adaptive and agile: elevate the response in acutely threatening situations in combat, but train it to be transient, so that it recedes in safe circumstances.

Again, we can put a Stoic gloss on this: train in advance to withhold *inappropriate* assent to impressions of threat by engraining alternative patterns of assent to impressions of calm and safety. In the classroom setting, think of this in terms of inculcating agile responses to live shooters or other grievous threats. We want students and teachers to be alert to threats. But we also want the classroom to be a safe haven and not a place of anxious hypervigilance or constant fear. We want to elevate the response to threat as appropriate by pre-rehearsal. But we want also to train agility in pivoting our focus so that pre-rehearsal exercises don't leave us traumatized, robbed of anything positive or more neutral to dwell on.

The Stoics go on to suggest that pre-rehearsal may reduce the compounding effects of secondary distress – or as Cicero reports, the distress that we were caught off guard and "might have been able to prevent" what happened (Cicero 2002: Bk. 3.58). Of course, "hindsight bias" can be magical thinking – a tendency, after the fact, to overestimate our ability to predict an outcome. "Should-have's" and "could-have's" can be grandiose ways of misattributing responsibility. Sometimes, they are ways of coping with grief or survivor guilt, as I learned in my work with military service members returning from deployments in Iraq and Afghanistan. We take moral responsibility in order to make sense of what seems senseless or what "shouldn't have happened."[5] We replace flukish luck with failed moral agency. Moral injury, the extreme moral distress of real or apparent moral transgression, as agent, victim, or bystander can result.[6] Conscientiousness becomes overwrought and anguished. But moral conscientiousness needn't always be anxious. Many ways of being prepared, and being responsible for being prepared, are far from irrational or overwrought. They are what good people, and especially those responsible for others, whether in a classroom, battlefield, or hospital, do to take care of themselves and others. This is consistent with Stoic notions of taking preparation seriously at a personal and societal level.

Still, Stoic pre-rehearsal, if it focuses only on the glass half-empty and not half-full, can seem a recipe for inducing anxiety. Reducing future distress comes at the cost of increasing present distress. Even if we are agile and poised to move quickly to positive scenarios, we still may find ourselves ruminating about worst possible cases, dwelling on how we would react to bad news, becoming preoccupied with adversity and loss. We are in battle-mode before there is a war to fight. But again, there are good and bad ways of being future-minded. Strategic thinking, risk analyses, long-term planning, coordinated and collaborative efforts, are all ways to mitigate disaster that help reduce the emotional overlay of individual debilitating fear or depression. They are not necessarily ways of being alarmist, but ways of being realistically prepared.

Anticipating a natural or medical disaster, such as extreme climate change or a pandemic, is a collective enterprise, managed, we hope, by enlightened institutions and public local and global structures. But anticipating profound personal loss is something else. And we all have different resilience levels, having to do with psychological, social, political, and historical factors and more.

Epictetus suggests we can train for personal loss of loved ones by gradually increasing the stakes: we move incrementally from rehearsing small potential disturbances to great ones: "In the case of everything that attracts you or has its uses or that you are fond of, keep in mind to tell yourself what it is like, starting with the most trivial things." He suggests we start with a jug: "If you are fond of a jug, say: "I am fond of a jug. Then, if it is broken, you will not be troubled." Again, the advice makes no sense if it's just a verbal incantation – tacit or expressed. Let's try to fill it out. We give ourselves advance warning. I say to my husband, as I recently did: "I really adore this Richard Batterham large fluted celadon crock. I'm going to be really upset if either one of us breaks it." What's unsaid but both of us are now cued up to think: "let's be careful." And that might lead to a conversation, again, half tacit, half spoken, about whether it's the end of the world if it breaks: "It's meant to be used." "Storing the bread in it now is a perfect use for it." "We'll be really careful." "Why have it if we don't use it?" "And if it breaks, well, it breaks."

Maybe something like that is what Epictetus is inviting us to rehearse. It's all too fast in his formulation. But, after all, we're not at his lectures in real time, milling around with other students, listening, analyzing, and interpreting. We're doing it now, some two thousand years later. We are putting into practice his therapeutic counsel: trying to imagine rehearsing loss at the same time as we think about recalibrating our values concerning what really matters. We're trying to test how Stoic we are. If we are in the classroom, and teaching about Stoic techniques of pre-rehearsal, we illustrate with examples that catch a student's interest, as I once did with a famed basketball player in my class. How does he rehearse the idea that he might get injured before a really important game, or have to sit out a season? What does the mental exercise look like? How does he prepare himself to cushion the blow?

Epictetus teaches that we pre-rehearse by gradually widening the sphere of practice. In his own exercises, he moves from breaking a jug to being around annoying people who could ruin your day:

"If you go out to bathe, picture what happens at the bathhouse – the people there who splash you or jostle you or talk rudely or steal your things" (Epictetus 2018: Ch. 4). Remind yourself about what you might expect. The case, again, hits close to home. I often think about going to the Y at the end of the day for an outdoor swim, in winter and summer, and in winter, in non-pandemic times, a post-swim warm-up in the hot tub or sauna. But the locker room is often crowded with screaming teens coming in from swim team practice. Are they going to be there today? Is it a practice day? Did I time my visit just right? If they're there, it's not what I want at the end of a tough day. But now, if I'm listening to Epictetus, he's telling me "If at the outset" I say to myself: "I want to bathe, but I also want to keep my will in harmony with nature," that is, in sync with how things turn out, then I'm less likely to "get angry about what is happening" (Ch. 4). It makes sense. I will have given myself an advance talking to. I'm armed. If the swim team girls are giggling and gossiping at high volume, then it won't be what I wanted initially, but I may be better poised to adjust expectations.

Epictetus then graduates from these relative triflings to what's most pressing in our lives. The now familiar anecdote gets embellished: "When you kiss your little child or your wife, say that you are kissing a human being. Then, if one of them dies, you will not be troubled" (Ch. 3).

Wait: This is a steep progression: from a broken jug to the loss of a loved one with an unruly throng at the bathhouse somewhere in between. Pre-rehearsal may give you a perspective on mortality, but to think that it averts grief suggests both the worst parts of Stoicism and psychologically unsound ways of dealing with loss.

Is there a way to humanize the view? The following may help. Stoic mental preparation involves working one's way up to tough tests that we might face and know we would if only we had fuller, divine-like knowledge of how things will unfold. Some of those future scenarios and counterfactual reactions to them (If this were to happen, then I would …) we might now find outright crazy. But if circumstances were really different – if, for example, I knew I was destined to be ill, explains Epictetus, then "I'd have an impulse to be ill." I'd want to be "in sync" with nature. And too, if my foot had a mind, there would be times, as absurd as it may seem, when it "would have an impulse to get muddy" (Epictetus 1925: Bk. 2.6.9; Long & Sedley 1987: 58J). That is, what are now "dispreferred indifferents" might in another context be preferred and appropriate to select. "Seeing that we do not know beforehand what is going to happen, it is appropriate to adhere to what is by nature more suited for selection" (Epictetus 1925: Bk. 2.10.5–6; Klein 2015: 267–268). Of course, we don't know what it is "to adhere to what is by nature" in the absence of knowing nature's full secrets and how and when they will be disclosed. But what we *can* do is train to be adaptive and prepare ourselves for what is hardest – the worst, even if we hope for the best.

Pandemics are again a salient case. With guidance from expert epidemiological and policy teams, economists and medical researchers, educators and technology experts working with teachers can take steps to prepare. They can begin to work out the implications of quarantines for teaching remotely, including wide disparities in technological equipment in homes and in broadband internet access. Full preparation for understanding the implications of a pandemic is impossible, as we know. The Stoics would argue that is why we also must prepare for the personal and emotional toll that comes with calamity. We all need to know the attitudes that travel with disaster – anxiety, dread, massive sorrow and grief, loneliness, dislocation, and more. And we need to know the sources of comfort and support that come from others and humane institutions.

There is no way we can be immune from psychological distress. Nor would we want to be. Moreover, any armor that claims to fully protect is a scam, a fool's errand. Still, there are Stoic lessons we can learn about possible ways of minimizing and managing distress both on a personal and institutional level. And pre-rehearsal is at its core: Try to make hardships that are distant and almost unthinkable real and proximate. And then imagine best responses in those hard cases – what is a pathway forward? That's a critical way to humanize the account.

Are there other Stoic techniques for preparing for uncertainty?

Hedges and Reservations

In addition to pre-rehearsal, the Stoics teach us to frame our plans and intentions in a way that mentally prepares us for the possibility that things might not work out as we'd like them to. They advise this technique: Tag on to your intentions, or as they say, impulses toward preferred indifferents, a tacit mental reservation: "if nothing happens to prevent it." We can think of the strategy as a way of hedging bets. Things may not work out. Always think of what you intend to do as tentative (Inwood 1985: 119–126). Again, be agile and flexible.

Here's Seneca illustrating the mental technique: Say to yourself: "I will set sail *unless* (*nisi si*) something interferes." "I shall become praetor [a Roman magistrate] *unless* something thwarts it." "My business will be successful *unless* something interferes" (Seneca 1932: Bk. 13.2–3, italics added). Epictetus invokes a similar idea, reminding his listeners about effective ways to modulate attitudes toward indifferents: Given we are not sages, what is "up to us which it would be fine to desire," are not now present to you. "So use only impulse and aversion, but lightly, with reservation and in a relaxed way" (Epictetus 2018; Brennan 2000: 151). Epictetus's points are compressed and in Stoic idiom. The gist is this: As non-sages, we don't yet have stable access to fine or noble desires directed at the only real good, virtue. Instead, what we have at our disposal are impulses (and aversions) directed at indifferents. In going "light" on those impulses, we avoid excess and strain, the ache of yearning and the anxiety of panicky avoidance. Mental reservation adds the thought like that of the cautious bather at the public bathhouse: It may be noisy there. Readjust your expectations. What you find may not be what you originally hoped for.

But what exactly is the advice here? Should we always qualify impulses so they become fail-proof? Impulses, on this gloss, would come with built-in cushions, a bit like car airbags that inflate upon impact in an accident. Formulated in the right way, impulses and desires can't disappoint. They come with psychological immunity. But do we really want to make ourselves, bullet proof, immune to loss?

Perhaps a better way of thinking about reservation is on the financial trading model. Most of us are familiar with the tagline that's standard in market prospectuses: "past performance is no guarantee of future results." It's a warning not to assume an investment will do well in the future just because it did well in the past. Market climates change. We have to be adaptive. But equally, what did poorly in the past may just as easily be an opportunity in the future. Either way, we have to be agile, not as market timers, but as investors poised to re-balance on a regular basis to meet target asset allocations as markets change.

This financial frame is actually a useful way of thinking about key Stoic texts on mental reservation. So, to return to Seneca's example: I'll go on a boat ride. But I'll change my plans (and intentions) if I notice that a storm is setting in. I plan to campaign for election. But I'll change my plan if my bid for election seems highly unlikely. I'll live in this beautiful family house until we both reach a ripe old age. But I'll change my plan if I notice I can't keep up with the upkeep or garden. And so on. We aim for responsiveness to new information.

We do this in our personal lives and our professional lives. In counseling our students, when they ask for our help when they apply to graduate or professional schools, we review their transcripts, the schools they want to apply to, the faculty there, their track record in placing gradates in jobs, etc. We try to get our students to be flexible, to think about what's next if they don't get into their dream schools or land the job they've trained for. We want them to be agile, to change course, if necessary, and especially so, in a world undergoing cataclysmic changes.

To sum up, the Stoics offer profound lessons for our times. If the fundamental point behind mental reservation is cognitive agility, facing facts squarely, trying to keep up with fluid informational landscapes, then the Stoic kernel idea is less about how to beat frustration than about how to change motivations in ways that align with new and reliably curated information. In a similar way, pre-rehearsal of bads is a way of training agility by not being stuck in the present. We need to "dwell" in the future, even and especially in imagining worst-case scenarios that otherwise we would prefer to avoid. The idea is not to become inured to what is distressing, but to give ourselves practice in facing it. Similarly, by monitoring patterns of assent, we review our repertoire of beliefs and actions, assessing where we should suspend assent when we may have assented too easily. All of these are mental exercises in becoming more adaptive and resilient in facing uncertain futures.

Resilience and the Social Fabric

I began this essay by saying that overall Stoic resilience will come not just from our strengthened will, or capacity to imagine worst-case scenarios, or mental reservation that teaches agility in our plans and strategies. We become resilient by reaching beyond ourselves and seeking and accepting the sustaining support of others. Marcus, the Stoic emperor on the battlefield, facing loss and death, knows that he commands a cadre, legions in a campaign, in fact, to connect more and more of humanity. His words are not empty when he reflects to himself that we are "woven together" by a "common bond." Aristotle, without the militarism or global reach, would say we are "social animals."

The Stoics never deny the social fabric. But they are acutely aware of our vulnerability in the face of it. Through their notion of preferred indifferents, and the recalibrated attitudes and behavior that go with it, they urge us to learn how to be connected and supported in ways that can mitigate paralyzing attachment or disabling chronic grief. We do this by exercising the very same pre-rehearsal and mental reservation techniques we reviewed earlier. We don't deny the sustaining role of others – of friendship, love, and healthy relationship – in our lives. Our development and well-being depend on them. But our resilience also depends on finding ways to adapt to the very vulnerability that comes with attachment. Here, too, the way to face that vulnerability is by pre-rehearsing loss – dwelling, proactively and calmly, in the future. And this includes the ultimate rehearsal of the mortality of those we love.

(Related Chapters: 3, 4, 10, 14, 35.)

Notes

1 For a wonderful discussion with insight into the current philosophical literature, see (Ward 2020). For critical work in this area, see (Fricker 2007).
2 The Greek term suggests this: *prosphatos*, rawness as in newly slaughtered, "fresh" meat (Long & Sedley 1987: 65B, Andronicus *On passions* 1: *SVF* Bk. 3.391).
3 That is the traditional and educative role of ancient tragedy – a *mimesis*, or imitation of life. See reflections on this and tragic accidents in Aristotle's *Poetics* (Sherman 1992).
4 Both Albert Ellis and Aaron Beck, founders of an early version of CBT, acknowledge the debt: (Ellis 1962; Beck 1975). Note, there has been a move within the military community to use the term posttraumatic stress (PTS), dropping the "D" for "disorder" which many find stigmatizing. One argument often made is that servicemembers don't come home from war with "limb disorders," but "limb injuries." Psychological injuries should be viewed with parity. Others argue that in so far as posttraumatic stress is a *normal* response to an *abnormal* situation of overwhelming life threat, the notion of a "disorder" gets the response wrong. I have used "PTSD" in the above discussion simply for consistency, because the literature I go on to cite on pre-exposure uses the term.
5 I call this "accident guilt" in Sherman (2010). See also Sherman (2011).
6 For extended discussion of this, see Sherman (2010, 2015).

References

Aurelius, M. (2011) *Meditations* (R. Hard, trans.). New York: Oxford University Press.
Badura-Brack, A. S., Naim, R., Ryan, T. J., Levy, O., Abend, R., Khanna, M. M., ...Bar-Haim, Y. (2015) "Effect of Attention Training on Attention Bias Variability and PTSD Symptoms: Randomized Controlled Trials in Israeli and U.S. Combat Veterans," *The American Journal of Psychiatry* 172(12): 1233–1241.

Beck, A. (1975) *Cognitive Therapy and the Emotional Disorders.* Madison, CT: International Universities Press.

Brennan, T. (2000) "Reservation in Stoic Ethics," *Archiv für Geschichte der Philosophie* 82: 149–177.

Cicero (2002) *Cicero on the Emotions: Tusculan Disputations 3 and 4* (Graver, M. ed.). Chicago: University of Chicago Press.

Ellis, A. (1962) *Reason and Emotion in Psychotherapy.* Oxford: Lyle Stuart.

Epictetus (1925) *The Discourses as Reported by Arrian, The Manual, and Fragments* (W. A. Oldfather, trans.). Cambridge, MA: Harvard University Press.

Epictetus (2018) *Encheiridion,* in *How to be Free: An Ancient Guide to Stoic Life. Encheiridion and Selections from Discourses* (A. A. Long, trans.). Princeton: Princeton University Press.

Fricker, M. (2007) *Epistemic Injustice: Power and the Ethics of Knowing.* New York: Oxford University Press.

Hendriks, L., de Kleine, R. A., Broekman, T. G., Hendriks, G.-J., & van Minnen, A. (2018) "Intensive Prolonged Exposure Therapy for Chronic PTSD Patients following Multiple Trauma and Multiple Treatment Attempts," *European Journal of Psychotraumatology* 9(1): 1425574–1425574.

Inwood, B. (1985) *Ethics and Human Action in Early Stoicism.* Oxford: Oxford University Press.

Klein, J. (2015) "Making Sense of Stoic Indifferents," *Oxford Studies in Ancient Philosophy* 49: 227–281.

Lazarov, A., Suarez-Jimenez, B., Abend, R., Naim, R., Shvil, E., Helpman, L., ...Neria, Y. (2019) "Bias-contingent Attention Bias Modification and Attention Control Training in Treatment of PTSD: A Randomized Control Trial," *Psychological Medicine* 49(14): 2432–2440.

Long, A. A., & Sedley, D. N. (1987) *The Hellenistic Philosophers,* Vol. 2. Cambridge: Cambridge University Press.

Seneca (1932) "On Tranquility of Mind" (J. W. Basore, trans.), in *Moral Essays,* Vol. 2. Cambridge, MA: Harvard University Press.

Seneca (1995) "On Anger" (J. M. Cooper & J. F. Procope, trans.), in *Moral and Political Essays.* New York: Cambridge University Press.

Sherman, N. (1992) "Hamartia and Virtue," in A. O. Rorty (ed.) *Essays on Aristotle's Poetics.* Princeton, NJ: Princeton University Press, 177–196.

Sherman, N. (2010) *The Untold War: Inside the Hearts, Minds, and Souls of Our Soldiers.* New York: W. W. Norton & Company.

Sherman, N. (2011) "War and the Moral Logic of Survivor Guilt," *New York Times.* Retrieved from https://opinionator.blogs.nytimes.com/2011/07/03/war-and-the-moral-logic-of-survivor-guilt/

Sherman, N. (2015) *Afterwar: Healing the Moral Injuries of Our Soldiers.* New York: Oxford University Press.

Sherman, N. (2021) *Stoic Wisdom: Ancient Lessons for Modern Resilience.* New York: Oxford University Press.

Wald, I., Degnan, K. A., Gorodetsky, E., Charney, D. S., Fox, N. A., Fruchter, E., ...Bar-Haim, Y. (2013) "Attention to Threats and Combat-related Posttraumatic Stress Symptoms: Prospective Associations and Moderation by the Serotonin Transporter Gene," *JAMA Psychiatry* 70(4): 401–408.

Wald, I., Fruchter, E., Ginat, K., Stolin, E., Dagan, D., Bliese, P. D., ...Bar-Haim, Y. (2016) "Selective Prevention of Combat-related Post-traumatic Stress Disorder using Attention Bias Modification Training: A Randomized Controlled Trial," *Psychological Medicine* 46(12): 2627–2636.

Ward, K. (2020) *Standpoint Phenomenology* (Ph.D. dissertation). Washington, D.C.: Georgetown Univeresity.

14
CHARACTER EDUCATION

Paul Watts and Kristján Kristjánsson

The Nature, Importance, and Current State of Character Education

We understand the term "character education" in this chapter to encompass any form of holistic moral education focusing on the systematic development of virtues as stable traits of character, with the aim of promoting human flourishing (*qua* objective wellbeing) and founded on some general virtue theory, be it philosophical (about virtues as morally valuable universally) or psychological (about virtues as universally valued morally). On this understanding, character education forms a specific subset of moral education which, in turn, forms a subset of general values education. Character education has had a checkered and tumultuous history (Arthur 2020) and continues to accommodate fairly different theoretical, disciplinary, and practical perspectives. We want to do justice, as far as possible, to the multi-dimensionality of character education in what follows.

The most obvious answer to the question of why character education is important is: "because character is important." But why is character important? We know that people spend a lot of their time reflecting upon, discussing, and gossiping about other people's character; moral character traits like honesty register higher with users of dating sites than any of the amoral Big-Five personality traits; many employers are more interested in the potential character of employees than their formal qualifications; and character education at school has been shown to elicit (modest) increases in grade attainment (Berkowitz & Bier 2005). While these are practical considerations, recent academic work has also highlighted the way in which good character is both conducive to and constitutive of overall wellbeing, which is widely considered the "ungrounded grounder" of all human efforts, including educational ones (Aristotle 1985; Peterson & Seligman 2004).

While scholarly interest in character education has traditionally been confined mostly to specialists in Ancient Greek moral philosophy (Annas 2011), educational philosophers (Curren 2010), and educationists (Berkowitz 2002), psychology has recently become its greatest growth industry (Fowers et al. 2021; Wright et al. 2021). This retrieval of character-and-virtue research in psychology, referred to as a new "science of virtue" (Fowers et al. 2021), has been spurred on by the advent of positive psychology and in particular its research into universal character strengths (Peterson & Seligman 2004; McGrath 2015). Defying historic anti-virtue catechisms in psychology (Kohlberg 1981), positive psychologists have conducted extensive research into the role of good character in the flourishing life (Seligman 2011). However, renewed efforts at integrative and interdisciplinary work on character education have left various mines in the ground, to be excavated in subsequent sections. As an educational phenomenon, there has been something of a revival of character education in the past ten

DOI: 10.4324/9781003172246-17

years, including in Asia and South America where character education is underpinned by a variety of philosophical approaches and cultural contexts. Character education now has a place within school timetables as part of formal or informal education curricula – for example in Singapore, Japan, Korea, and the United Arab Emirates. Closer to the present authors, since 2012, character education has featured as a priority set out by Secretaries of State for Education in the U.K. An outcome of those efforts is that character education now features in government guidance for school leaders in England (Department for Education 2019) and within the school evaluation criteria set out for school inspectors (Ofsted 2019). Major funders such as the John Templeton Foundation and Kern Family Foundation have helped establish a strong research base for character education, both in the U.S.A. (where character education is also undergoing a retrieval) and internationally, and, as a result, approaches have become better grounded theoretically and empirically.

Some Key Concepts and Unique Features of Character Education

The key foundational concept in character education is typically not "character" but rather "flourishing" or "living well" (*eudaimonia*). Normative and empirical claims are then made about how flourishing requires (or at least is taken to require by most people) the actualization of certain traits or states of character, called virtues. Character is here understood to comprise a certain subset of more general personality traits: namely, that part of personality which is reason-responsive, morally evaluable, and educable. General personality traits, such as the Big-Five ones of openness, conscientiousness, extraversion, agreeableness, and neuroticism, are to a large extent genetic and not amenable to education; however the character traits are taken to be more malleable, context-sensitive, and responsive to coaching (Kristjánsson 2015). That said, the more general personality traits can facilitate or hinder the development of character traits. For instance, a person constitutionally prone to agreeableness may find it more difficult to develop the virtue of honesty but easier to exhibit compassion.

The most basic kinds of character traits are typically called "virtues" and "vices"; hence character education can be described as education "in" or "for" virtue. Virtues are here taken to be settled (stable and consistent) traits of character, concerned with praiseworthy conduct in specific (significant and distinguishable) spheres of human life. Each character trait of this sort typically comprises a unique set of attention, emotion, desire, behavior, and a certain comportment or style of expression. The compassionate person thus notices easily and attends to situations in which the lot of others has been undeservedly compromised, feels for the needs of those who have suffered this undeserved misfortune, desires that their misfortune be reversed, acts for the relevant (ethical) reasons in ways conducive to that goal, and exudes an aura of empathy and care (Kristjánsson 2015). The terms "virtue" and "vice" strike some people as old-fashioned, outdated, or even religiously tethered (Allen & Bull 2018). However, "virtue" can be replaced with words such as "character strength" or "positive character quality" if doing so is necessary to making it more linguistically palatable.

In traditional character-and-virtue theories, such as those of Aristotle and Confucius, each virtue is considered to form a medial state between two extremes of deficiency and excess (with courage *qua* golden mean between cowardice and foolhardy fearlessness given as the standard example). Moreover, at least in Aristotle, each virtue is contextualized vis-à-vis *developmental level, social position,* and *individual constitution.* For example, emulousness is a virtue for young people whereas adults ideally do not need to emulate role models. Magnanimity (*megalopsychia*) is a virtue for people blessed with unusually abundant material resources but not for ordinary folks. Temperance in eating is not the same for the Olympic athlete as for a novice athlete, because what is intermediate in virtue is relative to the individual, "not in the object" (Aristotle 1985: 43 [1106b1–7]). And, from an educational perspective, a boxing instructor will not "impose the same way of fighting on everyone"

(1985: 295 [1180b9–11]). When coupled with the Aristotelian thesis that each individual needs an intellectual meta-virtue to secure the successful integration of potentially conflicting moral virtues (Darnell et al. 2019), this concession about the individualization of one's virtuous make-up imports difficulties when trying to administer characterological interventions across groups of different individuals, such as all students in a given classroom.

Various different virtue taxonomies exist. One of the more prominent ones divides virtues into four categories of moral, civic, performative, and intellectual – with one of the intellectual virtues, namely *phronesis*, also accorded a special metacognitive place as a virtue adjudicator (Jubilee Centre for Character and Virtues 2017). This taxonomy derives strength from its historic grounding in Aristotle's distinction between moral virtues, intellectual virtues, and technical skills, although he did not distinguish as cleanly between moral and civic virtues. More recently, a 3-or-4 factor taxonomy along similar lines has garnered support from empirical analyses of millions of people's self-reported character strengths across the world (McGrath 2015), although the self-report instrument in question was originally built upon a different 6-factor taxonomy (Peterson & Seligman 2004).

Philosophically, character education is perhaps best described as the educational incarnation of virtue ethics. According to virtue ethics, an action is right not because it is required as one's duty in accordance with a formalistic principle (as in Kantianism) or because it has desirable overall consequences (as in utilitarianism) but because it exhibits good character. In contrast to other moral theories, the concept of good character is thus what is foundational in virtue ethics, rather than the concepts of duties or consequences, and what defines acting well is derivative or a matter of what is consistent with good character. However, the term "virtue ethics" needs to be understood quite permissively, as the term has been ascribed to philosophers as distinct as Plato, the natural-law Stoics, and Nietzsche. For present purposes, the sort of virtue ethics that need concern us is mainly of the Aristotelian kind, according to which an action is right when it enhances virtue and contributes to a flourishing (*eudaimonic*) life, or simply "living well" (Curren 2015) – as opposed to a languishing or floundering one. Here, the focus is no longer so much on the correctness of individual actions as on their role in the well-rounded life and their roots in the "inner world" of the agent: in stable states of character that incorporate motivational and emotional elements. What matters in the end for moral evaluation is not merely observable behavior, but the emotions with which an action is performed, the motivation behind it, and the manner in which it is performed. Since Aristotle-inspired character education is about the development and enhancement of virtue, it is not concerned with "prosociality" in the same sense as many other paradigms of moral education. "Prosociality" is a behavioral concept, and behavior can be prosocial without being virtuous (e.g., uncritically and unreflectively following another person's lead to do a good thing) and virtuous without being prosocial (e.g., showing justified anger which happens to upset and alienate people).

Although the recent surge of interest in character education coincides with the rising profile of virtue ethics, especially of the Aristotelian kind (Curren 2010), in moral philosophy (harking back to Anscombe 1958), it would not be far-fetched to design character-educational interventions also along the lines of the consequentialist Mill or the deontologist Kant, as neither theorist expunged virtues completely from their moral theories. Indeed, on closer inspection, the aforemetioned characterization of character education as the incarnation of Aristotelian virtue ethics invites various difficulties. First, the very idea of a moral theory informing and guiding a developmental/educational program is itself problematic (Curren 2015). Second, Aristotle never saw himself in the business of designing an ethical theory, with eliciting from it an educational theory as a subsequent independent task. He did not consider the task of ethical inquiry to be *theory*-construction in the first place, but rather considered it a branch of practical inquiry that he described as "political science" (1985: 2 [1094a27–28]).

Third, the characterization of Aristotelian virtue ethics as a "moral theory" and Aristotelian character education as a theory of "moral education" is misleading in various ways: most conspicuously because Aristotle did not have the term "moral" (on a modern understanding) at his disposal in the first place. He was interested in *ethical* (meaning, in ancient Greek, "having to do with character") and *civic* (social, communal) virtues, but he had no term like "moral" to either combine them under a single umbrella or to limit their meaning with respect to various other aspirations that moderns would consider non-moral (for example, related to psycho-physical health). Aristotelian character education is about "living well" in a much more general sense than that captured by most moral theories and theories of moral education. This is why Aristotle would find a modern minimalist justification of moral education (such as offered by Hand 2018) strangely limited at best, seriously misguided at worst. Every educator must, *ex hypothesi*, be in the business of helping students find ways to "live well." Such efforts will by necessity transcend the boundaries of what moderns call "moral"; they relate to character development in a more general sense, and as such they are not "optional"; rather, they are what education is all about. Only the most serviceable strategies to achieve this remain a matter of choice.

Notice also that the current interest in anything character-related in some pockets of social science is not rooted in virtue ethics in a philosophical sense at all, but rather in an empirical virtue theory, which simply states that it so happens that more or less the same virtues are valued universally – without taking a stand on whether such valuing is philosophically warranted or not, because that is seen as an inherently normative and hence an unscientific question (Peterson & Seligman 2004).

For philosophers of education, character education may be seen as an object of unique interest, as it combines insights from philosophy, education, and other areas of social science in ways that are fairly unusual in academia. However, here is the disappointing news for philosophically oriented readers. Given its historical provenance in Aristotle-derived virtue ethics, one would expect the critical discourse about character education in the West to revolve around questions of how an ontologically realist and epistemologically rationalist moral outlook (such as Aristotle's) can be justified practically, and how character educators will respond to the "self-centeredness" and "non-action-guiding" objections standardly lodged against virtue ethics. However, those issues are rarely elicited in the literature, and it is even moot whether some varieties of character education, such as the positive psychological one, are morally realist rather than anti-realist or – with regard to virtuous emotions – rationalist rather than sentimentalist. This does not mean that character education is uncontroversial academically (see subsequent section on controversies); it simply means that the areas of discord are not necessarily those that will be topmost in the minds of academic philosophers.

Different Approaches to Character Education

Some recent criticisms of character education assume that there is a single network or community of thinkers promoting this approach (Allen & Bull 2018). However, that is an over-simplification. Indeed, the divisions among proponents of character education are no less prominent than any common assumption that may seem to unite them under a single umbrella. Notably, each of the "varieties" or "approaches" on offer comes with its distinctive pros and cons. We only have space to address four approaches.

US-style Character Education in the 1980s–1990s

This approach, often associated with Thomas Lickona's influential work (1991), signaled the resuscitation of a characterological emphasis after decades of neglect, during which rationalist approaches ruled the roost in moral psychology and moral education (Kohlberg 1981). Lickona's book offers a treasure trove of methods for classroom implementations and in many ways paved the way for all subsequent efforts. Yet, this approach came under criticism for being behavioristically (rather than virtue ethically) grounded, conservative, individualistic, and religiously motivated (Kohn 1997).

Confucian Character Education

Character education along Confucian lines is rooted in an ancient Chinese tradition that has, recently and somewhat unexpectedly, been retrieved in mainland China. While similar in many ways to the Aristotelian approach to character education fleshed out later, Confucianism has more to say on moral learners' "spiritual" and "enchanted" attachments to abstract moral ideals (Yu 2007). On the other hand, it does not lend itself as easily to scientific inquiry as does Aristotelianism, nor does it account as well for the social determinants of virtuous conduct, assuming rather that no external exigencies can harm the morally good individual. Moreover, some concepts in Confucianism, such as "Heaven" and "the Way," will appear alien to non-Chinese educators and students.

Positive Education

Character education forms a substantial part of what is known as the educational incarnation of positive psychology, called positive education (Seligman 2011), although it also includes non-characterological elements. As it is meant to absorb the best of traditional approaches, positive education reproduces many of the merits of Confucianism and Aristotelianism. However, it makes do without any meta-virtue of *phronesis*, as well as without a theory of virtue as a golden mean, assuming rather that "the more is better" in any virtue. For example, gratitude as a virtue (on which a lot of positive psychological work has fastened) can and should evidently be boosted indiscriminately, without fear of any "gratitude excess." Moreover, positive psychologists' ambivalent attitude towards questions of normativity and their predominantly instrumentalist stance (see next section) tend to alienate philosophically oriented educationists (Kristjánsson 2015).

Aristotelian Character Education

Neo-Aristotelian thinking characterizes some of the most prominent and popular approaches to character education in recent times, as already indicated. Its appeal lies in various factors, such as (a) a naturalistic methodology according to which all moral and educational theorizing is answerable to empirical research and hence revisable; (b) its explicit grounding in a blueprint of the good life *qua* flourishing; (c) the nuanced developmental story it tells about how virtues are acquired; (d) its focus on critical thinking and reflection at the post-childhood stage of character development, hence deflecting worries about indoctrination and lack of autonomy; (e) its emphasis on the need for intellectual virtues (Roberts & Wood 2007), not least to oversee metacognitive virtue adjudications; (f) its sensitivity to socio-political contexts and its rejection of a purely individualist stance, hence offering a bridge from character education to civic education; (g) its highlighting of the emotional features of good character; and (h) its practical down-to-earth stance which resonates well with teachers and other practitioners (Curren 2010; Annas 2011; Kristjánsson 2015, 2020; Jubilee Centre for Character and Virtues 2017; Peterson 2020).

However, neo-Aristotelian character education also has its potential weaknesses: (a) Because of its early-years determinism about character cultivation, it may seem to have little to offer people "brought up in bad habits," nor be able to make sense of radical moral transformations later in life; (b) it leaves the transition from early-years habituation to subsequent critical *phronesis*-guided moral thinking explanatorily underdeveloped; (c) it does not account for the idea of personal authentic purpose as part of a flourishing life (because the concepts of a personal purpose and authenticity originated much later than Aristotle's time); and (d) it does not address questions about how virtue (development) can be evaluated.

It could be argued that those weaknesses only hit at traditional Aristotelian, rather than neo-Aristotelian, character education, as the earlier-mentioned naturalistic methodology should enable us to figure out contemporary solutions to them. Nevertheless, the discussion in this section is meant to alert readers to the fact that there are various approaches to character education competing for allegiance, and there is no reason to think that the "best" one has yet been developed fully.

Why is Character Education Controversial?

Character education remains controversial, both politically and academically. Politically, character education finds itself in a precarious position in the politico-educational landscape. More precisely, it often ends up in the squeezed-middle position of coming under attack from both the political left and the political right. Leftists accuse it of disregarding social structures and focusing instead, in politically naïve or even reactionary ways, on fixing individual students (Suissa 2015). Right-wingers renounce character education for importing one more brand of "psycho-babble" into classrooms, at the expense of pedagogic rigor (Young 2014). Interestingly, character education in the U.S.A. tended to be criticized more from the left (e.g., Kohn 1997), because of its association with conservative politics, but character education in the U.K. from the right (Young 2014), because of its historic links to left-wing politics. Recently, however, the U.K. has also seen criticisms emerge from the left, alleging that character education is grounded in a neoliberal ideology (Jerome & Kisby 2019).

Insofar as neo-Aristotelian approaches have gained traction recently both in the U.S.A. and the U.K., and insofar as the criticisms from the left and the right are targeted at those approaches, they seem curiously misdirected, however (Kristjánsson 2021). With regard to the former, Aristotelian politics has historically been criticized for being too collectivist rather than individualist, and it appears as more socially progressive than conservative by today's standards (Peterson 2020). With regard to the latter, neo-Aristotelian character education is not grounded in a paradigm of the fragile child who needs to be shielded from academic rigor, but rather in a paradigm of the flourishing child who needs to be challenged further (Walker et al. 2015).

To turn to academic debates, those are varied and concern a multiplicity of issues that are at the heart of character education (Kristjánsson 2015: chap. 2); we can only offer some glimpses here. To begin with debates that are *internal* to the character education camp – insofar as it can be seen as a single camp – those have recently become crystallized along a single main dividing line, separating a positive psychological model from a virtue ethical, Confucian, or Aristotelian, one. To summarize and simplify the differences between these models, the first one – which tends to be promoted by business organizations, civil servants, politicians, and many practically minded social scientists – understands character as encompassing the "non-cognitive" side of personality skills (so-called "soft skills"), whereas the virtue ethical model understands character in terms of the morally evaluable part of personality. The main substantive focus in the first model is on performance virtues such as grit, resilience, and self-confidence, and on how those broaden and build personal resources, whereas the second model prioritizes moral and civic virtues such as compassion, justice, and honesty. Accordingly, the first model considers the main value of the virtues to lie in their instrumental benefits for better behavior, higher grades, and better workplace performance, while the second model highlights the intrinsic value of the virtues for the flourishing life of which they are constitutive (although grades and performance will also supposedly improve as a happy side-effect). Finally, the positive psychological model assumes that a chain of virtues is as strong as its strongest link, with little attention paid to virtue conflicts, trade-offs, and painful adjudications. In contrast, the virtue ethical model assumes that too much of a virtue becomes a vice, just like too little, and that a chain is only as strong as its weakest link – with significant attention being paid to virtue conflicts (Kristjánsson 2015). To outsiders, at least, the relationship between these two "sub-camps" may appear confusing and ambivalent (Jerome & Kisby 2019). On the one hand, harsh critiques by one camp of the other are common (e.g., Arthur et al. 2016); on the other hand, efforts seem to be afoot to synthesize the insights of the two factions (e.g., Arthur et al. 2021).

External academic critiques of character education typically address the very construct of character. Two will be mentioned here briefly: the situationist and social intuitionist challenges. According to *situationism* (Doris 2002), grounded in famous social psychological experiments such as the Milgram and Stanford Prison ones, no stable character traits exist and all moral reactions are situationally determined. In response, some theorists partial to virtue ethics and character education emphasize cross-situational consistency as evidenced by "density distributions" of virtue-relevant actions (Jayawickreme & Fleeson 2017), while others insist on within-situation-type consistency only (Ng & Tay 2020). A common response is to point out that situationists (wrongly) understand virtues behavioristically. For example, they would record the sight of a person handing money to a beggar as "generous," while that of person refraining from giving as "ungenerous." However, as already explained, current character educationists (at least from the neo-Aristotelian camp) tend to have little interest in behavioral tendencies but rather in reason–action combinations. Someone might give money to a beggar for non-virtuous reasons that have nothing to do with generosity, while another could refrain from giving for reasons that are fully virtuous.

Social intuitionism understands moral reactions as determined by (mostly genetically determined) intuitive-emotional processes, with "reasons" only offered *post hoc* as rationalizations rather than serving as true motivations (Haidt 2001). Social intuitionists either deem those insights incompatible with the virtue theories underwriting character education, or actually compatible – on closer inspection – with the automaticity typically presupposed in accounts of how character motivates action. It must be said, however, that any potential resemblance of a dual-process social intuitionist model of moral decision-making (Haidt 2001) to (at least a neo-Aristotelian model of) character education is illusory. While *phronetic* decision-making will wind up being automatic to a large extent in a mature person encountering familiar situations, this is not because reason has been circumvented by irrational, intuitive emotional thrusts, but rather because the characterologically developed person has, through precedents and prospection, anticipated (most often unconsciously) the proper reactions to future scenarios (Railton 2016).

In general, external critiques of character education apply standard psychological misgivings about virtue ethical theories to the developmental and educational story character educationists like to tell, although more fundamental philosophical issues are often eschewed. The extent to which those critiques are considered to succeed depends largely on the extent to which one sees virtue ethics as painting a realistic and warranted picture of moral life.

How to Teach Character Education

There is no singular approach to teaching character education. While some countries have established a formal character-education curriculum for schools, there is no formal blueprint for "what works." In recent years, however, the creation of various research-informed character education models and frameworks (e.g., Character.org 2018; Berkowitz 2021; Jubilee Centre for Character and Virtues 2017; Seligman 2011) have helped to ensure that principles of effective practice are shared and commonly understood at various levels within education: primary, secondary, undergraduate, postgraduate, and professional.

While each model/framework outlines its own key principles of teaching character education, a common theme underpinning contemporary approaches is that character can be *caught* and *taught*, as well as *sought* by students themselves (Jubilee Centre for Character and Virtues 2017). Caught character education relates to the inspirational and positive ethos, culture, and vision of the school or organization and is highly reliant on the teachers (and wider school community) who model good character and influence students through emotional contagion and staff-student relationships (Arthur et al. 2017a; Harrison et al. 2016b; Jubilee Centre for Character and Virtues 2017, 2020; Sanderse 2013). Taught character education relates to the experiences that "equip students with the language, knowledge, understanding, skills and attributes that enable character development" (Jubilee Centre for Character and Virtues 2017: 9). Planned and intentional approaches to teaching character education are wide-ranging and we outline a few examples later. Approaches might target specific virtues (e.g., honesty or compassion) or components of virtue (e.g., virtue knowledge and understanding, virtue reasoning, etc.). To be effective, it is important that taught approaches to character education account for students' prior learning and experiences, providing opportunities for students to reflect on and relate the virtue(s) to their own lives and experiences (Watts et al. 2021). Sought character education relates to the "varied opportunities that help students over time to seek, desire, and freely pursue their character development" (Jubilee Centre for Character and Virtues 2017: 9). As such, sought character education is reliant on both school provision and students' internal motivation to develop their own character.

Teachers and other prominent adults in the school community are influential character educators. Though parents and care-givers in the home are regarded as children's most consistent and significant sources of moral and ethical guidance, teachers also share in this responsibility during schooling. Through their position and influence in students' lives, teachers naturally share responsibility for students' character development, as character is taught by, and essentially caught from, teachers who are role models and exemplars. The vast majority of teachers acknowledge their influence and responsibility as role models (Arthur et al. 2015); however, it is notable that explicit role modelling is rarely employed by teachers (Sanderse 2013). As such, teaching is often regarded as an implicit form of character education, where teachers influence students through their character and presence, behaviors, and relationships (Arthur et al. 2017b).

Increasingly, however, teachers are also tasked with teaching character education explicitly through the school curriculum. Character education can be taught through explicit lessons and programs, but also through integration within other subject lessons through a co/cross-curricular approach, the wider curriculum, and through extracurricular learning or "enrichment" opportunities, such as social action, or "service-learning" (Watts et al. 2021). While different curriculum models exist, a "spiral curriculum" model has been recommended for taught character education (Arthur et al. 2017b). A spiral curriculum model engages students in a process of "personal experience and practice, information gathering and documentation, reflection, analysis and internalization, and informed action, then round again, as if moving up a spiral" (Arthur et al. 2017b: 71). Based on this model, teachers are encouraged to teach students about different virtues and to revisit these regularly at differing levels of complexity, and through different activities, providing students with varied experiences and opportunities for reflection.

While the distinction between character caught, taught and, sought is analytically valuable, in practice approaches aimed at teaching character do not tend to target each in isolation. Case studies and examples of good practice, shared by teachers and researchers in the field, evidence various approaches through which character can be caught, taught, and sought in tandem (Arthur et al. 2017b; Berkowitz 2021; Harrison et al. 2016b; Watts et al. 2021). Common approaches to teaching character education across the curriculum include: seeking to inspire and motivate students by teaching about the lives and actions of role models and exemplars (Sanderse 2013); learning through others' experiences by discussing, debating, and reflecting on quandaries and problems faced by protagonists from literature and the arts (Bohlin 2005); and providing rich and meaningful experiences for students to enact and practice virtues, for example through enrichment and social action opportunities (Lamb et al. 2019).

Similar strategies are also employed and advocated in higher education with approaches aimed at cultivating character and creating "leaders of character" within the professions (Lamb et al. 2021). Within postgraduate character education, emphasis is also placed on providing experience and opportunities to reflect on professional practice; raising awareness of (professional/institutional) situational variables influencing character and behavior; encouraging or creating moral reminders (e.g., recalling moral commitments); and forming friendships with exemplars who are relevant and attainable (Lamb et al. 2021).

How to Evaluate Character Education

Philosophers tend to approach questions of practical evaluations in the field of character from a normative perspective. They are interested in the question of whether a given trait is admirable and worthy of emulation, and why – and should it pass that normative test, whether it is intrinsically or instrumentally valuable, or possibly both. Philosophers might also question whether good character – even if assessable in theory – should be measured at all for any (presumed) practical purposes. Would the disadvantages and potential hazards of doing so perhaps outweigh the benefits?

More practically oriented character educationists usually either sidestep those fundamental questions or take a positive answer to the general measurement question for granted. When evaluating character education in schools, those practically minded character educationists face two important subsidiary questions, however: whether evaluation should be formative or summative in nature, and whether evaluation should be focused at the level of individual students, or at that of the program/whole school. Due to the high-stakes nature of schooling, teachers may be tempted to undertake summative assessment, assigning character grades for individual students in order to track progress. However, while the holistic assessment of each student's character would be illuminating, the "messy theme" of virtue measurement (see Kristjánsson 2015: chap. 3) poses significant challenges. Furthermore, schools and teachers are advised to consider whether it is useful, or appropriate, to undertake summative assessments of character. Indeed, it may be more viable and appropriate to draw on indicative measures of character or components of virtue as part of ongoing and formative evaluation (Curren & Kotzee 2014).

Factors considered crucial to successful self-evaluation of character education include drawing on teachers' professional judgments and the perspectives of the wider school community, and the triangulation of data collected through mixed methods and through multiple sources of evidence (Harrison et al. 2016a). Watts and colleagues (2021) also outline numerous sources of evidence and tools that schools can use to inform evaluations of character education and understand their impact, including drawing on schools' academic, attendance, and behavior data.

To understand the efficacy of character education approaches, character educationists also require viable strategies to measure students' character development within the constructs targeted by specific programs. However, the measurement of character is regarded as "character education's profoundest problem" owing to the notable absence of "tried-and-tested instruments to concretise and measure moral virtue" (Kristjánsson 2015: 61) and an over-reliance on (subjective) self-reports. Within the fields of education, philosophy, and psychology, interest in various methods of virtue measurement has continued to increase (Fowers et al. 2021; Wright et al. 2021). While it is not our intention to provide a comprehensive overview of developments in measurement methods, we highlight some popular and commonly used approaches that can be used to measure changes in students' character virtues. For readers with a specific interest in virtue measurement, Wright and colleagues (2021) pay significant attention to virtue measurement, including that of single virtues, and virtue groups and clusters that are interrelated.

Self-report methods such as the Values in Action Inventory of Strengths (VIA-IS) (Peterson & Seligman 2004) and its youth adaptation (VIA-Youth Inventory) are commonly used to understand individuals' self-perceived character strengths (McGrath 2015; Park & Peterson 2006) and could be utilized in the evaluation of character education to identify changes in signature strengths. Another form of self-report, Experience Sampling Method (ESM) (Larson & Csikszentmihalyi 1983), involves self-reporting over time, typically multiple times each day. ESM may be particularly useful in providing an overall summary of a (self-reported) virtue (Jayawickreme & Fleeson 2017) and may help to partially address the limitations of standard self-reports through reducing self-perception biases and social-desirability biases (Wright et al. 2021).

More objective insight into individuals' character strengths may perhaps be provided by moral-dilemma tests and measures. Moral-dilemma tests offer "critical distance" from perceived virtue and enable insight into participants' judgments and reasoning when faced with multiple courses of action; hence, tracking moral performance rather than just self-beliefs (Kristjánsson 2015: 71). Moral-dilemma tests such as the Adolescent Intermediate Concept Measure (AD-icm) (Thoma et al. 2013) and Behavioral Defining Issues Test (bDIT) (Choi et al. 2019) can be used with students to help to understand developments in moral reasoning (Choi et al. 2019). Although the DIT and ICM measures are historically rooted in a Kohlbergian paradigm, unsympathetic to virtue development as part of moral education, Thoma et al. (2013) consider their developments away from the orthodox Kohlbergian paradigms to build bridges to character education and evaluations of virtue.

Does Character Education Work and Where Is It Headed?

Meta-analyses of research into the outcomes of character education suggest positive outcomes for students. Not only has character education been shown to be associated with increases in academic results, but also with improvements in student behavior, attitudes, and character strengths (Diggs & Akos 2016; Jeynes 2017), with stronger effects observed in programs that have been implemented for longer periods of time (Jeynes 2017). Notably, however, existing meta-analyses are limited to quantitative measures of academic performance, behavior, and attitudes. With a deeper (qualitative) insight, it is plausible that the observed effects may be even more pronounced. Indeed, case-study research employing a range of quantitative and qualitative measures suggests that targeted and intentional approaches to character education can lead to a multitude of benefits. These include improvements in students' character traits (Seider 2012) and the provision of a common language with which to discuss moral conduct and character development (Arthur et al. 2017a). Furthermore, students in schools recognized for their character-education provision have been shown to score higher in a measure of moral functioning than a comparison group (Arthur et al. 2017a).

Potentially more powerful than the collation of findings from research studies is anecdotal evidence offered by schools and organizations that have made character education a conscious and planned part of their provision. Case studies provided by schools (e.g., see Watts et al. 2021), suggest that character education can lead to improvements in: students' character virtues, wellbeing, behavior, attitudes, attendance, and even staff retention and job satisfaction. It must be admitted, however, that only in rare cases has empirical research into the effectiveness of character education included control groups receiving no instruction or an instruction in some alternative values-education program. Often, a Hawthorne effect cannot be excluded, therefore.

To conclude, in this chapter, we have taken readers on something of a rollercoaster ride of the topics that typically occupy the minds of character educationists: be those philosophers or social scientists. We hesitate, however, to prognosticate about the future of character education, either in our own country (U.K.) or internationally. It is well-known that the history of education is a history of fads, subject to the vicissitudes of time and circumstance. Global events, such as the COVID-19 pandemic, may determine where education heads next in search of the next Eldorado. The main hope for the future of character education lies, in our view, in the broadening of its remit to that of a more general paradigm of human flourishing as the aim of education (Walker et al. 2015; Kristjánsson 2020). Once flourishing is given pride of place in educational discourse, a deeper exploration of the human excellences that make up flourishing cannot be avoided, and those will include the virtues in which character educationists tends to be most interested.

As we have pointed out already, character education is in many ways a divisive field. Various historical and political reasons have made it more controversial – and more easily misinterpreted – than it need be. Its fundamental message is one that should have universal resonance: how can we help young people develop the excellences that enable them to live well? At the moment, the greatest surge of interest in character research is within psychology, rather than pure education, pure philosophy, or even educational philosophy. Readers may notice that few of the works cited in this chapter have appeared in traditional outlets of educational philosophy. Does this mean that philosophers of education are not sufficiently interested in questions of classroom applications of theories, or that character education is simply not sophisticated enough philosophically to interest philosophers? In any case, the recent psychological turn in character education has moved the center of gravity in the relevant research away from theoretical and conceptual issues towards empirical ones (of "what works" and how to evaluate it). While these developments have strengthened the practical side of character education, they have not resolved all the philosophical questions that might be addressed. There is more work to do.

(Related Chapters: 2, 3, 10, 11, 13, 27, 30, 31, 32.)

References

Allen, K., & Bull, A. (2018) "Following Policy: A Network Ethnography of the UK Character Education Policy Community," *Sociological Research Online* 23(2): 438–458.

Annas, J. (2011) *Intelligent Virtue*. Oxford: Oxford University Press.

Anscombe, G. E. M. (1958) "Modern Moral Philosophy," *Philosophy* 33(1): 1–19.

Aristotle (1985) *Nicomachean Ethics*, trans. T. Irwin. Indianapolis: Hackett Publishing.

Arthur, J. (2020) *The Formation of Character in Education: From Aristotle to the 21st Century*. London: Routledge.

Arthur, J., Cleverdon, J., Morgan, N., O'Shaughnessy, J., & Seldon, A. (2021) *Educating for a Characterful Society: Responsibility and the Public Good*. London: Routledge.

Arthur, J., Harrison, T., Burn, E., & Moller, F. (2017a) Schools of Virtue: Character Education in three Birmingham Schools. University of Birmingham, Jubilee Centre for Character and Virtues. http://www.jubileecentre.ac.uk/userfiles/jubileecentre/pdf/Research%20Reports/SchoolsOfVirtueResearchReport.pdf

Arthur, J., Kristjánsson, K., Harrison, T., Sanderse, W., & Wright, D. (2017b) *Teaching Character and Virtue in Schools*. London: Routledge.

Arthur, J., Kristjánsson, K., & Thoma, S. (2016) "Review of Angela Duckworth's *Grit*. University of Birmingham, Jubilee Centre for Character and Virtues," Insight Series. http://www.jubileecentre.ac.uk/userfiles/jubileecentre/pdf/insight-series/Is_Grit_the_Magic_Elixir_of_Good_Character_InsightSeries2016.pdf

Arthur, J., Kristjánsson, K., Walker, D., Sanderse, W., & Jones, C. (2015) *Character Education in UK Schools*. University of Birmingham, Jubilee Centre for Character and Virtues https://www.jubileecentre.ac.uk/userfiles/jubileecentre/pdf/Research%20Reports/Character_Education_in_UK_Schools.pdf

Berkowitz, M. W. (2002) "The Science of Character Education," in W. Damon (ed.) *Bringing in a New Era in Character Education*. Stanford: Hoover Institution Press.

Berkowitz, M. W. (2021) *PRIMED for Character Education: Six Design Principles for School Improvement*. London: Routledge.

Berkowitz, M. W., & Bier, M. C. (2005) *What Works in Character Education: A Research-driven Guide for Educators*. Character Education Partnership. https://www.researchgate.net/publication/251977043_What_Works_In_Character_Education

Bohlin, K. (2005) *Teaching Character Education through Literature: Awakening the Moral Imagination in Secondary Classrooms*. London: Routledge/Falmer.

Character.org (2018) *The 11 Principles of Character. A Validation Framework: For Inspiration, Validation and Certification, Introductory Guide, 2018–2020 Revision*. Character.org. https://www.character.org/11-principles-framework

Choi, Y-J., Han, H., Dawson, K. J., Thoma, S. J., & Glenn, A. L. (2019) "Measuring Moral Reasoning using Moral Dilemmas: Evaluating Reliability, Validity, and Differential Item functioning of the Behavioural Defining Issues Test (bDIT)," *European Journal of Developmental Psychology* 16(5): 622–631.

Curren, R. (2010) "Aristotle's Educational Politics and the Aristotelian Renaissance in Philosophy of Education," *Oxford Review of Education* 36(5): 543–559.

Curren, R. (2015) "Virtue Ethics and Moral Education," in M. Slote & L. Besser-Jones (eds.) *Routledge Companion to Virtue Ethics*. London: Routledge, 459–470.

Curren, R., & Kotzee, B. (2014) "Can Virtue be Measured?" *Theory and Research in Education* 12(3): 266–282.

Darnell, C., Gulliford, L., Kristjánsson, K., & Paris, P. (2019) "*Phronesis* and the Knowledge-action Gap in Moral Psychology and Moral Education: A New Synthesis?" *Human Development* 62(3): 101–129.

Department for Education (2019) *Character education framework guidance: November 2019*. https://assets.publishing.service.gov.uk/government/uploads/system/uploads/attachment_data/file/904333/Character_Education_Framework_Guidance.pdf

Diggs, C. R., & Akos, P. (2016) "The Promise of Character Education in Middle School: A Meta-analysis," *Middle Grades Review* 2(2): 1–19.

Doris, J. (2002) *Lack of Character: Personality and Moral Behavior*. Cambridge University Press.

Fowers, B. J., Carroll, J. S., Leonhardt, N. D., & Cokelet, B. (2021) "The Emerging Science of Virtue," *Perspectives on Psychological Science* 16(1): 118–147.

Haidt, J. (2001) "The Emotional Dog and its Rational Tail: A Social Intuitionist Approach to Moral Judgment," *Psychological Review* 108(4): 814–834.

Hand, M. (2018) *A Theory of Moral Education*. London: Routledge.

Harrison, T., Arthur, J., & Burn, E. (2016a) *Character Education Evaluation Handbook for Schools*. University of Birmingham, Jubilee Centre for Character and Virtues. http://jubileecentre.ac.uk/1721/character-education

Harrison, T., Morris, I., & Ryan, J. (2016b) *Teaching Character in the Primary Classroom*. London: Sage.

Jayawickreme, E., & Fleeson, W. (2017) "Does Whole Trait Theory Work for the Virtues?" in W. Sinnott-Armstrong & C. B. Miller (eds.) *Moral Psychology, vol. 5: Virtue and Happiness*. Cambridge, MA: MIT Press, 75–103.

Jerome, L., & Kisby, B. (2019) *The Rise of Character Education in Britain: Heroes, Dragons and the Myths of Character*. London: Palgrave-Macmillan.

Jeynes, W. H. (2017) "A Meta-analysis on the Relationship Between Character Education and Student Achievement and Behavioral Outcomes," *Education and Urban Society* 49(1): 1–39.

Jubilee Centre for Character and Virtues (2017) *A Framework for Character Education in Schools*. Jubilee Centre for Character and Virtues. http://www.jubileecentre.ac.uk/userfiles/jubileecentre/pdf/character-education/Framework%20for%20Character%20Education.pdf

Kohlberg, L. (1981) *Essays on Moral Development, vol. 1: The Philosophy of Moral Development*. New York: Harper & Row.

Kohn, A. (1997) "The Trouble with Character Education," in A. Molnar (ed.) *The Construction of Children's Character*. Chicago: University of Chicago Press, 154–162.

Kristjánsson, K. (2015) *Aristotelian Character Education*. London: Routledge.

Kristjánsson, K. (2020) *Flourishing as the Aim of Education: A Neo-Aristotelian View*. London: Routledge.

Kristjánsson, K. (2021) "Recent Attacks on Character Education in a UK Context: A Case of Mistaken Identities?" *Journal of Beliefs & Values*, in press.

Lamb, M., Brant, J., & Brooks, E. (2021) "How is Virtue Cultivated? Seven Strategies for Postgraduate Character Development," *Journal of Character Education* 17(1): 81–108.

Lamb, M., Taylor-Collins, E., & Silvergate, C. (2019) "Character Education for Social Action: A Conceptual Analysis of the #iwill Campaign," *Journal of Social Science Education* 18(1): 125–152.

Larson, R., & Csikszentmihalyi, M. (1983) "The Experience Sampling Method," *New Directions for Methodology of Social and Behavioral Science* 15(1): 41–56.

Lickona, T. (1991) *Educating for Character: How Our Schools Can Teach Respect and Responsibility*. New York: Bantam Books.

McGrath, R. E. (2015) "Character Strengths in 75 Nations: An Update," *Journal of Positive Psychology* 10(1): 41–52.

Ng, V., & Tay, L. (2020) "Lost in Translation: The Construct Representation of Character Virtues," *Perspectives on Psychological Science* 15(2): 300–326.

Ofsted (2019) *School Inspection Handbook: Handbook for Inspecting Schools in England*. https://assets.publishing.service.gov.uk/government/uploads/system/uploads/attachment_data/file/843108/School_inspection_handbook_-_section_5.pdf

Park, N., & Peterson, C. (2006) "Moral Competence and Character Strengths among Adolescents: The Development and Validation of the Values in Action Inventory of Strengths for Youth," *Journal of Adolescence* 29(6): 891–909.

Peterson, A. (2020) "Character Education, the Individual and the Political," *Journal of Moral Education* 49(2): 143–157.

Peterson, C., & Seligman, M. E. P. (2004) *Character Strengths and Virtues: A Classification and Handbook*. Washington, DC: APA.

Railton, P. (2016) "Morality and Prospection," in M. E. P. Seligman, P. Railton, R. F. Baumeister, & C. Sripade (eds.) *Homo Prospectus*. Oxford: Oxford University Press, 225–280.

Roberts, R. C., & Wood, W. J. (2007) *Intellectual Virtues: An Essay in Regulative Epistemology*. Oxford: Oxford University Press.
Sanderse, W. (2013) "The Meaning of Role Modelling in Moral and Character Education," *Journal of Moral Education* 42(1): 28–42.
Seider, S. (2012) *Character Compass: How Powerful School Culture Can Point Students Toward Success*. Cambridge, MA: Harvard Education Press.
Seligman, M. E. P. (2011) *Flourish: A Visionary new Understanding of Happiness and Well-being*. New York: Free Press.
Suissa, J. (2015) "Character Education and the Disappearance of the Political," *Ethics and Education* 10(1): 105–117.
Thoma, S., Derryberry, W. P., & Crowson, H. M. (2013) "Describing and Testing an Intermediate Concept Measure of Adolescent Moral Thinking," *Journal of Educational and Developmental Psychology* 10(2): 239–252.
Wagner, L., & Ruch, W. (2015) "Good Character at School: Positive Classroom Behavior Mediates the Link Between Character Strengths and School Achievement," *Frontiers in Psychology* 6(610): 1–13.
Walker, D. I., Roberts, M. P., & Kristjánsson, K. (2015) "Towards a New Era of Character Education in Theory and in Practice," *Educational Review* 67(1): 79–96.
Watts, P., Fullard, M., & Peterson, A. (2021) *Understanding Character Education: Approaches, Applications and Issues*. London: McGraw-Hill.
Wright, J., Warren, M., & Snow, N. (2021) *Understanding Virtue: Theory and Measurement*. Oxford: Oxford University Press.
Young, T. (2014) "Why Schools Can't Teach Character," *The Spectator*, Nov. 8. https://www.spectator.co.uk/article/why-schools-can-t-teach-character
Yu, J. (2007) *The Ethics of Confucius and Aristotle: Mirrors of Virtue*. London: Routledge.

PART III

Education and Justice

15

EQUAL EDUCATIONAL OPPORTUNITY: WHAT *SHOULD* IT MEAN?

Gina Schouten

On the face of things, the social ideal of equal educational opportunity is a broadly unifying one, especially in the United States. Many of us prize equal opportunity generally (McCall 2013), and education is integral to that ideal (Howe 1997). But, as others have pointed out, this appearance of unity is more apparent than real, and the broad commitment to equal educational opportunity masks deep *dis*agreement about just what that ideal calls for (Coleman 2012; Howe 1997; Jencks 1988; Temkin 2016). That's because there is no *one* social ideal to which fans of equal opportunity refer when they invoke that slogan. Instead, diverse ideals with widely divergent political implications go under that heading, such that those across the left-right spectrum can claim that their suite of policy commitments advances equal opportunity. This is no less true once we narrow in on education. This chapter considers some apparently plausible interpretations of equal educational opportunity and ultimately defends one – what I'll call "radical educational equality" – as an ideal of educational justice genuinely worth striving for.

We can distinguish conceptions of equal educational opportunity along several different dimensions (Westen 1985). I focus on two. First: *How demandingly egalitarian* is equal educational opportunity? Second: What does it favor equalizing opportunities *for*? By mapping it along these two dimensions, I stake out what I take to be a plausible and coherent interpretation of equal educational opportunity. That interpretation shifts our thinking about equal educational opportunity from a matter of equal opportunity *for* education to a matter of equal opportunity *through* education. I argue, finally, that we can make the ideal of equal educational opportunity helpfully action guiding by distinguishing between *what it is to realize educational justice* and *what reasons for action educational justice gives us here and now.*

I focus on primary and secondary schooling, and what equal educational opportunity should mean in that context. In considering equal educational opportunity as a family of *principles* or *ideals*, I don't definitively answer any normative questions about what *policies* we should embrace in those contexts. Such answers require not only ideals or principles but also *rich understandings of the facts on the ground.* This chapter is about the ideal of equal educational opportunity that I think should *guide* answers to normative policy questions, which questions also rely on empirics that this chapter will largely not engage. In closing, however, I do briefly address the question of how the ideal I defend can provide helpful guidance.

In actual political practice, the ideal of equal opportunity can often serve to excuse starkly *unequal outcomes.* For that reason, it's easy for leftists and progressives to get fed up with this ideal that can mean such different things to different people but seems almost never in practice to yield

DOI: 10.4324/9781003172246-19

*meaningful*equality. My brief is this: We should not give this ideal over; rather, we should fight for the *right* interpretation of it, and then fight to realize it.

15.1. How Demandingly Egalitarian?

A first tempting answer to the question of what equal educational opportunity requires invokes the democratic ideal that differential treatment requires justification (Jencks 1988). Assuming students are all *equally entitled* to the goods of education, equal educational opportunity might call for equal *treatment* understood to mean that *equal resources* should be invested in each. This "*equal inputs*" standard is more complicated than it seems, because the most educationally important resources are themselves complicated goods—difficult to quantify and measure, and imperfectly correlated with dollars spent. A teacher might prefer to work in a suburban school with relatively advantaged students even if she could (hypothetically) earn a higher salary at an urban school serving less advantaged students; if so, a fixed amount of funding will purchase a less valuable educational input at the disadvantaged school than it does at the privileged school. A further complication is that schools are unequally well-situated to exploit economies of scale. Several suburban schools might share an educational specialist – a music teacher, for example, or an expert in teaching non-native-English-speaking students – who rotates among schools over the course of the school day. Rural schools will have more trouble managing such arrangements because schools are farther apart. For these reasons, the measure of dollars spent per student is a quite rough proxy for valuable educational resource inputs.

In any case, the equal inputs ideal isn't an ultimately plausible understanding of equal educational opportunity. In very unequal societies like the United States, equalizing educational inputs across students does not translate to equal educational opportunity. Students arrive at school unequally prepared to make good use of educational resources. This unequal preparation is due in large part to differences in social class, which can give rise to educationally-salient differences among children in terms of their health, neighborhood structures, security, and stimulation outside of schools, and in the childrearing strategies their parents deploy (Lareau 2003; Rothstein 2004). For any set amount of per-student resources, then, some students will flourish and others will flounder, and this unequal preparation is due to unequal educationally-salient opportunities outside of schools. Against this backdrop, an equal inputs strategy of educational provision will do little more than reinforce unequal opportunities that already exist.

In an influential paper on educational justice, Christopher Jencks notes these problems with equal inputs as a conception of equal educational opportunity, and considers alternative construals of that ideal, all of which license some inequalities in *inputs* to respond to or offset differences among students in terms of their preparation to learn or other seemingly relevant criteria (Jencks 1988). One possibility is to allow educational resource allocation to track *students' effort*. Especially when we think about the most fine-grained level of resource allocation – teachers allocating their time and attention in individual classrooms – we might think that students who work hard should be rewarded with extra educational investment. This is a construal of equal educational opportunity because it directs us to *equalize* educational resources *conditional on* equal effort. And, to be sure, differences in effort are often salient considerations for the purposes of theorizing just allocations of resources. For example, plausibly, adults who spend relatively more time working and relatively less time on leisure are, other things equal, entitled to a greater share of the rewards of work than those who spend relatively *less* time on work and *more* on leisure. The idea that rewards should track effort is deeply embedded in much thinking about equal opportunity as a principle of justice: We want to equalize *opportunities*, not *outcomes*, precisely so that individuals can make their own tradeoffs between work and leisure. Separately, we might have the pragmatic aim of rewarding effort so as to *incentivize* it. But our commitment to equal opportunity is generally coupled with a principled conviction that those who work hard within a fair system of social rewards are *entitled to* the rewards they gain by virtue of their effort and deferral of leisure.

But, like equal inputs, this "*moralistic*" construal of equal educational opportunity is ultimately implausible. Whatever we think *generally* about conditionalizing access to social goods on effort, I've argued elsewhere that such conditionalization is misplaced when it comes to the social good of primary and secondary education (Schouten 2012a). Students are not fully-formed agents whom we are right to hold deeply responsible for their choices. They are *agents-in-formation*. Part of the purpose of education is to help them develop into adults who *can* rightly be held accountable for their choices. Sometimes, that will mean basing treatment on effort. For example, teachers might rightly praise students for working very hard, so that those students can come to value hard work. But teachers should do so only insofar as it serves *developmental* purposes – insofar as it constitutes an investment in students' development into mature agents.

This example relies on a distinction between principled and pragmatic cases for conditionalizing treatment on effort: We have a *principled* case only when effort really does influence what students are entitled to. We have a *pragmatic* case when rewarding effort serves extrinsic ends that we have reason to value. I am here denying that there is a good principled case, in primary and secondary education, for conditionalizing treatment on effort. But that denial is *consistent with* there being a *pragmatic* case. Teachers may praise hard work if habituating students to be hard workers serves the students' own interests. But pragmatic considerations justify conditionalizing treatment on effort only within the parameters set by students' *actual educational entitlements*. Withholding a privilege for developmental purposes is one thing. Withholding valuable educational resources, like instructional time and attention, is inappropriate assuming students are entitled to equal opportunity along *some* dimension or other.

Defenders of the moralistic construal of equal educational opportunity might rejoin that the principle calls for favoring hard-working students only when doing so comes at no cost to others. But this rejoinder is unsatisfactory. Schooling involves allocating scarce resources among students. Any allocation will impose costs on some – and confer benefits on others – relative to alternative feasible allocations. We can agitate for more funding for education, and teachers can work to make their instruction a positive sum game. But for any amount of resource or resource capacity, tradeoffs among students will need to be made. The task of a principle of educational justice is to guide us with respect to those tradeoffs. Moralistic equal opportunity allows allocation choices to be made on the basis of calculations about student effort, and in so doing fundamentally misunderstands a morally significant fact about childhood: Children should not be held responsible for converting educational resources into actual meaningful goods. To make this vivid, consider the fact that education is mandatory in our society until age sixteen. We do not allow children to choose to forego the life outcomes which education enables them to attain, because we deem the outcomes so important and judge that children under the age of sixteen lack the necessary degree of agency to be held responsible for converting – or failing to convert – educational opportunities into positive outcomes (Harel Ben-Shahar 2016; Schouten 2012b).

So moralistic equal opportunity fundamentally misunderstands the role of responsibility attributions in determining children's moral entitlements. It also fundamentally misunderstands the role of education in *shaping* students' intellectual values and dispositions, and thus in *developing* their fitness to bear responsibility attributions. Just like other forms of academic preparation, inclination to exert effort and to value educational opportunities is itself largely a product of students' social circumstances – including social circumstances that schools can affect. So, inclination to exert effort is also an *output* of education. Education should not treat student effort as a fixed point to justify unequal educational investment, but as an aim of education itself. Whether or not students are taught within their families and communities of origin to value education, the schooling process itself should help them to develop into hard workers disposed to recognize and utilize valuable opportunities, educational and otherwise. Whether students have these skills and dispositions coming *into* schooling is a circumstance largely beyond their control; as such, it does not license unequal educational investment.

In fact, a commitment to equal opportunity suggests not only that we should refrain from conditionalizing investment in students on factors outside of their control; it suggests that we should *offset* diminished educational opportunity due to factors outside their control. The intuitive pull of equal educational opportunity, after all, is that it's unfair for students to have less favorable life prospects due to unchosen social contingencies. This is just what makes *education* such an important site for thinking about justice in the first place: Schools are the institutions in society that seem best equipped to set students on equal footing with respect to all that will come after – to *equalize* life opportunities in the face of *un*equal starting points. This natural thought leads us to a conception of equal educational opportunity that favors *compensating* students for initial educational disadvantage: to put it colloquially, a construal that favors evening things out between students with educational advantages – for example, with lots of books at home and adults at leisure to read to them – and those without such advantages. This construal of equal educational opportunity is more progressive than those we have considered so far. To make it more precise, it directs us to invest educational inputs *un*equally so as to achieve more equal educational *outputs* – for example, to draw the most experienced teachers to the schools serving the most disadvantaged students so as to improve their access to learning compared to the students who are already – on average – relatively well set on that front. The aim is to break the link between social class background and subsequent educational achievement – in opportunity terms, to enhance the opportunities of disadvantaged students to attain the goods to which education serves as a gateway by offsetting the influence of social class background on learning.

At its heart, the ideal of equal opportunity reflects an aspiration for a social system in which individuals' position reflects the choices they make and the effort they exert – a system in which life prospects are less about circumstances beyond our control and more about the choices and behaviors that are in some morally relevant sense *due to us*. I think this aspiration captures the sense of equal opportunity *across* the political spectrum, but that upon reflection, it pushes us toward the more progressively egalitarian construal of that ideal just described. In describing that construal just now, I focused on the aim of offsetting *social* disadvantage – the educational disadvantage characteristic of kids whose caregivers must work long hours that limit time for play and reading, for example. But notice that, if we care about mitigating disadvantage due to circumstances beyond students' control, we have as much reason to mitigate *naturally-caused* disadvantage as *socially-caused* disadvantage. We have as much reason, for example, to act with special concern for a student who struggles in school due to a naturally-caused hearing impairment as we do to act with special concern for a student whose hearing impairment results from environmental injustice (Schouten 2012b). As John Rawls makes the case, "[t]here is no more reason to permit the distribution of income and wealth to be settled by the distribution of natural assets than by historical and social fortune" since social contingencies and natural abilities are "equally arbitrary" from a moral point of view (Rawls 1999: 64–65).

If Rawls is right that social contingencies and natural assets are equally morally arbitrary, that's plausibly because both equally fall outside of individuals' spheres of responsibility: We no more control our natural endowments than the social circumstances into which we're born. This suggests that a construal of equal educational opportunity that favors offsetting *only* social disadvantage is unstable: The equal opportunity case for offsetting social disadvantage *also* favors offsetting *natural* disadvantage, and on the same grounds. Insofar as we found the case for progressive equal educational opportunity compelling, then, we should feel compelled to go yet a step further. Equal educational opportunity favors offsetting social *and* natural disadvantage: investing extra resources *not only* in those students whose prospects are low due to their social class background, *but also* in those whose prospects are low due to their *natural* endowments, like innate intelligence.[1] Call this principle "radical educational equality": Educational resources should be distributed so as to favor disadvantaged students with disproportionally large shares of educational resources – whether those students' disadvantage is due to unearned social circumstances or unearned natural circumstances – so as to break the link between students' unchosen social and natural circumstances – including effort level – and their subsequent educational achievement (Brighouse & Swift 2014; Harel Ben-Shahar 2016).

In his audit of equal educational opportunity principles, Jencks considers a version of equal educational opportunity equivalent to radical educational equality, but he rejects it on the grounds that it constitutes a principle of equal educational *outcomes* rather than equal educational *opportunities*. He has a point. Once we acknowledge that among children, effort should be regarded as itself unearned – as due to just the sorts of background contingencies that equal opportunity directs us to neutralize in order to "level the playing field" – it does begin to look doubtful that radical educational opportunity approves any educational inequalities at all. But, contra Jencks, this observation is not a reason to reject radical educational equality as a construal of equal educational opportunity. Equal opportunity, and the motivating insight that it aims to codify, may simply be more stringently egalitarian than many have presumed (but see O'Neill 1976). Plausibly, *equal opportunity* for some goods requires competitors to be *equally positioned* at the outset of competition for those goods – and *equal positioning* entails some degree of equality of condition along some dimension. If this were true anywhere, it would be true along the dimension of primary and secondary education. As Harry Brighouse argues, "the intuition which gives this principle its appeal is the idea that it is unfair for some people, through no fault of their own, to have a worse start in life than others, especially with respect to the basic skills and information required for living a full and rewarding life in a modern society" (Brighouse 1995: 415; see also Cohen 2008: 60; Lippert-Rasmussen 2016; Temkin 2003; Arneson 1989). Educational justice matters in large part because education serves as a gateway to later life course goods including income and wealth, further (competitive) educational opportunities, secure jobs, health and longevity, and social status. Because of its position as a gateway to these rewards, a fair distribution of educational goods for students is one that promotes equal opportunity in the competition for the rewards that accrue *outside* of schooling.

Universal provision of education has long been regarded as crucial to ensuring that all have a fair shot to compete for unequally distributed social and economic rewards. If universal *provision* isn't enough to ensure fair competitions for those rewards, then we should conclude, not that something has gone wrong in our understanding of fair competitions, but that an ideal of fair competitions for life course goods turns out to have more robustly egalitarian implications for education than we might initially have thought. Indeed, our political discourse reflects this change, to an extent: In the domain of compulsory education, we no longer talk about equal access; instead, we talk about troubling inequalities in output: achievement gaps between students' learning, as measured by conventional indicators like standardized tests, along lines of race and social class. If educational justice consists in equalizing opportunities in the *subsequent* competition for social and economic advantage, then the fact that radical educational equality calls for equal educational outcomes is no grounds for rejecting that principle. Equal educational *outcomes* are crucial to ensuring equal *opportunities* in competitions subsequent to education.

15.2. In Defense of Radical Educational Equality

Suppose it is true that, even if equal opportunity turns out to be more demanding than we thought, we should not on that basis conclude that we have arrived at a misunderstanding of what equal opportunity calls for. Still, you might think – and plenty have argued – that under those circumstances we *should* start to doubt that ideal is worthy of pursuit (Wilson 1991). If equal educational opportunity really does require equal outcomes along some educational metric in order to secure equal opportunity for subsequent life course goods, perhaps we should reject the ideal of equal educational opportunity altogether. For one thing, it seems impossible to realize. So long as students arrive at school vastly unequally prepared to learn – as they will do so long as severe injustice outside of schools persists – schools cannot equalize their educational achievement (Rothstein 2004). Radical educational equality seems utterly unattainable.

But it is no mark against a principle of educational justice that it is not fully realizable so long as other social institutions remain deeply unjust. This is a fact that we must contend with in non-ideal theorizing. Compare social inequities and higher education admissions. One might sensibly think – I don't say it's true – that a just system of admissions for colleges and universities should ideally be fully race- gender- and class-blind *and* result in equal representation across race, gender, and class. But because of systemic social injustice, this is currently unattainable. We might favor one of these outcomes and sacrifice the other or aim for some balance that sacrifices a bit of each. That doesn't mean we were wrong about what we should want; it means only that some local ideals are unattainable when global injustice persists.

A deeper problem for radical educational equality lurks: Even granting that the ideal is impossible fully to realize, it calls for radically favoring disadvantaged students in the allocation of educational resources, up to the point at which students are equally well educated. This includes, plausibly, investing disproportionally in students with serious cognitive impairments and severe social disadvantage with the aim of *equalizing* educational outcomes between them and their more advantaged peers. At this extreme, disproportionate investment in the less advantaged appears tantamount to *depriving* the *more* advantaged. This can easily seem unfair to the more advantaged. Moreover, at some point, disproportional *educational* investments in disadvantaged students might not work to those very students' *ultimate* advantage. At some point, plausibly, it will be *ultimately* better for the worst off that education develop and orient the human capital of the most talented, whose later pursuits could benefit all of us.

Some theorists respond to these worries by giving up on equality – of opportunity or otherwise – and instead embracing *adequacy* principles of educational justice. Defenders of adequacy principles argue that we should not construe the justice aim of education as requiring that we *equalize* students' educationally; all that is required is that we educate all students so that their prospects are *good enough* (Anderson 2007; Gutmann 1999; Satz 2007; Tooley 1995). Adequacy theories demand that educational resources be distributed so that everyone has a level of educational success adequate for some specified level of functioning in society. Adequacy theorists differ in their criteria for an adequate education, but argue, against equal opportunity in education, that ensuring everyone is adequately educated is all that justice demands. Because adequacy is less demanding than equality, it avoids many of the worries that radical educational equality provokes. Above and below the threshold for an adequately good education, inequalities are irrelevant from the perspective of justice. What we owe to those students who have unfairly diminished prospects for attaining positive life course outcomes is not that we bring them up to the level of their more advantaged peers, but that we educate them *well enough*.

But the apparent objections to radical educational equality can be met without resorting to a less demanding adequacy principle. To see how, we need to distinguish between, first, the *considerations that inform* what we should do, and, second, *what we should do* once *all* relevant considerations are taken into account. Plausibly, promoting equal opportunity is only one part of what primary schooling should do, and thus only one among the considerations that should inform schooling policy (Brighouse & Swift 2008, 2009; Temkin 2016: 257). If that's right, then we can't point to cases in which *it would be bad* to promote equal educational opportunity without regard for other considerations and infer from those cases that equal educational opportunity doesn't matter. We can surely infer that it is not *all* that matters; we cannot infer, however, that it is not the right way to construe educational justice as one among the things that matter. Considered within this context, radical educational equality can simply disavow the apparent counterintuitive implications regarding over-demandingness (Brighouse & Swift 2009; Harel Ben-Shahar 2016). When educational justice comes into conflict with other values, it must be balanced against them. But observing that values can be in tension with one another under some circumstances does not compel us to reject any among those values. Equal educational opportunity may call for equal educational outcomes as radical educational equality holds, but the need to attend to other considerations constrains how far we should pursue that ideal.

Beyond equal opportunity, we should care about equipping students to serve capably and ethically in the positions of service and leadership throughout society (Anderson 2007; Callan 1997; Gutmann 1999). And we should care that all students are safe, cared for, and stimulated in school, and that schooling contributes to, rather than detracting from, their enjoyment of childhood wellbeing (Brighouse 2005; Macleod 2010, 2016). These considerations constrain the extent to which we should, all things considered, divert resources from the most advantaged students to the least advantaged. Radical educational equality may indeed require depriving advantaged students if we cared *only* about equal opportunity. But thinking about equal opportunity as *one among* the considerations of educational ethics enables us to defend radically demanding conceptions of equal educational opportunity without those conceptions shipwrecking on alleged implausible implications (Brighouse & Swift 2009).

15.3. Opportunities For What?

I wrote in the introduction of this chapter that I'd stake out a particular construal of equal educational opportunity by mapping it along two dimensions. In the first section, I considered the question of how demandingly egalitarian equal educational opportunity really is and argued that a radically egalitarian principle is most in keeping with the motivating insight of that ideal. I now want to consider the second dimension and explore its connections with the first. What are the opportunities that equal educational opportunity ought to be construed as regulating?

We *might* think of equal educational opportunity as demanding equal opportunities for *academic* outcomes. In embracing *radical* educational equality, we see that equal *opportunity* collapses in its demands into equal *outcomes* – and, given the motivation for it, that collapse is not a liability. This means that when we turn to the question of how to construe the opportunities, equal opportunity for *academic* outcomes effectively means *equal academic outcomes.*

But academic outcomes are an unappealing way to construe the opportunities that matter for equal educational opportunity. Even holding in mind that we're theorizing *only one consideration* bearing on normative questions about education, it's implausible that the value of equal educational opportunity fixates so narrowly on academic outcomes. And, properly construed, equal educational opportunity can call for equal *outcomes* without calling for equal *academic* outcomes. For the purposes of theorizing educational opportunity, we should measure advantage and disadvantage using a metric of all-things-considered life prospects, rather than short-term academic success (Brighouse 2000; Schouten 2012b). This includes prospects for realizing *all* the goods that add up to a flourishing life: for example, the ability to derive meaning and purpose from making a contribution to society, the ability to maintain social relationships that bring meaning and enjoyment, or the ability to devise and pursue personal projects that one finds stimulating and expansive or even just enjoyable (see Curren & Metzger 2017).

Like my case for radical educational equality, my case for construing opportunities in terms of all-things-considered life prospects draws on the motivating insight of the principle itself. A metric of all-things-considered life prospects coheres with our reasons for caring about equal educational opportunity. Justice in education matters because of the strong correlation between education and later life course outcomes. When we think about educational advantage and disadvantage, then, we should think beyond test scores and college readiness. We should think about the constituents of ultimately good lives to which education is a gateway.

This point helps us connect the question about the demandingness of equal opportunity with the question about the nature of the opportunities it regulates. On a metric of *academic* success, radical educational equality might indeed call for a tremendous redirection of resources away from the academically most gifted. After all, elevating the SAT scores of the most socially- and naturally- disadvantaged to the level of the most advantaged would fully exhaust educational resources and then some. But that's not the right way to think of the "equal outcomes" that radical educational equality calls for. If equal outcomes are to be construed instead as (roughly) equal prospects for leading good lives, then radical educational equality plausibly requires significant investment in the most academically gifted students. This investment may focus, for example, on expanding the skills of highly promising students and orienting them in ways that raise the likelihood that they will subsequently deploy their skillsets to the advantage of the least advantaged (Schouten 2012b). Meanwhile, direct educational investment in the least advantaged need not aim exclusively at elevating their academic outcomes. Raising their prospects for leading good lives might mean ensuring that their schooling be supportive of their emotional and social development, that they have opportunities to develop meaningful and rewarding friendships, and that they learn to enjoy intellectual pursuits. In short, by shifting our focus from equality of academic accomplishment to equal prospects for living good lives, we can expand the range of educational strategies on offer for investing meaningfully in the prospects of disadvantaged students (Schouten 2012b).

I argued in the previous section that radical educational equality does not have the implausible implications its opponents charge it with because equal educational opportunity is only *one* consideration bearing on normative questions about education. Now we can see that radical educational equality avoids many such alleged implications *even when equal educational opportunity is considered in isolation*. That's because students' life prospects are interdependent. If we cared only about equalizing *academic* success, we might have to invest massively in the disadvantaged to the point of depriving the better off. But if we care about equalizing life prospects *generally*, then insofar as *everyone's* life prospects are enhanced by investing in the more advantaged, equal educational opportunity, even taken alone, approves that investment.

15.4. Equal Opportunity *Through* Education

We have narrowed in on a particular construal of a principle that, in slogan form, commands near universal appeal. I have tried to motivate a principle of equal educational opportunity that regulates opportunities for living good lives and that effectively entails equal *outcomes* along that dimension. In short, I've endorsed a principle of equal educational opportunity that directs us to equalize students' prospects for living good lives.

My arguments for this construal effectively urge a particular re-orientation toward thinking about the value in question. Rather than thinking about equal educational opportunity in terms of equal opportunity *for* education, I've been nudging us toward seeing equal educational opportunity as equal opportunity *through* education: toward thinking of educational justice as a requirement for fairness in children's life prospects *generally* (see also Lazenby 2016; Temkin 2016). I now want to motivate that re-orientation directly. Equal educational opportunity is a crucial ingredient for realizing social justice broadly, and it requires radical educational equality.

At its heart, I've suggested, the appeal of equal opportunity lies in the conviction that it's somehow unfair when some enjoy considerably less favorable life prospects than others through no fault of their own. In the context of education, *all* disadvantage should be regarded as arising through no fault of the one suffering it: Even if children should be held responsible for *some* purposes, they should not be held responsible in any way that justifies withholding educational benefit. So, were we simply to implant the ideal of equal opportunity into education, we'd arrive at a construal of equal educational opportunity that demands equal academic outcomes.

But the appeal of equal educational opportunity is not redeemed simply by implanting that broad ideal into schools; rather, the appeal comes from appreciating the importance of education *for securing the broad ideal*. This distinction may seem to split hairs. But it suggests that, even independently of the arguments so far developed in this chapter, construing equal educational opportunity as equal opportunity *through* education is congruent with our reasons for caring about equal educational opportunity in the first place. Education equips students with the skills and dispositions to build valuable lives for themselves. Because the broad ideal of equal opportunity favors each of us enjoying equal opportunities to build valuable lives for ourselves, and because education is the common vehicle by way of which we're prepared to live valuable lives, equality of opportunity favors education equally preparing all students to live valuable lives. In this way, the broad ideal has radically egalitarian implications for education, but those implications do not amount to importing the value wholesale *into* education: They don't amount to requiring that schools preserve fair competitions *for academic outcomes*. Rather, equal educational opportunity – equal opportunity *through* education – means securing the educational prerequisites for equal opportunity to obtain broadly. That means pursuing radical educational equality *and* it means measuring educational equality in terms of prospects for living good lives.

Now, in urging us to consider equal educational opportunity as equal opportunity *through* education, I effectively introduce a new bit of work for us to do: Theorizing equal educational opportunity now requires a conception of *general* equal opportunity. We can find one such conception in John Rawls seminal theory of justice. In developing his account of equal opportunity, Rawls first considers a principle that he ultimately – and illuminatingly – rejects as too weak: a principle that he calls "careers open to talents." Careers open to talents is a minimal, legalistic construal of equal opportunity. It requires that all of us have "the same legal rights of access to all advantaged social positions" (Rawls 1999: 62) – that favorable positions are allocated even-handedly *given the existing distribution of qualification*. But careers open to talents imposes no requirements of fairness in opportunities to *become qualified* – it requires "no effort to preserve an equality, or similarity, of social conditions" (Rawls 1999: 62; see also Schaar 1967; Young 1994). If we award positions by merit but tolerate social obstacles to some people *acquiring* the kind of merit in question, then we won't have achieved genuine equal opportunity on the dimension we have reason to value. To put it more colloquially, if what we care about is neutralizing the effects of our undeserved "starting points" – "levelling the playing field" so that our prospects aren't so affected by the lot we're born into – then we have to care not only about opportunities *for positions* but also about *developmental* opportunities: opportunities to acquire the skills and dispositions that make us qualified for positions. *That* is why education is so crucially important for equal opportunity on the *right* construal.

Rawls rejects careers open to talents in favor of a more demanding construal of equal opportunity. On this construal, equal opportunity requires that "positions are to be not only open in a formal sense, but that all should have a fair chance to attain them" such that "those with similar abilities and skills should have similar life chances" (Rawls 1999: 63). Among other things, this requires "maintaining equal opportunities of education for all" (Rawls 1999: 63). To this end, Rawls goes on to say, "the school system, whether public or private, should be designed to even out class barriers (Rawls 1999: 63).

Rawls's principle of equal opportunity, which he calls "*fair* equality of opportunity," envisions mobility across social divisions. Importantly, achieving this vision requires contributions from different social sectors. Education plays a pivotal role in securing fair equality of opportunity. But, for Rawls, it can do that work *only if* inheritance and bequests are regulated to prevent large accumulations of wealth across generations. That's because of the role that intergenerational transfers of privilege play in sustaining educational advantage and disadvantage. As Rawls puts it, "the internal life and culture of the family influence, perhaps as much as anything else, a child's motivation and his capacity to gain from education" (Rawls 1999: 265). Only if wealth is broadly dispersed can educational institutions have any hope of educating students to enjoy fair equality of opportunity (see also Curren 2017). To recall, this is one reason we should not reject radical educational equality on grounds of its being impossible to realize: We can secure the educational prerequisites for equal opportunity *only if* other institutions are doing their share – share only if our inheritance and bequest law is broadly dispersing material and thus human capital. In capitalist societies wherein wealth and opportunities concentrate in the hands of a few, we should *expect* a principle of justice in education to be unrealizable. By contrast, in the institutional structure Rawls favors, "The emphasis [of institutional cooperation] falls on the steady dispersal over time of the ownership of capital and resources by the laws of inheritance and bequest, on fair equality of opportunity secured by provisions for education and training, and the like, as well as on institutions that support the fair value of the political liberties" (Rawls 1999: xv).

15.5. The Ideal to Realize and The Way to Realize It

For Rawls, it seems, a just society is one wherein early developmental inequalities are kept in check by various institutional mechanisms for distributive justice, and wherein egalitarian educational institutions render inert the developmental inequalities that remain. But plausibly, when other institutions fail, educational justice has yet more evening out to do. This means that, when we turn to the question of *what equal educational opportunity tells us to do*, we should expect the answer to depend strongly on facts on the ground: on what inequalities exist and what other institutions are doing about them. Equal opportunity *through* education means equalizing the educational prerequisites for leading good lives. So long as other institutions are unjust, that can't fully be accomplished, certainly not without running afoul of other values.

I think equal opportunity is the right ideal by which to measure educational injustice. But I think that when it comes to questions about *what we should do*, we'd be better guided – including guided in ways that help us come closer to realizing equal opportunity – by Rawls's *other* principle of distributive justice. The difference principle favors the social arrangement with the highest floor: the arrangement wherein the worst off are better off than they could be under any other arrangement. Practically speaking, and applied to schools, "the difference principle would allocate resources in education ... so as to improve the long-term expectation of the least favored" (Rawls 1999: 86–87; see also Parfit 1997). Rawls goes on:

> If this end is attained by giving more attention to the better endowed, it is permissible; otherwise not. And in making this decision, the value of education should not be assessed solely in terms of economic efficiency and social welfare. Equally if not more important is the role of education in enabling a person to enjoy the culture of his society and to take part in its affairs, and in this way to provide for each individual a secure sense of his own worth.
>
> *(Rawls 1999: 87)*

I don't endorse the difference principle on Rawls's terms exactly. In particular, I don't endorse the *absolute* priority of the *very* worst off relative to others who are nearly as badly off. But I think that any social sector that wants to promote egalitarian justice – and that must work against failures in other institutions, and that faces dire tradeoffs between egalitarian justice and other values – has good reason to adopt a prioritarian approach. Education is a social sector that *must* promote egalitarian justice broadly; educational justice is indispensable for social justice. Here, in sum, is how I think we should understand its role: Education *is just* when it equalizes students' prospects for leading good lives. This ideal is unattainable, at least for now. But we can pursue it – and we can pursue it in a way that is robust across changes in the (in)justice of other institutions – by working through education to improve the prospects of the least favored. In crafting and evaluating education policy, we should attach moral weight to students' interests in proportion to how badly off those students are, measured by their prospects for living good lives.

(Related Chapters: 3, 6, 16, 18, 19, 20, 21, 22, 23, 24, 25, 33, 34.)

Note

1 The principle I endorse here treats social class background and natural endowments as analytically distinct but morally equivalent, and thus as calling for the same response when it comes to educational justice. That means my principle avoids the problem of needing to distinguish among sources of educational disadvantage in practice. This is a welcome feature of the principle, because we lack broadly applicable measures for discriminating between acquired and innate aspects of intelligence. IQ scores do not reliably track differences in natural ability but are largely a product of cognitive exercise. See Flynn 1987; Neisser 1998.

References

Anderson, E. (2007) "Fair Opportunity in Education: A Democratic Equality Perspective," *Ethics* 117(4): 595–622.

Arneson, R. J. (1989) "Equality and Equal Opportunity for Welfare," *Philosophical Studies* 56(1): 77–93.

Brighouse, H. (1995) "In Defence of Educational Equality," *Journal of Philosophy of Education* 29(3): 415–420.

Brighouse, H. (2000) *School Choice and Social Justice*. Oxford: Oxford University Press.

Brighouse, H. (2005) *On Education*. 1st edition. New York: Routledge.

Brighouse, H. & Swift, A. (2008) "Putting Educational Equality in Its Place," *Education Finance and Policy* 3(4): 444–466.

Brighouse, H. & Swift, A. (2009) "Educational Equality versus Educational Adequacy: A Critique of Anderson and Satz," *Journal of Applied Philosophy* 26(2): 117–128.

Brighouse, H. & Swift, A. (2014) "The Place of Educational Equality in Educational Justice," in K. Meyer (ed.) *Education, Justice and the Human Good*. New York: Routledge, 14–33.

Callan, E. (1997) *Creating Citizens: Political Education and Liberal Democracy*. Oxford: Oxford University Press.

Cohen, G. A. (2008) *Rescuing Justice and Equality*. Cambridge, Mass: Harvard University Press.

Coleman, J. (2012) "The Concept of Equality of Educational Opportunity," *Harvard Educational Review* 38(1): 7–22.

Curren, R. (2017) "On the Arc of Opportunity: Education, Credentialism, and Employment," in K. P. Schaff (ed.) *Fair Work: Ethics, Social Policy, Globalization*. London: Rowman & Littlefield, 59–78.

Curren, R. & Metzger, E. (2017) *Living Well Now and in the Future: Why Sustainability Matters*. Cambridge, Mass: MIT Press.

Flynn, J. R. (1987) "Massive IQ Gains in 14 Nations: What IQ Tests Really Measure," *Psychological Bulletin* 101(2): 171–191.

Gutmann, A. (1999) *Democratic Education: Revised Edition*. Princeton: Princeton University Press.

Harel Ben-Shahar, T. (2016) "Equality in Education – Why We Must Go All the Way," *Ethical Theory and Moral Practice* 19(1): 83–100.

Howe, K. R. (1997) *Understanding Equal Educational Opportunity: Social Justice, Democracy, and Schooling*. New York: Teachers College Press.

Jencks, C. (1988) "Whom Must We Treat Equally for Educational Opportunity to Be Equal?" *Ethics* 98(3): 518–533.

Lareau, A. (2003) *Unequal Childhoods: Class, Race, and Family Life*. University of California Press.

Lazenby, H. (2016) "What Is Equality of Opportunity in Education?" *Theory and Research in Education* 14(1): 65–76.

Lippert-Rasmussen, K. (2016) *Luck Egalitarianism*. Bloomsbury Ethics Series. London: Bloomsbury.

Macleod, C. (2016) "Just Schools and Good Childhoods: Non-Preparatory Dimensions of Educational Justice," *Journal of Applied Philosophy* 35(S1), DOI:10.1111/japp.12227.

Macleod, C. (2010) "Primary Goods, Capabilities, and Children," in H. Brighouse & I. Robeyns (eds.) *Measuring Justice: Primary Goods and Capabilities*. Cambridge: Cambridge University Press, 174–192.

McCall, L. (2013) *The Undeserving Rich: American Beliefs about Inequality, Opportunity, and Redistribution*. Cambridge: Cambridge University Press.

Neisser, U. (ed.) (1998) *The Rising Curve: Long Term Gains in IQ and Related Measures*. Washington, D.C.: American Psychological Association.
O'Neill, O. (1976) "Opportunities, Equalities and Education," *Theory and Decision* 7(4): 275–295.
Parfit, D. (1997) "Equality and Priority," *Ratio* 10(3): 202–221.
Rawls, J. (1999) *A Theory of Justice, Revised Edition*. Cambridge, Mass: Harvard University Press.
Rothstein, R. (2004) *Class and Schools: Using Social, Economic, And Educational Reform to Close the Black-White Achievement Gap*. New York: Teachers College Press.
Satz, D. (2007) "Equality, Adequacy, and Education for Citizenship," *Ethics* 117(4): 623–648.
Schaar, J. (1967) "Equality of Opportunity and Beyond," in R. Pennock & J. Chapman (eds.) *Nomos IX, Equality*. New York: Atherton Press, 228–249.
Schouten, G. (2012a) "Educational Justice: Closing Gaps or Paying Debts?" *Journal of Applied Philosophy* 29(3): 231–242.
Schouten. G. (2012b) "Fair Educational Opportunity and the Distribution of Natural Ability: Toward a Prioritarian Principle of Educational Justice," *Journal of Philosophy of Education* 46(3): 472–491.
Temkin, L. S. (2016) "The Many Faces of Equal Opportunity," *Theory and Research in Education* 14(3): 255–276.
Temkin, L. S. (2003) "Egalitarianism Defended," *Ethics* 113(4): 764–782.
Tooley, J. (1995) *Disestablishing the School: De-Bunking Justifications for State Intervention in Education*. New York: Ashgate Publishing.
Westen, P. (1985) "The Concept of Equal Opportunity," *Ethics* 95(4): 837–850.
Wilson, J. (1991) "Does Equality (of Opportunity) Make Sense in Education?" *Journal of Philosophy of Education* 25(1): 27–32.
Young, M. (1994) *The Rise of the Meritocracy*. 2nd edition. New Brunswick, N.J: Routledge.

16

NON-PREPARATORY DIMENSIONS OF EDUCATIONAL JUSTICE

Colin M. Macleod

Introduction

This chapter addresses the nature of educational objectives and what objectives belong within the domain of educational justice. Schools and other educational institutions and arrangements do many things and there is contestation about what they should do. Scholars and citizens often disagree about how the various functions of education are best understood and interpreted. There is debate about what the appropriate aims of education are, what pedagogical strategies best advance these aims, and how resources and opportunities should be distributed so as to fairly and effectively advance the appropriate aims of education. Schools are not, of course, the only institutional arrangement through which educational objectives are pursued. Families, religious institutions, cultural communities, private clubs, the marketplace, and social media all influence education in a myriad of complex ways. This fact in turn generates important questions about the division of educational labor between different social institutions in realizing different aims of education. Here, there are familiar debates about what role, if any, public schools should play in providing religious education. Similarly, there are debates about who should bear various costs of education. Should parents or local municipalities or states pay the salaries of teachers or cover the costs of books, computers, and other educational materials? How these matters are resolved has a profound effect on the calibre of education that is available to people, the accessibility of education to different people, and the general distribution of educational resources and opportunities amongst people. Although issues of educational justice arise in many contexts and although children and adults are greatly affected by the character of educational institutions and arrangements, this chapter will primarily address a dimension of educational justice that pertains to children in primary and secondary schools.[1]

Against this background, the aim of this chapter is to illuminate and motivate the importance of an underappreciated but important facet of educational justice. This facet pertains primarily to the metric that should be employed in making judgements of justice about the manner in which educational institutions and policies distribute resources and opportunities to students in primary and secondary schools. The principal claim I advance is that accounts of educational justice should be sensitive to what I call *non-preparatory dimensions of education*. The precise character and importance of non-preparatory dimensions of education will be developed in the rest of the chapter. However, the key idea is reasonably simple. It is obvious that decent schools teach children skills, knowledge, and dispositions that contribute to many aspects of their development and maturation. But schools are also sites in which children conduct a great deal of their lives as children. Some dimensions of

DOI: 10.4324/9781003172246-20

children's experiences at school – grounded in the resources, opportunities, and activities to which they have access – may have little or no effect on their overall intellectual, moral, psychological, or physical development or their subsequent success in life as adults. Yet such experiences bear upon the quality of children's lives even if they play no, or only a negligible role, in preparing children for life after school. A comprehensive theory of justice should give consideration to the goods to which children have access as children and how such goods are distributed among children. Since many of the goods of childhood can be realized or frustrated by the kinds of resources and opportunities provided (or denied) to children within schools, this facet of justice arguably lies substantially within the domain of educational justice.

In what follows, I shall try to illuminate the nature and importance of non-preparatory facets of educational justice. First, I will review the principal educational issues that are routinely emphasized in discussions of education justice and explain the manner in which they reflect a largely preparatory conception of education. I will offer an explanation of the strong orientation toward a wholly preparatory conception of educational objectives. Second, I will offer an explanation of why a wholly preparatory conception of educational justice is incomplete and indicate how it should be supplemented by attention to non-preparatory dimensions of education. Third, I will identify some implications for debates about the distribution of educational resources and opportunities that arise from recognition of the non-preparatory dimensions of education.

Dimensions of Educational Justice

From a fairly abstract vantage, we can identify two broad aims of accounts educational justice. First, there is a concern to determine what properly lies within the domain of educational justice. Here we may ask: what does a proper education provide to students and what resources and opportunities are essential or pertinent to realizing the appropriate aims of education? Second, there is a concern to illuminate the principles that should regulate the kind of access that students have to educational resources and opportunities. These principles largely provide an account of what a just distribution of educational resources and opportunities consists in. Egalitarian views hold that all students should have equal access to education resources and opportunities (Brighouse & Swift 2009, 2014; Macleod 2012). Sufficientarian views claim that justice in education is secured by ensuring that all students have access to a certain minimum quality of education but that beyond this threshold, substantial inequalities between students are just (Anderson 2007; Satz 2007). Libertarian views hold that access to education should be determined primarily by the choices parents make in private educational markets (Narveson 2001). Prioritarians favour distributions that work to the greatest advantage of the least advantaged students (Schouten 2012). And so on.[2]

The articulation of distributive principles of educational justice may also broach special considerations that affect the manner in which different aspects of education may be made accessible to students. We can see this at work in discussions of the place of perfectionist considerations in education. As I use the term here, perfectionism authorizes the state to draw upon and promote normatively rich but potentially contentious ideals about what constitutes a good or flourishing life for humans. Anti-perfectionism sharply circumscribes the role of such ideals in state policy.[3] This distinction can complicate our understanding of educational justice in various ways. For instance, an egalitarian but anti-perfectionist conception of educational justice could endorse the view that students should have equal access to educational resources but hold that educational institutions operated by the state may not orient education towards the promotion of controversial ideals of human excellence or flourishing. John Rawls' variety of political liberalism takes educational justice in this direction. On Rawls' view, state schools must not only refrain from promoting religion, they must not try to foster "the values of autonomy and individuality as ideals to govern much if not all of life" (Rawls 2005: 199). Yet a view like Rawls' that restricts state promotion of such ideals can allow that they are permissibly pursued by non-state educational institutions (e.g., via churches that promote religious views or clubs that advance secular ideals of human excellence). A more comprehensively anti-perfectionist position holds that even non-state institutions should not orient education towards the encouragement or promotion of particular conceptions of the good or ideals of human excellence. For instance, Matthew Clayton argues that legitimate education of children, whether by the state or parents, must not promote specific conceptions of the good or ideals or aim at securing children's allegiance to them (Clayton 2006). By contrast, an egalitarian and broadly perfectionist conception of justice could hold that students should have equal access to resources and that state provided education should be expressly orientated toward the advancement of specific, and perhaps contentious, conceptions of human flourishing (e.g., a broadly Aristotelian conception of eudaimonia; Curren 2013). Here the promotion of at least some distinctive ideals of human excellence is part of the appropriate mission of state schools and presumably non-state may join in this mission.

As the foregoing points illustrate, the partition between domain and distributive issues is not always sharp. Nonetheless, the distinction provides a useful preliminary framework for analyzing matters of educational justice since there is often broader agreement about domain issues than about distributive issues. For instance, there is widespread acceptance of the idea that education should foster literacy, numeracy, and other skills relevant to participating in the political community and economy. Most also agree that education should provide students with knowledge and understanding of material in a wide variety of fields such as science, history, literature, and politics. There is controversy, of course, both about the precise character of these objectives and the specific content that should be addressed in various subject areas. For example, there have long been controversies about the appropriate content of sex education. Currently, there are heated disputes about the place of 'critical race theory' in the curriculum of schools. Even when there is broad agreement about curriculum content matters, there are frequently disagreements about what pedagogical techniques are effective and appropriate in realizing curriculum objectives.

In addition to the broad issues of domain and distributive questions, there are a host of other more specific matters that arise in discussions of educational justice. For example, theorists address the issue of what forms of institutional design best achieve educational justice – e.g., whether primary and secondary schools should be wholly or primarily public. Similarly, there are important questions about how a just system of education should accommodate and respond to the distinct needs and interests of particular groups of students such as persons with disabilities and linguistic, cultural, and religious minorities. There are also interesting issues about the internal organization and governance of school and about the degree to which students themselves should exercise democratic control over significant features of the schools they attend. Finally, there are many difficult issues concerning the programs and policies that should be pursued to remedy or mitigate the longstanding injustices. What policies of remedial justice, for instance, should be adopted to address the legacy of racist segregation in education or the grossly unjust system of residential schools that were imposed on many Indigenous communities? Addressing all these facets of education justice is enormously challenging not just because there is rather deep normative contestation about basic principles of justice but also because of the complex interaction between different considerations at different levels of application. It is not surprising, therefore, that there is great contestation about education justice. Despite this contestation, there is a general tendency in the literature to conceptualize education as orientated primarily towards preparation of children for successful participation in projects and activities that have meaning and significance for adults.

Conceptions of Childhood and Education

As noted below, the orientation towards the preparatory dimensions of education can be seen both in how educational objectives are articulated and how educational quality is measured. However, the orientation arguably reflects and perhaps is rooted in a general conception of the nature and value of childhood that is embraced, at least implicitly, in a great deal of contemporary political philosophy. For many theorists, the articulation of ideals of justice is dominated by the assumption that ideals of justice principally focus on regulating the interactions of autonomous persons and delineating their rights and the share of resources and opportunities to which they have a justice-based entitlement. In this picture, children are not fully constituted selves and childhood is, as Tamar Schapiro puts is, a "predicament" (Schapiro 1999): a diminished normative state characterized mainly by the absence of the developed cognitive powers and rational capacities that are constitutive of mature agency.[4] Successful child rearing facilitates children's exit from this predicament so that they can join the world of mature, autonomous, moral agents who formulate and pursue the conceptions of the good that confer meaning on their lives.

This kind of 'agency assumption' (Macleod 2010) is quite ubiquitous. It is central, for instance, to the Rawlsian approach to justice in which the participants in the scheme of mutually advantageous cooperation that principles of justice regulate are depicted as free and equal persons in virtue of their possession of the two moral powers (Rawls 2003). In a different but related vein, relational egalitarians conceive of justice as concerned with facilitating the social and pollical conditions in which mature citizens can interact respectfully with one another as equals (Anderson 1999). Libertarianism gives center stage to recognition and protection of the private property rights of self-owning persons capable of making authoritative choices about how to conduct themselves and control their property (Nozick 1974). Even the Capability Approach, pioneered by Amartya Sen (1999) and Martha Nussbaum (2006), in which justice concerns the provision of opportunities to individuals to achieve valuable 'functionings' – intrinsically valuable human activities or states of being – adopts an agency assumption. For on this view, whether a person is unjustly disadvantaged or not depends on the responsible choices that were available to them to achieve a functioning.[5] The agency assumption at work in so much theorizing about justice underpins a 'mature project achievement view' (Macleod 2018) of human well-being and flourishing in which "the principal projects or activities that confer goodness on a person's life are those adopted and pursued by mature rational agents" (Macleod 2018: 77). It is notable, for instance, that the list of primary goods that John Rawls takes to be central to justice are ones that have value for agents who already possess the two moral powers. The basic political liberties he prioritizes along with income and wealth have significance for him mainly because they are conducive to the formulation and pursuit of conceptions of the good by adult citizens. The mature project achievement view valorizes adulthood over childhood and treats childhood as a life phase that is mainly oriented toward development of the capacities and skills requisite to leading a successful life as an adult.

Developmental Objectives of Education

Against the background of this general conceptualization of childhood, it is not surprising that articulation of educational objectives typically focuses on the important developmental and transformational effects of education. Education is oriented toward the future and "the value of an education is constituted in large part by the future benefits for which education serves as a gateway" (Schouten 2012: 472). Students begin school lacking literacy, numeracy, skills, and knowledge and acquire understanding and competencies in a variety of areas through processes of education. Although, as I have noted, there are disagreements about the precise preparatory objectives of education, the appropriate aim of education is to facilitate children's development so that they can, as adults, successfully participate in the economy as well as social and political life as responsible, reasonably informed, citizens. Education is also conceived as playing an essential role in moral development. For Rawlsians, for instance, it should contribute to the development of the two moral powers – a sense of justice and a capacity for a conception of the good. Theorists who endorse children's rights to an autonomy facilitating upbringing emphasize the ways education should equip children with capacities for reflective consideration of conceptions of the good and other fundamental moral commitments. Those who doubt that children have a claim to robust development of autonomy insist that moral education is sufficient if it provides citizens with a basic understanding of democratic rights and processes and readies them to interact respectfully with other citizens. For instance, in her influential treatment of democratic education Amy Gutmann places emphasis on "fostering the conditions that facilitate the development of capacities for personal choice and democratic citizenship" (Gutmann 1980: 351). More ambitious depictions of educational objectives hold that education should promote various human excellences that are conducive to flourishing or eudaimonia. But even these views have a strong preparatory tilt. Thus on Randall Curren's broadly Aristotelian view the main function of education is "to *promote forms of development conducive to living well, in circumstances conducive to students achieving the essential goods* of truth, understanding, knowledge, good judgment, and self-governance in accordance with good judgment; relationships of mutual goodwill in which virtues of character are displayed; and goods associated with diverse forms of competence or excellence in arts of performance, production, and other forms of endeavor" (Curren 2013: 241). This preparatory focus is not incompatible with recognition that it is important that students have good experiences while at school. Indeed, successful development of children is typically facilitated by such experiences so a good path to adult flourishing will no doubt usually include some childhood flourishing. But we cannot assume that the full importance and character of childhood flourishing is supplied by understanding its role in successful development.

Measuring Educational Quality

Once key educational objectives have been identified, it is important to have ways of determining how well schools are performing in fulfilling their educational mission. Standard approaches to measuring or gauging the quality of education also focus on the degree to which schools succeed in achieving preparatory objectives. Ladd and Loeb observe that there are three main techniques that are standardly employed to measure and compare education quality: (1) analyses of the amount of spending per pupil in different schools or jurisdictions; (2) analyses of observations of teaching and classroom environments by external reviewers; and (3) analyses of student outcomes as tracked through various kinds of achievement data (e.g., test scores, graduation rates, post-secondary educational attainment, employment and earnings) (Ladd & Loeb 2013). Although many complex issues arise about the development and deployment of these metrics to track educational quality, the preparatory focus of the standard tools used in this area is clear. Ultimately, the measures attempt to track how well or poorly schools have done in equipping students for future success in life. The data that is compiled employing these measures will be employed in turn in making judgements about the degree to which educational justice in various contexts is realized.

Beyond Preparation: The Goods of Childhood

The preparatory dimensions of education are clearly very important, and it is quite understandable that discussions of educational justice give them a lot of attention. Education is a transformative process, and we have every reason to be concerned about the outcomes at which it is appropriately directed. Moreover, if childhood is conceived as a diminished normative state from which children need to be rescued then endorsement of a wholly preparatory conception of educational justice can seem appropriate. If the important parts of one's life lie primarily with one's well-being and achievements as a mature agent, then it makes sense for education to be oriented towards preparing one for success in the part of one's life that really matters. However, if the value of childhood is not located solely or even primarily in how features of childhood contribute to life as an adult, but has normative significance in its own right, then there is room for acknowledging non-preparatory dimensions of educational justice.

The idea that there are distinct goods of childhood and that recognition of these goods has salience for theories of justice has recently been advanced by a variety of theorists (Macleod 2010; Brennan 2014; Gheaus 2015). The central idea is that there are good-making features of children's lives whose value does not lie in the contribution they make to maturation and the development of cognitive, psychological, and moral capacities of mature agents. Indeed, children's access to such 'intrinsic goods of childhood' depends to a large degree on the absence of fully mature agential powers. This is not to deny that children, in various complex ways at different ages and states, display forms of agency. Even quite young children formulate preferences and make choices that merit acknowledgement and respect from the adults who care for them and who exercise authority over them. But the form of juvenile agency displayed by children is quite different from mature agency and arguably provides children special, and perhaps unique, access to goods that can enrich their lives as children. Moreover, we need not characterize childhood as a diminished normative state. As Sigal Ben-Porath notes, childhood "has its own characteristics which should be regarded not as deficiencies – in relation to adulthood – but rather as qualities relevant to this part of life, some of which tend to dissolve or evolve into other traits as time passes" (Ben-Porath 2003: 133). The distinct characteristics of childhood arguably give rise to distinct goods of childhood.

There are various ways of elaborating this claim about the distinct goods of childhood but goods related to children's capacities for play, imagination, and innocence merit consideration. "The unbridled and unselfconscious delight children can exhibit when they engage in various forms of play provides strong evidence of the value of play. Similarly, children have remarkable capacities of imagination that permit them to engage with the world and others in creative ways not readily accessible (or perhaps not accessible at all) to adults. Finally, children's innocence also permits them to have special intimate caring relationships and to experience the world with a sense of wonderment and awe" (Macleod 2018: 79).

Three general features of the distinct goods of childhood need emphasis. First, the presence or absence of these goods in the lives of children will have a significant impact on the quality of children's lives as children and also with respect to the overall success of a person's lifetime. The badness of a bad childhood diminishes the overall goodness of person's life even if that badness is overcome in adulthood and even if the badness does not impede successful pursuit of a conception of the good as an adult. Second, although there will often be connections between children's access to the goods of childhood and the heathy development of the various skills, capacities, and dispositions that are crucial to flourishing as an adult, the value of goods of childhood does not lie solely in their contribution to healthy maturation. For example, play may contribute to the development of children's sense of self (Schapiro 1999) and play has been recognized as crucial to cognitive development (Piaget 1962). But the full value of play for children is not exhausted by its developmental role. Even if play contributed little to cognitive or moral development, it is important to the well-being of children for them to have access to play. Similarly, even if robbing children of their innocence did not scar them emotionally or impede their capacities to form and pursue intimate relations as adults, it would be bad to deprive them of the conditions conducive to childhood innocence. Third, although children's access the goods of childhood is grounded in features of their capacities as children, meaningful access to goods of childhood is affected by material and social conditions external to children. Some ways of structuring institutions and distributing resources are hospitable to children accessing these goods and some arrangements impede or eliminate children's access to the goods. Children need time and space to play, their opportunities to engage the world imaginatively can be enhanced through access to artistic materials and avenues of aesthetic exploration, and their innocence can be disrupted by exposure to violence, sex, and other harsh (but perhaps unavoidable) aspects of the world of adults. The maturation of children does, of course, influence what sorts of resources and opportunities contribute to realization of the goods of childhood. Baby toys, for example, will not usefully facilitate the play of young teens. So, the precise way in which resources and social structures can be distributed and organized so as to be conducive to the promotion of the goods of childhood needs to be sensitive to the different ages and stages of children.

Education and Access to Goods of Childhood

The recognition of childhood goods with these features has general implications for theorizing about justice. All credible theories of justice acknowledge that considerations of justice extend to children. So, accounts of justice need to consider not only how the distribution of resources and the structuring of social institutions affect the prospects of children qua future adults. They need also to address how such matters influence children's access to the distinct goods of childhood. This point, in turn, opens the door to recognition of non-preparatory dimensions of educational justice. Three simple observations are pertinent here. First, childhood is a significant and valuable part of a human life in which distinct goods can be realized. For an average person, as much of one quarter of one's life is spent in childhood and adolescence. Second, children, at least in the developed world, typically spend large portions of their childhood at schools. Most children in developed countries attend school for 10 to 12 years and they are in school roughly half of the year. This means that a great deal of the quality of a person's life as a child will be influenced by the character of their school experiences. Third, the manner in which schools are structured and provisioned can facilitate or frustrate children's access to goods of childhood. Some schools have elaborate playgrounds in which children can safely engage in carefree play and have fun before, during, and after school. Other schools have few or no such facilities. Some schools have extensive music, sports, arts and aesthetic programs in which children can engage in creative activities that engage their imaginations. In other schools such programs are largely or completely absent. Some schools are located in safe, pleasant environments in which children have a measure of insulation from disturbing features of the outside world that are corrosive to childhood innocence. Other schools are located in dangerous areas in which serious crime is common. Some schools offer their students trips and outings that are entertaining or adventuresome. Many do not. And so on. A line from a letter that a third-grade student from the Bronx sent to educational researcher Jonathan Kozol grimly but aptly captures the issue: "We don't have no gardens," and "no Music or Art," and "no fun places to play" (Kozol 2005).

The enormous inequalities between schools that bear upon children's experiences at school are often associated with differences in student achievement that matter in even a wholly preparatory conception of educational justice. Children who have better access to play and a wide variety of athletic, aesthetic, recreational activities and whose schools are safe and pleasant will often be better placed to succeed academically than those whose opportunities along these lines are poor. So, it might be contended that non-preparatory dimensions of education overlap sufficiently with preparatory concerns such that just provision of resources to schools in the pursuit of preparatory objectives will secure non-preparatory dimensions of justice. Perhaps, for instance, an education that prepares students for citizenship, equips them to pursue careers and their mature conceptions of the good is an education in which the goods of childhood are amply and fairly supplied to children at school. It is plausible to suppose that there is a degree of overlap between securing preparatory objectives and providing children access to goods of childhood.

But the degree of overlap is not likely to be complete. The absence of a rich program of extracurricular activities at an otherwise decent school probably does not put students who attend such a school at an unfair disadvantage in the pursuit of careers and conceptions of the good as adults compared with students who enjoyed access to excellent extracurricular programs. Rather, the main differences between students will concern the character of their childhood and the goods they accessed as children.

Given this possible and indeed probable divergence, it is appropriate to address the non-preparatory dimensions of educational justice directly. Even if there is, in many contexts, a harmony between achievement of preparatory and non-preparatory educational objectives, it is important to understand the rationale for displaying sensitivity to non-preparatory features of education. That rationale lies in the significance of a person's entire life, including what they experience, achieve, and do as children. We need to prepare children for success as adults but a good childhood, whether or not it contributes to adult success, matters in its own right. As Gina Schouten observes in her discussion of educational justice: we "must recognize benefits conferred on two fronts: increases in children's attainment of actually valuable outcomes, and increases in their prospects for flourishing as adults" (Schouten 2012: 480).

Some Implications

Broadening the domain of educational justice to include sensitivity to the impact of educational arrangements on children's access to goods of childhood has a number of implications that merit brief mention. First, although the standard academic objectives of education remain vital to educational justice, we have reason to resist simplistic accounts of the distinction between core and peripheral elements of schooling in which programs, whether in the official curriculum or school sponsored extracurricular activities, in music, arts, athletics are treated as optional and, perhaps luxurious, add-ons that lie outside the essential educational mission of schools. If, as seems likely, such programs are sites of flourishing for children, *as children*, then we have reason to view them as falling within the core of the educational mission. Children's justice-based entitlement to access goods of childhood afforded by such programs can render fair access to such programs by children a matter of justice.

Second, reconfiguring the domain of education justice suggests that the metrics used to measure and assess the quality of education and the success of schools need to be developed so as to track the access that children, in different educational settings, have to the goods of childhood.

Third, standard accounts of the just distribution of educational resources and opportunities need to be interpreted with a view to accommodating the non-preparatory objectives. For instance, egalitarians frequently raise objections to the manner in which elite private schools confer unjust advantages on the children who attend them. The unjust inequalities emphasized by egalitarians largely fall within the preparatory domain and concern the ways in which some students are better prepared for college or careers. If the ambit of distributive equality includes non-preparatory matters then the egalitarian case against private education may be more powerful.

Yet, egalitarians will also have to develop a more nuanced understanding of the manner in which the structure of families and the opportunities that they can provide children upset distributive equality in the non-preparatory realm. After all, the main avenue through which many children have access to non-preparatory goods (e.g., via recreational activities, music lessons, stimulating trips and outings) is the family and there are significant inequalities between the capacities that different families have to provide such resources and opportunities to their children. Such inequalities arguably fall within the general domain of egalitarian justice since they reflect arbitrary and unfair differences in the access that children from different families have to important goods of childhood. But such inequalities also seem to be relevant, at least indirectly, to educational justice. After all, they reflect ways in which inequalities in access to childhood goods in schools can be compounded. Children who are deprived of access to decent opportunities for recreation and play both at school and at home are doubly disadvantaged compared to children who enjoy excellent opportunities for play and recreation at school and at home. Efforts to remedy such injustice might reasonably direct more recreational resources to schools attended by children from economically disadvantaged families. Just as with the familiar preparatory dimensions of educational justice, we cannot determine whether justice in access to education is achieved by focusing narrowly on the educational resources provided to children in schools. This general point extends even to relational conceptions of educational justice that reject egalitarian distributive principles. Even sufficientarian accounts of educational justice will need to determine what constitutes sufficient access, on the part of children, to non-preparatory facets of education. And a proper determination of whether a decent standard of sufficiency is achieved will require attention to conditions for children at school and at home.

It is possible, especially against the background of the relative scarcity of resources for the provision of education, that there will be tensions between fully securing the preparatory objectives of education and fully securing non-preparatory objectives. The foregoing discussion does not demonstrate that preparatory and non-preparatory educational objectives have equal normative weight. For instance, ensuring that children become literate and numerate is likely to be more important than furnishing them with good playgrounds and a pleasant school environment. However, assigning greater normative gravity to preparatory objectives when proper pursuit of them conflicts with advancement of non-preparatory objectives does not establish either that non-preparatory objectives are unimportant or that they lie outside the domain of educational justice. The foregoing discussion does not address how possible trade-offs between different facets of educational justice should be interpreted and resolved. Rather the principal aim has been to explain why a wholly preparatory account of educational justice is incomplete and why it should be supplemented by attention to non-preparatory educational objectives.

(Related Chapters: 3, 8, 15, 17, 19, 32, 34.)

Notes

1 Homeschooling is a very important phenomenon and the general issues I raise here are pertinent to evaluating homeschooling arrangements, but I shall not directly explore them.
2 See Culp 2020 for a helpful survey of a range of contemporary views of educational justice.
3 There is contestation about the proper characterization of perfectionism and its relation to other positions including liberalism, which is itself a highly contested concept. On some construals, perfectionism is hostile to the accommodation of the idea that there is a plurality of reasonable but divergent conceptions of the good. This gives perfectionism a potentially illiberal cast since state promotion of a conception of the good or human flourishing may seem in tension with respecting the freedom of persons to pursue diverse conceptions of a good life. Yet, since human flourishing is, on many accounts, multiply realizable and since the promotion of perfectionist ideals need not involve the coercive imposition of a single, narrow construal of flourishing, perfectionism need not clash with respect for pluralism about the good life. Tim Fowler embraces the label of perfectionism in describing his view that the proper upbringing of children is expressly aimed at securing specific, though broadly characterized, objective goods for children (Fowler 2021). Fowler's variety of perfectionism for children is not illiberal. Similarly, although he eschews the label 'perfectionism,' Randall Curren's form of eudaimonic justice certainly favors education that cultivates and promotes forms of human excellence but in a manner compatible with diversity and core liberal freedoms (Curren 2022).
4 Hannan 2018 goes even further and holds that childhood is bad for children.
5 A familiar example concerns the valuable state functioning of being well-nourished. A person who has access to a nutritious diet but deliberately forgoes it because they are engaging in a hunger strike is not disadvantaged when compared to the person who chose to consume nutritious food. With respect to the functioning of being well-nourished these people enjoy equal capabilities since the difference in the actual functioning they achieve is grounded in different ways of exercising agency.

References

Anderson, E. (1999) "What is the Point of Equality?" *Ethics* 109(2): 287–337.
Anderson, E. (2007) "Fair Opportunity in Education: A Democratic Equality Perspective," *Ethics* 117(4): 595–622.
Brennan, S. (2014) "The Goods of Childhood, Children's Rights, and the Role of Parents as Advocates and Interpreters," in F. Baylis & C. McLeod (eds.) *Family-Making: Contemporary Ethical Challenges*. Oxford, UK: Oxford University Press, 29–45.

Brighouse, H., & Swift, A. (2009) "Educational Equality Versus Educational Adequacy: A Critique of Anderson and Satz," *Journal of Applied Philosophy* 26(2): 117–128.
Brighouse, H., & Swift, A. (2014) "The Place of Educational Equality in Educational Justice," in K. Meyer (ed.) *Education, Justice and the Human Good. Fairness and Equality in the Educational System*. London, UK: Routledge, 14–33.
Ben-Porath, S. (2003) "Autonomy and Vulnerability: On Just Relations between Adults and Children," *Journal of Philosophy of Education* 37(1): 127–145.
Clayton, M. (2006) *Justice and Legitimacy in Upbringing*. Oxford: Oxford University Press.
Culp, J. (2020) "Educational Justice," *Philosophy Compass* 15(12): 1–12.
Curren, R. (2013) "A neo-Aristotelian Account of Education, Justice, and the Human Good," *Theory and Research in Education* 11(3): 231–249.
Curren, R. (2022) "Social Issues: A Self-Determination Theory Perspective" in R. Ryan (ed.) *Handbook of Self-Determination Theory*. Oxford: Oxford University Press.
Fowler, T. (2021) *Liberalism, Childhood and Justice: Ethical Issues in Upbringing*. Bristol: Bristol University Press.
Gheaus, A. (2015) "The Intrinsic Goods of Childhood and the Good Society," in A. Bagattini & C. Macleod (eds.) *The Wellbeing of Children in Theory and Practice*. Dordrecht: Springer, 35–52.
Gutmann, A. (1980) "Children, Paternalism and Education: A Liberal Argument," *Philosophy and Public Affairs* 9(4): 338–358.
Gutmann, A. (1998) *Democratic Education*. Princeton: Princeton University Press.
Hannan, S. (2018) "Why Childhood is Bad for Children," Journal of Applied Philosophy 35(S1): 11–28.
Kozol, J. (2005) *The Shame of the Nation: The Restoration of Apartheid in America*. New York: Crown.
Ladd, H. & Loeb, S. (2013) "The Challenges of Measuring School Quality Implications for Educational Equity," in D. Allen & R. Reich (eds.) *Education, Justice and Democracy*. Chicago: University of Chicago Press, 43–61.
Macleod, C. (2010) "Primary Goods, Capabilities, and Children," in H. Brighouse and I. Robeyns (eds.) *Measuring Justice: Primary Goods and Capabilities*. Cambridge: Cambridge University Press, 174–192.
Macleod, C. (2012) "Justice, Educational Equality and Sufficiency," in C. Macleod (ed.) *Justice and Equality*. Calgary: University of Calgary Press, 151–175.
Macleod, C. (2015) "Agency, Authority and the Vulnerability of Children," in A. Bagattini & C. Macleod (eds.) *The Wellbeing of Children in Theory and Practice*. Dordrecht: Springer, 53–64.
Macleod, C. (2018) "Just Schools and Good Childhoods: Non-preparatory Dimensions of Educational Justice," *Journal of Applied Philosophy* 35(S1): 76–89.
Narveson, J. (2001) *The Libertarian Idea*. Guelph, Ontario: Broadview Press.
Nozick, R. (1974) *Anarchy, State, and Utopia*. New York: Basic Books.
Nussbaum, M. (2006) *Frontiers of Justice: Disability, Nationality, Species Membership*. Cambridge, MA: Harvard University Press.
Piaget, J. (1962) *Play, Dreams and Imitation in Childhood*. New York: Norton.
Rawls, J. (2003) *Justice as Fairness: A Restatement*, Cambridge, MA: Harvard University Press.
Rawls, J. (2005) *Political Liberalism: Expanded Edition*. New York: Columbia University Press.
Reich, R. (2013) "Equality, Adequacy, and K-12 Education," in D. Allen & R. Reich (eds.) *Education, Justice and Democracy*. Chicago, IL: University of Chicago Press, 43–61.
Satz, D. (2007) "Equality, Adequacy, And Education for Citizenship," *Ethics* 117(4): 623–648.
Schapiro, T. (1999) "What is a Child?" *Ethics* 109: 715–738.
Schouten, G. (2012) "Fair Educational Opportunity and the Distribution of Natural Ability: Toward a Prioritarian Principle of Educational Justice," *Journal of Philosophy of Education* 46(3): 472–491.
Sen, A. (1999) *Development as Freedom*. Oxford: Oxford University Press.

17

CHILD WORK AND EDUCATION, A GLOBAL PERSPECTIVE

Nico Brando

Introduction

In the contemporary Western world, the standard view of children's rightful place is that they should be in school. Children's task as children is to learn and develop skills so they can become active contributing members in their society. This life at school does not exist for many children, however. An estimated 260 million children worldwide are out-of-school, many of them because their time is spent working (UIS 2019).

How can the idea that children have a right to an education be reconciled with the reality that almost one-fifth of the world's school-aged children currently do not go to school and many of them are engaged in economic and caring activities that conflict with their interest in getting an education?[1] This chapter provides an overview of the core issues that arise from the dyad of children's education and work. How are these concepts understood in the literature? What are the tensions between work and education? How can they be addressed? And what problems arise from current attempts to eliminate these tensions? A global perspective, relying on examples from across the globe, will allow us to explore the common patterns of interaction between children's work and education, while also highlighting the radical variation and diversity that exists in the manifestations of child work and education globally.

First, I introduce the core concepts and the basic data on education and child work globally. Second, I present the main arguments in the literature on the morality of child labor. Third, I explain how a child's right to an education relates to the debate on child labor. Fourth, I introduce the standard approach in the literature used to address the dyad of child labor and out-of-school children (the compulsion-and-ban approach). Finally, I address four problems that arise from this approach (diversity, causality, source, and inclusivity).

Core Definitions

Let us start by clarifying the use of the terms "child work" and "education" in this chapter. Since the 1990s, international organizations (particularly, the International Labor Organization [ILO]) have emphasized the need to distinguish between what they term "child work" and "child labor" (ILO 2021). "Child work/employment" is an umbrella category that encompasses all activities engaged in by children that produce economic benefits, be it in the market itself, or indirectly, such as by acting as caretakers, or doing household chores. Child work can be formal or informal, it can be

DOI: 10.4324/9781003172246-21

remunerated or not, and it can happen within and outside the family. "Child labor" is a specific manifestation of child work, defined as one that "deprives children of their childhood, their potential and their dignity, and that is harmful to physical and mental development" (ILO 2021). This refers to all work that can be mentally, physically, or emotionally harmful to the child, and all those that interfere with schooling.[2] "Child labor" is a normative category that refers to morally problematic economic activities engaged in by children.

This categorization of certain forms of children's work as invariably "wrong" has been strongly criticized by researchers who work with child workers themselves, as it oversimplifies the variety of ways in which children themselves relate to their work, and the variable harms and benefits that children's engagement in economic activities may entail (Bourdillon 2011; Liebel 2004: Ch. 2). This chapter addresses child work, broadly understood, in order to explore its diverse relationships with education.

As with "child labor," "education" is defined very narrowly in the legal and policy literature, especially when applied to research on child work. It refers, in short, to education in its institutionalized form; that is, formal schooling (e.g., Brown 2012). When education is mentioned in relation to child work, it refers to children's (lack of) access to the school system, and to the years of formal education an individual has received. This definition is problematic, as it already prefigures the scope of options available to provide children with access to an education. Informal educational settings (including the education that exists in the workplace) are, thus, excluded from the definition of "education" in this literature. This chapter uses the term "schooling" to refer to the institutionalized form, and "education" to refer to all forms of formal or informal learning.

Basic Data

Global estimates indicate that around 160 million children were in child labor at the beginning of 2020. This accounts for almost 10 percent of the child population globally. Nearly half of these are in hazardous labor, and at least 5 million are engaged in the worst forms of child labor. This data shows a rise of 8 million in comparison to 2012, and around 9 million more are expected by 2022 due to poverty caused by the COVID-19 pandemic (ILO-UNICEF 2021: 8).

As for access to education, it is estimated that 260 million children are out-of-school. The worst figures come from children aged 15–17, 35 percent of whom are out-of-school. Sixteen percent of 12–14-year-olds are out-of-school, and 8 percent of 5–11-year-olds do not go to school (UIS 2019: 2–3). Child workers account for around 20 percent of the total out-of-school population, with child workers making up almost 50 percent of the out-of-school population for the 5–11 age group (ILO-UNICEF 2021: 47–48).

What Is Wrong with Child Labor?

We tend to respond negatively to the idea of children working. But what grounds our moral impulses regarding child labor? There are various economic, consequentialist, and deontological arguments against child labor. First, children working can be considered as inefficient for the labor market (Basu and Hoang Van 1998; Ray 2009). If a population starts working full-time at a very young age and children do not develop fundamental skills at school, human capital formation will be limited, and countries will have generations of mostly unskilled workers. Moreover, enlarging the labor force would lead to lower wages and higher unemployment for the rest of the working population. But child labor is frowned upon for reasons beyond its economic impact on society. More importantly, children are subjects of moral concern, and allowing them to work may be inconsistent with protecting their fundamental interests.

Regardless of the metric used to assess what children's fundamental interests are (be it human rights, capabilities, primary goods, resources), and regardless of the threshold used to assess what is owed to children (equality, sufficiency, priority), child labor is standardly considered a direct affront to protecting children's fundamental interests. According to Philip Cook's taxonomy (2018), harm, exploitation, and failure-to-benefit are the three main arguments used to show that child labor is wrong. The *Harm argument* holds that children's condition as mentally and physically developing beings makes them especially vulnerable to harms (in general). Working conditions can threaten children's short- and long-term interests; long hours, harsh conditions in the workplace, contact with hazardous materials, and use of complex machinery threaten children's well-being (Satz 2010: 159–161). All employment that can negatively affect children's well-being is a moral wrong, according to this argument.

The *Exploitation argument* appeals to the moral relevance of children's condition as "weak agents" (Satz 2010: 157–158), which makes them especially vulnerable to exploitation in the labor market. Children's assumed lack of understanding of the implications of their choices, their limited capacity to foresee the consequences of their decisions regarding work, and their limited social and economic skills puts them in a weak position vis-à-vis employers. The conclusion drawn is that this makes children wrong for the labor market, as they will always be vulnerable to exploitation due to their weak agency.

The *Fail-to-benefit argument* claims that working conditions not only harm children (in the sense of reducing their well-being as compared to not working), but also arrest their potential development. The time children spend working instead of being at school limits their opportunity to develop fundamental abilities, motivations, and skills that would allow them to reap ample benefits in the future (Pierik and Houwerzijl 2006; Jonas 2016: 390–391). Thus, all work that conflicts with children's schooling is wrong, and should be abolished, according to this argument.

How Does Education Fit into The Equation?

Consensus exists on the fundamental role played by education in fostering human and economic development. Access to education is a structural resource for individuals to develop the skills necessary to live in our social and economic world. Its value in promoting human development is the reason why education is enshrined as a human right, and as a special right for children (UNGA 1989: Art. 28, 29). International law obliges states to ensure free and compulsory primary education for all children, and secondary and higher education accessible to all.

Various reasons are given in the philosophical literature to justify the right to education, and the duty to be educated. First, education is a structural prerequisite to securing equality of opportunity within a society (Brighouse & Swift 2006); it should establish a level playing field for individuals from different socioeconomic strata by providing equalizing (equal, adequate, or compensatory) access to the resources and skills needed to compete for positional goods and attain social mobility. Second, education is fundamental for the development of autonomy and self-government (Feinberg 1980; Brighouse 2000; Curren 2009): it provides individuals contact with and access to a variety of options and life-choices, enabling their development as autonomous individuals. Education is, moreover, a foundational factor for the development of most human capabilities required for flourishing (Nussbaum 1997; McCowan 2011). It develops and strengthens our understanding of ourselves and others, our capacities for practical reasoning, our relationship to our sociopolitical world, and the skills required to act as economic agents.

Beyond individual benefits, education is also a fundamental resource for producing collective goods (Schouten 2018). Education can provide certain goods that are socially valuable and required for a society to function well. An education can be foundational for economic development and stability, and for promoting the virtues and values of citizenship (Gutmann 2003). A well-functioning economy requires a skilled and educated workforce to ensure economic growth and stability (Basu & Hoang Van 1998; Ray 2009). Moreover, educated democratic citizens can be necessary for the stability and sustainability of political systems (Gutmann 1999). A society's right to secure these collective goods through education may add a duty to be educated, beyond a right to be educated.

Research on education and education policy, especially that targeted towards the least advantaged children, requires studying the sources and manifestations of child work owing to the impact that children's economic activities can have on their educational interests. Children who work have less time to go to school, less energy to study in their free time, and, in many cases, no time or energy to either go to school or study. For many children, working implies not going to school at all. For others, it implies very long days working and studying, or being enrolled at school but barely going. Some children find a balance between their work and their studying, but this is not always an easy task, as most school systems are not sufficiently accommodating to the particular needs and schedules of working children (Boyden 1994).

Regardless of whether the work done by children harms them in a physical or emotional sense, child work is considered morally problematic as it is a direct threat to children's right to an education; it is a threat to a society's economic development; and it is a threat to the civic health and political stability of a country (Hindman & Smith 1999). If states have a duty to protect children's interest in having an education, and if work conflicts with the possibility of securing this right for all children, then child work can be considered a source of harm to children that states have a duty to prevent (Jonas 2016: 397).

The Incompatibility View

Child work and education are generally conceptualized as categorically incompatible. The modern conception of childhood that started getting traction at the end of the 19th century establishes the school as the primary space in which children should dwell and studying as their primary social responsibility (Fyfe 2015). Despite it deriving from WEIRD (Western, Educated, Industrialized, Rich Democracies) social and political discourses, the conception of childhood as a preparatory stage of life in which individuals are protected and separated from the adult world has become the standard through which childhood is studied, and policy and law enacted (Schapiro 1999; Wells 2015: 15–21). As child work interferes with the objective of keeping children within the sphere of the school, law and policy are required to ensure children's access to an education, and their protection from the harms of the labor market (Hindman & Smith 1999).

The International Labor Organization (ILO) is the main institution in charge of managing and determining the course of international discourses on child work. Child work is regulated by international law not only to protect children from physical and exploitative harms, but also to ensure a better fulfilment of children's right to an education. For example, the ILO Convention 138 (1976), establishes minimum ages of employment, not only relating to how certain types of work can harm children due to their developmental state (see Article 3 in relation to hazardous labor, i.e., mining, dangerous machinery, chemicals or substances, or sexual work), but also in relation to their right to an education. C138 establishes that the minimum age for working "shall not be less than the age of completion of compulsory schooling" (ILO 1976: Art. 2.3). This means that, regardless of the age and developmental capacities of an individual, the right to work is directly conditioned by an individual's duty to enroll in and complete compulsory schooling.

The tandem of legislation on the right to an education and the restriction on child labor structures this notion of a descriptive and normative incompatibility between child work and education. It claims that work inevitably interferes with the realization of children's rights to an education (in the sense that it affects their chances of attending school, forces them to drop out, and restricts their study time). Education and work are, thus, seen as mutually exclusive activities.

There is, of course, an element of truth in this normative claim: child work interferes with children's rights to an education by imposing obstacles to their access and progress in formal schooling. This claim tends to lead to what are termed "compulsion-and-ban policies" on child labor and education (Boyden 1994). By banning children from working, and by making schooling compulsory, these policies attempt to solve the dual moral issue posed by children working and not getting an education. Compulsion-and-ban policies aim to protect children from the harms of working and ensure access to the benefits that schooling has for their short and long-term interests. A co-dependent normative relationship is thereby established between protecting children from work and ensuring their access to schools: by banning child labor, access to schools can be improved, and by making schooling compulsory, children are forced to leave the labor market.

Issues with Compulsion-And-Ban

Notwithstanding the seeming straightforwardness of a compulsion-and-ban approach to addressing the dual issues of child labor and out-of-school children, there are various problems with its operationalization. Despite the reliance of policymakers and economists on this approach, there is little proof that it can achieve its dual objective. It does not address the roots of the dual problem, and there are obstacles to legitimizing the imposition of these regulatory norms on diverse populations. Critics of compulsion-and-ban approaches argue that the relationship between school and work is extremely complex and varies depending on the sundry cultural, social, and economic circumstances of different groups of children (Boyden 1994: 3). Regulatory solutions should take this variability into account.

There are four problems, in particular, that compulsion-and-ban approaches to the abolition of child labor and the protection of the right to education encounter. First, the problem of addressing *intersectionality and diversity* when developing international norms and regulations; second, the question of *causality* between children working and not attending schools; third, the problem of not addressing the actual *source* of this dual problem (usually, poverty); finally, a concern that it is the *lack of inclusivity* of formal schooling systems that restricts working children's access to an education, rather than their work.

Diversity and Intersectionality

Compulsion-and-ban policies depend on an assumption that the child working population is homogeneous with respect to their reasons for working, and for not going to school. They also depend on the assumption that child workers are not agents in themselves, but rather passive actors who are controlled by others, usually parents or the larger family. These two assumptions are deeply flawed, however. An intersectional analysis of children's diverse relationships with school and work shows that the homogeneity assumption is not uniformly correct. There are many factors tied to the individual child's condition, the working conditions, and the schooling conditions that affect a child's relationship to school and work. Moreover, not accounting for children's role as active agents fosters biased understandings of children's relationships to their work and education.

Research on child labor grounded in a postcolonial standpoint (e.g., Nieuwenhuys 2013; Balagopalan 2018) has put into question the validity of universalist ontologies that rely on generalized understandings of how human societies function. What is "childhood," what is good for children, and how to ensure justice for children are questions that do not have straightforward answers (Nieuwenhuys 2013: 6). David Lancy's expansive anthropological research has shown that the conceptualization of "childhood" as a protected and innocent life-stage when humans must be educated and pampered is mostly a modern and Western construct (Lancy 2015: Ch. 2). Moreover, he shows that in most contemporary societies (not to say in earlier ones) work, and providing economic support in the household, are considered fundamental aspects of the child's development, and are not only encouraged but sometimes mandated (Lancy 2015: Ch. 7). Children in many parts of the world are not only individuals with rights, but also understood as duty-bearers with responsibilities towards their families and to give their share for their household's needs (Letuka 1998).[3] The universalist appeal of compulsion-and-ban policies, to abolish child labor and force children into schools, is interpreted as an act of cultural and epistemic domination by the Global North for other regions of the world that do not endorse the Western conception of childhood or its prescriptions for how to secure justice for children.

One could argue that the postcolonial critique, while empirically accurate, is not normatively compelling. The fact of cultural variation regarding the status and role of children in diverse societies should not affect our normative assessment of what harms children and what they are owed as a matter of justice. Following the UNCRC, if getting an education and being protected from exploitative work is in the child's best interests, a child's rights should be taken as trumps over their societal traditions so those interests are protected.[4] If endorsers of the incompatibility view can justify the claim that cultural environments that foster children's work at the expense of education are sources of oppression and domination of children, they may have a strong argument for implementing universal guidelines on how to police children's education and work (Brando 2019). However, this argument still depends on the validity of the assumption that the child working population is mostly homogenous and passive.

Of course, that is not the case. The incompatible relationship between child work and schooling is conditional on many variables, including the specific job the child has, number of hours working, gender, and access to schools in her area, among many others. Research in Lima (Peru) shows that domestic workers or children who work at their own home have higher attendance and success rates than children who have salaried work in factories or building sites (Ennew & Milne 1989). However, this is strongly affected by whether children work in rural or urban areas. In general, rural children are less likely to attend school than children working in an urban setting. Various explanations for this have been offered: first, even if rural children have more time and flexibility than salaried urban workers, the lower accessibility of schools in rural areas makes mixing work and school more difficult (Boyden 1994: 16–18). Moreover, education is generally perceived as less valuable than work in rural environments, as children are expected to stay in agriculture when they grow up (Ornert 2018: 5).

A crucial variable in the relationship between work and school is gender. Gender bias entails that, if a family has limited resources to send children to schools, they will prioritize boys over the girls in the family. As education is commonly linked to skilled productive activities rather than domestic work, and as women in many regions of the world are socially encouraged to prioritize domestic work, schooling (especially secondary education and beyond) is not a high family priority for their girls. ILO research in Andra Pradesh (India), showed that, after schooling for basic literacy and numeracy (around 8 years-old), the gap between boys' and girls' access to school increases exponentially (Singh & Khan 2016: 9). Similar results were found in Ethiopia by the Young Lives project, where another relevant variable for girls' access to school was their marriage status (Tafere & Chuta 2016).

Variation in children's work and education experiences is not only conditioned by factors that children themselves cannot control (their location, gender, parental incentives, etc.), but, very importantly, by children's own understanding of their role in society and their choices as autonomous agents themselves. Much research on child labor and education assumes children's lack of choice over their work, and over how they combine (if they do) working and studying. It is assumed that adults are the only agents who make decisions over children's lives, and that children, as "weak agents," are simply forced to fulfil their adult guardians' wills (Satz 2010; Ray 2009).

However, for many children, working rather than going to school is an autonomous choice taken due to difficult circumstances, or due to the perceived benefits that economic independence gives. For many girls, for example, leaving home and finding work may be their only option to avoid early marriage and a life of child-rearing and homemaking (Liebel 2004: 167–168). Moreover, for many children, earning money, contributing to household earnings and/or saving money for themselves are valuable in themselves as status symbols of adulthood. Research in Brazil and in Jamaica highlighted changes in teenagers' conceptions of themselves and their value when they are active economic contributors (Boyden 1994: 13). It is also stressed that child workers in these countries valued their improved status within the household, of their decision-making powers, and of their self-determination due to their working condition.

This is all to say that diversity in the why, how, and where of child work are important variables to consider when thinking about children's relationship to their work and education. Considering any work that conflicts with schooling as necessarily wrong is an over-generalization; not considering how certain intersectionalities may affect our moral judgement, or how children's own agency and choice may change our understanding of what is best for them can lead to regulative solutions that cause more harm than good.

Causality of Harm

Besides its assumption of homogeneity, the compulsion-and-ban approaches depend on an empirical assumption about causality. For child work to be labelled as harmful (and thus wrong), it must cause children to have less access to schooling and less achievement in school than they would otherwise have. In terms of efficacy, for compulsion-and-ban policies to achieve their dual aim of reducing harm caused by child labor, and increasing school attendance and achievement, there must be a causal link between children working and not going to school.

While the literature generally agrees that children who work tend to have lower achievement rates at school than those who do not work (Woldehanna & Gebremedhin 2015), the wider question of whether working interferes with children's schooling, causing lower achievement, is a more difficult question to answer (Ornert 2018). On the one hand, ample evidence from studies in different regions, and of children in radically different circumstances, show scarce correlation between not attending school and working; on the other hand, while it is assumed that children do not go to school because they work, in many instances the reasons for not going to school may point in the direction of the schooling system itself. Lack of incentives and lack of supports, regardless of whether they work or not, are often the cause of large numbers of children being out-of-school.

There must be strong evidence showing that work is a significant obstacle to attending school to justify asserting causality between these variables. Although child work does have a strong negative effect on tests scores and school completion, it does not have the same effect on enrollment (Betcherman et al. 2004). A recent participatory project, *It's Time to Talk!,* led by Terre des Hommes (O'Kane et al. 2018), showed that 76 percent of the child workers consulted were studying (in formal and informal schooling settings). Data from different regions of the world point to similar results. In Sri Lanka, the average time spent studying by working and non-working children is similar until the teenage years arrive (Ray 2009: 123). That is, up to the age of 13, children who work and who do not work spend similar amounts of time studying. From 13 onwards, the gap between the two groups starts to grow exponentially. This seems to show that the negative effect of work on children's study time is not exclusively tied to the fact that they work but to their life-stage. Data from Cambodia showed no radical variation between working and non-working children's ability to read and write (Ray 2009). Just as in the Sri Lankan research, no variation exists until children turn 13; after that, the gap between working and non-working is around 5 percent.

Studies in Latin America also show significant percentages of working children who also go to school. A survey conducted in Colombia showed literacy rates of almost 100 percent in child workers between 12 and 14-years-old, with many not only completing primary school, but also attending secondary school while working (Boyden 1994: 6). A further large-scale study with almost

400.000 children, between 7 and 14 years old, in Bogotá (Colombia) showed that out of this ample sample of the city's child population, 87 percent worked in some way or another (either in the formal or informal sector) (Boyden 1994: 7). This means that a very large section of the student population in this city belonged to the working population as well. If work is a core cause for not attending school, how can one account for such high percentages of child workers in the school system?

Combining work with schooling seems to be a standard practice for child workers all around the world. Compulsion-and-ban policies may be a relevant reason why child workers go to school, but it does little to deter their engagement in the labor market. The choice in child workers' hands does not seem to be between school or work, "but rather how much time and effort should be given to each activity" (Boyden et al 2016: 11). This is because children (and their families) have little incentive to stop working, regardless of whether it is against the law. For many children, it is their work which allows them (or their siblings) to have an education (to pay for fees, books, through earn-and-learn schemes) (Bourdillon et al. 2010: Ch. 6); not only is their work not incompatible with the schooling, in many cases it is the reason why they are able to go to school.

Moreover, research shows that a core cause of children not going to school is not that work conflicts with them attending, but that schools themselves are inaccessible (either due to distance or cost) or, very importantly, the quality of accessible schools is so low that parents (or children themselves) do not have an incentive to lose time going to a school that cannot ensure any economic returns (either short- or long-term) (Betcherman et al. 2004). The Young Lives project in Ethiopia, India, Peru, and Vietnam found that poor quality education in schools was in most cases a stronger determinant of the interruption of a child's schooling than children's work (Morrow & Boyden 2018; Boyden et al. 2016). Development agencies' narrow focus on increasing access to education in the developing world while disregarding the quality of the education provided has proven to be a well-intentioned but futile attempt to improve children's access to school (Banerjee & Duflo 2011: 56–74).

School systems function, primarily, as institutions for the creation of human capital. If parents and children see meagre potential returns from the time spent in school, there is little incentive for households to lose out on the extra income provided by the child just so they can go to school. Incentives are a fundamental phenomenon that compulsion-and-ban policies cannot fully address (Betcherman et al 2004: 3). Forcing children to go to school and restricting their access to the labor market merely through coercion is insufficient for improving their quality of life. As long as the education provided in school does not ensure sufficient returns, and as long as the family (and the child) require the child's time for other economic activities, there is little that coercion alone can do to force them to change. Creating incentives for families and children is, thus, a structural matter that policies on child work and education should address (Boyden et al. 2016). Earn-and-learn schemes in Zimbabwe have proven extremely effective in moving the child working population into schools (Bourdillon et al. 2010: 109–111), while cash transfers to parents (mothers usually) conditioned on children's enrollment and attendance in schools have had positive effects in countries like Mexico, Brazil, and Bangladesh (Betcherman et al. 2004: 23–24; Baird et al. 2014). If the source of child labor is need for a child's time and work, then it is need we should focus on in order to provide better regulative proposals.

Work and Need

Although many children do manage to combine work and schooling, many others do not. Yet, banning child labor has not worked as a solution to these children being out-of-school. The reason for this is simple: most children who work and do not go to school do so because they need to. They do not have an alternative. Even in households where getting an education is valued, if a child's income is required to maintain subsistence, if their time is needed to care for others or to take on responsibilities at home, both parents and children may have to forgo the long-term benefits that an education can provide, to ensure their short-term subsistence (Betcherman et al. 2004: 15; Jonas 2016).

Banning children from working, when children and their families need a child's income and time to survive, not only does not protect children from the potential harms of labor, it can force them to work in even more exploitative conditions, with fewer protections, and for lower economic returns. Economic deprivation and need lead children to work and not go to school because the relative value of a child's education is conditioned by hers and her family's needs and requirements. Scarcity and deprivation imply that any choice on how one uses one's time has high opportunity costs, and household decisions on making children work rather than study can be rational, in fact (Betcherman et al. 2004: 14–15). It is not irresponsibility that leads parents to encourage (or compel) their children to take on economic activities; it is a tragic choice that must be made to secure the short-term well-being of the family unit (Wolff 2019).

The relative value of a child's formal education is conditioned by the perceived value of a child's time for income-generating activities, and by the relative value of the household income for other needs. A deprived household's income is highly limited, and the costs of schooling (even if not high) may not be a priority when other perceived needs are considered more urgent. Moreover, a child's time may be perceived as more valuable if she obtains her own income, supports the family trade, provides domestic work, or performs caring duties, so that other members of the household can have more time to earn an income.

Not surprisingly, the top two reasons given for working by children interviewed in the *It's Time to Talk!* project were to help and support their family, and to meet urgent basic needs associated with poverty (O'Kane et al. 2018: 11). This shows children's awareness of their role and responsibilities to sustain and support of their family members. Even households that value a child's education may not be able to afford sending them to school, as there are more urgent issues to address. It does not matter how stringent compulsion-and-ban policies are; when in need, there is no incentive for a child to go to school if her time and income can be put to better use. Families dodge infringing compulsion-and-ban legislation by registering children in school but rarely allowing them to go (dodging compulsion) and making use of their time by either working at the margins of the legal market, or by carrying out work at home, such as caring for other family members. If a family is in need, and can barely achieve subsistence, there are no incentives to having a mouth to feed that does not generate an economic benefit. Compulsion-and-ban policies are, in this sense, insufficient to address the actual root of the problem that affects many children who work and do not go to school: poverty.

Awareness of the reality in which children live implies exploring solutions that account for their situated selves (Liebel 2004). This requires going in two different directions: first, focusing on redistribution of resources, on providing safety nets, cash transfers, increasing minimum wages, and in the state and businesses taking a more engaged and responsibility-based role in the welfare of children. Moreover, as has been noted, for many children the school system is actually a significant reason why they work. Some need to work to pay for their tuition fees, textbooks, materials, while others start working because they are disappointed by the school system. Waiving fees, providing resources, and improving the quality of schools can provide valuable incentives for children to enroll.

Formal Schooling and Inclusivity

Compulsion-and-ban policies consider that the education that is owed to children is the one provided by formal schools. It implies that a child's development process is benefited by a child's space and time being restricted to formal schools and to studying. But as Cook argues: "it is unclear that development is a benefit and, second, it is unclear that schooling is a benefit" (Cook 2018: 298). Liberationist theorists of childhood have argued that this binding of the child's life to the institution of schools and to a "developing" understanding of childhood is a coercive, oppressive, and unjust practice (Illich 1970; Firestone 1970; Farson 1974).

On the one hand, the concept of "development" in itself can be considered a problematic notion, one that promotes a specific understanding of who "children" are, by reifying them as passive, incapable and vulnerable actors, without agency or will of their own (Burman 1994; Nieuwenhuys 2013: 5). It has been argued that this "becoming" understanding of childhood (Uprichard 2008; Gheaus 2015) is harmful as it does not count children as beings in the present who have particular interests, and who may participate as active social and economic agents. Critical theorists have argued that formal schooling is the institution through which this harmful understanding of children as "developing beings" is operationalized (Illich 1970: Ch. 2; Firestone 1970: Ch. 4), by limiting children's potential societal contributions and coercing them to behave as developing beings, rather than as full human beings.

The problem of the institutionalization of children as "developing beings" can be exemplified by how compulsion-and-ban approaches restrict the definition of "education" to that provided by the formal schooling system. In this scenario, an important issue must be raised: just because "education" is beneficial and a fundamental interest of children, does this mean that "schooling" is necessarily beneficial and fundamental for children as well? (Cook 2018: 299). Schooling is a specific institution through which a formal and organized form of education is provided to children; children are expected to adapt themselves and their time to what the organized system of a school requires from them. This compulsion need not be harmful or an unjust imposition on children (Schouten 2018: 351–352); in fact, a homogenous curriculum with predetermined timeframes and requirements may be necessary and beneficial to protect the interest of many children (Purdy 1992: Ch. 5). The question is, however, are working children benefited, and are their interests protected and promoted, by being forced to go to compulsory formal schools?

While compulsion-and-ban policies claim that children's work conflicts with their education; advocates of child workers, and child workers themselves, claim that it is the rigidity and lack of inclusivity of the current school system which conflicts with both their education and their work (Liebel 2004: Ch. 10; O'Kane et al. 2018). As mentioned above, a primary reason why children work is because they need to do so. It does not matter how accessible schools are; if children need to make use of their time to support themselves and their famlies, work is still going to be a part of their lives. Forcing them to attend a rigid system of schooling, which conflicts with their working or care obligations, will require them to prioritise some facets of their lives over others, potentially affecting all of them.

For many children, the work environment is an invaluable source of education. However, an understanding of "education" as "formal schooling" omits the possibility of accepting the fact that children are often being educated and socialized at work (Ornert 2018: 9–10). Children in rural areas, who work in farms, reap the greatest educative benefits from practicing the trade on which their household depends (Bourdillon et al. 2010). Of course, for children's work experience to be educative it must support their development of skills, aptitudes, and general flourishing. Banning children from work has the consequence of marginalising the work of children into illegal, non-formative, and potentially exploitative labor. Protecting their rights as workers can have a highly positive impact on the kind of work they do, the wage they receive, and the hours they work, which means they can better control and balance their schooling and work responsibilities.

To expand working children's access to an education, the current restrictive, understanding of education as "formal schooling" may have to be either abolished, as some have suggested (Illich 1970; Cook 2018: 299), or at least, radically revised for it to accommodate and adapt to the needs and interests of the child working population (Boyden et al 2016; Morrow & Boyden 2018). Flexible schedules, part-time schools, and adapted curricula are some of the best practices that are considered effective in promoting child workers' access to an education.

(Related Chapters: 3, 8, 15, 16, 18, 21, 23, 34.)

Notes

1 I follow the standard definition of the Convention on the Rights of the Child (UNCRC) which defines a "child" as "every human being below the age of eighteen years unless under the law applicable to the child, majority is attained earlier" (UNGA 1989: Art.1).
2 Child labor is further divided into three sub-categories: child labor, hazardous labor, and worst forms of child labor.
3 This, in fact, is enshrined in Article 31 of the African Charter on the Rights and Welfare of the Child. Article 31 claims that children have a duty "to work for the cohesion of the family, to respect his parents, superiors and elders at all times and to assist them in case of need" (OAU 1990: Art. 31a).
4 The UNCRC (UNGA 1989), ratified by every country but the United States, claims that all children have a right to free primary education (Art. 28), a right against economic exploitation (Art. 32), and to have their best interest taken as primary consideration on any action that affects them (Art. 3.1)

References

Baird, S., Ferreira, F. H. G., Özler, B., & Woolcock, M. (2014) "Conditional, Unconditional and Everything in Between," *Journal of Development Effectiveness* 6(1): 1–43.
Balagopalan, S. (2018) "Afterschool and During Vacations: On Labour and Schooling in the Postcolony," *Children's Geographies* 17(2): 231–245.
Banerjee, A. V. & Duflo, E. (2011) *Poor Economics. A Radical Rethinking of the Way to Fight Global Poverty*. New York: Public Affairs
Basu, K. & Hoang Van, P. (1998) "The Economics of Child Labor," *The American Economic Review* 88 (3): 412–427.
Betcherman, G., Fares, J., Luinstra, A. & Prouty, R. (2004) "Child Labor, Education, and Children's Rights," *World Bank: Social Protection Discussion Paper Series* No.0412.
Bourdillon, M. (2011) *A Place for Work in Children's Lives?* Ottawa: Plan International - Canada.
Bourdillon, M., Levinson, D., Myers, W. & White, B. (2010) *Rights and Wrongs of Children's Work*. New Brunswick: Rutgers University Press.
Boyden, J. (1994) "The Relationship between Education and Child Work," *Innocenti Occasional Papers* 9: 1–37.
Boyden, J., Porter, C., Zharkevich, I. & Heissler, K. (2016) "Balancing School and Work with New Opportunities: Changes in Children's Gendered Time Use in Ethiopia (2006–2013)," *Working Paper 161*, Oxford: Young Lives.
Brando, N. (2019) "Universalism, Embeddedness and Domination: An Analysis of the Convention on the Rights of the Child," *Journal of Global Ethics* 15(3): 270–286.
Brighouse, H. (2000) *School Choice and Social Justice*. Oxford: Oxford University Press.
Brighouse, H., & Swift, A., (2006) "Equality, Priority, and Positional Goods," *Ethics* 116: 471–497.
Brown, G. (2012) *Child labour and educational disadvantage: Breaking the link, building opportunity*. London: The Office of the UN Special Envoy for Global Education.
Burman, E. (1994) *Deconstructing Developmental Psychology*. London: Routledge.
Cook, P. (2018) "What's Wrong with Child Labor?" in A. Gheaus, G. Calder & J. De Wispelaere (eds.) *The Routledge Handbook of the Philosophy of Childhood and Children*. New York: Routledge, 294–303.
Curren, R. (2009) "Education as a Social Right in a Diverse Society," *Journal of Philosophy of Education* 43(1): 45–56.
Ennew, J. & Milne, B. (1989) *The Next Generation: Lives of Third World Children*. London: Zed Books.
Farson, R. (1974) *Birthrights*. New York: Macmillan Publishers.
Feinberg, J. (1980) "The Child's Right to an Open Future," in *Freedom and Fulfillment. Philosophical Essays*. Princeton: Princeton University Press, 124–153.
Firestone, S. (1970) *The Dialectics of Sex*. New York: Bantam Books.
Fyfe, A. (2015) "Coming to Terms with Child Labor: The Historical Role of Education," in H. Hindman (ed.) *The World of Child Labor: A Historical and Regional Survey*. London: Routledge, 49–52.
Gheaus, A. (2015) "Unfinished Adults and Defective Children: On the Nature and Value of Childhood," *Journal of Ethics and Social Philosophy* 9 (1): 1–21.
Gutmann, A. (1999) *Democratic Education*. Princeton: Princeton University Press.
Gutmann, A. (2003) "The Authority and Responsibility to Educate," in R. Curren (ed.) *A Companion to the Philosophy of Education*. Oxford: Blackwell, 397–411.
Hindman, H. & Smith, C. (1999) "Cross-Cultural Ethics and the Child Labor Problem," *Journal of Business Ethics* 19: 21–33.

Illich, I. (1970) *Deschooling Society*. London: Marion Boyars.
International Labor Organization, (ILO) (1976) *Convention 138 Concerning Minimum Age for Admission to Employment*. C138.
International Labor Organization (ILO) (2021) *What is Child Labour*. Geneva: International Labor Organization.
ILO-UNICEF (2021) *Child Labour: Global Estimates 2020, Trends and the Road Forward*. New York/Geneva: ILO-UNICEF Reports.
Jonas, M. (2016) "Assessing Baselines for Identifying Harm: Tricky Cases and Childhood," *Res Publica* 22 (4): 387–404.
Lancy, D. F. (2015) *The Anthropology of Childhood*. Cambridge: Cambridge University Press.
Letuka, P. (1998) "The Best Interests of the Child and Child Labour in Lesotho," in W. Ncube (ed.) *Law, Culture, Tradition and Children's Rights in Eastern and Southern Africa*. Aldershot: Ashgate Publishing, 203–224.
Liebel, M. (2004) *A Will of Their Own: Cross-Cultural Perspectives on Working Children*. London: Zed Books.
McCowan, T. (2011) "Human Rights, Capabilities and the Normative basis of 'Education for All'," *Theory and Research in Education* 9(3): 283–298
Morrow, V. & Boyden, J. (2018) *Responding to Children's Work: Evidence from the Young Lives Study in Ethiopia, India, Peru and Vietnam*. Summative Report. Oxford: Young Lives.
Nieuwenhuys, O. (2013) "Theorizing Childhood(s): Why We Need Postcolonial Perspectives," *Childhood* 20 (1): 3–8.
Nussbaum, M. C. (1997) *Cultivating Humanity*. Cambridge, MA: Harvard University Press.
O'Kane, C., Barros, O. & Maslaoui, N. (2018) *It's Time to Talk! Children's Views on Children's Work*. Dusseldorf: Kindernothilfe/Terre des hommes.
Organization of African Unity (OAU) (1990) *African Charter on the Rights and Welfare of the Child*. Doc. CAB/LEG/24.9/49.
Ornert, A. (2018) "Evidence on Links between Child Labour and Education," *K4D Helpdesk Reports*. Brighton: Institute of Development Studies.
Pierik, R. & Houwerzijl, M. (2006) "Western Policies on Child Labor Abroad," *Ethics and International Affairs* 20(2): 193–218.
Purdy, L. M. (1992) *In Their Best Interest?* Ithaca: Cornell University Press.
Ray, R. (2009) "Education and Child Labor: A Global Perspective," in H. Hindman (ed.) *The World of Child Labor: A Historical and Regional Survey*. London: Routledge, 118–126.
Satz, D. (2010) *Why Some Things Should Not Be for Sale*. Oxford: Oxford University Press.
Schouten, G. (2018) "Schooling," in A. Gheaus, G. Calder & J. De Wispelaere (eds.) *The Routledge Handbook of the Philosophy of Childhood and Children*. New York: Routledge, 351–361.
Schapiro, T. (1999) "What Is a Child?" *Ethics* 109: 715–738.
Singh, R. & Khan, S. (2016) "Perspectives on Children's Work and Schooling: Evidence from a Longitudinal Study in Andhra Pradesh and Telangana, India," ILO Asia-Pacific Working Paper Series: International Labor Organization.
Tafere, Y. & Chuta, N. (2016) "Gendered Trajectories of Young People through School, Work and Marriage in Ethiopia," *Working Paper 155*. Oxford: Young Lives.
UNESCO Institute for Statistics (UIS) (2019) "Out-of-school Children and Youth," http://uis.unesco.org/en/topic/out-school-children-and-youth. New York: UNESCO.
UN General Assembly (UNGA) (1989) *Convention on the Rights of the Child*. Resolution 44/25 of November 20, 1989.
Uprichard, E. (2008) "Children as 'Being and Becomings': Children, Childhood and Temporality," *Children & Society* 22: 303–313.
Wells, Karen. (2015) *Childhood in a Global Perspective*. Cambridge: Polity.
Woldehanna, T. & Gebremedhin, A. (2015) "Is Child Work Detrimental to the Educational Achievements of Children?" *Working Paper 140*. Oxford: Young Lives.
Wolff, J. (2019) "Poverty, Social Expectations, and the Family," in N. Brando & G. Schweiger (eds.) *Philosophy and Child Poverty*. Dordrecht: Springer, 69–90

18
EDUCATIONAL PROBLEMS OF MASS MIGRATION

Danielle Zwarthoed

Introduction

Educational problems of mass migration pertain to both education and migration. Broadly construed, education refers to all the processes that modify children and adults' beliefs, knowledge, desires, values, habits, capabilities, competences and actions. Normative discourses about education, such as this chapter, tend to think of education as an intentional process that constructively engages and develops a learner's mental and other capabilities, with the aim of benefiting society, the educated person, or both. According to R. S. Peters, education develops the mind by initiating learners into activities or forms of knowledge in such a way that they "know what they are doing" (Peters 1965). Hence ideological manipulation, commercial advertising and brainwashing do not count as education in this sense. Normative discourses with prescriptive ambitions also tend to regard education as a process under the responsibility of well-identified organizations such as schools, universities, or families, to which moral responsibilities and duties can be ascribed. Yet we could include the news media as well as state programs and NGOs that facilitate the integration of new immigrants by providing language courses, for instance.

Migration is a subgenre of geographical mobility. It is the mobility of humans who aim to change residence. Our contemporary world is divided in sovereign states and most people take for granted that sovereignty includes the right to control one's own borders and to decide who can get in.[1] Hence, we generally take migration to be *international* migration. Migration thus refers to the mobility of humans who cross international borders with the aim of changing residence. The so-called "migration crisis" of 2015, when the war in Syria caused an increase in the number of asylum seekers in the European Union and in North America, nurtured the perception that we live in an era of unprecedented mass migrations. However, historians call for caution (e.g., Lucassen & Lucassen 2017). Migrations seem to have been a structural feature of many past human societies, although the Industrial Revolution and the transport revolutions of the 19th and 20th centuries probably contributed to an increase of long-distance mobility. Yet the one million migrants who crossed the Mediterranean Sea in 2015[2] seems quite a small number of people to accommodate for wealthy countries, compared to the 40 million European civilians displaced during and after the Second World War (Gatrell 2013: 89) or to the five and a half million refugees who left Afghanistan for Pakistan and Iran following the wars that started with the Soviet invasion in 1979 (Gatrell 2013: 255). The Afghan case reminds us that South-North migratory movements are but a fraction of global migrations. Eighty percent of refugees live in low- or

DOI: 10.4324/9781003172246-22

intermediate-income countries. In Europe, 70% of international migrants originate in European countries (UN 2020).

Bearing these facts in mind, this chapter will argue that philosophy of education should avoid the *sedentary* assumption that those who are educated will stay and live in the country and society in which they were educated (Culp & Zwarthoed 2020: 6). This cannot be a valid *empirical* assumption, since it is invalidated by the very fact that significant numbers of people migrate and that this phenomenon it is not just an anomality of our times, but a structural feature of human societies throughout history. If it is a *normative* assumption, that is, if philosophers of education have good reasons to believe that sedentary ways of living are superior to nomadic ones, then we (and especially those of us who are international migrants) are owed a reasonable explanation as to why this is the case. Pending this reasonable explanation, an account of philosophy of education that takes for granted that education should prepare humans to live in the country in which they receive most of their education would suffer from a *sedentary bias*.

Three methodological comments are in order. First, this chapter is an exercise in non-ideal theory understood as "realistic theory" (Valentini 2012), that is, normative theorizing that takes into account feasibility constraints. More precisely, two feasibility constraints will be accounted for. First, although strong justice-based arguments support open borders (e.g., Carens 1987, 2013: 225–254; Oberman 2016; Sager 2016), in the near future states are unlikely to give up the right to control their own borders and decide who should get in. Second, despite the fact that states have the *right* to control their borders, most do not have the capacity to fully prevent migrants from illegally crossing their borders, which involves very high financial and human costs. A world of closed borders is nearly as utopian as a world of open borders. Our world is a world of semi-open borders. Second, the approach expounded here is value pluralist. More specifically, it suggests that educational systems should be shaped by the following rather uncontroversial values: justice, reciprocity, care, compassion, feeling of belonging, and absence of alienation. Third, this chapter will expound reasons supporting the existence of *pro tanto* moral obligations regarding education and migration, but these *pro tanto* reasons could be overcome by other reasons in favor of other moral obligations. For its conclusions to be prescriptive, other moral considerations should be taken into account.

International migration poses at least three challenging issues for philosophy of education. Tackling these challenges may be a first step in avoiding the sedentary bias, that is, the view that education should only prepare humans to live in the place in which they received most of their education. The first challenge is the relevance of citizenship education for children and teenagers who, once they reach adulthood, won't get citizenship in their country of residence. The second challenge is equality of opportunity for students whose families do not possess the linguistic and cultural capital needed to succeed in the country of arrival. The third challenge is the problem of the fair distribution of educational costs and benefits in a world in which people do not always work and pay taxes in the countries that paid for their education. These challenges are discussed in the sections that follow.

Citizenship Education and Migration

I shall start with an anecdote. On October 16, 2020 a French History and Civics teacher named Samuel Paty was assassinated by a terrorist after showing satirical cartoons depicting the Prophet of Islam, Muhammad, during a Civics lesson on freedom of expression.[3] Commemorations were to be held in all French schools on the first school day after the attack. The French Minister of Education selected a letter of Jean Jaurès, a famous French Socialist politician from the beginning of the 20th century, to be read to students. The letter is titled *Lettres aux instituteurs et institutrices* ("Letter to primary school teachers"). I teach History and Civics in a public high school in the suburbs of Paris and I remember colleagues gathered to read and discuss the letter before class. Many of them had previous experience teaching in so-called "tough" high schools and were concerned with students' reactions. A colleague read Jaurès's letter loudly and stopped at the italicized sentence:

> Children in your care will not only have to write and decipher a letter, read a sign in a street corner, add and multiply. *They are French* and must know France, its geography and its History, its body and its soul.
>
> *(Jaurès 1888)*

My colleague added the following comment: "Well, at this point, half of the students won't listen to us anymore." He was pointing to the fact that a significant proportion of our students either do not have French citizenship or come from families whose members are not French.

The letter was chosen with, I believe, well-meaning intentions. The idea was to reconcile students with their teachers and, beyond that, to reconciliate French society. Yet the very choice of this document, as my colleague's comment emphasizes, shows that such an idea of French society really is an *idea*. This is the normative ideal of the nation-state characterized by ethnic homogeneity and little human mobility. Migrants are not unwelcome, but they are expected to settle for good and to integrate or assimilate so as not to disrupt the ethnic homogeneity deemed necessary for the stability of democratic institutions.[4] Integration and assimilation involve the rapid acquisition of citizenship.

There are several problems with this view. These problems point mostly to the discrepancy between this utopian view and the real-world composition and history of our societies. *In abstracto,* this view is beautifully consistent. Yet holding such a view requires being blind to the historical fact that many nation-states such as France, Great Britain, or the Netherlands, to name a few, did conquer colonies whose inhabitants had a language, a culture and a religion that was different from the conquering nation's one. Moreover, it seems many colonial powers never really tried to assimilate the colonized population so as to make them full members of the metropole's national community. France, which is often seen as the successful outcome of a policy of integrating newcomers into an ethnically homogeneous nation state since the 19th century, did implement unabashedly multiculturalist policies in its colonies. The *sharia,* the Islamic law, was part of the French legal system in colonial Algeria (1830–1962) and applied to all the Muslim subjects (Blévis 2003; Schacht 1964: 97). A remnant of these multiculturalist policies is the institution of Islamic polygamy, which was maintained until 2013 in the French territory of Mayotte. Now, colonization facilitates circulation between the metropole and its colonies. Hence a high proportion of working immigrants after World War II originated in the colonies or the former colonies, colonies whose culture did not only happen to be different from the culture of the metropole but had been deliberately preserved as such. A second problem with the normative ideal of the nation-state is that the economy, and especially the ageing European and East Asian economies, needs immigrants who may have foreign cultural backgrounds to maintain decent dependency ratios. According to the European Commission:

> The EU is ... facing a series of long-term economic and demographic challenges. Its population is ageing, while its economy is increasingly dependent on highly skilled jobs. Furthermore, without migration the EU's working age population will decline by 17.5 million in the next decade. Migration will increasingly be an important way to enhance the sustainability of our welfare system and to ensure sustainable growth of the EU economy.
>
> *(European Commission 2015: 14)*

Unless patriotic sentiments are strong enough for people to accept raising an additional child for the sake of the sustainability of the welfare state, to accept the dirty, dangerous and demeaning work that immigrants often do, or to give up retirement before the age of 76, it is very likely the economy will continue to rely on international immigrants, documented or not. Besides economic factors, human beings must often rely on migration to address their problems of security, poverty, love, dissatisfaction, and so on.

A third problem is that immigration is not always followed by the rapid acquisition of citizenship. Some immigrants are undocumented. Others do not fulfil the requirements to become a citizen. In countries such as Switzerland, acquiring citizenship is a long and difficult process. Some migrants cannot legally obtain two citizenships, and many legitimately hesitate to give up citizenship in their country of origin. Some are unsure of the long-term economic prospects in the receiving countries. Others plan to return to the country of origin after accumulating enough capital. Some war refugees wish to return once the conflict ends, which may happen sooner or later.

If we accept that some students are unlikely to acquire citizenship once they reach adulthood, what are we to do with citizenship education? Answering this question requires defining what citizenship is. So far, I have assumed that citizenship is (i) attached to a particular nation state and (ii) primarily defined by a set of legal rights (such as the right to vote or the unconditional right to stay) and obligations (such as mandatory military service wherever it still exists). Both assumptions can be dropped. Against defenders of more or less liberal patriotic and particularistic education, such as William Galston and Eamon Callan (e.g., Callan 1999; Galston 1989), some philosophers support programs of cosmopolitan education based on a moral rather than legal understanding of citizenship. Martha Nussbaum grounds her view of cosmopolitan education on a version of moral universalism combining Kantianism with a moral psychology that emphasizes compassion (Nussbaum 1996, 2019). Randall Curren defends an ethic of universal respect which, combined with the fact of our interdependence, implies that moral agents have a responsibility to cooperate at a global level to address world scale issues such as climate change. A program of global citizenship education should prepare children and teenagers to become apt members of the global community (Curren & Dorn 2018).

The facts of migration call for cosmopolitan education with content overlapping the global civic education advocated by Nussbaum and Curren, but the justification is different. The argument is that it may be wrong to teach national citizenship education to children who are not and may not become nationals in the future. It is wrong, first, because it wastes these children's time as well as taxpayers' money for no good reason, time and money that could be used for more useful educational enterprises such as language courses. Second, it makes these children feel *alienated*.[5] Teaching national citizenship to foreigners makes them feel that they do not belong. Such feeling, especially for teenagers whose self-esteem is often quite fragile, may be destructive. It would not be in the interest of the student, who would be deprived of a very basic need, the need to belong, as well as a sense of her self-worth, because teaching her something she does not need implicitly conveys the message that she is a second-class student. Such education might not be in society's interest either, since alienated teenagers and young people might be more likely to adopt antisocial behaviors (other things being equal).

This argument does not imply that programs of citizenship education aimed at *all* children should be suppressed or restricted to cosmopolitan education. Cosmopolitan education could substitute for particularistic forms of education as far as the cultivation of feelings of belonging and of moral sentiments is concerned. The goal is to make students feel that, wherever they come from and wherever they may go, they *belong*. Immigrant children deserve as much as anyone else an education that makes them feel they can be full members of a community and that accumulating identities need not be an issue (on multiple identities, see Sen 2007).

This argument does not imply that multicultural education should replace patriotic education either. Multicultural education, understood as an education aiming at teaching students the culture of a particular, subnational, community, so as to strengthen feelings of belonging to this community (perhaps at the costs of patriotic feelings), also suffers from a sedentary bias. Migrants do not just cross national borders. They also cross cultural borders and should be prepared to navigate between different cultural worlds, which is an educational experience in itself. An immigrant child might genuinely wish to assimilate into the culture of the receiving society and thus feel alienated if she is taught that her parents' national identity defines her. Hence, there are reasons to believe multicultural education as defined above should also be optional.

This argument, finally, does not imply that migrant students should not be taught useful knowledge and skills needed to pursue opportunities in their receiving countries, some of these knowledge and skills being often part of programs of civic education. Knowledge of the receiving country's history (but pointing to the fact that this history is connected to the history of other geographical areas), geography and institutions (including those that deal with migrants such as asylum offices or the European Union), mastering the language and the cultural codes, and acquiring critical thinking skills, are examples of such educational contents. In other words, citizenship education is morally acceptable as long as it does not make immigrant students feel that they do not belong.

Such education would have implications for the education of sedentary students too. It could foster decentration, that is, the "intellectual process of overcoming positional biases, combatting egocentrism and questioning one's prejudices" (Vandamme 2020). It could encourage students to base their self-esteem and self-respect not on the fact that they are nationals of the country they live in, but on their potential and capacities as human beings. It could equip these students with the tools they need to critically assess media discourses on immigration and migratory policies.

Equality of Opportunity and Migration

The sedentary bias poses a second challenge for philosophy of education, pertaining to equality of opportunity. Equality of opportunity is a principle of educational justice endorsed by many philosophers of education, policy makers and lay citizens. Philosophers of education have outlined and discussed various understandings of this principle (see Culp 2020; Jencks 1988). Rather than defend a particular account of educational justice in this chapter, I will assume that societies owe their members a fair share of educational resources to secure adequate or equal social and economic opportunities. An implication of such a view is that the arbitrary effects of students' social and economic backgrounds on educational outcomes should be mitigated. This may concern what governments should do as a matter of justice, but also parental rights and duties. Regarding parental rights and duties, Harry Brighouse and Adam Swift have discussed (and partially rejected) the controversial implication that socially and culturally advantaged parents may have no right to give their children unfair advantages in educational opportunities, such as by reading them bedtime stories (which can be justified as an aspect of intimate family relationships) or sending them to elite schools (which are specifically designed to provide competitive advantages and cannot be defended on the basis of parental rights) (Brighouse & Swift 2014). Applying this discussion to the case of immigrant students raises the issue of whether their personal experience with migration disadvantages or benefits them (Stojanov 2020).

In what follows, I shall investigate two crucial features of migrants' experiences that may hamper their educational opportunities: language and migratory status. The *pro tanto* reason to believe the influence of these features on students' opportunities ought to be mitigated is that immigrant students who are still minor children are not responsible for the fact that their background may turn out to be disadvantageous in terms of educational opportunities. As Stojanov puts it, from a responsibility-sensitive view of justice, in the case of minor children, the distinction between voluntary and forced migration is morally irrelevant to define the justice-based obligations society owes them, since children did not choose to leave (or stay in) their home country (Stojanov 2020: 36). If migration imposes morally arbitrary disadvantages on children, they may be owed some forms of compensatory education as a matter of justice.

Students whose parents are foreign immigrants may not speak the *language* of the receiving country in their homes. Some immigrant students arrive in the receiving country without knowing its language. If they are of school age, they will have started their studies in another language and may struggle to catch up in the receiving country. Moreover, if it turns out that they live in a socially disadvantaged neighborhood, the version of the national language they will speak with their friends is likely to significantly differ from the school's standardized and written language, and they may not have the cultural codes needed to know in which context slang is or is not appropriate.

Such issues attracted the attention of sociolinguists in the 1970s. Two diverging accounts of the causes of students' difficulties suggested two diverging paths of action (Bautier 1998). The first account, which, following sociolinguist Elisabeth Bautier, may be termed the *relativist* one, assumes that all languages and all language forms are equally valuable. Whether fluency in a language and a language form happen to be an advantage in the pursuit of educational and socioeconomic success is the arbitrary outcome of power relationships. The prescriptions that follow from such diagnosis may be interpreted in two ways. First, one could argue that the world in which some languages and some language forms arbitrarily dominate others should not exist anymore. However, a world free of such linguistic domination is certainly not in the immediate reach of educational agents. Thus, a less ambitious recommendation may be to avoid stigmatizing migrant (or socially disadvantaged) children's language and language forms and to avoid imposing the school's form of language. Such an approach is (in the short run) beneficial to immigrant children's self-esteem. However, one can imagine that, in our competitive educational system and labor market, this is highly counterproductive as far as equality of opportunity is concerned.

The second account, in its most extreme form, views the linguistic background of immigrants as well as socially disadvantaged children as a "sociocultural disability." The practical implication is that these children should be taught to replace the language they speak at home with the school's language and language form. If serious efforts are invested in this endeavor, the linguistic obstacle to equal opportunities for immigrant children will be lifted. However, the *sociocultural disability* account raises a couple of problems. First, it does not question the fact that one specific language and one specific language form is dominant. Arbitrary power relationships between native speakers and newcomers remain intact. Not to mention the additional perversity that not all native languages of immigrant students (and, henceforth, not all immigrant students) are treated equally. English-speaking, French-speaking, and German-speaking parents living abroad often proudly boast that they speak their native language at home with their children, thus conferring on them an enormous advantage in the global competition for interesting and well-paid jobs. This is not the case with Bambara-speaking, Berber-speaking or Pashto-speaking parents. Even Arabic, Chinese or Russian, which might turn out to be significant languages for success in the global job market, are rarely considered as such by the educational institutions of receiving countries. As Jim Cummins puts it, "Bilinguism was good for the rich and bad for the poor" (Cummins 2000).

Second, the *sociocultural disability* premise that children should be taught to replace the language they speak at home with the school's language and language form may alienate immigrant students from their families because it implicitly (and sometimes explicitly) conveys the message that it is not worth investing time in perfecting their mother tongue. However, possessing a rich and nuanced language is a crucial constituent of loving and affectionate relationships. Language provides irreplaceable tools to formulate and add nuance to ideas, to defend one's perspective, to affirm one's values, to end conflicts, to express feelings and emotions, and so on. Hence, by treating immigrants' mother tongue as a "handicap," this approach may deprive immigrants of the family relationship goods emphasized by Brighouse and Swift (Brighouse & Swift 2014). Third, since language is closely connected to identity, a policy that disparages immigrant students' mother tongue may negatively affect their self-esteem and their self-respect.

These criticisms of the *sociocultural disability account* do not necessarily imply that schools should teach children in their native language. In places in which children arrive speaking dozens of different languages, this would be too costly. However, these criticisms suggest that the attitude of schools towards speakers of non-dominant languages should evolve. These languages should not be labelled as an obstacle to learning and instructors should be encouraged (and helped) to train and adapt their teaching methods to this particular context.

To address this dilemma, sociolinguists like Elisabeth Bautier recommend explicitly teaching students that the uses and values of languages and language forms are context-dependent. In the school context as well as in the labor market, students should be taught that the school's standardized and written language is the most valuable and that mastering it is a decisive advantage. They should be taught that *written* language is not *spoken language put down in writing*. Its conventions are different and more exacting than those of spoken language. In other contexts, however, other languages and language forms may be more valuable.

More generally, recent research in sociology and linguistics suggests that a crucial explanation of educational failure is that culturally and socially disadvantaged students do not fully understand educational institutions' culture, codes, methods and expectations (Bonnéry 2007). Immigrant and working-class parents often endorse so-called "traditional" pedagogies and their children do not always grasp the logic underlying pedagogical methods such as discovery learning or inquiry-based approaches. Stéphane Bonnéry cites the telling example of an 11-year old immigrant student, Amidou. Students are taught for the first time how to draw a geography map: mountains must be colored brown, lowlands green. Amidou, who has been told by his parents, who are West African immigrants, to be obedient and hard-working at school, applies himself to reproducing the teacher's map as accurately and neatly as possible. The day of the graded assessment, he has worked hard to learn the teacher's map by heart. But the teacher, who wants to verify whether students grasped what she takes to be the most important point, that is, learning the cartographic language, assigns *another map* to be colored according to geographic relief. Amidou is outraged and feels a deep sense of injustice. He even wonders whether the teacher is racist.

Such situations are rather frequent in classrooms that welcome students whose parents are not acquainted with the school's language, codes and culture. It is labelled by sociolinguists as a "socio-cognitive misunderstanding." Amidou's feelings signal there is also an injustice going on there, although the teacher cannot be held responsible for that. She genuinely wanted her students to succeed and tried her best. The injustice here is not really an injustice in the distribution of resources either, although decreasing class sizes and improving continuing education for teachers would surely help. This is more an issue of justice *in* education, "that is, in teaching, curriculum development, assessment and classroom interactions" (Stojanov 2020: 35). Addressing this injustice requires adequate teacher training. Teachers can fulfil their caring responsibilities towards immigrant students if they are equipped with the tools and capacities needed to distance themselves from the way they conceive the learning process (which they often model on their own) and understand the way their students conceive this learning process. This requires a mix of theoretical knowledge, classroom observation, moral imagination and compassion.

As to *migratory status,* in our world migrants do not have an unconditional right to stay, unless they are permanent residents. Some forms of migratory status, such as the status of undocumented migrants, are extremely fragile. However, migratory status is not a valid reason to deprive a person her right to education. Yet when undocumented migrants are summarily deported, those who are students are deprived of the continuity of learning, which is crucial for educational success and access to adequate social and economic opportunities. Securing an adequate level of educational opportunities for migrant students therefore provides a *pro tanto* moral reason to provide them with a stable migratory status until they complete the level of education they are entitled to. When states fail to fulfil this obligation, schools may have to take up the slack and engage in proactive protection of their immigrant students by undertaking whatever course of action is needed to slow or hamper the deportation process (Geron & Levinson 2020).

The Funding of Education and Migration

Securing immigrant students' fair share of opportunities may involve additional costs for receiving societies. To put it briefly, there are three potential views as to how immigrant children's education should be financed. The first view (call it the *universalist* view) is that the allocation of educational benefits should be blind to whether students are citizens or not. This view may be grounded on a universalist ethic that affirms that migrants are owed their fair share of educational opportunities on the mere ground that they are human beings. According to the "ought implies can" principle, the receiving state owes them these opportunities insofar as it is capable of delivering them. The second view (call it the *dual treatment view)* stipulates that the state owes only its citizens their fair share of educational opportunities. Migrant students may be owed just enough educational opportunities to fulfil their basic human needs. Note that an implication of this view is that migrants' country of citizenship should continue funding their education abroad so as to secure them their fair share of educational opportunities. This is in line with the practices of some wealthy countries that subsidize high-quality education for expatriates (think about the *lycée français)*, but not with the practices of less advantaged countries. The third view (call it the *reciprocity-based* view) stipulates that, insofar as non-citizen migrants are liable to the same level of taxation as citizens, and thus contribute to the financing of public education, they and their children are owed the same level of publicly funded educational opportunities. The moral intuition underlying this view is captured by the fairness principle (Rawls 1999: 96). This principle states that, when agents contribute to a joint cooperative venture, they are entitled to the same level of advantage as other participants. How contributions and advantages are to be distributed depends on the justice principles that regulate the cooperative scheme. The important point is that entitlements to benefits are grounded on contribution rather than citizenship. This *reciprocity-based* view is an interesting compromise between the first and the second views and might be the most likely to seem reasonable to both citizens and migrants. But this is a hypothesis that has yet to be proven, and detailed discussion of the relative merits of these views is beyond the scope of this chapter.

So far, we have discussed whether states should fund the education of immigrants so as to secure their fair share of educational resources and thereby access to a fair level of social and economic opportunities. Another issue is that, in a world characterized by high levels of international mobility, states may subsidize the education of nationals who emigrate abroad once they become adult and are capable of contributing to the cooperative scheme. Brain drain – the emigration of high-skilled professionals who, had they stayed, might have contributed to the improvement of the economic and social conditions of their compatriots – seems highly problematic from a justice perspective.

The empirical picture is, however, perhaps more complicated than that.[6] The presence of a significant highly educated population can benefit its compatriots in various ways. Critiques of brain drain argue that the departure of highly educated people imposes negative externalities on those who remain (Bhagwati & Hamada 1974). However, recent evidence suggests "brain drain" may benefit countries of emigration under some conditions (Docquier & Rapoport 2012: 683). Immigrant workers' remittances contribute to the mitigation of poverty. Potential emigration prospects incentivize citizens of low-income and intermediate-income countries to invest more in education, which is beneficial if they end up staying (Beine et al. 2001, 2008; Docquier & Rapoport 2012: 699). Educated diasporas facilitate technology transfers and foreign investments, and they may favor improvements of the quality of governance and political institutions in their country of origin

(Docquier & Rapoport 2012: 709). The extent to which brain drain is beneficial or detrimental also depends on emigration rates. According to economists, the net effect of brain drain is positive for countries whose emigration rate is lower than 15–20%. However, it is negative when emigration rates are higher (Beine et al. 2008; Docquier 2007).

Let us move from the empirical facts to normative issues. Reciprocity is a key issue when discussing brain drain. In countries of emigration, families, educational institutions, taxpayers, and others bear significant material and non-material costs to educate future emigrants. Do countries of immigration owe something to countries of emigration in virtue of these countries' contribution? Once again, the moral intuition at stake is captured by the fairness principle. If different countries jointly participate in a potentially mutually advantageous cooperative migration scheme, those who have contributed their share have a legitimate claim to a similar contribution on the part of those who benefit from the fact that immigrants have been educated elsewhere. The fairness principle prohibits violations of reciprocity such as free-riding and exploitation.

Free-riding or exploitation occurs in specific conditions (Olsaretti 2013). First, for someone to be a free-rider, she must be a *net* beneficiary of the cooperative venture – in this case the international migration and education scheme. In other words, countries of immigration free-ride on the educational system of countries of emigration if they are all-things considered better off than if they had not accepted those highly-skilled immigrants. This seems plausible enough.

Second, participation in a joint cooperative venture – a migration scheme – should be voluntary (otherwise, this is not cooperation but "theft"). If the educational efforts of countries of emigration purport to benefit destination countries, then they can be deemed voluntary. This is generally not the case, although there are exceptions. For instance, the Philippines deliberately train more nurses than the country needs so as to send them abroad and benefit from their remittances. Investments in English language courses may serve the same purpose. The voluntariness condition can also be interpreted in a weaker sense. One could say that, insofar as education systems aim at educating the young, *whoever the ultimate beneficiary is*, this is sufficient to deem voluntary their participation in any migration scheme involving the mobility of educated people. In other words, they are said to voluntarily participate in this migration scheme just because they choose to educate children, and in a world of semi-open borders such choice may involve the possibility that these children could use their talents and skills abroad.

The third condition is that the joint product of the cooperative venture be a public or a socialized good. Thus, fairness assessments of brain drain situations actually consider educated migrants as a public good. This may sound bizarre. Public goods are non-excludable and often non-rivalrous. A non-excludable good is a good anyone can access and consume. A non-rivalrous good is a good whose supply is not affected by people's consumption. Fresh air is a non-excludable and non-rivalrous good. Now, migrants are not a public good in the way air is, because institutional interventions are required for the product of their labor to benefit the society they live in. Therefore, in the same way as children are "socialized goods" rather than "public goods" (Olsaretti 2013: 252), migrants may be considered a "socialized good." The social and institutional interventions that turn migrants into "socialized goods" are, first, the welfare system and, second, the way the crossing of borders is organized. The welfare system involves states paying for a more or less significant part of the education of its population. The money mostly comes from taxpayers, although states can also benefit from international aid, borrow money, or even constrain central banks to "create" it. It is thus extremely difficult to trace and identify the exact person who actually paid for a person's education. As to the way the crossing of borders is organized, receiving countries enjoy a high level of discretion to admit or exclude immigrants, whilst sending countries are, in principle, not allowed to prevent their people from emigrating.

This results from the asymmetric treatment of exit and entry by international law. But this also results from the asymmetry of power between immigration and emigration countries. Countries of immigration enjoy greater control insofar as they have the capacity to sanction undesired immigrants by denying them a stable legal status, which renders these undocumented migrants vulnerable to various kinds of abuse. Countries of emigration often do not have the capacity to sanction emigrants. Countries of immigration are thus able to purposely set up a social security system and open their borders to additional workers and taxpayers, while sending countries are unable to prevent the redirection of the product of their efforts to foreign countries and their residents.

Brain drain is a violation of the fairness principle if it amounts to free-riding. If the international migration scheme at stake results in sending countries being net contributors to the education of receiving countries' population, we have a situation of free-riding. And if the international migration scheme additionally makes sending countries worse off than they would have been otherwise, we have a situation of exploitation. The normative implication of the fairness principle is that countries that receive educated migrants who contribute to their wealth should compensate sending countries' educational efforts. International "welfare state" agreements stipulating that receiving countries should participate in the funding of education in sending countries may solve the issue without depriving educated people of their right to emigrate.

So far, I have assumed that the sole beneficiaries of the educational system in countries of emigration are countries of immigration, that is, their citizens and residents. However, the migrants themselves benefit from the education they received. From this observation, one could infer that emigration restrictions are justified. However, emigration restrictions are a morally acceptable solution to brain drain only in very limited circumstances, for instance when there are good reasons to believe emigrants owe their compatriots their labor and that they could not adequately compensate them otherwise (Oberman 2013). An alternative approach would be to argue that compensation is all that can be expected of educated migrants. This is Gillian Brock's view (Brock & Blake 2015). This compensation could be in cash (taxes) or labor (public service). Michael Blake, however, argues in the same book that compensation in labor is impermissible from a liberal-minded perspective. According to Blake, labor is more akin to organs and body parts than to money. Requiring emigrants to compensate for the education they receive with additional years of public service would thus threaten their bodily integrity.

There are, however, no good reasons to believe that only migrants owe monetary compensation for the education they received in their country of emigration. This is so because education has positive spillover effects on the society they live in as well as on the society they come from. In other words, the beneficiaries of migrants' education are not just the migrants themselves, but also the receiving society and, in some cases, the sending society. The receiving society should therefore compensate the sending society that educated these migrants. Migrants might also be expected to compensate for the education they received, but this compensation might not necessarily be paid in the form of a specific tax such as the famous Bhagwati tax. Insofar as immigrants pay taxes in their country of residence, if this country were ready to compensate sending countries for the net benefits they derive from the education of foreign residents, immigrants would actually indirectly contribute to the educational system they benefited from.

Conclusion

This chapter has argued that philosophy of education must set aside the assumption that people will stay in the society in which they receive their education. Citizenship education solely aimed at prospective citizens may wrong immigrant students who may not stay by triggering feelings of alienation. Insofar as immigrant children did not choose their country of residence, they are owed the same share of educational resources as well as the same level of economic and social opportunities as the citizens of their country of residence. The mitigation of the effects of immigrant students' background on their opportunities and educational outcome raises difficult moral issues. The discrepancy between the school's language and cultural codes, on the one hand, and those of the migrants' family, on the other hand, may estrange successful migrant students from their relatives. The sovereign right of states to determine migrants' legal status (and thus to deport them) may be in tension with the continuity of learning required for access to adequate educational opportunities. Finally, the complex issue of brain drain shows that, given the structural mobility of human beings, the normative theorizing of the funding of education should not limit itself to national borders.[7]

(Related Chapters: 2, 15, 17, 19, 20.)

Notes

1 I shall not address the issue of whether borders should be open, which is beyond the scope of this chapter. Joseph Carens (1987) presents a classic case for open borders.
2 In 2015, 1,015,078 migrants reached Europe by crossing the Mediterranean Sea (216,054 in 2014). Cf. HCR, Operational Portal. Mediterranean Situation., 2018. https://data2.unhcr.org/en/situations/mediterranean, consulted on October 27th, 2018.
3 The terrorist was not one of Paty's 8th grade's students, but a radicalized 18-year-old Muslim who wanted to become a "martyr" and learned about Samuel Paty from an angry parent connected to him through social media.
4 For a philosophical argument in favor of such a view, see for instance the works of Michael Walzer and David Miller (Miller 2016; Walzer 1983).
5 For an analysis of immigrant children's feelings of alienation and estrangement in L. Cantet's film *Entre les murs* (2008), based on the autobiographical novel of a French teacher, see Fonseca de Carvalho (Fonseca de Carvalho 2020).
6 What follows is an adaptation of a section in a chapter co-written with Axel Gosseries (Gosseries & Zwarthoed 2016).
7 I am grateful to Randall Curren for his careful reading and pertinent comments and suggestions. Remaining errors are my own.

References

Bautier, E. (1998) "Maîtriser la langue, mais pourquoi (en) faire," *XY ZEP*, 2.
Beine, M., Docquier, F., & Rapoport, H. (2001) "Brain Drain and Economic Growth: Theory and Evidence," *Journal of Development Economics* 64(1): 275–289.
Beine, M., Docquier, F., & Rapoport, H. (2008) "Brain Drain and Human Capital Formation in Developing Countries: Winners and Losers," *The Economic Journal* 118(528): 631–652.
Bhagwati, J., & Hamada, K. (1974) "The Brain Drain, International Integration of Markets for Professionals and Unemployment: A Theoretical Analysis," *Journal of Development Economics* 1(1): 19–42.
Blévis, L. (2003) "La citoyenneté française au miroir de la colonization," *Geneses* 53(4): 25–47.
Bonnéry, S. (2007) *Comprendre l'échec scolaire: Elèves en difficultés et dispositifs pédagogiques*. Paris: La Dispute.
Brighouse, H., & Swift, A. (2014) *Family Values: The Ethics of Parent-Child Relationships*. Princeton: Princeton University Press.
Brock, G., & Blake, M. (2015) *Debating Brain Drain: May Governments Restrict Emigration?* Oxford: Oxford University Press.
Callan, E. (1999) "A Note on Patriotism and Utopianism: Response to Schrag," *Studies in Philosophy and Education* 18(3): 197–201.
Carens, J. (1987) "Aliens and Citizens," *Review of Politics* 49(2): 251–273.
Carens, J. (2013) *The Ethics of Immigration*. Oxford: Oxford University Press.
Culp, J. (2020) "Educational Justice," *Philosophy Compass* 15(12): 1–12.
Culp, J., & Zwarthoed, D. (eds.) (2020) *Education and Migration*. New York: Routledge.
Cummins, J. (2000) "Language, Power and Pedagogy," in *Language, Power and Pedagogy*. Multilingual Matters. https://www.degruyter.com/document/doi/10.21832/9781853596773/html
Curren, R., & Dorn, C. (2018) *Patriotic Education in a Global Age*. Chicago: University of Chicago Press.
Docquier, F. (2007) "Fuite des cerveaux et inégalités entre pays," *Revue d'economie du developpement* 15(2): 49–88.
Docquier, F., & Rapoport, H. (2012) "Globalization, Brain Drain, and Development," *Journal of Economic Literature* 50(3): 681–730.

European Commission. (2015) *Communication on the European Agenda on Migration'*. https://eur-lex.europa.eu/legal-content/EN/TXT/?uri=celex%3A52015DC0240 (Consulted on September 19th, 2021)
Fonseca de Carvalho, J. S. (2020) "Education as Hospitality: Welcoming Foreigners into a Common World," in J. Culp & D. Zwarthoed (eds.) *Education and Migration*. New York: Routledge, 11–22.
Galston, W. (1989) "Civic Education in the Liberal State," in N. L. Rosenblum (ed.) *Liberalism and the Moral Life*. Cambridge, MA: Harvard University Press, 89–101.
Gatrell, P. (2013) *The Making of the Modern Refugee*. Oxford: Oxford University Press.
Geron, T., & Levinson, M. (2020) "Intentional Collaboration, Predictable Complicity, and Proactive Intervention: U. S. Schools' Ethical Responsibilities in Slowing the School-to-Deportation Pipeline," in J. Culp & D. Zwarthoed (eds.) *Education and Migration*. New York: Routledge, 23–33.
Gosseries, A., & Zwarthoed, D. (2016) "Generations and Global Justice," in D. Held & P. Maffettone (eds.) *Global Political Theory*. London: Polity Press, 281–304.
Jaurès, J. (1888) "Lettres aux instituteurs et aux institutrices," *La Dépêche, Journal de La Démocratie Du Midi*. 15 January 1888.
Jencks, C. (1988) "Whom Must We Treat Equally for Educational Opportunity to be Equal?" *Ethics* 98(3): 518–533.
Lucassen, J., & Lucassen, L. (2017) "Theorizing Cross-Cultural Migrations: The Case of Eurasia Since 1500," *Social Science History* 41(3): 445–475.
Miller, D. (2016) *Strangers in Our Midst: The Political Philosophy of Immigration*. Cambridge, MA: Cambridge, MA: Harvard University Press.
Nussbaum, M. C. (1996) "Cosmopolitanism and Patriotism," in J. Cohen (ed.) *For Love of Country*. Boston: Beacon Press, 3–17.
Nussbaum, M. C. (2019) *The Cosmopolitan Tradition: A Noble but Flawed Ideal*. Cambridge, MA: The Belknap Press.
Oberman, K. (2013) "Can Brain Drain Justify Emigration Restrictions?" *Ethics* 123(3): 427–455.
Oberman, K. (2016) "Immigration as a Human Right," in S. Fine & L. Ypi (eds.) *Migration in Political Theory: The Ethics of Movement and Membership*. Oxford: Oxford University Press, 32–56.
Olsaretti, S. (2013) Children as Public Goods? *Philosophy & Public Affairs 41*(3): 226–258.
Peters, R. S. (1965) "Education as Initiation," in R. D. Archambault (ed.), *Philosophical Analysis and Education*. New York: The Humanities Press, 87–111. Reprinted in R. Curren (ed.) *Philosophy of Education: An Anthology*. Oxford: Blackwell, 55–67.
Rawls, J. (1999) *A Theory of Justice* (Revised edition). Cambridge, MA: Harvard University Press.
Sager, A. (2016) "Immigration Enforcement and Domination: An Indirect Argument for Much More Open Borders," *Political Research Quarterly* 1(1): 1–13.
Schacht, J. (1964) *An Introduction to Islamic Law*. Oxford: Clarendon Press.
Sen, A. (2007) *Identity and Violence: The Illusion of Destiny*. London: Penguin.
Stojanov, K. (2020) "Educational Justice and Transnational Migration," in J. Culp & D. Zwarthoed (eds.) *Education and Migration*. New York: Routledge, 34–46.
UN. (2020) *Division of Economic and Social Affairs, International Migrations 2020 Highlights*. https://reliefweb.int/sites/reliefweb.int/files/resources/International%20Migration%202020%20Highlights.pdf (Consulted on September 19th, 2021)
Valentini, L. (2012) "Ideal vs. Non-Ideal Theory: A Conceptual Map," *Philosophy Compass* 7(9): 654–664.
Vandamme, P.-E. (2020) "Indirect Cosmopolitan Education: On the Contribution of National Education to Attitudes Towards Foreigners," in J. Culp & D. Zwarthoed (eds.) *Education and Migration*. New York: Routledge, 114–129.
Walzer, M. (1983) *Spheres of Justice*. New York: Basic Books.

19
THE POLITICAL ETHICS OF BILINGUAL EDUCATION

Daniel M. Weinstock

"Bilingual education" refers to educational systems in which curricular elements are presented to pupils in two languages.[1] The contrast is with educational systems in which children are exposed to other languages in language classes (and of course, with systems in which children receive no exposure to languages other than the one in which they receive their education in math, history, and so on).

On the face of it, bilingual education would seem to be a "motherhood and apple pie" issue. From the point of view of children there are multiple advantages to being educated in more than one language, and no obvious downside.[2] There are numerous benefits to being fluent in more than one language. It increases the range of persons with whom one can interact for commercial, cultural, romantic, and many other purposes. To the extent that different languages embody different conceptual repertoires, multilingualism allows us to see the world in different ways, and thus to problematize some of the taken-for-granted implicit valuations that are part of any one such repertoire. There have clearly been multilingual bigots, but there is reason to think that, all things equal, an ability to speak a number of languages is contingently related to a higher tolerance for difference. And a bilingual education is clearly an effective tool with which to achieve bilingualism. Children in bilingual schools actually use the languages in which they are taught to think, speak, and write about a variety of issues. This is more likely to give rise to fluency than is an education in which instruction in another language is confined to designated language classes.

This chapter therefore starts with the assumption that there are very strong reasons, where possible, for children to be educated bilingually. It then asks whether there can in certain very specific contexts be considerations that defeat that very strong presumption. I will consider two such contexts. The first is that of asymmetrical bilingualism, that is, of contexts in which the two languages in which bilingual educational systems purport to educate children differ in terms of their capacity to attract speakers. The second is that of "nation-building," that is, of contexts in which it is deemed important that a single language establish itself firmly across an entire territory. I will argue that, in some contexts, there are valid moral considerations that tell in favor of unilingual education, even where the empirical conditions exist for bilingual education. In many contexts, however, the considerations that are put forward do not pass ethical muster. I'll begin, however, with a brief summary of the debates that have only recently been joined in the field of political philosophy over the question of what a *just* language regime looks like. This will serve as a useful backdrop for the discussions of the normative dimensions of bilingual education that will occupy us later.

DOI: 10.4324/9781003172246-23

I

Political philosophers only really became sensitive to the need for a theory of justice as regards language with the writings of the Belgian philosopher Philippe Van Parijs (Van Parijs 2011). The work of Will Kymlicka and of others who had previously argued for minority cultural rights can be seen as a forerunner to Van Parijs' work on linguistic justice (Kymlicka 1995), but it is important to note that language and culture do not denote the same thing, and thus that they raise different sets of normative issues. Many very different cultures after all share the same language (think of the very different cultures that are anglophone, francophone, hispanophone, lusophone, and so on). One can thus clearly protect a language without protecting a culture. And a culture can arguably survive language change (think of the persistence of Ashkenazi Jewish culture despite the disappearance of Yiddish as a widely spoken language, or of Scotland despite the increasingly anglophone nature of that society). It is thus possible, at least in principle, to protect a distinctive culture without protecting its language. Language and culture overlap contingently, but the distribution of languages in the world does not map out perfectly onto the distribution of cultures.

One of the questions that theorists of language rights and language policy have had to contend with has to do with the specific values that languages embody, that are distinct from the values that are embodied in cultures more generally. Are there reasons to worry about languages as a matter of justice that do not simply reduce to reasons to worry about cultures more broadly?

Van Parijs' argument in his pioneering work begins with the obvious point that languages are mediums of exchange and communication that make the achievement of a wide range of collaborative goods possible. A philosophy seminar is an event in which, one hopes, participants come away more enlightened about some question of philosophical interest than they had been going in, and that increase in enlightenment is the result of a linguistically mediated process. Languages allow people to do things together. This is not obviously true of other aspects of culture worth saving for other reasons, perhaps to do with identity and tradition.

The next observation in the argument is to observe that the historical spread of languages has situated people differently with respect to languages. Some people are raised speaking languages that are used by a great many people, and that are therefore very useful in achieving the kinds of goods that are at issue, whereas others speak languages that are only spoken by a small number of people. What's more, this unequal distribution is from the point of view of individual speakers the result of the operation of luck rather than the result of decisions that people can take credit for. If you're born in the U.S., it's likely that you will grow up speaking what has become the global *lingua franca*, whereas if you are born in Tartu, it's likely that your mother tongue will be a fiendishly complicated language spoken by very few people.

Readers familiar with recent debates about distributive justice will recognize a central concern being triggered. According to what has become the dominant paradigm of theories of distributive justice, it is unjust that people's holdings of particularly important resources be determined by luck. According to such theories, it's one thing if people become unequal because of choices that they make, and for which they can be held responsible; it is quite another when that inequality comes about through the operation of "brute luck" (Cohen 1999).

Van Parijs' principal argument is that speakers of "smaller" languages face what is in effect an economic hardship. They can either forego the benefits of linguistically mediated cooperation and stick to the range of relationships that their language makes possible; or they can invest resources in acquiring competency in a "larger" language. Such investments come with opportunity costs, of course. The time and money that native speakers of smaller languages devote to acquiring a second "larger" language is devoted by native speakers of "larger" languages to more directly productive pursuits.

There are two kinds of injustice that this analysis, very summarily described here, give rise to. The first has to do with the costs involved in acquiring a more communicatively effective language, costs that in a *laissez faire* environment are borne by speakers of "smaller" languages themselves.[3] The second has to do with the greater vulnerability of smaller languages. There is a sociolinguistic tendency for speakers of smaller languages to linguistically assimilate to the bigger ones, and over time to lose their patrimonial language entirely. There is always more reason for speakers of a smaller language to make use of the larger language than the reverse. If this tendency is allowed to play itself out in an unregulated manner, there will be a tendency for there to be fewer and fewer public contexts in which smaller languages will be used, culminating with linguistic extinction (Laponce 1990).

Van Parijs has proposals about how to respond to these injustices. Larger languages such as English provide non-native speakers with many resources that can be "plundered" in order to acquire proficiency. The domination of English – on the Internet, in popular culture, etc. – makes it the case that people can be provided with the tools with which to learn English for free, as it were. And Van Parijs also suggests that speakers of vulnerable languages "grab a territory" in order to stabilize their languages, by creating public contexts in which the language is imposed by force of law.

I have written elsewhere on the strengths and limitations of Van Parijs' arguments for these solutions (Weinstock 2015), and I don't want to rehearse them here. The question I want to ask is how, in general, educational systems can contribute to the resolution of these problems of linguistic justice, and how bilingual education, in particular, can in various specific contexts serve or disserve the cause of linguistic justice. Now one can, of course, deny that language is the kind of thing that can appropriately be considered as an object of concern for theories of justice, that there is something about language that is too mercurial to fit neatly into distributive schemes (Wee 2010). But those of us who find the kinds of concerns raised by Van Parijs compelling will want to know if bilingual education serves the cause of justice (notwithstanding the fact that it benefits children, a fact that I have stipulated for the purposes of the present paper).

II

Though this chapter operates on the assumption (contestable in the light of relevant empirical research[4]) that bilingual education is good for children, there are circumstances in which it is not good for linguistic communities. These are cases of asymmetrical bilingualism.

Asymmetrical bilingualism refers to cases in which the members of two linguistic communities interact, but in which one of these two communities is significantly more likely to attract speakers when linguistic choices are being made. These choices involve everything from the choice of which language to educate one's children in, to what language to speak when a group of friends gets together. This could be the case in virtue of mere numbers. One linguistic community may simply have a far greater number of speakers than the others. The larger language is more attractive because it opens a greater number of channels of communication, and thus a greater number of opportunities of all kinds. It can also have to do with the fact that in certain sets of circumstances, the use of one language rather than another is linked to higher status and greater access to positions of economic and political power.

In situations of asymmetrical bilingualism, there is a greater incentive for people to choose the more numerous and/or the more powerful language. This greater attractiveness can occur in a number of contexts. For example, immigrants arriving to the polity and having to make choices about where it is most efficient to expend resources in order to integrate into the society will, absent special circumstances, tend to choose to learn the language that gives them greater numbers of opportunities across the full range of the socio-economic spectrum, and, perhaps more significantly, to have their children educated in it. Among members of the polity in question, there is greater incentive for speakers of the numerically smaller and/or less powerful language to acquire proficiency in the larger and/or more powerful language than the reverse. This, in turn, will give rise to a situation in which communication among native speakers of the two languages will tend to occur in the language that is more successful at attracting speakers, as communication will be more effective the higher the degree of fluency among interlocutors. The more powerful language will then tend to get used increasingly in public contexts, with the less "successful" language being consigned increasingly to private contexts. It is only a step toward the "folklorization" of the language in question (i.e., its relegation to purely private contexts), and, in the most extreme cases, its extinction.

Though the processes just briefly sketched rest on powerful sociolinguistic laws, they are not inexorable. Especially when the speakers of a smaller language manage to heed the imperative put forward by Van Parijs to "grab a territory" (either by becoming fully sovereign or by securing group rights within a federal or quasi-federal system), they can enact legislation that can effectively counteract these laws. Thus, for example, they can require of immigrants that they pass a language test as a condition of admission. They can require of the children of immigrants, and indeed of all children, that they be educated in the language. They can make the otherwise weaker language into the language of official communication between public institutions and citizens. They can require that commercial signage be predominantly or exclusively in the language for which protection is being sought. There is a broad range of policy measures that can be, and indeed that have been, successfully used in order to arrest the processes whereby a language that possesses a greater number of speakers and/or that is associated with greater social status comes to dominate in a space of linguistic interaction that it shares with a language that has fewer speakers and/or is associated with lesser social status.

Educational policy is quite clearly one of the main levers employed by speakers of smaller and less powerful languages that have "grabbed a territory" in order to stabilize their languages in the face of powerful sociolinguistic forces. They can make instruction in the smaller language mandatory, thus ensuring that the next generation of citizens will achieve fluency in a language that might otherwise be threatened. This has been done in federal states such as Canada, where education policy is one of the primary policy tools that has been used by successive governments in order to ensure the protection of the French language. But it has also characterized quasi-federal and even unitary states such as Spain and the United Kingdom, where similar (though not identical[5]) protections exist to protect Catalan and Welsh.

If we attend closely to the description of the linguistic dynamics that have briefly been described above, it becomes clear however that in contexts of asymmetrical bilingualism, making instruction in the vulnerable language mandatory may not be sufficient to ensure the required protection. Indeed, what places some languages at risk is not just lack of linguistic proficiency in the smaller language, but also the absence of the required incentive structure. To recall, asymmetrical bilingual contexts are ones in which there is always more reason for people to revert to the larger and more powerful languages in institutional contexts since, even given equal linguistic proficiency, there is a greater incentive on the part of all interlocutors to speak the larger, more powerful language. The threat in such contexts, therefore, is bilingualism itself.

One way in which to attempt to protect a vulnerable language while at the same time ensuring that speakers of that language as well as immigrants nonetheless have access to the stronger language is by engineering a kind of quasi-bilingualism through the school system. Schools can, for example, delay the introduction of the larger language to the curriculum to a point in the pedagogical trajectory of children at which they are unlikely to become fully bilingual. Another way is to restrict the larger language to language classes, and therefore to prescind from introducing bilingual education proper. If children emerge from the school system more comfortable in the vulnerable language than they are in the larger language, then the incentive structure that we have been describing shifts. It will no longer be the case that ease of communication among speakers of weaker and stronger languages will tend to favour communication in the latter, or at least, not to the same degree.

This is the strategy that has been adopted in the Canadian province of Quebec. The children of immigrants and of francophones are required to attend French schools, where English is introduced toward the middle of elementary school years. The only children who are permitted to attend English schools are those whose parents were educated in English in Canada. *De jure* English schools are often bilingual "immersion" schools, in which anglophone children are taught subjects throughout the curriculum in both English and French. The hoped-for result is one in which francophone children and the children of immigrants emerge from the public school system somewhat more proficient in French than in English, and anglophone children come out of it sufficiently proficient in French to be able to interact with their fellow citizens in French. This delicate balance is one that would shift the incentives sufficiently to ensure that it is not just the case that people in Québec are fluent in French but also, crucially, that they are incentivized to use it rather than English in public settings.

How should this way of using policy levers be evaluated from an ethics standpoint? On the one hand, if one locates oneself within an individualist framework in which individuals are the only loci of moral value in the universe, there seems to be something morally amiss here. Indeed, to the extent that children benefit from being educated bilingually, as I have assumed for the purposes of this chapter, this seems to be a case in which their rights and interests are being subordinated in order to protect a collective entity, namely, a language. But, again on individualist moral grounds, shouldn't the degree to which we expend resources to protect a language depend on what it is worth to individuals? And isn't the best way in which to gauge the worth of a language to attend to the degree to which it is, in fact, chosen as a medium of communication?[6]

Things are not so simple, however, even if we remain (as I believe we ought) within an individualist moral framework.[7] Plainly, liberal-democratic states often circumscribe individual rights in order to secure benefits to individuals. One of the contexts in which they do so has to do with collective action problems. Collective action problems are situations in which we can all see what would need to be done in order to achieve an important social good, but it is not rational for any of us to act so as to achieve the good in question. It would only make sense to do so if others did so as well. If they do not, we end up in the worst of all possible worlds, having been made the "patsies" of other people's defections from the common good. Situations such as these pervade social life. They were memorably dramatized by Thomas Hobbes in his *Leviathan* and formalized by game theorists in the 20th century. One of the core functions of states is to help us to avoid such self-defeating situations (Heath 2001).

The maintenance of a vulnerable language is arguably a collective action problem. We can assume that people want to preserve their language, but it is only rational for them to take steps to do so if they know that a sufficient number of their fellows will do so as well. If they cannot have this assurance, the second-best strategy is to defect from any policy that will tend to protect the vulnerable language. The state's role, as in other contexts of collective action problems, is to take the defecting option off the table, as it were. This is precisely what the kinds of educational policies I have described above purport to do.

Now, the plausibility of this response depends upon an argument to the effect that it is rational for agents to want to preserve their language, rather than simply assimilating linguistically into the larger and more powerful language. Instrumentalists about language would claim that this is in fact not the case. On their view, people have an interest in being able to communicate with one another effectively, and rationality dictates that they choose the most efficient tools with which to do so. However, instrumentalism ignores that languages are also sources of identity and self-respect (Robichaud & De Schutter 2012). People define who they are at least in part on the basis of the languages that they speak. What's more, the maintenance of a language allows people to maintain a connection with the historical sources of their linguistically mediated identities. The situation is therefore much more complicated than instrumentalists allow. A full reckoning of the relevant normative considerations far exceeds the limits of this chapter. The limited point that I want to make here is that situations of asymmetrical bilingualism are at least *prima facie* cases in which there is a moral case against educating children bilingually, as this would tend ultimately to benefit the dominant language within the pair.

III

Linguistic uniformity has been seen both by some politicians and by a number of political theorists as a pre-condition of successful nation-building (Gellner 1983). Many of the nations that presently constitute the European Union were at the outset linguistic crazy quilts. Efficient communication among citizens of the various regions of France, Italy, Germany, and so on, were made possible through the imposition of a common vernacular. This often was felt to require that the central state take over the education of children throughout a given territory and prohibit teaching in regional languages.

Thus, a second context in which some have felt that there was reason to prohibit bilingual education is that of nation-building. According to this view, a common language is an absolutely essential part of a national identity, and a stable, cohesive national identity is central to the stability of modern nation-states.

There is *prima facie* empirical plausibility to this claim. Countries with two official languages are notoriously fractious. Consider the cases of Belgium and of Canada, both of them beset with secessionist politics.

But what is the normative case for insisting upon unilingual education on nation-building grounds? After all, national building often consists not in the creation of a "neutral" national identity, one that would be equally situated relative to the cultures and languages of the groups making up a nation. Rather, it often is the result of the imposition of an economically and politically dominant group's cultural and linguistic identity upon non-consenting minority groups (Weinstock 2004). In the cases of nation-states established in the context of settler colonialism, the creation of nation-states has represented the culmination of the colonial extinguishing of indigenous cultures and languages.

In the light of this morally shabby history, is there anything that can be said positively in favour of nation building, and of the linguistic requirements thereof? Many "liberal nationalists" have in recent years claimed that in spite of this ethically spotty historical record, nations can under certain sets of circumstances perform morally admirable functions. In particular, they claim that the successful establishment of a shared national identity has been the empirical condition for the creation of broad solidarities among people who will never encounter one another in any face-to-face setting, and whose connection is therefore entirely mediated by "imagined" national communities. Thinkers as different as David Miller, Will Kymlicka, Philippe Van Parijs, and others have observed that for all the claims that have been made on behalf of supra-national, and even global solidarities, the construction of the modern mass nation-state is in reality the only successful example we know of a successful construction of enlarged sympathy and solidarity (Kymlicka 2001; Miller 1995; Van Parijs 2004).

According to these authors, this is particularly true in the domain of distributive justice. The equitable sharing of the fruits of social cooperation under market conditions requires that those that are successful in market transactions wilfully part with some of their resources in order to benefit the less well-off. No matter how philosophically dubious is the claim that people's pre-tax income is in any real sense "theirs," such that to part with some of it is to be viewed as a case of supererogatory largesse (Murphy & Nagel 2004), it is nonetheless the case that real-world welfare states need to be able to rely at least to some degree on the unforced consent of the rich in order to fund redistribution and welfare state programs. The claim made by some of these authors is that this is much harder to do in societies that view themselves as "multicultural." To put it in a more positive formulation: the practice of distributive justice is greatly facilitated when the well-off view themselves as making sacrifices for the benefit of people that they recognize as "one of us." The further claim might therefore be that when people are allowed, and perhaps even encouraged, to continue living according to the tenets of their cultures, and in particular, to live as minority linguistic enclaves, this makes the business of distributive justice harder to put in place.

A related argument, focussing on those whose minority languages would figure in bilingual education schemes (the latter argument focussing on the motivations of members of the linguistic and cultural majority), is put forward by Thomas Pogge, who has argued that educating minority children in their patrimonial tongue is bad *for children themselves*, since providing them with the ability to form minority linguistic enclaves unwittingly deprives them of the range of opportunities that they would have were they to assimilate linguistically to the language of the majority (Pogge 2003).

What are we to make of such arguments? Are we really faced with a tragic dilemma between, on the one hand, achieving the kind of national solidarity that will enable robust schemes of distributive justice, and, on the other hand, the granting of language rights to minority language groups whose languages might be allowed to survive by the adoption of bilingual education schemes?

I believe that the range of cases in which this might be true is much narrower than the range of cases covered in the previous section. There are many reasons for this. First, the empirical evidence for the claim that multiculturalism is an obstacle to generous welfare state provision is not univocal. Keith Banting and Will Kymlicka have for years now been testing the empirical hypothesis that this argument relies on, and they have reached the conclusion that it is quite difficult to generalize. They have not found a straight causal arrow between increased multiculturalism on the one hand and decreases in support for the welfare state on the other (Banting & Kymlicka 2006).

Second, there is a risk of equivocation as to what the linguistic correlate of the claim under consideration really is. Is the claim regarding language that national solidarity requires that people only speak the majority language, or that the majority language be firmly established as a *lingua franca*, that is, as a language fluently spoken by all, predominant in the public sphere, and that allows for unimpeded communication? Bilingual education schemes are of course fully compatible with the perceived need to establish a national *lingua franca*.

But the normative consideration that I want to draw specific attention to has to do with the moral evaluation of the social processes that are putatively in play in the present argument. Recall the sociolinguistic laws that were adduced in the previous section. The claim was that the mere coexistence of two linguistic groups of very different sizes suffices to put in place a set of incentives that make the smaller of the two languages vulnerable. Members of the larger language group are not to blame when the sociolinguistic laws and regularities pointed to by sociolinguists are set in motion. Now, to be sure, the fact that certain languages have risen to their present numerical status, while others have receded in some cases to the point of extinction, often results from past injustices (Ives 2015). It is clearly not an accident that global languages such as English, French, Spanish, and to a lesser degree Dutch and Portuguese, have been languages of empire. And of course, in the case of settler colonial societies, the injustices that have led to extreme cultural and linguistic vulnerability are still very much present. The refusal by governments of such societies to take positive steps to undo these oppressive cultural and linguistic regimes and to correct their linguistic consequences is clearly morally condemnable.

But in cases in which, say, two imperial languages such as English and French confront one another in asymmetrical contexts, it is possible to imagine processes rendering one of these languages vulnerable without any present speakers of the larger language being to blame. In other work, I have referred to these as "mere number cases" (Weinstock 2020).

The social mechanism that underpins the refusal of bilingual education schemes on the grounds that they might erode social solidarity is more deeply problematic, and it is difficult to imagine cases in which it could be morally vindicated. G. A. Cohen has in another context put his finger on what is so morally problematic about this kind of argument (Cohen 2006). Cohen has pointed out that there is something deeply problematic about John Rawls' claim in *Theory of Justice* that the more productive members of society need incentives in order to produce to their full capacity. When considered not as a third-personal, social scientific claim, but as a claim hypothetically made by the more productive toward their less productive fellow citizens, it amounts to making something like the following, morally dubious claim: "we will not produce as much as we can unless we can draw unequally from the exercise of our productive capacities." What seems morally tenable as an objectively stated claim becomes morally problematic when expressed from the first-person standpoint. Now, some may be willing to bite the moral bullet that consists in saying that it is morally permissible for people to be principally motivated to produce by the incentive of financial reward, but at the very least we can agree that it is not morally admirable.

Something similar is at work in the argument we are considering here. It has some *prima facie* plausibility when it is stated in a "third-personal," objective manner. From this standpoint, the claim amounts to saying something like "multilingual societies are less likely than monolingual ones to sustain robust redistributive schemes." This sounds like a morally neutral, empirically testable proposition. But when it is transformed into a "first personal" claim made by a member of the majority culture and of the larger linguistic group to a member of a minority linguistic group, it amounts to saying something that is as morally problematic as is the claim that was inferred by Cohen in his consideration of Rawls' argument. Indeed, it amounts to saying something like "we will only wilfully include you within the scope of our redistributive arrangements if you divest yourself of core dimensions of your identities, such as your languages." Needless to say, this is a much more difficult moral claim to vindicate. It amounts to defending a rather extreme form of ethno-cultural national partiality.

To bring together these two discussions, the claim that I am making is that it is much more difficult in the case of arguments from national identity and solidarity to identify a class of morally acceptable cases, as we had done in the case of asymmetrical bilingual scenarios by identifying what I referred to as "mere number cases." Now, it might be claimed that such a limited range of cases actually exists, and that it corresponds precisely to the limited set of cases that we have identified in the foregoing section. These are cases in which the very survival of a smaller national group depends upon its enacting what might on the face of it seem like fairly illiberal policies such as the prohibition of bilingual education schemes, especially in situations where the second of the languages within that scheme is that of the larger and more powerful linguistic group. It might apply to Quebec's prohibitions on English-language education, or to the prohibition in the tiny Baltic states of education in Russian.

But the argument as I have just reframed it abandons the normative terrain of solidarity to take up that of cultural and linguistic survival. Proportionality considerations will properly view certain policy measures as permissible if they can be shown to be required to secure the very existence of a culture and language, whereas they would not be acceptable were they put forward as required in order to ensure a requisite level of social solidarity as among majorities and minorities.

I conclude this section by claiming that it is much more difficult to justify the prohibition of bilingual education schemes on the grounds of national solidarity than it is in cases of the kind of extreme linguistic vulnerability that is generated by situations of asymmetrical bilingualism.

IV

I have in this chapter assumed, *arguendo* that bilingual education benefits children. This creates a very strong *prima facie* case for bilingual education schemes, one that, I have argued, can only be defeated in a very limited range of cases, namely, ones in which bilingual education risks reenforcing sociolinguistic laws that make "smaller" languages vulnerable. In such cases, following Van Parijs, I have argued that it can be morally defensible, where more moderate policies are not effective, to limit bilingual education that exposes children both to the vulnerable and to the dominant language.

In this concluding section, I want to further limit the range of cases in which it might be appropriate to prohibit or limit access to bilingual education. From the fact that bilingual education schemes that educate children in a vulnerable and in a dominant language can be limited for the sake of the more vulnerable language, it does not follow that bilingual education schemes that educate children in two smaller and more vulnerable languages can also be prohibited. In the section on asymmetrical bilingualism, I've followed Van Parijs' exhortation that speakers of smaller languages should "grab a territory" in order to enact legislation, in the educational sphere and elsewhere, that will reduce the vulnerability of their language. An unstated assumption here is that the language (or languages) that serve as the impetus of such a prohibition is (or are) locally or globally dominant.

But could prohibitions on bilingual education be framed in a selective manner? That is, could such policies be restricted to the languages that do, as a matter of fact, pose a threat to the survival of a language? To return to the case of Québec, while bilingual education schemes that would educate children in French and in English might pose a threat to the survival of the French linguistic community in North America, having immigrant parents from, say, Sweden decide to educate their children in French and Swedish would pose no such threat. Can one imagine a prohibition that targeted only the languages that did pose a threat?

This is actually a more difficult question to answer than might seem at first blush. On the one hand, prohibiting instruction in a regionally or globally dominant language whilst allowing such instruction in languages that pose no sociolinguistic threat might seem a case of clear discrimination. However, to claim that if bilingual instruction featuring as part of the pair a language possessing quite particular sociolinguistic features is to be prohibited, then all bilingual education is to be prohibited, is arguably a case of levelling down. What's more, a dominant language is likely to be acquired at least to a certain level of proficiency even if it is not a language in which children are educated, in virtue of its dominant status on the internet, in popular media and culture, and so on. Equality requires treating like cases alike, as Aristotle taught us, but in the case I have been considering Swedish and a regionally and globally dominant language such as English are not like cases in the ethically relevant sense.

There is clearly more to be said about the general issue of the permissibility of targeted as opposed to blanket prohibitions in asymmetrical bilingual contexts. But let me assume, for the sake of argument, that there are no *a priori* grounds for such blanket prohibitions. I want to distinguish three kinds of cases, that seem to me to possess quite different moral valences.

Consider, first, the kind of case that I introduced in order to stimulate reflection on the issue of blanket vs. targeted prohibitions. Imagine a group of Swedish immigrants were to set up a school that educated their children in Quebec in Swedish and French. I see no reason not to allow our hypothetical group of parents to do so. Swedish does not in the North American context represent a sociolinguistic threat to French. I do not however believe that there would be an obligation on the part of the state to fund such a school. Immigrants don't have a right against the state that it fund education in their patrimonial language, but it would also be an abuse of the coercive power of the state were it to prohibit parents from doing so, as long as other curricular conditions are satisfied.

A second case concerns established linguistic minorities that are neither speakers of a dominant language, nor recent immigrants. As Joseph Carens has argued, the amount of time that groups have settled makes a difference to the moral status of their claims (Carens 2009). Vulnerable linguistic minorities that are successful in heeding the imperative put forward by Van Parijs of "grabbing a territory" (whether through the achievement of national sovereignty or within federal or quasi-federal arrangements), and thus, of determining the way in which the educational system on that territory is set up, will rarely, if ever, find a linguistically homogeneous population there. There will be members of linguistic minorities speaking the regionally dominant language from which protection is being sought. But there will also be long established vulnerable linguistic minorities, who might be made even more vulnerable by state policies aimed at increasing the viability of a linguistic group that has been successful in "grabbing a territory."

In such cases, it seems to me that parity of reasoning would make it the case that the state not only may, but must, aid the community in question to stabilize its language, if necessary through the funding of bilingual language schemes. As an example, consider the Yiddish-speaking community that has been present in Québec's largest city, Montreal, for over a century. While unilingual Yiddish education would deprive the children of such communities of access to the province's *lingua franca*, bilingual education would allow them both to participate in the broader society's attempt to ensure the viability of the local *lingua franca*, while ensuring that this does not occur at the cost of a language that is subject to many of the same threats of erosion that French would be subjected to in an entirely *laissez faire* linguistic environment.

A third case is that of indigenous populations whose languages and cultures have been made vulnerable by deliberate colonial policies. If anything, the obligation on the part of the state to help indigenous people to set up bilingual educational schemes is even stronger. Policies aimed at reclaiming indigenous languages are a requirement of corrective justice. Their goal is not to establish as even a playing field between linguistic groups as is possible within a context marked by sociolinguistic laws that can render certain languages more vulnerable in unregulated contexts than others, but to attempt to correct the lasting effects of deliberate acts of oppression. Where this is consonant with the goal of reclaiming indigenous languages that have been harmed as a result of colonialism, bilingual education is a requirement of justice more urgent than in the case considered a moment ago (Borrows 2018). There is indeed no obligation more urgent for settler colonial states than to recognize and to endeavour to correct the effects of the cultural genocide that was an integral part of colonialism, and which received its most morally catastrophic expression in the residential schools in which indigenous children were abused and killed, and the intention of which was to eradicate indigenous cultures (Truth and Reconciliation Commission of Canada 2016; Adams 1995).

The upshot of this final section is to suggest that even in the case of linguistic communities that have a *prima facie* moral case to prohibit bilingual education, this case is subject to a range of limitations. First, they cannot prohibit groups from setting up bilingual education where languages that do not pose sociolinguistic threats are involved, and where the groups in question are willing to incur the costs involved in setting up the bilingual education system. Second, they must as a matter of justice participate in the institution of bilingual education schemes where such schemes are taken to be required to protect long established languages that are placed at greater risk by policies aimed at reducing the larger group's linguistic vulnerability. Third, they must as a matter of urgent corrective justice participate in the funding and setting up of schemes aimed at undoing the cultural and linguistic harms of past malfeasance, of which colonialism is a particularly egregious example. If this is seen by the communities that have been victims of colonial oppression as requiring bilingual education in a native language and in the local *lingua franca*, such schemes pose a further limit on the ability of groups that have "grabbed a territory" to use unilingual education in order to protect their own language.

V

In this chapter, I have considered the question of bilingual education through the narrow but important lens of *linguistic justice*. I have asked under what circumstances bilingual education serves, and in some circumstances might actually disserve, the cause of linguistic justice. There are of course a number of other relevant ethical questions that can be posed in considering not only *whether*, but *how* a bilingual curriculum ought to be implemented. If the present chapter has made anything clear, it is that bilingual education never occurs in a political vacuum. Rather, whether intentionally or not, it has effects both foreseeable and adventitious on what is often a linguistic field rife with conflict and division. This realization, as we have seen, can sometimes lead us to the conclusion that bilingual education would hinder rather than promote the cause of linguistic justice. That same realization about the contextual nature of any existing system of bilingual education should have an impact on not just the political but also the interpersonal ethics involved. There is clearly a rich research agenda here, of which this brief chapter merely scratched the surface.

(Related Chapters: 2, 15, 18, 20, 22, 23.)

Notes

1 For an overview of debates about bilingual education, see Baker 2010.
2 I set aside concerns that it may be bad for the linguistic and cognitive development of children that they be exposed to too many languages at too young an age. I find much of the evidence for this claim to be less than compelling. What's more, and most importantly for present purposes, a significant period in the education of children and adolescents occurs after the threshold which those who hold this position view as delimiting the period of a child's life during which they ought to be shielded from multilingual contexts. The question of bilingual education arises even for those who believe that it is in their interest that they have a single mother tongue.
3 Van Parijs is principally concerned with the global *lingua franca*, English, but the point can be made about smaller languages and regionally dominant languages.
4 For a survey of recent empirical research, see Byers-Heinlein and Lew-Williams (2013).
5 For example, the Spanish state imposes by law a minimum of 25% instruction in Spanish, though this is being actively resisted by Catalan local authorities. See https://www.euronews.com/2021/12/18/thousands-of-catalans-protest-against-decision-for-more-spanish-in-schools
6 I consider this range of considerations in Weinstock (2003).
7 The next paragraphs summarize an argument I develop at greater length in Weinstock (2020).

References

Adams, D. W. (1995) *Educating for Extinction. American Indians and the Boarding School Experience*. Lawrence: University of Kansas Press.
Baker, C. (2010) "Bilingual Education," in R. B. Kaplan (ed.) *Oxford Handbook of Applied Linguistics*. Oxford: Oxford University Press, 294–304.
Banting, K. & Kymlicka, W. (2006) *Multiculturalism and the Welfare State*. Oxford: Oxford University Press.
Borrows, L. K. (2018) *Otter's Journey through Indigenous Languages and Law*. Vancouver: The UBC Press.
Byers-Heinlein, K. and Lew-Williams, C. (2013) "Bilingualism in the Early Years: What the Science Says," in *Learning Landscapes* 7(1): 95–112.
Carens, J. (2009) "The Case for Amnesty?" *Boston Review* 34(3) 7–10.
Cohen, G. A. (1989) "On the Currency of Egalitarian Justice," *Ethics* 99(4): 906–944.
Cohen, G. A. (2006) *Rescuing Justice and Equality*. Cambridge, MA: Harvard University Press.
Gellner, E. (1983) *Nations and Nationalism*. Ithaca, NY: Cornell University Press.
Heath, J. (2001) *The Efficient Society*. Toronto: Penguin Books.
Ives, P. (2015) "Global English and Inequality," in R. Tupas (ed.) *Unequal Englishes. The Politics of Englishes Today*. London: Palgrave-MacMillan, 74–91.
Kymlicka, W. (1995) *Multicultural Citizenship. A Liberal Theory of Minority Rights*. Oxford: Oxford University Press.
Kymlicka, W. (2001) *Politics in the Vernacular*. Oxford: Oxford University Press.
Laponce, J. (1990) *Langue et Territoire*. Ste. Foy: Presses de l'Université Laval.
Miller, D. (1995) *On Nationalism*. Oxford: Oxford University Press.
Murphy, L., & Nagel, T. (2004) *The Myth of Ownership*. Oxford: Oxford University Press.
Pogge, T. (2003) "Accommodation Rights for Hispanics in the United States," W. Kymlicka & A. Patten (eds.) *Language Rights and Political Theory*. Oxford: Oxford University Press, 105–122.
Robichaud, D., & De Schutter, H. (2012) "Language is Just a Tool! On the Instrumentalist Approach to Language," in B. Spolsky (ed.) *The Cambridge Handbook of Language Policy*. Cambridge: Cambridge University Press, 124–145.
Truth and Reconciliation Commission of Canada (2016) *Canada's Residential Schools: Missing Children and Unmarked Burials. The Final Report of the Truth and Reconciliation Commission of Canada, Vol. 4*. Montreal: McGill-Queens Press.

Van Parijs, P. (2004) "Cultural Diversity against Economic Solidarity?" in P. Van Parijs (ed.) *Cultural Diversity versus Economic Solidarity*. Brussels: De Boeck, 371–396.

Van Parijs, P. (2011) *Linguistic Justice for Europe and the World*. Oxford: Oxford University Press.

Wee, L. (2010) *Language without Rights*. Oxford: Oxford University Rights.

Weinstock, D. (2003) "The Antinomy of Language Policy," in W. Kymlicka & A. Patten (eds.) *Language Rights and Political Theory*. Oxford: Oxford University Press, 250–270.

Weinstock, D. (2004) "Four Types of (Post-) Nation Building," in M. Seymour (ed.) *The Fate of the Nation State*. Montreal: McGill-Queens, 51–68.

Weinstock, D. (2015) "Can Parity of Self-Esteem Serve as the Basis for the Principle of Linguistic Territoriality?" *Critical Review of International Social and Political Philosophy* 18(2): 199–211.

Weinstock, D. (2016) "The Politics of Language: Philosophical Reflections on the Case of Quebec," in S. Gervais, C. Kirkey, & J. Rudy (eds.) *Quebec Questions: Quebec Studies for the XXIst Century"*, 2nd edition. Oxford: Oxford University Press, 197–207.

Weinstock, D. (2020) "Liberalism and Language Policy in 'Mere Number Cases'," in Y. Peled & D. Weinstock (eds.) *Language Ethics*. Montreal: McGill-Queens Press, 178–201.

20
GLOBAL DEMOCRATIC EDUCATIONAL JUSTICE*

Julian Culp

Introduction

Philosophical work on educational justice has had an overwhelmingly domestic focus.[1] It was largely shaped by theories of domestic justice in the era before political philosophers were thinking about global justice or human rights. The intense and wide-ranging debates on global justice within contemporary political philosophy have hardly influenced the current debates on educational justice. We now have theories of global justice and so it is time to think about global justice and education.[2] Indeed, several philosophers and educational theorists have already recognized the need for a cosmopolitan or global form of citizenship education that would enable future citizens to live up to the national-border transcending responsibilities that they have in a globalized world (Nussbaum 1996, 1997; Suárez-Orozco 2007; Sander & Scheunpflug 2011; Gaudelli 2016). In that way they already affirm a central premise of the global justice discourse, which is that all persons enjoy rights that deserve recognition not only from co-citizens and national governments but also from citizens of other states as well as from inter- and transnational actors such as international organizations or multinational corporations. Socio-economic rights to be free from extreme poverty, for example, are often conceived in this way (Pogge 2007). Nevertheless, philosophers and educational theorists have paid only scant attention to the question as to which rights to education, if any, can be justified as a matter of global justice. Their discourse on educational justice has remained domestic in its scope and focused mainly on the question of which rights to education co-citizens must mutually recognize.

The aim of this chapter is to transcend the domestic framing of the current discussion on educational justice by presenting a democratic conception of global educational justice. The next two sections situate this democratic conception of global educational justice within the philosophical discourses on educational and global justice. More specifically, they present the "cosmopolitan plateau" of the contemporary discourse on global justice as well as the domestic focus of the existing conceptions of educational justice. Following that, the chapter will lay out my conception of global democratic educational justice, by first explaining the democratic conception of global justice on which it relies.

* Earlier versions of this chapter were presented at the Catholic University of Louvain-la-Neuve in March 2017, at the Katholike Universitet Leuven in May 2017, and at the Technical University Dortmund in July 2021. I would like to thank Axel Gosseries, Katharina Fragoso Pitasse, Hervé Pourtois, Pierre-Etienne Vandamme, Vanderheiden, Nicolás Brando, Helder de Schutter, Johannes Drerup, Douglas Yacek, as well as the audiences for their valuable comments. In addition, I have also benefitted from valuable written comments from Randall Curren and Danielle Zwarthoed.

DOI: 10.4324/9781003172246-24

The Cosmopolitan Plateau of Global Justice Theorizing

Criticisms of the domestic framing of John Rawls's (1971) conception of justice as fairness have been an important focus of the debate on global justice.[3] Rawls limited the validity of his liberal egalitarian principles of justice – the equal liberties principle, the fair equality of opportunity principle, and the difference principle – to the national basic structure of a liberal democratic state.[4] Rawls did not justify principles of justice for the global basic structure but maintained merely that in international affairs "natural duties … hold between persons irrespective of their institutional relationships … [which should inform] the conduct of states" (Rawls 1971: 115). Charles Beitz argued, however, that Rawls's understanding of justice as fairness gives it global rather than merely domestic applicability; his account of fair terms of social cooperation applies to global society because 20th century economic and political globalization has given rise to a global basic structure that could only count as a fair system of cooperation if it were regulated by Rawls's principles of justice as fairness (Beitz 1999: 150–153).

Accordingly, Beitz insisted that Rawls's methodological device of the original position should be used and modified so that principles of global justice for the global basic structure would be chosen behind an appropriately adapted veil of ignorance (150–153). As in Rawls's theory, the point of this veil of ignorance thought experiment is to simulate a fair choice of principles by imagining that parties who choose the principles know nothing about themselves, such as their natural talents or social background. In addition, however, Beitz argued that in a *global* original position scenario the parties should be conceived as not knowing their national citizenship. In that way, he maintained, the principles that would be chosen in such a global original position would not unduly favor the members of any nation-state over those of any other. And while Beitz held that the parties of such a global original position would also select Rawls's principles of justice as fairness, he insisted that the scope of these principles would have to be global, as their purpose was to regulate the global basic structure. Beitz thereby justified the conclusion that lack of basic liberties, global fair equality of opportunity, and global economic inequalities that are not to the greatest advantage of the least well off should count as global injustices. Hence, moral problems in international affairs should not only be answered by drawing on "natural duties … [that] hold between persons irrespective of their institutional relationships," as Rawls had suggested (Rawls 1971: 115). The global basic structure should also be assessed on the same principles of justice that Rawls applied within individual societies.

In recent years, the contemporary discourse on global justice has become much more diversified. The major positions in this discourse, which I will outline below, are national or statist conceptions, globalist conceptions, as well as inter- and transnational conceptions (cf. Culp 2014). What is more, the discourse has now reached – following Mathias Risse's terminology – a "cosmopolitan plateau" (Risse 2012: 10).[5] It has reached such a plateau in the sense that all the major positions within the global justice debate – including Rawls's (1999) conception of global justice in *The Law of Peoples* – accept that there are some universally valid, human rights that all persons possess no matter where they reside. What is distinctive about these rights is that they are, as Beitz observes, "a matter of international concern" (2009: 105–106).[6] They entail responsibilities of justice to contribute to their realization not only on the part of the respective national governments, but also on the part of the international community. Thus, there is no longer any major position within the current global justice debate that would limit the scope of justice to the confines of the nation-state.

The most minimal of these positions are national or statist positions, according to which *sufficientarian* principles of justice are globally valid, whereas *egalitarian* principles of justice are valid only within states. Michael Blake (2001), David Miller (2007), and Gillian Brock (2009) recognize, for example, that all states and the international community have responsibilities of justice to ensure that a sufficientarian threshold of justice is met in all countries so that nobody, no matter where they reside, suffers from the under-fulfillment of basic needs or a lack of personal autonomy. Yet global socio-economic inequalities of opportunity or outcome do not count as global injustices according to these positions. By contrast, the globalist conceptions of Beitz (1999), Gosepath (2001), Pogge (2002), Moellendorf (2002), Tan (2004), and Caney (2005) affirm that egalitarian principles of distributive justice have global validity and that the relations among all persons globally must be such that there is no justice-relevant interpersonal inequality. On Caney's (2005: 122) luck-egalitarian understanding of global justice, for example, this means that no person, no matter where that person resides, should be worse off than any other person through no fault of her own.[7]

Furthermore, there are also inter- and transnationalist conceptions of global justice, according to which the question of global justice is not only whether all persons are entitled to some sufficientarian or some egalitarian entitlement of justice. In addition, further central questions of global justice are how to arrange justly the relations between states (Rawls 1999; Pettit 2010; Culp 2014), as well as the relations between states and non-state actors such as multinational corporations (cf., O'Neill 1991; Forst 2001; Fraser 2009). These inter- and transnationalist positions do not disagree with the national or statist positions that some sufficientarian threshold of justice must be met globally. Yet they add that there are also inter- or transnational principles of justice that should govern the relations between states and non-states actors. Rawls (1999: 65, 71–78), for example, has accepted in *The Law of Peoples* that all societies need to accept a set of basic human rights and that the international community has a duty to work towards the fulfillment of these rights whenever they remain unmet. In addition, Rawls (1999: 42n) has also recognized the need for principles of international justice that regulate the global background structure that shapes the interactions among states.

The Domestic Focus of Theories of Educational Justice

Despite this *global turn* in the theorizing of justice, however, conceptions of educational justice have remained mainly state-centered in their orientation. Theorists of educational justice have relied on domestically conceived conceptions of social justice and have used them as normative foundations for their respective conceptions of educational justice. As an illustration of this, consider that Harry Brighouse and Adam Swift have defended their respective and joint conceptions of equal educational opportunity (Brighouse 2000; Swift 2003; Brighouse & Swift 2006, 2009, 2014) based on alternative interpretations of the fair equality of opportunity principle that Rawls has defended as a principle regulating access to occupational opportunities within (relevant) nation-states.[8] Likewise, Elizabeth Anderson (2004, 2007) and Debra Satz (2007) rely on a relational or democratic conception of social justice that Anderson (1999) and Samuel Scheffler (2003) initially developed for conceptualizing the demands of social justice within the nation-state.[9] Similarly, Gina Schouten (2012) unfolds her prioritarian conception of educational justice by way of explaining what the demands of an interpretation of Rawls's difference principle are within education and schooling. And as I have already mentioned, Rawls defends his difference principle as a requirement of social justice within a liberal-democratic nation-state and not as a requirement of global distributive justice. Finally, Krassimir Stojanov's (2011) recognition-theoretic conception of educational justice is based on Axel Honneth's Hegelian understanding of what justice requires within the nation-state.

The domestic orientation of the contemporary debate on educational justice does not imply that the theorists of educational justice deny there are principles of global justice or hold that considerations of justice are only relevant within the confines of the nation-state. Theorists of educational justice may or may not have settled views about which proposed principles of global justice are the most defensible, and they may or may not have settled views about whether their preferred accounts of educational justice are globally applicable.[10]

Due to this domestic basis of the existing conceptions of educational justice it is high time to reflect on how to understand principles of *global* educational justice that have conceptions of global justice as their normative foundations. The next section makes a step in that direction by way of presenting one distinctively democratic conception of global educational justice that is based on a democratic conception of global justice. The breadth of conceptions of global justice makes it possible to lay out various related conceptions of global educational justice.[11] Accordingly, my presentation of just one conception of global educational education in the next section does not at all exhaust the conceptual possibilities of articulating global educational justice. Nevertheless, my presentation clearly demonstrates the possibility of conceiving educational justice in a global as opposed to a domestic manner. It also reveals important questions that such a global conception of educational justice must answer, and which have thus far been neglected due to the domestic framing of the debate on educational justice. Above all, this is the question of how important the realization of domestic educational justice within a single state is relative to the realization of global educational justice within all states.[12]

A Democratic Conception of Global Justice[13]

In this section I outline the basic ideas of a democratic conception of global justice, which I employ as the foundation for developing a democratic conception of global educational justice in the next section.[14] In a nutshell, the most important requirement of a democratic conception of global justice is to establish structures of justification that allow everyone to veto or block the justifications that are given within political discourses for how to go about addressing political conflicts and problems.[15] The central demands of global educational justice that follow from this conception are the formation of personal moral and public autonomy through educational public policy so that persons are not dominated in their personal development and can effectively participate in political decision-making processes.

One important point of departure of the democratic conception of justice is Iris Young's challenge of what she refers to as the "distributive paradigm" in theorizing justice (Young 1990: ch. 1; 2000). Instead of focusing on how resources are distributed, she argues, it is necessary to focus on the structure of the decision-making processes that lead to a distribution of resources in the first place. Young calls for displacing "the distributive paradigm in favor of a wider, process-oriented understanding of society, which focuses on power [and] decision-making" (1990: 37). Similarly, Rainer Forst urges avoiding a purely distributive "picture" of justice and highlights the importance of recognizing a political "picture," as well (2012: ch. 12; 2014: ch. 1). This political picture relies on the idea that all moral persons possess a *basic moral right to justification* that entitles them "to demand and provide justifications" for how they are treated and "to challenge false legitimations" of their social and political orders (Forst 2011: 9). This basic right relies on a conception of moral respect for persons, according to which morally respecting persons means behaving towards them in ways that are *morally justifiable* to them.

Forst's account, which draws on Jürgen Habermas's discourse theory of morality, states that the standards of a moral justification consist of the criteria of *generality* and *reciprocity*.[16] Generality means that a moral justification must not be justifiable solely to those persons who share a specific socio-political context and particular conceptions of the good. Rather, generality requires the justification to be justifiable to all persons, regardless of whether they belong to the same socio-political contexts and endorse the same conception of the good. Further, reciprocity requires that the justifications given must not be one sided. Justifications should not be articulated in a manner that privileges certain persons by exempting them from certain moral requirements. Nor must justifications regard the interests of certain persons as facts of nature and thus beyond reasonable criticism. The two criteria of generality and reciprocity, then, express more concretely what it means to show respect to others "by treating them," as Rawls once put it, "in ways that they can see to be justified" (1971: 516).

Arguably, this means that social and political institutions must be justifiable to their members in such a way that they can come to see themselves as *authors* of *their* institutions. Therefore, such institutions must be perceivable as the result of a reasoning process in which nobody has been arbitrarily excluded and nobody has enjoyed the privilege of counting as a greater justificatory authority than anyone else. On a more practical level, this means that fundamentally just social and political orders must afford all their members appropriate social and political roles through which they can encounter one another on an equal footing in the exchange of reasons concerning which norms should underlie their common institutions. Accordingly, a theory of justice must provide an account of the effective social and political *structures of justification* that enable persons to call into question the justifications that are given for certain social and political contexts that, among other things, lead to a specific distribution of goods and scheme of production. The demand for such basic structures of justification is the most fundamental requirement of a democratic or discourse theory of justice (Forst 2001: 174, 176; 2012: *passim*).

Building on Forst's discourse theory of justice, I endorse an *internationalist* conception of global democratic justice. It holds that basic or fundamental global democratic justice requires that the national representatives of internally sufficiently just states ought to have sufficient justificatory power in international processes of opinion and will formation that affect the lives of their members (cf. Culp 2014: ch. 5).[17] These international processes of opinion and will formation are international political discourses in which official or formally recognized political agents deliberate and negotiate empirical and normative questions that have an effect not only on their respective national political communities but also on the world at large.

More specifically, those who represent states that are internally sufficiently just must participate in the construction of the material or substantive principles of justice that will count as internationally valid. Accordingly, state representatives must be capable of partaking in discursively determining the substantive principles that will serve as normative building blocks for a just international order.[18] While such international processes must transmit the viewpoints of the members of the respective national population, it is also necessary that, additionally, citizens from various states can voice their demands through *transnational* processes of opinion and will formation. In this way these citizens will be able to co-determine international decision making.[19]

Furthermore, this internationalist conception of global democratic justice requires institutionalizing basic structures of justification at the *intra*national or domestic level. The reason for this is that the justifications for any kind of global order must be justifiable to citizens in their capacity as normative authorities. Otherwise, the international processes of opinion and will-formation cannot be properly thought of as being justifiable to all those who are impacted by the decisions reached in these processes. Those who are impacted in such ways must also become politically capable of critically examining the choices that the representatives of states made.

Global Democratic Educational Justice[20]

Democratic educational justice requires that educational public policies are democratically adequate (cf. Anderson 2004, 2007; Satz 2007), and to count as such, these policies must form persons' personal moral and public autonomy.[21] Public autonomy refers to persons as public subjects who can participate in public decision-making processes by cooperating with others in reasoning critically about the public ends of their respective political communities. This reasoning concerns the understanding, the application, and the construction of mutually justifiable principles of justice. From the perspective of democratic educational justice such public autonomy is of fundamental importance because it is through public deliberation that persons determine how to arrange their social and political order.

Among other things, this requires that persons learn to accept the fact of reasonable pluralism about conceptions of the good. They must recognize that securing basic civic and political liberties such as liberty of thought, liberty of speech and liberty of assembly unavoidably leads to a situation in which citizens come to endorse different conceptions of the good. For if persons are free to use these liberties, then the exercise of reason makes it the case that they will come to formulate and adhere to different conceptions of the good. After all, they have different kinds of experiences in their lives and interpret in different ways the concepts that they use in order to render these experiences sensible to them in relation to their understanding of themselves and members of groups.[22] In addition, they must also be "reasonable" in the sense of being able to be properly motivated to comply with the institutional rules that correspond to the principles that they have justified intersubjectively. According to this ideal of public autonomy, individuals therefore should become joint authors of the social and political orders that they inhabit, and they should be willing to maintain "their" normative orders by following these orders' political rules.[23] So they must also feel bound by a responsibility of justice to follow those norms that have been intersubjectively justified.

But in addition to furthering public autonomy, democratic educational justice also demands that educational public policies promote personal moral autonomy. Personal moral autonomy refers to the capacity to act morally in the sense of being able to act according to moral norms that are justified by the criteria of reciprocity and generality (cf. Forst 2002: 268). This idea of personal moral autonomy demands that persons should be aware that they have an individual right to reason about which ends they would like to pursue in their private lives. After all, the criterion of generality requires that all practical norms are justifiable to all persons, and the criterion of reciprocity holds that persons need not accept any conception of the good simply because someone else has proposed this conception. All persons count as equally authoritative concerning "ethical" questions of what the good life involves.

The basic idea of personal moral autonomy is thus also that of non-domination, according to which others must not arbitrarily interfere in one's life (cf. Costa 2011: 86). Like public autonomy, personal moral autonomy is inextricably linked to the moral right to justification because this right means that no individual is entitled to decide for another individual how to lead his or her life. Accordingly, the possession of this right requires the development of personal moral autonomy through educational public policy so that persons are not subject to the arbitrary imposition of other persons' will regarding what conception of the good to accept and follow.

Recall that the fundamental political requirement of this democratic conception of global justice is to build appropriately arranged basic structures of justification at the domestic and at the international levels. These structures must enable domestic and international political discourses that discursively determine further principles of global justice. When recognizing this conception as the normative ground of educational public policy, the educational rights to public and to personal moral autonomy that constitute my global conception of democratic educational justice should have two features. First, the *scope* of validity of fundamental – or "primary" – rights to democratically adequate education that ensures the enjoyment of both public autonomy and personal moral autonomy must be viewed as global or universal. These rights to democratically adequate education must be fully realized within all states. Second, the *content* of these fundamental rights to democratically adequate education must not be limited to an education that is merely effective in facilitating participation in democratic decision making domestically. Rather, educational public policies must also enable citizens to participate in international decision-making. This means that such policies must contribute to the realization of citizens' capabilities of partaking in transnational political discourses, since these discourses are one central mechanism through which citizens can shape international decision making.

One way in which to emphasize this specific content of the rights to democratically adequate education is to differentiate between the right to *domestically* democratically adequate education and the right to *internationally* democratically adequate education. A global conception of democratic educational justice requires the realization of both rights. Curren and Metzger argue that the preparation for participation in international decision-making procedures through appropriate forms of educational public policy is crucial on grounds of legitimacy (2017: ch. 6). They maintain that "legitimacy rests on transparency, which requires understanding of what is at stake, hence a wealth of relevant education for all who may directly or indirectly be parties to the negotiation or subject to the terms of cooperation it yields – in short, everyone in the world" (2017: 170).

Yet in addition to these fundamental rights to domestically and internationally democratically adequate education, my conception also includes further – "secondary" – rights to those kinds of education that are justified within properly arranged basic structures of justification. Thus, it also consists of these further rights to education that are justified within such structures of justification at the domestic as well as at the international levels. So relative to the way in which appropriately structured domestic and international deliberations justify further rights to education, these further or secondary rights also constitute demands of global democratic educational justice. These further or secondary rights might be certain rights to equal educational opportunity or rights to education that benefit the least well off.[24]

Since this conception of global democratic educational justice consists of fundamental (or primary) and further (or secondary) rights to education that must be realized not only domestically but within all states, the question arises of how to rank these rights in terms of their moral importance. In particular, the question arises as to whether a state, once the fundamental rights to democratically adequate education have been entirely realized in this state, should pursue the domestic realization of further, secondary rights to education, or whether the state should rather aim at realizing the fundamental rights to education of citizens from other states.[25] In my view, in such a case the fundamental rights to democratically adequate education of citizens from other states are in principle morally more important than the domestic realization of any further or secondary rights to education domestically.

For example, consider a state in which democratically adequate education already has been achieved. Should the state now use additionally available educational resources for realizing equal educational opportunity domestically rather than supporting the realization of fundamental rights to democratically adequate education in other states? My conception maintains that, other things being equal, the available educational resources should be employed for realizing the fundamental rights to democratically adequate education in other states rather than for realizing domestic equal educational opportunity.

Finally, when it comes to determining in greater detail which agents should prioritize the realization of the fundamental rights to democratically adequate education that my global conception of democratic educational justice defends, my first answer is that those who can, should. Thus, I claim that all states that have already fulfilled the primary rights to education domestically as well as the educationally relevant international organizations – such as, above all, the OECD, UNESCO, and UNICEF – bear the moral responsibility for realizing the fundamental rights to democratically adequate education of all citizens within all states. The reasoning underlying this claim is that these are especially powerful actors that have the capacity for assuming such responsibility without having to sacrifice other goods of greater moral importance. In addition, those who benefit or contribute to a global institutional order that reproduces global educational injustices also bear moral responsibilities for reducing these injustices (cf. Pogge 2002; Young 2007, 2011). It is difficult to identify with precision the agents that benefit and contribute in this way, yet it is reasonable to assume that those who belong to upper echelons of the income and wealth distributions and those who occupy influential roles in culture, economy, and politics are the bearers of such responsibility.

These general answers do not offer determinate replies to further questions about moral responsibility for realizing the fundamental rights to democratically adequate education. These questions include: Are there any other reasons for ascribing responsibility to certain actors for realizing global educational justice – reasons that are based on considerations of international law? How should the moral responsibility for achieving global democratic educational justice be divided among states? Are there any actors other than states that bear a similar kind of moral responsibility? If yes, how should the moral responsibility for global democratic educational justice be divided among these various kinds of actors? Although my initial answers do not offer detailed replies to these questions, they offer a determinate approach for answering these questions. For the kind of basic structures of justification that it argues should be erected are also meant to facilitate democratic deliberation within domestic and international political discourses about how to allocate justly the responsibilities for achieving global democratic educational justice.[26]

Conclusion

Conceptions of educational justice are closely connected to more far-reaching conceptions of social justice that usually serve as their normative foundations.[27] Hence, it does not come as a surprise that the diversity and subtlety of conceptions of social justice that has emerged since the last quarter of the 20th century has given rise to a corresponding variety of conceptions of educational justice. These latter conceptions include liberal egalitarian, democratic, prioritarian, and recognition-theoretic perspectives. However, whereas the discourse on social justice has been globalized since the 1990s, the debate on educational justice has remained mainly domestic, or state-centered, in its normative orientation. To overcome the curious neglect of the philosophical debate on global justice that is underlying this domestic orientation, this chapter has presented a democratic conception of global justice as well as a corresponding conception of global democratic educational justice. In that way this chapter has shown but one way in which the global justice discourse can inform the debate on educational justice. Given the diversity of conceptions of global justice, many other conceptions of global educational justice are also conceivable.

This chapter has also maintained that the exploration of the concept of global educational justice has overlooked normative importance, since the demands of educational justice at the domestic level need to be understood in the context of the demands of educational justice at the global level. It is unreasonable to bracket the discussion of global education justice on the presumption that fulfilling demands of global educational justice is of negligible normative relevance for as long as an ideal of a domestically conceived conception of educational justice is not yet fully fulfilled. It is normatively more appropriate to hold, as I have done in the case of my democratic conception of global educational justice, that states and their citizens should seriously concern themselves with furthering educational justice in other states once they have reached a basic or fundamental level of educational justice at the domestic level. Yet it is only through conceiving educational justice from a global perspective that the relative weight or priority of domestic rights to education vis-à-vis global rights to education elsewhere becomes clearly visible.

In addition, the discussion of my democratic conception of global educational justice has revealed that a global perspective provides insights concerning the appropriate formulation of the contents of rights to education. In the case of my democratic conception, one of these insights has been that educational public policies must also prepare persons for their participation in international decision-making processes. This is because they have a right to justification that entitles them to challenge false legitimations, regardless of whether they occur at the domestic or at the global level. And so, it is of paramount importance to pursue this *global turn* in the theorizing of educational justice.

(Related Chapters: 1, 2, 6, 8, 9, 15, 16, 17, 18, 19, 20, 34.)

Notes

1 Cf. Culp (2020) for an overview of the contemporary philosophical debate on educational justice.
2 Unless specified otherwise, the central focus of this chapter is *school education*.
3 Work on rights of succession and the ethics of humanitarian intervention, e.g., by Buchanan (1991), were early steps toward addressing larger questions of global justice, starting around 1990.
4 See Rawls (2001: 42–43) for the ultimate formulation of these three principles.

5 Risse's terminology is itself an adaptation of the term "egalitarian plateau" that Kymlicka (2000) uses to describe the competing conceptions of social justice.
6 As Beitz (2009: 105–106) puts it: "Whatever else is true of human rights, they are supposed to be matters of international concern in the sense that a society's failure to respect its people's human rights on a sufficiently large scale may provide a reason for outside agents to do something."
7 Caney (2005:122) explains this as follows: "The point can be put in more colloquial terms: in recent years the term 'postcode lottery' has been employed in Britain to criticize the situation in which people who lived in the jurisdictions of different councils have very unequal access to health and education. This, it was said, was unfair for it is wrong that someone should get less simply because he or she lives in one place rather than another. The cosmopolitan point is simply to radicalize this and to see through its logic at the global level."
8 Cf. also Gosepath (2014). There are strong and weak versions of the conception of educational justice as equal educational opportunity, which Brighouse and Swift (2009, 2014) call the meritocratic conception and the radical one, respectively. The weak version states that all citizens with equal (natural) talents and equal motivation to use their talents should have equal chances for formal educational achievement. By contrast, the strong version holds that all citizens with equal motivation to use their talents, but irrespective of the relative level of their talents, should have equal chances for formal educational achievement.
9 See also Randall Curren (1994) and John White (1994) for threshold conceptions of educational justice.
10 Brighouse and Swift (2011: 122), for example, have recognized the moral importance of supporting members of other nation-states by arguing that "even if national relationship goods were very valuable, we'd still need to know the opportunity cost of their production as far as other goods are concerned, and why an individual could legitimately pursue them for herself and her fellow nationals rather than helping others to realize them."
11 Zwarthoed (2019), for example, has analyzed whether it is justifiable to defend autonomy as an educational aim at the global level. In addition, Schwartz (2019) has focused on the question of what is owed to children of primary and secondary school age who are living outside their country of origin.
12 Again, while many theorists of educational justice, like Brighouse and Swift (2011), are likely to recognize this point, they have not yet fleshed out its theoretical and normative implications.
13 This section heavily draws on ch. 2 of my book *Democratic Education in a Globalized World – A Normative Theory* (2019: 33–44).
14 My defense of the democratic or discourse-theoretic conception of justice follows the ground-breaking work of Forst (2002, 2012), as I will further explain in the remainder of this chapter. In Culp (2015), I offer a critical comparison between this democratic way of conceiving justice and the luck-egalitarian conception of justice that Cohen (2008) defends.
15 I follow Peters' (2007: 217) definition of the term "discourse," which I use interchangeably with the term "deliberation," and which emphasizes that claims that are part of a discourse claim to be grounded on appropriate reasons: "*Discourse*," he explains, "occurs if empirical statements, descriptions or reports, explanations, interpretations, proposals prescriptions, normative judgments or evaluations are supported by some kind of justification, by some argumentative backing, or by some presentation of evidence."
16 For an explication of the criteria of reciprocity and generality, see, Forst (2002: 68–69, 133–134; 2012: 80–81); on the research program of a discourse-theoretical moral philosophy, see Habermas (1990).
17 For other internationalist accounts, see Buchanan (2004), Ronzoni (2009), Christiano (2010), Pettit (2010).
18 See also Habermas (2008: 334) for his proposal for a transnational negotiation system among states. For similar internationalist accounts, see Christiano (2010), Pettit (2010).
19 Despite the importance of transnational social movements and political discourses for my conception of global democratic justice, I nevertheless refer to it as an *internationalist* rather than a transnational conception. There are three features of my conception of global justice that make it appropriate to label it as an internationalist one. One such feature of my conception of global justice is that it assumes that the international system of states can in principle realize fundamental global justice. It neither calls for anarchy nor for world government, but for a democratic international system. Another relevant feature is that my conception of global justice holds that (democratic) states and (democratically constructed) international law are central bearers of rights and responsibilities of global justice. States and international law play a central role for both conceptualizing and realizing global justice. Finally, my conception of global justice is compatible with the view that different states will domestically realize certain conceptions of social justice in different ways. It recognizes the importance of issues of justice across, between, and beyond states, but also maintains that social justice needs to be realized in context-specific ways in different states.
20 This section heavily draws on ch. 2 and 3 of my book *Democratic Education in a Globalized World – A Normative Theory* (2019: 33–44, 77–79).

21 Other philosophers of education who put particular emphasis on the public autonomy to participate in processes of democratic decision making are De Wijze (1999) and Costa (2004).
22 See Rawls (2005: 54–58) on what he calls the "burdens of judgment."
23 This metaphor of joint authorship does not mean that my conception of public autonomy assumes that all individuals will eventually gather and decide together which laws should be put in place and which policies should be implemented. That would be an unrealistic utopian claim. "Joint authorship" can, however, play the role of a regulative idea that practically informs actions and policies even if not everyone participates in collective decision making and even if there is no unanimous agreement on how to decide.
24 To clarify, by arguing philosophically for the moral primacy of rights to democratic education I do not mean to suggest that the political discourses about how to achieve democratic education will become superfluous. For example, it is necessary to spell out in greater detail what is meant by a right to democratic education that is "adequate."
25 One can question whether states are entitled to realize first the rights to democratic education of their citizens, before attempting to realize the rights to democratic education of citizens from other states. One reason why states have this entitlement is the consideration that the most efficient way for realizing all rights to democratic education is to ascribe primary responsibility for realizing citizens' rights to democratic education to their respective states. Another reason is that using a state's resources to realize rights to democratic education elsewhere cannot be legitimately decided unless that state's citizens already enjoy democratic rights.
26 See Culp (2016) on why this is an adequate way to allocate responsibility for global justice.
27 Forst (2017) has coined the term, a "normatively dependent concept," in order to describe this kind of relationship between two normative concepts such as educational justice and social justice.

References

Anderson, E. (1999) "What's the Point of Equality?" *Ethics* 109(2): 287–337.

Anderson, E. (2004) "Rethinking Equality of Opportunity: Comment on Adam Swift's *How Not to Be a Hypocrite*," *Theory and Research in Education* 2(2): 99–110.

Anderson, E. (2007) "Fair Opportunity in Education: A Democratic Equality Perspective," *Ethics* 117(4): 595–622.

Beitz, C. (1999 [1979]) *Political Theory and International Relations*. 2nd edn. Princeton: Princeton University Press.

Beitz, C. (2009) *The Idea of Human Rights*. Oxford: Oxford University Press.

Blake, M. (2001) "Distributive Justice, State Coercion, and Autonomy," *Philosophy & Public Affairs* 30(3): 257–296.

Brighouse, H. (2000) *School Choice and Social Justice*. Oxford: Oxford University Press.

Brighouse, H. & Swift, A. (2006) "Equality, Priority, and Positional Goods," *Ethics* 116(3): 471–497.

Brighouse, H. & Swift, A. (2009) "Educational Equality versus Educational Adequacy: A Critique of Anderson and Satz," *Journal of Applied Philosophy* 26(2): 117–218.

Brighouse, H. & Swift, A. (2011) "Legitimate Partiality, Parents, and Patriots," in A. Gosseries & P. Vanderborght (eds.) *Arguing about Justice. Essays in Honor of Philippe van Parijs*. Louvain: Presses Universitaires de Louvain, 115–123.

Brighouse, H. & Swift, A. (2014) "The Place of Educational Equality in Educational Justice," in K. Meyer (ed.) *Education, Justice and the Human Good. Fairness and Equality in the Educational System*. London: Routledge, 14–33.

Brock, G. (2009) *Global Justice – A Cosmopolitan Account*. New York: Oxford University Press.

Buchanan, A. (1991) *Secession: The Morality of Political Divorce from Fort Sumter to Lithuania and Quebec*. Boulder: Westview Press.

Buchanan, A. (2004) *Justice, Legitimacy and Self-Determination*. New York: Oxford University Press.

Caney, S. (2005) *Justice Beyond Borders*. Oxford: Oxford University Press.

Christiano, T. (2010) "Democratic Legitimacy and International Institutions," in S. Besson & J. Tasioulas (eds.) *The Philosophy of International Law*. Oxford: Oxford University Press, 119–137.

Cohen, G. A. (2008) *Rescuing Justice and Equality*. Cambridge, MA: Harvard University Press.

Costa, V. (2004) "Rawlsian Civic Education: Political not Minimal," *Journal of Applied Philosophy* 21(1): 1–14.

Costa, V. (2011) *Rawls, Citizenship, and Education*. London: Routledge.

Culp, J. (2014) *Global Justice and Development*. London: Palgrave Macmillan.

Culp, J. (2015) "G. A. Cohen, Constructivism, and the Fact of Reasonable Pluralism," *Analyse & Kritik* 35(1–2): 131–147.
Culp, J. (2016) "How Irresponsible Are Rising Powers?" *Third World Quarterly* 37(9): 1525–1536.
Culp, J. (2019) *Democratic Education in a Globalized World. A Normative Theory*. London: Routledge.
Culp, J. (2020) "Educational Justice," *Philosophy Compass* 15(12): 1–12.
Curren, R. (1994) "Justice and the Threshold of Educational Equality," in M. Katz (ed.) *Philosophy of Education*. Urbana: Philosophy of Education Society, 239–248.
Curren, R. & E. Metzger (2017) *Living Well Now and in the Future: Why Sustainability Matters*. Cambridge, MA: The MIT Press.
De Wijze, S. (1999) "Rawls and Civic Education," *Cogito* 13(2): 87–93.
Forst, R. (2001) "Towards a Critical Theory of Transnational Justice," *Metaphilosophy* 32(1–2): 160–179.
Forst, R. (2002) *Contexts of Justice*. Berkeley: University of California Press.
Forst, R. (2017) "Toleration," in E. Zalta (ed.) *The Stanford Encyclopedia of Philosophy* (Fall 2017 Edition), URL = <https://plato.stanford.edu/archives/fall2017/entries/toleration/>.
Forst, R. (2011) "Transnational Justice and Democracy," *The Formation of Normative Orders Working Papers* 4: 1–18.
Forst, R. (2012) *The Right to Justification: Elements of a Constructivist Theory of Justice*. New York: Columbia University Press.
Fraser, N. (2009) *Scales of Justice – Reimagining Political Space in a Globalizing World*. New York: Columbia University Press.
Gaudelli, W. (2016) *Global Citizenship Education. Everyday Transcendence*. London: Routledge.
Gosepath, S. (2001) "The Global Scope of Justice," *Metaphilosophy* 32(1–2): 135–159.
Gosepath, S. (2014) "What Does Equality in Education Mean?" in K. Meyer (ed.) *Education, Justice and the Human Good. Fairness and Equality in the Educational System*. London: Routledge, 100–113.
Gutmann, A. (1987) *Democratic Education*. Princeton: Princeton University Press.
Habermas, J. (1990 [1983]) *Moral Consciousness and Communicative Action*. Cambridge: MIT Press.
Habermas, J. (2008) "A Political Constitution for the Pluralist World Society?" in *Between Naturalism and Religion*. Cambridge: Polity Press, 312–353.
Kymlicka, W. (2000) *Contemporary Political Philosophy. An Introduction. 2nd edn*. Oxford: Oxford University Press.
Miller, D. (2005) "Against Global Egalitarianism," *The Journal of Ethics* 9(1–2): 55–79.
Miller, D. (2007) *National Responsibility and Global Justice*. Oxford: Oxford University Press.
Moellendorf, D. (2002) *Cosmopolitan Justice*. Boulder, CO: Westview Press.
Moellendorf, D. (2009) *Global Inequality Matters*. Basingstoke: Palgrave.
Nussbaum, M. (1996) "Patriotism and Cosmopolitanism," in J. Cohen (ed.) *For Love of Country*. Boston: Beacon Press, 3–20.
Nussbaum, M. (1997) *Cultivating Humanity*. Cambridge, MA: Harvard University Press.
O'Neill, O. (1991) "Transnational Justice," in D. Held (ed.) *Political Theory Today*. Cambridge: Polity Press, 276–304.
Peters, B. (2007) *Public Deliberation and Public Culture*. Basingstoke: Palgrave Macmillan.
Pogge, T. (2002) *World Poverty and Human Rights*. Cambridge: Polity Press.
Pogge, T. (ed.) (2007) *Freedom from Poverty as a Human Right*. Oxford: Oxford University Press.
Rawls, J. (1971) *A Theory of Justice*. Cambridge, MA: Harvard University Press.
Rawls, J. (1999) *The Law of Peoples*. Cambridge, MA: Harvard University Press.
Rawls, J. (2001) *Justice as Fairness*. Cambridge, MA: Harvard University Press.
Rawls, J. (2005 [1993]) *Political Liberalism*. Expanded paperback edition. New York: Columbia University Press.
Risse, M. (2012) *On Global Justice*. Princeton: Princeton University Press.
Ronzoni, M. (2009) "The Global Order – A Case of Background Injustice?" *Philosophy & Public Affairs* 37(3): 229–256.
Pettit, P. (2010) "A Republican Law of Peoples," *European Journal of Political Theory* 9: 70–94.
Scheffler, S. (2003) "What is Egalitarianism?" *Philosophy & Public Affairs* 31(1): 5–39.
Sander, W. & Scheunpflug, A. (eds.) (2011) *Politische Bildung in der Weltgesellschaft*. Bonn: Bundeszentrale für Politische Bildung.
Satz, D. (2007) "Equality, Adequacy, and Education for Citizenship," *Ethics* 117(4): 623–648.
Schouten, G. (2012) "Fair Educational Opportunity and the Distribution of Natural Ability: Toward a Prioritarian Conception of Educational Justice," *Journal of Philosophy of Education* 46(3): 472–491.
Schwartz, L. (2019) "International Educational Justice: Educational Resources for Students Living Abroad," *Global Justice: Theory Practice Rhetoric* 12/1: 78–99.

Stojanov, K. (2011) *Bildungsgerechtigkeit. Rekonstruktionen eines umkämpften Begriffs*. Wiesbaden: Verlag für Sozialwissenschaften.
Swift, A. (2003) *How Not to Be a Hypocrite: School Choice for the Morally Perplexed Parent*. New York: Routledge.
Suárez-Orozco, M. (ed.) (2007) *Learning in the Global Era: International Perspectives on Globalization and Education*. Berkeley: University of California Press.
Tan, K.-C. (2004) *Justice Without Borders. Cosmopolitanism, Nationalism and Patriotism*. Cambridge: Cambridge University Press.
White, J. (1994) "The Dishwasher's Child: Education and the End of Egalitarianism," *Journal of Philosophy of Education* 28: 173–182.
Young, I. (1990) *Justice and the Politics of Difference*. Princeton: Princeton University Press.
Young, I. (2000) *Inclusion and Democracy*. Oxford: Oxford University Press.
Young, I. (2007) *Global Challenges. War, Self-Determination and Responsibility for Justice*. Cambridge: Polity.
Young, I. (2011) *Responsibility for Justice*. Oxford: Oxford University Press.
Zwarthoed, D. (2019) "Autonomy Education Beyond Borders," *Global Justice: Theory Practice Rhetoric* 12/1: 100–120.

21
NEOLIBERALISM AND EDUCATION

Lawrence Blum

Neoliberalism has been a significant force in the world of education, and of social policy more broadly, for several decades. Neoliberalism is a developed political philosophy. But its influence is also as a more general, not-necessarily-systematized, outlook, a set of policy tendencies, and a set of evaluative orientations (in sum, an "imaginary") some of which shape "common sense" so that people do not recognize them to be a part of a distinct political/evaluative outlook. Neoliberalism has affected education through all of these modalities.

Origins of Neoliberal Thought

The origins of what is now understood to be "neoliberalism" are quite clear. It began with a group of German, Austrian, and American economists in the 1930s and '40s. They were looking to design an economic and social order as an alternative to communist and Nazi collectivism, but also to the Keynesian-influenced economic orders of the United States (in the Roosevelt era) and Great Britain, with their strong role for state intervention in the economy, in part to support welfare states. The Austrian Friedrich Hayek, a philosophically minded economist (who became a British citizen in 1938), and an American, Milton Friedman, were the most prominent, and were instrumental in setting up an international network of "free market" theorists (the Mont Pèlerin Society), eventually establishing a beachhead at the University of Chicago. "Neoliberal" was understood as an attempt to retrieve classical liberalism from the social liberalism and state interventionism that had taken over in the United States and Western Europe, seen as only different in degree from collectivist totalitarianism, as expressed in Hayek's influential 1944 call to arms, *The Road to Serfdom*.

The social liberal and social democratic orders of the 1950s and 1960s with their robust welfare states and strong unions were not hospitable to neoliberal ideas in that period. But Hayek, Friedman, and their colleagues saw themselves as public intellectuals and intellectual activists, promoting classical liberal and free market ideas to intellectual elites (partly through think tanks funded by wealthy capitalists who agreed with their ideas). Their ideas began to take hold in the 1970s; both Hayek and Friedman received Nobel Prizes in Economics in the '70s. The elections of conservatives Margaret Thatcher in the U.K. in 1979 and Ronald Reagan in the United States in 1980 provided fertile soil for neoliberal ideas to influence public policy, an influence that very much continued in the Democratic as well as Republican US governments and Labor and Conservative governments in the UK in the '90s, '00s and '10s. Neoliberalism came to dominate economic thinking in international financial and trade organizations such as the IMF and WTO.

DOI: 10.4324/9781003172246-25

As its influence increased, neoliberalism around the globe retained, and retains, a strong commitment to introducing market mechanisms and approaches in all areas of social life – health care, housing, education, and (public) transportation – not only the economic. In addition, neoliberalism encourages using business approaches and metrics for organizations, agencies, and practices delivering public services; a preference for private over public modalities; a competitive ethos in service and public goods provision, generally tied to, but existing apart from, the preference of private over public; a tendency to see all value as having an economic character; a valorizing of "entrepreneurial" modalities regarded as underpinning business thinking; a "consumerist" way of assessing the value of a public good; and hostility to regulation of private and business entities. This congeries of policy proposals, initiatives, and evaluative orientations is not always entirely self-consistent, but is plausibly regarded as "neoliberalism."

At the same time, neoliberals also accord the state an important role in supporting a market-structured social order, with strong protections for property rights and market transactions. Earlier neoliberals like Hayek and Friedman also favored a role for a minimal welfare order; but in general neoliberalism joined classical liberalism in hostility to the state as a guarantor of public welfare in the face of the market's failure to provide for it. However, neoliberals much more than libertarians see a definite role for the state in protecting the market, market processes, and market values. The market is not something that will naturally arise and flower if only the government gets out of the way, but a social order that requires construction and protection by a strong state.

Neoliberalism and Education

The terminology of "neoliberalism" can be confusing to Americans. For Americans "liberalism" has come to mean a capitalist society with a central role for state intervention to promote public welfare and public goods that cannot be adequately supplied by a market. It is similar to the European idea of "social democracy," though with a somewhat less robust welfarist regime. In Europe, by contrast, "liberalism" is seen in the classic liberal, or "economic liberal," mode, and this tendency has been strengthened in the post-Soviet period when to "liberalize" a society means to make it more marketist, and also more civil libertarian, but not more socially liberal in the welfarist sense.

Neoliberalism, Freedom, and Grounding Values

It is sometimes said that for neoliberals, "freedom" is the fundamental value underlying all its other evaluative and policy commitments and tendencies. This view assimilates neoliberalism to libertarianism, in that libertarianism is officially defined as using "freedom" or "liberty" as the ultimate source and criterion of all valid policy positions. Whether or not all traditional elements of libertarianism can be so understood, neoliberalism does not lend itself to this analysis. The commitment to "marketizing everything" that is fundamental to neoliberalism only partially rests on a commitment to freedom. It sometimes (also) rests on the idea that markets are the most efficient device for satisfying human needs and desires. Hayek particularly argues that markets organize and co-ordinate the information needed to ensure that the products surviving in a market society are those maximally suited to meet human/consumer desires in a way that can never be accomplished by state entities. A more general point is that the drive to marketize often functions in neoliberalism as a fundamental goal in its own right, not necessarily connected in the market advocate's mind with any further value served by it.

Neoliberalism, The Market, and Monopoly Power

A tension within neoliberalism showed itself early on in the history of the Mont Pèlerin group. In the absence of regulation, the freedom to pursue private profit through capitalist enterprise can lead to a concentration of corporate power, in particular economic sectors or even across sectors. Some neoliberals did not object to this development since it arose from the activity of purportedly free agents in a market context. But others thought it contrary to a true market philosophy, since monopolization prevented new aspiring market agents from gaining entry to the market where they could ply their wares within a competitive framework. The latter theorists saw unfettered market competition at one stage as often leading to the stifling of competition at a later stage. Monopolistic power thus ended up apparently squelching competition, entrepreneurialism, and consumer choice.

Adherents of the anti-monopolistic view thought the state should regulate markets to ensure that barriers to market entry were not too great, and such regulation would have to be ongoing, preventing excessive concentrations of power. So, the two sides of this debate took quite different views of the role of the state in relation to the market. However, by and large they held to the other elements of neoliberal philosophy and evaluative sensibility. CEOs of mammoth, monopolistic corporations laud the "free market," entrepreneurialism, consumerism, a preference for public over private, and so forth. Moreover, the two sides also agreed that the state should have no more than a minimal role in social provision for the vulnerable and needy in society, or for providing for public goods not readily provided for by the market, such as parks and road systems. Neoliberalism often presents itself, like libertarianism, as opposing a strong state overall. This is misleading as both views with respect to corporate concentration believe the state should play a strong role in upholding markets, market relations, and property rights; and the anti-monopolists further favor a strong state's role in preventing corporate concentration.

Education

Advocates of market-based neoliberal reform tend to see the traditional public school system as captive of the 'dead hand of bureaucracy,' monopoly, and the power of teachers' unions. My analysis will focus primarily on the charter sector in the United States, a prominent manifestation of neoliberal reform. Globally, neoliberalism takes other forms as well, such as contracting out educational services to private firms, incentives for parents to use the private school system, and vouchers for private schools (Verger et al 2016).

Charter Schools as Private of Public

Charter schools come into existence through a process in which some entity proposes starting a school (or taking over an existing school) and is then granted a charter by an authorizing agent, often a state education department. The school is run by a private operator that must abide by the terms of the charter, which generally specifies certain student outcomes. But the school has leeway as to how to achieve those results. Charter schools do not belong to their districts and are not governed by district rules. They are funded by the state with a formula, largely dependent on enrollment, that draws funds from the districts served by the school. Charter schools differ from private schools in not being permitted to charge tuition.

Charter schools (generally referred to, as I will, as "charters") generally claim to be public schools, and, as publicly funded and free to students, one might wonder whether they are appropriate to consider as exemplifying neoliberalism. In reply, first, public entities can exemplify neoliberal principles, for example, by operating more like businesses or outsourcing to private operators. We noted that in contrast to libertarianism, neoliberalism provides for a substantial role for the state, though a state that operates according to neoliberal principles.

Second, though they are not "private schools" as standardly understood, charter schools do possess some traditionally "private" characteristics when compared with traditional public schools (hereafter "TPS"). They are run by and generally started by private operators. Their state-level authorization involves some degree of public accountability but nothing like the level of traditional local school boards. They are generally not bound by strictures of public disclosure; they are not required to open their records to the public. Many charter schools, especially those run by charter management organizations (CMOs), receive private money in a way not permitted by public schools.

Charter schools often say they are "open to all," implying that this is part of what makes them public. But "open to all" is ambiguous. Charter schools are "open to all" in the sense that any parent may apply to one. The public system is open to all in the much more substantial sense that anyone of appropriate age must be accepted by the public school system of the district in which they live. By contrast no one is guaranteed a spot in either a particular charter school or charter schools as a sector. If a student is expelled from a TPS school, they still remain the local TPS system's responsibility to educate. But if a student is expelled, or edged out, of a charter school, no other charter school is required to admit them, but the TPS system is.

Thus, TPSs are governed by a public logic of "universal provision," in line with the egalitarian aspect of the normatively informed idea of "public," that charter schools are not.

Individual Threads within Neoliberalism

I will now examine several distinct, though related, threads in neoliberalism; look at whether and how they are manifested in educational institutions, policies, and practices; and give a brief normative assessment of that thread. I will then examine neoliberalism's relation to inequality in general and race in particular.

Competition

This neoliberal principle is invoked to favor charter schools and vouchers as introducing competition into a public school system largely lacking it, on the premise that it will improve the schools as a whole. If districts lose funding to the extent that district students choose to attend charter schools, they will have an incentive to improve their schools. Charter advocates tend to assume or claim that lacking that competition-based incentive, districts and district schools experience no incentive to improve the education delivered to students.

In their earliest incarnation, as proposed by Albert Shanker, then head of the American Federation of Teachers, one of the two large, national teachers' unions in the United States, charter schools were not viewed in this competitive way. Shanker proposed that groups of teachers and parents be permitted to create schools that were tied to the district but were freed from some regulations. The purpose was to serve students not being well-served by the current regime in those districts. If the schools were successful, their lessons would be adopted by district schools. In this way, charter schools were more like an experiment run by a district than an alternative structure putting competitive pressure on the district (Kahlenberg & Potter 2014: 7–16).

But from early on, charters took on an identity as competition with district schools. State charter laws seldom required that they maintain any connection with district schools that would facilitate the "lessons" of (the successful among the) charter schools being adopted by district schools. They tended to be run by outside agents who, unlike Shanker's envisioned operators, had no knowledge of or ties to schools and personnel in the district.

Charter advocates see this model of competition as one (neoliberal) foundation for the value of charter schools. It is an empirical question whether charter schools actually have the desired competition-based effects on existing district schools, that is, whether district schools keep track of what charter schools are doing and try to mine their successes for their own programs out of a concern about losing the competition. But for the enhanced-quality-through-competition argument to work it would not in any case be sufficient that traditional public schools adopt practices from charter schools. Schools might adopt practices of other schools that are not particularly educationally valuable but do help with their competitive position in their particular education marketplace. For example, they might put funds into the physical plant for their athletic program that has no educational benefit.

Note also that a school might adopt a practice engaged in by another school but not for a competition-based reason. As Shanker envisioned, it could be because the former school, having come to recognize the latter school's practice, thinks adopting it would improve their school. The teachers or administrators at the former school might have learned of the practices in question through their professional networks in or out of the district. The idea of professionally-driven motivation to improve one's own practice, or the practice of institutions of which one is a part, is plausibly regarded as a source of educational improvement, and is also manifested in the professionally-informed desire of a teacher to improve how they serve their students. But this motivation is not credited in the neoliberal centering of competition as the primary motive for improvement.

Consumerism

Another thread in neoliberalism is that consumer behavior is the appropriate measure of value; a product that satisfies consumer preferences in a competitive marketplace is the product that should prevail. The kind of value represented by consumer preference is not value assessable from an impartial standpoint, like the value of beauty or knowledge. A full neoliberal philosophy rejects this robust sense of value. The power of the market way of assessing value is precisely that it does not rely on (allegedly) disputable views of what has value.

In educational contexts, who exactly is the "consumer"? In one sense it is the child, as the child will "consume" the good of education. But we do not think younger children should have the full responsibility of choosing important and complex life goods. So, in market approaches to education, parents' preferences are the ones the education market should be aggregating and responding to, in driving the array of educational options – public, private, religious ("parochial"), charter – generated thereby.

But making parental preferences the linchpin of an education system is problematic. First, parents' desires for their children do not always align with children's actual interests. Parents may be overly invested in ensuring that their children embrace their own value system (religious or not) at the expense of the child developing the autonomous ability to choose for themselves.[1] Or parents may mis-assess what it would take for a school to foster their child's cognitive and emotional growth and may therefore prefer a less than optimal school for their child.

Second, studies have shown that parents do not always select, or express preferences for, schools based on (their understanding of) their child's interests. This is one manifestation of a larger point that agents behave less rationally than some market models of "agent rationality" suppose (Ben-Porath & Johanek 2019: 94–96). For example, parents may accord the racial composition of a school or the type of uniforms required (or not) in the school undue importance in their overall assessment of the school.

Third, parents may not be aware of or know how to find the information about particular schools it would be rational of them to take account of. Knowledge about a given school's average achievement levels, for example, would not take a parent very far towards what they need to know about how their particular child would fare in that school. There are also class differences in parent time and wherewithal to undertake the project of locating and understanding this information.

A fourth problem with consumerism concerns aggregate versus individual-level goals. For example, from an individual parent's perspective it is better for her child to be in classes with as few disruptive students as possible. If an individual school treats this preference in the aggregate as an incentive for it to try to keep disruptive students out, rather than to figure out how best to accommodate and educate such students in the context of classes with non-disruptive students, this will result in disruptive students not receiving a quality, or any, education (Brighouse 2020: 190).

A fifth concern with consumerism is that society has a stake in the school's producing knowledgeable and civically competent students who will become productive citizens in the democratic society that they inherit. This vital public function of schools is not derived from, and by no means always aligns with, parental preferences for what they want their individual child to learn in school.[2] Civic education serves a common, public good out of reach of marketist consumerism.

A final problem with the consumerist strand in educational neoliberalism concerns schools' needing to attract parent-customers. A school in a marketplace is viable only if it has customers/ students to attend it. But according parents-as-consumers that kind of power in a school's success invites schools to do whatever it can to attract those parents, including misrepresenting the school's program, offerings, and character in ways that parent-consumers cannot readily discern. If the market challenge is to bring the potential customer to their product, producing the objectively best product is not the only way to accomplish this goal. Misrepresenting the truth about one's, or a rival's, product will often accomplish it.

For all these reasons, it would not be wise for a school and a school system to rely overly much on parental preferences for their individual child's education to drive educational programming, to sort students into particular schools or to decide what sorts of schools should be created. Other educational philosophies, founded on democratic participation, provide an essential role for parental input, deriving from the parent's role as a member of the school community, not only as guardians of their own child's educational welfare. Neoliberalism does not have a monopoly on parental voice, as it portrays itself as having because it sees the only alternative to neoliberalism as an ossified state bureaucracy (including teacher unions) running the schools (Friedman 2020).

Choice

Advocates of charter schools and vouchers often tout "choice" as an important value exemplified by these neoliberal reforms. It is often said that poor families should have as much choice to find a good school for their child as a wealthy family, that zip code should not affect the quality of school a child attends.

"Choice" in relation to schools is not a conceptually or morally uniform category. Not all choice plans have a market character. "Controlled choice" involves a district allowing parents to rank their preference for schools within the district, then its striving to give as many of the parents one of their top preferences as possible. To do so, the schools in the district have to be seen as relatively equal in quality, differing only in specific focus, such as arts or science, or pedagogical approaches all of which can be seen as valuable by different groups of parents. If there were to be a widely shared sense among parents in the district that certain schools are "bad" and others "good," satisfying the large majority of parental preferences, as controlled choice seeks to do, would not be possible.

Thus, controlled choice does not leave it to the market to supply schools, nor to employ competitive effects in weeding out some schools and incentivizing others to improve. So, this form of choice is utilized in a framework structured by attempts by the district to ensure relatively equal quality, thus differing fundamentally from a market system in which families exit the perceived inferior traditional system for the perceived superior charter or voucher system. Therefore "choice" by itself does not provide an argument in favor of a neoliberal system of education.

Moreover, even confining ourselves to choice in the specific context of a market system including charter, voucher, and traditional public schools, it is not clear that "choice" is an important value for most parents in seeking schools. It depends on what "choice" means. If it means the provision of a school the parent regards as high quality, of course most parents will want "choice" in that sense, as in the idea that wealthy parents have the "choice" of a high-quality school. But if it refers to the processes a parent is required to engage in to research different schools in an option set available to the parent, and then to go through the often-demanding process of making applications to schools (without a guarantee of securing one's preferred placement), it is much less clear that parents across the class spectrum would desire "choice" in this sense. We saw that there are serious barriers to gaining adequate information about individual schools, and also that working-class parents often do not have the time or resources to engage in the "choice activities" required for doing so. It is far from clear that the choice activities required by a market system are generally valued by parents.[3] Finally, one might question whether accessing a public good to which citizens are entitled should require such exceptional efforts.

Equality

Let us now turn to the relation of neoliberalism to equality, as the charter sector is often defended as serving a disadvantaged population. I will start by looking at the comparative success of charter schools and TPSs. Unfortunately, it is not entirely easy to make the comparison.

Comparing Charter and Traditional Public Schools

Several respected studies have compared the two types of school on standardized test scores. Harry Brighouse summarizes the overall finding: "The evidence on charter school achievement effects suggests that they are not, on average, better than traditional public schools in the respects that social scientists measure" (Brighouse 2020: 139). The last qualification is important. On the one hand, as Brighouse points out, charter schools want to establish their superiority or at least their quality, according to readily recognized and accepted criteria, so they generally use standardized test scores, and in any case are often required by the chartering agreement to do so. So, a comparison with TPS is possible in this respect. On the other hand, standardized tests do not, or do not yet, capture important aspects of the complex learning process that we are interested in, including moral and civic education, and education for personal flourishing (Curren & Kotzee 2014).

A second problem is how to take account of differences in advantage and disadvantage in the populations served by the different types of school. Studies have shown that charter schools serve a smaller percentage of special needs students (and some smaller studies suggests that among special needs students, they serve ones with less severe disabilities), and a smaller proportion of ELL students (White 2015: 137; Blum 2017: n. 45). This disparity is partly due to charter schools' often not being required to serve these populations by providing disability services in their schools.

Charter schools and TPSs serving the same income-defined areas have also been compared. A limitation of those studies is that "free and reduced lunch" is generally the criterion used to define income level, as that is a measure the schools must keep records of, in regard to their qualifying for Title I (poverty-related) funds. But that category runs from 0% to 185% of poverty level income ("free" is 0–130%, "reduced" 130–185%), so students in different tiers of this category are bringing quite different levels of poverty-related disadvantage to the school.[4]

Many charter schools aim to serve a low-income, disadvantaged population, almost always students of color in urban centers. One subset of such schools is referred to as "no excuses" schools to emphasize both a strict behavioral regimen and also a philosophy that neither teachers nor students can use a student's poverty as an "excuse" for not making educational progress. But these schools engage in a form of unofficial selectivity that leaves them with easier-to-educate students within the low-income category. Chester Finn, Bruno Manno, and Brandon Wright, prominent charter school advocates, concede that "the no-excuses model … does in fact lead to self-selection and a form of creaming, whether voluntary or school-driven" (Finn et al. 2016: 163). The schools are not allowed to select students according to their previous grades, and (if oversubscribed) they must select among applicants according to a lottery, but as already mentioned, the admission process makes it challenging for low-income parents to do the work necessary to find out about the process, visit schools (which is sometimes required), and submit applications. These demands effectively exclude dysfunctional parents and many who do not have the time or capital to engage in all aspects of this process, and in that way favoring the easier-to-educate students among the disadvantaged target population.

In addition, once students are admitted, the schools' strict behavioral regimen, and the requirement that parents sign on to help enforce this regimen, means that students can be excluded or "counseled out" (i.e., encouraged to consider leaving the school) because they are not perceived as adhering to the regimen, or because the parents are not perceived as adhering to their agreement. One study of the KIPP (Knowledge is Power Program), the best known of the "no excuses" schools, found that a "typical KIPP grade cohort shrunk by about 30% between grades 6 and 8" (Kahlenberg & Potter 2014: 79).

These processes, acknowledged by the charter advocates mentioned, mean that even if charter schools do show greater success with a student population defined by "free and reduced lunch," this is not sufficient evidence that they are more successful at educating disadvantaged students who are relevantly comparable to TPS students.

Notice that even if (contrary to the argument just presented) KIPP schools were superior to TPS, this would not show the superiority of charter schools in general to TPS, since KIPP schools are only one segment of the overall charter sector. Moreover, experience shows that charter schools that are superior by some standard measure do not have the effect of driving out "lesser quality" charter schools. Finally, market logic requires the possibility of continual entry by new educational entrepreneurs into the education market, and ongoing subjection of the new and the old to market processes ("market discipline").

KIPP and other CMOs also raise the issue of controversy in the neoliberal movement mentioned earlier, concerning the impact of large, well-funded charter chains driving out and making entry difficult for smaller "mom and pop" charter schools, and violating market principles in this sense. In her study of charter schools in Harlem, Terrenda White also claims that in contrast to the early community-based charters, the later-arriving chains tend to have leadership remote from the schools' communities, to be overly invested in standardization in the service of expansion, and to be beholden to the views of overwhelmingly white wealthy donors (White 2018).

Neoliberalism, Inequality, and Wealthy Foundation Funding

Neoliberalism as a political philosophy does not object to inequalities in life conditions. Its market fundamentalism expects such disparities because a market must have winners and losers, that is, producers whose goods are given uptake by the population and those that are not. Its competitive ethos requires substantial disparities of reward. These inequalities can be quite extreme, as in our current highly neoliberalist order with its reduced taxes, weakening of progressivity in taxes, and deregulation of corporate practices.

It is no accident that a substantial part of the charter sector is funded to a significant degree by foundations explicitly embracing a neoliberal, marketist philosophy, advocating low taxes on the wealthy, minimal state regulation (except to preserve the market) and hostility to unions. The Walton Foundation (funded by the family that owns Walmart), Broad Foundation, Gates Foundation, and the Koch Brothers networks are the prime exemplars. This private largesse toward schools meant to be and claiming to be public is a significant aspect of the charter school scene, involving a mammoth public relations and advocacy apparatus for the charter sector in general, as well as for specific charter networks. These donors regard charter schools as a sector as entirely consistent with the overall inequalities fundamental to neoliberalism.

In addition, the substantial private funds from these sources enable charter schools to employ costly educational improvements like longer school days and years, that throw further into doubt the relevance of higher test scores in KIPP and similar schools to the superiority of the educational regimen of KIPP to TPS schools. Moreover, this funding is often undisclosed, making it even more difficult to track the relevant variables in comparing the two types of schools. In addition, there is of course no guarantee that the private funding would continue if the supported schools succeeding in driving competitor schools out of the market. Finally, there is indeed reason to be concerned that well-funded CMOs backed by market-promoting foundations will drive out the smaller charter operators without providing higher quality offerings, just as the early strand of neoliberalism feared about monopolies created through initial market processes.

Charter Schools, Race, and Inequality

Yet it might seem that the charter sector's educational philosophy does not align with neoliberalism's embrace of inequality in that a significant segment of the charter sector sees itself as exemplifying the fight for racial justice, often asserting that "education is the civil rights issue of our time" and seeing themselves as part of that struggle for civil rights (Cunningham 2021: 30; King 2017[5]). Nevertheless, the neoliberal influence in the world in which these charter sector agents operate greatly constrains and often distorts their vision of social justice.

First, the charter sector does not challenge the extreme inequalities in American society today. It aspires only to provide its own students with the educational wherewithal to avoid the lower rungs of the socio-economic hierarchy. As schools, networks, or a whole sector, it does not put forward the message that this system of inequities is unjust and needs change, and that their education should be part of that change – a message increasing numbers of districts and schools are adopting and seeing as continuous with an implied justice mission of the public school system (Blum & Burkholder 2021: 147–149).

This failure to challenge inequality is partly due to charter schools' generally embracing a "human capital" way of conceiving of education and its value. This approach aims to provide students with what they need to become successful market agents in the society as it is currently structured, with its vast reward disparities along both racial and class axes. Sidelined are other often quite traditional educational values at odds with this economistic and inequality-accepting focus. These include an emphasis on *personal flourishing* in which students would be taught to work out their own life path with the understanding that doing so would not necessarily be reflected in society's reward structure; an emphasis on developing students' capacities for *thinking critically* about their own society and its traditions, goals, and institutions; and a *civic perspective*, educating students to be knowledgeable citizens in society, working toward a common good that would provide a vantage point for criticizing racial and socio-economic disparities. All three of these educational purposes are at odds with a human capital view of education's purpose.

A second limitation of charter agents' understanding of the social justice they imagine themselves to be seeking concerns the "creaming," mentioned above, of the easier-to-educate from among the wider group of disadvantaged students. The limitation is partly that the charter supporters portray themselves as helping disadvantaged black and brown students in general while their practices draw students with "hidden" sources of advantage among the disadvantaged. But in addition, by removing the more advantaged from the TPS pool of students, they further disadvantage the comparatively-harder-to-educate students remaining in TPS by increasing that group's percentage of the overall TPS population. Doing so has this effect because individual students' educational progress is affected not only by their own disadvantaging characteristics but, independently, by those of their peers as well.[6]

In their 2016 call for a moratorium on new charter schools, the National Association for the Advancement of Colored People (NAACP), a leading US civil rights organization, mentioned this feature of charter schools specifically, claiming that charters perpetuate de facto segregation of the highest-performing children, compared to those whose aspirations may be high but whose talents are not yet as obvious (NAACP 2017). Apart from these resonances with traditional Jim Crow Segregation, this heightening of disparity within the disadvantaged population is in line with neoliberalism's and the charter sector's overall lack of a critical stance toward inequalities.[7]

A third neoliberalism-related limitation on charter agents' sense of social justice is a denial of the educational significance of poverty, especially prominent in the "no excuses" schools. These see the invoking of poverty in explaining educational deficits as an evasion of the educator's responsibility, and the student's own responsibility, to advance the student's learning. This is neoliberal (and libertarian) in denying systemic barriers to individuals' potential for advancement, in the offloading of responsibility purely to individuals (and families) and in the withdrawal of a norm of public responsibility for provision.[8]

A fourth limitation is the in-school normative environment promoted by the no-excuses schools. The schools regard the students' home cultures, including their ethnoracially-based ancestral cultures as channeled through the family's cultural traditions, as at odds with the schools' stringent class- and culturally-slanted behavioral demands. The school does want buy-in and support from the parents, but their way of understanding what this support involves disrespects those parents' cultures. This disrespect is racialized not only in that when the school's leadership is white and the parent is Black or Brown, it smacks of a racist paternalism; but also because the charter philosophy views the student very much in racial terms and sees their home culture, through a racial lens, as an important part of what educationally disadvantages the student. The student is regarded as immersed in a culture not conducive to success in the white middle-class world, implied to be the standard the school is preparing the student to meet (White 2015).

For all these reasons whatever sense of social and racial justice animates charter school actors, the sector's (especially its "no excuses" wing's) beholdenness to neoliberal inegalitarianism seriously constrains the conception of justice involved.

Neoliberalism, School Closings, Race, and Community

A different though related manifestation of neoliberalism in relation to race concerns the shuttering of schools that fall below a certain measurable standard, generally in its students' test scores. Students are then generally reassigned to various other schools. Sometimes the school is reconstituted under different, often charter, management. The schools in question are almost always situated in low-income Black and Brown communities.

Parents and communities served by these schools have sometimes organized to try to keep the schools open, citing the importance of the school as a neighborhood hub; as a safe and home-like space for its students, especially homeless ones; as a symbol of and tribute to a historical institution important to black education in general, and in a particular location; and as an affirmation of the voice of a marginalized community in its attempt to keep the school alive.[9]

Such school closings offend against educational justice for low-income students of color, channeling neoliberalism's privileging of test scores over a range of other educational considerations. But the protests against the closings reveal constrictions in neoliberalism's valuational framework that go beyond justice. Its individualistic orientation, embedded in its market philosophy, is unable to see or appreciate the communal values asserted by the community protesters – the sense of community within and toward the school itself; the wider neighborhood community seeing the school as a valuable institution serving that community; and the historical dimension of the school as expressing an historical commitment to black education. These communal values are not recognized in neoliberalism's economism of educational value. Finally, neoliberalism is blind to the specifically racial aspect of these communal values – the way communal affirmation and assertion is a resistance to racism, racial devaluing, and racial marginalizing.[10]

Challenges to Neoliberalism from the Right and Left

Neoliberalism is alive and well in the United States and the world, both in society in general and in the world of education specifically. It continues to have its stable of wealthy foundation support. The Trump administration passed the most wealth-friendly tax cut in recent history.

But the Trump years also saw some important pushback against some aspects of the neoliberal agenda. Trump's economic nationalism, echoed by the rise of ethnonationalist forces in Europe and elsewhere, counters "free trade." The "populist" aspect of right-wing ethnonationalism, though politically allied with corporate hegemony, nevertheless results in at least a small counterweight to that hegemony, resulting in greater popular support for taxing wealth and corporate excess, that left populism can pick up on.

Progressive forces on the left have also become stronger in this same period. The Democratic party agenda is the most anti-neoliberal one since the Johnson administration, with a much greater willingness to use the tools of government to promote the general welfare and the plight of the disadvantaged, and to recognize that the market and market approaches do not solve many of the major problems of society.

This economic populism has a direct bearing on education in that inequality and poverty are significant drivers of educational failure and class and race disparities. Serious reductions or blunting of poverty, as in the Covid relief measures in the United States in 2020–21, have a salutary impact on student educational performance. So, in contrast to right-wing populism, left-wing populism has implications for education independent of direct changes to educational policy itself.[11] In addition, there has been pushback against various aspects of neoliberalism: teachers unions have engaged in labor actions to support on-site services for low-income students, and for greater funding for such schools; parents and students have boycotted high-stakes standardized tests; low income parents have protested the closing of schools in their neighborhoods slated for "takeover," mentioned earlier. The Supreme Court of the State of Washington declared charter schools not to be "public" in that state's understanding (Higgins 2015). A highly visible campaign to increase the charter presence in the liberal state of Massachusetts was soundly defeated on a popular referendum in 2016 (Cunningham 2021; Blum 2017). President Trump's Secretary of Education, Betsy DeVos, was such an extreme opponent of public schools that, together with her being associated with an administration that came to be anathema to liberal Democrats, served to weaken the liberal and Democratic support for the neoliberal educational agenda the Obama administration had encouraged.

There are further signs, some stemming from the Covid crisis and the perceived need for government action to deal with it, that neoliberalism does not have the unchallenged hegemony it once had across the West and imposed on the rest of the world. Nevertheless, it remains a potent force in society and education more generally.[12]

(Related Chapters: 1, 6, 8, 17, 20, 22, 34, 35.)

Notes

1 I have worded this point so as not to assume that autonomy is the central goal in education, having lexical priority over all others. I am taking the weaker position that autonomy is one plausible educational goal, that can run up against parental preference for a child to adopt the parent's value system (which I am not here assessing as a worthy educational goal or not).

2 To be sure, many parents do in fact want their children to learn civic competence in school.

3 One study of parents in a low-income African American neighborhood found that parents felt more disempowered than empowered by a school choice program involving charter schools. "Not one parent [out of 77] expressed positive enthusiasm for or a personal desire to search for such schools" (Pattillo 2015: 54).

4 A study of Boston-based charter school showed that 44.8% of students fell into "free lunch" category compared to 74.6% in Boston Public School (Levinson 2016: 182).

5 King was Secretary of Education in the Obama administration in its last year and civil rights language was often used by that administration (but also by the previous Bush administration) for, among other things, the promotion of charter schools in poor Black and Brown communities.
6 One study showed that introducing an academically selective magnet school into a district found that "removing higher performing students from nonmagnet schools not only lowered the mean achievement of the sending schools but also lowered the actual performance level of the students in that school" (Mickelson et al. 2012: 186).
7 At least some parents think of charter schools as private or selective (Pattillo 2015: 57), reinforcing the idea that the charter sector fosters hierarchy in the way parents think about schools. My argument does not deny that many Black families support their charter schools and charter schools in general. See valuable discussion of this support in Pedroni 2007.
8 For further discussion of the denial or deliberate ignoring of poverty as an educational barrier, see Blum & Burkholder 2021:111-116.
9 Eve Ewing (2018) documents an extended community effort to keep an historically important school in an historic black neighborhood in Chicago. She also mentions other such efforts elsewhere.
10 This racial aspect of the protests is emphasized in Ewing's account.
11 Wendy Brown makes a case that neoliberalism and ethnonationalism/authoritarianism are not as far apart as generally thought (Brown 2019).
12 But see Goldberg 2021. Some neoliberal critics of public schools have found the COVID-19 era to be fertile ground for promoting school privatization and charter schools.

References

Apple, M. W. (2006) *Educating the 'Right' Way: Markets, Standards, God, and Inequality*, 2nd edition. New York: Routledge.

Ben-Porath, S. & Johanek, M. (2019) *Making Up Our Mind: What School Choice is Really About.* Chicago, IL: University of Chicago Press.

Blum, L. (2016) "Charter Schools, Education Markets, and Democracy," in M. Levinson & J. Fay (eds.) *Dilemmas of Educational Ethics: Cases and Commentaries.* Cambridge, MA: Harvard Education Press, 202–205.

Blum, L., & Burkholder, Z. (2021) *Integrations: The Struggle for Racial Equality and Civic Renewal in Public Education.* Chicago, IL: University of Chicago Press.

Blum, L. (March 2017) "What We Can Learn from the Massachusetts Ballot Question Campaign on Charter School Expansion," *National Education Policy Center.*

Brighouse, H. (2020) "Debating Markets in Education," in D. Schmitz & H. Brighouse (eds.) *Debating Education: Is There a Role for Markets?* New York: Oxford University Press.

Brown, W. (2015) *Undoing the Demos: Neoliberalism's Stealth Revolution.* Brooklyn, NY: Zone Books.

Brown, W. (2019) *In the Ruins of Neoliberalism: The Rise of Antidemocratic Politics in the West.* New York: Columbia University Press.

Chubb, J. & Moe, T. (1990) *Politics, Markets, and America's Schools.* Washington, DC: Brookings Institution Press.

Crouch, C. (2007) "Commercialization or Citizenship: The Case of Education," in R. Curren (ed.) *Philosophy of Education: An Anthology.* Oxford: Blackwell Publishing, 200–207.

Crouch, C. (2011) *The Strange Non-Death of Neoliberalism.* Malden, MA: Polity Press.

Cunningham, M. T. (2021) *Dark Money and the Politics of School Privatization.* Cham, Switzerland: Palgrave Macmillan.

Curren, R. & Kotzee, B. (2014) "Can Virtue be Measured?" *Theory and Research in Education* 12(3): 266–283

Davies, W. & Gane, N. (Sept 15, 2021) "Post-Neoliberalism? An Introduction," *Theory, Culture, and Society.* 10.1177/02632764211036722

Day, M. (July 25, 2021) "Elites Profit From 'Nonprofit' Charter Schools—An Interview with Carol Burris," National Education Policy Center, https://nepc.colorado.edu/blog/elites-profit

Ewing, E. L. (2018) *Ghosts in the Schoolyard: Racism and School Closings on Chicago's South Side.* Chicago, IL: University of Chicago Press.

Fink, B. (2016) "How Neoliberalism Got Organized: A Usable History for Resisters, With Special Reference to Education," *The Good Society* 25(2–3): 158–171.

Finn, C. E., Jr., Manno, B., & Wright, B. L. (2016) *Charter Schools at the Crossroads: Predicaments, Paradoxes, Possibilities.* Cambridge, MA: Harvard Education Press.

Friedman, M. (2020 [1962]) *Capitalism and Freedom.* Chicago, IL: University of Chicago Press.

Goldberg, M. (Dec. 17, 2021) "We Desperately Need Schools to Get Back to Normal" *The New York Times*, https://www.nytimes.com/2021/12/17/opinion/randi-weingarten-schools.html?smid=em-share

Harvey, D. (2005) *A Brief History of Neoliberalism*. New York: Oxford University Press.
Hastings, M. (May 2019) "Neoliberalism and Education," *Oxford Research Encyclopedia of Education*, 10.1093/ACREFORE%2F9780190264093.013.404
Hayek, F. A. (1976) *Law, Legislation and Liberty, volume 2: The Mirage of Social Justice*. Chicago, IL: University of Chicago Press.
Hayek, F. (2005 [1949]) *The Road to Serfdom*. London UK: Institute of Economic Affairs.
Higgins, C. & Abowitz, K. K. (2011) "What Makes a Public School Public? A Framework for Evaluating the Civic Substance of Schooling," *Educational Theory* 61(4): 365–380.
Higgins, J. (September 2015) "State Supreme Court: Charter Schools are Unconstitutional," *The Seattle Times*, https://www.seattletimes.com/seattle-news/education/state-supreme-court-charter-schools-are-unconstitutional/
Kahlenberg, R. D. & Potter, H. (2014) *A Smarter Charter: Finding What Works for Charter Schools and Public Education*. New York: Teachers College Press.
King, J., Jr. (May 2017) "Education Remains the Civil Rights Issue of Our Time," *The Education Trust*. Washington DC: The Education Trust.
Levinson, M. (2016) "How, if at all, Should Charters Be Compared to Local Districts," in M. Levinson & J. Fay (eds.) *Dilemmas of Educational Ethics: Cases and Commentaries*. Cambridge, MA: Harvard Education Press, 179–185.
Lipman, P. (2011) *The New Political Economy of Urban Education*. New York: Routledge
Lubienski, C., & Lubienski, S. (2013) *The Public School Advantage: Why Public Schools Outperform Private Schools*. Chicago, IL: University of Chicago Press.
Mickelson, R., Bottia, M., & Southworth, S. (2012) "School Choice and Segregation by Race, Ethnicity, Class, and Achievement," in G. Miron, K. Welner, P. Hinchey, & W. Mathis (eds.) *Exploring the School Choice Universe: Evidence and Recommendations*. Charlotte, NC: Information Age Publishing, 167–192.
NAACP Task Force on Quality Education (July 2017) "Quality Education for All: One School at a Time," NAACP, https://educationvotes.nea.org/wp-content/uploads/2017/07/Task_ForceReport_final2.pdf
Pattillo, M. (2015) "Everyday Politics of School Choice in the Black Community," *Du Bois Review* 12(1): 41–71.
Pedroni, T. (2007) *Market Movements: African American Involvement in School Voucher Reform*. New York: Routledge.
Plant, R. (2009) *The Neo-liberal State*. New York: Oxford University Press.
Rooks, N. (2020) *Cutting School: The Segrenomics of American Education*. New York: The New Press.
Schneider, M. K. (2016) *School Choice: The End of Public Education?* New York: Teachers College Press.
Strauss, V. (July 26, 2017) "NAACP Sticks By its Call for Charter School Moratorium, Says, 'They are not a Substitute' for Traditional Public Schools," *Washington Post*.
Stedman-Jones, D. (2014) *Masters of the Universe: Hayek, Friedman, and the Birth of Neoliberal Politics*, updated edition. Princeton, NJ: Princeton University Press.
Stitzlein, S. (2013) "For-Profit Charter Schools and Threats to the Publicness of Public Schools," *Ohio Valley Philosophy of Education Society*: 88–99. https://files.eric.ed.gov/fulltext/EJ1015716.pdf
Vallier, K. (June 2021) "Neoliberalism," *Stanford Encyclopedia of Philosophy* (summer 2021 edition), Edward N. Zalta (ed.) https://plato.stanford.edu/archives/sum2021/entries/neoliberalism/
Verger, A., Fontdevila, C., & Zancajo, A. (2016) *The Privatization of Education: A Political Economy of Global Education Reform*. New York: Teachers College Press.
Weiner, L. (April 10, 2021) "Heads up! Chins down! Resisting the New Bipartisan Neoliberal Project in Education," *NewPolitics*.
Wheeler-Bell, Q. (2018) "Broken Glass: The Social Evil of Urban Poverty and a Liberatory Education," *Educational Policy* 33(7): 1076–1102.
White, T. (2015) "Charter Schools: Demystifying Whiteness in a Market of 'No Excuses' Corporate-Styled Charter Schools," in B. Picower & E. Mayorga (eds.) *What's Race Got to Do With It? How Current School Reform Policy Maintains Racial and Economic Inequality*. New York: Peter Lang Publishing, 121–146.
White, T. (2018) "From Community Schools to Charter Chains: New York's Unequal Educational Landscape," in R. Sanders, D. Stovall, & T. White (eds.) *Twenty-First-Century Jim Crow Schools: The Impact of Charters on Public Education*. Boston, MA: Beacon Press, 69–106.

22

RACIAL DOMINATION IN EDUCATION

Quentin Wheeler-Bell

Racial domination within society greatly impacts racial domination in schools, and vice-versa. Understanding the nature of racial domination or injustice in education thus requires a more general understanding of racial domination in the society and how it shapes education. To understand what racial justice in education would be also requires a more general understanding of what racial justice or non-domination in the society would be and how education could promote it. In this chapter, I will address the nature of racial domination and three misconceptions about racial justice and how education can promote it. I will then present a critical approach to addressing racial domination in and through education.

What Is Racial Domination?

We need to begin with a clear definition of race. *Race is a symbolic category of domination based on false or misrecognized ideas of racial phenotype or ancestry that is socially mobilized to undermine a racialized group's democratic social power.* This definition is dense, so let me unpack the four distinct features of race. First, race is socially constructed, which means the symbolic categories defining "race" are not natural attributes but human creations. Second, racial categories are embedded within sociohistorical contexts, so they will differ from one sociohistorical period to another. Third, racial categories operate by being misrecognized as natural attributes. Finally, race is fundamentally a form of domination because it operates by creating norms, habits, and institutional arrangements that misrecognize racial groups, limiting the democratic social power of some groups while giving other groups power over them. Each of these features of race requires some explanation.

Race as a Social Construct

Saying that race is socially constructed means the ideas, notions, and values that define a racial group are human creations, rather than natural attributes. This implies that race categories are given meaning through human activities; our individual and collective activities create and recreate racial categories. In this sense, we should not view racial categories as natural. Instead, race categories are based upon false distinctions between individuals that become socially misrecognized as natural. The naturalization of racial categories is one of the distinct ways in which false racial distinctions are produced and maintained. As Matthew Desmond and Mustafa Emirbayer explain, the invention of "whiteness" in North America began to form out of a group of Europeans who had never before

DOI: 10.4324/9781003172246-26

seen themselves as having anything in common (Desmond & Emirbayer 2009; Emirbayer & Desmond 2015). This formation was not a natural process; it was a deliberate racial project. The early racial project of white supremacy aimed to create an imagined white and black identity wherein Europeans became classified as "white" and Africans, who represented hundreds of different tribes, were classified as "black." The purpose of these racial classifications was to construct a system of racial domination that would justify treating "non-whites" as less than human and would seem like a "natural order."

Race and Social-Historical Context

Since race is a social construct, racial categories are always embedded within a sociohistorical context, and they differ across different sociohistorical periods. Racial identities gain meaning only within a larger system of racial classifications in a specific sociocultural context. Consequently, understanding racial classifications requires analyzing what Michael Omi and Howard Winant call *racial formations*, which are "the sociohistorical process[s] by which racial identities are created, lived out, transformed, and destroyed" (Omi & Winant 2014: 109). Because racial identities are defined within larger systems of racial classifications, racial identities are always *relationally formed*. This means that racial identities are created, lived out, transformed, and destroyed within a system of racial supremacy. For example, the creation and formation of racialized identities in the U.S., such as Native American, Latinx, Black, and Asian-American, mutually depend upon the creation and formation of whiteness. These racial identities only have meaning within a larger system of racial domination and white supremacy. Thus, we have to analyze the socio-historical circumstances that create and reproduce a system of white supremacy in order to understand how these racial identities are created and recreated.

Race and Misrecognition

What makes race a unique social construction is that it depends upon a system of racial misrecognition. *Racial misrecognition* occurs when symbolic categories are created and reproduced through social, material, economic, political, and psychological practices that attribute false phenotypic and ancestral attributes to racialized groups. As Desmond and Emirbayer argue, "racial domination survives by covering its tracks, by erasing its own history. It encourages us to think of the mystic boundaries separating, say West from East, white from black, black from Asian, or Asian from Hispanic, as timeless separations – divisions that have always been and will always be" (Desmond & Emirbayer 2009: 51).

To explain why race requires misrecognition, let us look at the conservative culture of poverty thesis. This thesis claims that poor people – people of color – perform less well in school owing to cultural attributes, such as poor family structures, poor study habits, or oppositional cultural norms (Moynihan 1968; McWhorter 2000; Wax 2008). This thesis exemplifies racial misrecognition because it attributes a gap in academic achievement to cultural attributes, without acknowledging the circumstances of poverty and racism to which the attitudes and behaviors of members of black communities are adaptive or rational (Fordham & Ogbu 1986; Anderson 2012; Lewis 2012; Morton 2022). This exemplifies racial misrecognition because it falsely attributes phenotypic or ancestral attributes (i.e., the culture of poverty) to a racialized group. What gets misrecognized in this assessment is the nature of the individual attributes involved and their relationship to poverty; attributes that are rational adaptations to the conditions of poverty are misidentified as causes of poverty, and this misrecognition is integral to a system of racial domination that has disproportionately and unjustly locked people of color into poverty with little prospect of escaping it.

Race and Domination

The construction of racial categories is inherently the construction of a system of domination, so domination is an essential feature of race. Racial categories and symbols are fundamentally categories that place individuals within an oppressive hierarchical system. This means racial categories *only* gain meaning because of how they operate within a system that misrecognizes the equal moral standing of racialized groups. Race thereby entails forms of misrecognition that prevent racialized groups from having the democratic social power to create non-dominating conditions. Clarifying this point requires an explanation of the connections between three ideas: *justice as a right to justification, democratic social power, and racial domination.* In brief, racial domination involves unjust violations of a racialized group's equal right to justification, robbing it of democratic social power.

Justice is about ensuring all social practices and power relations affecting an individual's life are reasonably justified to the individual affected, and democracy is the process through which these justifications are established. Justice rests on a *right to justification.* As Rainer Forst explains, "the demand for justice is an emancipatory demand ... Its basis is the claim to be respected as an agent of justification, that is, in one's dignity as a being who can ask for and give justifications" (Forst 2011: 2). This emancipatory demand aims to ensure that all social relationships affecting an individual are democratically determined, and all individuals are able to take part in civic dialogues that respect their right to justification. Racialized others would thus be treated as moral equals when they are given equal standing within the democracy.

Erik Olin Wright describes *social power* as "power rooted in the capacity to mobilize people for cooperative and voluntary collective actions of various sorts in civil society" (Wright 2010: 121). Such power is implicitly democratic, in being cooperative, voluntary, and as such predicated on mutual justification and agreement on common goals. *Democratic social power* is thus essentially the ability to democratically organize collective efforts to secure common goods, such as creating non-dominating conditions of life or ensuring that social institutions and practices are justly structured to promote human flourishing.

One reason justice and democracy are coextensive is that both require establishing relations of non-domination. As Forst (2008) explains, "justice is first and foremost about ending domination and unjustifiable arbitrary rule, whether political or social in a broad sense" (Forst 2008: 315). *Domination* exists when individuals are subjected to the arbitrary rule of power, which occurs when the principles of *generality* and *reciprocity* that should govern processes of public justification and exercises of authority are systematically ignored or undermined. These principles (*generality* and *reciprocity of reasons*) ensure that the diverse members of a society have adequate grounds for accepting as authoritative the reasons that count as providing justification, and (*reciprocity of content*) require that everyone accept what those justifying reasons demand of themselves while expecting no more than they demand of others.

Racial domination occurs when people of color are subjected to a system of white supremacy or, in other words, an arbitrary rule of power that systematically privileges whiteness and disadvantages people of color. This means that *white supremacy* is the arbitrary system of racial categories that ensure whites and whiteness receive unjustifiable recognition and advantages, while people of color are systematically misrecognized and disadvantaged in ways that prevent them from using their democratic social power.

For brevity, I will focus on two aspects of the complex process through which racial domination prevents people of color from exercising democratic social power: *democratic exclusion* and *democratic disempowerment. Democratic exclusion* occurs when unjust laws, social practices, and institutional arrangements are designed to systematically exclude people of color from participating in a democratic society as moral equals and from securing acceptable living conditions. For example, in *Unjustifiably Oppressed*, Roderick Van Daniel explains how Mississippi, and other southern states of the U.S., established Black Codes in the 1860s that limited the freedom of African Americans and ensured their availability as a cheap labor force after slavery was abolished during the Civil War (Van Daniel 2018). Under Black Codes, many states required Black people to sign yearly labor contracts; if they refused, they risked being arrested, fined, and forced into unpaid labor. Black Codes are an example of democratic exclusion in two respects. First, the creation of Blacks Codes was unjust and undemocratic because blacks were excluded from the democratic processes through which the Codes were created. Second, by excluding blacks from the democratic process, white southerners were able to construct labor laws that further excluded blacks from participating as equals in the labor market. The construction of an unjustifiable system of white supremacy was thus facilitated by denying people of color their right to justification and limiting their democratic social power.

Another way in which racial domination is (re)produced is through *democratic disempowerment*. This may occur even when people of color (and others) are not categorically excluded from participation in democratic processes but lack real and effective opportunities to advance their collective well-being or transform the system of racial domination. For example, one aspect of Black Codes is that they prevented blacks from acquiring wealth, land, and other forms of capital, and an enduring effect of these laws – and a host of other unjust practices – is the current black-white wealth gap in the United States. One measure of this is that the net worth of a typical white family in the U.S. in 2016 was $171,000, which was nearly ten times greater than that of a Black family ($17,150) (McIntosh, et al. 2020). This wealth gap has consequences for opportunities, including the relative social power of groups to advance their well-being. It is an ongoing aspect and consequence of the ways people of color have systematically been denied the democratic social power needed to overcome a system of racial domination, even as they are no longer categorically excluded from participation in democratic processes.

Three Misconceptions about Racial Justice in Education

Having explained what racial domination is, I want to critique three misconceptions about education and racial justice. These misconceptions are that: 1) *Multicultural* education is the key to racial justice in and through education; 2) *Equal Educational Opportunity* is the key to racial justice in and through education; 3) *Integrating schools* is the key to racial justice in and through education.

Multicultural Education Is the Key to Racial Justice in and through Education

One educational misconception about race is that multicultural education is the embodiment of racial justice in education. Multicultural education in the U.S. has been based on the idea that schools should respect the various ethnic cultural traditions present in the society and not seek to assimilate all students into a homogenous American culture, suppressing or extinguishing their distinctive cultural heritages. The focus of multicultural education initiatives has often been the correction of curricular omissions and misrepresentations in order to accurately represent the contributions that different ethnic cultural groups have made to the society and world, and to encourage tolerance of, or respect for, cultural differences (Banks 1995; Lopez and Vogel 1979; NCSS 1976). Understood in this way, multicultural education is fundamentally opposed to such practices as the coercive education for cultural extinction that was long imposed on Native Americans (Blum & Burkholder 2021: 23–31, 64–73; Adams 1995; Subcommittee on Indian Education of the Senate Committee on Labor and Public Welfare 1969). It may also have some value in correcting negative cultural stereotypes or prejudice.

If false or misrecognized ideas of *racial* phenotype or ancestry are *cultural* stereotypes, and these ideas are an aspect of racial domination, then multicultural education might have some value in addressing racial domination. Nevertheless, the assumption that multicultural education is the key to racial justice is misguided. It relies on the premise that race can be equated with ethnicity or culture, and it is at best a partial remedy for racial domination. As Charles Mills argues,

> Replacing race by culture, or assuming that race and a particular culture are always linked, is problematic for the simple reason that there is no essentialist one-to-one correspondence between the two. Race has been historically created through discriminatory legislation and social custom, but this does not mean that people uniformly categorized across different regions, classes, and educational levels as members of one "race" are similarly uniform in their cultures, even if they are similarly structurally subordinated.
>
> *(Mills 2007: 100–101)*

We can see the problem with equating race with culture or ethnicity by looking at the term "Asian" or "Asian-American." No "Asian culture" exists. Instead, the concept "Asian-American" is an externally imposed grouping of Chinese, Japanese, Cambodian, Indian, Laotian, and other peoples under an invented category "Asian-American" that is presumed to be justified by similarities of culture or ethnicity. This category only has meaning within a system of racial domination, and the creation of this racialized group is a non-voluntary imposition on the disparate peoples who did not choose to be grouped together in this way. Claiming to create an education that respects "Asian-Americans" is problematic because it is the very creation of this subordinating category that is the problem. It is not a problem that can be rectified by encouraging respect for an "Asian" culture that does not exist.

Before proceeding, let me address two potential misconceptions. First, I am not saying that cultures and ethnicities cannot exist within systems of racial domination. Chinese, Japanese, Cambodian, and other peoples all have cultures before (and after) being racialized. Racial domination does not inherently erase culture, rather one way it operates is by reconfiguring how we define various cultures to make it seem they are all the same. Second, I am not saying that cultures cannot develop within a system of racial domination. For example, the African-American culture developed within a system of racial domination, such that blacks now have a unique history, tradition, and body of cultural practices. What ties African-American culture together (and other cultures that developed within systems of racial domination) are the various ways people make sense of themselves and their world within a system of white supremacy.

I note these misconceptions to help distinguish a broadly multicultural education from an anti-racist education.[1] Multicultural education focuses on pluralism, i.e., on respecting different cultures and ethnicities. An anti-racist education, on the other hand, focuses on oppression – i.e., analysis of the complex relationships between a system of racial domination, the formation and reformation of racial categories and how these categories are treated as natural or cultural attributes. Multicultural education could present actual cultures of members of racialized groups (not generic non-cultures) in a positive light – a good thing, if done well – but this is no substitute for the analytical insights about racial domination that anti-racist education should convey. Multicultural education is not equivalent to education that promotes racial justice because race is not culture and presenting diverse cultures in a positive light is not sufficient to overcome racial domination.

Multicultural education is focused on tolerating and respecting different cultures, but race is a system of domination that should not be tolerated or respected. Instead, race must be dismantled and transformed. While a multicultural education might assume we should teach students how to respect "Asians," an education focused on racial domination would focus on the system of racial domination (i.e., white supremacy), rather than distinct cultures and ethnicities. It would teach children how a diverse group of people from different countries are even classified as "Asian." Such an education might focus on issues like: "What are the historical and current reasons for constructing the term "Asian"? Why are people who are classified as "Asian" targeted for specific harms and injustices?

And how are these harms, injustices, and racial classifications operating within a larger system of white supremacy?

Equal Educational Opportunity Is the Key to Racial Justice in and through Education

Another misconception is that racial justice in education is equivalent to equal educational opportunity and racial justice would be achieved if people of color were provided with equal educational opportunity. *Equal opportunity* is an ethical ideal concerning the *fairness of competitions* through which valuable things are distributed. It is an ideal of distributive justice concerned with who gets what, when, and why. *Equal educational opportunity* is a complex and disputed form of equal opportunity because it pertains both to access to education – opportunities to be educated – and to the role of education in selection for jobs and other roles through which further goods are distributed (Jacobs 2016; Jencks 1988; Coleman 1968; Coleman, et al. 1966). Racial domination has involved both denying people of color access to education essential to competing for positions in the society (Blum & Burkholder 2021; Darby & Rury 2018) and violating the ideal of equal opportunity by denying people of color equal access to positions for which they are qualified. Against this background, it is not surprising that struggles for racial justice have often focused on the provision of equal educational opportunity and regulation of employment practices to ensure as far as possible that hiring is strictly on the basis of *bona fide* job qualifications, i.e., ones that are relevant to job performance (Ezorsky 1991).

Nevertheless, it is a mistake to equate equal educational opportunity with racial justice in education or to think that racial justice would be achieved if people of color were provided with equal educational opportunity. As important as equal opportunity is, a singular focus on it obscures essential aspects of racial domination. For example, racial domination has prevented, and continues to prevent, people of color from democratically determining answers to the following questions: How are the relevant goods produced, and by whom? Who determines the structures of production and distribution? Who determines what counts as a good, and why? These questions precede concerns about fairness in competition-based distributions because they are questions about democratic social power – i.e., the right to collectively determine how to structure all aspects of our lives. A distributive justice focus on the fairness of competitions undervalues these questions and does not fully engage the injustices resulting from people of color lacking the democratic social power to reasonably shape the society they live within.

A fundamental limitation of the ideal of equal educational opportunity is that it takes the nature of basic institutions, such as the economy, more or less for granted, and focuses primarily on *procedural fairness* or what would be fair principles for determining winners and losers in competitive struggles to secure favorable outcomes, such as opportunities for more advanced learning or for jobs. Such fairness might require that all children within a local school district receive instruction in the same curriculum by equally qualified teachers, regardless of race of family resources, it might require equalization of the quality of instruction across the entire society (Wheeler-Bell 2018a), or it might require differentiated instruction to better meet students' individual needs (Coleman 1968). Since the 1960s, and especially since the publication of John Rawls's *A Theory of Justice* in (Rawls 1971), concern for procedural fairness has been supplemented by concern for *background fairness*, or the importance of creating a "level playing field for all competitors" (Jacobs 2016: 325). Rawls frames this in terms of *fair equality of opportunity*, which requires that all children have equal chances (not just at school but in their lives as a whole) to develop their talents and qualify for higher learning and the most coveted occupations and positions (Rawls 1971: 83–90).

As difficult as achieving fair equality of opportunity might be, it would not create a just society or eliminate racial domination. One reason it would not is that it is consistent with competitions being structured in ways that put most people at great risk and ensure they will lose. Equal opportunity regulates the fairness of competition for whatever positions in society there are, not the quality of the positions themselves or how much of what people need is only accessible through paid employment. It is silent as to whether (capitalist) labor markets are a justifiable way of distributing what people need to live good lives, and it is silent as to what may be needed to overcome racial domination. Instituting equal educational opportunity of the kind that would be required for fair equality of opportunity may be helpful to reducing the gap in democratic social power, but education focused on labor market success would not directly challenge racial domination.

The misconception that racial justice in education is equivalent to equal educational opportunity may rest on the assumption that racial injustice is primarily a matter of people of color lacking equal access to (capitalist) labor markets. If so, this misconception rests on two questionable ideas. The first is that capitalist labor markets are justly structured, relatively speaking. The second is that having equal access to capitalist labor markets is desirable and feasible. Advocates of racial justice have developed critiques of capitalism that are reasonable enough to warrant consideration. While one might not agree with these critiques, a theory of racial justice must adequately address their concerns. For example, radicals, like Adolph Reed Jr. and Angela Davis, argue that equalizing opportunity within capitalism is morally undesirable, because it presumes that racial justice is about ensuring the capitalist class structure is diverse (Reed 2001; Davis 1998). However, the capitalist system is based upon class domination and exploitation, so racially equalizing capitalist class structure is simply trying to prove that people of color have an equal opportunity to compete in a capitalist system of domination and exploitation.

Integrating Schools Is the Key to Racial Justice in and through Education

The final misconception is the belief that racial justice is achieved through the *racial integration* of schools. In the U.S., this belief has been associated with the 1954 U.S. Supreme Court ruling in *Brown v. Board of Education* that the system of racial apartheid in schooling that existed at that time could not be justified as "separate but equal" schooling, because the education of those forcibly separated from the "mainstream" of society was inherently unequal. Separate schooling was understood to be an impediment to both economic and civic equality, and integrated schooling was understood to facilitate both forms of equality, as explained in a 1967 U.S. Commission on Civil Rights report, *Racial Isolation in the Public Schools*:

> The public schools traditionally have provided a means by which those newly arrived in the cities – the immigrant, and the impoverished – have been able to join the American mainstream. The hope for public education always has been that it would be a means of assuring equal opportunity and of strengthening and unifying American society.
>
> *(Commission on Civil Rights 1967: 1)*

This reference to public schools being a means of joining the "mainstream" implies that integrated schooling has often sufficed to enable those outside the "mainstream" to achieve *civic equality* or truly equal citizenship in the society as well as equal (economic) opportunity. The report proposes steps to racially integrate public schools, and it is reasonable to interpret this as implying that racial integration of schools would constitute racial justice with respect to education and would go a long way toward establishing racial justice in the society. A view widely held by liberal educational theorists is that integrated schooling would facilitate civic equality both by reducing racial prejudice through inter-group contact in schools and by elevating people of color to high-status professions.

Elizabeth Anderson prioritizes civic equality (also known as *democratic equality*) in her contemporary defense of integrated schooling, but she echoes the 1967 Commission's view of integration in closely linking the achievement of democratic equality – the ability to function as a fully equal citizen – to economic opportunity and to integrated schooling's potential to shift the beliefs about people of color held by those in the "mainstream" (Anderson 2010).[2] The goal of racial integration of schools, as she describes it, is to provide blacks with "opportunities for human, social, and cultural capital formation needed to compete on a par with whites" (64) and to foster inter-racial ease, cooperation, and friendship. Regarding the former, success in competition for high-status positions in the society is seen as instrumental to being able to function as civic equals. Regarding the latter, Anderson describes the stages of integration as moving from existing "on terms of equality" in the same space (*spatial integration*), to accepting ground rules that require cooperation as equals (*formal social integration*), to inter-racial friendships, trust, and cooperation that go beyond what the ground rules require (*informal social integration*) (116).

This view of racial justice has at least two shortcomings. First, to the extent that it envisions the path to democratic equality running through equalization of economic opportunity, it replicates one of the shortcomings of the second misconception about racial justice in education. As already noted, black Marxists claim that integration into the "mainstream" is undesirable because capitalism is inherently a system of exploitation and domination. A second shortcoming is that the integrationist view fails to consider alternatives to integration and the concern that integration may deny people of color the advantages of educational self-determination, as it did Native Americans. The fact that ethnically integrated public schools were a traditional path to economic and civic integration into the society is not a sufficient ground for assuming that it the only or best remedy for racial injustice.

The integrationist view dismisses the argument made by people of color that racial separation and social transformation are required to achieve racial justice. For example, black nationalists argue that white supremacy is built into the basic structures of society, and whites have too much of a vested interest in its preservation. Consequently, integration is not a viable means, and separation is the only means, for achieving racial justice.

A related argument is that integration reinforces white supremacy and Eurocentrism. By Eurocentrism I mean the belief that the European and American modernization project would have been organized as currently structured even without racial domination. An example of Eurocentrism is the idea that the educational system would have been organized in relatively the same manner even if people of color had been given the power to collectively determine how the educational system developed. The integration approach reinforces this Eurocentrism by assuming that the "mainstream" institutions that people of color should integrate into are (or would have been) justifiable to people of color. However, people of color have questioned this Eurocentric view of schools and society. For example, the independent school movements led by African-Americans, Latinx, and Native Americans advocated for collective self-determination over their own education, not for integration into pre-established schools.

Collective self-determination concerns the democratic right to determine how schools are structured, what counts as an educational good, who gets to determine what is an educational good, and how to structure the relationship between schools and the larger society. The radical independent schools movement was concerned with educating children in the *face of oppression*, not integrating pre-established systems. In fact, the educational radicals leading this movement argued that the basic structure of education was designed to reproduce racial domination. Again, integrationists may disagree with this charge of Eurocentrism. The point remains that racial domination has prevented people of color from having the democratic social power to reasonably participate in structuring the educational system. Therefore, when scholars equate racial justice with integration, they presume people of color find (or would have found) the current structure of the educational system justifiable. Consequently, integrationists inadequately confront a fact about racial domination: people were denied adequate democratic power to structure or restructure the institution they assume should be integrated. Therefore, they are unable to explain why the institutions they hope to integrate are democratically justifiable to people of color. A viable account of racial justice in education must begin from a well-developed and thorough critique of racial domination.

Racial Domination Within Education: A Critical Approach

A critical approach to racial justice in education differs from traditional distributive justice approaches in two key respects. First, the critical approach focuses not on multiculturalism, equal opportunity, or integration, but on democratic empowerment. Second, this focus on democratic empowerment involves equipping students with morally reflective understanding of structures of power and how to deepen democracy (Wheeler-Bell 2018b). As a form of critical pedagogy, the critical approach to education for racial justice is focused on promoting conversations and inquiry concerning the nature of power and oppression and advancement of human emancipation. This involves cultivating students' autonomous capacities of diagnostic understanding and moral reflection, which would ideally be grounded in moral philosophical principles (Wheeler-Bell 2018b, 2020). Children should learn to diagnose and accurately frame moral judgments about racial domination, and they should learn to identify effective approaches to building democratic social power and advancing social transformation. A critical approach does not neglect students' capabilities and opportunities of access to "mainstream" institutions, but it equips them with the understanding and capability to use the forms of capital they acquire in the cause of democratic empowerment.

As noted above, justice as justification involves democratic processes predicated on a right to justification – a right to participate in processes of public justification guided by principles of *reciprocity* (regarding what count as justifying reasons and regarding obligations to provide justifications and accept what they demand of one) and *generality* (regarding the justifying basis for basic norms) (Forst 2011). *Reciprocity of reasons* entails that no one may simply assume that others have the same values and interests as oneself or make recourse to "higher truths" that are not shared, and *generality* requires that reasons for generally valid basic norms must be shareable by all those affected.

Racial justice requires that people of color have real, effective, and equal possibilities for assuming active roles in directing the social affairs in which they take part. This means that racial justice requires racialized groups to have the democratic social power to determine: (1) what ought to be the purpose(s) of education; (2) what educational goods should be valued, and why; (3) how the school system is structured around said educational goods; (4) how resources are constructed and distributed.

Educating for Racial Justice

Educating for racial justice is primarily focused on the content of the curriculum, specifically what students need to understand and be able to do to challenge racial domination. A philosophical example of educating for racial justice is recounted by Lawrence Blum in *High School, Race, and America's Future* (Blum 2012). In this book, Blum reflects upon his teaching of race in a multiracial high school classroom. He tackles a number of issues related to race, including the historical construction of race, morality and racism, complications around racial identities, and white supremacy. A key aspect of Blum's approach is the importance he places upon morality and racism. This is essential because race is a form of domination; therefore, to teach children about race we also need to help them understand what makes race and racism immoral. Blum's attention to the construction of race, white supremacy, and morality make it an example of a critical approach to racial justice education that equips students with diagnostic understanding of race and domination and related capacities of moral judgment, though it does not address approaches to overcoming racial domination and achieving democratic disempowerment.

Other examples of educating for racial justice could be offered, but this example is sufficient to make the point that a comprehensive critical approach to racial justice education would require teachers to have expertise that many do not have. It would be unfair to expect teachers to be well-versed in the philosophical and sociological complexities of racial domination. The ideal teacher would have the education and professional development needed to adequately teach about race, but this is not the reality we live within. Therefore, I believe it's best to encourage teachers to begin having discussions about race with their students, even if these are imperfect.

The more students are used to talking about race, in various classroom and educational settings, the more they will learn how to think more critically about the complexities of race. Educators should not think about "getting the racial discussion right," but rather about getting the racial conversation started. As teachers and students become more comfortable with an education for racial justice, they also learn more about race, how to discuss the complexities of race, and hopefully will desire to learn more about race themselves. This desire to learn more about race is what will help individuals develop the intellectual tools to think through the complexity of racial domination.

Structuring Education for Racial Justice

Structuring education for racial justice concerns the democratic process of organizing the educational system in a way that advances racial justice. When focused on the structure of education the central concern is *democratic empowerment*: empowering racialized groups to have more democratic social power to define what counts as educational goods, how goods are distributed, and by whom. The critical approach focuses on democratic empowerment, avoiding the three misunderstandings discussed in the previous section.

The critical approach avoids the problem of equating race with culture and ethnicity by focusing on power. Race is inherently a system of domination, so advancing racial justice requires more than respecting cultures or ensuring that racial groups are adequately represented in the curriculum. While racial representation matters and cultures should be respected, neither of these goals sufficiently challenges the system of racial domination. Challenging the system of racial domination requires transforming power relationships, dismantling the social norms and institutional arrangements that prevent people of color from democratically determining how to (re)structure the educational system. This involves a focus on power, which is to say the social norms and structures that limit racialized groups from having real and effective opportunities to participate in the democratic process and determine how the school system is structured and how other institutions function.

One aspect of the structure of the school system to which the critical approach is relevant is the racial diversity of the teaching force. When race is equated with culture, a racially just teaching force is interpreted as one in which all racial groups are equally represented. From a critical perspective, this approach leaves unquestioned what knowledge is taught and who would be most qualified to teach. A requirement that all students receive an anti-racist education would transform what knowledge is taught, who is qualified to teach, and how they become qualified. Moreover, with such a change in the curriculum it might be the case that people of color are more qualified to teach and should therefore be overrepresented within the teaching profession.

Neoliberal restructuring of school systems provides another illustration of how a critical approach to structuring education would differ from other approaches. Consider that after the devastation caused by Hurricane Katrina, New Orleans had an opportunity to radically restructure how it organized its school system. As Kristen Buras illustrates, instead of restructuring the governance structure to provide the black community with more democratic control, schools were restructured along neoliberal lines (Buras, et al. 2010). This neoliberal restructuring had the negative effect of further excluding the black community, including black teachers and activists, from the school governance process. The adoption of a neoliberal model decreased the social power of the communities of color, while racial justice in education would demand the opposite.

A third illustration of the structural distinctiveness of the critical approach it how it avoids the problem of racial essentialism, which is the belief in an essential nature that defines all members of a racial group. One kind of belief or tacit assumption about a shared racial nature is that a particular racialized group shares (or ought to share) the same beliefs or desires. For example, the integrationist approach may be seen as essentialist, if it assumes all blacks want (or ought to want) to integrate – i.e., that they share a common desire to belong to the same "mainstream" that whites want to belong to. The critical approach avoids this problem through the principle of reciprocity. This democratic principle states that no one may simply assume that others have the same values and interests as oneself or make recourse to "higher truths" that are not shared (reciprocity of reasons). This principle is respected by creating more inclusive democratic deliberations. Rather than assuming that individuals within the same racial group hold the same values and principles, it is through the deliberative process that we learn about the diversity of opinions and perspectives within a racial group, while respecting each individual's opinions and perspectives.

Conclusion

This chapter has defended an account of race as a socially constructed form of domination that involves misrecognition of racial groups, and that limits the democratic social power of some groups while giving other groups power over them. This understanding of race implies that none of the three common understandings of racial justice in education is adequate; multicultural, equal opportunity, and integrationist approaches all fall short of directly addressing the realities of race as an unjust system of domination that can only be remedied through an equalization of democratic social power. I have sketched all too briefly the critical alternative to these familiar approaches, outlining its aims of democratic empowerment and social transformation, its essential content, and some of its challenges and implications for how education is structured. A critical pedagogy of racial justice must provide students with the sociological and moral understanding essential to autonomously navigating unjust institutions and working collectively to advance democratic equality and human flourishing.

(Related Chapters: 2, 15, 21, 23, 25, 31, 32, 35.)

Notes

1 In distinguishing anti-racist education from broadly multicultural education, I do not mean to deny that anti-racist education has been embraced *as a focus of* multicultural education by some prominent advocates of both. James Banks argued in 1977 that multicultural education should be focused on "groups which experience discrimination in American society" (Banks, 1977: 3), and Sonia Nieto later argued that "Antiracism … [and] antidiscrimination in general, is at the very core of a multicultural perspective" and requires "teaching young people skills in confronting racism" (Nieto 2000: 305, 307).

2 For more on the centrality of economic opportunity to Anderson's defense of integration, see Wheeler-Bell 2018b.

References

Adams, D. W. (1995) *Educating for Extinction. American Indians and the Boarding School Experience*. Lawrence: University of Kansas Press.

Anderson, E. (2010) *The Imperative of Integration*. Princeton: Princeton University Press.

Anderson, E. (2012) "Race, Culture, and Educational Opportunity," *Theory and Research in Education* 10(2): 105–129.

Banks, J. A. (ed.) (1995) *Handbook of Research on Multicultural Education*. New York: Macmillan.

Banks, J. A. (1977) "The Implications of Multicultural Education for Teacher Education," in F. H. Klassen & D. Golnick (eds.) *Pluralism and the American Teacher: Issues and Case Studies*. Washington, D.C.: American Association of Colleges of Teacher Education, 1–30.

Blum, L. (2012) *High School, Race, and America's Future: What Students Can Teach Us About Morality, Diversity, and Community*. Cambridge, MA: Harvard Education Press.
Blum, L., & Burkholder, Z. (2021) *Integrations: The Struggle for Racial Equality and Civic Renewal in Public Education*. Chicago, IL: University of Chicago Press.
Brown v. Board of Education, 347 U.S. 483 (1954).
Buras, K. L., with Randels, J., Salaam, K. Y., and Students at the Center (2010) *Pedagogy, Policy, and the Privatized City: Stories of Dispossession and Defiance from New Orleans*. New York: Teachers College Press.
Coleman, J. (1968) "The Concept of Equality of Educational Opportunity," *Harvard Educational Review* 38(1): 7–22.
Coleman, J., Campbell, E. Q., Hobson, C. J., McPartland, J., Mood, A. M., Weinfeld, F. D., et al. (1966) *Equality of Educational Opportunity*. Washington, D.C.: US Government Printing Office.
Darby, D. & Rury, J. L. (2018) *The Color of Mind: Why the Origins of the Achievement Gap Matter for Justice*. Chicago: University of Chicago Press.
Davis, A. Y. (1998) *The Angela Y. Davis Reader*, J. James (ed.). Malden, MA: Blackwell.
Desmond, M., & Emirbayer, M. (2009) *Racial Domination, Racial Progress: The Sociology of Race in America*, 1st ed. New York: McGraw-Hill.
Emirbayer, M. & Desmond, M. (2015) *The Racial Order*. Chicago: University of Chicago Press.
Ezorsky, G. (1991) *Racism & Justice: The Case for Affirmative Action, 5thed*. Ithaca, NY: Cornell University Press.
Fordham, S. & Ogbu, J. (1986) "Black Students' School Success: Coping with the 'Burden of Acting White'," *The Urban Review* 18(3): 176–206.
Forst, R. (2008) "First Things First: Redistribution, Recognition and Justification," in N. Fraser (ed.) *Adding Insult to Injury: Nancy Fraser Debates her Critics*. New York, NY: Verso, 310–326.
Forst, R. (2011) *The Right to Justification: Elements of a Constructivist Theory of Justice*, J. Flynn (trans.). New York: Columbia University Press.
Jacobs, L. A. (2016) "Dealing Fairly with Winners and Losers in School: Reframing how to Think about Equality of Educational Opportunity 50 Years after the Coleman Report," *Theory and Research in Education* 14(3): 313–332.
Jencks, C. (1988) "Whom Must We Treat Equally for Educational Opportunity to be Equal?" *Ethics* 98: 518–533.
Lewis, C. (2012) "Oppositional Culture and Educational Opportunity," *Theory and Research in Education* 10(2): 131–154.
Lopez, T. R. & Vogel, A. W. (eds.) (1979) *No One Model American*. Toledo, OH: College of Education, University of Toledo.
McIntosh, K., Moss, E., Nunn, R., & Shambaugh, J. (2020) "Examining the Black-White Wealth Gap," *Brookings* Feb. 27, https://www.brookings.edu/blog/up-front/2020/02/27/examining-the-black-white-wealth-gap/ (accessed Dec.12, 2021).
McWhorter, J. (2000) *Losing the Race: Self-Sabotage in Black America*. New York: The Free Press.
Mills, C. W. (2007) "Multiculturalism as/and/or Anti-Racism?" in A. S. Laden, & D. Owen (eds.) *Multiculturalism and Political Theory*. Cambridge: Cambridge University Press, 89–114.
Morton, J. M. (2022) "A Moral Psychology of Poverty?" in M. Vargas & J. Doris (eds.) *The Oxford Handbook of Moral Psychology*. Oxford: Oxford University Press.
Moynihan, D. (1968) "Sources of Resistance to the Coleman Report," *Harvard Educational Review* 38: 23–36.
National Council for the Social Studies (NCSS) (1976) "Curriculum Guidelines for Multiethnic Education," *Social Education* 55: 274–294.
Nieto, S. (2000) *Affirming Diversity: The Sociopolitical Context of Multicultural Education*, 3rd ed. New York: Longman.
Omi, M. & Winant H. (2014) *Racial Formation in the United States 3rdEdition*. New York: Routledge.
Rawls, J. (1971) *A Theory of Justice*. Cambridge, MA: Harvard University Press.
Reed, A. (2001) *Without Justice for All: The New Liberalism and Our Retreat from Racial Equality, 1st Ed*. New York: Routledge.
Subcommittee on Indian Education of the Senate Committee on Labor and Public Welfare (1969) *Indian Education: A National Tragedy – A National Challenge*. Washington, D.C.: Government Printing Office.
U.S. Commission on Civil Rights. (1967) *Racial Isolation in the Public Schools*. Washington, D.C.: U.S. Gov. Printing Office.
Van Daniel, R. (2018) *Unjustifiably Oppressed: Black Codes of Mississippi (1865)*. Virginia Beach, VA: CreateSpace Independent Publishing Platform.
Wax, A. (2008) *Race, Wrongs, and Remedies*. Stanford, CA: Hoover Institution Press.

Wheeler-Bell, Q. (2018a) "Bring the State Back into Focus: Civil Society, The State, and Education," in N. Levinson (ed.) *Philosophy of Education Society Yearbook*. Urbana, IL: Philosophy of Education Society, 126–134.

Wheeler-Bell, Q. (2018b) "Broken Glass: The Social Evil of Urban Poverty and a Liberatory Education," *Educational Policy* 33(7): 1076–1102.

Wheeler-Bell, Q. (2020) "An Immanent Critique of Critical Pedagogy," *Educational Theory* 69(3): 265–281.

Wright, E. O. (2010) *Envisioning Real Utopias*. London New York: Verso.

23
THE COSTS OF UPWARD MOBILITY[1]

Jennifer M. Morton

A core ideal to which many of us subscribe is that the opportunities available to a citizen should be determined by that person's motivation, talent, and perseverance rather than by the family into which she was born. Even though spelling out this ideal in a broadly appealing way is no easy task, we aim to have our educational institutions embody it. Mobility, both upward and downward, is seen as a sign that we are living up to this ideal. If a child born into a family at the bottom of the income scale can emerge at a higher socioeconomic level than their parents due to the educational opportunities available to them, we take the system to have worked as it should.

Much like other societies that profess to embody the ideal of equality of opportunity, the United States falls dramatically short of it. A child's future earnings, a flawed but widespread mobility measure, is more likely to be determined by her family's zip code than by her talent or motivation (Chetty et al. 2014). The story is now familiar to many. Families with resources tend to buy into neighborhoods with other families from similar socioeconomic and racial backgrounds, thus segregating themselves away from lower-income families and, often, Black and Latinx families (Orfield & Lee 2005). Schools in such neighborhoods tend to be better resourced and enjoy higher test scores, higher rates of graduation, more experienced teachers, and higher rates of college attendance (Darling-Hammond 2013). Outside of school, better-resourced families also invest in their child's educational development through extracurricular activities and other forms of academic enrichment (Lareau 2011). As Richard Reeves (2018) has argued, families who can afford to do so will "hoard opportunity" for their children, thus cementing intergenerational advantages (and disadvantages). Once a child is poised to apply for college, much of their educational trajectory has been determined by factors outside their control: family income, parents' education, neighborhood, and school (Chetty et al. 2014).

Despite, or perhaps because of, these facts, we uphold university as the educational institution that can and should mitigate inequalities by propelling low-income students out of a trajectory that seems destined to leave them behind. Economist Raj Chetty's (2017) work has been influential in making the case that we should judge higher education institutions based on a "Mobility Report Card" that awards its highest grades to those colleges and universities that admit more low-income students and successfully move them up the economic ladder. On this measure, the most selective private institutions fare much worse than less-selective public institutions. The mobility report card has reified upward mobility as an ideal for the higher education sector, but should it be? In this essay, I ask us to reconsider upward mobility as an ideal. I will make the case that upward mobility has significant costs to the higher education sector, the individuals who experience it, and our society. This is not to say that we should give up on equal

DOI: 10.4324/9781003172246-27

opportunity, but it means that we need to think more deeply about the role that colleges and universities should play in its pursuit.

The Knowledge Aim

The role that colleges and universities play in society has changed over time. In many countries, a college education is becoming necessary to achieve middle-class employment. Enrollment numbers reflect this. Whereas a minuscule proportion of high school graduates considered attending college in the early part of the 20th century, by 2018 69% of graduating seniors in the United States enrolled in some sort of postsecondary education (NCES 2019). Though in the United Kingdom the numbers are lower (37.9%), there too have we seen a significant increase in the number of 18-year-olds enrolling in postsecondary education (UCAS 2021). According to UNESCO (2017), between 2000 and 2014 the number of students enrolled in higher education across the world doubled. While some might applaud this trend as constituting an expansion of access to higher education and thus opportunity, others are concerned that this is evidence of an "arms race" of credentials that deepens inequality. For example, Randall Curren (2017) worries that our focus on university and college attendance as a way to mitigate inequality has led us to ignore alternative non-academic postsecondary pathways to good employment and flourishing lives. He suggests that such alternatives might be a better way of mitigating inequality. Peter Cappelli (2015) argues that the returns on a college degree are not as high as they might initially seem. It depends on the institution one attends, the amount of debt one takes on, and degree type. Notwithstanding these skeptical voices, much of the recent debate around higher education has focused on upward mobility, often at the expense of other dimensions of education that are equally important.

Given that a college degree affects access to good employment, a livable wage, and the goods that usually flow from them, many have come to think of the university's task as "leveling the playing field." Kotzee and Martin (2013) label this the "distributive" conception of the university. According to this view, the university's role is to "redistribute life-chances in some egalitarian fashion" (628). Kotzee and Martin argue that this view of the university is too thin to account for much of what a university education does. To drive their point across, they ask us to consider alternatives to redistribution, such as compensating people born into disadvantage with a sum of money equal to the value of the education they missed or making it illegal to consider a university degree in hiring admissions (634). They admit that these are outlandish alternatives. However, the argument allows us to see that if students were offered these alternative forms of compensation, they would be missing out on a critical part of higher education – the knowledge and understanding that constitute the university's educational and research aim. Kotzee and Martin label this the "knowledge" aim and argue that this is the university's central mission.

Kotzee and Martin's argument focuses on an essential role that the university plays – enriching our knowledge and understanding. A college or university that conferred degrees to mitigate inequalities without educating the disadvantaged students it admitted would be doing a disservice to them even if it allowed them access to opportunities for employment they would not have had otherwise. However, this does not show that considerations of equality are irrelevant to thinking about who should have access to a college education. Even if an institution's essential aim is orthogonal to equality, it might still play such a significant role in exacerbating inequalities that the state is permitted to interfere in its inner workings to make its effects more equal.

David O'Brien (forthcoming) offers an argument against this line of thinking. He argues that liberal egalitarians might be committed to thinking of the university as a special institution similarly to how they conceive of the family. Briefly, the family is a social institution that serves an essential political function and that is central to many conceptions of the good life. According to O'Brien's interpretation of Rawlsian liberalism, these features protect the family from political interventions aimed at altering its inner workings for the sake of equalizing opportunity. Even though well-functioning families exacerbate inequality, liberal egalitarians are committed to finding other ways to mitigate these inequalities that do not involve political intervention into family life because such intervention would alter the character of this essential institution. O'Brien suggests that universities are also social institutions that serve an important political function – discovering, promoting, and communicating knowledge – and that their existence is a central element of reasonable, good lives. In virtue of this, they too are protected from political intervention.

O'Brien's argument is compelling, but it is important to note that it is a conditional argument. It tells us that if we are committed to liberal egalitarianism, it follows that some institutions are shielded from state intervention. Some might take this argument to speak against political liberalism rather than in favor of the sanctity of the higher education sector. Furthermore, one might argue that under non-ideal conditions, such interference is warranted even if we want to preserve something like the sanctity of the university under more ideal conditions. For example, Brighouse and Swift (2014) have made compelling arguments about why considerations of equality apply to what families are allowed to do in our non-ideal circumstances, even if these constraints are limited by the internal goods families provide. Similarly, we might argue that there is much we could do to make higher education institutions more equal even while we respect the internal goods that these institutions provide.

The problem with focusing only on the distributive effects of higher education is that it instrumentalizes education. We end up thinking of higher education as a tool for the achievement of certain egalitarian goals, but in doing so miss the deeper transformative potential of the educational experience. In her essay "Liberal Education and The Possibility of Valuational Progress" Agnes Callard (2017) puts forward a vigorous defense of a liberal arts education. She suggests that colleges and universities are uniquely well-positioned to offer "access to a distinct domain of aesthetic, scientific, [and] literary value" (14). On her view, a liberal arts education offers students the opportunity to fall in love with a domain of value to which they might not have been exposed until they arrived on campus. This is another dimension of education that we miss if we're only focused on mobility.

Some might dismiss this as a romantic conception of education. Students from low-income families might be taking on enormous amounts of debt to get through college (Goldrick-Rab 2021). For them, the socioeconomic payoff might be quite important. This kind of valuational progress view of education might seem like a luxury that they cannot afford. This is an important point. It's not clear, though, that it should push us to ignore the dimension of the educational experience that Callard stresses. Instead, we might consider the possibility that everyone should have access to this kind of educational experience for free (Martin 2021).

These arguments help us see that the focus on mobility is too narrow to encompass the many things that universities and colleges do. We want to know not only whether students are "moving up" but how their lives are being transformed and enriched through education. We want universities to not only be places that enable students to move up the socioeconomic ladder, but also places that enable students to pursue knowledge. Many students attend college to discover new sources of value, not just to increase their socioeconomic standing. Whether all these aims can be coherently satisfied is not a question I can address here, but the preceding discussion shows us that we impoverish the conversation about higher education by focusing only on socioeconomic mobility.

The Ethical and Health Costs of Upward Mobility for Strivers

Education is meant to be transformative. Eager students arrive on campus ready to deepen their interests or to discover new passions. They make friends, meet their future partners, and develop mentorship relationships with professors and older students. If all goes as advertised, a college degree positions a student to have an engaging career, an interesting group of friends, and a rich intellectual life. Yet, for some low-income or first-generation students – strivers, as I call them – higher education brings different kinds of transformations. Some of them are welcome. As we have discussed, college degrees hold for strivers the promise of upward mobility. This means that, if they succeed, their class and social standing in society will change and they will be able to access certain goods that they might previously have been prevented from accessing – valuable expertise, well-paid and interesting jobs, and different professional and social circles. Yet this potential transformation of their life trajectories comes with steep costs. First, as I will argue, many strivers find that accessing mobility often means joining communities where opportunities reside and distancing themselves from their home communities. This distancing changes their position with respect to important goods in their lives – relationships with family, friends, and other community members with whom they have close ties. Second, as Brody et al. (2020) show, upward mobility can undermine strivers' physical health. Even as strivers succeed, they increase the likelihood that they will suffer from heart disease and diabetes.

As I argue in my book *Moving Up Without Losing Your Way* (Morton 2019), many strivers face a conflict between pursuing opportunities for advancement and remaining connected to their family, friends, and community. Due to socioeconomic segregation in housing, schooling, and social life in the United States, disadvantage tends to be concentrated. Those communities in which low-income and first-generation students tend to grow up will often have underfunded schools, low-paying jobs, and fewer opportunities for advancement. Furthermore, because of neighborhood segregation, those born into well-off families tend to go to school, work, and socialize with other people from similar families, while those with fewer resources tend to do the same. Finally, the safety net in the United States often leaves many people behind. The families of students born into disadvantage have to contend with lack of access to suitable healthcare, childcare, eldercare, and the like. As a result, a striver seeking upward mobility through education will often have to leave their home and enter those communities where opportunities and resources are available. In doing so, strivers feel torn, especially if they are playing critical support roles within their families. These sources of value that strivers potentially put on the line to pursue mobility are what I call "the ethical costs" because they are critical elements of a well-lived life.

Many of the strivers I interviewed in the book talked about how hard it was to prioritize their education over supporting their families. Henry, a white middle-aged academic, grew up with his mother and sister in poverty. At times, they had no electricity or hot water. They relied on food stamps. As Henry found himself climbing the ladder of opportunity, his sister fell into drugs, but he was unable to help her while simultaneously pursuing his degree. Reflecting on his experience of mobility, Henry wrote to me that "When I think about them [his mother and sister] I feel like I have no soul. I keep walking away" (31). Furthermore, the more a striver inhabits these new communities, the more likely they are to become proficient in the norms and expectations of those communities (Jack 2019). This enables them to navigate these spaces in increasingly successful ways, but it might also make them feel more distant from those with whom they grew up. Strivers describe feeling like visitors in their home communities and like outsiders in the communities they seek to enter.

To be clear, not all strivers face the same choice situations or make the same choices. Some strivers grow up in diverse communities to which they remain connected even as they climb the ladder of opportunity. Other strivers might reject upward mobility in favor of remaining connected to those for whom they care. Moreover, others never feel connected to their community of origin and are glad to find more welcoming communities. This might be especially true of those who grow up in communities with sexist, racist, or homophobic ideologies. Finally, some strivers might find that the trade-offs they make are not quite as sharp. However, for many strivers, the transformation that higher education promises is ethically fraught.

Mobility is not only ethically difficult for strivers; research suggests it also negatively affects their health. Brody et al. (2020) looked at 368 low-income rural African American youths. They found that those who exhibited higher levels of planning and self-control during childhood were more likely to attend college, have lower symptoms of depression, and have better social adjustment. However, that group also exhibited an increase in factors contributing to heart disease (metabolic syndrome or MetS) and higher levels of insulin resistance (IR) levels than their counterparts who had not attended college and had stayed in poverty. The authors write:

> What is it about striving for upward mobility that undermines the health of skin-deep resilient young adults? In this study, most participants were the first in their families to attend college. They feel tremendous pressure to succeed to ensure their parents' sacrifices have been worthwhile. Many feel socially isolated and disconnected from peers from different backgrounds. They may encounter racism and discrimination. Against this backdrop, striving for success in the face of interpersonal, community, and institutional challenges is likely to occasion frequent activation of stress responses from the hypothalamic-pituitary-adrenal axis and the sympathetic nervous system … . Sustained exposure to high levels of these hormones can promote weight gain, elevate blood pressure, dysregulate lipids, and promote inflammation, all of which could hasten MetS and IR.
>
> *(Brody et al. 2020: 924)*

Given that the comparison group that did not make it out of poverty did not see the same health effects, the research appears to show that it is striving that leads to the adverse effects on strivers' health, not poverty itself. This is a striking finding. Strivers who are succeeding by the measures that we focus on – mobility – are endangering their health in doing so. Health, arguably, is also an important ethical good – one that is central to a flourishing life.

When we consider the costs of mobility for strivers, we start to understand why upward mobility is not an unalloyed good. It is arguably better for those born into poverty to be able to strive despite these costs. We cannot deny the value of having an education that enables one to have well-paying, stable employment and to be able to offer one's own family a good life. Nevertheless, strivers undermine critical aspects of their flourishing in this pursuit. This should lead us to rethink the structure of opportunity and our focus on mobility as the standard by which we judge its success.

The Costs to Community

A problem with looking at higher education as an institutional mechanism to increase mobility is that it ignores the costs that this imposes on our communities and civic relationships. The first kind of cost involves the loss of valuable relational social goods we have discussed in the previous section. Striving does not only undermine these essential relational goods for strivers but also for those with whom strivers have these relationships. The second kind of cost derives from the competitive nature that underlies much of the higher education system. By making admissions into university competitive, we encourage students to approach their education in a way that estranges them from each other.

As we saw in the previous section, for some strivers, college is not only a place to deepen their understanding of the world and develop skills that will serve them as they move through the world – it is also a place that threatens to siphon them off from their families and home communities. The ethical costs strivers pay is the result of the geography of inequality and the structure of opportunity. These two factors, in effect, incentivize individuals that wish to pursue avenues for economic advancement to do so at the expense of remaining connected to their communities. The process of mobility threatens to make family relationships, friendships, and tight community bonds ever more fragile. Increasingly, the institution that has taken on the role of facilitating this process is the university.

In the previous section, I argued that these costs were ethical because they concerned essential aspects of a flourishing life. In effect, strivers need to prioritize their education over other elements of their lives that they cherish for the sake of mobility. Here I would like to suggest that this system undermines goods that are central to flourishing communities. In effect, it poses a dilemma for communities – either some of their talented and motivated members attain opportunities for socioeconomic advancement elsewhere, or those members stay and contribute to their community at the expense of attaining mobility. This situation undermines the bonds of care between families, neighbors, schoolmates, and friends that bind communities together. In all communities, these bonds constitute the forms of solidarity critical to social flourishing. Poverty challenges these bonds, but the pressure of mobility threatens them further.

When a striver leaves, this is a loss both for the striver and for those with whom she has a relationship. Neighbors, friends, and community members lose someone they loved or cared for. The community loses a potentially contributing member. Some strivers might reject opportunities for mobility, preferring to stay connected to those they love. But, in doing so, they opt out of economic advancement and the benefits that such opportunities might bring to them and their families. This also undermines communities in which lower educational attainment, joblessness, and other ills of poverty are already concentrated.

Another way in which mobility frustrates important societal values is that it undermines solidarity among citizens pursuing higher education. Mobility is often understood positionally. Chetty et al. (2017), for example, measures how many people from the bottom quartile make it into the top. This means that if someone moves up, someone else must move down. More concretely, if universities are sites for upward mobility, we must acknowledge that those who do not gain admissions will lose out when they are competing with others who do hold those degrees. In countries like the United States, where accessing employment opportunities with job security, health benefits, and the like often requires a college degree, university admissions at those campuses that provide mobility is an increasingly fraught, high-stakes competition. Those who can secure those admissions spots significantly increase their likelihood of not just earning a degree but of accessing the kind of stable, well-paid employment that is out of reach for many. According to Cappelli (2015), the college wage premium is partially the result of declining wages for those who do not attend college. He writes, "it paid to have a college degree because the wages if you didn't have one were awful" (90). Consequently, even for students who grow up with a fair amount of socioeconomic privilege, gaining admissions at selective college campuses has become increasingly competitive (Tough 2019).

Waheed Hussain (2020) argues that institutions can mistreat people by defining a normative framework that "pit[s] people against each other" (80). Competition, Hussain argues, is vital, but some institutional arrangements increase the stakes in a way that undermines solidarity between citizens. Hussain argues that such institutional arrangements lead to estrangement because citizens see each other as potential obstacles to the attainment of goods essential to a good life. For example, applying for a job that offers health care in an environment in which healthcare is expensive and few jobs offer it becomes a high-stakes competition that pits the health of one applicant against that of another.

Arguably this is happening in higher education. There are few alternatives to a college education that offer a pathway to the kind of work that will offer retirement savings, healthcare, and a good enough salary to be comfortably middle class. As the gap between those with a degree and those without is not just about salary but about access to elements central to good lives – healthcare, housing, and access to good schools for one's children – the competition is ever more fraught. This makes the competition for college access one that threatens to undermine solidarity between citizens.

A similar critique is leveled by Michael Sandel (2020) in his book on meritocracy. As Sandel sees it, the problem is that meritocracy depends on the idea that those who earn positions through talent and hard work deserve it. A society that operates under the illusion that it is pursuing a meritocratic ideal is liable to fall prey to a kind of hierarchy of "smarts." Those who are the beneficiaries of meritocracy end up buying into the idea that their success is earned, which leads them to act with a kind of entitlement that breeds resentment. Those on the bottom resent the power garnered by those on the top. Even as we know that those who do "win out" in this meritocratic race started with the privileges that stem from being born into well-off families in wealthy neighborhoods, the system continues to bestow admiration on the "winners" and contempt on the "losers." The fact that some students from less well-resourced backgrounds manage to make it in this system only reinforces the entitlement of those who make it. According to Sandel, this erodes civic relationships and creates distrust of elites.

Sandel's critique focuses on how the idea of meritocracy validates a system of "winners and losers" tied to educational achievement. He proposes that it is this idea that is to blame for the erosion of solidarity among citizens. However, Hussain's analysis offers an alternative theory – the high-stakes nature of the competition, not the justification we offer for it, leads to estrangement between citizens. Regardless of whether we think it is the entitlement of those at the top or the increasingly high-stakes nature of the educational divide, higher education has the potential to exacerbate the deterioration of critical civic bonds.

According to the argument I have laid out, the problem with looking at higher education as an institutional mechanism to increase mobility and equalize opportunity is that it ignores the costs that this imposes on communities. An individual who has access to the opportunity to go to a good school to obtain a degree that will lead to a good job is doing better in some ways than many of those who do not even have that opportunity. However, if what this means is that we, in effect, have created a high-stakes competition that undermines the bonds that hold communities together and offers few good options for those who do not "win," then we have failed to organize our society in a way that reflects what we value.

Conclusion

Equality of opportunity is an ideal because we want to make sure that the lives of citizens are not determined by the accidents of birth but by their own talent, effort, and choices. In our non-ideal circumstances, in which children born into poverty do not fall far from the tree into which they were born (Bowles et al. 2009), equalizing opportunity means increasing the likelihood that those children will be able to transcend the circumstances of their birth. This has led us to focus on mobility as an important measure of how well we are achieving opportunity. In this essay, I have made a case for why upward mobility is not the panacea that we should be after. The pursuit of a college degree has become a high-stakes competition with high costs to our educational institutions, strivers, and to our communities. Focusing on mobility obscures these negative effects. Shifting the focus away from mobility would allow the university to focus on delivering the educational goods that are inherent to this mission – knowledge, personal transformation, and value acquisition. However, we must ensure that these goods are available to all who wish to pursue them and that those who would like to pursue other opportunities have equally good alternative paths to a flourishing life. What we should be after is a system of educational opportunities that lifts us all. Such a system would not focus on mobility, but on the flourishing of all who are touched by it.

(Related Chapters: 15, 19, 24, 25, 28.)

Note

1 Thanks to Dustin Webster and Monika Greco for their feedback on this piece.

References

Bowles, S., Gintis, H., & Groves, M. O. (eds.) (2009) *Unequal Chances: Family Background and Economic Success.* Princeton: Princeton University Press.

Brighouse, H., & Swift, A. (2014) *Family Values: The Ethics of Parent-Child Relationships.* Princeton: Princeton University Press.

Brody, G. H., Yu, T., Chen, E., & Miller, G. E. (2020) "Persistence of Skin-deep Resilience in African American Adults," *Health Psychology* 39(10): 921–926.

Callard, A. (2017) "Liberal Education and the Possibility of Valuational Progress," *Social Philosophy and Policy* 34(2): 1–22.

Cappelli, P. (2015) *Will College Pay Off? A Guide to the Most Important Financial Decision You'll Ever Make.* New York: PublicAffairs.

Chetty, R., Friedman, J., Saez, E., Turner, N., & Yagan, D. (2017) "Mobility Report Cards: The Role of Colleges in Intergenerational Mobility," *NBER*, Working Paper 23618. doi: 10.3386/w23618

Chetty, R., Hendren, N., Kline, P., Saez, E., & Turner, N. (2014) "Is the United States still a Land of Opportunity? Recent Trends in Intergenerational Mobility," *American Economic Review* 104(5): 141–147.

Curren, R. (2017) "On the Arc of Opportunity: Education, Credentialism, and Employment," in K. Schaff (ed.) *Fair Work: Ethics, Social Policy, Globalization.* London: Rowman & Littlefield, 59–77.

Darling-Hammond, L. (2013) "Inequality and School Resources: What It Will Take to Close the Opportunity Gap," in Welner, K. Grant, & Carter, P. L. (eds.) *Closing the Opportunity Gap: What America Must Do to Give Every Child an Even Chance.* Oxford: Oxford University Press, 77–97.

Goldrick-Rab, S. (2021) *Paying the Price: College Costs, Financial Aid, and the Betrayal of the American Dream.* Chicago: University of Chicago Press.

Jack, A. A. (2019) *The Privileged Poor: How Elite Colleges are Failing Disadvantaged Students.* Cambridge, MA: Harvard University Press.

Kotzee, B. & Martin, C. (2013) "Who Should go to University? Justice in University Admissions," *Journal of Philosophy of Education* 47(4): 623–641.

Lareau, A. (2011) *Unequal Childhoods: Class, Race, and Family Life.* Oakland, CA: University of California Press.

Martin, C. (2021) *The Right to Higher Education: A Political Theory.* Oxford: Oxford University Press.

Morton, J. (2019) *Moving up Without Losing Your Way: The Ethical Costs of Upward Mobility.* Princeton: Princeton University Press.

National Center for Educational Statistics (2019) "Recent High School Completers and Their Enrollment in College, by Sex and Level of Institution: 1960 through 2018," (Table 302.10). Retrieved from https://nces.ed.gov/programs/digest/d19/tables/dt19_302.10.asp

O'Brien, D. (forthcoming) "How Far can Political Liberalism Support Reforms in Higher Education? *Social Theory and Practice.*

Orfield, G., & Lee, C. (2005) "Why Segregation Matters: Poverty and Educational Inequality," UCLA: The Civil Rights Project/Proyecto Derechos Civiles. Retrieved from https://escholarship.org/uc/item/4xr8z4wb

Reeves, R. V. (2018) *Dream Hoarders: How the American Upper Middle Class is Leaving Everyone else in the Dust, Why That is a Problem, and What to Do About It.* Washington, D.C.: Brookings Institution Press.

Sandel, M. (2020) *The Tyranny of Merit: What's Become of the Common Good?* New York: Farrar, Straus and Giroux.

Tough, P. (2019) *The Years That Matter Most: How College Makes or Breaks Us.* New York: Houghton Mifflin Court.

UCAS (2021) "Record Levels of Young People Accepted to University," Retrieved from https://www.ucas.com/corporate/news-and-key-documents/news/record-levels-young-people-accepted-university

UNESCO (2017) Six Ways to Ensure Higher Education Leaves No One Behind, https://unesdoc.unesco.org/ark:/48223/pf0000247862

UNESDOC (2017) "Six Ways to Ensure Higher Education Leaves No One Behind," Retrieved from https://unesdoc.unesco.org/ark:/48223/pf0000247862

Waheed, W. (2020) "Pitting People Against Each Other," *Philosophy & Public Affairs* 48(1): 79–113.

24

WHO SHOULD PAY FOR HIGHER EDUCATION? AN EDUCATIONAL AIMS PERSPECTIVE

Christopher Martin

Introduction

The debate over who should be responsible for the costs of higher education provision – generally divided between students and the state or taxpayer[1] – brings to bear important considerations of distributive fairness. By "distributive fairness" we mean, broadly, claims about the fair sharing of benefits and burdens arising from a given cooperative scheme. An apartment can be subject to distributive fairness, for example. Sharing an apartment is a cooperative project. Occupants invest labor (housecleaning) in the upkeep of a shared space, and the occupants benefit from these investments. Distributive fairness comes into play when we endeavour to decide who should be expected to invest, and how much. When one roommate gripes about the messiness of the other, intuitions about distributive fairness are surely at play.

Higher education systems are not at all like rental apartments, but they share many of the formal characteristics that make them subject to fair distribution. First, we can understand higher education as a cooperative scheme (albeit a more complex one). People come together to combine their efforts and resources, directly and indirectly, in support of the higher education system. They do so directly, for example, by attending a higher education institution and paying fees. And they do so indirectly through taxation. Second, there are different benefits and burdens that arise from that cooperative scheme. The aforementioned taxation, for example, is one burden. The opportunity costs for those who study at a university instead of working full time is another. But there are also benefits. Individually speaking, graduates usually experience an increase in lifetime income. Society may also benefit. For example, when a large enough number of people receive a higher education the larger community experiences public goods such as lower crime and increased civic engagement.[2]

"Who should pay for higher education?" asks what kind of funding regime for higher education would make it a distributively fair cooperative arrangement. When we claim that the person attending should bear the full costs themselves, for example, we presuppose a certain view of how (and how much) the person benefits and the burdens that it is reasonable for them to shoulder in light of these benefits.

We might therefore be led to think that answering the question of "who should pay?" is a simple matter of accounting for all of the benefits and all of the burdens, plugging these benefits and burdens into some distributive ideal that best captures what any fair arrangement should look like, and forging public policy on that basis.

My aim in this chapter is to show why the answer is not that straightforward.[3] One way that it might not be straightforward, of course, is that people will disagree about distributive ideals more

DOI: 10.4324/9781003172246-28

generally. I have a different complication in view. *The central aims or purposes* of higher education play a significant, if not fundamental, role in how we should *weight* the benefits and burdens under consideration. Our understanding of these purposes – the nature of the cooperative scheme, we might say – directly bears on what distributive fairness requires.[4] Getting a better grasp of them is therefore essential to any attempt at resolving the question of "who should pay?"

Why Educational Aims?

Some might take a focus on educational aims to be irrelevant. One can point out that most young people know that they can reliably earn more if they graduate from a university. This "college premium" is a driving force behind a lot of the modern expansion of higher education irrespective of any other educational goals it might harbor. And it's not as if a person could successfully argue, "Look, my aim in getting a university education is to expand my mind. I should not be held responsible for the fact that my lifetime income will increase if I successfully graduate. It is a benefit that I should not be made to account for." The aggregate economic benefits and burdens of higher education are undeniable.

Economic realities such as the "college premium" and rising institutional costs certainly bear on the question of who should pay for higher education. My point is that the *moral significance* we assign to the college premium and other benefits and burdens requires some prior understanding of the purposes that make higher education what it is. Put simply, we need to direct our attention both to *what* is being distributed as well as how it is distributed (Sen 1980).

In order to understand how the nature of a cooperative arrangement bears on the moral significance of the various benefits and burdens arising from that scheme, consider again the example of the rented apartment. Suppose I lose patience with my roommate's lack of due regard for the benefits they experience from my taking on all of the household cleaning. Suppose further that my roommate and I are married. The fact that we are married does not take us outside the realm of distributive fairness.[5] But it surely changes the nature and scope of our cooperation, and it alters the significance of the benefits and the burdens considerably. It may even introduce benefits and burdens that would not be morally relevant if we were simply roommates. For example, my partner's refusal to contribute could be experienced as an emotional, as well as a physical, burden for me.

Perhaps the example is misleading because the aims of higher education are stable. It cannot be one kind of cooperative scheme one day (roommates), and something different the next (romantic partners).

Yet, higher education *has* undergone some dramatic transformations. In the last 100 years it has expanded from a select training ground for a small minority to enrollment near and above 50% of the population in some jurisdictions (a threshold percentage that the sociologist of higher education, Martin Trow (1973), referred to as "universal higher education"). Over the course of these years, university qualifications have come to play a much greater role in job markets. We can list other changes. My point is that higher education has experienced a major transformation in the purposes that the cooperative scheme serves (or that people expect it to serve). This mutability suggests that we cannot take the benefits and burdens of higher education as a given. Rather, the *justification* of higher education purposes is logically connected to the *justice* of higher education

Aims of Higher Education: Benefits and Burdens of Socioeconomic Mobility

In order to track the extent to which, and ways in which, different conceptions of the aims and purposes of higher education bear on judgements of distributive fairness, we should start with an aim widely recognized as central to modern higher education policy: that it should aim to help disadvantaged people achieve upward social mobility by increasing their employability.[6] How might this aim influence our reasoning about the fair distribution of benefits and burdens?

It would be unjust if the private costs of higher education prevented people that desired upward social mobility from accessing the system. These costs would frustrate upward social mobility because the less well off – the very people that the system should aim to support – will not be able to access that system in the first place.

This might look like a good reason to shift the burden of higher education entirely to the public, thereby eliminating the barrier of private costs. However, as the costs of higher education rise it looks increasingly unfair to require the public to match those rising costs. For example, public funding would require people who never opted for a higher education – or never qualified for admission – to shoulder a greater tax burden so that others who benefit from attendance can escape the costs. It may even involve shifting public funding away from goods that are presumptively beneficial for all, such as health care. On top of this, graduates will likely experience the aforementioned college premium – an increase in average earning power after graduation - while those who helped to pay for them will not.

It is unfair to prevent those less well off from accessing a higher education. It is unfair to require those that do not receive a higher education to shoulder the entire burden. How do we navigate between these two different, and entirely reasonable, distributive concerns? Harry Brighouse (2004) provides a way forward over the course of his argument for "means-tested" public provision. "Means-tested" refers to the idea that a person is eligible to have their access to a good funded by the public if they do not have the economic means to access that good through their own efforts. His argument runs like this. First, we have to realize that adult students should be responsible for their choices, and because the economic benefits of higher education mainly go to the student, it is in principle entirely reasonable to require them to pay. Second, we also have to consider the fact that there are many students who will be discouraged from attending if they have to pay upfront, either because they do not have the money in the first place, or because taking on student debt is too risky an investment. Therefore, fairness requires that relatively well-off students pay, while those less well-off should receive public support.

In this context, students who are so poorly off that private costs are a barrier to accessing the system should qualify for public funding. These students are clearly worse off than many people and receiving higher education as a benefit will help to level the socioeconomic playing field. But there are some students who are not especially wealthy and cannot afford to pay the upfront costs of higher education yet are well off *enough* that if the public paid for their attendance it would go beyond what is "fair," because these students are already better off than many of the people who would be asked to help fund their access. However, these students of middle-class background can have access to higher education through loans. Debt financing is a distributively fair policy. It enables people of average income (or family backgrounds with average income) to access the system without placing an unfair burden on the public.

Brighouse's analysis sets out principled grounds on which the public should financially support individual access to higher education while also recognizing the burdens of such support. For example, when resources are scarce and the costs of higher education are rising, the aim of fair socioeconomic mobility rules against policies that shift too much of the cost to students. Higher education has become an important gateway to improved socioeconomic fortunes, and so it is unjust to ask low-income students to pay or borrow in order to enter. However, a concern for socioeconomic equality rules against policies that redistribute too much of the burden on the public. Full public funding, for example, would involve paying for students who are already quite well off in socioeconomic terms.

The aim of fair socioeconomic mobility gives us reason to allocate at least some public funding for higher education. But is this the *only* reason why the public should pay? Perhaps there are other reasons why people should contribute. If so, could these reasons justify public funding above and beyond what socioeconomic mobility alone requires, or perhaps a different arrangement altogether?

Cooperative Schemes, Educational Goods, and Justice

Many of the candidate non-economic reasons for the public to pay for higher education are based on the idea that education should promote the development and cultivation of knowledge and understanding. This would imply that higher education has value independent of any role it may happen to play in increasing employability. One could perhaps argue, then, that the public should support higher education because society benefits from the production of good thinkers (where "good" is construed widely). We might say that an educated democracy is an important aim of higher education, for example, and so the public should contribute more funding than what socioeconomic reasons alone call for.

But we need to be cautious about the mere *assertion* of an educational aim as a reason for compelling others to contribute. For, even if the aim of producing more able thinkers were desirable in and of itself, *obligating* the public to pay for the production of such thinkers is a different matter. Here is why: People sometimes gripe about being taxed for public health care and basic schooling. And while these complaints are not usually seen as strong enough to undermine the political legitimacy of publicly funding these goods, it isn't always clear when it is reasonable to require people to contribute to a cooperative scheme and when it is unreasonable.

When it is obvious that everyone will benefit from the funding of a good, the requirement seems easier to justify. For example, there are some goods that are beneficial to everyone but undersupplied by the market. And some of these undersupplied goods serve an interest shared by all. These are *presumptive public goods* (Klosko 1987). Health care is a paradigmatic case. Each person has an individual interest in health care and supplying health care to others benefits the individual supplying it (by reducing communicable diseases, for example). This makes it reasonable to shift some of the funding burden to the public.

However, some goods that rely on large-scale cooperation are not of interest to every individual. Think of the libraries and sport facilities, both of which have value but are discretionary. Individual people are free not to observe an interest in *discretionary public goods*, even when they are widely recognized by others as having value (Klosko 1990).

And so, a case needs to be made for why a particular good ought to be provided by the state and, given the role that forced taxation typically plays in such provision, this case must include reasons why it is fair to impose an additional financial burden on individual people in exchange for that good. For goods that are presumptively beneficial, these reasons will be relatively easy to come by. People across the board have a hard-to-deny interest in them. However, in cases where many people really do have no interest ("I don't want the city using my taxes in order to build an NHL hockey arena!") a much stronger argument for why they should pay for the good in question is needed.

This is why the justification of higher education aims is part and parcel with the justification of who should pay. Many of our claims about the value of higher education are claims about its discretionary value. They reflect goods that some will surely find to be worthwhile, but certainly not all. I say that higher education aims to contribute to high culture, but you do not really care that much for high culture. As such, my claim does not serve as a convincing basis for shifting the funding burden to the public (and to you).

But the presumptive/discretionary distinction also points a way forward. Brighouse's argument, for example, does not rest on the discretionary value of higher education. It rests on higher education's role in supporting the presumptive good of socioeconomic justice. If someone asks why they should support higher education at all, one can argue that it is an essential means to a good that all can benefit from: a more socioeconomically fair community. Higher education is discretionary for the individual, to be sure, but it aims to produce something presumptively good for *all* of society.

We can surely debate the claim that maximizing the socioeconomic fairness of society is something that higher education institutions are essential to and should be politically responsible for.[7] But that debate, no matter where it lands, abides by the general terms that *any* argument from educational aims must satisfy if it is to justify a shift away from payment by the individual student and toward the public. These justifying reasons must demonstrate how that aim is essential to some presumptive public good – a good that all people will benefit from and therefore have an obligation to contribute towards. That is to say, reasons of *justice* are required in order to motivate such a shift.

I will next argue that personal autonomy as an educational aim, much like the argument from socioeconomic mobility, can satisfy these general terms. On this view, an adult's personal autonomy is a presumptive good for any liberally just society, and so we therefore have reasons of justice to allocate public resources to its fair promotion among free and equal people. I will also show how recognizing this aim changes, in a noteworthy way, the moral assessment of the benefits and burdens that the scheme generates.

Aims of Higher Education: Benefits and Burdens of Personal Autonomy

Many philosophers working in the liberal tradition have focused on personal autonomy as an essential educational aim owed to all persons on grounds of political justice (Brighouse 1998; White 1990; Schouten 2018). Broadly speaking, by "personal autonomy" we are referring to a person's capacity to decide on self-determined goals that give meaning and purpose to their life (Raz 1986). The successful pursuit of these goals contributes to a person's well-being, or human flourishing. When we say that personal autonomy ought to be a central aim of education, then, we mean that education should cultivate the knowledge, understanding, dispositions, and skills that will enable students to decide amongst a range of possible self-determined goals available in a free and open society, as well as enable those students to *succeed* in the pursuit of such self-determined goals.

If I cannot commit to a particular goal or goals in life – if I am unable to give my life any kind of direction – I lack a degree of personal autonomy relative to those who can. But it might also be the case that I have a variety of worthwhile goals in view and cannot make good on any of them because I lack the knowledge or skill required to successfully pursue these goals or to participate in the social form or practice that the goal represents. For example, I might have a passion for restoring old homes and resolve that this activity should give shape and direction to my life. But I possess neither the practical skills nor an understanding of the norms and values that constitute restoration work.

Autonomy-based arguments for the public funding of education are almost exclusively marshalled in support of the compulsory education of children.[8] Why should we think that such arguments have any bearing on the distributive fairness of higher education? Higher education students are presumed to be adults. Autonomy-based reasons are unlikely to justify public funding for the "already autonomous." Nor are adults (legitimately) compelled by the state to get a higher education, and some would-be students are turned away or do not qualify. So even if we *could* identify such reasons, they are unlikely to take us very far before running afoul of an unfair distribution of benefits and burdens.

Let us take on both of these limitations by first setting out how exactly it is that autonomy-based reasons could motivate public funding for higher education *at all*. Then we can see *how far* these kinds of reasons can take us before they run into the problem of distributive unfairness.

First, higher education goods do not simply support a person's access to desired jobs but the realization of self-directed goals, more generally. Higher education does this by providing students with knowledge, understanding, and skills that make certain self-directed goals more achievable. Think, for example, of those who take up a university education relatively late in life because they want to take their life in a different direction. On this view, higher education is essential to at least some people's free pursuit of the good life. Second, we can claim that everyone benefits from a society in which a person's pursuit of their self-directed goals is not arbitrarily constrained by a lack of economic resources. An education for personal autonomy is essential to the presumptive good of a society characterized by *equal* freedom, so autonomy-grounds for public funding can also be reasons of justice.

Now envisage a scenario where those who choose a higher education are deemed fully responsible for the upfront costs. We can quickly see why some public funding would be warranted. Many people would be unable to realize their self-determined goals for the morally arbitrary reason that they do not have the resources to pay these up-front costs. Therefore, autonomy-based reasons justify at least *some* public funding.

What about students from middle-class families? These students and families lack the resources to cover the up-front costs of attending, but they have relatively more resources than others in society, and as such they are already in a better position to exercise their basic liberties in the pursuit of the good life. They have the money, the cultural capital, and the leisure time to exercise personal autonomy in directions that many others do not. But an unjust constraint on autonomy would remain. There are certain options in life that may only be accessible through some form of post-compulsory education, and the fact that a person is not rich *enough* to merit public funding should not get in the way of their pursuit of such options. One might propose a by-now familiar solution: these individuals can borrow the money from the public and pay it back after graduation.

This line of reasoning puts autonomy-based arguments for public funding in roughly the same place as arguments grounded in socioeconomic mobility, and it does not bode well for my claim that educational aims have differential impacts on distributive fairness. Perhaps every justice-promoting, higher educational aim converges on the same distributive arrangement. This is not the last word, however, because the argument from personal autonomy adds a perspective on benefits and burdens that the socioeconomic argument misses.

First, consider the consequences of debt-financing for autonomy. Suppose higher education is free for the individual, and I choose to study creative writing. I have no realistic expectation of making very much money from my writing, but I don't mind. I will probably have to pick up casual employment after graduation. It is unfortunate that my personal goals are not likely to be financially rewarding, but it is not unjust. I will be doing what I want with my life, and I will do so without taking on burdens beyond those I am willing to accept as part of that life.

But now suppose my higher education must be debt-financed. Now I must decide whether a creative writing degree is an investment that will enable me to pay off the debt that I anticipate on graduation. The prospect of this debt imposes a significant constraint on my goals. I must be mindful of my repayment obligations. I might fail to meet my debt obligation. And the consequences of this failure, such as accumulating interest and being saddled with a lower credit rating, will undermine many of the other goals that I might have in view. I am therefore inclined to judge that I would be better off pursuing a more lucrative program of study, if I pursue study at all.

The constraints on personal autonomy imposed by debt financing are profoundly different from those brought about through our own, freely undertaken choices about the kind of life we want to live. We have a degree of control over the latter. We can recognize that different choices bring different mixes of costs and benefits, and we can accept responsibility for the mix we choose. But borrowing incurs a hardship that impacts on *all of our other choices*. That is to say, the spectre of a significant debt repayment forces the borrower to assess their goals primarily with a view to their economic consequences for many other spheres of life. Compare this with the situation of those who make the same educational decisions free of debt: higher education supports the autonomy of these people more effectively than others for the morally arbitrary reason that they can leave the institution without being followed by choice-constraining debt.

Recall that upfront costs frustrate higher education's efforts at socioeconomic equality by closing off valuable opportunities to those with little or no resources. This is unjust, and so it is reasonable to obligate the public to fund some places and permit loans for others. But loans also frustrate higher education's efforts by subverting its autonomy-promoting value for those that lack the resources to pay up front. This is unjust, and so it is reasonable to obligate the public to fund places for both lower-class *and* at least some middle-class students. For example, a student who would not qualify for student loans on socioeconomic grounds might qualify for funding on autonomy grounds for the reason that the borrowing they will have to engage in to access the system would unjustly constrain their range of options.

Full Public Funding for Higher Education and Distributive Fairness

In the last section, I used the example of personal autonomy to show how arguments about the aims of higher education can broaden our understanding of the cooperative scheme of higher education and, in so doing, disclose reasons regarding "who should pay" that differ from – and in some cases may justify public funding beyond – what is warranted by the view that higher education's core purpose is fair socioeconomic mobility.

However, there is a significant threshold that the argument from educational aims has yet to cross: could such an account, either from personal autonomy or socioeconomic mobility or some other aim, ever justify higher education as a *universal benefit*?[9] That is, could such an aim ever justify full public funding with no cost for the individual? For it to be reasonable to expect everyone (i.e., the public) to pay, higher education must have an aim that benefits every individual. It must be a cooperative scheme closer to compulsory schooling or health care (in Canada), where the public bears the full burden of funding (or overwhelming majority of it).

Before getting to the question of aims, we need to find out what distributive conditions would have to be satisfied in order to avoid the charge of distributive unfairness. This is because a funding model for higher education that is destined to be crassly unequal in terms of the benefits that it provides and the burdens that it imposes, no matter the aim, would bring considerable doubt to the idea that higher education can be plausibly understood as a universal benefit. It would lead us to suspect, perhaps rightly, that the stated aim is simply there to function as a *post hoc* justification for a distributively unfair policy.

We can distinguish between two versions of these distributive conditions. One version says that the distribution must benefit each individual member of the society by putting goods or resources directly into everyone's pocket (a child tax benefit, for example). We can see how this way of thinking about distribution is a prima facie obstacle to regarding higher education as a universal benefit: people are free not to attend, and so asking them to carry the burden of full public funding would be unreasonable. We could never satisfy such a condition unless we forced everyone to receive a higher education.

But we can also say that a distribution can benefit people by ensuring that there is a pool of resources available for them *should the need for those goods arise*. In fact, knowing that such a pool of resources is there for me to dip into if I need to is itself a benefit, even if I am not actually availing myself of those resources. A social insurance scheme is a good example. I pay into an employment insurance scheme even when I may never come to require the benefits that the scheme makes available. But the fact that the benefit is there to claim, should I need it, militates against the claim that those who are legitimately in need of employment insurance are benefitting unfairly.

Perhaps we could think of higher education in similar terms. From a universal benefits perspective, this would mean that higher education provides goods that any adult should be free to avail themselves of when they judge that they can benefit from them.

Consider by contrast a conception of higher education focused on fair access to socioeconomic opportunities. As we have already seen, full public funding of such a system is very much open to the charge of distributive unfairness. And for good reason. Even when the availability of such opportunities satisfies commonly recognized requirements of fair equality of opportunity, many of the people forced to contribute to the funding of such opportunities are also excluded from the individual benefits those opportunities confer.

First, these people may be deemed not to merit the receipt of those benefits because they lack the requisite talent. But there is a second form of exclusion to consider. Some may not opt to access a higher education because they do not desire it. One way to account for this lack of desire is that such people have no appreciation of a formal education beyond what they are required to undertake. Explanations of this kind are superficial at best. At least part of the reason that some people do not desire a higher education is because the opportunities it provides do not fit with their self-directed goals. They are excluded, either unintentionally or by design, because the cooperative scheme of higher education is structured in such a way that these people will *not* desire a higher education, not because they do not desire educational goods in general.[10]

Imagine a health insurance scheme where everyone must pay in, but you can only make an insurance claim if you were hurt while participating in professional sports. The majority would not be able to claim such benefits because they do not have the talent to become a professional athlete, and while all people can benefit from free health care few may desire to be professional athletes. It is obvious that a "ProCare" insurance scheme of this kind would be unfair from a distributive point of view. Similarly, a fully funded system of higher education that excluded many who pay into it on the grounds that they do not "deserve" access, or because the nature of the benefit only applies to those who value further education for a fairly narrow set of goals, looks to be little different.

In order for a higher education fully funded by the public to avoid the problem of unequal benefits – in order to for it to be less like ProCare – it would need to satisfy two additional distributive criteria *alongside* full public funding.

First, higher education should be *non-exclusive*. It may not prevent people from accessing that system on the grounds that they are insufficiently talented. To deny access to higher education goods, at least as universal benefit, would be the equivalent of requiring people to *become* professional athletes in order to benefit from a health care scheme that they are required to pay into. Second, it should support *a broad range* of self-directed goals suitable for people in a plural liberal society with diverse talents, interests, and at various stages of life. To deny access to higher education goods on these grounds would be the equivalent of requiring them to have an *interest* in professional athletics in order to benefit from a health care scheme that they are required to pay into.

With these distributive conditions in view, we can now return to the question of aims. What educational aim or purpose could justify a higher education system that aspires to satisfy such conditions? In what follows I argue that personal autonomy is an educational aim *compatible* with allocating higher education as a universal benefit. But I stress that I am not arguing (here)[11] that this aim supplies the most favorable grounds for the justification of this benefit. There is a difference between the claim that frustrating a person's pursuit of their self-determined goals on economic grounds is arbitrary and unjust (as I argued in the last section) and the claim that every single person ought to have their pursuit of self-determined goals supported by a system of higher education. But let us assume that the aim justifies the entitlement, all the same. Relevant to our purposes is how an educational aim should align, conceptually, with the fair distributive conditions to which a fully funded model of higher education would need to conform.

First, *non-exclusion* on grounds of talent is compatible with an education for personal autonomy. There is nothing in the concept of an education aimed at helping people to facilitate their goals that requires admission on the basis of talent. To be sure, a university could decide who can attend based on a judgement about whether or not someone is able to benefit from what that the university has to offer. But the judgement that a person is not ready to benefit from a particular educational pathway does not justify (or require) their exclusion from higher education goods across the board.

Second, *a broad range of self-directed goals* is also compatible with an education for personal autonomy. Unlike children receiving a basic education, adults are in a position to specify (and take responsibility for) their educational goals. A higher education devoted to the promotion of autonomy would therefore have to organize the transmission of knowledge, understanding, and skill in a manner that facilitates a variety of self-determined goals for people at different stages of adult life. It would need to be as open to the high school graduate as it would be to the retired senior, and support people who have revised, or wish to radically alter, one or more of their self-determined goals.

These three distributive conditions (non-exclusivity; support for diverse conceptions of the good; costless for the individual) must all be met for all people to have access to higher education as a universal benefit and to counter the charge that it would involve an unfair distribution of benefits and burdens. These distributive criteria also align with autonomy as an aim of higher education. A higher education for personal autonomy does not necessitate exclusion on grounds of talent, different conceptions of the good,[12] or a lack of economic resources. I take this to be no coincidence: educational institutions should aim to facilitate free and equal people's pursuit of the good life and combat morally arbitrary constraints on that pursuit.[13]

Finally, while we can assess the nature and scope of distributive fairness as it pertains to a cooperative scheme of higher education taken by itself, we should keep in mind that higher education plays but a part within a much broader cooperative scheme: that of a free, open, and fair political community. Other institutions such as health care and the legal system also play an important role in this broader scheme, and so any analysis of the question 'who should pay for higher education' will eventually have to take into account the funding of these other institutions, as well. Of course, in a world of unlimited economic growth and resources one could imagine that every sufficiently important institution could be fully funded by the state. However, it is important to remember that debates about distributive fairness proceed under assumed[14] conditions of relative scarcity. Therefore, the higher education funding debate will also need to account for the priority and importance of higher education in people's lives relative to other institutions, and this will require some further thinking about the social vision of society at which these institutions ought to aim.

Conclusion

Understanding the nature of higher education as a cooperative scheme is a necessary antecedent to determining who should pay and who should benefit. To be sure, the aims of higher education as conventionally understood – socioeconomic mobility in particular – might well be the best account of this scheme. Here we have in view a certain optimal mix of private individual and public financing. But we can also think of social mobility as but one of a number of self-determined goals that higher education institutions should be responsible for supporting. Here we can admit reasons why it is desirable for students to graduate without significant debt, and this may warrant greater public funding than the socioeconomic view does. Finally, we can structure higher education provision as a universal benefit where the public ought to pay the full costs, provided that certain distributive values are satisfied. The key to this, however, is an educational aim or aims that warrant viewing higher education as a universal benefit to begin with. Personal autonomy could be one such aim, and it has the advantage of aligning with what political philosophers have argued is central to education in a free and open society more generally.

(Related Chapters: 15, 20, 21, 23, 25.)

Notes

1 We can make many further distinctions within the public/private spheres. I have elsewhere argued that the state has grounds for taxing larger corporations in particular and using those resources to fund access to a higher education, to the extent that higher education qualifications provide a valuable signal to employers about where they can find labor. For the purposes of this chapter, we can include corporate taxation as part of the larger stock of public resources that would be (re)allocated to higher education systems. See Martin (2019).
2 Economists refer to these as "positive externalities" of higher education. For an overview of economic arguments for state support of higher education see Toutkoushian and Shafiq (2010).
3 Sections of this chapter are adapted from Martin (2021), Chapter Six.
4 In this chapter I focus on higher education as a cooperative scheme. However, we can understand higher education as part of a larger cooperative scheme of basic institutions within a liberal society writ large, with institutions having distinct functions or purposes, which together work to promote liberal aims and values. For example, educational institutions should play a key role in cultivating certain norms, skills, and dispositions. But the legal system and health care system have equally important, but also distinctive, roles to play. The philosopher John Rawls referred to this range of institutions as "the basic structure." For an account of the basic structure that has influenced my analysis of higher education see Hodgson (2012).
5 As many feminist scholars have pointed out, the family is not exempt from questions of political justice. See Okin (2015) and Schouten (2017).
6 See Curren (2017) who argues that a growing reliance on a hierarchical, credential-conferring system of education responsible for providing meaningful opportunities may "bend the arc of opportunity" away from justice. See also McCowan (2015) for an account of the nature (and limits) of employability as an aim of higher education.
7 See David O'Brien (forthcoming) for an analysis of the potential nature and limits of such an aim.
8 The particular conception of personal autonomy – that is, what an autonomous life must consist in for it to *be* an autonomous one – can differ between these various accounts. For example, some philosophers define autonomy in terms of "procedural-independence," in which it is sufficient for autonomy that a person is able to independently and freely reflect and decide on different values and goals. Other accounts emphasize tolerance of different ways of life. The Razian conception that I proffer further requires that the person have access to a range of options from which to choose, to be able to participate successfully in the social forms and practices that define these goals, and that those options be valuable in an objective sense. See also Curren (2009) on the connection between the right to education and human flourishing.
9 The fact that a good could be fairly allocated like a universal benefit does not necessarily mean that people have a right to that good. People might vote for a political party that makes the allocation of a good a universal benefit as a matter of social policy, even if there is no prior right to that good. However, in Martin (2021) I make a stronger claim: that higher education is indeed a right. On this account, access to educational goods over a life is key to a political conception of the person understood as free and equal and is therefore owed to all as a matter of basic political justice. Higher education is here understood as the institution, broadly conceived, responsible for the provision of such educational goods across adulthood. In this chapter, I focus on the distributive conditions of higher education that would have to be satisfied if it is to be fairly allocated as a universal benefit. But these distributive conditions would also apply in the context of a right to higher education.
10 See Voigt (2017).
11 See Martin (2021).
12 Anti-perfectionist liberals might object that a higher education structured around personal autonomy would exclude conceptions of the good that do not take self-determined goals to be essential to their flourishing. Rebutting this argument would go beyond the scope of this chapter, but see Martin (2018).
13 For a more detailed justification of this approach to thinking about basic institutions see Chapter Four of *The Right to Higher Education* (Martin 2021).
14 I say "assumed" because the claim that federal and state/provincial budgets cannot afford to fully fund certain key institutions warrants careful scrutiny. For example, the defense budget of the United States may well cover the public funding of higher education several times over.

References

Brighouse, H. (1998) "Civic Education and Liberal Legitimacy," *Ethics* 108(4): 719–745.
Brighouse, H. (2004) "Paying for Higher Education: Are Top-up Fees Fair?" *Éthique et Économique* 2(1): 1–11.
Curren, R. (2009) "Education as a Social Right in a Diverse Society," *Journal of Philosophy of Education* 43(1): 45–56.

Curren, R. (2017) "On the Arc of Opportunity: Education, Credentialism, and Employment," in K. Schaff (ed.) *Fair Work: Ethics, Social Policy, Globalization*. London: Rowman & Littlefield International, 59–77.
Hodgson, L. P. (2012) "Why the Basic Structure?" *Canadian Journal of Philosophy* 42(3–4): 303–334.
Klosko, G. (1987) "Presumptive Benefit, Fairness, and Political Obligation," *Philosophy & Public Affairs* 16(3): 241–259.
Klosko, G. (1990) "The Obligation to Contribute to Discretionary Public Goods," *Political Studies* 38(2): 196–214.
McCowan, T. (2015) "Should Universities Promote Employability?" *Theory and Research in Education* 13(3): 267–285.
Martin. C. (2018) "Political Authority, Personal Autonomy and Higher Education," *Philosophical Inquiry in Education* 25(2): 154–170.
Martin, C. (2019) "The Case Against (Actually Existing) Higher Education: Human Capital, Educational Signalling, and Justice," *On Education. Journal for Research and Debate* 2(6), https://www.oneducation.net/no-06_december-2019/the-case-against-actually-existing-higher-education-human-capital-educational-signaling-and-justice/
Martin, C. (2021) *The Right to Higher Education: A Political Theory*. Oxford: Oxford University Press.
O'Brien, D. (forthcoming) "How far can Political Liberalism Support Reforms in Higher Education?" *Social Theory and Practice*.
Okin, S. M. (2015) *Justice, Gender, and the Family*. London: Routledge.
Raz, J. (1986) *The Morality of Freedom*. Oxford: Clarendon Press.
Sen, A. (1980) "Equality of What?" in S. McMurrin (ed.) *Tanner Lectures on Human Values, Vol. 1*. Cambridge: Cambridge University Press, 197–220.
Schouten, G. (2017) "Citizenship, Reciprocity, and the Gendered Division of Labor: A Stability Argument for Gender Egalitarian Political Interventions," *Politics, Philosophy & Economics* 16(2): 174–209.
Schouten, G. (2018) "Political Liberalism and Autonomy Education: Are Citizenship-based Arguments Enough?" *Philosophical Studies* 175(5): 1071–1093.
Toutkoushian, R. K., & Shafiq, M. N. (2010) "A Conceptual Analysis of State Support for Higher Education: Appropriations versus Need-based Financial Aid," *Research in Higher Education* 51(1): 40–64.
Trow, M. (1973) *Problems in the Transition from Elite to Mass Higher Education*. Berkeley, CA: Carnegie Commission on Higher Education.
Voigt, K. (2017) "Distributive Equality, Relational Equality and Preferences about Higher Education," *Theory and Research in Education* 15(2): 109–128.
White, J. (1990) *Education and the Good Life: Beyond the National Curriculum*. London: Kogan Page.

25

TOWARD A POST-PANDEMIC HIGHER EDUCATION SYSTEM

Ariel C. Armony and Ann E. Cudd[1]

In early March 2020, in response to the rapidly spreading coronavirus, the University of Pittsburgh decided to upend the normal course of the semester by ending on-campus, in-person teaching and closing our dormitories. We prepared to lockdown all our campus buildings and shutter our research labs within three days. Similar decisions took place at every university, college, and community college in the country. We did not know then, and a year-and-a-half later we still did not know, when and under what conditions we would fully return to our campuses. We were forced to change plans often based on limited information and rapidly changing conditions. But a year into the pandemic we knew that there had been massive losses in terms of life, jobs, financial security, research, and that nothing would ever be the same in higher education.

With a new perspective gleaned from loss and physical distance, we also saw more clearly the things that were utterly erroneous about what we had been doing in higher education prior to the pandemic, as well as how absolutely central education – including higher education – is to modern civic life. Several of the wrongs had been obvious for many years: systemic racism, structural impediments to career advancement for faculty and staff, a weak commitment by universities to invest in the well-being and inclusive economic development of their communities, and unequal access to technology for minorities and other underserved members of the university community, among other injustices. As we muddled through the pandemic and tried to visualize the end of the global disease, we began to see opportunities for change in a new light.

In this chapter, we explore the fundamental tensions that we face in our work as educators and researchers and ask how higher education should transform itself to right the wrongs that we, as leaders and faculty in institutions of higher learning in the United States, have been complicit in and that have been laid bare by the crisis brought about by COVID-19. Attention will be paid to the role of technology, which has acquired a central place in education.

Three Tensions

Above everything else, the loss of lives has been a common denominator of these times. It has touched every single member of our communities, locally and globally. There has been an epidemic of loneliness, anxiety, and mental illness. Staff, particularly front-line workers who kept universities running, endured angst, uncertainty, and job insecurity. Faculty put in enormous, time-consuming, anxiety-ridden efforts to transform their pedagogy with varying degrees of support and success. Jobs became more precarious, and institutional budget cuts were demoralizing. Many colleges and

 DOI: 10.4324/9781003172246-29

universities faced declining enrollments, teetering on the brink of financial collapse. Students complained about having to pay for a lower quality education and some even sued institutions for lower tuition and fees. At the same time, rising costs associated with technology, workplace health protection, and other requirements deepened financial hardship and uncertainty.

Trust in leadership flagged. Presidents and provosts were retiring, resigning, or being fired in much greater numbers than before the pandemic. Public trust in educational institutions, already slumping prior to the pandemic, continued a downward trend. According to a 2021 Pew Research Center survey, 57% of adults in the United States believed that colleges and universities had a positive effect on the country's situation, a 12-point decrease compared to 2015 (Van Green 2021). Public perception of colleges and universities as detached from society deepened as many Americans believed that institutions of higher education were worried only about revenues and were sacrificing the health of students, faculty, and the communities they resided in to preserve their own financial well-being. Forty percent of interviewees in a 2021 survey by the Association of American Colleges and Universities and the Bipartisan Policy Center expressed doubts about the real value of a college degree (Burt 2021). A survey of US college and university presidents revealed that 82% of leaders in higher education agreed that most Americans do not have "an accurate view of the purpose of higher education in general" and 73% of those interviewed stated that this view has been shaped by a perception that the institutions' priorities – for instance, investment in amenities to attract students – are misplaced (Inside Higher Ed 2021).

In these difficult times, we have learned – by necessity and through painful experiences – some important lessons that are shaping the future of higher education. There is increasing realization that gender, racial, and other disparities are systemic in the way we have configured the academic enterprise and how we conduct research. Universities now face the monumental task of dismantling long-standing structures that impose an unfair burden on minorities that hinder their careers and professional success.

The pandemic also exposed serious vulnerabilities in our risk, health, and safety infrastructures. Many universities were slow to react to the key signs of the COVID-19 pandemic, a disease exacerbated by globalized transportation and the unparalleled mobility of people around the world. Important gaps in coordination and communication slowed down decision making in the onset of the pandemic.

Still, we learned that institutions of higher education, as they were forced to react for their own survival, showed a high level of resilience, flexibility, and creativity. Many colleges and universities exhibited a moral commitment to protect vulnerable employees and students, expanding their efforts to keep people safe and preserve their jobs even when they could not do any useful work during lockdown. Institutions created funding mechanisms to support graduate students, international students, and others in need. Faculty demonstrated that they could pivot rapidly and completely to remote teaching. The demand to confront a new reality in the workplace sparked a groundbreaking debate on the competencies that students needed to advance "a human-centered agenda for the future of work, with increasing investments in people's capabilities, in the institutions of work ... and in decent and sustainable work" (Dede 2020: 11).

In many respects, we now are better equipped to ask questions that can guide a serious conversation about the future of higher education. On one hand, we ought to rethink higher education when considering technology, costs, and maximization of access. On the other hand, we must reorient debates on how universities should train students for the future of work and to be effective and engaged citizens, and how our institutions can lessen inequalities on campus and in communities. This agenda requires crafting a new vision that redefines the proposed value of higher education.

These challenges point to three fundamental tensions that map out the landscape of higher education in the 21st century. One is a tension between embracing competition and elite education for the most talented against creating more equality through emphasizing access to education – meritocracy versus democratization of education. A second tension is between free speech for all to openly debate and express their views with the opposing view that universities must provide safe spaces, where minorities are protected from the insults and threats from majority students and faculty and where they can enjoy their culture as dominant. A third tension is between the university as an ivory tower with its own separate norms and values versus the university as a shared social institution for the common good. This tension also speaks about the university as a place-based institution committed to its local community and the university as a global enterprise that extends its reach beyond national borders.

These tensions share some common elements, which involve questions about lifelong learning, the relationship between universities and employers, and the role of institutions of higher education beyond their campuses. The promises and perils of technology is also a theme that permeates all three tensions in ways that were not so evident prior to the pandemic. These tensions expose deep fault lines that require concerted actions not only from administrators, but also from faculty, students, staff, and members of the communities that are home to our institutions. These tensions and, to an important extent the contradictions embedded in these tensions, cannot be resolved by simply choosing a single alternative. The challenge is to find new, creative, unconventional ways to capitalize on the innovative power of higher education.

Elite Education and Equality through Access

Higher education is an ecosystem with several levels of access and opportunity. These levels have been rigidly separated in the past. At the lowest, entry level there are two-year community colleges easily accessible by virtually anyone who can pay the low fee for a course or a term. In the middle, regional and state colleges and universities that teach masses of students in four-year degree programs, accessible by students who took a college prep curriculum in high school and who can afford tuition that roughly equates to buying a nice car over four years, as well as room and board. At the top are the elite research universities that are selective and allow only elite students, often the most affluent and White, to enter, but are frequently made affordable with scholarships for the low-income students who are selected. For the most part, these latter types of institutions have been designed with a traditional age range, 18–24-year-old students, in mind. While the higher education ecosystem has expanded somewhat with for-profit colleges and online programs, these have almost exclusively been marketed towards non-traditionally aged, adult learners or learners who did not have the credentials to access a traditional four-year institution.

The rapid adoption of technology as was needed by the COVID-19 pandemic has unleashed a new ecosystem of higher learning with the potential to expand and diversify. Because of the newfound capacity for online education, even traditional campuses can expand geographically, as students choose to study remotely around the world and faculty likewise can choose to teach and collaborate with colleagues from distant locations. The growth of online education can make college much more accessible in response to growing demand, the allure of increased revenue, and the ever-increasing ability to automate and scale aspects of teaching. This transformation can create greater access to elite education, which will open many doors of opportunity for learners of all ages and abilities.

Today's marketplace requires significant investments on the part of universities to incorporate advances in AI, virtual reality, robotics, learning analytics, digital badging, and blockchain. While technology may offer the ability to automate and scale aspects of teaching – expanding access to education by reducing costs while maintaining instructional quality – there are still some key limitations.

First, designing digital material and training professors to effectively deliver it is costly, and many institutions are not able to adequately do either. Richer colleges and universities may be able to take advantage of blended teaching and thus incorporate innovative pedagogical approaches in tandem with digital tools and platforms, while maintaining traditional courses and supporting in person interactions between professors and students. This hybrid approach can more effectively use class time and help prepare students for engagement and participation, but financially it may be unavailable to institutions with scant resources. Few of the institutions already at a high market risk have the capital required to finance the investment in an online teaching modality. As a result, technology could be helping to increase existing gaps in higher education, rather than the opposite, reinforcing a "winner's market" in which wealthy institutions get wealthier and large institutions get larger, specifically four-year public and four-year private non-for-profit colleges and universities, while two-year community colleges and four-year private for-profit institutions suffer significant losses in enrollment (Kim 2018; Zemsky et al. 2020).

Second, the expansion of access through educational technology does not guarantee the democratization of high-quality education. Institutions of higher education continue to struggle with determining how meritocratic or egalitarian access to education should be. The global demand for creative workers with advanced cognitive competencies to process information and symbols has increased the competition among universities to attract the most talented from around the globe. The transformation of the work environment drives corporations to focus on acquiring, developing, and retaining creative workers, and universities are major sources of such talent. As such, they are expected not only to provide their graduates with the set of competencies required to join a "new creative class," but also to devise strategies to cluster innovation and create an ecosystem that attracts the best doers and thinkers from around the world (Haskel & Westlake 2017; Anderson et al. 2015; Florida 2006).

The ensuing competition has resulted in an increasingly selective process and less equitable access to higher education as those coming from higher income brackets typically have greater access to the educational resources that prepare and position them as a part of this aspiring creative class. A report in 2017 found that, in the U.S., "children whose parents are in the top 1% of the income distribution are 77 times more likely to attend an Ivy League college than those whose parents are in the bottom income quintile" (Chetty et al. 2017). Moreover, while in 1992 "there were 20 colleges that admitted fewer than one-third of applicants ... today there are 75 to 80. There were two colleges that admitted fewer than 20%, and today that number is closer to 40" (Jaschik 2021).

This runs counter to the stated aims of universities to expand educational access to include minorities and underserved populations, not only to attract talent but also to train and produce talent from those with varied backgrounds, providing mobility for individuals from lower income brackets. For instance, while the percentage of immigrant-origin students enrolled in US institutions of higher education represented nearly 30% in 2018, a ten-point increase from 2000, "they are likely to face barriers and limits on resources that many other students do not" (Jordan 2020; see Batalova & Feldblum 2020). The tension between the democratization of an elite education through increased access to instruction and the need to preserve rigor, high quality and continuous innovation is central to the future of higher education (Hughes 2021). If diversity is celebrated as an important goal, the competition for top talent will often frustrate this aim. It is also important to consider that "access alone is not enough for fostering inclusion and generating mobility," as Anthony A. Jack argued (2019: 22). Lower-income students may be given access to elite institutions, but policies and practices at these institutions often fail them – these are the new "privileged poor" in US higher education (Jack 2019).

Third, institutions must address questions regarding the equitable use of technology for different groups, how technology may reinforce unequal opportunities, how technology will impact disadvantaged groups of the campus community, and how this reflects the institution's view on the role of technology in society more broadly. Technologies are not neutral instruments, not just in terms of their use and impact, but also because of their very design (Papendieck 2018). While educational technologies are adopted as tools to fulfil goals that advance social goods, such as expanding access to education, adopters need to understand that such technologies "black-box sociopolitical assumptions and agendas, and smuggle dominant ways of knowing, understanding the world into classrooms" (Latour 1987, as cited in Papendieck 2018). Contrary to the "techno-idealistic" assumption that technology necessarily improves society – for instance, by democratizing education – technology may in fact exclude and marginalize disadvantaged groups, by deepening existing inequalities and mechanisms of oppression as well as by creating new inequities and reinforcing and/or reproducing existing power structures (Papendieck 2018). "Even where discrimination is not intended," the Office of the UN High Commissioner for Human Rights argues, "indirect discrimination can result from using innocuous and genuinely relevant criteria that also operate as proxies for race and ethnicity." Furthermore, "the use of and reliance on predictive models that incorporate historical data – data often reflecting discriminatory biases and inaccurate profiling – including in contexts such as law enforcement, national security and immigration" reproduce patterns of discrimination and exclusion (OHCHR 2020).

As institutions address the tension between elite education and expanded access, they must engage in new conversations around the potential of technologies to advance goals of equity and social justice. This is a potentially transformative agenda. Institutions of higher education can influence how technology is designed, how it interacts with society, and what impact it has on marginalized communities and other vulnerable groups. Also, expanded access to digital knowledge can empower university students to support their community, facilitating the positioning of underserved populations in the dynamics of the technological phenomenon as agents of change and not only as spectators, through practices of digital solidarity. These practices can involve digital literacy initiatives and the development of applications, programs, and software based on diverse worldviews and cultural heritages.

The adoption of technology to expand access to education does not have to be shaped by the dichotomy elitism/democratization if colleges and universities acknowledge the embedded inequities of the exclusionary design of digital products and virtual environments. Institutions of higher education are uniquely positioned to reinvent the interactions that we create with technology, advancing a new paradigm that recognizes and values the range of human experience and backgrounds (Jeffrey & Jimenez 2021). As the labor market demand for diversely-skilled workers grows, technology-enhanced learning should be implemented equitably to benefit all – beginning with the most marginalized and excluded populations. An inclusive agenda can leverage technology to personalize education, enhance college readiness, and create pathways for retraining and new skill acquisition, thereby narrowing socio-economic, gender, ethnic, racial, and other achievement gaps.

Free Speech and Safe Spaces

A second tension speaks about one of the most contentious dimensions in higher education, namely, the tension between the university as a place where free speech for all is secured and, at the same time, where under-represented groups are safeguarded from threats, harm, and aggression and have their own spaces where they can express their own shared culture. This tension has become compounded by the recent eruption of racial conflicts and a drastic loss of trust in our government, political and social divisions, and a poisonous climate of incivility, xenophobia, and toxic masculinity.

It has been argued that the tension between free speech and protection of minorities can be resolved by making campuses "safe enough" for members of the university community to feel empowered to leave their comfort zones and hear viewpoints they did not anticipate hearing (Roth 2019). This requires creating a place "where students know that, if they espouse unpopular views, they will not be attacked, that there will be no reprisals" and where it is possible "to explore difference, to have one's ways of thinking tested – not just protected" (Roth 2019: 103, 124).

Colleges and universities have taken increasingly activist approaches to eradicating expressions of discrimination and hate – in large part because of changing demographics and a much stronger demand from minority students for university leadership to address the issue (Nossel 2018; Cudd 2019). College students support free speech on their campuses, while they think that the rights and concerns of minorities against speech deemed threatening should not be ignored. A 2020 poll by Gallup found that "close to 7 in 10 college students (68%) regard citizens' free speech rights as being 'extremely important' to democracy. Nearly the same percentage (69%) believe an inclusive society that is welcoming to diverse groups is 'extremely important.'" Students do not support curbing controversial speech as "nearly three-quarters believe colleges should not be able to restrict expression of political views that are upsetting or offensive to certain groups" (Gallup 2021). Still, there is significant support for actions that foster a strong sense of belonging. As Gallup's 2020 survey showed, "78% of college students favor colleges providing safe spaces, or areas of campus that are designed to be free from threatening actions, ideas or conversations" (Gallup 2021).

Studies on the synergies between diversity and innovation stress the imperative to create an environment where minority views can be expressed and given due consideration. Otherwise, diversity may lead to lower levels of cohesiveness, trust, and communication. If group members do not feel psychologically safe to express their viewpoints, or if conflict is poorly managed, creativity is often hampered, and innovative outcomes are less likely to emerge (Bassett-Jones 2005; Phillips et al. 2014; Kurtzberg 2005; Post et al. 2009; Paulus & Dzindolet 2008). In higher education, synergies between diversity and innovation benefit students in numerous ways, including engaging them in higher forms of cognitive learning such as critical thinking and problem-solving, deepening their conceptual competencies, and providing opportunities to learn from dynamic creative processes (Sharif 2019). In particular, the process of creativity is nurtured by environments that involve "diversity, openness, mutual respect, and communication" (Glăveanu & Clapp 2018: 54). On one hand, the diversity of cultural experiences nurtures creativity "by diversifying the range of experiences possible for both self and others" (54). On the other hand, a creativity that acknowledges people and their context requires understanding one's own positionality within a system, making an honest conversation about issues of power an essential one whenever alterity and diversity are also being discussed (Glăveanu & Clapp 2018).

Some have argued that university campuses should be treated as "unregulated markets" of ideas. However, an unregulated market approach tolerates injury and insult, and it is likely to harm historically marginalized and vulnerable groups (Roth 2019: 99). In recent years, university campuses have been important battlegrounds in the contentious debate over whether to allow all sorts of speech, even if the espoused views counter university aims of inclusion and diversity.[2] The ACLU (2021), for instance, has adopted the position that "speech that deeply offends our morality or is hostile to our way of life warrants the same constitutional protection as other speech because the right of free speech is indivisible" and "historically, restrictions on speech have proven at best ineffective, and at worst counter-productive, in the fight against bigotry." The ACLU's position does not neglect the interests of groups that have been historically vulnerable, but it emphasizes the importance of placing power in the hands of "those seeking to question or dismantle existing power structures" rather than in the hands of "authority figures – the government or a college administration" (ACLU 2021).

The complex relationship between learning and belonging lies at the heart of the tension between free speech and safe spaces. This relationship also matters as we seek to understand the experience of belonging in virtual learning environments, an important theme for further research. Higher education aims to develop "self-awareness, subtlety of thought, and openness to the possibility of learning from others" (Roth 2019: 8). However, if efforts are limited to highlighting the values of diversity and inclusion – mostly through rhetorical devices – the tension between learning and belonging cannot be properly addressed and we will fail to advance the mission of our institutions (Roth 2019). This points to the imperative of dismantling structures that sustain racial and other inequities in higher education. Addressing the question of belonging demands, for instance, an antiracist agenda. This is an agenda that requires identifying "racial inequity in all its intersections and manifestations" (in particular, policies causing racial injustice), dismantling assimilationist ideas, untying "the idea of a culture from the idea of behavior," and cultivating difference while underscoring the fact that "racial groups are equals in all the ways they are different" (Kendi 2019: 17–18, 28, 31, 95, 231).

An antiracist project in higher education should decolonize both the pedagogical and curricular framework that dominates most institutions of higher education in the United States. The necessary decolonization of knowledge is a daunting task because it requires action at the theoretical, epistemological, analytical, and methodological levels (de Sousa Santos 2021). This is an endeavor that requires identifying and dismantling "theories gleaned from European subjects masquerading as universal theories" (Kendi 2019: 167). It involves the "identification, reconstruction and validation" of knowledges deemed to be "non-scientific" that have been vital in struggles against colonialism and domination (de Sousa Santos 2021: 251). It is impossible to conceive the creation of safe spaces at colleges and universities, where encounters with diversities are effectively encouraged and protected, if the notion of "civilization" continues to define dominant paradigms and cultural difference is subject to long-established cognitive hierarchies (Roth 2019; Kendi 2019).

Eurocentric knowledge continues to underpin our cognitive hierarchies. The construction of Western "expertise" was intertwined with the colonial enterprise, which extracted local knowledge (for example, adopting indigenous agricultural practices) while asserting both intellectual and political domination. "The claim to invention, like the claim to discovery in the patent charters of colonial conquest, is the justification for the takeover of market systems and economic systems through globalized patent regimes," Vanda Shiva argued (2008: 274). The extraction and patenting of local people's traditional knowledge in drug development, agriculture, and other fields is well known. Therefore, decolonizing Western science involves questioning its colonial nature (such as the exploitation of cultures through the forceful and/or illicit appropriation of local knowledge), its patriarchal character (the devaluation of women's life and work), and the global mercantilization of labor and nature (de Sousa Santos 2021; see Deb Roy 2017, 2018).

Colleges and universities have nurtured spaces of intercultural dialogue not dominated by Eurocentric knowledge systems (de Sousa Santos 2021: 258). Programs on Black Studies, Chicano Studies, Indigenous Studies, Women's Studies, and Ethnic Studies founded in the United States in the 1960s and 1970s played a fundamental role in "the struggles for the recognition of cultural diversity." These struggles have "gradually destabilized epistemological and monocultural hegemony through the introduction of new problems and new types of epistemological approaches" (de Sousa Santos 2021: 251). Still, the efforts to advance cognitive justice face multiple obstacles from hidebound disciplinary traditions (de Sousa Santos 2021: 267, 282; Visvanathan 2021).

Another dimension of an antiracist project geared toward resolving the tension between free speech and safe spaces should prioritize the creation of culturally integrated spaces. Such spaces should emphasize the equality of difference and champion difference across diverse groups. This approach fuses, as Kendi (2019) proposes, "desegregation with a form of integration and racial solidarity" (180). Attaining new modes of solidarity is important to creating intersectional coalitions. Calls for general solidarity, however, cannot ignore nor diminish the concerns, interests, and demands of different diversities under the pretext that moving away from "narrow identities" of race and gender, for example, is beneficial for marginalized groups (Roth 2019: 108). Indeed, antiracism calls for both intersectional solidarity and group-specific recognition by demanding concerted efforts to eliminate "not only the hierarchy of races but of race-genders," as well as ethnic racism and other forms of systemic exclusion and discrimination (Kendi 2019: 63–64, 188–189).

Addressing social justice also involves several aspects related to technology, including digital equity, accessibility for students with disabilities, and targeted efforts to leverage educational technology to meet the needs of underprivileged students (see, for instance, Brown 2020). Attention must also be given to the expansion of surveillance capacity to respond to security breaches, and how it can impair the creation of safe spaces in colleges and universities. Also, because of the pandemic, "new tracking and surveillance technologies have flooded the campus securitization market, including access control systems that create 'a digital record of who accessed a space on a specific day or time' and 'robots and drones [that] ... can provide live video and bidirectional audio'" (Watkins 2020). How these technologies may be used disproportionally against minority groups is a rising concern. Members of these groups "are those most likely to be surveilled and stopped by campus officers," so the introduction of additional methods of control – prompted by the enforcement of "a host of new social distancing-related offenses," for example – is likely to negatively impact the creation of safe spaces on university campuses (Watkins 2020).[3]

In sum, institutions of higher education can resolve the tension between free speech and safe spaces, but there is a real danger of doing so in ways that segregate and divide if we are not careful and intentional. It is important to promote the institutional mission-centered case for diversity and education in cultural competency, followed by the argument for social justice, in order to build broad support and solidarity. Diversity benefits the knowledge creation and educational missions both by creating more and better ideas and discussions and by equipping students to interact successfully in a global, multicultural world. Education for cultural competency will inevitably involve creating empathy and understanding of difference. This will create allies among the majority and feelings of belonging among minorities. There will still be disagreement and even sometimes hurt feelings, but these are tolerable if one feels that one belongs in an accepting, inclusive environment that values diversity.

Ivory Tower versus Shared Social Institution

Finally, and connected to the resolution of the first two tensions, universities need to be of their communities and not tower above them if they are to lead positive transformative change. Our institutions need to engage and collaborate with the communities in which we live. First, we owe it to them for the support we get as non-profits, a status our institutions receive because we are working toward a common interest, not special interest. Second, this is the way to expand access to education for our local communities. Third, the feeling of belonging to a university community can only be enhanced if the community trusts the university and the university demonstrates accountability to the community. By collaborating with our local communities on questions of interest to them, and providing a space for community-university discussions, our faculty and students will expand the problem-solving and methodological approaches needed to address major challenges with local impact. Engaged scholarship will lead to better science and deeper scholarship about questions that matter, resulting in solutions that improve lives.

Institutions of higher education can play a key role in advancing the common good if they leverage their resources in a strategic manner and engage with the community in mutually beneficial ways. Universities can share resources, align with local economic development agendas through hiring, purchasing, and procurement, and provide the community real opportunities to influence and leverage the work of institutions of higher education. Universities are experimenting with new approaches to the science of learning (Brown, et al. 2014). The use of behavioral variables at the individual level and new inroads in cognitive science have significant potential to serve greater social equity. Universities can collaborate on grand challenges, particularly if they listen to communities, ask the right questions, and build teams endowed with cognitive diversity. Universities have the connections and networks to co-create solutions with their communities and address global imbalances.

Universities have the capacity to play a "place-based" role and help facilitate social justice, but only if they can successfully maximize the benefits of economic investments and opportunities for their communities, to ensure that under-resourced, vulnerable, and underserved populations do not continue to be left behind. The so-called civic university, whose purpose involves making a positive community impact, can act as a driver of more just, equal, and sustainable places (Goddard & Vallance 2013; UPP Foundation 2019). However, the view of the university as a social institution for the common good has been questioned, particularly by those who argue that the rise of the university as a corporate structure can create major roadblocks to socially just urban planning and the ability of cities to become places for more equitable economic and social outcomes. This is a major dimension of higher education's future agenda, as cities and their surrounding regions are being reimagined in the context of a post-pandemic era, a generalized crisis of representation, legacies of racism and colonialism, climate change, health disparities, and long-standing challenges in housing, food supply, and other basic needs.

The tension between the civic university and the corporate university involves the role that universities play in their places, for example, in cities impacted by de-industrialization. In the United States, many post-industrial cities have come to rely on their existing educational institutions as key economic drivers. Attracting the start-ups, incubators, and new talent to their cities was needed to help the cities and their surrounding regions to restart their economies following the collapse of their local economies. These cities are now considered crucibles of reinvention and innovation and, as the narrative goes, they have successfully navigated the sunsetting of industrial production and creatively reoriented to intellectual technology, advanced manufacturing, business services, and life science innovations. This is often known as the "eds and meds" model.

However, this narrative has come under heavy criticism considering protracted socioeconomic inequalities across racial and other cleavages in many cities. While universities, especially when situated in higher concentrations, often have a positive economic impact for their region, and even show spillover effects with neighboring regions, their role in advancing social justice – effectively working to promote more equitable growth in their communities – has become a focus of concern (Valero & Van Reenen 2019). For example, a study by Bloomberg CityLab found that "metros with at least one research university have considerably higher levels of income segregation than those with none. And income segregation is roughly 10% higher in metros with a research university that is ranked among the top 100 in the world" (Florida 2018).

Critics stress that institutions of higher education have significantly expanded their influence, becoming a powerful actor in urban governance. In major cities across the United States, the university is often the dominant employer, real estate holder, health-care provider, and even agent of policing (Baldwin 2021). In New York, Saint Louis, Phoenix, and other cities, universities have accumulated a significant degree of power, for example, by flouting or rewriting zoning laws (Baldwin 2021; see Day 2021). The physical expansion of universities results in higher housing costs and the displacement of lower-income residents. The investments made in constructing new campuses or expanding their urban footprint (such as Columbia University's Manhattanville campus) have resulted in rising prices and inequalities that force out many of the long term, often poorer, inhabitants from the community, replaced by tech startups and boutique stores catering to young professionals (Kensinger 2018). Critics have also noted that, in many cases, the university's claim to advance a social justice mission is in contradiction to the institution's position vis-à-vis demands by their employees for better working conditions and against austerity programs (Benneworth 2021).

The notion of the civic university speaks to both "a utilitarian ideal of mutually beneficial links between cities and universities" as well as "an ethical ideal of serving the cities in which universities are located and directly responding to the needs of local communities" (Todd et al. 2021: 147). Linking the utilitarian and ethical ideals requires universities to design strategies for engagement that address both the imperatives posed by today's knowledge economy – in which universities serve "as engines of 'smart growth,' driving the urban economy" – and their commitment to extend prosperity and wellbeing to their surrounding communities through access to affordable housing and health care, decent labor conditions, enhancement of energy efficiency systems, and democratization of arts and culture. This is further complicated in the case of global universities that have adopted the "city-as-campus model" in locations around the world where regulatory environments fail to protect the rights of the local, often migrant labor force (Baldwin 2021: 20–23; UPP Foundation 2019; Zilahy & Huisingh 2009).

Strengthening the connection between universities and their places brings up the question of the tension between the local and global, and whether a university that claims commitment to the needs of its local community and economy can embrace a global agenda, with an emphasis on addressing the demands of international students, devoting resources to public good projects in other countries, and partnering with businesses and other organizations around the world. While it is easy to make the case that universities can leverage their global networks and their capacity to attract global talent for the benefit of local economic development, it is also true that universities in the global North contribute to brain drain, exert a stark domination in the international research community, and often extend their global reach while failing to engage in activities that are locally relevant and responsive to local community and government goals (Branković et al, 2014; Yang 2003).

The benefits of educational technology are not equally distributed, locally and globally. Digital divides in US higher education are primarily driven by economic inequality, reinforcing a vicious cycle in which lesser-resourced colleges and universities struggle to support a digital enhanced learning environment. These are the very institutions serving poorer students, who experience significant obstacles to accessing online education (Alexander 2017). The global digital divide cannot be ignored either. A one-hour Zoom call in Malawi would cost nearly three times the cost in the United States, using mobile data, which represents almost a week's salary in that African country (Wilcox 2021). Universities in the United States and Europe could support public-private partnerships, encourage competition among internet providers, foster open access to the internet, partner to democratize "digital governance," and contribute to teaching digital skills to reduce gaps in access by social status, gender, and income level (Wilcox 2021; OHCHR 2020).

Universities can cooperate with governments and the private sector on initiatives oriented to addressing structural inequities in the digital technology domain, including the expansion of representation of racial, ethnic, and national groups in all aspects of decision-making, research, and knowledge production in the design and use of emerging digital technologies (OHCHR 2020). The magnitude of the global digital divide is especially relevant when we consider, for instance, that the future for Africa in the 21st century is inextricably linked to the continent's technological transformation of higher education, a requirement for inclusive development in a region where 60% of the population is below the age of 25. As Zeleza and Okanda (2021) put it, "The danger of remaining peripheral to the Fourth Industrial Revolution for Africa is not exploitation and marginalisation, but historical irrelevance ... becoming a landmass of disposable people." A truly global agenda of cooperation in higher education could not ignore the unprecedented opportunities for transformation that inclusive technological development could bring to the global South. This is part of an agenda that requires new alliances based on democratic access, a new ecology of knowledges, participatory methodologies and evaluation, and the creation of networks that reject cognitive and patriarchal colonialisms and respect differences across ways of knowing.

Conclusion

The tensions discussed in this essay are tied together by three common elements. One is the new reality of an integrated lifelong learning approach, what has been described as a conversion "from a lifetime career to a lifetime of careers" (Richards 2020: 143). Institutions of higher education are expected to meet the demand for a workforce with constant skill acquisition, reskilling, and upskilling to match the pace of technological advancements and organizational innovations. The new reality of "a lifetime of careers" involves training people how to learn in diverse environments and in multicultural teams. The fourth industrial revolution demands that workers be flexible, adaptable, creative, and have skills in metacognition, collaboration, global mindset, critical thinking, and an awareness of personal and social responsibility, while still being fluent in broader digital competencies (International Labour Organization 2021). This represents a momentous shift from an education-centered approach to one focused on learnability, conceived as a process that is continual and not linear. The key goal is to develop "the ability to learn" (Scott 2020; Infosys 2021). Digital environments, which allow learners to upskill at any time or place, and inclusionary institutions, which provide learners the opportunity to learn how to collaborate across and benefit intellectually from diverse perspectives, are integral components of this agenda.

A second element is the framing of a new kind of engagement between higher education and employers. From the employer perspective, higher education has been too slow in responding to the rapidly changing environment in industry. Employers want continuous curriculum development and more skill-focused training for the workplace – more important, they want a stronger voice in shaping curricula, credentials, and pedagogies (Wingard & Farrugia 2020). From the university perspective, there is a strong incentive to bridge the higher education-employer gap to prepare students for career adaptability, especially in the digital economy (Richards 2020). Universities have also the capacity to shape the workplace by training the talent that will innovate and change how industry operates. Still, some argue that there is risk in defining higher education's mission as satisfying the need for technically skilled employees, no matter what these skills are, which could lead to the reduction of democratic deliberation, utilization of remote education to cut personnel costs, and a widespread mercantilization of universities at the expense of the cultivation of civic virtue, particularly a global civic education (de Sousa Santos 2021; Curren & Dorn 2018). There are no doubt two-way pressures between industry and higher education, which are at the core of future engagements between universities and employers.

The third element highlights the importance of moving "beyond campus walls to understand the full impact of universities" and their role as research and innovation powerhouses and key intermediaries between government and corporations (Baldwin 2021: 20–22). Universities have the capacity to influence and transform the urban economy and shape digital technologies and other areas of innovation, which, in turn, can reinforce patterns of racial, ethnic, and gendered inequities within and across nations. On a global scale, the technologies that universities have helped create may displace human labor through automation, contribute to a destabilization of the ecosystems on which human life depends, and deepen geopolitical inequalities by expanding the dominance of technology produced by the Global North (see OHCHR 2020). Addressing questions of access to higher education, inclusivity and belonging, and the university as a fundamental civic actor requires a comprehensive framework that places our institutions within the multiple networks and relationships that define their work, impact, and identity.

There are ways to resolve these tensions, but it will require rethinking the model of the university, that worked well for centuries, but now must adapt to new local, national, and global realities. We are witnessing an ecosystem of higher education that is expanding and diversifying to an enormous degree, and colleges and universities can become engines of social, cognitive, and climate justice, reinventing learning, and embracing innovative academic digital strategies. However, there is a serious risk that the gap between institutions will deepen within and across countries, solidifying an environment where non-research institutions with fewer resources – particularly those serving poorer students – will focus on job training and certification at the expense of "building transferable skills for future career growth and career change" (Alexander 2017; Dede 2020: 3).

The resolution of these tensions also demands that institutions of higher education, not only the elite ones, equip their students with the competencies to interact successfully in a global, multicultural world. Education for cultural competency will inevitably involve producing empathy and understanding of difference. This will create allies among the majority and feelings of belonging among minorities. It will also help colleges and universities to fully accept the moral imperative to educate global citizens, a generation that embraces the idea that global interdependence is unavoidable and that "the imposition of risk on one another" calls for global cooperation under fair terms. As the global pandemic and climate change have underscored, "global problems are largely problems whose solution or management requires forms and norms of governance that do not yet exist" (Curren & Dorn 2018: 125, 130). It is vital that those designing new governance frameworks come from a broad spectrum of individuals representing diverse backgrounds and identities. Higher education should emerge as a place where diversity produces the knowledge creation that will support the kind of environment necessary for building a cooperative global community.

Despite many challenges, the present environment offers unique opportunities to collectively design a new future for higher education, working together with our places, locally and globally, to create a better, more inclusive, and just university and through it, a better democracy and civic life.

(Related Chapters: 1, 15, 20, 21, 22, 23, 24, 26, 27, 28.)

Notes

1 We thank Rosa Hassan De Ferrari, Anthony Ocepek, and Rachel Travis for their excellent research assistance.

2 There is an intense debate around "cancel culture," which has extended beyond academic circles. See, for example, Applebaum (2021); Goldberg (2021).

3 Now that institutions have invested in technology that gives them broader access to monitoring their communities, it is unlikely that they will do away with it after the pandemic. Thus, the question of privacy rights and how data can be used in other instances after the pandemic becomes an important consideration.

References

ACLU (2021) *Speech on Campus.* https://www.aclu.org/other/speech-campus

Applebaum, A. (2021, August 31) "The New Puritans," *The Atlantic.* https://www.theatlantic.com/magazine/archive/2021/10/new-puritans-mob-justice-canceled/619818/

Alexander, B. (2017, October 23) "Higher Education, Digital Divides, and a Balkanized Internet," *Educause Review* 52(6). https://er.educause.edu/articles/2017/10/higher-education-digital-divides-and-a-balkanized-internet

Anderson, T., Prasad, K., Robie, A., Esber, D., & Gregg, B. (2015, October 1) "Discussions on Digital: The New War for Talent [Audio podcast episode]," in *The Digital Transformation.* McKinsey. https://www.mckinsey.com/business-functions/organization/our-insights/discussions-on-digital-the-new-war-for-talent

Baldwin, D. L. (2021) *In the Shadow of the Ivory Tower: How Universities Are Plundering Our Cities.* New York: Bold Type Books.

Bassett-Jones, N. (2005) "The Paradox of Diversity Management, Creativity and Innovation," *Creativity and Innovation Management* 14(2): 169–175.

Batalova, J., & Feldblum, M. (2020) *Immigrant-Origin Students in U.S. Higher Education: A Data Profile.* Washington, D.C.: Migration Policy Institute. https://www.migrationpolicy.org/sites/default/files/publications/immigrant-origin-students-postsecondary-ed-final.pdf

Benneworth, P. (2021) "So What is a University in Any Case? A Grass-roots Perspective on the University and Urban Social Justice," in M. Steer & B. Davoudi (eds.) *Hope Under Neoliberal Austerity: Responses from Civil Society and Civic Universities.* Bristol, UK: Bristol University Press, 251–256.

Branković, J., Klemencic, M., Lazetic, P., & Zgaga, P. (2014) *Global Challenges, Local Responses in Higher Education: The Contemporary Issues in National and Comparative Perspective.* Rotterdam, The Netherlands: Sense Publishers.

Brown, P. C., Roediger, H. L., & McDaniel, M. A. (2014) *Make It Stick: The Science of Successful Learning.* Cambridge, MA: Harvard University Press.

Brown, L. (2020, July 20) "How to Center Disability in the Tech Response to COVID-19," *Brookings.* https://www.brookings.edu/techstream/how-to-center-disability-in-the-tech-response-to-covid-19/

Burt, C. (2021, September 13) "Does a College Education Have Value? Only 60% of Americans Say Yes," *University Business.* https://universitybusiness.com/does-a-college-education-have-value-only-60-of-americans-say-yes/?eml=20210917&oly_enc_id=1461H9017034G6V

Chetty, R., Friedman, J., Saez, E., Turner, N., & Yagan, C. (2017) "Mobility Report Cards: The Role of Colleges in Intergenerational Mobility," *NBER Working Paper* No. 23618. https://opportunityinsights.org/paper/mobilityreportcards/

Cudd, A. E. (2019) "Harassment, Bias, and the Evolving Politics of Free Speech on Campus," *Journal of Social Philosophy* 50(4): 425–446.

Curren, R., & Dorn, C. (2018) *Patriotic Education in a Global Age*. Chicago: University of Chicago Press.

Day, M. (2021, September 2) "The Rise of the University: An Interview with Davarian L. Baldwin," *Jacobin*. https://jacobinmag.com/2021/09/university-cities-urban-development-gentrification?fbclid=IwAR3SKnADx4qhMbBg7GHkPc-E5ciYF21jiyZhGIof1dCdHpWl_Jq5NtRFQvY

de Sousa Santos, B. (2021) *Descolonizar la Universidad: El Desafío de la Justiciar Cognitiva Global*. Buenos Aires, Argentina: CLACSO.

Deb Roy, R. (2018) *Malarial Subjects: Empire, Medicine, and Nonhumans in British India, 1820-1909*. Cambridge, UK: Cambridge University Press.

Deb Roy, R. (2017, April 5) "Decolonise Science – Time to End Another Imperial Era," *The Conversation*. https://theconversation.com/decolonise-science-time-to-end-another-imperial-era-89189?xid=PS_smithsonian

Dede, C. J. (2020) "Introduction: Reconceptualizing Higher Education and Lifelong Learning in the Era of the Synergistic Digital Economy," in C. J. Dede & J. Richards (eds.) *The 60-Year Curriculum: New Models for Lifelong Learning in the Digital Economy*. New York: Routledge, 1–24.

Florida, R. (2018, June 5) "The Paradox of Prosperity at America's Universities," *Bloomberg CityLab*. https://www.bloomberg.com/news/articles/2018-06-05/u-s-universities-fuel-both-urban-growth-and-inequality

Florida, R. (2006) "The Flight of the Creative Class: The New Global Competition for Talent," *Liberal Education* 92(3).

Gallup. (2021) *The First Amendment on Campus 2020 Report: College Students' Views of Free Expression*. https://knightfoundation.org/wp-content/uploads/2020/05/First-Amendment-on-Campus-2020.pdf

Glăveanu, V. P., & Clapp, E. (2018) "Distributed and Participatory Creativity as a Form of Cultural Empowerment: The Role of Alterity, Difference and Collaboration," in A. U. Branco & M. C. Lopes-de-Oliveira (eds.) *Alterity, Values and Socialization: Human Development within Educational Contexts*. Cham, Switzerland: Springer, 51–63.

Goddard, J. & Vallance, P. (2013) *The University and the City*. London: Routledge.

Goldberg, M. (2021, September 20) "The Middle-Aged Sadness Behind the Cancel Culture Panic," *New York Times*. https://www.nytimes.com/2021/09/20/opinion/generation-cancel-culture.html

Haskel, J., & Westlake, S. (2017) *Capitalism without Capital: The Rise of the Intangible Economy*. Princeton, NJ: Princeton University Press.

Hughes, C. (2021) *Education and Elitism: Challenges and Opportunities*. London: Routledge.

Inside Higher Ed (2021) *2021 Survey of College and University Presidents*. https://www.readyeducation.com/hubfs/Ready-Education_IHE-2021-Presidents-Survey.pdf?hsCtaTracking=4678cd65–9765-478c-962e-ef7495c7fa58%7Cf2328357-a0e8–48df-b22a-a199a29a8db4

International Labour Organization (2021) *The Future of Work in the Education Sector in the Context of Lifelong Learning for All, Skills and the Decent Work Agenda* (TMDWA/2021). https://www.tandf.co.uk//journals/authors/style/reference/tf_apa.pdf

Jack, A. (2019) *The Privileged Poor: How Elite Colleges Are Failing Disadvantaged Students*. Cambridge, MA: Harvard University Press.

Jaschik, S. (2021, May 3) "Should Competitive Colleges Admit More Students?," *Inside Higher Ed*. https://www.insidehighered.com/admissions/article/2021/05/03/some-say-most-competitive-colleges-admissions-should-increase-size

Jeffrey, A., & Jimenez, L. (2021, April 22) *Preparing Students of Color for the Future Workforce*. Washington, D.C.: Center for American Progress. https://www.americanprogress.org/issues/education-k-12/reports/2021/04/22/498408/preparing-students-color-future-workforce/

Jordan, M. (2020, October 15) "Children from Immigrant Families are Increasingly the Face of Higher Education," *The New York Times*. https://www.nytimes.com/2020/10/15/us/immigrant-families-students-college.html

Kendi, I. X. (2019) *How to Be an Antiracist*. New York: Random House.

Kensinger, N. (2018, March 8) "As Columbia University Moves into Manhattanville, Its Industrial Past is Erased," *Vox Media*. https://ny.curbed.com/2018/3/8/17095838/manhattanville-columbia-university-expansion-photo-essay

Kim, J. (2018, October 10) "Is Technology Driving Educational Inequality?" *Inside Higher Ed*. https://www.insidehighered.com/digital-learning/blogs/technology-and-learning/technology-driving-educational-inequality

Kurtzberg, T. R. (2005) "Feeling Creative, Being Creative: An Empirical Study of Diversity and Creativity in Teams," *Creativity Research Journal* 17(1): 51–65.

Latour, B. (1987) *Science in Action: How to Follow Scientists and Engineers through Society*. Maidenhead, UK: Open University Press.

Nossel, S. (2018, May 25) "You Can Only Protect Campus Speech if You Acknowledge Racism," *The Washington Post*. https://www.washingtonpost.com/outlook/you-can-only-protect-campus-speech-if-you-acknowledge-racism/2018/05/25/5c26bbcc-59ed-11e8-b656-a5f8c2a9295d_story.html

OHCHR. (2020) "Racial Discrimination and Emerging Digital Technologies: A Human Rights Analysis," *United Nations Human Rights Council Forty-Fourth Session*, 15 June–3 July 2020. https://undocs.org/en/A/HRC/44/57

Papendieck, A. (2018) "Technology for Equity and Social Justice in Education: A Critical Issue Overview," *Texas Education Review* 6(1): 1–9.

Paulus, P. B., & Dzindolet, M. (2008) "Social Influence, Creativity and Innovation," *Social Influence* 3(4): 228–247.

Phillips, K. W., Medin, D., Lee, C. D., Bang, M., Bishop, S., & Lee, D. N. (2014) "How Diversity Works," *Scientific American* 311(4): 42–47.

Post, C., De Lia, E., DiTomaso, N., Tirpak, T. M., & Borwankar, R. (2009) "Capitalizing on Thought Diversity for Innovation," *Research-Technology Management* 52(6): 14–25.

Richards, J. (2020) "Assessment of the Current State of the 60-Year Curriculum and Research Agenda for the Future," in C. J. Dede & J. Richards (eds.) *The 60-Year Curriculum: New Models for Lifelong Learning in the Digital Economy*. New York: Routledge, 142–155.

Roth, M. S. (2019) *Safe Enough Spaces: A Pragmatist's Approach to Inclusion, Free Speech, and Political Correctness on College Campuses*. New Haven, CT: Yale University Press.

Scott, A. (2020) "Education, Age, and the Machine.," in C. J. Dede & J. Richards (eds.) *The 60-Year Curriculum: New Models for Lifelong Learning in the Digital Economy*. New York: Routledge, 25–40.

Sharif, R. (2019) "The Relations between Acculturation and Creativity and Innovation in Higher Education: A Systematic Literature Review," *Educational Research Review* 28: 100287. doi:10.1016/j.edurev.2019.100287

Shiva, V. (2008) "Biodiversity, Intellectual Property Rights, and Globalization," in B. de Sousa Santos (ed.) *Another Knowledge is Possible: Beyond Northern Epistemologies*. London: Verso, 272–287.

Todd, L., Davoudi, S., Shucksmith, M., & Steer, M. (2021) "The Civic University: Introduction," in M. Steer, S. Davoudi, M. Shucksmith & L. Todd (eds.) *Hope Under Neoliberal Austerity: Responses from Civil Society and Civic Universities*. Bristol, UK: Policy Press, 147–152.

UPP Foundation (2019) *Truly Civic: Strengthening the Connection between Universities and Their Places*. https://upp-foundation.org/about-us/civic-university-network/

Valero, A., & Van Reenen, J. (2019) "The Economic Impact of Universities: Evidence from Across the Globe," *Economics of Education Review* 68: 53–67.

Van Green, T. (2021, August 20) "Republicans Increasingly Critical of Several Major U.S. Institutions, Including Big Corporations and Banks," *Pew Research Center*. https://www.pewresearch.org/fact-tank/2021/08/20/republicans-increasingly-critical-of-several-major-u-s-institutions-including-big-corporations-and-banks/

Visvanathan, S. (2021, April 26) "Plurality is More Than Tolerance or Liberalism; It is an Active Recognition of the Need for Diversity," *The ACU Review*. https://www.acu.ac.uk/the-acu-review/the-search-for-cognitive-justice/

Watkins, G. (2020, September 14) "The Dark Side of Campus Efforts to Stop COVID-19," *The Washington Post*. https://www.washingtonpost.com/outlook/2020/09/14/dark-side-campus-efforts-stop-covid-19/

Wilcox, O. (2021, March 4) "Visualizing the Global Digital Divide," *DT Global*. https://dt-global.com/company/blog/march-4th–2021/visualizing-digital-divide

Wingard, J., & Farrugia, C. (2020) "Market-Driven Education: The Imperative for Responsive Design and Application," in C. J. Dede & J. Richards (eds.) *The 60-Year Curriculum: New Models for Lifelong Learning in the Digital Economy*. New York: Routledge, 104–118.

Yang, R. (2003) "Globalisation and Higher Education Development: A Critical Analysis," *International Review of Education* 49(3): 269–291.

Zeleza, P. T., & Okanda, P. M. (2021, February 9) "Enhancing the Digital Transformation of African Universities: COVID-19 as Accelerator," *The Elephant*. https://www.theelephant.info/long-reads/2021/02/09/enhancing-the-digital-transformation-of-african-universities-covid-19-as-accelerator/

Zemsky, R., Shaman, S., & Campbell Baldridge, S. (2020) *The College Stress Test: Tracking Institutional Futures across a Crowded Market*. Baltimore, MD: Johns Hopkins University Press.

Zilahy, G., & Huisingh, D. (2009) "The Roles of Academia in Regional Sustainability Initiatives," *Journal of Cleaner Production* 17(12): 1057–1066.

PART IV

Educational Practices

26
FREE SPEECH AND EDUCATION

Sigal Ben-Porath and Dustin Webster

In perhaps the most well-known American student free speech ruling, the Vietnam-era case of *Tinker v. Des Moines* (1969), Justice Abe Fortas, writing for the majority, struggled to strike a balance between protecting the rights of students who engage in war protest, and leaving school officials the latitude to manage their institutions. The Court decided that student speech should be protected unless it "materially and substantially" interfered with the school day and with its constructive learning environment (505). In this case the school failed to show that the speech in question – wearing black armbands – created such an interference. Since the ruling, the protections of *Tinker* may have eroded, but this central tension has remained as a powerful way to understand how free speech functions in educational institutions.

Speech protections and restrictions in educational institutions are distinct from the general protection of speech in a democracy: the latter reflects the dignity of all participants, and the humility necessitated by their equal fallibility in the search for truth; but in educational settings, in addition, speech regulations need to align with the institutional mission. To do so, the regulation of speech is considered against the broader demands of an institution operating within a democratic legal, constitutional, and political context. These sometimes conflicting pressures, and the diverse ways in which some of them are interpreted by policy-makers, educational practitioners, citizens, and courts, all contribute to the struggle over the boundaries of speech in education.

Advocates of unalloyed free speech tend to present restrictions on speech as inimical to the purposes of education, as well as to the foundations and rules of democracy. Their views are sometimes described as the "marketplace of ideas" model (Chemerinsky & Gillman 2017; Strossen 2018), and are firmly grounded in John Stuart Mill's sweeping defense of free speech. Mill puts forward his arguments for not merely tolerating but actually embracing freedom of expression because nobody is infallible, and we should thus remain open to the possibility of finding truth in marginal views; even an opinion that is generally erroneous may contain either a grain of truth that would enrich prevailing opinions, or when it is wholly misguided, can challenge those who hold correct views to examine the reasons for their beliefs. The rational grounds of our views are more readily discernible when our views are challenged, even by false critiques. In the absence of vigorous debate, "the meaning of the doctrine itself will be in danger of being lost, or enfeebled, and deprived of its vital effect on the character and conduct" (Mill 1859/1947: 59). This view informs contemporary liberal scholarship and jurisprudence, laying ground for the liberal argument for the inclusion of even false and harmful views in the marketplace of ideas.

DOI: 10.4324/9781003172246-31

This approach frames much of the scholarship on free speech in education. Two preeminent legal scholars in the field, Erwin Chemerinsky and Howard Gillman (2017) argue that "campuses never can censor or punish the expression of ideas, however offensive, because otherwise they cannot perform their function of promoting inquiry, discovery, and the dissemination of new knowledge" (Chemerinsky & Gillman 2017: 19). The unrestricted free and open exchange of ideas is for liberal champions of free speech important enough so as to include a defense of hate speech in educational institutions, since the difficulty in defining the boundaries of hate speech are such that attempts to regulate it will remain overly broad, and "risk punishing people based on political viewpoint or worldview" (104).

At the other side of the spectrum, advocates of inclusion and civility make the case for speech restrictions that preserve a constructive learning environment by preventing harms which speech might potentially cause. While notable scholars like Alexander Meiklejohn (1948) hold that the democratic interest in both individual and institutional speech stems from their epistemic contributions to self-government, public discussion on protecting free expression and some key court cases have focused on defending hateful and exclusionary forms of expression. Rejecting the unregulated marketplace of ideas, some contemporary scholars see little reason to protect within the context of education expression that can readily be recognized as hateful, bigoted, or patently false. This type of speech, they suggest, clashes with the goals of learning: epistemically, it clashes with the prioritization of truth; and socially, it clashes with the inclusion of all members of the learning community (Scott 2019; Roth 2019). Miranda Fricker sees harms and lies as often overlapping in this context: "prejudice presents an obstacle to truth, either directly by causing the hearer to miss out on a particular truth, or indirectly by creating blockages in the circulation of critical ideas" (Fricker 2007: 32). This implies that bias and prejudice can often be silenced with little cost, contrary to the "counterspeech doctrine" articulated by Justice Louis Brandeis, who argued in *Whitney v. California* (1927) that, "if there be time to expose through discussion the falsehood and fallacies, to avert the evil by the processes of education, the remedy to be applied is more speech, not enforced silence" (377). For Fricker and others (Dotson 2011; Solorzano et al. 2000) who observe that words can also cause harm, Brandeis's vision still requires differentiating between ideas that merit a response and those that have so little value or cause such harm that they should be restricted rather than engaged, particularly in educational settings.

We focus this chapter first on the value, purpose, and justifications for protecting free speech in education. We identify two core values to protecting speech in educational settings: an epistemic value, or value based on the mission of schools and universities to produce, introduce, and disseminate knowledge; and a civic value, or value anchored in the social and democratic mission of education. We then consider the justifications for setting general boundaries for speech, as well as specific ones first in K-12 (or primary and secondary) schools, and then in higher (or post-secondary) educational institutions. The context of K-12 education intensifies tensions around speech regulation. In the K-12 years children are compelled by law to attend school, and the adults supervising them in public schools are agents of the state. Young children do not enjoy the same rights and privileges afforded to adults, and even in higher education students are often considered to be citizens in formation rather than full social participants. Epistemic and democratic ideals require that in these circumstances, knowledge production and dissemination organize the regulation of speech in ways that facilitate open inquiry and exchange, prioritize evidentiary practices and rigorous study, and aim to include all members in an ongoing conversation.

The Value of Free Speech in Education

Speech in education is protected in different ways, and for different reasons, from the general protection of speech in a democracy. The defense of free speech in schools and universities is broadly justified by two core arguments: first, that speech in education has an epistemic value, or value related to the process of intellectual development; and second, that speech in education has a social and civic value, or value related to the cultivation of democratic citizens. While the two types of values – the epistemic and the democratic – are related, and in some aspects rely on each other, it is useful to consider them in turn to clarify the ways in which free speech enables each of them.

Epistemic Value of Free Speech in Education

Mill famously notes that, "However unwillingly a person who has a strong opinion may admit the possibility that his opinion may be false, he ought to be moved by the consideration that however true it may be, if it is not fully, frequently, and fearlessly discussed, it will be held as a dead dogma, not living truth" (Mill 1859/1947: 34). Continuous examination of views and beliefs with an open mind is necessary for learning and growth. Even those ideas which may be wrong or objectionable, when allowed to enter into the discourse, present challenges that enable rethinking, refreshing one's arguments in opposition, and a thoughtful rejection. This aspirational liberal perspective presents the exchange of views as central to an educational institution or a learning community, in which the expansion of one's mind, and the critical and considerate assessment of facts and arguments, are core aspects of the mission. It assumes that educational institutions operate as reliable and equitable epistemic communities, in which learning is cooperative and symmetrical, and evidentiary practices guide everyone's epistemic efforts (assumptions that can readily be challenged in non-ideal unequal, discriminatory environments, or ones in which misleading information is propagated). As epistemic institutions, schools and colleges need to provide the conditions for empowering students to expand their minds, and these rely on the critical assessment of beliefs. Encountering a broad range of ideas, theories, and visions is a significant aspect of helping students become careful critical thinkers, with a basic knowledge of the world and society around them. Such encounters are made possible and accessible to students when they take place within an atmosphere that encourages an honest and equitable engagement. Many of the protections of free speech in education are crafted so as to allow these epistemic and cognitive processes to take place.

The epistemic benefits of free speech in education are hence accrued through the introduction of diverse views in the curriculum or syllabus, as well as through maintaining an atmosphere of open inquiry in the classroom, where students and instructors feel welcome to share their views, interpretations, knowledge, and questions. The breadth of perspectives represented in both school and college courses is a matter of continual debate. Notably, ongoing "history wars" pull curricula between glorified and critical versions of national history (Taylor & Guyver 2012; Zimmerman 2005), while legislative and administrative efforts aim to regulate or restrict discussion about "divisive" or "corrupting" topics. The selection of subjects and perspectives reflects a set of evolving professional, political, and moral considerations. In teaching basic skills like reading, the same tensions arise, using literary texts or nonfiction paragraphs which represent views and experiences that would be familiar to some and new to others. Books are promoted or censored by political and administrative decisions (Berkowitz 2021); scientific theories are centered or discarded, sometimes with the advancement of knowledge, and sometimes not (Laats & Siegel 2021). The freedom of instructors to represent diverse views and voices in the curriculum is always bound by political and administrative guidance, but given the significance of representing a diverse set of perspectives in the curriculum and on syllabi, it is critical to the epistemic mission of education to preserve the freedom of curriculum developers, teachers, and instructors to use their professional judgement and expertise about these matters (Maxwell et al. 2019).

The importance of freedom in selecting class materials and facilitating discussion is easy to recognize when considered against contexts in which these are absent. In the United States, some Christian Evangelical schools teach books which decry American moral decline and celebrate Christian nationalism as the moral alternative to "immoral philosophies" such as multiculturalism, globalism, and environmentalism (Greenawalt 2005: 174–176). These schools may be successful in limiting their students' exposure to values that they find harmful, at the cost of the opportunity to develop independent thinking. Other religious schools limit instruction to worksheets, eliminating the open exchange of views among students (Dwyer 2001: 194), whereas some "no excuses" schools control student speech to the point of silencing (Golann 2021). These illustrations of restricted curriculum and discussion highlight the epistemic significance of freedom of speech in the classroom: absent such freedom for both teachers and students, the epistemic benefits of education dwindle, leaving students ill-informed and lacking in the skills and attitudes required for conscientiously and critically assessing views and perspectives, and for developing independent thinking.

Exposure to a broad range of ideas is a core aspect of the epistemic development of students at all levels of education. This process might generate discomfort and intellectual challenges, which are juxtaposed by some with the sense of safety that students demand (Lukianoff & Haidt 2019). However, such safety is often a precondition to students' ability to participate in the learning community with its opportunities for growth and evolution of thought (Ben-Porath 2017; Callan 2016).

An atmosphere that supports the positive epistemic development of students starts with treating all students as "knowers" to a similar degree, namely, as people who have some knowledge, whose knowledge may be worth sharing or considering, and who are capable of obtaining further knowledge through learning. Accruing the epistemic benefits of learning in educational institutions thus requires avoiding common forms of epistemic injustice, particularly the replication of power imbalances through presuppositions about the capacity of members of some groups to know or learn (Fricker 2007).

Academic Freedom and the Epistemic Value of Free Speech

Academic freedom, as defined and defended by the American Association of University Professors (AAUP), is established to bolster instructors' protection in sharing their knowledge to the benefit of their students' epistemic development. It is meant to protect researchers from political, institutional, and other pressures or threats as they work to contribute to the advancement of knowledge. The value and necessity of such freedom was articulated by the AAUP formally in a document known as the *1915 Declaration of Principles on Academic Freedom and Academic Tenure*, which was prompted by the dismissal of two faculty at the University of Utah. John Dewey, president of the newly formed organization, saw it as imperative that faculty be provided with these protections.

Academic freedom protections reflect the established view that the epistemic value of free speech in education is beneficial not solely to students, who gain opportunities to expand their knowledge and challenge their beliefs. It is also essential to scholars and researchers, who rely on it as part of an infrastructure that protects open inquiry, as they expand the boundaries of knowledge to the benefit of society at large. Free inquiry is necessary for the search for knowledge, and academic freedom uses administrative mechanisms, like tenure, to protect scholars from being penalized for pursuing controversial lines of work and expressing unpopular views.

The AAUP (1915) declaration outlines three broad areas that are protected under academic freedom. These are: "freedom of inquiry and research; freedom of teaching within the university or college; and freedom of extramural utterance and action" (AAUP 1915: 20). The first two areas offer protections along with professional responsibilities related to the pursuit of knowledge. Freedom of research operates along with disciplinary standards and evidentiary practices; classroom speech and conduct are similarly constrained by professional norms and the mission of the institution. Hence, the value of academic freedom implies boundaries to its application. It might be tempting to think about academic freedom as functioning to protect the "marketplace of ideas" by allowing unpopular or unorthodox views to be presented, but at the same time it sets limits by not allowing certain types of speech. In this way, academic freedom is not entirely compatible with the marketplace framework (Reichman 2019).

The boundaries of protected ideas and actions are negotiated within the community of researchers, in a discipline or an institution. Academic freedom thereby maintains the autonomy of scholarly researchers. Yet, this autonomy does not come without tension, as deciding whether or not some speech or idea conforms to the standard of a discipline can also have a conservative or stifling influence. "Disciplinary communities provide the consensus necessary to justify academic freedom as a special freedom for faculty. But the inseparable other side of this regulatory and enabling authority is that it can suppress innovative thinking in the name of defending immutable standards" (Scott 2019: 52).

Perhaps where the tension between free speech and academic freedom becomes most apparent is when it comes to faculty engaging in extramural speech, or speech outside of their official capacity as a researcher and educator. These often reflect political tensions. For decades, "frequent and fierce debates about the nature of academic freedom have resulted from a systematic and sustained effort to discipline what some regard as an out of control liberal professoriate" (Finkin & Post 2009: 2). Ideological expression can raise difficult questions, particularly when a faculty member is speaking outside of their discipline or area of expertise, or engages in "epistemic trespassing" (Ballantyne 2019). When considering a controversial instance of such speech, Joan Scott (2019) says we must ask questions like, "Was there a responsibility to behave in a certain 'academic' manner even when one was exercising one's rights as a citizen? Did the special right of academic freedom entail limits on the public right of free speech?" (Scott: 57). It seems likely that the public will in many cases assign more credence to the words of an academic with advanced degrees, regardless of the relationship of those words to that individual's areas of expertise. Although Scott notes that thus far few argue that this means academics have a responsibility to restrict their extramural speech, it still raises difficult questions about the position of academic speakers and institutions in the public debate.

The Civic Value of Free Speech in Education

Presenting diverse ideologies, perspectives, and identities in the curriculum is not sufficient for fulfilling the aims of free speech in education, if discussion about them is stifled. The benefits of freedom of speech in education accrue not just from protections for teachers and instructors presenting diverse views, or simply from students sharing theirs, but also from the opportunity to consider, reflect, and debate these diverse views in the structured context of the classroom (Hess 2009). In the early grades, students are introduced to the idea of a "persuasive essay" and taught how to express their opinions in a clear and compelling way. They learn about the scientific method and how information about the world is gathered and assessed. In the older grades, students are introduced to more advanced forms of rhetoric and the way in which the discourse of competing ideas functions for knowledge production. Higher education continues this mission by exposing students to a broader array of perspectives and methods of inquiry. All of these developmental opportunities require that students be exposed to new and diverse ideas, and also that they be able to freely express, try out, and revise their views.

An atmosphere of open inquiry, open expression, and open dialogue in education contributes to the development of key democratic civic traits, attitudes, and relations, which can be understood together as the civic value of free speech. Hess and McAvoy (2015) argue that the benefits of such open discussion extend even to the inclusion of issues in the classroom that might otherwise be considered "empirically closed," or no longer the subject of meaningful debate within the relevant community of experts. They provide the example of a student who may deny the reality of climate change. Rather than censor such views immediately, the teacher can use the situation as an opportunity to engage students in a discussion around the difference between political and empirical questions and how empirical questions are settled, even if they ultimately do not entertain an actual debate about whether climate change is real or not in the classroom (McAvoy & Hess 2013: 39).

During primary and secondary education, civic education is one of the explicit aims of schooling (Coleman 1998), an aim that can be advanced by focusing on democratic pedagogical practices as well as training students in the deliberative skills that are necessary to participate in a democracy (Gutmann 1999). This aim also extends to higher education where, as students develop into young adults, they are able to more independently engage in the habits and routines that mark being a citizen in a democratic, pluralist society.

Strengthening students' capacities to make their voices heard in the democratic context in an informed and effective way is both pressing and feasible. Yet, in the United States as in some other democracies, the erosion of speech protections for students (Ross 2015) and teachers (Maxwell et al. 2019) intensifies the challenges to implementing proven democratic pedagogical practices that sustain free speech in service of its civic value. Since no one is born with the skills and knowledge required to be an engaged citizen, political content, speech, and debate are needed to sustain this unique form of government (Hess & McAvoy 2014). Democracies everywhere easily slip into trouble: they become polarized, steeped in disinformation, their civic infrastructure erodes, and their citizens become distrustful of government and of each other. We need "active citizens who care about democracy and are willing to work for it," but this requires cultivation of "the requisite traits" (Hart & Youniss 2018: 57).

In *Our Common Purpose* the authors indicate that beyond "names and dates ... The American citizen today must be prepared to acknowledge our nation's mistakes, to recognize that we have grappled over time to improve our imperfect union, to find pride in those struggles, and to recognize that, at our best, everyone is included ... citizens today must be able to deal with ongoing debate and argument, be able to engage in debate, find compromise ..." (AAAS 2020: 63). The centrality of open expression, as a broad commitment by the school rather than as a topic for a lesson plan, is the key to this type of civic education. Students could be taught about this directly, particularly by learning the history of student open expression. This exposure to the evolving boundaries of their own speech could begin to illustrate to them why it is important. But students also need the ability to exercise this right themselves.

The habits of democracy, which are shared, civic, and social, must be developed through a shared process of truth-seeking and open discussion, so that students can overcome the single-minded pursuit of conspiracy theories, and the polarizing effects of self-segregation and mistrust. Sharing the process of information production, assessment, and distribution – sharing the judgement of what is reliable and what should be shared – can produce trust, if done within broad and clear norms of speech and exchange. To enable the development of democratic civic skills, schools need to maintain a robust context for students to voice and share their views. Strict and punitive boundaries that focus on strict hierarchical structures of authority do not allow students to develop the connections and the capacity and inclination to engage across differences, which is necessary for democratic revitalization.

While student speech on political and scholarly topics might be most evidently important, other speech is similarly deserving of protection. Criticizing school and other institutions, and forming social relations through an open exchange of views and sharing of experiences, both contribute to the civic attitudes and skills that sustain democracy.

Public schools serve the vast majority of students in many democracies, so protecting speech in these institutions facilitates the development of civic skills across students from all backgrounds and walks of life, although notable differences exist in the quality of civic instruction and outcomes. Meira Levinson describes what she calls a "civic empowerment gap": the alignment of active participation in democracy with citizens' class, whereby upper classes participate more in voting and other formal civic practices; and similarly with race and educational level, which themselves are aligned with class background (Levinson 2012). One of the vectors that expresses and exacerbates the difference in civic skills development is the more open and discursive schools typical of upper and middle class neighborhoods, and the more restrictive and authoritative contexts available to most poor, minority, and working class children (Anyon 1981; Ben-Porath 2007; Golann 2021). In post-secondary or higher education, students further develop their political voices and civic skills. In this context, broad speech protections are necessary for unpopular and unorthodox views to be voiced and considered, allowing mainstream, popular, and orthodox views to be questioned and tested. Contemporary struggles regarding the boundaries of legitimate expression at universities need to be understood and addressed in light of the expansion of this mission, and the changing social and political environment in which it takes place. Polarization and the geographic separation of different groups results in limited exposure of young people to competing worldviews and to increased distrust of those who hold them. Higher education continues to carry the torch of developing young citizens, which is handed off to them after the high school years.

The Educational Boundaries of Speech

The right to speak freely, like all rights, has boundaries, enshrined in laws and legal precedents as well as institutional practices and social norms. In many democracies, libel and defamation, breaches of intellectual property, harassment, and incitement to violence are among the impermissible forms of expression. In educational settings, additional considerations can reasonably curtail speech. Such limitations are most commonly based on three types of considerations: administrative requirements; harm and exclusion; and the goal of seeking true knowledge.

Administratively, speech regulation can result from professional and institutional expectations: teachers in public schools can be compelled to speak to the curriculum that is prescribed to them, regardless of general legal protections against government compelled speech; student newspapers can be censored by administrators, thus not benefitting from press freedom protections; professors can be required to read attendance, or abide by other administrative practices, regardless of free speech or academic freedom protections. While administrative regulations on speech are sometimes taken as technical and often go without a challenge (Fish 1994), they can also create public and normative complications, as with the case of requiring that instructors use students' correct pronouns in class (Meriwether v. Hartop 2021).

Hence, administrative boundaries sometimes arise in reference to the core mission of the institution and relate to the key normative considerations relating to the core mission of educational institutions: including all members in the process of learning and expanding true knowledge. Consequently, speech can be organized so as to prioritize true or reliable speech over inaccurate, misleading, or fraudulent speech; and speech that undermines the ability of some students to participate as equal members of the learning community might be regulated. Note that we say "prioritize" and "regulate" rather than prevent, censor, or punish. There are many options short of hardline restrictions that are available to educational institutions when dealing with acts of speech that might be seen as challenging or in some way harmful. Considerations related to truth and to inclusion need to be weighed against their costs, and enacted, within the boundaries of local laws, in a way that aims to maintain both a commitment to an expansive and open exchange of views, and to ensuring that this exchange is grounded in disciplinary evidentiary practices (or, is advancing true knowledge), and is accessible to all students, allowing them to engage with it and respond to it (or, is inclusive).

Arguments for limiting speech rely on the foundational idea that for some speech, the harm it causes is enough to justify its restriction. The notion of harm has been central to the liberal debate at least since it was articulated by Mill, who notes that "the only purpose for which power can be rightfully exercised over any member of a civilized community, against his will, is to prevent harm to others" (Mill 1859/1947: 9). With this, Mill provides both the suggestion that speech is capable of doing harm, and also that harm is a reasonable justification for its restriction. While this articulation may seem quite broad in that the case can be made that all sorts of speech cause some kind of "harm," it should be noted that Mill is sometimes understood to have envisioned "harm" as a more limited concept, and thus to have claimed that the right to speak freely is not necessarily limited even when words cause harm (Jacobson 2000; D'Orazio 2020).

But what qualifies as "harm" that justifies restricting speech? The answer is highly contested, even in the case of extreme and hateful speech (Post 2009). Hate speech – protected in the United States under the First Amendment, but legally restricted in most other democracies – is commonly perceived as causing harm. Some argue that this epistemic and social harm is reason enough to restrict it, especially in educational settings: "In evaluating hate speech, we are not just weighing the civil standing and dignity of victims against the supposed self-revealing autonomy of hate speakers. We are weighing an illusory gain in autonomy for hate speakers, against a very real loss in autonomy for their targets. Hate speech is bad for everyone's autonomy: the speakers, and the spoken against" (Langton 2016: 868). Beyond preserving one's autonomy, perceiving all members of a learning community as equal in their capacity to make contributions as knowers and speakers is the foundation of true inclusion in a school or campus. In this way, the unique harm of hate speech in the context of education, especially that which is aimed at a particular group, is that it can undermine a group member's ability to fully participate in the social or educational community, effectively limiting their access to learning. Paradoxically, the protection of expressions of hateful rhetoric can function as a restriction on the ability of others to express themselves in an equal way.

Beyond inclusion, the educational mission of learning and knowledge production also suggests possible limitations on speech. Cornel West and Robert P. George, two eminent scholars who represent opposing ideological views, claim that "All of us should be willing – even eager – to engage with anyone who is prepared to do business in the currency of truth-seeking discourse by offering reasons, marshaling evidence, and making arguments" (George & West 2017). In this, West and George aim to prioritize truth, and to permit speech that might be hurtful, if it is part of the truth-seeking mission of the institutions. Prioritizing truth in educational settings is in itself a principle that can justify restrictions on speech. Some have argued that patent lies and distortions have no room in the classroom, and that misleading views – holocaust denial, anti-science stances, and the like – should not be represented in the curriculum or in educational settings. Universities' truth-seeking mission implies that they have a responsibility to restrict certain ideas or to not welcome certain speakers. "Every day, universities exclude some ideas from debate while inviting others. Before we look at which kind of speech gets invited, we need to understand that this vetting process in the university is not a secondary matter in the speech debates, but essential to everything we value in education" (Baer 2019: 11).

In sum, beyond the administrative regulation of speech in classrooms, educational institutions regulate speech in alignment with their mission: they aim to protect inclusive environments and to avoid harm, so that all members are able to equally participate in the learning community; and they prioritize truth-seeking over the spreading of falsehoods and misinformation. The specific boundaries of each of these limitations continue to be contested. Below we look at some of these contests, first in K-12 and then in higher education.

Boundaries of Speech in K-12 Schools

The boundaries of K-12 speech as reflected in Court decisions as well as in policy and practice are influenced by the fact that students are children, and thus are not afforded the same speech (and other) rights as adults. That allows for further regulation of speech, beyond what is acceptable in higher education or in broader society. Children are perceived to have less knowledge, and to need greater protection from harm than adults, therefore expanding the reach of both justifications for regulation.

The rich legal history of speech in education cannot be explored in full here, but it is useful to outline the arc of legal decisions about speech in schools to frame the role that core values play in the process, from bringing a case to court, to the court's decision, and on to its impact on education policy. The legal treatment of free speech in schools varies across countries: in the United States, the contemporary history of how the courts have dealt with speech in education, particularly in K-12 education, provides an example of how "mission" can imply boundaries. As noted above, the *Tinker* test set by the Court decided that speech which would "materially and substantially interfere with the requirements of appropriate discipline in the operation of the school" could be prohibited. The school's mission is to educate its students, and thus, interfering with that mission by sufficiently disrupting the conditions in which that education occurred established the "learning environment" boundary. In *Tinker*, speech won the day, but since then, the courts have continuously restricted students' speech rights by expanding the scope of what is required for a suitable learning environment. In that, the Courts have generally not taken minors to be citizens deserving of full constitutional protections, and whose views deserve to be heard. The Court in the decades since *Tinker* has restricted a student's right to engage in an innuendo laden political campaign speech for a classmate (*Bethel School District v. Fraser*, 1986); students' rights to cover controversial topics such as teen pregnancy and divorce in their school newspaper *(Hazelwood School District v. Kuhlmeier*, 1988); and nonsensical student pranks, such as a student unfurling a banner at an out-of-school event reading "BONG HiTS 4 JESUS" (*Morse v. Frederick* 2007). The most recent decision at the time of drafting this chapter, however, represented a departure from this trend. In 2021, the Court upheld a student's right to use profanity on social media outside of school in expressing her frustration with her club sport placement (*Mahanoy Area School District v. B.L.)*. This decision was narrow, and the Court left the door open for other out-of-school speech to be regulated, but significantly, for the first time since *Tinker* the Court sided with student speech, limiting the learning environment argument for school speech regulation.

Students may be young and often in need of greater protection and greater exposure to knowledge, but supporting the development of their voices is essential to the practice of education. As Paulo Freire (1970/1996) recognized, children should take part in the production of knowledge and not simply be seen as passive recipients. Freedom of speech in the classroom is foundational to this endeavor. The shifting boundaries of speech in schools reflect evolving social views on the capacity of children and youth to participate in knowledge production, and on the responsibility of schools to prepare them for their civic roles.

Boundaries of Speech in Higher Education

In 2014, the University of Chicago released their "Report of the Committee on Freedom of Expression" (Zimmer & Isaacs 2014), which has since become known as simply "the Chicago Statement." The report was prepared in response to incidents involving controversial speakers on various campuses, and briefly affirms the university's general commitment to free speech and open expression on campus. Based firmly in the marketplace of ideas defense of free speech, the report says in part that,

> The University's fundamental commitment is to the principle that debate or deliberation may not be suppressed because the ideas put forth are thought by some or even by most members of the University community to be offensive, unwise, immoral, or wrong-headed. It is for the individual members of the University community, not for the University as an institution, to make those judgments for themselves, and to act on those judgments not by seeking to suppress speech, but by openly and vigorously contesting the ideas that they oppose.
>
> *(Zimmer & Isaacs 2014)*

It further expresses that though the right to protest speech is also protected, such protest cannot "obstruct or otherwise interfere" with the expression that the protestors find objectionable. The report was lauded by many who worried that in the effort to embrace inclusion and avoid harm to students, institutions of higher education had leaned too far toward restricting speech, for example by cancelling events and speakers, or enacting speech codes. The Chicago Statement, while seen as controversial by some (Whittington 2019: 55–56), was embraced by various organizations committed to free speech in higher education, including the Foundation for Individual Rights in Education (FIRE),[1] which tracks the dozens of institutions that have adopted it. It has also been embraced by some local governments in the United States and Canada that demand its endorsement by public institutions.

The implementation of free speech principles such as Chicago's in higher education is complicated by the fact that many of these institutions are residential, and therefore function not only as learning environments but also as homes to their students. The regulation of speech in classrooms is distinct from that in dorms, and the understanding of speech in these contexts is often expanded to include expression in the naming of buildings, more broadly in the built environment, and in the social and civic meaning that those exude (Barczak & Thompson 2021). In class, the epistemic goals of free speech organize the boundaries of expression by prioritizing the production and dissemination of true knowledge. Outside of class, the social and civic benefits of free speech inform the boundaries of expression around the goal of maintaining an inclusive atmosphere.

As with other educational contexts, higher education institutions regulate speech according to their mission, and set boundaries related to the search for knowledge and truth, and to the aims of diversity and inclusion (and the related prevention of harm). It is commonly acknowledged in many institutions' mission statements and practices that freedom of speech can be realized through the rejection of intolerance and through openness to dialogue. The freedom to express intolerant views remains a matter of struggle: universities are challenged to consider the price that some of their members pay for expressing controversial views, particularly on matters that are of ideological or cultural concern. As places where knowledge is developed and disseminated, universities require the freedom to inquire, question, and probe established views and new visions without fear of retribution or silencing. This freedom is central to research, to teaching, and to learning. Speech protections are therefore necessary if researchers and their students are to make the kinds of contributions that society expects them to make, and for which they join the university. At the same time, universities need to consider the uneven costs of hateful speech borne by some members of the community, and that the same groups tend to be the targets of such speech again and again (Roth 2019: 99).

It is notable that speech itself is a matter of ideological controversy, pushing some American undergraduates to argue that First Amendment rights are secure (Gallup 2020), while still nearly half of the surveyed students support some restrictions on speech. Many frame their concern around the threat that certain views pose to themselves or their peers, contrary to the common concerns in the late 60s, when students were mostly concerned about threats to their ability to express their dissenting views. Students "increasingly favor restrictions on speech that targets minority groups," but also believe that "colleges should not be able to restrict expression of political views that are upsetting or offensive to certain groups" (Gallup 2020: 1). The diminished value students attach to the protection of speech indicates for some a dangerous slide toward authoritarian control of opinions, or a retreat to comfort that prefers to avoid challenges to the orthodoxy of the day. However, they might simply reflect a generational shift in focus, away from taking free speech as an orthodoxy in itself, and toward voicing greater concern regarding potential harms caused by open expression particularly on college campuses, especially in response to the politicization of the speech struggle in public, on social media, and in the courts. In this way, the concerns raised about the liberal vision of speech (as reflected by the Chicago Statement for example) might be misguided: free speech could be strengthened and expanded by incorporating the diverse views of members of groups that were excluded either formally or effectively in the past, and ensuring that they enjoy a constructive learning environment.

That could mean that expressing certain views, particularly those that undermine participation in the campus discourse, can be justifiably restricted: "A campus visitor who argues that some students are inherently inferior, materially undermines the conditions that make speech free" (Baer 2019: 80). For leaders in higher education, a host of responses to such speech are possible, from prohibiting or censoring speech, to clearly expressing their opposing values, and to actively supporting speech by students or other visitors who better reflect those values. In cases of bigoted, biased, and otherwise controversial views, speech can legitimately be seen as exclusionary and thus as undermining the equal standing of diverse members of the community. Focusing on these marginal cases can be helpful to improving a university's practice and its climate, but it also distracts from the fact that for the most part the two values go hand in hand, especially in the higher education context. In these marginal cases, a framework of inclusive freedom distinguishes between speech that is based in an effort to take intellectual risks, and to explore new (even unpopular) ideas, and on the other hand, speech that is causing dignitary harms by expressing ideas that are silencing and marginalizing, compounding existing forms of exclusion and discrimination (Callan 2016).

Conclusion

Freedom of speech in education has both epistemic and civic-social value and this value justifies broad protection of diverse ideas and forms of expression at all levels of education. The boundaries of speech in education include administrative, democratic, and legal restrictions, and incorporate additional regulations aimed at maintaining a constructive learning environment, as appropriate to the mission of the educational institution. The commitment to open expression and the commitment to inclusion are commonly portrayed as being in tension with one another, and indeed they sometimes collide, particularly around the expression of biased views that threaten to harm some members of the community. But overall, this exaggerated dichotomy contributes to the politicization of speech, and fails to reflect the ways in which schools and colleges regularly incorporate commitments to inclusion into their open expression practices. Educational institutions honor both inclusion and open expression by ensuring a robust and open inquiry in which all can equally participate, or, through a commitment to inclusive freedom. The aims of education are tightly linked with the value and practice of free and open exchange of ideas, in which all can be seen as contributors, and all can participate in the production and dissemination of knowledge. Free speech in education, with its epistemic and civic benefits, is thus a foundational aspect of education theory, policy, and practice.

(Related Chapters: 10, 11, 25, 27, 28, 29, 31.)

Note

1 https://www.thefire.org/

References

American Academy of Arts and Sciences (AAAS) (2020) *Our Common Purpose: Reinventing American Democracy for the 21st Century*. Cambridge, MA: AAAS. https://www.amacad.org/ourcommonpurpose

American Association of University Professors (AAUP) (1915) "General Report of the Committee on Academic Freedom and Academic Tenure," *AAUP Bulletin* 1(1): 20–43.

Anyon, J. (1981) "Social Class and School Knowledge," *Curriculum Inquiry* 11(1): 3–42.

Baer, U. (2019) *What Snowflakes Get Right: Free Speech and Truth on Campus*. Oxford: Oxford University Press.
Barczak, T. J., & Thompson, W. C. (2021) "Monumental Changes: The Civic Harm Argument for the Removal of Confederate Monuments," *Journal of Philosophy of Education* 55(3): 437–452.
Ballantyne, N. (2019) "Epistemic Trespassing," *Mind* 128(510): 367–395.
Ben-Porath, S. R. (2007) "Civic Virtue out of Necessity: Patriotism and Democratic Education," *Theory and Research in Education* 5(1): 41–59.
Ben-Porath, S. R. (2017) *Free Speech on Campus*. Philadelphia: University of Pennsylvania Press.
Berkowitz, E. (2021) *Dangerous Ideas: A Brief History of Censorship in the West, from the Ancients to Fake News*. London: Saqi Books.
Bethel School District No. 403 v. Fraser, 478 U.S. 675 (1986).
Callan, E. (2016) "Education in Safe and Unsafe Spaces," *Philosophical Inquiry in Education* 24(1): 64–78.
Chemerinsky, E., & Gillman, H. (2017) *Free Speech on Campus*. New Haven, CT: Yale University Press.
Coleman, J. (1998) "Civic Pedagogies and Liberal-Democratic Curricula," *Ethics* 108(4): 746–761.
Dotson, K. (2011) "Tracking Epistemic Violence, Tracking Practices of Silencing," *Hypatia* 26(2): 236–257.
D'Orazio, D. (2020) "Expressive Freedom on Campus and the Conceptual Elasticity of Harm," *Canadian Journal of Political Science* 53(4): 755–776.
Dwyer, J. G. (2001) *Vouchers Within Reason*. Ithaca, NY: Cornell University Press.
Finkin, M. W., & Post, R. C. (2009) *For the Common Good: Principles of American Academic Freedom*. New Haven, CT: Yale University Press.
Fish, S. (1994) *There's No Such thing as Free Speech: And it's a Good Thing, Too*. Oxford: Oxford University Press.
Freire, P. (1970/1996) *Pedagogy of the Oppressed (revised)*. New York: Continuum.
Fricker, M. (2007) *Epistemic Injustice: Power and the Ethics of Knowing*. Oxford: Oxford University Press.
Gallup, Inc. in collaboration with the Knight Foundation (2020) *The First Amendment on Campus 2020 Report: College Students' Views of Free Expression*. https://knightfoundation.org/wp-content/uploads/2020/05/First-Amendment-on-Campus-2020.pdf
George, R. P., & West, C. (2017) *Truth Seeking, Democracy, and Freedom of Thought and Expression*. Princeton, NJ: James Madison Program in Ideals and Institutions, Princeton University. https://jmp.princeton.edu/statement
Golann, J. W. (2021) *Scripting the Moves: Culture and Control in a "No-excuses" Charter School*. Princeton: Princeton University Press.
Greenawalt, K. (2005) *Does God belong in Public Schools?* Princeton: Princeton University Press.
Gutmann, A. (1999) *Democratic Education*. Princeton: Princeton University Press.
Hart, D., & Youniss, J. (2018) *Renewing Democracy in Young America*. Oxford: Oxford University Press.
Hazelwood School District v. Kuhlmeier, 484 U.S. 260 (1988).
Hess, D. E. (2009) *Controversy in the Classroom: The Democratic Power of Discussion*. London: Routledge.
Hess, D. E., & McAvoy, P. (2015) *The Political Classroom: Evidence and Ethics in Democratic Education*. London: Routledge.
Jacobson, D. (2000) "Mill on Liberty, Speech, and the Free Society," *Philosophy and Public Affairs* 29(3): 276–309.
Laats, A., & Siegel, H. (2021) *Teaching Evolution in a Creation Nation*. Chicago: University of Chicago Press.
Langton, R. (2016) "Hate Speech and the Epistemology of Justice," *Criminal Law and Philosophy* 10(4): 865–873.
Levinson, M. (2012) *No Citizen Left Behind*. Cambridge, MA: Harvard University Press.
Lukianoff, G., & Haidt, J. (2019) *The Coddling of the American Mind: How Good Intentions and Bad Ideas are Setting up a Generation for Failure*. London: Penguin Books.
Mahanoy Area School District v. B.L. 141 S. Ct. 2038 (2021).
Maxwell, B., Waddington, D. I., & McDonough, K. (2019) "Academic Freedom in Primary and Secondary School Teaching," *Theory and Research in Education* 17(2): 119–138.
McAvoy, P., & Hess, D. (2013) "Classroom Deliberation in an Era of Political Polarization," *Curriculum Inquiry* 43(1): 14–47.
Meiklejohn, A. (1948) *Free Speech and its Relation to Self-Government*. New York: Harpers Brothers.
Meriwether v. Hartop, 992 F.3d 492 (6th Cir. 2021).
Mill, J. S. (1859/1847) *On Liberty*. Wheeling, IL: Harlan Davidson.
Morse v. Frederick, 551 U.S. 393 (2007).
Post, R. (2009) "Hate Speech," in I. Hare & J. Weinstein (eds.) *Extreme Speech and Democracy*. Oxford: Oxford University Press, 123–138.
Reichman, H. (2019) *The Future of Academic Freedom*. Baltimore: Johns Hopkins University Press.
Ross, C. J. (2015) *Lessons in Censorship*. Cambridge, MA: Harvard University Press.

Roth, M. S. (2019) *Safe Enough Spaces*. New Haven, CT: Yale University Press.
Solorzano, D., Ceja, M., & Yosso, T. (2000) "Critical Race Theory, Racial Microaggressions, and Campus Racial Climate: The Experiences of African American College Students," *Journal of Negro Education* 69(1–2): 60–73.
Strossen, N. (2018) *Hate: Why We Should Resist It with Free Speech, not Censorship*. Oxford: Oxford University Press.
Scott, J. W. (2019) *Knowledge, Power, and Academic Freedom*. New York: Columbia University Press.
Taylor, T., & Guyver, R. (eds.) (2012) *History Wars and the Classroom: Global Perspectives*. Charlotte, NC: IAP.
Tinker v. Des Moines Independent Community School District, 393 U.S. 503 (1969).
Whitney v. California, 274 U.S. 357 (1927)
Whittington, K. E. (2019) *Speak Freely*. Princeton: Princeton University Press.
Zimmer, P. R. J., & Isaacs, P. E. D. (2014) *Report of the Committee on Freedom of Expression*. Unpublished manuscript.
Zimmerman, J. (2005) *Whose America? Culture Wars in the Public Schools*. Cambridge, MA: Harvard University Press.

27

DEMOCRATIC EDUCATION AND THE CONTROVERSY OVER CONTROVERSIAL ISSUES

Johannes Drerup

Introduction

Debating controversial issues in schools is considered one of the central practical means of realizing the aims of democratic education. Yet, which issues should count as controversial is itself contested, both in increasingly polarized political debates and in classrooms across the world (Pace 2021). This makes the task of dealing with controversial issues in the classroom a politically fraught and practically complex challenge for teachers. As representatives of the liberal state and as educators in polarized political environments, teachers have to find ways to reconcile the necessity of impartiality in democratic education with the equally important goal of cultivating concrete civic dispositions and virtues in students that will make them active stewards of democratic life (Hess & McAvoy 2015; Journell 2016). In this vein, teachers have been increasingly exposed to allegations of political partiality or even indoctrination by political movements, parties and parents. In a variety of countries (e.g., Germany, the Netherlands), right-wing political parties have filed complaints against teachers for being non-neutral with respect to the former's political agendas. These developments have resulted in considerable insecurity among teachers concerning what should legitimately count as controversial in educational contexts.

In what follows I will first provide an outline of major aims of democratic education. Second, I will reconstruct some of the contextual factors (e.g., sociopolitical contexts) that should be taken into account in debates about controversial issues in schools. Third, I will engage with the controversy over controversial issues in the philosophy of education and examine two of the most important criteria that have been put forward for the classification of issues as controversial or non-controversial. I will argue that for teachers and students these criteria – the criterion of political authenticity and the epistemic criterion – can fulfill the normative and epistemic functions attributed to them only to a limited extent and are therefore in need of revision. Based on my critique of these criteria, I will develop an alternative pluralistic framework for deciding which issues should count as controversial in the classroom and will defend it against a common objection.[1]

The Aims of Democratic Education

The idea that a functioning and flourishing democracy is essentially dependent on (democratically) educated citizens who are able to take an informed and critical stance on public controversies is anchored in a variety of traditions of democratic education (Honneth 2020). It is based on the

DOI: 10.4324/9781003172246-32

normative ideal of a mutual justificatory relationship between the institutions of liberal democracy, a critical and not merely receptive public sphere (Habermas 1962), and institutionalized practices of democratic education that are geared towards enabling future citizens to participate in collective processes of democratic decision-making and self-determination (Drerup 2020). In this context, democratic education can be understood as an initiation into basic values, norms, and practices that are conducive to the intergenerational reproduction of liberal democracies. It is by no means necessarily geared towards maintaining the societal status quo, nor is it incompatible with the critique and transformation of existing social orders, at least insofar as the critique does not amount to an abolition and radical questioning of basic liberal and democratic values. Education in and for liberal democracy aims to establish a democratic culture of discussion in which individuals – despite disagreements – do not regard and treat each other as enemies, but as dialogue partners, co-shapers of democratic political reality, and sometimes political opponents (Levitsky & Ziblatt 2018), who respect each other as persons with equal rights and freedoms. Children have to learn that in democratic procedures and discussions losses and defeats are unavoidable and have to be endured (Allen 2004) and people must nevertheless deal with each other in a civil, responsive, and tolerant manner (Warnick et al. 2018; Drerup 2018b; Laden 2012).

The central aims of democratic education include the acceptance of basic freedoms, human rights, and other fundamental principles of liberal democracies (such as the separation of powers and pluralism). They also include, above all, personal and political autonomy: the individual ability and willingness to critically and reflexively question one´s own lifestyle and convictions and to develop well-founded and informed positions on politically relevant issues.[2] It follows from its own guiding principles that democratic education also aims at cultivating forms of solidarity that relate to the promotion of the autonomy of *others* and to the dismantling and critique of restrictions of their autonomy in the context of unjustified relations of power and domination. What it can concretely mean to take into account the needs, interests and perspectives of others, however, should not be prescribed in schools, but generally speaking should itself be treated as an object of controversy (except, perhaps, in cases of serious breaches of justice).

Beyond these broad educational ideals, democratic education as a form of *general education* involves instruction in several important domains of knowledge. These include, first, a sufficiently broad spectrum of knowledge about the political world, including knowledge about political institutions and their functions, political traditions, ideals, ideas, and utopias. A second important domain of knowledge and skills concerns dealing appropriately with different forms of arguments and associated validity claims (including a basic form of scientific literacy). A third is knowledge about alternative conceptions of the good, their differences, and justification; and a fourth is knowledge about concrete political disputes and controversies about politics and political concepts and ideas. Examples would include controversies about "democracy" itself, as well as about different ways in which conflicts and dissent concerning politically relevant issues have been dealt with in liberal democracies.

Moreover, democratic education can also be seen as a form of *character education*. As such, it is generally argued that democratic education should be geared towards the cultivation of various communicative and epistemic virtues in addition to the domains of knowledge described above. These include the ability and willingness to articulate one´s own views rationally, to justify them discursively, and to examine and, if necessary, revise them in confrontation with counter-arguments and evidence. Among the epistemic virtues that are crucial for democratic education are respect for evidence, objectivity, epistemic humility, impartiality, and truthfulness, which have an indirect ethical and also political relevance due to their significance for the quality of our judgements (Reichenbach 2017: 196). Fostering these epistemic virtues is important for democratic education because they can counteract epistemic vices – such as dogmatism, excessive deference to authority, and uncritical acceptance of questionable stereotypes and prejudices – which tend to go along with political intolerance (Drerup 2021c).

In light of these aims, the discussion of controversial issues in classrooms can be regarded as one of the central educational means to realizing democratic education's various purposes. Through the practice of discussion, students can become better acquainted with the epistemic contours of issues and with positions different from their own. This can lead them to a better understanding of the premises of their own views and, if necessary, to reflexively question them, or to form a well-founded view in the first place (Hand & Levinson 2012: 617). Classroom debates and the encounters with a plurality of views that go along with them can thus trigger reflective and learning processes that enable students to broaden their personal and political perspectives and contribute to the transcendence of their own self-interest in favor of an orientation towards the common good.[3] In the next section, I will outline some of these ideas in more depth and discuss some of the important contextual features that teachers face in using controversial issues in their classrooms.

Political Classrooms in Context

The challenges of determining which issues should be taught as controversial in schools, and if so how, are significant for different aspects of the school system. These include the *curriculum* and *syllabus* (what issues are present and how are they framed), *textbooks* and *teaching materials* (what issues are included and how they are presented), the design of the *learning environment*, and how *classroom interactions* are shaped by pedagogical arrangements (how issues are introduced and dealt with by teachers). Whether and how certain topics are discussed in class depends on a number of factors. These include the relevant attitudes and knowledge of teachers and the composition of the student body (e.g., socio-economically or politically heterogeneous or homogeneous; age, prior knowledge, and interests; individual sensitivities and vulnerabilities). They also include ethical, legal, and political guidelines and regulations, school ethos and climate, and the socio-political context (which may involve polarized political debates in digital public spheres and political pressure from parents).

One of the most difficult challenges that teachers confront when grappling with controversial issues in the contemporary classroom is the fact that what is considered controversial or not controversial in schools can vary greatly at different times and in different sociopolitical constellations. In other words, what appears controversial depends in part on political power struggles and conflicts outside the classroom (Zimmermann & Robertson 2017; Ho et al. 2017; Wilson 2020). The occasions and objects of controversies thus change with changing social conditions. In some cases, due to rapidly changing norms and societal crises (Levinson & Reid 2018) or dissonances between legal jurisprudence and changing attitudes in the population, it remains unclear and controversial whether and in what respect a topic is still, or should no longer be regarded, as the subject of a genuine socio-political controversy (Hess 2009).

Thus, topics and questions should not be seen as controversial as such, but only as framed by the specific and contingent social-political contexts in which they emerge. Think, for example, of debates about the curricular role of evolutionary theory in the United States, which no longer have any significant relevance in Germany. A related fact about contexts is that teaching controversial issues poses different challenges and risks depending on the circumstances. In highly polarized socio-political contexts, addressing a controversy can cause and intensify already-existing conflicts. Where this is the case, it can be difficult to initiate a genuine controversy at all, if "initiating controversy" is understood as encouraging students to appreciate the epistemic pull of positions other than their own (Yacek 2018). In such circumstances, it might be advisable for teachers to point out the political *relevance* of a debate or the problematic lack of such a debate rather than engage in the debate themselves. In many cases the question is not so much *how* an issue (or a controversy) should be prepared and discussed in class, as *whether* the issue should come up at all. Moreover, there is always the danger that teachers may reproduce questionable discourses, associated stereotypes and prejudices, and one-sided representations of debates (e.g., incorporated in school textbooks) when dealing with controversial issues, instead of putting them up for discussion and scrutiny together with the students. Teachers should therefore be aware of the fact that dialogic practices of democratic education in some cases may (re-)produce and cement the very problems they claim to resolve (Merry 2020). In order to avoid these and related problems, it is of pivotal importance to think about the criteria teachers should use to decide whether an issue should be taught as controversial or not, and what it means to properly treat an issue *as* controversial.

The Controversy Over Controversial Issues

The controversy over controversial issues in the philosophy of education is concerned with various – more or less inclusive – criteria for distinguishing between issues that should be taught as controversial in classrooms and those that should not be taught as controversial. One of the central – though also contested (Warnick & Smith 2014; Gregory 2014) – assumptions of the debate is that all topics that should be discussed openly as controversial should be taught in a non-directive manner, i.e. without intention to compel belief and without using educational means adapted to this aim (such as the use of particular examples to guide the discussion). Such issues should be presented as impartially as possible by taking into account a variety of perspectives. For all issues to which this does not apply, directive forms of teaching are generally considered legitimate. Such methods have the "aim of persuading pupils that a matter is settled, a claim true or a standard justified" (Hand 2020: 14). On this view, if an issue that should be taught controversially is, nevertheless, taught directively, the teacher justifiably faces the charge that she is manipulating or indoctrinating students. In this context, it is important to note that the treatment of a topic as non-controversial does not necessarily imply that the issue should not be discussed in class. It only means that it should not be treated as a controversial issue on which different equally valid and legitimate perspectives exist. The following section will first discuss two of the most important criteria for marking out the realms of directive and non-directive teaching and will then develop an alternative, pluralistic approach to the criteria debate.

The Criterion of Political Authenticity

Diana Hess and Paula McAvoy, in their extensive empirical study of teaching controversial issues in schools, locate their approach in the tradition of deliberative democratic theory. They advocate a contextualist and pragmatic approach to determining which issues count as controversial; emphasizing that teachers must deal with controversial issues on the basis of their professional judgement. They introduce the criterion of political authenticity as follows: "The politically authentic criterion distinguishes between what is bandied about in general society as a matter of controversy and that which has entered the authentic political sphere of decision-making. Using this standard, political issues are controversial when they have traction in the public sphere, appearing on ballots, in courts, within political platforms, in legislative chambers, and as part of political movements" (2015: 168–169). Thus, according to this criterion, the public sphere and the political system have a filter function, which can be relied on to distinguish between controversies that are to be taken seriously in schools and those that are not. However, Hess and McAvoy also acknowledge the problem that controversies are sometimes downplayed or ignored in the public sphere and that sometimes pseudo-controversies are staged so as to increase political polarization (Grammes 2014: 268). Since it is not very productive to discuss empirically false, pseudo-scientific and discriminatory positions as legitimate and equally valid, they introduce an additional distinction between empirical and political questions that should be taken into account when applying the criterion. Empirical questions with regard to which there is no sufficient consensus they call open questions, and those for which there is sufficient consensus they call closed or settled. The same applies to political questions concerning decisions on concrete policies. Apart from the unavoidable problem that it may be unclear how this important distinction should be understood in individual cases, Hess and McAvoy´s proposal has the advantage of being relatively open to different interpretations. Thus, unlike approaches based on epistemically and politically more exclusive criteria, it allows teachers more leeway in including a plurality of real political debates.

Although Hess and McAvoy's methodological realism convincingly acknowledges the many dilemmas associated with teaching controversial issues, it comes nonetheless at the price of too much political and epistemic flexibility, in my view. The criterion of political authenticity is in danger of being strained, for instance, when right- or left-wing populist parties sit in parliament, or when Holocaust deniers hold positions in the ministries and decide what is to be regarded as controversial in the classroom and what is not (which is, unfortunately, the case in Germany at the moment). While these developments speak to the validity and importance of the distinction between facts and political opinions, they also indicate that, depending on the context, it may be an ethos of discontinuity (Brighouse 2007; or non-authenticity) with the goings-on of the public sphere that must be emphasized as a corrective. Such an ethos does not exclude discussing real political debates and policies in class, but it requires that the selection of debates and their educational representation should be handled more restrictively than the criterion of political authenticity suggests. This also applies to the question of the basic political values that should guide democratic education. For example, when it comes to the question of same-sex marriage, Hess and McAvoy ultimately make too great a concession to ideological opponents of democratic ideals of equality, allowing the issue to be considered controversial when it is not one in fact. They do acknowledge though that it can be problematic for teachers to discuss this issue openly and controversially (as they suggest) because framing it this way can seem to discriminate against certain students.

One should think, however, that – despite the advocacy of defenders of traditional conceptions of marriage – this issue *should* be regarded as settled in the 21st century within the context of liberal democracies and that, accordingly, the boundaries of discursive tolerance must be drawn more narrowly (Hand 2007; Drerup 2019). Even if one concedes that trade-offs must always be made in dealing with controversial issues in class (e.g., due to political pressure by parents), the question remains how students are supposed to interact with each other as political equals when the political and empirical reasons for granting or denying them equal rights are discussed in the classroom. One must also ask what positive learning effects these interactions might have for *them*. Some controversies that involve denying equal rights to certain groups are not worth continuing and teachers should be supported in approaching the controversy as closed, if the issue comes up in classroom discussion (Mayo 2016). To justify this, however, one needs more exclusive criteria, such as the epistemic criterion proposed by R. F. Dearden, Michael Hand, and John Tillson.

The Epistemic Criterion

Dearden's epistemic criterion holds that, "a matter is controversial if contrary views can be held on it without those views being contrary to reason. By 'reason' here is not meant something timeless and unhistorical but the body of public knowledge, criteria of truth, critical standards and verification procedures which at any given time has been so far developed" (Dearden 1981: 85). In other words, "A matter is controversial when contrary views can be held on it without being contrary to reason" (Hand 2007: 6). Hand (2007, 2008) argues that when teachers violate this criterion by promoting a position as the only correct one, even though the evidence allows for different rationally defensible positions, they fail to adhere to the overarching aim of helping students develop the capacity for rational reflection. Hand starts from the perfectionist premise that rationality is not only instrumentally valuable but constitutive for a good life, from which he infers that "teachers have an obligation to endorse views for which the relevant evidence and argument is decisive, regardless of whether there are people who sincerely hold contrary views" (Hand 2014: 79). With his interpretation of the criterion, Hand also claims to be able to clarify and settle moral-political questions. Thus, from this perspective, the aforementioned debate on same-sex marriage is not to be treated as controversial, since it is not rationally justifiable to deny people equal rights.

One objection to the criterion is that it amounts to a problematic parallelization of the logic of political argumentation and the logic of scientific argumentation, the former of which generally has lower standards of justification than the latter. Such a treatment of political debates seems to conflate the realities of political discussion and power struggles with the ideals of a philosophical seminar. According to this view, this results in a depoliticization of political debates and in a conception of controversiality that is too narrow and distant from everyday life and excludes too many political debates (Hess & McAvoy 2015: 168). This criticism is supported by arguments against expansionist ideals of critical rationality – standards that teachers could practically never really meet – and an associated rationalistic narrowing of the goals of democratic education. Anti-perfectionist critiques assume that the focus on rational forms of discussion and problem-solving (also in questions of individual lifestyles that are considered private) amounts to an illegitimate octroi because it is not sufficiently neutral (Giesinger 2019), for instance with respect to religious orientations (Cooling 2014).

Hand is certainly right in assuming that an overly broad version of the "controversial" can lead to moral skepticism and relativism on the part of students and can downplay the central importance of good reasons and justifications – especially with respect to moral-political questions – for a healthy democratic culture. Moreover, applying the rationalist orientation associated with the epistemic criterion to questions of the individual good life seems educationally sound and legitimate in light of the many irrationalities to which pupils are exposed outside the school. If, for example, they are told at home that submission to religious or secular authorities should always be uncritically accepted, that COVID-19 is punishment from God, or that Bill Gates is planning compulsory vaccinations for the purpose of mind control, then the boundaries between privately and politically relevant issues often become blurred. It is then advisable and pedagogically required to call these irrationalities by their names instead of respecting them as expressions of privately cultivated doctrines. It is also indeed reasonable to assume with Hand that moral-political positions based on nonsensical empirical assumptions become themselves questionable.

Hand is therefore also right in assuming that there are, of course, nonsensical and empirically wrong positions that cannot be accepted into the classroom other than as unreasonable or irrational and therefore as neither epistemically nor morally justifiable. However, the class of cases where this can be established beyond doubt on *epistemic grounds alone* is certainly smaller in political contexts than he assumes. It is thus not plausible and amounts to a form of "criterion-stretching" to assume that in order to defend basic *political* values it is sufficient to put forward epistemic reasons alone and not also decidedly normative, political and moral reasons (cf. Bogner 2021). Epistemic considerations are certainly of crucial importance when dealing with controversial political issues in educational contexts, in part to provide the relevant facts as a basis for a reasonable debate. To justify decisions concerning what should be taught as controversial with respect to distinctively *political* debates and value conflicts, however, a purely *a*political criterion does not suffice (Clayton 2021). In such decisions both epistemic *and* political reasons and values and hence more than just one criterion will have to be taken into account.

An Alternative Framework

A major theoretical problem of the debate about the pros and cons of the epistemic and the politically authentic criterion ultimately consists in the implausible assumption that one can derive from a *single criterion* for *all* possible cases and issues what is to be taught as controversial or not. In what follows, therefore, an alternative, pluralistic framework is proposed. It offers a third way between the criterion of political authenticity, which leaves too much leeway when it comes to the determination of legitimate limits of political controversiality in educational contexts, and the epistemic criterion, which lacks a substantive political value basis to provide sufficient orientation for the proper evaluation of political controversies. The framework is pluralistic in the sense that it consists of two equally valid and important criteria, a political criterion *and* a "science-oriented" criterion, defined as follows:

1. A politically relevant question should be discussed controversially, if no clear answer can be derived with respect to it on the basis of central political values and principles that are foundational for a good personal and political life in liberal-democratic states (i.e., central fundamental and human rights; personal and political autonomy, value pluralism; as well as separation of powers, protection of minorities, rule of law, etc.).[4]
2. A politically relevant issue should be discussed controversially if there are different reasonable, i.e., well-founded and empirically best substantiated views on this issue and if the relevant issue is considered genuinely controversial in the relevant scientific or research disciplines – according to their own standards of rationality, methods, forms of argumentation and bodies of knowledge. Decisions about whether an issue should be considered controversial should be based on the intellectual and discursive standards – "the intellectual life" (Yacek 2020) and the associated expertise (Tillson 2017; Zimmermann & Robertson 2017) – of scientific disciplines.

These criteria are not to be understood as schematized templates that enable comprehensive interpretations and evaluations of educational situations and simple normative deductions adapted to them. They should rather be understood as pragmatic principles that describe relevant normative limitations of legitimate controversiality, which can be weighted and interpreted differently by educators depending on their particular situations (without thereby losing their fundamental, context-transcending validity). The moderately particularistic thrust of this approach is not to be confused with a radical situationism that considers the criteria debate superfluous (Saetra 2019). It is directed against the naïve assumption of the possibility of simply deducing proper pedagogical action from general criteria that do not sufficiently take into account the relevant contexts of application and reception (e.g., by teachers).

Both criteria should be taken into account in deciding whether an issue should or should not be taught controversially. When it comes to their application, it has to be considered that from the fact that there is a broad scientific consensus on a topic, it does not follow that this also holds for all questions of how to deal with this topic politically (e.g., in the case of climate change or the COVID-19 pandemic). Likewise, from the fact that a topic is largely uncontroversial in political terms it does not necessarily follow that there is no scientific controversy pertaining to it that should be discussed. Thus, the combination of the political criterion and the science-oriented criterion does not imply that all political issues and conflicts could be resolved by referring to the results of scientific research or that the absence of political conflict implies there is no need for scientific research to determine the "facts." Moreover, in many cases it will not be easy (though certainly not impossible) to disentangle matters of fact from political value judgments in political controversies. Despite these difficulties, in order for future citizens to be able to participate in democratic discussions in an informed and critical as well as tolerant and civil way, it is of pivotal importance that teachers adhere to both criteria when they teach controversial issues.

Two major aims should be accomplished when coupling these two criteria: (1) an epistemic civilizing of debates to counteract a politically motivated subordination of reality (McIntyre 2018), and (2) a political civilizing of debates by clarifying and enforcing the limits of tolerance and pluralism in a liberal democracy. This dual – epistemic and political – orientation therefore does not lead to skepticism with regard to moral questions, as Hand argues in his critique of the political criterion (2008), since rational argumentation and the defense of basic democratic values do not rule each other out. At the same time, the justification of political norms – *pace* Hand – requires its own value basis beyond purely epistemic norms, i.e., an independent normative justification – in the case of this approach, a liberal perfectionist justification[5] – which establishes a normative common ground to make civilized and reasonable debates possible in the first place.

When it comes to the presentation of controversies in the classroom, this framework requires educators to draw clear boundaries between what is legitimately negotiable in terms of basic rights and "factual truth(s)" (Arendt 2006: 23) and what is not. For example, the position of the Turkish government on the genocide of the Armenians should provide just as little reason for a genuinely open controversy as the question of whether Angela Merkel is planning to replace the European population with refugees. Corresponding forms of reality distortion, as they are also expressed in political constructions or fictions propagated by right-wing authoritarian movements (e.g., the German "Volksgemeinschaft"), should therefore provide grounds for criticism and directive forms of teaching, but not for an open controversy. An orientation towards truth and truthfulness is constitutive for democratic education; it applies to the way students (who are not to be manipulated and deceived) are treated, to the way students treat each other, and to the discursive practices in which they learn to justify their claims rationally and with reference to relevant scientific evidence (Giesinger 2018). As a cross-curricular task, democratic education is also based on the teaching of basic forms of scientific literacy, i.e., basic aspects of dealing with scientific knowledge in an appropriate and responsible way. Students should understand the fallibility and provisional status of scientific knowledge, but also the necessity of an epistemic division of labor and a certain trust in scientific expertise (cf. the proposals by Benner 2002 and Oulton et al. 2004). Democratic education also requires the cultivation of epistemic virtues, which ideally should enable students to critically question, examine, and correct their beliefs when dealing with political controversies. While this certainly does not protect them against political aberrations per se, nor guarantee political tolerance and civility, it can at least indirectly contribute to a rationalization of political debates in and outside the classroom by creating the conditions for a sufficiently informed and constructive exchange of views and arguments.

The *science-oriented criterion* is not based on the unrealistic and overly demanding assumption that teachers – who are usually not themselves scientists or researchers – can or should reproduce scholarly debates 1-to-1 in the classroom, nor does it imply an overly rationalistic narrowing of the practices and aims of democratic education. It only means that in the selection and presentation of positions and controversies, teachers *ideally* have to orient themselves by the standards and results of scientific and academic debates (Tillson 2017). When applying the science-related criterion, problems of selection and presentation of complex contents inevitably have to be taken into account. The necessity of methodological preparation always entails the risk that relevant positions may be excluded and that – relative to the students´ level of development and knowledge and to the respective state of academic discussion – controversies may be presented in an overly simplified or even distorted way. However, the limits of a "complete" presentation of controversies, which is in any case an unrealistic target not only in pedagogical contexts, can be made explicit and it can be justified (also to students) that certain positions are not addressed for pragmatic reasons (for example, lack of time) (Grammes 2014).

With regard to the application of the *political criterion*, it is obvious that in many cases there are grey areas whose appropriate interpretation can and should be legitimately disputed. What follows from the political criterion is not always clear – in part because basic values can themselves come into conflict with each other – and must therefore in many cases be discussed in open controversies. For example, on issues of migration policy there are a number of defensible positions that cannot easily be described as non-controversial for political reasons. This naturally applies to a bulk of conflicts over ethical, moral, political, and religious issues, which cannot be easily resolved, although the values and principles associated with the political criterion must nevertheless be adhered to in the way these conflicts are dealt with. A central challenge and task of democratic education is that students must learn to tolerate different politically acceptable views and at the same time to draw boundaries of tolerance, i.e., to see what is definitely not compatible with basic fundamental values of liberal democracy (such as racist positions). Apart from all legitimate discussions about grey areas and boundary cases, it must thus be clear that in political questions not *every* case is a boundary case; there are also clear cases where there should be no open and impartially organized controversy. A critical orientation towards and identification with basic political values thus represents the starting point for dealing with controversies in the classroom and for defining the limits of controversy.

Objection

One of the most common objections to more exclusive and demanding criteria is the charge that they result in a form of indoctrination. The term indoctrination is often used in a highly ambiguous way, especially in the public debate, so that sometimes even the mere discussion of a question is considered indoctrination (see the critique of such positions in Hess 2004). With regard to the two criteria discussed above, a central problem is whether democratic education itself produces the consent to the normative requirements and basic values associated with its legitimacy (cf. the discussion in Merry 2020), which could then be evaluated as a form of "manufacturing consent" or indoctrination.

The following responses can be formulated against this objection, the first of which is based on a clarification of the concept of indoctrination: Indoctrination can be understood as a system of practices and arrangements that is usually geared towards enforcing doctrinally justified exercises of power. It is based on forms of justification that are aimed at immunizing themselves as well as the reasons for their supposed validity against criticism. With respect to students or those at the receiving end of indoctrinatory practices, it thereby aims at irreversibly pre-structuring the space of reasons reflexively accessible to them, contrary to the available evidence and on the basis of primarily power-political and not scientifically justified criteria (Drerup 2018b: 15).

The *science-oriented criterion* can be understood as a threefold barrier to indoctrination. *First*, its orientation to subject-specific scientific rationality standards has been shown through historical analyses to have anti-indoctrinary effects (Tenorth 2008). You cannot, for instance, provide a reasonable and sound education for engineers and at the same time expect them to not question claims such as, "Smog does not exist in the DDR, because it is a capitalist phenomenon." *Second*, its orientation to appropriate epistemic-scientific justification of positions excludes attempts at self-immunization against criticism.[6] *Third*, its orientation to methods and contents that accommodate these standards, such as practices of explanation and rational persuasion in dealing with scientifically justified claims about the world, are incompatible with the suppression of critical attitudes (Hand 2020).

Furthermore, the appropriate educational application of the *political criterion* should be oriented towards the aims of personal and political autonomy, which are also to be respected in the educational process. The associated desideratum of minimizing coercion and designing directive educational practices and arrangements in conformity with the educational aim of autonomy is also justified by the fact that authoritarian forms and styles of education tend to result in attitudes and views that can be qualified as anti-democratic and anti-liberal. Liberal democracies, however, depend on the intergenerational reproduction of forms of life and of education that incorporate democratic values (Brumlik 2018: 46). The focus on personal and political autonomy does not imply that there should be no steering towards the justified acceptance of liberal-democratic basic values, whose rational criticism – in whatever form – should nevertheless not be excluded per se. The aim of reducing restrictions on personal and political autonomy that are neither educationally nor politically justified and the simultaneous promotion of the basic values of liberal democracies via democratic education do not rule each other out. They represent overarching aims of democratic education that should be enforced in the educational systems of liberal democracies.

The political criterion and the science-oriented criterion may leave less interpretive leeway and openness with regard to what should be treated as controversial than other criteria (such as the criterion of political authenticity) and this certainly entails a variety of other problems and conflicts (e.g., with members of more traditional communities), but it allows us to draw clear normative boundaries for opponents of liberal democracies who tend to instrumentalize accusations of indoctrination as Trojan horses to reenforce illiberal doctrines.

Conclusion

This proposed approach to dealing with controversy in the classroom suggests three research desiderata worth considering in future work. First, there is still a lack of (representative) quantitative and qualitative studies that contribute to overcoming the normative-empirical divide in the field of democratic education (Gronostay 2019), for example, by taking into account and integrating the philosophical controversy over controversial issues in the context of theory-based empirical research (e.g., the approach of Hess & McAvoy 2015). Of particular interest are the criteria teachers of different subjects[7] actually use when selecting controversial issues, how they justify these decisions and what follows (or does not follow) from this for the practice of discussion as well as its short- and long-term effects on students. Second, and closely related to this, more research is needed about country-specific differences and similarities in the discussion of controversial issues as well as about the effects of different sociopolitical contexts on classroom discussions (see, e.g., Ho et al. 2017; Pace 2021). Third, both to theoretically clarify the status of controversies from different perspectives (of scholars, politicians, practitioners, etc.) and to better prepare educational practitioners for the practice of discussing controversial issues, it will be important to advance the development of models based on normative case studies that reconstruct the complexity of teaching controversial issues in the classroom (Levinson & Fay 2019).

(Related Chapters: 1, 2, 25, 26, 28, 29, 30, 31.)

Notes

1 The following approach to the controversy over controversial issues is based on the comprehensive analysis developed in Drerup (2021a, b), which focus specifically, but not exclusively, on the German debate. I would like to thank Randall Curren and Douglas Yacek for their helpful comments.
2 In the approach defended here, the educational *ideals* of personal and political autonomy entail the cultivation of critical thinking as well as the fostering of other epistemic virtues. For a detailed discussion of critical thinking as an educational aim in its relation to epistemic virtues, see Siegel (2017).
3 A body of quantitative and qualitative research suggests that in classroom discussions children not only learn to discuss matters with each other, but also acquire and cultivate a variety of epistemic, communicative and political attitudes, skills, virtues, and associated bodies of knowledge on which democratic societies depend. These include knowledge about and interest in political issues, critical thinking skills, motivation for political engagement, as well as acceptance of basic democratic values and principles (equality, tolerance, pluralism, etc.) and the ability to deal with conflict in a civil and peaceful way (cf. the overviews in Hess 2002, 2009; Hess & McAvoy 2015; Gronostay 2019; Pace 2021).
4 For related conceptions of a political criterion, see Archard (2002); Petrovic (2013).
5 This liberal perfectionist orientation holds that the promotion of personal and not only political autonomy should be a guiding aim of (democratic) education in liberal democracies and should be promoted and enforced by the public school system as *constitutive* elements of a good personal and political life (Drerup 2018a). This is a central respect in which it differs from politically liberal (Nussbaum 2011), radical democratic (Westphal 2018), and deliberative (Hess & McAvoy 2015) conceptions and justifications of democracy and democratic education. According to this approach, personal autonomy and, similarly, basic forms of science orientation should remain central guiding ideas of the public school system even if this is not acceptable to many parents and communities, e.g. for religious or other reasons, and if majority conditions

change and politicians are in power who ignore scientifically approved facts. The associated liberal perfectionist order of justification of democratic education thus narrows the space of what should be regarded as controversial in political, educational, and epistemic terms (see 4.). At the same time, due to the relatively open formulation of its guiding principles and aims, it remains compatible with a plurality of other positions in democratic theory that can, at least to a certain extent, complement each other (Reichenbach 2020).

6 While it is correct that indoctrination must not necessarily imply the inculcation of "doctrines" and that attempts to indoctrinate in many cases make references to scientific claims (Siegel 2017), these references are usually ideologically motivated and not themselves scientifically justified. Thus, even though it is not per se impossible to indoctrinate scientifically justified content and associated beliefs, in most relevant historical cases of systems of indoctrination it is doctrinal ideologies and not properly justified scientific contents that are major elements and driving forces of indoctrination.

7 Here it would be interesting to learn more about differences (if there are any) between the way teachers of different subjects deal with controversial issues. Moreover, future research should focus less (even though this is important as well) on "best practices" and more on "ordinary" practices of teachers who are less experienced in teaching controversial issues.

References

Allen, D. (2004) *Talking to Strangers*. Chicago: University of Chicago Press.

Archard, D. (2002) "How Should We Teach Sex?" *Journal of Philosophy of Education* 32(3): 437–450.

Arendt, H. (2006) *Wahrheit und Politik*. Berlin: Wagenbach.

Benner, D. (2002) "Die Struktur der Allgemeinbildung im Kerncurriculum moderner Bildungssysteme," *Zeitschrift für Pädagogik* 48(1): 68–90.

Bogner, A. (2021) *Die Epistemisierung des Politischen*. Ditzingen: Reclam.

Brighouse, H. (2007) "Channel One, the Anti-Commercial Principle, and the Discontinuous Ethos," in R. Curren (ed.) *Philosophy of Education: An Anthology*. Oxford: Blackwell, 208–220.

Brumlik, M. (2018) *Demokratie und Bildung*. Berlin: Neofelis.

Clayton, M. (2021) "Against Religious Schools". Unpublished manuscript.

Cooling, T. (2014) "The Epistemic Criterion: A Response to Michael Hand," *Journal of Beliefs & Values* 35(1): 86–89.

Dearden, R. (1981) "Controversial Issues and the Curriculum," *Journal of Curriculum Studies* 13(1): 37–44.

Drerup, J. (2018a) "Zwei und zwei macht vier," Über Indoktrination und Erziehung,"*Diskurs Kindheits- und Jugendforschung* 1: 7–24.

Drerup, J. (2018b) "Education for Democratic Tolerance, Respect and the Limits of Political Liberalism," *Journal of Philosophy of Education* 52(3): 515–532.

Drerup, J. (2019) "Sexualerziehung, staatliche Neutralität und der Wert der Vielfalt," in J. Drerup & G. Schweiger (eds.) *Handbuch Philosophie der Kindheit*. Stuttgart: J. B. Metzler, 430–437.

Drerup, J. (2020) "Demokratische Bildung in und für digitale Öffentlichkeiten. Zeitdiagnosen – Problemvorgaben – Herausforderungen," in U. Binder & J. Drerup (eds.) *Demokratieerziehung und die Bildung digitaler Öffentlichkeiten*. Berlin: Springer VS, 29–53.

Drerup, J. (2021a) *Kontroverse Themen im Unterricht*. Ditzingen: Reclam.

Drerup, J. (2021b) "Demokratieerziehung und die Kontroverse über Kontroversitätsgebote," *Zeitschrift für Pädagogik* 67(4): 480–496.

Drerup, J. (2021c) "Education, Epistemic Virtues, and the Power of Toleration," *Critical Review of International Social and Political Philosophy* 24(1): 108–131.

Giesinger, J. (2018) "The Independence of Education," *On Education. Journal for Research and Debate* 1(1). doi: 10.17899/on_ed.2018.1.4

Giesinger, J. (2019) *Zur Kontroverse um das Kontroversitätsgebot. Ein politisch liberales Kriterium*. https://www.praefaktisch.de/bildung/zur-kontroverse-um-das-kontroversitaetsgebot-ein-politisch-liberales-kriterium/

Grammes, T. (2014) "Kontroversität," in W. Sander (ed.) *Handbuch der politischen Bildung*. Frankfurt am Main: Wochenschau Verlag, 266–274.

Gregory, M. (2014) "The Procedurally Directive Approach to Teaching Controversial Issues," *Educational Theory* 64(6): 627–648.

Gronostay, D. (2019) *Argumentative Lehr-Lern-Prozesse im Politikunterricht. Eine Videostudie*. Wiesbaden: Springer VS.

Habermas, J. (1962) *Strukturwandel der Öffentlichkeit*. Berlin: Suhrkamp.

Hand, M. (2007) "Should We Teach Homosexuality as a Controversial Issue?" *Theory and Research in Education* 5(1): 69–86.

Hand, M. (2008) "What Should We Teach as Controversial? A Defense of the Epistemic Criterion," *Educational Theory* 58(2): 213–228.
Hand, M. (2014) "Religion, Reason and Non-directive Teaching: A Reply to Trevor Cooling," *Journal of Beliefs & Values* 35(1): 79–85.
Hand, M. (2020) "Moral Education and the Community of Inquiry," *Journal of Philosophy in Schools* 7(2): 4–20.
Hand, M. & Levinson, R. (2012) "Discussing Controversial Issues in the Classroom," *Educational Philosophy and Theory* 44(6): 615–629.
Hess, D. (2002) "Discussing Controversial Public Issues in Secondary Social Studies Classrooms: Learning from Skilled Teachers," *Theory and Research in Social Education* 30(1): 10–41.
Hess, D. (2004) "Controversies about Controversial Issues in Democratic Education," *Political Science & Politics* 37(2): 257–261.
Hess, D. (2009) *Controversy in the Classroom: The Democratic Power of Discussion*. London: Routledge.
Hess, D. & McAvoy, P. (2015) *The Political Classroom*. London: Routledge.
Ho, L., McAvoy, P., Hess, D. & Gibbs, B. (2017) "Teaching and Learning about Controversial Issues and Topics in the Social Studies: A Review of the Research," in M. McGlinn Manfra & C. Mason Bolick (eds.) *The Wiley Handbook of Social Studies Research*. Oxford: Wiley-Blackwell, 321–335.
Honneth, A. (2020) *Die Armut unserer Freiheit*. Berlin: Suhrkamp.
Journell, W. (ed.) (2016) *Teaching Social Studies in an Era of Divisiveness*. Lanham, MD: Rowman & Littlefield.
Laden, A. S. (2012) *Reasoning: A Social Picture*. Oxford: Oxford University Press.
Levinson, M. & Reid, E. (2018) "The Paradox of Partisanship," *On Education. Journal for Research and Debate* 1(1). doi: 10.17899/on_ed.2018.1.3
Levinson, M. & Fay, J. (2019) *Democratic Discord in Schools*. Cambridge, MA: Harvard Education Press.
Levitsky, S. & Ziblatt, D. (2018) *How Democracies Die*. New York: Broadway Books.
Mayo, J. B. (2016) "The Imperative to Teach Marriage Equality in the Social Studies Classroom: A History, Rationale, and Classroom Practice for a More Inclusive Democracy," in W. Journell (ed.) *Teaching Social Studies in an Era of Divisiveness*. Lanham, MD: Rowman & Littlefield, 79–92.
McIntyre, L. (2018) *Post-Truth*. Cambridge, MA: MIT Press.
Merry, M. (2020) *Educational Justice*. London: Palgrave.
Nussbaum, M. (2011) "Perfectionist Liberalism and Political Liberalism," *Philosophy and Public Affairs* 39(1): 3–45.
Oulton, C., Dillon, J., & Grace, M. (2004) "Reconceptualizing the Teaching of Controversial Issues," *International Journal of Social Science Education* 26(4): 411–423.
Pace, J. (2021) *Hard Questions*. Lanham, MD: Rowman & Littlefield.
Petrovic, J. (2013) "Reason, Liberalism and Democratic Education: A Deweyan Approach to Teaching about Homosexuality," *Educational Theory* 63(5): 525–541.
Reichenbach, R. (2017) "Lernen im Kollektiv – Schule und Demokratie," in R. Reichenbach & Bühler, P. (eds.) *Fragmente zu einer pädagogischen Theorie der Schule*. Weinheim: Beltz, 196–207.
Reichenbach, R. (2020) *Bildungsferne*. Zürich: Diaphanes.
Saetra, E. (2019) "Teaching Controversial Issues: A Pragmatic View of the Criterion Debate," *Journal of Philosophy of Education* 53(2): 323–339.
Siegel, H. (2017) *Education's Epistemology: Rationality, Diversity, and Critical Thinking*. Oxford: Oxford University Press.
Tenorth, H.-E. (2008) "Unterwerfung und Beharrungskraft – Schule unter den Bedingungen deutscher Diktaturen," *Schweizerische Zeitschrift für Bildungswissenschaft* 30(2): 275–297.
Tillson, J. (2017) "When to Teach for Belief: A Tempered Defense of the Epistemic Criterion," *Educational Theory* 67(2): 173–191.
Warnick, B. & Smith, S. (2014) "The Controversy over Controversies: A Plea for Flexibility and for 'soft-directive' Teaching," *Educational Theory* 64(3): 227–244.
Warnick, B., Yacek, D. W., & Robinson, S. (2018) "Learning to be Moved: The Modes of Democratic Responsiveness," *Philosophical Inquiry in Education* 25(1): 31–46.
Westphal, M. (2018) "Kritik- und Konfliktkompetenz," *APuZ* 68(13–14): 12–17.
Wilson, T. (2020) "Contesting Public Education: Opting Out, Dissent, and Activism," *Educational Theory* 70(3): 247–254.
Yacek, D. (2018) "Thinking Controversially: The Psychological Condition for Teaching Controversial Issues," *Journal of Philosophy of Education* 52(1): 71–86.
Yacek, D. (2020) *The Criterion of Disciplinary Authenticity for Teaching Controversial Issues*. Unpublished manuscript.
Zimmermann, J. & Robertson, E. (2017) *The Case for Contention*. Chicago: University of Chicago Press.

28

COLLEGE TEACHING, INDOCTRINATION, AND TRUST

Anthony Simon Laden

According to a standard conservative talking point, US colleges and universities, overrun by left-leaning faculty, are indoctrinating their students. The implication is that college teachers have abdicated their responsibility to transmit useful and civically valuable knowledge and teach various intellectual skills in favor of a program of ideological conversion to some ungodly mix of socialism, secular humanism, feminism, queer liberation, and critical race theory. As with most of the live fronts in the culture wars, this line of criticism manages to both give expression to a genuine anxiety many parents feel about sending their children to college while at the same time calling forth strident defenses from its target that fail to address that very anxiety. The result is that colleges and their faculty, in defending themselves against what they understand the charge to be, only serve to reinforce the impression that generates the anxiety in the first place. In this essay, I diagnose this failure to adequately respond to the charge of indoctrination as the result of a conceptual mistake, and so propose that the way forward starts with some philosophy. In particular, I argue that the failure begins when college teachers and those defending them hear the charge of indoctrination as one about beliefs – how they are formed and potentially transformed. I suggest, instead, that the underlying concern is not so much about what students come to believe, but rather who and what they trust.

The Conventional Debate

Although there is debate about how, precisely, to characterize indoctrination and to locate its epistemic and moral deficiencies, debates on the topic in political philosophy and the philosophy of education tend to focus on beliefs. It is commonly held that indoctrinating someone, like brainwashing them, involves not merely leading them to form new beliefs, but doing so in an epistemically (and perhaps, morally) inappropriate manner. The debate concerns how to characterize that manner.[1] Thus, indoctrination is said by some to be the inculcation of beliefs that are either false or that are inculcated with no regard to their truth. Others argue that it is a process of belief transmission that in various ways by-passes rational processes of belief formation. A third position holds that the distinctive feature of indoctrination lies in the sort of believing it cultivates, one that aims for the close-minded adherence to the indoctrinated beliefs. All these positions support a background picture whereby those doing the indoctrinating somehow plug a set of beliefs into others directly, so that their efforts cannot be resisted or later rejected. According to this common picture, coming to hold beliefs via indoctrination is different from coming to hold them as a result of a genuinely educative process that includes reflection or the availability of new information. It is this

 DOI: 10.4324/9781003172246-33

understanding of what is distinctive about indoctrination that explains why the charge that faculty are indoctrinating their students packs such a rhetorical punch while the otherwise similar charge that faculty are teaching students left-wing world views does not.

Some common replies to the charge of indoctrination suggest that this is how the charge is understood by those who deny it. Consider, for examples, the following three lines of defense:

1 College instructors could not directly impart questionable beliefs because they do not have that kind of effectiveness or power. A student in a college classroom will spend 30–40 hours spread out over several months with an instructor, and at most a couple of hundred more engaged in the material of the class, chosen by that instructor. Compared to the 18 or more years that the student has spent at home, with her parents and in a particular community, the time in a single class is completely marginal. Besides, if college teachers had the power to mold their students' beliefs, they would certainly use it to impart beliefs about study habits or class attendance as important paths to success and better grades. Since that seems to be beyond most of our abilities, it is hard to think we are radically transforming students' more deep-seated moral, religious, or political beliefs.
2 College instructors are not trying to implant beliefs, but to encourage critical thinking. Even instructors who consciously choose to teach left-wing points of view on controversial topics (as I have done), are not aiming to convert their students, but to make them think hard and well about difficult issues. We consider our teaching a success if the student does that critical and reflective work, regardless of the beliefs they leave the class with.
3 To the extent that college teachers are trying consciously to mold their students' values and attitudes, it is not in order to shape them toward partisan positions. Rather, we are concerned to cultivate values that citizens need to sustain the fabric of democracy. That is, even if some of what happens in a university classroom aims at value transformation, it is merely training into democratic citizenship, which is among the legitimate purposes of a university in a democratic society. All of us (not just left-leaning faculty) should want students to learn to respect all other people as political equals, to listen respectfully, and to be committed to basic democratic ideals and norms.

These replies are, in one sense, perfectly good defenses against the charge of indoctrination. First, they by and large accurately describe what goes on in college classrooms: faculty have a lot less sway over the political beliefs of their students than it is often suggested they have; they are not, for the most part, trying to convert anyone; and they are concerned with making their students better citizens, along with their other educational aims. Moreover, these are also defensible things for university teachers to be doing: the society at large should want us to be helping students become more careful and critical thinkers and better citizens. Nevertheless, these replies rarely assuage those making the charge.[2] That suggests that the heart of the problem to which the charge is giving expression lies elsewhere. Before exploring where the real problem lies, we need a detour into social epistemology and in particular, the role of trust in the acquisition, production, and transmission of knowledge.

Trust and Knowledge

Social epistemology is a somewhat heterogenous field that investigates the role of social relations, institutions, and contexts in knowledge production, acquisition, and transmission. To a large extent, philosophers who work in social epistemology have been interested in trust insofar as it seems to play a role in the transmission and production of knowledge. For instance, it seems that in order to understand how we form beliefs on the basis of other people telling us things, we need to understand the role trust plays in that process. In what follows, I am mostly concerned with something like the reverse direction: How does the transmission, acquisition, and production of knowledge shape vectors of trust? I argue that it is the transformation of these vectors of trust in the course of a college education that spurs the charge of indoctrination.

To make that thought clearer, we need to see trust in a particular light. In a recent paper, C. Thi Nguyen argues that trust, in at least one of its more ubiquitous forms, can be understood as taking an "unquestioning attitude" toward someone or something (Nguyen forthcoming). When I look at my watch and it says 3:10, I accept that this is the time. I do not try to verify it or look into the watch's mechanics to make sure its springs are properly calibrated. I enter the information it gives me directly into my thinking processes. In doing so, I take an unquestioning attitude to my watch: I trust what it tells me. We trust the deliverances of our senses and the solidity of the physical objects around us in a similar manner. Think here of the difference in how you walk along a solid sidewalk, and how you walk when feeling your way across marshy ground or crusted snow. Turning closer to the cases that interest us here, we can also trust people and what they tell us in this way. When I trust the stranger in an unfamiliar city to give me directions when I ask, I just take off in the direction she points without hesitation or a quick look at my map. If I trust the *New York Times* to accurately report the monthly unemployment rate, then I do not check their figure against those of other news organizations or government agencies, or spot check the raw data coming out of the Bureau of Labor Statistics. In trusting these sources, I give the information I receive from them direct access to my cognitive processes. This allows me to use what they tell me as the material for my thinking rather than the subject of my thinking.[3] Because my watch says 3:10, I rush out of my office, suddenly realizing that I am late to pick up my child at school. Because the *New York Times* reported that the unemployment rate is rising sharply, I reconsider leaving my job just now, and begin to worry whether the party currently in power will be able to stay there at the next election.

Nguyen points out that trust of this sort is a necessary form of agency extension: given that we are finite beings and have both finite abilities and particularly finite mental space and processing capacity, we of necessity have to off-load a certain amount of thinking. Trust allows us to do that by letting us take on board directly certain kinds of already processed information, or by otherwise relieving us of the need to verify every step. That means that we cannot survive without a rather large amount of trust.

We misunderstand just how prevalent and complex trust is to our capacity for knowledge if we focus solely on direct testimony and our trust in particular sources. Consider what lies behind my trust in the *New York Times* report about the monthly unemployment rate. If I believe and consider myself justified in believing that the unemployment rate in the United States in December of 2021 was 3.9% because I read it in *The New York Times,* this involves several chains of trust. In order to trust the figure, I have to trust the journalist who reports it. But my trust in her is likely not to be based on any direct knowledge of her. Rather, I trust her because I trust a range of other processes and structures: the hiring process that landed her at the paper, and the editorial process that put this figure on the page. This is what it means for me to trust *The New York Times* more generally. But even those processes do not end the role of trust here. The hiring process trusts the various people who recommended her and the credentialing institutions that certify her competence to report on economic news. She, in turn, trusts, at least to some degree, the Bureau of Labor Statistics to report its finding accurately, and the Bureau trusts its processes of gathering information, those charged with gathering it, and the theories that generate a single figure out of a mess of data. And so forth. If I lose faith in any link along that chain – if I come to think that universities are handing out degrees in journalism or economics without cause or that the basic theoretical work that guides economic modelling is flawed, or that the Bureau has been captured by political interests and is no longer a neutral assembler of data but a partisan actor – then I will not take an unquestioning attitude to the figure I read in my morning paper.

Moreover, in addition to all these chains that lead back from this figure, I rely on another range of watchdog agencies that check up on the reliability of all these connections. Part of what supports my trust that the Bureau has not been corrupted or that the *Times* has not started hiring bad journalists is that I trust that such agencies would ferret this out and make it publicly known. Thus, I can continue to trust these links because I have heard nothing that would tell me to stop doing so. A lot of our beliefs about the world, and practically all of those that we might acquire in a college classroom, rest on these complex webs of institutions that I will call a trust network. When people say that they "believe in facts" or "believe in science," what they actually mean is that they trust a certain set of institutions and procedures. When others are skeptical of the facts or scientific findings they are exhorted to believe, this is often a result of not trusting those same institutions and procedures.[4] What we know and believe is a function of which trust networks we inhabit. One way, then, to change someone's epistemic capacities is to change the trust networks she inhabits.

Trust is also a form of intimacy. When I trust, I give someone or something direct and unmediated access to my judgments, removing the barriers and filters that come from being critical and questioning information that I receive. Trusting involves allowing the trusted in past the walls of my thoughts and psyche, as it were. That is, after all, why it is both necessary and valuable. But, like other forms of intimacy, taking up the unquestioning attitude of trust leaves us vulnerable: to making mistakes and bad judgments, and to being manipulated, among other things. Moreover, because trust is a form of intimacy, the trust networks we inhabit shape not only our epistemic position but our social one. And the connection trust forges between our epistemic and social positions goes both ways. I am more likely to trust what those with whom I am socially connected tell me, but I am also more able to form social connections with people who inhabit the same trust networks as I do. When two people inhabit the same or at least overlapping trust networks, then they have points of reference in common, and this will make it easier for them to talk with one another. For people who occupy different trust networks, easy conversation may be difficult, and this can make forging or sustaining social ties more challenging.

College and the Engineering of Trust Networks

Students enter college with a particular trust network; they accept in an unquestioning way the information they receive from certain people and institutions, and not from others. They can take input from certain kinds of information sources in a fluent way, but not others. Though this may be reflected in the beliefs they hold or the political and moral positions they take, it goes beyond this to capture their networks of intimacy. The trust networks they inhabit are shaped by but also help to sustain their social ties to their families, friends, and communities. Over the course of their time in college, however, the shape of that network changes, sometimes in profound and radical ways. Moreover, these changes are not incidental to the education they receive in college, nor are they the results of educational malpractice.

College classes not only aim to provide their students with new information, but to train them within a discipline. That involves teaching students to understand and access information from certain specialized sources and import that information into their thinking processes directly. Forms of information become legible to students through this training and the result of that legibility is that while they may question certain findings and claims within a discipline, large swaths of the background that informs the discipline is taken on board unquestioningly. In other words, students learn to add various disciplinary sources to their trust networks. So, for instance, although a history student may learn to question the expert claims of an eminent historian, that very questioning will be made possible by an ability to assimilate all sorts of other material directly: information that surrounds the claim, but also information about how historical claims are made and debated, what archival processes are reliable and what counts as evidence for what. Learning all this greatly expands the student's cognitive reach by extending her trust networks.

Disciplinary training extends both cognitive reach and critical capacities by extending and preserving the epistemic integrity of certain trust networks. But beyond this sort of training of critical capacities, colleges and their instructors aim to teach broader skills of critical thinking. In developing these broader skills, teachers train students to raise questions about a wide variety of things they previously left unquestioned. Training in this sort of critical thinking thus serves to prune students' trust networks. Note that this pruning takes place even if the students' beliefs remain unchanged. A student who learns to subject the beliefs she brought from home to critical scrutiny and decides to affirm them may nevertheless stand in a different relation to those beliefs than she once did. She may hold them, but no longer because she trusts the sources on which she previously relied.

Next, consider what happens in the training for citizenship that college teachers also claim to do. Developing democratic habits involves, among other things, learning to regard those of your fellow citizens who are different or unfamiliar with respect as equals. One aspect of treating others as equals is not to dismiss them and their points of view in an unquestioning way. In other words, learning to treat others equally involves no longer automatically excluding them from the possibility of becoming part of your trust network. Perhaps even more important, a great deal of what gets included under the guise of learning the rules, norms, and values of civic reasoning and civic behavior involves putting trust in certain kinds of authorities and expertise. It involves trusting those with academic and university credentials: the scientific community, published research, the expertise of those with law and medical and engineering degrees, and certain kinds of journalism. It is their trust in these sorts of institutions that ground some people's comfortable claim that they "believe in facts."

Finally, leaving the classroom for a minute, note that when students come to college, they also meet new people, forge new friendships, and attenuate or drop ties to former social circles and friends. College changes their social environment, and this also affects what they trust.[5]

Note, moreover, that in doing this work, college teachers do more than merely give our students the tools to exercise greater and more deliberate control over their trust networks. We actively aim to develop a particular trust network and train our students to rely on it: one that relies on the sort of complex institutional web that allows me to trust the mainstream media, the reports of government agencies, and the knowledge produced by credentialed expertise. We do not just arbitrarily choose these networks and they are not merely the ones we happen to inhabit, although, by and large, we do inhabit them. We think that they are epistemically advantageous: they help us and others know more and more deeply and surely about the world. We have reason to think that inhabiting them improves our understanding. One reason to think so is that the networks themselves are structured to be open to criticism and subject to the discipline of reason.

But even if there are good reasons to inhabit such a network, and so good reasons for college teachers to help their students do so, we should not lose sight of the effect that a transformation of their trust network has on some of our students. Although some students arrive in our classrooms inhabiting more or less the same trust network that we aim to build for them, many others do not. Maybe they trust more fully in religious authorities or the wisdom and passed-down knowledge of their communities. They may be skeptical of the good will or reliability of the sources and institutions we teach them to trust. Perhaps they come from communities who have suffered harm at the hands of those very institutions, or on whom the inhabitants of these trust networks look with a certain condescension or contempt. For those students, a university education not only serves to give them control over their trust networks but aims to radically change their content and shape.[6] If it succeeds, however, it risks leaving them alienated from the communities and families from which they came, even if it does not change the content of their beliefs and values.

So, even if there are good reasons to build new trust networks for these students in an effort to improve their epistemic standing, in doing so, we also change who they are and which social networks they can comfortably inhabit. In particular, we make it harder for them to fit into the social networks from which they came. Such changes may be reflected in a change in their beliefs, the sources of those beliefs, or the ways those beliefs are held, but they need not be. And so, the mere fact that college teachers are not converting our students to new beliefs about fundamental matters or manipulating their thought processes in some insidious manner, does not mean we are not changing where they stand, epistemically and socially.

Indoctrination, Revisited

Consider, then, what such a transformation looks like to those with whom a student was originally intimate. A student goes off to college and then starts to take an unquestioning attitude to things and people who they did not trust previously and who those back home may still not trust. They begin to stand at a certain distance from those in whom their families, friends, and communities place their trust. When those we love or care about begin to trust people and sources that we do not, and they begin forming new social ties with people we may not trust, and distancing themselves from their old social ties, it will not look like they have been taught or convinced or have otherwise reflectively changed their beliefs. It will look as if they have been indoctrinated. These are all tell-tale signs that someone is in an abusive relationship, for instance.

This suggests that the basic worry to which the criticism that colleges are indoctrinating students gives expression concerns this transformation of trust networks. So understood, it gives voice to a basic anxiety that comes with being a parent or standing in any intimate relation with others: the fear that the intimacy will be damaged, that one's intimates will drift away, become distant. It also arises from a recognition of an undeniable and central part of what colleges deliberately aim to do, and so it does not miss its mark in the way that the charge of indoctrination understood in terms of belief manipulation is thought to do. This is a charge, then, that warrants not merely a defensive reply, but a genuine response.

If, however, we want to respond and not merely reply to the charge of indoctrination, I think we need to consider head-on just what it is about a college education that can be alienating, and what to do about it. When we ask this question, it turns out that there is an interesting overlap between criticisms of university education from the left and the right. Whereas the criticism on the right is often framed in terms of indoctrination, the one from the left is framed around an idea of inclusion. If the analysis of the charge of indoctrination presented here is on the right track, however, those are versions of the same worry.

Concerns with inclusion center on the need for colleges to recognize the subtle and not-so-subtle ways they are structured to be welcoming to members of various dominant groups while being hostile or unwelcoming to those from marginalized groups or with marginalized identities. Some forms of failures of inclusion involve unstated assumptions that colleges and universities make about their students and faculty: the resources they have access to, or the training in certain forms of social interaction and relation to authority figures (Jack 2019). Others involve a failure to realize the kinds of ethical costs students from marginalized communities end up paying to fit into the cultural world of college and college graduates (Morton 2019). Finally, these critics challenge the assumptions colleges and their faculty tend to make that the trust networks they inhabit and develop for their students are, in fact, trustworthy. The critics point out that when they point out the problems with these assumptions, they are often met with an attitude of dismissive arrogance. They point to the similarity between this attitude and that which colonizers routinely take to colonized populations. Note, however, that all three of these charges point to the potential costs imposed on students and their communities when colleges transform their trust networks, along with charges that the trust networks colleges cultivate may not be as trustworthy as they are made out to be.

The rhetoric of inclusion tends to focus on bases of marginalization like class, disability, race, gender, and sexuality. That of indoctrination tends to focus on political ideology and religiosity. But in both cases, a sound basis of the concern lies with the particular trust networks that colleges aim to develop for their students: such trust networks are not universal or neutral, and they tend not to align well with the trust networks of communities and populations that do not have a widespread history of college education or commitments to, or a positive history with, the trust networks in which universities and their faculties are anchored. The concurrence between criticisms of indoctrination and of failure to be inclusive are obscured because each side accuses the other of being part of the problem they are criticizing. Among the ideologies colleges are supposed to be indoctrinating their students into are those like radical feminism and anti-racism that developed in part in response to a recognition that mainstream social institutions like colleges were not inclusive. It is thus thought that the primary driver of policies and practices that aim to indoctrinate conservative students are those demanding that colleges be more inclusive.

If, however, we focus less on the content of ideology and belief, and more on the structure of trust networks, the two complaints line up well. Both charges start from the recognition that a college education is designed in part to enmesh students into a certain kind of trust network. They also both recognize that this network is not neutral or universal; it is already the home of some students but not others, and its degree of compatibility with their home networks varies quite a bit. Finally, they both raise genuine concerns about the content of the trust network that colleges develop in their students, even if the content of those concerns is not always the same. In both cases, they perceive that some students are essentially presented a choice in college: to move into the newly acquired trust networks and abandon those from home, or to reject what college offers in an effort to preserve the ties of home.

What, then, might a more adequate response to the charge of indoctrination look like? Here I focus on how it might shape or re-shape what happens in college classrooms, and how college teachers approach their work.[7] We could start by being more open, honest, and transparent about what the hoped-for effects of our teaching are. Although we should not be trying to convert our students or manipulate them into having beliefs we favor, we can be doing none of that and still working to re-shape their trust networks. Approaching what we do as the engineering of trust networks makes it easier for us to accept the effects of our teaching and to then begin to confront the fact that what we are doing can impose ethical and other costs on our students. Unlike the mere transmission of information or training in particular useful skills, re-engineering someone's trust networks, even in ways that benefit them, is an intimate and awesome task. Teachers can begin to respond to charges of indoctrination by accepting the responsibility that comes with such a task. It would, for instance, make it harder to resort to polly-annish comments about transformation or to deflect our responsibility by down-playing the deep effects of what we, collectively, do.

Owning up to this description of what we try to do in our classrooms makes it easier as well to see the trust that is placed in us by the students who sit in our classrooms and the families that send them to us. Having trust placed in you calls for a certain kind of response: a mix of gratitude, care, and reciprocity. When someone trusts you, they honor you in regarding you as trustworthy, and that calls for gratitude in response. At the very least, showing students and families gratitude for the trust they place in us would rule out treating them with contempt or derision, deriding their values or ways of life as merely something to be overcome or escaped. Beyond that, we can show gratitude for the trust that is placed in us by showing due care for that which is entrusted to us. In the case of our students and their trust networks this means several things. First, we need to be attentive to whether or not we are in fact improving our students' trust networks through our efforts at re-engineering them. College teachers can become complacent in our beliefs in the superiority of our own trust networks and ways of knowing, and merely assume that initiating others into those networks will mark an epistemic improvement for them. Most of what gets taught in college classes and most of the transformations in trust networks that happen there no doubt do improve the epistemic position of students, but taking seriously the trust placed in us means being attentive to whether that is always the case and being able to articulate to those who ask how and why it is.

Second, seeing the epistemic position of our students in terms of trust networks helps us see that we are being entrusted with more than their epistemic standing. Showing due care for the trust networks of our students as we work to improve their epistemic standing requires being aware of and concerned about the social effects and costs that such improvement might impose on them, and either not imposing it unnecessarily or helping them address and shoulder those costs when they are inevitable. Teaching them not only how to inhabit a new trust network, but how to build bridges between their new and old trust networks can help them mitigate the social and ethical costs that may come with epistemic improvement. Finally, when we are entrusted with something's care, we also incur obligations toward those who place their trust in us. If you trust me to take care of your prized Ming vase, I should not juggle with it, even if my skills as a juggler mean that I am not putting the vase at any risk. That is because I owe you care as well: not to exploit the anxieties and fears that may come with entrusting something you value to another's care. So, similarly, we should be mindful of what we owe to our students' families and communities who entrust their children's trust networks to us. I do not think we owe them complete deference or help in cementing their own values into our students' networks. But we owe them something like a manifest attentiveness to our students' value and values and, in particular, the role those values play in fortifying their social ties. One way to do that is to work to ensure that our classrooms are safe spaces for doing this kind of work. Safety here does not require freedom from challenge or criticism, but it does require some level of assurance that in the course of making oneself vulnerable to changing, one is not thereby put in danger, whether of failure, ridicule, or condemnation.

The third aspect of an appropriate response to trust is reciprocity. We repay someone's trust in us both by being trustworthy and by returning their trust. Being trustworthy involves more than being competent at the task you have been trusted to do. It also requires a certain manifest responsiveness to the vulnerability and dependence that the trusting person's trust creates for them. One way to manifest such responsiveness is to not ignore or dismiss their challenges and criticisms. In the case of being trustworthy in our efforts to engineer our students' trust networks, this means demonstrating when called on that our own trust networks are worthy of habitation and open to being questioned and challenged. Taking another's challenges seriously and being open to the possibility of their challenges involves accepting a certain kind of vulnerability towards and dependence on them. In other words, we can demonstrate our own trustworthiness by being willing to trust our students with our own trust networks. This need not involve letting our students convert us any more than we expect their trust in us involves them submitting to being converted by us. What it requires is that what they say can change how we think, both about them, and about the world we are helping them figure out and understand. In other words, it turns out that to teach them well, and not indoctrinate them, we also have to be willing to learn from them.[8]

(Related Chapters: 4, 5, 11, 12, 23, 26, 27, 29.)

Notes

1 For an overview see Callan and Arena (2009).

2 In some cases, the reply fails because the charge is not made in good faith in the first place. Since the person making the charge is trying to score political points or demonize an institution, she is happy to focus on an unrepresentative sample of classroom behaviors that even most faculty would consider educational malpractice. Since I think there is a form of the charge that is made in good faith and is worth engaging with, I am going to ignore the bad faith version of the charge here, even if it is common.

3 This is not to say that I cannot at any time turn my attention to the trusted source and investigate it. But then I am no longer treating it as a trusted source.

4 This does not imply that facts are subjective or that we are entitled to our own version of the facts. Some trust networks are epistemically better than others, some institutions are more trustworthy than others. The point is that in order to compare epistemic positions, we have to investigate a more subtle and complex social web that centrally involves relations of trust and questions of trustworthiness.
5 I explore this avenue by which a college education can transform a trust network in more detail in Laden 2022. For a discussion of the role of friends in working our way out of certain kinds of dysfunctional trust networks, see Nguyen 2020.
6 I note here in passing that this suggests that the divide that is sometimes drawn between treating a college education as an opportunity to develop knowledge and skills and treating it as a potentially transformative experience is merely apparent. Insofar as the development of knowledge and skills requires a re-engineering of a student's trust networks, it will also be transformative.
7 See Laden 2022 for a broader range of strategies.
8 This chapter was prompted by engaging with some work by Gina Schouten, and it has greatly benefitted from conversations and feedback from her, Harry Brighouse, Carrie Welsh, Annette Martín, Sam Fleischacker, Anne Eaton, Paula McAvoy, Jennifer Morton, Sarah Stitzlein, and the members of the Center for Ethics and Education's 2020–21 Summer Graduate Institute. I am grateful to Randall Curren for the opportunity to include it here, and for his final editorial and philosophical suggestions.

References

Callan, E., & Arena, D. (2009) "Indoctrination," in H. Siegel (ed.) *The Oxford Handbook of Philosophy of Education*. Oxford University Press, 104–121.
Jack, A. (2019) *The Privileged Poor.* Cambridge, MA: Harvard University Press.
Laden, A. (2022) "The Social Costs of a College Education" in S. Cahn (ed.) *Academic Ethics Today*. Lanham, MD: Rowman and Littlefield, 231–239.
Morton, J. (2019) *Moving Up Without Losing Your Way*. Princeton: Princeton University Press.
Nguyen, C. T. (2020) "Echo Chambers and Epistemic Bubbles," *Episteme* 17(2): 141–161.
Nguyen, C. T. (forthcoming) "Trust as an Unquestioning Attitude," in T. S. Gendler & J. Hawthorne (eds.) *Oxford Studies in Epistemology*, vol. 7. Oxford: Oxford University Press.

29

CLIMATE, SCIENCE, AND SUSTAINABILITY EDUCATION

Matt Ferkany

Introduction

In recent years, debates about lay cognition of scientific information and science communication have been at the forefront of debates about climate communication and education, and to a lesser extent, sustainability education (McCaffrey & Rosenau 2012; Priest 2013; Bedford 2016; Plutzer et al. 2016; Ranney & Clark 2016). Theories and evidence concerning especially the motivated cognition of scientific information, and about the frailty of human cognition generally (such as *dual systems* and *argumentative theories of reasoning*), have been taken to suggest that *science literacy* – in the sense of knowing some basic results or methods of the sciences – will be insufficient to ensure that citizens form beliefs and attitudes consistent with consensus climate (and other) science (Suldovsky 2018), and in particular with the thesis that observed global warming in the past 50–100 years is primarily anthropogenic (the AGW or anthropogenic global warming thesis).

Climate contrarians indeed have self-reported high levels of general science literacy (Kahan et al. 2012) and climate literacy (McCright & Dunlap 2011). Many researchers have thus concluded that climate communicators and educators should move away from teaching that reflects a *deficit model* of the causes of science ignorance/denialism and of the methods of remediating it, namely, ignorance of relevant scientific knowledge or methods, or other misunderstanding of science, and teaching designed to remedy such ignorance and misunderstanding (Priest 2013; Bardon 2019; Feinstein & Waddington 2020).

What to put in its place has been a matter of some disagreement. But widely discussed strategies include careful framing of the climate change issue in educator language (Nisbet and Mooney 2007); teaching key ideas about the nature of science (NOS), such as the epistemic status of scientific claims (i.e., they are reliable truths, not certainties) (Feinstein & Waddington 2020); or "inoculating" the learner against fallacious anti-science arguments by exposing them to the scientific consensus or to past examples and showing why they are fallacies (e.g., "The evidence linking smoking to cancer remains uncertain, therefore more research is needed before action is taken") (Linden et al. 2017). Whatever the particular strategy, it is widely agreed that, because science *comprehension* (understanding, knowledge) does not determine a capacity (or will) to recognize and give due credit to trustworthy science, science communicators and educators should alter their purposes to prioritize teaching a capacity to *recognize* and make use of reliable science, i.e., institutionalized consensus science, and so deprioritize teaching for science comprehension (Priest 2013; Kahan 2017; Feinstein & Waddington 2020). In other words, the ability to identify and trust reliable science *independently of*

DOI: 10.4324/9781003172246-34

any capacity to understand it should be the focal purpose of civic science education, i.e., the learning citizens of a democracy need to competently make decisions about science-laden social issues (*socio-scientific issues*).

This chapter examines the meaning of this debate for the teaching of climate science – and indirectly sustainability – in formal settings, especially K-16 science classrooms. Is it urgent that school and university *science teachers* deprioritize teaching for comprehension and worry more (than they have to date) about how they frame the climate issue, teach the NOS, or inoculate students against fallacious anti-science arguments? Should they in general be less concerned to teach for science comprehension and more concerned to teach for reliable science recognition as they attempt to promote civic science learning?

I critically discuss some oft-cited evidence supporting a "Yes" answer to these questions, the *Humean diagnosis* of the causes of climate contrarianism. Some reforms suggested by this evidence are not obviously very relevant for formal science educators; others make sense independently of it. The latter are dubiously contrasted with *science literacy*, and I will argue that the *Humean diagnosis* is a potentially unhelpful lens for teaching the value dimensions of socially relevant sciences like climate science in science classrooms.

The Humean Diagnosis

It will be helpful to organize the reasoning at issue into the following *argument from the Humean diagnosis*:

1. If general or climate science literacy do not correlate with and predict concern for AGW (or other due trust in consensus climate science), then the *deficit model* is false; climate beliefs are not a function of scientific knowledge or comprehension.
2. If the *deficit model* is false, then increasing general or climate science literacy will be (at best) insufficient if science educators/communicators aim to increase belief in AGW or trust in climate science.
3. (*The Humean Diagnosis*) Because of the cultural cognition of scientific information, together with the biased nature of human cognition, including moral cognition, general science or climate literacy do not predict/correlate with concern for AGW.
4. Therefore, the *deficit model* is false.
5. Therefore, increasing general science or climate literacy will be insufficient if educators aim to improve belief in AGW or boost trust.

The Humean diagnosis itself consists of a few components. These include (a) the *cultural cognition thesis*, (b) an *argumentative theory of reasoning*, and (c) a *social intuitionist account* of moral reasoning and judgment. This set of ideas embody a Humean diagnosis in that they analyze denial not in terms of epistemic standards of evidence or warranted belief, but in terms of what causes or explains belief (Bardon 2019: 4). The postulated causes, moreover, are certain desires, such as for social inclusion, as well as associated emotions and gut-level moral reactions. Altogether they embody a certain skepticism concerning moral reasoning in particular.

Cultural cognition is a species of motivated cognition (or reasoning). *Motivated cognition* is any process of belief formation that serves some end other than true or warranted belief (Bardon 2019; Kahan et al. 2012). By hypothesis, motivated cognition is fallacious reasoning that is fallacious because of some factor other than ignorance of relevant information, faulty premises, or faulty cognitive faculties (e.g., memory loss, clinical paranoia). These factors can obviously interact. But motivated cognition is thought to independently explain reasoning that turns on or yields ignorance or false beliefs; the reasoning turns on or yields these because the reasoner is motivated to ignore relevant true information.

Because belief is involuntary, motivated cognition can seem mysterious. In nonmotivated reasoning, evidence that T is true compels belief that T. Motivated reasoners are aware of the evidence that T, yet deny that T; some research subjects who score high on science literacy nevertheless deny the findings of climate scientists. Thus, some mechanism of rationalization or self-deception must be involved. According to the cultural cognition hypothesis, that mechanism is a reasoner's desire to signal and protect their status as a member of a valued cultural group, especially one defining their political identification (Bardon 2019; Kahan et al. 2007, 2012). So, it is sometimes also called *identity-protective cognition,* though it would be more accurate to call it *group identity-protective cognition* (or "GIP cognition"). What is protected through cultural cognition is not just any identification, e.g., "jogger" or "native Pennsylvanian." What is protected is membership in a *political culture* identifying group. Thus, conservatives deny the scientific consensus on anthropogenic climate change because they fear that affirming it would be counter to their status as conservatives; liberals deny the science supporting GM food safety because affirming it would threaten their status as liberals.

Relative to science denial, defenders of cultural cognition are egalitarians of a certain sort. They believe that susceptibility to science denial is human. Conservatives and liberals, scientists and nonscientists, are all equally liable to deny some bit of science depending upon its perceived sociopolitical consequences (Bardon 2019; Kahan 2017). If those consequences fit with the ways conservatives prefer to frame social issues, conservatives are more likely to affirm, whereas liberals are more likely to deny, the relevant science, and *vice versa.* So, conservatives deny whereas liberals affirm climate science because it is perceived to fit with a "big government" framing of this social issue. Conversely liberals deny whereas conservatives affirm the science supporting GM food safety because it fits with a "big ag" framing of food politics. If this is correct, susceptibility to denial of scientific information is symmetrical between liberals and conservatives. Some critics reject this egalitarianism, arguing that conservatives are demonstrably more susceptible to science denial, given factors such as personality and the tendency of new science to disrupt the social *status quo* (Jost 2017).

In a Humean analysis, the cultural cognition thesis is combined with the *argumentative theory of reasoning* and the *social intuitionist* theory of moral judgment. According to the argumentative theory of reasoning, human practices of argumentation, and the faculties of cognition underlying them, are not evolved for the purpose of uncovering truth. Rather they evolved for the purpose of coordinating social action, which they do primarily by helping us identify reasons that will persuade others to see things as we do (Mercier & Sperber 2019). Consequently, humans are bad at reasoning, and they prefer to draw conclusions based on intuitive shortcuts or gut feelings, heuristics, and biases. Jay Odenbaugh has noted that many of these – including availability bias and anchoring, loss aversion, and temporal discounting heuristics – "are relevant to how we think and act regarding climate change": "Our pro-environmental behaviors depend on the options we consider, their anchoring, their being represented as losses or gains, and how close or remote their impacts in time are" (Odenbaugh 2017: 27).

Social intuitionists apply this thinking to moral belief, claiming that it is generally conditioned by the emotions (Haidt 2013). Moral beliefs are governed by intuitive, emotional reactions to situations, and changes in our feelings are regulative for our moral thinking – and not *vice versa* – even when the grounds of these feelings are irrelevant to the moral issue at hand. Thus, one study found that induced feelings of disgust can bias moral judgment (Wheatley and Haidt 2005) and that moral reasoning frequently appears to occur *post hoc,* in order to justify beliefs antecedently adopted on the basis of gut reactions.[1] To this, social intuitionists add that differences in moral, and even political, beliefs reflect different prioritizations of several intuitive *moral foundations*, i.e., foundational moral values, including care/harm, fairness/cheating, loyalty/betrayal, deference to authority/subversion of authority, purity/degradation, and liberty/oppression. Whereas liberals tend to prioritize care, fairness, and liberty, conservatives tend also to give weight – more so than liberals – to loyalty, deference to authority, and purity (Haidt 2013).

Together with the politicization of climate science, these ideas make for a powerful explanation of American climate denialism. As is known, special interests opposed to climate mitigation (fossil fuel industry, free market ideologues, "small government" libertarians, and deregulation advocates) have used their power and influence to make climate change a partisan political issue while circulating misinformation designed to undermine confidence in climate science (Oreskes & Conway 2011). They capitalized, in other words, on the psychology, using misinformation to reinforce heuristic thinking (rather than deliberate reasoning) and partisan political identification to stoke tribal defenses and shut down reasoning and reflection. Combining these forces, we would expect denialism to track partisan political affiliation and to be unrelated to knowledge of climate science. In the now-famous study "The Cultural Cognition of Scientific Consensus," Kahan *et al.* found nearly that (2012). Conservative subjects who self-reported greater science literacy more strongly rejected consensus climate science. Other research has found that conservative white men account for the great majority of climate deniers, and that those who self-reported understanding global warming "very well" more strongly denied the consensus science of it (McCright & Dunlap 2011).

The State of Climate and Sustainability Education

To fully evaluate the argument from the Humean diagnosis, we need to appreciate the current state of climate education. As climate is perhaps the world's most pressing sustainability problem, the state of sustainability education is one aspect of the state of climate education. At the K-12 level, the news is not very good in either case, though arguably worse relative to general sustainability.

Climate literacy has been defined in terms of many fundamental principles, too numerous to specify here. Focal principles concern the role of the Sun and solar radiation in climate; the role of Earth systems, such as carbon cycling and oceans; the impact of human activities and natural sources of climate variability; and the impact of climate change for Earth systems and human life (USGCRP 2009).

The news is not all bad. According to research by Plutzer et al. (2016), it is now nearly impossible for students in the United States to leave K-12 schooling having received no instruction at all on climate change. In general, concern for climate change among students is also high, even in conservative states, such as Texas (Foss & Ko 2019). And nearly all teachers teach something about climate change.

Still, a convergence of evidence suggests that few students are leaving schools in the United States with basic climate literacy. Standards mandating instruction in anthropogenic climate change are a relatively recent development and they have apparently been implemented ineffectively, on the whole (Holland 2020; NCSE 2020). Reformed standards for science education that include climate science – the Next Generation Science Standards (NGSS) – were first introduced only in 2013. Many states were slow to adopt the standards, and many implemented their own variation. These variations frequently dilute the NGSS standards relating to Weather and Climate, including standards requiring the teaching the AGW thesis (NCSE 2020).

At the high school level (ages 14–18), the NGSS standards for Weather and Climate crucially include the following (NGSS Lead States, 2013):

> HS-ESS2.D3: Changes in the atmosphere due to human activity have increased carbon dioxide concentrations and thus affect climate.
>
> HS-ESS2.D4: Current models predict that, although future regional climate changes will be complex and varied, average global temperatures will continue to rise. The outcomes predicted by global climate models strongly depend on the amounts of human-generated greenhouse gases added to the atmosphere each year and by [sic] the ways in which these gases are absorbed by the ocean and biosphere.

HS-ESS2.A3: The geological record shows that changes to global and regional climate can be caused by interactions among changes in the sun's energy output or Earth's orbit, tectonic events, ocean circulation, volcanic activity, glaciers, vegetation, and human activities. These changes can occur on a variety of time scales from sudden (e.g., volcanic ash clouds) to intermediate (ice ages) to very long-term tectonic cycles.

These standards reflect the fundamental ideas of climate literacy, including those that would require knowledge of the chemical/physical mechanism of global warming and of the impact of human activity on climate. However, these particular standards are not among those governing climate education in many NGSS states, such as Michigan. Instead, one finds more vague standards, such as (Michigan State Board of Education, 2015):

MS-ESS3–5 Ask questions to clarify evidence of the factors that have caused the rise in global temperatures over the past century.

HS-ESS2–4 Use a model to describe how variations in the flow of energy into and out of Earth's systems result in changes in climate.

HS-ESS3–5 Analyze geoscience data and the results from global climate models to make an evidence-based forecast of the current rate of global or regional climate change and associated future impacts to Earth systems.

Any education imparting understanding meeting such standards will require students to consider many of the fundamental concepts of climate literacy, including the human impact on climate. They stop short, however, of directing educators to teach the truth that human activity is the answer to the questions students will presumably ask in curricula built around standard MS-ESS3–5.

This is shocking. But unfortunately, it is consistent with other shortcomings of post-NGSS climate education. Studies of the state of teacher preparation in climate education and climate teaching in schools find that climate is frequently not addressed at all (Foss & Ko 2019; Plutzer et al. 2016). Teachers lack knowledge as well as resources, time, and support (not least, and as just indicated, the support provided by curricular standards that authorize their teaching of the subject) (Colston & Ivey 2015). When it is addressed, as much as 80% of K-12 educators significantly underestimate the degree of consensus among climatologists about the anthropogenic causes of recent global warming and 30% take a "both sides" approach to teaching this focal issue (Plutzer et al. 2016).

The NGSS are not the only relevant set of standards governing science education. For many educators the Common Core State Standards and C3 Framework apply to their work. Concepts relating to climate change appear in guidelines for geography in the C3 Framework (NCSS 2013). Concepts relating to sustainability are implicit there and in other dimensions as well. They are, however, quite sparse. More importantly, they are absent from standards and guidelines for relevant subjects like social studies and even economics. This later omission is especially remarkable given the influence of economic ideas in early prominent articulations of "sustainability" as a concept for global politics, such as the Brundtland definition of sustainable development: "development that meets the needs of the present without compromising the capacity of future generations to meet their needs" (WCED 1987).

Climate change and sustainability are interdisciplinary problems requiring a capacity for reasoning that integrates scientific information and the civic reasoning skills taught – in theory, anyway – in the humanities and social sciences. The absence of sustainability concepts outside the domain of science is both troubling and a potential source of hope. Given the obvious urgency of these topics over the past couple of decades, how can our institutions still have failed to address them at this late stage? At the same time, the humanities and social sciences offer an array of promising approaches to correcting possible sources of error, confusion, maybe even vice, in socio-scientific reasoning. A few of these approaches will be briefly discussed in the penultimate section of this chapter.

Teaching that badly frames the climate issue or misrepresents the NOS may be important obstacles to a citizenry that can recognize and credit consensus climate science. But basic climate literacy is not being effectively taught in K-12 schools and materials and methods from outside the sciences are both apt and underappreciated for teaching sound socio-scientific reasoning. It is hardly clear that science teachers at present should prioritize the former to simply teaching sound climate science.

The Epistemic Aims of Science Education and Framing

Ensuring belief in the AGW thesis and general trust in consensus climate (and other) science is a legitimate purpose of formal science education. The AGW thesis is true, given the best available evidence, and it is the business of educators to teach what is known to be true. Educators also have a responsibility to prepare future citizens to cope with the world they will (likely) inherit so that they may make informed, reasoned choices about how best to flourish in it (Curren & Metzger 2017). Unmitigated climate change will seriously impact the world they will inherit, mostly for the worse.

Let's suppose, then, that the Humean diagnosis is accurate. Does it follow that *science teachers* should prioritize recognition to comprehension? It is not evident that it does. The criticism of the deficit model and science literacy approach is that they are *insufficient* to remediate misunderstanding of and resistance to consensus climate science, especially concerning AGW (Suldovsky 2018). The full meaning of this criticism for formal education might be easily misunderstood. It is standardly a claim about the efficacy of supplying information to the general public; increasing people's knowledge of science or supplying more, or more accurate, information does not (often enough) improve their beliefs. From here it may be tempting to draw the following conclusion: The educational value of science literacy, if any, must be independent of its impact on better civic decision-making with respect to socio-scientific issues. The tempting conclusion is, in other words, that science literacy is not educationally valuable as a component of better socio-scientific citizenship.

This would clearly be an absurd conclusion to draw. It can be true both that merely sharing new information with the public is not (commonly) persuasive and that the same audience would be even less capable of recognizing consensus science absent basic science literacy acquired through formal science education. Indeed, contra the evidence supporting the thesis of cultural cognition of climate science, other research finds that climate science literacy is exceptionally low across all political groups and that climate science literacy is highest among those most concerned for anthropogenic global warming and lowest for those least concerned (AGW) (Bedford 2016; Ballew et al. 2019).

Overall low climate literacy across all political groups has been taken as evidence that concern (or lack thereof) for AGW is rooted in "elite cues or the views of family and friends," not a lack of understanding of climate science (Bedford 2016: 195). In studies of concern for AGW among the American general public, researchers have found that only about 8% of subjects receive climate literacy scores of A or B (on an A–F, school-style grading scale) whereas about 80% score a D or an F (Leiserowitz & Smith 2010; Libarkin et al. 2013). However, those with higher climate literacy scores constitute the majority of the most concerned about climate change, whereas those with the lowest scores constitute the majority of the least concerned (Leiserowitz & Smith 2010; Ranney & Clark 2016: 54). In a study of concern about AGW among undergraduates, Bedford also found that:

> … basic climate literacy appears to reduce polarization between Republicans and Democrats by increasing the chances that Republicans will become more concerned about

> AGW (Democrats are already concerned, more or less regardless of their level of climate literacy). Thus, *the specific type of knowledge examined seems to matter when considering how different groups respond to information.* While increased levels of education (Hamilton 2012) or of scientific/quantitative literacy (Kahan et al. 2012) can simply better equip individuals to seek out information that accords with their existing views, increased levels of climate literacy appear to have the opposite effect.
>
> *(Bedford 2016: 195, emphasis added)*

The form of climate literacy perhaps most relevant to the problem of concern for AGW is knowledge relating to solar radiation and the chemical/physical mechanism through which global warming occurs. In a study of the effect of this knowledge on climate belief, Ranney and Clark (2016) found that virtually no subjects could produce a short, accurate explanation of this mechanism, such as this: "Earth transforms sunlight's visible light energy into infrared light energy, which leaves Earth slowly because it is absorbed by greenhouse gases. When people produce greenhouse gases, energy leaves Earth even more slowly—raising Earth's temperature" (2016: 52). However, being provided with and taught to produce such a simple explanation resulted in increased acceptance of anthropogenic climate change across the political spectrum (2016: 59).

The precise meaning of this research is debatable. However, as Ranney and Clark observe, such basic climate knowledge could be expected to ensure an appropriate burden of proof surrounding the AGW controversy:

> … if asserting that increased greenhouse gas emissions is not problematic, one who denies global warming ought to explain either flaws in the scientific consensus's mechanism, an alternative mechanism, or how the scientific mechanism is parametrically inconsequential (e.g., that climate sensitivity is low). The mechanism essentially demands a denier to answer this: "If nonnatural greenhouse gases chemically increase Earth's temperature, how can anthropogenic additions be negligible?"
>
> *(Ranney & Clark 2016: 52)*

That this burden of proof will be difficult for most climate science laypersons to meet may explain findings (by some studies) that the most vehement climate contrarians include those reporting the highest rates of numeracy or science literacy. Sustaining denialism while in possession of basic climate literacy requires considerable resources and capacity for rationalization, resources, and capacity that only those highly educated or motivated will possess. From this it obviously does not follow that high science literacy is *the reason* they deny, nor that we should expect that knowing more about climate change will have no effect whatever on the ordinary layperson's ability to recognize the climatological consensus on AGW. Moreover, GIP cognition is only one explanation of the will to rationalize among such people – the motivation to deny, that is. Others include naked self-interest, not knowing how to know, genuine (if wrongheaded) moral disagreement, fear or hopelessness, or any number of folk-scientific confusions about the NOS (Barzilai & Chinn 2020; Shtulman 2015). GIP cognition also does not explain how the needed rationalization works. More illuminating in such cases are failures to appreciate some aspect of the NOS (such as its social nature and the role of norms of trust), inability to evaluate the reliability of testimonial information, relative unconcern for truth, or genuine disagreement about how to know (Barzilai & Chinn 2020).

An education ensuring that citizens can appreciate the full weight of the burden of justifying climate beliefs is crucial to overcoming climate contrarianism. Basic science literacy has crucial value here. In this regard, the preoccupation with framing in climate communication arguably is of relatively little significance for formal climate education. School and university educators should probably be aware of some of the most hazardous ways of framing the climate change issue in their presentation of it. Beginning a climate change unit with Al Gore's *An Inconvenient Truth* is very likely to alienate denialist students. Activist framings in general are likely to induce a "boomerang effect" (Hart & Nisbet 2012). However, research on framing reveals many and very subtle effects that it would be unreasonable to expect teachers to know or avoid. Republicans are known to recoil more at use of the term "global warming" than to "climate change." However, discussion of global warming cannot be eliminated from teaching that would address the AGW thesis.

Framing operates on the learner's cognition implicitly, moreover, and it is designed to solicit endorsement independently of argument or evidence. Careful framing is not for that reason improperly manipulative; framing is inevitable and a theory of legitimate *versus* illegitimate framing is required. However, because it operates behind reasoning, framing "would be unlikely to accomplish very much in the way of encouraging deeper thought about the NOS – or thoughtful views on particular controversies" (Priest 2013: 141).

Communication researchers do not in general assume that sharing relevant facts and information is unimportant or unnecessary for enhancing receptivity to publicly contested science.[2] However, so far as pragmatics are concerned, once a deficit model is abandoned, one could ask why any information used to build trust in socially relevant science has to be *accurate* at all. One obvious theory is not obviously compelling: Communication that is inconsistent with consensus science might be a counterproductive way to enhance trust in that science. In fact, much might be done or said that could, potentially, both effectively increase confidence in the socially relevant claims of climate science *and* be false, misleading, or otherwise inconsistent with climate science or science generally. A statistic that 90% of male Republican ornithologists believe that humans are causing climate change might be an effective frame for communicating consensus information to conservative white males. But if it is false (I just made it up) or very misleading (perhaps there are only 10 in the world), strategic grounds for refusing to use it are not plainly available. The need for a careful science of science communication arises partly because the public are not well-positioned to evaluate such claims for themselves. Unscrupulous science communicators might craft effective but entirely misleading messaging that increase trust in institutional climate science.

Such *merely* instrumental, strategic thinking is incompatible with the values and epistemic aims of liberal science education. The success of institutional science depends heavily on the sincerity and trustworthiness of scientists as they collectively build knowledge. Ultimately such values are important because scientists aim to uncover truths about our world, i.e., because, at their best, they are lovers of truth (Pennock 2019). Whatever other principles or values should guide our thinking about how to reform science education for the "post-truth era," this value should be paramount.

Problems for the Humean Diagnosis

Citizens, including scientists, have limited capacity to comprehend and evaluate the claims and evidence of new scientific information. Evaluating evidence (for any given claim in some field of science) requires expertise, and this expertise requires judgment acquired partly through experience working in the relevant field. Thus, even scientists in one field of study – climatology, say – will lack sufficient expertise to authoritatively evaluate new information in another field – epidemiology, say. Nonscientist citizens are obviously in a worse position.

For these reasons, it is essential that citizens acquire capacities to recognize credible new science, independently of any capacity to comprehend that science. Alas, as in many other parts of the formal school curriculum, science educators have tended to prioritize college and career readiness over civic science literacy (Tytler 2007). Among other undesirable consequences, this tendency seems to have made science unattractive to most K-12 learners, who have limited tolerance for very technical science.

To reach the conclusion that school science educators should make a significant priority of teaching students how to recognize credible science, it is not necessary to hypothesize that cultural/GIP cognition governs citizens' processing of scientific information. It is certainly not necessary to hypothesize, as social intuitionists do, that moral reasoning is little more than adherence to a set of intuitive, emotionally charged and partisan, foundational moral commitments. It may be educationally edifying to understand and teach human tendencies toward myside bias (evaluating and generating evidence in a manner favorable to prior beliefs), "satisficing" (settling for enough evidence when it is favorable to one's existing beliefs while demanding ever more when it is not), and the like. But the prospects for successful debiasing are unclear; part of the bite of cognitive bias research is that even knowledgeable researchers make these mistakes in research studies (Kahneman 2011). And it is neither clearly true nor helpful to suppose that reasoning does not exist or evolved for the purpose of social coordination – as opposed to the purpose of helping us to know and understand the world or solve the problems we face. Nor is it clear what this theory has to do with the many and various sorts of cognitive bias educators may wish to know and teach, such as anchoring bias (evaluating the next piece of information in terms of a perspective set by the first we encounter), fundamental attribution error (selectively overestimating the role of personality or character relative to situational factors in the successes/failures of others), or myside bias.

In formal settings, a focus on cultural/GIP cognition as the underlying cause of incapacity to recognize credible science would be unhelpful in other ways. At least in the short term, educators certainly cannot do much to remediate students' cultural (or political) identifications, and it is not, within certain legitimate constraints, clearly their business to do so. Teaching for democratic citizenship is a legitimate educator aim. But this aim is sufficiently capacious to accommodate partisan identities that may be at odds with the results of any given science. Climate contrarianism is strongly linked to free market ideology (more so, apparently, than to climate literacy). Unfettered markets are known to be inefficient, especially relative to common pool resource management and pollution. Educators may legitimately teach these facts and may even use methods designed to recruit students' sympathetic identification with them. But they may not teach students that they cannot be libertarians or Republicans. As noted in the prior section, however, education in sustainable economics at the K-12 level essentially does not exist.

A focus on cultural cognition and biased reasoning also obscures other important causes of science denialism. Some have argued it is unclear to what extent the cultural cognition thesis is explanatory at all. What we wish to understand is why citizens rely so heavily on social cues for deciding which information to trust; citing the influence of those social cues is circular (van der Linden 2016). Some explanations cite further social causes, such as misinformation campaigns (Oreskes & Conway 2011). But here again we are left to wonder why such social causes have such force.

Plausible further explanations redirect us back toward the epistemic. In doing so, they both re-establish a linkage between citizen comprehension of science and capacity to recognize credible science, i.e., between *science literacy* and recognition. They also point to areas of the curriculum *outside* of the hard and environmental sciences where reforms could contribute significantly to building learner capacity to recognize credible science.

With regard to climate science, and as discussed earlier, ignorance of the basic mechanism of anthropogenic global warming is one further explanation. In addition, public misunderstanding of (or disbelief in) the degree of scientific consensus is arguably rooted in ignorance of the methods, and especially social–collaborative nature, of scientific knowledge building. This is a failure to comprehend the NOS, and as such is appropriately regarded as a form of science literacy. In general, further *epistemic* explanations of science denialism include not knowing how to know; a host of confusions about the NOS, its scope, limitations, and institutional practices, and about the science and values relationship; genuine disagreement about how to know; naked self-interest; and fear, hopelessness, and paralysis (Barzilai & Chinn 2020).

Individuals may look to social cues for determining what information to trust simply because they do not know how to know. In the realm of science, this sort of ignorance will frequently reflect ignorance of the methods and practices of institutional science, especially of the collaborative nature of scientific knowledge building and the corresponding role of institutions of epistemic interdependence and trust, peer review, reproducibility, transparency of procedures and data, and accountability (Elgin 2011; Priest 2013; Elliott 2017).

But the linkage between factual information, such as science provides, and value judgment is likely another obstacle to knowing how to know. Motivated reasoning involves resistance to factual information perceived to have undesirable consequences given a person's normative worldview. Arguably, susceptibility to this sort of reasoning would be heightened in those who believe that factual information determines reasonable social policy, i.e., if there were no logical distance between facts and values. However factual information does not determine reasonable social policy, or what one ought to do. In having no understanding of this, nor having ever been taught ethics – let alone ethics relating specifically to sustainability – citizens use disagreement about scientific information as a proxy for disagreement about morals or politics (Hicks 2017). Such a state of affairs is precisely what one would expect when disputants do not know how to engage in moral reasoning – reasoning about values and policy directly.

This situation is very unlikely to be fully mitigated absent more and better instruction in science and sustainability history and ethics, as well as STS (science, technology, and society), in the humanities and social sciences. Teachers of these disciplines are tasked, after all, with teaching socially relevant history, ethics, civics, and the like, and the problems of science in a democratic society are urgent social problems. Many of these teachers are also trained in methods appropriate to normative thinking, more so at least than their science teacher counterparts. This favorably positions them to handle, with due depth and subtlety, relevant subjects, such as the fact/value distinction and the limited role of scientific information in normative inquiry; history of civilizations and their collapse; the philosophy of science, and of science in society, through its history; and fundamental principles of ethical and political reasoning, as well as their application to sustainability ethics.[3] We should hardly be surprised that citizens cannot engage in appropriate socio-scientific reasoning – including knowing how to recognize credible science – when topics like these are not being addressed much at all during the years of compulsory schooling.

Promising approaches to all of these kinds of instruction exist and might serve as models for the development of improved standards and curriculum for science and sustainability ethics.[4] Worthy of special mention are approaches that merge insights in sustainability ethics and game theory to teach commons problems and the coordinated action structure of problems like climate change (Sadowski et al. 2013). In *sustainability ethics gaming*, students role-play the decision-making of actors in collective action dilemmas to experience the rewards of cooperating and the hazards of competing. Approaches like these have the potential to address not only sources of error or confusion in sustainability ethical reasoning, but maybe even vice.

Conclusion

As it stands, schools have only just begun to teach basic climate literacy, and it would be premature to abandon as a failure an approach to climate education that has barely been implemented. The evidence supporting the Humean diagnosis of the causes of climate contrarianism is equivocal. Even if it is correct, it does not follow that science teachers in science classrooms should rush to rebuild curriculum in an effort to deprioritize teaching for science comprehension. Moreover, sustainability problems like climate change can be addressed only through the exercise of integrated values-and-science moral reasoning skills. These skills call upon knowledge and practice typically conveyed, when taught at all, in the humanities and social sciences. However, schools and many universities do not prioritize teaching these skills through appropriate instruction in sustainability ethics and socio-scientific reasoning *within* the humanities and social sciences. Overall, it is arguably less important that science teachers spend countless hours fretting over the framing of their climate teaching, or learning how to teach the philosophy of science, and more important that educational institutions update the whole curriculum, and especially the humanities and social sciences, to infuse sustainability and values-and-science moral reasoning into them.

(Related Chapters: 1, 4, 5, 10, 11, 26, 27, 28.)

Notes

1 But see May (2018): chap. 2, for skeptical analysis of this research. In brief, the effect of induced disgust on moral belief is slight. In 7 of 8 cases, it only strengthened commitment to an existing moral position; it resulted in a *change* of moral positions in only 1.
2 Although see Sarewitz (2011), for a bald assertion that it is not.
3 Although see Bialystok et al. (2019), for valuable research on some significant difficulties that arise when high school teachers are pressed into service as philosophy instructors.
4 On sustainability history, ethics, and politics, see Curren & Metzger (2017). On the history and philosophy of science, see Matthews 2014.

References

Ballew, M. T., Leiserowitz, A., Roser-Renauf, C., Rosenthal, S. A., Kotcher, J. E., Marlon, J. R., Lyon, E., Goldberg, M. H. & Maibach, E. W. (2019) "Climate Change in the American Mind: Data, Tools, and Trends," *Environment: Science and Policy for Sustainable Development* 61(3): 4–18.
Bardon, A. (2019) *The Truth About Denial*. Oxford: Oxford University Press.
Barzilai, S. & Chinn, C. A. (2020) "A Review of Educational Responses to the "Post-truth" Condition: Four Lenses on "Post-truth" Problems," *Educational Psychologist* 55(3): 107–119.
Bedford, D. (2016) "Does Climate Literacy Matter? A Case Study of U.S. Students' Level of Concern about Anthropogenic Global Warming," *Journal of Geography* 115(5): 187–197.
Bialystok, L., Norris, T. & Pinto, L. E. (2019) "Teaching and Learning Philosophy in Ontario High Schools," *Journal of Curriculum Studies* 51(5): 678–697.
Colston, N., & Ivey, T. (2015) "(un)Doing the Next Generation Science Standards: Climate Change Education Actor-networks in Oklahoma," *Journal of Education Policy* 30(6): 773–795.
Curren, R. & Metzger, E. (2017) *Living Well Now and in the Future: Why Sustainability Matters*. Cambridge, MA: MIT Press.
Elgin, C. (2011) "Science, Ethics, and Education," *Theory and Research in Education* 9(3): 251–263.
Elliott, K. C. (2017) *A Tapestry of Values: An Introduction to Values in Science*. New York: Oxford University Press.
Feinstein, N. W. & Waddington, D. I. (2020) "Individual Truth Judgments or Purposeful, Collective Sensemaking? Rethinking Science Education's Response to the Post-truth Era," *Educational Psychologist* 55(3): 155–166.
Foss, A. W. & Ko, Y. (2019) "Barriers and Opportunities for Climate Change Education: The Case of Dallas-Fort Worth in Texas," *The Journal of Environmental Education* 50(3): 145–159.
Haidt, J. (2013) *The Righteous Mind: Why Good People Are Divided by Politics and Religion*. New York: Random House.
Hamilton, L. (2012) "Did the Arctic Ice Recover? Demographics of True and False Climate Facts," *Weather, Climate, and Society* 4(4): 236–249.
Hart, P. S. & Nisbet, E. C. (2012) "Boomerang Effects in Science Communication: How Motivated Reasoning and Identity Cues Amplify Opinion Polarization About Climate Mitigation Policies," *Communication Research* 39(6): 701–723.
Hicks, D. J. (2017) "Scientific Controversies as Proxy Politics," *Issues in Science and Technology* 23 January. Available at: https://issues.org/scientific-controversies-as-proxy-politics/ (Accessed: 5 July 2021).
Holland, C. T. (2020) "The Implementation of the Next Generation Science Standards and the Tumultuous Fight to Implement Climate Change Awareness in Science Curricula," *Brock Education Journal* 29(1): 35–35.
Jost, J. T. (2017) "Ideological Asymmetries and the Essence of Political Psychology," *Political Psychology* 38(2): 67–208.
Kahan, D. M. et al. (2012) "The Polarizing Impact of Science Literacy and Numeracy on Perceived Climate Change Risks," *Nature Climate Change* 2(10): 732–735.

Kahan, D. M. (2017) "On the Sources of Ordinary Science Knowledge and Extraordinary Science Ignorance," in K. H. Jamieson, D. Kahan, & D. A. Scheufele (eds) *The Oxford Handbook of the Science of Science Communication*. Oxford: Oxford University Press, 35–50.
Kahneman, D. (2011) *Thinking, Fast and Slow*. New York: Farrar, Strauss and Giroux.
Leiserowitz, A. & Smith, N. (2010) *Knowledge of Climate Change Across Global Warming's Six Americas*. New Haven, CT: Yale Project on Climate Change Communication.
Libarkin, J. C., Miller, H. & Thomas, S. R. (2013) "Scientists' Internal Models of the Greenhouse Effect," *American Geophysical Union*, Fall Meeting 2013, abstract id. ED32A-05.
Linden, S. van der. (2016) "A Conceptual Critique of the Cultural Cognition Thesis," *Science Communication* 38(1): 128–138.
Linden, S. van der, Leiserowitz, A., Rosenthal, S. & Maibach, E. (2017) "Inoculating the Public against Misinformation About Climate Change," *Global Challenges* 1(2): 1600008.
Matthews, M. R. (2014) *Science Teaching: The Contribution of History and Philosophy of Science*. 2nd edn. New York: Routledge.
May, J. (2018) *Regard for Reason in the Moral Mind*. New York: Oxford University Press.
McCaffrey, M. & Rosenau, J. (2012) "Science Literacy Still Matters," *Nature Climate Change* 2(9): 636–636.
McCright, A. M. & Dunlap, R. E. (2011) "Cool Dudes: The Denial of Climate Change among Conservative White Males in the United States [electronic resource]," *Global Environmental Change* 21(4): 1163–1172.
Mercier, H. & Sperber, D. (2019) *The Enigma of Reason*. Cambridge, MA: Harvard University Press.
Michigan State Board of Education (2015) "Michigan K-12 Science Standards," *Michigan Department of Education*.
NCSS (2013) *College, Career, & Civic Life C3 Framework for Social Studies State Standards: Guidance for Enhancing the Rigor of K-12 Civics, Economics, Geography, and History*. Silver Spring, MD: National Council for the Social Studies.
NCSE (2020) *Making the Grade: How State Public School Science Standards Address Climate Change*. National Center for Science Education and Texas Freedom Network Education Fund. Available at: https://climategrades.org/MakingTheGradeReport.pdf.
NGSS Lead States (2013) *Next Generation Science Standards: For States, By States*. Available at: http://www.nextgenscience.org/ (Accessed: 26 August 2015).
Nisbet, M. C., & Mooney, C. (2007) "Science and Society. Framing Science," *Science* 316(5821): 56.
Odenbaugh, J. (2017) "On the Contrary: How to Think About Climate Skepticism," unpublished manuscript.
Oreskes, N. & Conway, E. (2011) *Merchants of Doubt*. New York: Bloomsbury Press.
Pennock, R. (2019) *An Instinct for Truth*. Cambridge, MA: MIT Press.
Plutzer, E. et al. (2016) "Climate Confusion Among U.S. Teachers," *Science* 351(6274): 664–665.
Priest, S. (2013) "Critical Science Literacy: What Citizens and Journalists Need to Know to Make Sense of Science," *Bulletin of Science, Technology & Society* 33(5–6): 138–145.
Ranney, M. A. & Clark, D. (2016) "Climate Change Conceptual Change: Scientific Information Can Transform Attitudes," *Topics in Cognitive Science* 8(1): 49–75.
Sadowski, J., Seager, T., Selinger, E., Spierre, S., & Whyte, K. P. (2013) "An Experiential, Game-Theoretic Pedagogy for Sustainability Ethics," *Science and Engineering Ethics* 19(3): 1323–1339.
Sarewitz, D. (2011) "Does Climate Change Knowledge really Matter?," *WIREs Climate Change* 2(4): 475–481.
Shtulman, A. (2015) "How Lay Cognition Constrains Scientific Cognition," *Philosophy Compass* 10(11): 785–798.
Suldovsky, B. S. (2018) "The Information Deficit Model and Climate Change Communication," in *The Oxford Encyclopedia of Climate Change Communication*. Oxford: Oxford University Press.
Tytler, R. (2007) *Re-imagining Science Education*. Camberwell, Victoria: Australian Council for Educational Research.
USGCRP (2009) *Climate Literacy: The Essential Principles of Climate Science*. Washington, DC: U.S. Global Change Research Program. Available at: https://www.globalchange.gov/browse/reports/climate-literacy-essential-principles-climate-science-high-resolution-booklet (Accessed: 8 November 2021).
WCED (1987) *Our Common Future*. Available at: http://www.un-documents.net/wced-ocf.htm (Accessed: 12 April 2011).
Wheatley, T., & Haidt, J. (2005) "Hypnotic Disgust Makes Moral Judgments More Severe," *Psychological Science* 16(10): 780–784.

30

IS "SEX EDUCATION" AN INTELLIGIBLE CONCEPT?

Lauren Bialystok

There is no sex education in schools. This statement is not shorthand for the liberal's lamentation that sex education is too shallow, too scarce, or so watered down as to be ridiculous, although these things are all true. In the United States as of 2020, twenty states did not require any sex education, twenty-eight states did not require that any information provided be medically accurate, and thirty-six states allowed parents to opt their children out of sex education entirely (NCSL 2020). These policies translate into unsurprising gaps; for example, in one study, "among sexually experienced female teens, 83.3% … did not receive formal sex education before first sex" (Cox et al. 2014: 3).

The statement is, rather, intended to be taken at face value. Even when schools conduct "sex education," they are not teaching sex. Consider that the CDC-published study just cited, which established a glaring deficit of formal sex education among sexually experienced teen girls, defined "sex education" as "information on birth control" and "how to say no to sex" (Cox et al. 2014). How did these narrow forms of instruction come to stand in for knowledge about sex?

When opponents turn up to protest a new curriculum, it is common to hear that sex education will instruct students in sexual positions, invite them to masturbate or expose themselves in the classroom, or encourage them to experiment sexually. These claims are demonstrably false and amusingly absurd, but you could forgive some onlookers for taking the phrase "sex education" literally. When we say that we will teach *x* in schools, we usually mean that we will teach students to understand and practise *x* as fully and authentically as possible. Indeed, under the influence of constructivist educational philosophy and the present fervour for "authenticity" in education, progressive educators strive to synchronize the classroom as much as possible with the "real world," helping students become not just observers, but practitioners, of curricular content. Science education is supposed to involve doing science; Spanish instruction is supposed to involve immersing students in Spanish language and culture. Despite neoliberal imperatives to convert education into testable outcomes, progressives continue to strive for a version of education that resembles Dewey's ontology of the classroom as a site of genuine discovery, creation, and social life.

The same progressives teach sex education completely differently. The way we teach sex is more akin to Spanish instruction that says, "some people speak Spanish, and one day you will, but right now stay as far away as possible from all things Spanish." The approach is largely one of fomenting apprehension. Even when we teach young people about sex in more honest terms, the envisioned role of the school is usually to be a buffer between them and the sex-saturated culture we know they inhabit and the activities we know they will pursue outside the classroom. It is analogous to the message, "You may accidentally hear Spanish on television, but you should know that those are

DOI: 10.4324/9781003172246-35

actors and real Spanish speakers don't sound like that. If you must speak Spanish, proceed with the utmost caution."

Most of the tired public controversies over "sex education" can be reframed by attending to the stark contrast between sex and other subjects on the curriculum. Although opponents disagree on some bedrock values and what sex education *should* be, there is little disagreement about what sex education *cannot* be. In the United States and much of the world since the 1990s, the repertoire of approaches to sex education has been construed on a very narrow continuum, with "Abstinence-Only-Until-Marriage Education" (AOUME) on one end and "Comprehensive Sex Education" (CSE) (which is usually nowhere near comprehensive) on the other. In both cases, the emphasis has been on risk avoidance and keeping most types of sex at bay – the pedagogical antithesis of teaching Spanish; in no case is the practice of sex taught in schools. Although the most forward-thinking and innovative curricula interpret "sex education" to include critical conversations about such topics as gender identity, consent, and social media, there are built-in limits to the presence of sex in schools that no one truly calls into question. "Sex education" is incendiary because adults associate "sex" with sexual activity, and the activity has no place in a classroom. The failure to appreciate the discrepancy between referent and signifier stifles some debates over how to teach sex education almost before they can get started. In reality, schools can do very little to impart meaningful knowledge about sex. Nor can they do much to shelter students from unwanted information about sex; that ship has long sailed, with the current school-aged generation accessing any content they want (and a lot they do not) with the touch of a screen. What we are arguing about is not sex in school, but something else.

Philosophers have contributed to our thinking about the relentless controversy over sex education, with its obvious connections to ethics, philosophy of education, and political philosophy. Behind the strident positions of parents, community activists, religious leaders, and other stakeholders lie normative commitments that are amenable to philosophical analysis and argumentative testing. Most philosophers of education have argued for a classically liberal approach to sex education, in which the promotion of student autonomy and respect for sexual diversity are paramount (Archard 2000; McKay 1998; Reiss 1995). These values typically advise a comprehensive curriculum based on evidence and delivered in a non-ideological setting. More granular debates concern the details of negotiating between competing values and interest groups. These debates highlight that even liberal-minded philosophers can disagree about the ethics of how to broach this touchy subject in schools, while still largely adhering to the structural parameters of schools, curriculum, and political culture that generate our meagre options.

I want to enter the philosophical debates from a different angle here. Drawing on Foucault and the work of many contemporary sex education scholars, I want to dwell on the question of how to combine sex and education in the context of 21st Century Western schooling. Where and how do young people learn about sex? What do we want from school-based sex education? Or, as philosopher of education Alan Harris asked in a 1971 article that has aged disturbingly well, "Is sex education an intelligible concept?" (Harris 1971: 8).

"Two Great Procedures for Producing the Truth About Sex"[1]

In his intellectual genealogy *The History of Sexuality*, Michel Foucault (1976) identified two primary approaches to thinking and teaching about sex. The first, *scientia sexualis* (the science/knowledge of sex), views sex as a series of facts and injunctions (Foucault 1976: 58). Emerging in the 18th Century in Western Europe, this approach to sexual knowledge emphasized the identification and monitoring of sexual norms, the discursive control over sexual "truths" (especially through the process of confession), and the pathologization of sexual types. Although these impulses have obvious roots in Western Judaeo-Christian morality and especially the hierarchical Christian institutions of the

Renaissance, they were amplified by the vast social and political changes that followed the Enlightenment: urbanization, industrialization, rapid scientific progress, the early codification of Western medicine, and new state apparatus for engineering and disciplining populations. In this era, for the first time, "[i]t was essential that the state know what was happening with its citizens' sex, and the use they made of it, but also that each individual be capable of controlling the use he made of it" (Foucault 1976: 26). Public health and epidemiology were born. Along with scientific and philosophical breakthroughs came new hierarchies of expertise, their sexist and racist conceits conveniently deflected by the assertion of objectivity. Contrary to received wisdom, Foucault argues, Victorian sexuality was not repressed so much as it was policed.

By explaining the origins of modern Western attitudes toward sex, Foucault revealed that the attitude of *scientia sexualis* is a cultural aberration. Most civilizations have conceptualized sex in more private and less clinical terms. In *ars amoris* (the art of love), which Foucault associates with ancient Eastern traditions, the value of sex is precisely its refusal to submit to public circulation (1976: 57). Pleasure is regarded as its own purpose, "not considered in relation to an absolute law of the permitted and the forbidden, nor by reference to a criterion of utility" (Foucault 1976: 57). In this paradigm, sexual knowledge is a "masterful art" that is learned through sexual activity itself, "understood as a practice and accumulated as experience" (Foucault 1976: 57).

Common schooling originates in the same time period and social context as *scientia sexualis*. In the 18th Century, the "ponderous silence" (Foucault 1976: 29) about sexuality in schools was ominously accompanied by design choices intended to thwart children's sexual curiosity and inculcate docility (Foucault 1976: 27–29). Foucault (1976) refers to this as "a pedagogization of children's sex" (104). When sex made its way into formal curriculum in the 20th Century, it still obeyed the principles of *scientia sexualis*: sexual "truths" were linked to prohibitions and conveyed in the moralizing language of medicine and middle-class White values. To learn about sex was to learn about society's strictures and expectations. The earliest efforts to introduce sex education in schools came from advocates of social hygiene, "an area of study that ... focused on the diagnosis and reporting of sexually transmitted infections, genital and bodily cleanliness, eugenics, and [preventing] masturbation" (Bialystok & Andersen, 2022).

Sex education has evolved since the mid-20th Century, but the parameters in which it is delivered are effectively the same. Students learn about "sex" in rigidly organized classrooms under the glare of fluorescent lights – an environment that is itself designed to be as unsexy as possible – where a designated adult, who has the "knowledge," imparts and then tests students on a predetermined battery of facts. Regardless of how parsimonious or comprehensive a curriculum may be, our conception of schooling requires sexual content to be funneled into a curricular model with limited inputs and outputs.[2] It is about as epistemically distant from *ars amoris* as one could imagine. Reduced to propositional knowledge, sex, like other subjects, is construed as something that students can get "right" or "wrong." In our contemporary audit culture, in which educational programs must be amenable to widespread standardized testing in order to be judged valuable, sex education must sometimes contort itself into a species of science education or risk being eliminated completely.

If the meaning and place of sex in our social epistemology looked more like what Foucault calls *ars amoris*, sex education would look completely different – and perhaps much closer to what staunch opponents fear we mean by "sex education" today. The transmission of knowledge about sex in *ars amoris* is indivisible from sex itself, and indeed, sex has, in some civilizations, been used as a medium for broader relationships of education.[3] Where sexual pleasure is its own truth, "only [the master], working alone, can transmit this art in an esoteric manner and as the culmination of an initiation in which he guides the disciple's progress ... " (Foucault 1976: 57). This might mean that there is no collective or formal instruction about sex, but also less anxiety about young people pursuing their own sexual awakening through informal and private channels.

By comparing these two very different regimes of sexual knowledge, Foucault offers some macro perspective on the day-to-day battles over sex education that may seem all-important in a particular context. Whatever the relative merits of each of these two (and there are probably more than two) paradigms for producing sexual knowledge, we can be fairly certain that North American schools are still largely in the grip of a regime that resembles *scientia sexualis*. In spite of significant liberalization at the level of policy and culture, ours is still a society in which the modern European concern for population health and general Judaeo-Christian morality conditions most approaches to youth sexuality. This observation need not lead us to bemoan our epistemic heritage, much less to appropriate the attitudes of *ars amoris* – which, undoubtedly, can be linked to sexism and worrying opportunities for abuse. Rather, the point is to appreciate how beliefs about sexual knowledge correspond to particular attitudes about the meaning of "sex education" – who can provide it, what it entails, where and when (or whether) it should occur. Our debates remain surprisingly confined by the premises of certain modern Western attitudes to sexual knowledge and the function of schools.

Let's (Not) Talk About Sex

So, is there sex education in schools? What we designate as "sex education" in schools is perhaps intelligible only as a product of a civilization in which sex is categorically different from other potential subjects of education. It is intelligible as an exception, a warning, a grudging inclusion in the otherwise G-rated curriculum. Although it exists – often under the umbrella of "health education" or a more general course title – the epistemology of its role in education stands apart from most other subjects. As alluded to earlier, in a climate of progressive educational theory still under the sway of constructivism, pre-service teachers are taught to believe that good teaching requires immersing students in first-hand discovery of a subject. The value of the subject is taken for granted, as is the desire for students to become competent practitioners of it. The classroom, further, is supposed to be made as seamless with the rest of the world as possible in order for student learning to be "authentic."[4] But when it comes to sex, the classroom is conceived more as a bulwark against the rest of the world than a microcosm of it. "Authentic" sex education that mirrors the pedagogical tenets of Spanish and other subjects would have to involve explicit exposure, guidance, and perhaps in-class practice – a nightmare to adults of all persuasions.

The place where young people receive such explicit guidance about sex is undoubtedly pornography. In the Western tradition, sexually explicit artefacts have of course always been circulated, along with sex work and erotica; but, in keeping with Foucault's analysis of power and knowledge, they have been policed and stigmatized, at least in public, despite being an open secret among men. The Comstock Act of 1873 outlawed sending "obscene" or "lascivious" materials, including medical information about contraception and any images depicting gay sexuality, through the mail – a prelude to the Nazis' destruction of "degenerate" art. Through the 20th Century, American boys' first exposure to sexually explicit information may have come from a *Penthouse* or *Playboy* magazine surreptitiously shared among friends, or, perhaps, cribbed from their father.

The advent of global digital culture and smart phones has rendered all such attempts to regulate unofficial sex education pathetically moot. It is not only that young people have easier access to pornography now than ever before. The material itself is increasingly varied, violent, and designed to generate "clicks" for profiteering platforms. Studies show that young people are accessing pornography younger and more frequently than ever, with traceable impacts on their sexual beliefs (Horvath et al. 2013). Moreover, pornographic tropes are affecting young people's sexual behaviours: young women in particular are liable to take them as instruction manuals and to judge their sexual normalcy in reference to them (Goldsmith et al. 2017; Rogala & Tyden 2003). This is what experts mean when they declare, non-hysterically, that pornography *is* sex education (Orenstein 2016). It is mostly very bad education, but it provides young people in particular with the unmediated access to sexual knowledge that they evidently crave.[5]

The ineluctable difference between the sex education we provide in formal settings and the education afforded by pornography can be mapped, approximately, onto the difference between *scientia sexualis* and *ars amoris*. In official sex education, no matter how comprehensive, knowledge is the mastery of social rules and biological information, with the aim of self-regulation – *scientia*. In pornography, knowledge is pleasure, with the aim of self-abandon – *ars*. The problem, as any progressive educator or feminist scholar will be quick to point out, is that the "pleasure" that is featured and normalized in mainstream pornography is what a massive industry takes to be pleasurable for heterosexual cis-males. This regularly involves the domination of women, degrading and at times painful activities, and a preoccupation with male orgasm – the "money shot" – in a decontextualized narrative where consent is never explicitly attained (Bridges et al. 2010; Williams 1989). Pornography is perhaps the closest thing that most young people have to *ars amoris*, though it is corrupted and limited at every turn by the pathologies of patriarchy and capitalism.

Nor is pornography the only medium that gives young people unfettered exposure to sex acts and invitations to be sexually active. Mainstream culture, including cable television, music videos, and advertising, inundates young people with references to and depictions of all kinds of sexual activity and sexual relationships, from the profane and abusive to the erotic and queer. Words that could never be spoken out loud in a classroom are blasted into students' earbuds within the walls of the school. Although students are sanctioned for exposing a shoulder or thigh, pop stars pose nearly naked and discuss their sexual escapades in public. Surely this is closer to learning about sex than what the average embarrassed gym teacher can provide.

And, lest it be forgotten, students are *having sex*.[6] Formal sex education since the early 20th Century has been imagined as pre-empting young adults' sexual debut. Under the sexual epistemology of *scientia*, pleasure is to be accessed only within a regime of power and scientific expertise: children learn from authority figures, enter into socially sanctioned intimate relationships, and only *then* experience sexual pleasure. Of course, it's never worked reliably in this order. Importantly, the amount of teen sexual activity has actually declined, but the amount of sexual information exchange is climbing, largely thanks to social media and cell phones. In one study, "twenty percent of [middle-school] students [grades 6–8] with text-capable cell phone access reported receiving a sext and 5% reported sending a sext" (Rice et al. 2014). These forms of sexual exchange are increasingly the norm among tech-equipped adolescents. In a study of Dutch 12–18-year-old, many participants described doing something sexual in front of a webcam or sharing porn with peers as "arousing," "funny," "fun," or "informative"; the majority considered such activities "normal" or positive (Naezer 2018: 720).

In a bizarre homage to constructivism, students are actually learning about sex by using the educational tools at their disposal to experience, create, and share sexual knowledge. (Imagine if they studied all their subjects so diligently!) Ironically, sex education *is* happening in school, right under teachers' noses; but students are learning from each other more than from officially sanctioned instructors. Their sexual knowledge, as in *ars amoris*, is "understood as a practice and accumulated as experience" (Foucault 1976: 57).

In response, formal sex education is already shedding some of its traditional naiveté. Many educators recognize that we need to equip young people to navigate this unprecedented panoply of sexual opportunities and misinformation, offering positive models of sexual pleasure and ethical relationships. "Porn literacy," consent education, and other frontiers in progressive sex education are developing methods for talking to young people about this brave new world, using insights from ethics, media education, and gender studies, among other lenses (Jones 2018; Lamb 2010). These types of education buffer and contextualize student learning about sex. They belong on the explicit curriculum. But, to press my point, they are not teaching students sex itself, in the way that erotic materials and lived experience teach them. Besides, most curricula still shy away from anything remotely as honest as porn literacy.

Furthermore, as Foucault also reminds us, students receive myriad lessons from school alongside, and sometimes despite, the curriculum – especially about sex. Educational researchers today call this the "informal curriculum" or the "hidden curriculum" (Connelly & Connelly 2010). In the tradition of *scientia sexualis*, schools remain institutions in which information and behavior are regulated through everything from architectural layout to the rhythmic ringing of bells, from dress codes to choices made about topics for special assemblies and announcements. Even at institutions where students might be lucky enough to encounter something like a pilot program in porn literacy, they are inundated with messages about the place of sex in their lives and the expected comportment of their sexed bodies.

In other words, schools need not articulate everything in the language of curricular expectations to enforce various norms about sex and gender (Gilbert 2014; Kendall 2013; Fields 2008; Pascoe 2007; Trudell 1993). There is always a parallel curriculum that may reinforce or undermine whatever the designated "sex" teacher communicates. Whether a teacher intervenes upon hearing homophobic epithets in the hallway is part of this curriculum. How girls are censured for, or complimented on, their sartorial choices is part of this curriculum. Whether interactions are coded as "sexual assault" or "horseplay" is part of this curriculum.[7] The availability (or unavailability) of condoms is, too. At school, the overriding project of cultivating particular kinds of members of society invokes sexual embodiment and sexual values at every turn (Murray 2019).

Therefore, although the structure of schools and the formal curriculum – the functions and parameters of formal education in our contemporary society – make some sex education impossible, and even unthinkable, they also insert learning about sex into the places where we are trained not to look for it. These unacknowledged sources of (mis)education usually escape philosophical and public arguments about what belongs in "sex education," even as they work on students' developing beliefs and knowledge.

Sex, Para-Sex, and Meta-Sex Education

The preceding considerations complicate my initial assertion that there is no sex education in schools. Rather than a surprising absence, there is a contradiction: schools never teach sex, and constantly teach sex. Real learning about sex does not, and cannot, happen in schools as they are currently conceived. Yet, schools do have an obligation to help students acquire a meaningful sex education that is compatible with ethics, pleasure, and liberal democracy. Put differently, teaching about sex is both impossible and unavoidable. When we refer to "sex education" as the embattled object of curriculum policy, we are imprecise about what we mean by both "sex" and "education."

I propose that we clarify "sex education" in a way that makes it more intelligible and more conducive to progress in the interminable political debates that the subject seems to generate. There are two kinds of learning in schools that are adjacent to sex education: *para-sex education* and *meta-sex education*. Together, they form a penumbra around the kind of sexual knowledge that remains properly bracketed from schools. Para-sex education is the learning about topics relating to sex that can and ought to be delivered in a conventional school setting. This includes most of the topics on the curricula designed as "comprehensive" and advised by the likes of UNESCO (2018) and the WHO (2010): growth and sexual development, contraception, sexually transmitted infections, pregnancy and reproduction, and gender equality. It also includes things that have nothing intrinsic to do with sex, such as democratic citizenship, critical thinking, respect for others, mental health, and general self-care. These topics deserve the prefix "para" because they surround knowledge of sex itself. They are essential to lifelong sexual health and the collective well-being of a liberal society, but they do not immerse students in the practice of sex.

"Meta-sex education" refers to the learning that students need to make sense of their extra-scholastic sex education and personal sexual experiences. It is "meta" because it is education about the practice of sex. This type of learning has until recently played but a sheepish role in even the most comprehensive and liberal of programs. Inviting young people to reflect on where they receive actual sex education and the messages contained therein requires trespassing on some of the universal taboos of teaching in our *scientia*-inspired school culture. It requires naming the limits of school even as it uses schools to counteract and complement other institutions' influences on young people. It also translates into precisely the kinds of learning that feminist, queer, and critical sex education researchers have long called for: critical media literacy, including pornography literacy; inclusive explorations of gender identity and sexual orientation; practical strategies for negotiating consent and reducing violence; and discussions about sexual pleasure and desire – including how they are produced and manipulated by cultural norms. These lessons acknowledge that students already are learning about the mechanics, politics, and cultural tropes of sexuality outside the classroom, and that no amount of testing on the transmission of STIs will set them on a path of lifelong health and fulfilment. Meta-education comes as close to sex education as possible while respecting its distinctiveness as an academic subject. Rather than teaching students about sex in the manner of constructive developmental pedagogy, progressive educators should aim help students approach their own sexual practice thoughtfully, autonomously, and ethically. The outcomes of such lessons will never be explicitly recognizable or assessable within the formal education system, but potentially decisive in young people's lives.

Neither of these types of education – "para-" or "meta-" – is sex education in the strict sense.[8] They are intelligible as educational projects only because they put sex in relation to topics, and into pedagogical forms, that we believe (maybe) can be taught and learned in schools. They provide a structure into which students can insert their own, most intimate, sexual learning and development.

They also highlight that students receive education pertaining to sex regardless of what we put on the formal curriculum. Not all para- or meta-sex education is *good* education, and much of it may in fact undermine the very goals to which para- and meta-sex education should be oriented. As sex education researchers have pointed out, protocols at school dances, body-shaming in gym class, the selection of novels in language classes, and countless other events in school life contribute to the learning that conditions and surrounds students' first-order sexual learning. Para- and meta-sex education cut across the formal and implicit curricula. Until we stop thinking about sex education as a specific category on the curriculum that can be cordoned off from everything else, we will fail to grasp the penumbra of sex education and our obligations regarding it.

Beyond the Liberal Debates

In the face of unremitting public controversy and vexed decisions by policy makers and educators, philosophers have proposed rational bases for adjudicating disagreements about how to teach sex in schools. Rarely, though, is the possibility of teaching sex called into question, either in public discourse or in academic philosophy. Most of the controversy over "sex education" assumes it is possible and dwells on the details of what to include or omit, what to make optional and what to make mandatory. The implied premise is that students may not learn what they are not formally taught. Likewise, the structure of contemporary curriculum is treated as a non-negotiable framework into which sex education must be fitted.

Approaching the controversies over sex education through the filter of intelligibility and para-sex education may enable us to reframe, or possibly transcend, some of the conventional sticking points. In this section I will briefly revisit three of the major philosophical questions about sex education to show what they miss about the intelligibility of the practice. These questions concern the content of sex education (abstinence-only or more), authority over sex education (the state vs. parents), and value neutrality in sex education. The liberal perspectives that are standard fare among philosophers of education still provide the best answers to concrete questions of educational policy and curriculum. But, as I hope to show, they remain devoted to a conception of the place of sex in education that we should regard as contingent and incomplete.

AOUME vs. CSE

Judging by media coverage and policy battles in the United States and elsewhere, one could easily conclude that "sex education" must be either exclusively committed to preaching abstinence until marriage, or cautiously "comprehensive" about birth control and select other topics related to sexual health. This false dichotomy between AOUME and CSE is reflected in some of the defining philosophical debates about sex education curriculum – whether it should be "restrictive" or "permissive" (McKay 1998), whether it should cover only "plumbing" and "basics" (Archard 2000: 28) or "the full range of possible sexual behaviour" (Harris 1971: 9). Contemporary disagreements turn on the inclusion of more specific components of so-called CSE, such as information about abortion and the inclusion of trans or non-binary gender identity. It is important to articulate the rationale for providing students with information about any of these topics in schools, as well as the ethical criteria by which we may make decisions about the timing and content of such instruction in an environment where some people are hostile to the very prospect of teaching children the proper names for their genitals (Shahzad 2016). Some medical agencies and non-governmental organizations have identified CSE as a requirement of children's rights, arguing that anything less deprives young people of their human right to bodily integrity and self-determination (UNESCO 2018; WHO 2010; Malone & Rodriguez 2011). Liberal philosophers have, characteristically, stressed the connection between the aim of autonomy and the necessity of providing young people with the information to make choices about their sexual behavior and reproduction, thus favoring more comprehensive approaches to curriculum content (Archard 2000; McKay 1998; Reiss 1995). As Harris (1971) argued more than half a century ago, "*The more educated a person is the better he [sic] is able to make a responsible and informed choice between possible courses of behaviour. The more aware he is of these possibilities, the more freedom he has in the way he conducts his life*" (7; original italics).

These philosophers of education and broadly liberal-minded organizations are right to insist that young people are entitled to information that supports healthy and autonomous sexual behavior.[9] But such ideals overestimate the significance of curriculum content, assuming that "sex education" can be transmitted via the top–down pedagogical methods enshrined in modern Western institutions. As we have seen, this is a peculiar conception of sexual knowledge – as a set of facts and propositions – that is regularly overshadowed by students' engagement with more explicit sexual materials. Furthermore, beholden to *scientia sexualis*, advocates for comprehensive curriculum construe the possibilities for "sex education" within existing education structures that are intrinsically incompatible with sex and, at times, autonomy: the formal curriculum, vertical governance structures, and the surveillance of students' bodies, among other things. Regardless of what they are told in sex education classes, students experience school as a series of constraints on their physical freedom, as well as on what they can say, ask, and learn.[10] A truly autonomy-promoting and comprehensive vision of sex education would have to think outside these boundaries and, indeed, acknowledge the "freedom" that young people already have outside the classroom, for better or for worse.

Whose Job is It?

A second longstanding controversy over sex education concerns the question of educational authority. Across educational domains, there are important ethical questions about which adults can decide what children should be exposed to or protected from, what they should or should not learn to believe, to do, and to be. Invoking the famous Supreme Court decision in *Mozert v Hawkins* (1987), American scholars have typically parsed curriculum controversies as a tension between parents and the state, with the task being to set appropriate limits on each. Unsurprisingly, sex education has provoked substantive debate about educational authority, with philosophers debating the justification of state-mandated learning and the pros and cons of allowing parental opt-outs from controversial curriculum (Bialystok 2018; Gutmann 1987). Liberals are divided on the ethics of using state force to override parental objections. As long as we are steeped in a formal schooling model where sex education must be incorporated into the curriculum, these choices have consequences.[11]

Nonetheless, these positions are conditioned by what we think schools can actually accomplish without parental interference and whether we think parents can control what happens outside of schools. As I have been arguing, school-based "sex education," and especially one-off lessons in a brick-and-mortar classroom, are not where students learn *sex*. Rather than haggling *ad nauseam* over which adults and state institutions have the honor (or burden) of teaching young people about sex, it would be more productive to proceed from the recognition that young people are already learning about sex, whether the adults in their lives approve or not. What they need is para- and meta-sex education. The education that most liberals would like to see guaranteed in schools would then better complement the types of sexual knowledge and modes of learning that are actually precluded by schools, and which young people access without either parents' or teachers' blessing. Adult authorities have far less control over young people's sexual learning than is typically believed, rendering the old "state vs. parents" debate something of a red herring. At the same time, the recognition of how we do not and cannot provide young people with most of their sex education helpfully illuminates what we can and must provide them with. Both the family and the state have important roles to play in scaffolding young people's learning about sex.

Value Neutrality

A third longstanding area of philosophical work with evident applicability to sex education concerns the value of neutrality. Liberal theorists disagree on the limits of state neutrality with respect to views of the good life in the context of irreducible pluralism, and educational philosophers have wrestled with the ethics of addressing such pluralism in the classroom. Although most philosophers writing about sex education adhere to generally liberal values, there is ongoing debate about the scope of neutrality in such a context (Corngold 2013; Archard 1998; McKay 1998), including whether hot-button issues, such as homosexuality should be taught as controversial (Hand 2007), what role religion should play in sex education (Halstead & Reiss 2003), and whether the fact-value gap is as clear-cut as it has been claimed to be (Lamb 2013).

The familiar lines of disagreement over whether and how to teach "controversial" topics relating to sexuality rest on a mistake. The disagreement arises from an unintelligible conception of "sex education." Once we recognize that the classroom is not where students are really learning *sex*, and that sheltering them from such learning is hopeless, we can re-assign these debates to less inflammatory areas of the curriculum and ask what is necessary from the perspective of citizenship and social belonging. Some options rapidly lose any currency in this light. First, the posture of silent avoidance is simply untenable; in many cases, students now know more than their teachers about sexual politics, culture wars, reproductive rights, sexual diversity, and other "controversial" topics. Second, the classical liberal pretension to neutrality, where this means "unbiased ... accounts of evaluative views about various sexual practices (with no tendentious asides about their prevalence or which cite features strictly irrelevant to their defensibility)" (Archard 1998: 445–446), may express liberal values but places too much confidence in the role of the school as a gatekeeping institution.[12] By the time students are considered old enough to debate complex social issues in class, they have absorbed countless ideas about sexual practices that are anything but neutral.

Only some thick version of controversial issues education survives the reality check. Recognizing that school is the place for para- and meta-sex education, rather than first-order sex education, clarifies the necessity of teaching students critical thinking, media literacy, and ethical reasoning, among other skills, in order to negotiate the controversies and challenges to their value systems that they will inevitably confront in their personal lives. None of these topics amounts to learning *sex* or results in young people having sex that they would not otherwise have had; still less does it change anyone's sexual orientation or gender identity. Without such learning, however, the sex education that students access on their own time is far more likely to be bewildering or harmful. Once again, the general liberal intuitions regarding sex education are right, but this is best appreciated by problematizing the premise that schools are offering "sex education" in the first place.

Conclusion: What's in a Name?

The problems I have laid out here regarding our conceptualization of sex education are not merely semantic.[13] It might be appropriate to replace the term "sex education" with other labels – and in official curriculum documents, many jurisdictions have. "Relationships and Sex Education" (formerly "Sex and Relationships Education") was made statutory in the United Kingdom in 2020; in the United States, "Teen Pregnancy Prevention" replaced federally endorsed AOUME in 2010; in Ontario, Canada, a years-long debacle concerned a sub-unit of the Physical Education curriculum called "Sexual Health and Human Development." Scholars tend to favor the term "sexuality education" because it provides a more holistic perspective on the place of sex in a person's life (Fields et al. 2015). Each of these terms has advantages, and all are more accurate than the blunt phrase "sex education," while not yet correcting widespread confusion about what is and can be taught in schools. Regardless of the name used in a given school system, and regardless of the intentions of the educators within it, we tend to revert to the misleading concept of "sex education" as a placeholder for all adult anxieties about what students learn – or do not.

Due to the constant tension between the subject and the institution, sex is different from other subjects we find on the curriculum. "Sex education" is not intelligible in the way that, for instance, Spanish education is intelligible. It is, rather, a convenient proxy for some subject matter and educational goals that are intelligible, and in some cases necessary. But it elides the type of sex education that may matter most to young people (Allen 2005) – better para- and meta-sex education – and encourages endless controversy and distortion.

I have argued here that we must be clearer about what students actually learn about sex in schools and elsewhere. Schools deliver para- and meta-sex education, both in formal curriculum and in all the other features of the institution. Such education is not always intentional, productive, or consistent, but it follows from the conceptions of knowledge and sexual truth that are descended from *scientia sexualis*. Meanwhile, sex education that more closely resembles *ars amoris* occurs outside of institutional education, increasingly with the assistance of digital communications, and with similarly mixed effects on young people. Understanding this context can guide us in improving what happens at schools under the auspices of "sex education." I have elsewhere argued for a school-based model called Democratic Humanistic Sex Education (Bialystok & Andersen 2022: ch. 6). Among other things, this form of para- and meta-sex education would be cross-curricular, ongoing, unflinchingly informed by students' real lives, and separated from most formal assessment processes.

One might hope that a paradigm shift of this nature will help to deflate the high-pitched discourse over sex education in schools. After all, once we recognize that sex is not like Spanish and no one ever pretended it was, some anxieties about schools corrupting young people should abate. I am not optimistic that our political discourse will realign itself so rationally. Nonetheless, philosophy can help societies better define areas of disagreement over the role of schools in sex education and imagine more inventive alternatives.

(Related Chapters: 3, 6, 7, 8, 14, 16, 26, 27.)

Notes

1 Foucault 1976: 57.
2 In some cases, sex education is provided in schools by outside instructors – whether sex education specialists, medical providers, or religious/abstinence-only leaders – and thereby sidesteps some of the constraints of formal curriculum, especially where assessment is concerned. However, the lessons remain ensconced in an institutional environment that perpetuates the model of *scientia sexualis* and may exacerbate the pedagogical tensions explored here. For more discussion, see Bialystok and Andersen (2022), Chapter 6, and Andersen and Bialystok (forthcoming).
3 We see evidence for this in the Platonic dialogues, especially *Symposium*. As Foucault (1976) explains, "[i]n [ancient] Greece, truth and sex were linked, in the form of pedagogy, by the transmission of a precious knowledge from one body to another; sex served as a medium for initiations into learning" (61).
4 On the tension between constructivism and authenticity, see Bialystok (2017).
5 Pornography, of course, is intended to be sexually *stimulating* more than (or as well as) instructive. The fact that it may be stimulating does not detract from its efficacy as a means of instruction; on the contrary, "we learn better using images than words" and "we also learn better when aroused" (Layden 2010: 57).
6 About 40% of high school students report having had sex (NCSL 2020). The imprecision of the phrase "having sex" and the fallibility of self-reporting are well-known to researchers.
7 On this distinction, see Trudell (1993): 51–53.
8 These two categories are not intended to be rigidly delineated or mutually exclusive; certain types of learning will no doubt count as both. The exact relationship between para- and meta-sex education is a topic for another time.
9 There are also good reasons to be skeptical of autonomy as the overriding value in sex education (McAvoy 2013).
10 Moreover, these constraints are unequally enforced and regularly overlaid with sexist and racist values, especially when it comes to sex (Kendall 2013; Fields 2008; Allen 2005).
11 The consequences matter symbolically even if, as my analysis suggests, they have less direct practical effect than is commonly assumed. The state's choices about opt-out policies and mandatory curriculum communicate its values and priorities.
12 For another liberal defense of neutrality in sex education, see Reiss (1995): 381.
13 See Fields et al. (2015): 371.

References

Allen, L. (2005) *Sexual Subjects: Young People, Sexuality and Education.* Houndsmills & New York: Palgrave Macmillan.

Andersen, L. & Bialystok, L. (forthcoming) "Assessing a Touchy Subject."

Archard, D. (1998) "How Should We Teach Sex?" *Journal of Philosophy of Education* 32(3): 437–449.

Archard, D. (2000) *Sex Education. Impact* 7. London: Philosophy of Education Society of Great Britain.

Bialystok, L. (2017) "Authenticity in Education" in G. Noblit (ed.) *The Oxford Research Encyclopedia of Education.* Oxford: Oxford University Press. http://education.oxfordre.com/view/10.1093/acrefore/9780190264093.001.0001/acrefore-9780190264093-e-168

Bialystok, L. (2018) "My Child, My Choice? Mandatory Curriculum, Sex, and the Conscience of Parents," *Educational Theory* 68(1): 11–29.

Bialystok, L. & Andersen, L. (2022) *Touchy Subject: The History and Philosophy of Sex Education.* Chicago: University of Chicago Press.

Bridges, A. J., Wosnitzer, R., Scharrer, E., Sun, C., & Liberman, R. (2010) "Aggression and Sexual Behavior in Best-Selling Pornography Videos: A Content Analysis Update," *Violence Against Women* 16(10): 1065–1085.

Connelly, F. M. & Connelly, G. (2010) "Curriculum Policy," in C. A. Kridel (ed.) *Encyclopedia of Curriculum Studies.* California: Sage, 225–227.

Corngold, J. (2013) "Moral Pluralism and Sex Education," *Educational Theory* 63(5): 461–482.

Cox, S., Pazol, K., Warner, L., Romero, L., Spitz, A., Gavin, L., & Barfield, W. (2014, April 8). "Vital Signs: Births to Teens Aged 15–17 Years – United States, 1991–2012," *Centers for Disease Control and Prevention Morbidity and Mortality Weekly Report* 63: 1–7.

Fields, J. (2008) *Risky Lessons: Sex Education and Social Inequality.* New York: Rutgers University Press.

Fields, J., Gilbert, J., & Miller, M. (2015) "Sexuality and Education: Toward the Promise of Ambiguity," in J. DeLamater & R. F. Plante (eds.) *Handbook of the Sociology of Sexualities.* New York: Springer, 371–387.

Foucault, M. (1976) *A History of Sexuality, Volume 1.* Trans. R. Hurley. New York: Vintage.

Gilbert, J. (2014) *Sexuality in School: The Limits of Education.* Minneapolis: University of Minnesota Press.

Goldsmith, K., Dunkley, C., Dang, S., & Gorzalka, B. (2017) "Pornography Consumption and its Association with Sexual Concerns and Expectations among Young Men and Women," *The Canadian Journal of Human Sexuality* 26(2): 151–162.

Gutmann, A. (1987) *Democratic Education*. Princeton, NJ: Princeton University Press.

Halstead, M. & Reiss, M. (2003) *Values in Sex Education: From Principles to Practice*. London; New York: Routledge Falmer.

Hand, M. (2007) "Should We Teach Homosexuality as a Controversial Issue?" *Theory and Research in Education* 5(1): 69–86.

Harris, A. (1971) "What Does 'Sex Education' Mean?" *Journal of Moral Education* 1(1): 7–11.

Horvath, M., Alys, L., Massey, K., Pina, A., Scally, M., & Adler, J. (2013) *Basically … Porn Is Everywhere: A Rapid Evidence Assessment on the Effects that Access and Exposure to Pornography Has on Children and Young People*. Project Report. London, UK: Office of the Children's Commissioner for England.

Jones, M. (2018) "What Teenagers Are Learning from Online Porn," *The New York Times Magazine* Feb. 7. https://www.nytimes.com/2018/02/07/magazine/teenagers-learning-online-porn-literacy-sex-education.html

Kendall, N. (2013) *The Sex Education Debates*. Chicago: University of Chicago Press.

Lamb, S. (2010) "Toward a Sexual Ethics Curriculum: Bringing Philosophy and Society to Bear on Individual Development," *Harvard Educational Review* 80(1): 81–105.

Lamb, S. (2013) "Just the Facts? The Separation of Sex Education from Moral Education," *Educational Theory* 63(5): 443–460.

Layden, M. A. (2010) "Pornography and Violence: A New Look at the Research" in J. Stoner & D. Hughes (eds.) *The Social Costs of Pornography: A Collection of Papers*. Princeton, NJ: Witherspoon Institute, 57–68.

Malone, P. & Rodriguez, M. (2011) "Comprehensive Sex Education vs. Abstinence-Only-Until-Marriage Programs," *American Bar Association*. https://www.americanbar.org/groups/crsj/publications/human_rights_magazine_home/human_rights_vol38_2011/human_rights_spring2011/comprehensive_sex_education_vs_abstinence_only_until_marriage_programs/

McAvoy, P. (2013) "The Aims of Sex Education: Demoting Autonomy and Promoting Mutuality," *Educational Theory* 63(5): 483–496.

McKay, A. (1998) *Sexual Ideology and Schooling: Toward Democratic Sexuality Education*. London, ON: Althouse Press.

Murray, M. (2019) "Sex and the Schoolhouse," *Harvard Law Review* 132: 1445–1488.

Naezer, M. (2018) "From Risky Behaviour to Sexy Adventures: Reconceptualising Young People's Online Sexual Activities," *Culture, Health & Sexuality* 20(6): 715–729.

National Conference of State Legislatures (NCSL) (2010, October 1) "State Polices on Sex Education in Schools." https://www.ncsl.org/research/health/state-policies-on-sex-education-in-schools.aspx

Orenstein, P. (2016) "When Did Porn Become Sex Ed?" *The New York Times March 19*. https://www.nytimes.com/2016/03/20/opinion/sunday/when-did-porn-become-sex-ed.html

Pascoe, C. J. (2007) *Dude, You're a Fag: Masculinity and Sexuality in High School*. Berkeley, CA: University of California Press.

Reiss, M. (1995) "Conflicting Philosophies of School Sex Education," *Journal of Moral Education* 24(4): 371–382.

Rice, E., Gibbs, J., Winetrobe, H., Rhoades, H., Plant, A., Montoya, J., & Kordic, T. (2014) "Sexting and Sexual Behavior among Middle School Students," *Pediatrics* 134(1): e21–e28.

Rogala, C. & Tyden, T. (2003) "Does Pornography Influence Young Women's Sexual Behavior?" *Women's Health Issues* 13(1): 39–43.

Shahzad, R. (2016) "Thorncliffe Park School Offers 'Sanitized Version' of Sex Ed for Grade 1 Students." *CBC News* May 13. https://www.cbc.ca/news/canada/toronto/sanitized-curriculum-sex-ed-1.3581710

Trudell, B. (1993) *Doing Sex Education: Gender Politics and Schooling*. New York: Routledge.

United Nations Educational, Scientific and Cultural Organization (UNESCO) (2018) *International Technical Guidance on Sexuality Education: An Evidence-informed Approach. Revised Edition*. Paris, France: United Nations. https://www.unfpa.org/publications/international-technical-guidance-sexuality-education

Williams, L. (1989) *Hard Core: Power, Pleasure, and the Frenzy of the Visible*. Berkeley, CA: University of California Press.

World Health Organization (WHO) Regional Office for Europe and BZgA (2010) *Standards for Sexuality Education in Europe: A Framework for Policy Makers, Educational and Health Authorities and Specialists*. Cologne, Germany: World Health Organization. https://www.bzga-whocc.de/fileadmin/user_upload/WHO_BZgA_Standards_English.pdf

31

RACIAL IDENTITY FORMATION AND ANTIRACIST EDUCATION

Winston C. Thompson

The focus of this chapter is race as a potential *subject* of instruction across varied formal and informal educational spaces. Analyses of the ethical contours of race as an explicit subject of instruction will be explored, with considerable attention given to abiding perceptions of the social weightiness and moral complexity of racial categories. The teaching of race has been an especially thorny matter within educational contexts in the United States and elsewhere, and it has been accompanied by much handwringing, deliberation, and doubt (Reddick 1934; Givens 2019). Questions about the teaching of race are just one aspect of recent philosophical debate regarding racial justice in education (Blum 2017; Merriweather 2018), but they warrant a chapter of their own.

Despite the enduring presence of public and private hesitations regarding race as a subject of instruction, reference to it continues across several scholarly contexts.[1] Given this, the relative paucity of sustained analysis of the defensibility of teaching race is striking. What is the most ethically coherent stance regarding race as a subject of instruction? This chapter will engage this question, cataloguing a few of the ways in which educational actors might navigate portions of the competing concerns and conceptual positions related to the topic. In doing so, it highlights the possibility of coherence between some of the more popular approaches to teaching race as a subject. At its core, the chapter considers whether and how these approaches to race as a subject of instruction might be compatible with one another. In doing so, it will explore varied understandings of race and the complexity of racial identity formation as a pedagogical goal. Given the bounty of existing work on the subject, it will also provide a brief overview of arguments for and against what is commonly understood as antiracist education. Engaging its central question, the chapter will then close with some remarks on the conceptual and normative tensions pertaining to race as a subject of instruction.

A few preliminary remarks are warranted. First, it should be noted that much of what is discussed in this chapter operates on the assumptions of the English-speaking western world. Conceptualizations of race and criteria of (and demarcations between) racial group membership are but a few of the differences that might be found across contexts. Articulated differently, the analyses of race (generally, and as pedagogical subject) in this chapter are based within a specific historical, cultural, political, and social network of understandings about race, reflected in the discourses referenced and cited. This should not be read as suggesting that other conceptualizations or operationalizations of race are less valuable, impactful, or complex. The chapter offers no statement about the applicability of its analyses to those contexts in which race and racial identity groupings function in saliently dissimilar ways.

DOI: 10.4324/9781003172246-36

Contextualizing Race

Historical Context

Before directly engaging race as a subject of educational interest, it is helpful to place this chapter's understanding of race in a social, historical, and conceptual context. "Race" might be understood as a system of organizing persons into groups or kinds on the basis of shared physical and/or ethno-cultural characteristics (Outlaw 2005; Haslanger 2000). Chief among these defining racial characteristics has been skin color, but other criteria have surely been salient (Spencer 2015). Although similar characteristics were likely perceived across far distant periods of human history, those perceptions of difference did not constitute criteria for racial (in the contemporary usage of the concept) categorization until the 17th Century (McCarthy 2009).

Historians of race point to this period of time as the era within which "scientifically" articulated accounts of deep differences between human populations began to resemble what is now identified as "race" (McCarthy 2009; Blum 2012). These accounts were put forward by members of the growing scientific community as they sought to catalogue – and hierarchically organize – human populations, suggesting some inherent differences between them (Darby & Rury 2018). The ontological significance of these categorizations will be discussed below, but the economic significance of this modern account of race (during a period when Europe's colonial ambitions were in full manifestation) deserves mention. Race, and its implications regarding degrees of civilization and rationality, served as a legitimating rationale for much of Europe's expansionary and dominating practices. The understanding that some individual persons were members of scientifically demonstrable subordinate groups (i.e., ones less intelligent, less caring, more brutal, etc.) operated in the background of much of the historical period in which race came to be known as it is today (Darby & Rury 2018). Arguably, much of these perceptions and categorizations continue to attach to understandings of race in the contemporary context.

Even so, philosophers have developed rich analyses of the concept of race. These serve to identify precisely what is intended and implied by the use of race as a conceptual category within contemporary society, and they can be helpful in determining whether and how race might be taught.

Conceptual Context

As various theories and analyses of race might provide insight into different dimensions of its practical and ontological statuses, prioritizing any one of them might lead to an idiosyncratic exploration. The purposes of this chapter are consequently best served by an overview of the competing conceptualizations of race, focusing on the broad categories of views that exist within the field. This overview is not intended to be exhaustive. Instead, it will sketch a number of the major accounts of race that might be under discussion in debates concerning race as an educational subject.

A widely discredited view of race, still implicitly endorsed by many, is that it is entirely a *natural kind*. On this natural kind view, there exist objective biological facts about race, and these identify differences that are fully inclusive of all members of a given race (and exclusive of non-members), explaining group and individual dispositions and characteristics. The presumed biological differences are understood to be genetic (Mallon 2007), and an implication of these views is that races existed before people began referring to them in the 17th Century. Again, despite the fact that this cluster of views has been discredited by science, versions of this biological account of race persist in the present era. Other philosophical positions on race are by and large responses to the "natural kind" view of race.

One such alternative philosophical view of race is *racial skepticism*. In the wake of the biological view of race having been discredited, it might be the case that "race" has no objective referent. Since race is not a natural kind, it may not mark any real thing in the world. Racial skeptics, such as

Kwame Anthony Appiah and Orlando Patterson hold the view that such skepticism is largely warranted and that race ought to be understood as largely a fiction.

By contrast, *racial population naturalism* involves some limited acceptance of the biological account of race. It argues that while race might not be a natural kind, a vague biological view of race is defensible since "race" can be understood to overlap with biological characteristics according to the definitions of race that have been socially endorsed. This account does not identify exclusive or essential traits of a given race and has rather little to say about how race might manifest in behavior traits of individual persons. Some have suggested that a minimal account of racial population naturalism is evidenced in US census categories as these mark populations that are physically (i.e., phenotypically) dissimilar. As such, the concept of race might be understood as referring to something objective in ways that the racial skepticism view would reject (Spencer 2019).

Finally, *racial constructivism*, the view that race is a socially constructed phenomenon, is perhaps the most popular of explicitly defended views on race. (Arguably, among implicitly enacted views, a "natural kind" approach might still hold this title.) Especially popular among scholars in the social sciences (including education), this family of accounts rejects the biological "natural kind" view of race. According to these views, it would be entirely incorrect to understand races as having any existence before humans began referring to them in the 17th Century; races exist only as social constructs. Although a "thin" version of the constructivist account of race might grant that there exist some ancestral and/or genetic differences between groups of human populations – an allowance that is in many ways similar to some varieties of racial population naturalism – the constructivist view of race concludes that the fact that these are conceptualized as "racial" is a matter of social choice (Mills 1998; Outlaw 1996; Gooding-Williams 2006). Another strand of constructivism distances itself from granting the necessity of any shared physical characteristics among members of a race, arguing that the essential shared experience of having been racialized (that is, perceived and treated as though one is a member of a racial group) is the defining trait of a race's members (Shelby 2007). Across the varied constructivist accounts of race is much disagreement and nuance premised on the implications of race's ontological status as a social phenomenon. Some hold the view that race (and racial identity) can be a source of sustained joy or an ethical identity (and need not be linked to forms of oppressive power), whereas others hold that race is necessarily an expression of social power and caution should thus be exercised regarding race's present value, beyond its potential for facilitating collective social action in the service of its own elimination (West 1994; Jeffers 2019; Haslanger 2019).

Consistent with this observation, it should be noted that each of the major ontological views on race might lead an adherent to either preserve the concept of race in social practice or seek to eliminate it. These alternatives represent the major normative stances on race across the ontological categories sketched above. Again, there are nuances across the range of approaches that one might hold on the spectrum between these two poles (i.e., *conservationism* on the one end and *eliminativism* on the other) but the implications of these social aims being partially expressed as educational aims in a given curriculum cannot be overlooked.

Race as a Subject of Instruction?

Given the range of philosophical positions outlined above, one might expect that the potential justifications for or against including race on the curriculum are plentiful. Using these philosophical positions as a foundation for analyzing ontological views and normative commitments to the concept of race, the remainder of the chapter will engage the question of whether to teach race. As that question is generally understood in the contexts earlier stipulated, it might be read to imply at least three distinct questions. The chapter will focus on two of them.

First, in asking whether to teach race, one might intend to ask whether the fact (be it understood as biological, social, or otherwise) of race ought to be a subject of instruction. This might be understood as the most basic question at stake, as answers to it are presupposed by the other two questions. For this reason, much of the analysis to follow will not directly address it.

Second, in asking whether to teach race, one might intend to ask whether students should be taught that they have a racial identity. Should a curriculum communicate and endorse the view that the student has a race to be known and with which to identify? This is a question of the appropriateness of what might be called racial identity formation. It seems to be the intended focus of some who pose the general question of the legitimacy of race as an educational subject.

Finally, in asking whether to teach race, one might intend to ask whether students should be taught that they have normative obligations arising from the existence of the concept of "race" and its role in unjust systems of oppressive power.[2] This is the question of whether antiracist education is justified. Here, as is also the case for the question of whether racial identity should be taught, one might readily invoke the various ontological views or normative positions described above. These questions of racial identity formation and antiracist education will be addressed at length in the sections that follow.

Teaching Racial Identity

In its most basic form, racial identity formation can be described as the process by which a person comes to identify with (and potentially internalize) a racial identity – which potentially, though not necessarily, may include some normative guidance on how the person ought to act and interpret themselves in relation to others (Appiah & Gutmann 1996; Gooding-Williams 2001). As a phenomenon studied across disciplines, this process can be understood as developmental or educational in nature (Cross 1991; Kim 2001). It can also be fruitfully explored from a sociological perspective (Omi & Winant 2014). Philosophical attention to the various components and dimensions of such an education may also reveal non-obvious consequences (Thompson 2018). Of course, across these approaches, it is clear that one's identification as a member of a racial group may occur alongside salient development of other dimensions of a person's identity (e.g., gender expression, sexuality, ethnicity, etc.). Despite this intersectional observation, the present discussion of racial identity formation will proceed in relatively abstracted terms, with little reference to these complex and interconnected dimensions of identity.

At present, racial identity formation is rarely identified as an explicit educational aim in schools. Notable exceptions to this are potentially found in educational institutions with race-sensitive missions; for example, schools within the afro-centric education movement in the United States might (though do not necessarily) make such goals explicit. Still, despite the rarity of explicit statements of goals regarding racial identity formation, there exists much handwringing among detractors regarding the outcome (Hill 2017).

Learning to be Racialized

Asking whether racial identity formation *should* be an educational goal presupposes that the question is, in some sense, live. For, if one holds the view that persons will inevitably come to racial identities, regardless of any educational activity, the question of education's role would seem to be a miscategorization or misunderstanding of racial identity. Resistance to or acceptance of racial identity formation as an educational goal must, in any case, grapple with the various contexts within which racial identity formation might occur.

Racial identity formation might occur within formal educational contexts, including public, private, and other schools, colleges, and universities. Racial identity formation as a pedagogical goal within these institutions might manifest as an explicit portion of the curriculum either appearing on syllabi or as a part of the general ethos of the institution's mission, embodied within its culture. It might also exist in less formal ways, conducted in *ad hoc*, but no less educationally significant, ways.

Indeed, another context for racial identity formation is the informal educational practices of a student's experience. By this, one might surely recognize the informal (i.e., not officially sanctioned) lattice of intentional practices and interactions within, say, a school that (despite their having no fully predetermined design) lead to the pedagogical outcome of racial identification or internalization. Additionally, one might also recognize the informal education that occurs within a family, neighborhood, or broader community; social arrangements can greatly shape the ways in which persons come to understand, interpret, and (less-cognitively) embody the validity of their racial identity (Haslanger 2005). Arguably, much racial identity formation can occur within these informal educational contexts in ways either intentional (e.g., a parent seeking to instill a positive sense of racial group membership in a child) or unintentional-yet-predictable (e.g., a child's pattern of interactions with clerks at various shops in their town may suggest to the child some salient and potentially internalizable differences between them and their racially dissimilar peers).[3]

The question of the appropriateness of racial identity formation as curriculum (broadly construed) might be coherently analyzed across these contexts.

Potential Problems with Teaching Racial Identity

Across the various contexts in which racial identity formation might be a pedagogical goal, a number of argument types might be pursued in opposition or support. Below are a couple of the stronger categories of these.

Racial identity formation might fail to meet general pedagogical standards. Broadly applied to potential subject matter, the question of what ought to be included on any curriculum might rest upon epistemic standards (Tillson 2020; Hand 2008). More specifically, one might hold the view that racial identity formation simply fails to meet these. A racial skeptic, for instance, might hold this pedagogical view and conclude that any attempt to educate a student toward embracing a racial identity is tantamount to a form of educational malpractice, on the grounds that it involves teaching a false belief (Hill 2017). Of course, racial skeptics could also advocate for the inclusion of racial identity formation on the curriculum. For example, they might reject the above implied epistemic standards or replace them with other, more permissive, standards (e.g., by holding the position that some "falsehoods" might be justifiably taught if they are useful in further educational and/or social goals).

Similarly, though within a separate category, one might object to the curricular inclusion of racial identity formation on normative conceptual grounds. One might simply hold an eliminativist normative stance regarding race, such that ethical engagement with the idea of "race" would be aimed at weakening and/or destroying the present version of the concept (Haslanger 2000, 2019). This might be pursued by neither facilitating racial identity formation nor encouraging students to internalize a specific racial identity, with this resistance representing a meaningful step in that larger eliminativist project.

Of course, natural kind, racial population naturalism, and constructivist views can all accommodate the inclusion of racial identity formation on the curriculum. On the grounds that race represents some objective or intersubjective fact of the world, these views can perceive understanding race and identifying with a racial group as a desirable educational outcome that allows students to navigate a racially complex present and future.

Further Complications of Race and Power

A major facet of approaching the question of racial identity formation in the curriculum is the analysis of power. As some accounts of race build power into the very concept of race, power, and its hierarchical manifestations may seem essential (Haslanger 2000, 2019). Against the backdrop of the aforementioned categories of argumentation and the earlier-invoked framings of how race might be understood and racial identity might be learned, sensitivity to power and hierarchy can give rise to the case-types below. In each of these case-types, it is helpful to note that racial "up" groups (i.e., those racial identities that are placed comparatively higher in a social hierarchy than the presently relevant alternative group) have greater power than any "down" group (i.e., those racial identities that are placed comparatively lower in a social hierarchy than the presently relevant alternative group) with which they are engaged. These relationships of power can be explored across varied understandings of race and racial identity formation. In what follows, a few of the critical arguments within each case-type of student/teacher pairings will be presented.

Case 1: Up/Up

When members of the "up" group are taught their racial identity by other members of their "up" group, one might worry that an interest in reinforcing the status quo of the hierarchical structure would undermine objectivity in the educational project. Consider the potential for an education in racial identity occurring during a period of strict segregation in the United States or apartheid South Africa. The racial awareness most often communicated among members of the racial elite in such societies likely asserted the rightness of existing social positions; this might often have been done in rejection of, or indifference to, the pursuit of truth as an educational standard, but there are many more subtle ways in which shared Up-group membership might undermine objectivity. The concern here is that this case-type does not present a promising scenario for racial identity formation that challenges students' presumed superiority.

Of course, such unreflective replication of social conditions need not be the only racial identity formation that might occur within this case-type. "Up" group members might subscribe to a strain of eliminativism that results in their teaching a racial identity in the service of those aims.[4] This could entail the acceptance of a racial identity as a condition for recognizing an abiding responsibility to pursue ameliorative goals. Of course, to some extent this could be true given an eliminativist orientation in any of the case-types described below.

Case 2: Up/Down

When members of the "up" group are taught their racial identity by members of the "down" group, one might worry about the potential for harm to "down" group members.

If, on the one hand, the presumption is that "down" group members are teaching "up" group members to hold a racial identity that confirms the legitimacy of existing power arrangements, "down" group members would seem to be working against their own benefit. Arguably, by endorsing the legitimacy of the hierarchy, these "down" group members could be understood as doing greater service to the maintenance of the power structure than their "up" group peers in the previous case-type. Their endorsement of the racial structure, despite the detriments it visits upon them, can be seen as a more impartial statement of the validity of the status quo.

If, on the other hand, the presumption is that "down" group members are teaching "up" group members to hold a racial identity that disrupts the legitimacy of existing power arrangements, "down" group members might be unduly burdened by the task of leading "up" group members to analyses of racialized power. Consider the frustration of BIPOC (Black, Indigenous, and People of Color) educators who, despite being formally listened to, feel deeply unheard by their White audiences (Delpit 1988). The emotional exhaustion of this enterprise (i.e., being a member of a "down" group while attempting to educate members of an "up" group about their racial identity and race, more broadly) has been well described in popular outlets (Eddo-Lodge 2017).

Case 3: Down/Up

When members of the "down" group are taught their racial identity by members of the "up" group a number of concerns might surface.

First, worries similar to those outlined above might be present as "up" group members have power-based interests in maintaining the status quo and varying degrees of failure to grasp the realities of race. Even if motivated by truth rather than the maintenance of power privilege, "up" group members might be in relatively disadvantageous epistemic positions in comparison to their "down" group students. Given the ways in which social power operates in regard to knowledge creation and access, "down" group members might be in a position to more clearly "see" racial realities than their "up" group colleagues. Learning their racial identity via "up" group members might obscure aspects of their own experiences and/or constitute further epistemic or moral wrongs (Fricker 2007; Dotson 2018).

Finally, even if "up" group members are motivated by pursuit of truth and sufficiently informed about race, their work in teaching a racial identity to "down" group students may constitute a type of condescension. This is a concern of analyses that question the appropriateness of "up" group members' participation in this work on the grounds that, even if well qualified, there exist "down" group members who are similarly (or better) qualified for the work. A conclusion of these analyses is that the most appropriate task for "up" group members is to listen rather than instruct, as their efforts at instruction are a further exercise of unduly held racial power.

Case 4: Down/Down

When members of the "down" group are taught by members of their own "down" group, one might worry that they are passing along internalized identities that serve the existing racial power structure. This may occur not because they are passing along "down" group member's alleged moral shortcomings, but because they share understandings that reflect the epistemic obstacles they have had to navigate in their own process of coming to a racialized identity. Here, one might imagine that the dominant epistemic frameworks for understanding themselves via the concept of race are hermeneutically unjust, such that their educational efforts are marked by that injustice and visit the same upon their students.

On the other hand, the racial identity formation that occurs within this case-type might be genuinely empowering (as may be the case for the previous case-types involving "down" group members as well). Here one might think of the racial identity formed within a "down" group majority social or educational context, like those of Historically Black Colleges and Universities in the United States (Coates 2015).

Across the various conceptual categories, arguments, and cases-types, questions of how best to engage the realities of race (be they metaphysical, social, both, or neither) and the potential formation of a racial identity in educational contexts are challenging. Still, these questions about the place of racial identity formation represent only a small subset of the broader conversation about race as a curricular subject. Far more widely discussed are disputes regarding the teaching of normative responses to race. The chapter now turns its attention to these matters, which are often referred to collectively as antiracist education.

Antiracist Education

Beyond asking what duties might exist to educate students on the subject of (their) race, one might also wonder about what learnable duties, if any, follow from those more fundamental understandings. At its core, this is to ask whether students ought to be taught that they have normative obligations arising from their and others' race. For many, this question places race within a social–historical context, asking about the moral significance of its manifestations and operations. In societies in which race is (at least partially) defined by patterns of power and hierarchy, this social contextualization of race must address racism. Racism can be understood here to refer to instances of the unjust exercise of power contingent upon race; these exercises can be individual or group-based and can be either intentional or unintentional (Bonilla-Silva 2017). What, if anything, should students be taught about race and racism in such contexts?

Conceptual Distinctions

Although antiracist education is widely discussed in the media and, more specifically, within academic and practitioner-focused educational contexts, the distinction between non-racist and antiracist education may not be clear. *Non-racist education* encompasses educational projects that do not promote racist aims or ends. This would include, among other things, educational projects that are merely neutral with respect to race and power or offer no normative guidance regarding matters of racism.[5] In addition to education that is neutral with respect to race and power, the category of *non-racist education* could also be understood to include education that actively resists or opposes racism. *Antiracist education* might thus constitute a sub-class of non-racist education that, like the broader category, does not advance racist aims. By contrast with non-racist education that is merely neutral, however, antiracist education aims to resist racism, taking positive steps to advocate for and advance student awareness of and subscription to actions that would remove the unjust exercise of power contingent upon race.[6]

Recalling the earlier distinction between poles of racial *conservationism* and *eliminativism*, it is clear that strong and weak positions on this spectrum would lend support to different views on antiracist education. For example, a strong racial conservationist might hold the view (defended on instrumental and/or inherent considerations) that students ought to be taught that they have a strong obligation to maintain racial concepts within their society. By contrast, a weak racial eliminativist might be relatively agnostic about whether students are taught to engage in projects aimed at resisting the continued use of the concept of race (though they might have strong views about obligations to act in response to a racialized reality). Indeed, the range of normative arguments regarding race-sensitive moral obligations is wide. Most of these arguments tie the question of what ought to be taught regarding racial obligations to visions of social maintenance or improvement. Across these accounts of what is socially desirable, there are many reasonable views that might be considered antiracist.[7]

Antiracist education might take many forms across the educational contexts invoked earlier in this chapter. For present purposes, only a few arguments in support of an antiracist curriculum will be offered. This will be followed by a brief overview of some potential concerns.

Categories of Arguments in Support

As the literature regarding antiracist education is plentiful, this section will aggregate insights from that discourse in order to offer a few broad categories of arguments in support of pursuing antiracist education.

First, one popular category of argument asserts that antiracist education is the pedagogical expression of an abiding social/political project of antiracism. Against the backdrop of a broadly structurally corrective or ameliorative project, antiracists often defend the pursuit of their aims in and through the educational domain (Kendi 2019). There are at least two subcategories of argument that adopt this perspective. The first holds that education is simply one area, equal to many others, in an ongoing antiracist project. Perspectives within this view might regard antiracist education as no more or less desirable than antiracist practices in the areas of, say, employment, healthcare, or socializing. Another sub-categorical view might regard education as especially important to the underlying antiracist project. Perspectives within this view might regard antiracist education as a foundational cornerstone of pursuing antiracist ends. Education, broadly construed, might therefore be an area of special and prioritized attention for the antiracist project. In either case, under this broad category, students who receive an antiracist education participate in a desirable social/political project.

Related to the view that education has special significance, is the category of argument that sees racism as, in some crucial sense, a failure of education. This category of views need not be attached to a larger social/political project of antiracism. For example, one could advance arguments within this category, focusing on, say, the shortcomings of individuals and their intentions, while remaining uncommitted to addressing what is sometimes referred to as "systemic" forms of racism. At their core, arguments within this category see antiracist education as addressing a looming potential for miseducation, understood as cognitive, dispositional, epistemic, motivational, or myriad other forms of educational failure that may be associated with racism. Students who receive an antiracist education participate in an educational project that is desirable according to education's own standards.

Finally, a small but growing category of argument relies on the notion that antiracist education need not justify itself by reference to outcomes (be they social/political or educational). Instead, this category of argument holds that there is inherent or expressive value in pursuing antiracist education even if such efforts are unlikely to result in meaningful social/political improvement or meaningfully less educational failure.[8] Under this category of argument, the practice of antiracist education is desirable without reference to any outcome-oriented value for students.

Categories of Arguments in Opposition

Despite the range of arguments in support of antiracist education, arguments against it have received considerable public attention.[9] These arguments take multiple forms. Below are a few of the salient issues that tend to recur across these invocations.[10]

First, detractors worry about the degree to which certain forms of antiracist education might impress upon students either a sense of guilt regarding racism (if they are members of a racial "up" group) or might erode a sense of self-worth (if they are members of a racial "down" group) (Douthat 2021). Regarding the former, arguments linked to culpability tend to object to what they perceive as persons being saddled with responsibility for correcting racial wrongs, solely on account of their race. They argue that this onus (real or not) ought not be placed on students. Regarding the latter, arguments predicated on risk to self-worth tend to object to students being taught to view the world in a way that necessarily locates them as disadvantaged, oppressed, or victimized by racism.

Related to these issues is the view that antiracist education does reify racial identities. Even without utilizing the value-based dimensions referenced above, some hold the view that an explicitly antiracist education promotes race as a prioritized identity. According to these critics, rather than allowing students to come to racial understandings and identities on their own timeline, this curricular focus draws student attention to race in a way that is (socially, politically, educationally, etc.) undesirable.

Sometimes, the alleged undesirability of antiracist education is predicated on claims that it is too ideological a perspective to be taught in many educational contexts. Here, critics might advance the view that education ought to be relatively neutral or objective in regards to normative matters like race/racism, lest it constitute a form of indoctrination. It is incumbent upon those who take this position to explain how such arguments might align with the presence of other normative curricular content (Erickson & Thompson 2019, 2021).

Coherence, Racial Identity Formation, and Antiracist Education

Given the analyses of the arguments and observations in the previous sections, the chapter now turns its attention to consider potential alignment between perspectives on race as a curricular subject, expressed as racial identity education and/or antiracist education. In doing this, the chapter considers a handful of examples of how support or opposition for either of these two approaches to race as a pedagogical project might cohere with support for or opposition to the other.[11]

Anti-ARE/Pro-RIF

First, consider the potential coherence between opposition to antiracist education (Anti-ARE) and support for racial identity formation (Pro-RIF) in educational contexts. Stated plainly, the Anti-ARE and Pro-RIF approaches can exist in harmony. For example, an adherent to both perspectives might conclude that students need to learn about race, say, on the grounds that it is social fact; this education could also aim at students accepting their racialized identity.[12] In recognizing the social truth of race, this adherent to the Pro-RIF view need not also commit to any normative stance regarding the desirability of shifts in the default social circumstances of race and power. In some sense this position (Anti-ARE and Pro-RIF) represents a fairly traditional configuration of views regarding race as educational subject (i.e., relatively minimally descriptive without much normative content).

Anti-ARE/Anti-RIF

Second, consider the potential coherence between opposition to antiracist education (Anti-ARE) and opposition to racial identity formation (Anti-RIF) in educational contexts. Again, this configuration of views holds together relatively well. Though a number of examples could be explored under this banner, perhaps of particular salience (given the frequency of its invocation) is a variant of the "color blind" approach to race. An adherent to this colorblind view might hold that acting indifferent to race (being blind to "color", as it were) is a sufficiently ameliorative approach to racialized forms of power. Under this view, students should not be taught that they have a racial identity (Anti-RIF) as doing so is perceived by adherents as reifying the oppressive structures of racialized power. An adherent of this view might claim: "If students are no longer taught that there is any truth to their (or others) having a racial identity, race will soon lose any salience in our world." As such, the adherents' view need not lead students to commit to any response to race/racism (Anti-ARE); the absence of attention to race (in education and beyond) is understood as sufficient.[13]

Pro-ARE/Pro-RIF

Third, consider the potential coherence between support for antiracist education (Pro-ARE) and support for racial identity formation (Pro-RIF) in educational contexts. Though coherence is possible, the potential for tension within this view is worthy of attention.

On one hand, support for antiracist education (Pro-ARE) could entail a (at least) weak commitment to racial identities being held by persons, implying some degree of support for racial identity formation (Pro-RIF). That is, one might think that without such commitment (i.e., to persons holding racial identities), it may become rather challenging (though certainly not impossible) to unpack what antiracist education aims to address. Effectively, one would need to educate for antiracist ends within a context in which racialized patterns of power operate without persons endorsing the view that they or others have racialized identities.[14]

On the other hand, and more directly impactful for educators, is an interpretation of this view (i.e., the Pro-ARE and Pro-RIF view) that an antiracist education might necessarily result in a racial identity, formed either formally or informally via some educational activity (Thompson 2018). On this view, one might be reluctantly Pro-RIF, anticipating that engaging antiracist content is likely to lead a given student to accepting and endorsing a racial identity within that larger struggle against racism's effects. A racial eliminativist educator, say, might therefore be resigned to support racial identity formation (Pro-RIF), with the understanding that the potential intrapersonal harm of coming to hold a racial identity is a necessary or largely unavoidable component of realizing the greater goods of antiracist education.[15]

Pro-ARE/Anti-RIF

Finally, consider the potential coherence between support for antiracist education (Pro-ARE) and opposition to racial identity formation (Anti-RIF) in educational contexts. The potential for tension within this view is significant.

One way in which this view could be coherent might be found in adherents asserting that a full commitment to antiracist education (Pro-ARE) requires that no racial identity formation take place. A person nearly identical to the earlier exampled racial eliminativist educator could hold this view and, concluding that racial identity formation is itself an instance of the unjust exercise of power contingent upon race, resist the resigned acceptance of racial identity formation (i.e., be Anti-RIF). This person might hold that students could study and commit to antiracism with only a general or relatively impersonal sense of racial awareness (rather than an internalized endorsement of their having racialized identities). This position requires that the antiracist educator be careful to avoid even unintentionally visiting racial identification (here understood as a form of racism) upon their students.

Another way in which this view (i.e., Pro-ARE and Anti-RIF) could be coherent might be found in the earlier description of a systemic understanding of racism (i.e., in which racialized patterns of power can operate without persons endorsing the view that they or others have racialized identities). Again, this perspective might conclude that racial identity formation is a form of racism and that resisting it is a necessary but insufficient response to the injustice it represents (unlike the "colorblind" approach which views such resistance as sufficient). Even if successful in that goal (i.e., ending racial identity formation), adherents might expect that racism will continue to operate in the absence of any personal identification with race. As such, antiracist education continues to be desirable, under even those circumstances. Opposition to racial identity formation (Anti-RIF) does not make the antiracist educational project (Pro-ARE) obsolete.

Conclusion

This chapter has provided an overview of some common perspectives on race as an educational subject. It first explored foundational positions on the nature of race, providing a context for educationally sensitive views. Following this, the chapter focused attention on two specific approaches to engaging race as a subject of instruction: racial identity formation and antiracist education. Following sections exploring each of these approaches to race in curricula, the chapter offered examples and analyses of ways in which the commitments undergirding views on these approaches might be integrated into internally coherent perspectives on race as a subject of instruction.

Of course, given general and pervasive views on race, the popular senses of discomfort and/or uncertainty regarding race as a subject of instruction will likely persist unless relatively fundamental social transformations occur. Still, this chapter has offered some examples and clarifications regarding the ways in which consistent views on the subject can incorporate a wide range of commitments and values. Simultaneously, the chapter has provided a context within which additional analyses might be undertaken. These might involve further permutations of underlying conceptual or normative commitments and/or address other approaches to race as a subject of instruction. Surely, though the constituent matters might continue to be regarded as contentious, thoughtful analyses of race as an educational subject may, even if only incrementally, increase clarity and contribute to more productive deliberations ahead.

(Related Chapters: 2, 21, 22, 27, 33, 35.)

Notes

1 An especially thoughtful and nuanced study is undertaken in Blum (2012).
2 As discussed in Section 4, this interpretation may or may not also imply answers to questions of racial identity formation.
3 Though unintentional-yet-predictable lessons may not seem attached to educational goals, per se, I assert (but do not here argue) that they represent systemic goals even if unrecognized as such by those who enact them.
4 This position is often implied but rarely explicitly stated in educational literature.
5 Although non-racist education is a conceptual possibility, the existence of fully non-racist education may be a matter of some debate.
6 On some intersectional accounts of anti-racism, this resistance work extends beyond only race, as engagement with other identity categories is believed to be necessary for advancing the race-related aims.
7 Many approaches to teaching obligations regarding race could be classified as racist (and indefensible), such as teaching young children to disdain members of specific racial groups understood as subordinate to their own.
8 For example, afro-pessimist accounts of race and racism can support this view. Arguably, Ta-Nehisi Coates (2015) provides an afro-pessimist's view on antiracist parenting/education.
9 Much of this attention is owed to political disputations regarding the appropriateness of critical race theory (CRT) as public educational curricula.
10 I owe Sin Guanci and Jamie Herman thanks for their clear thinking and helpful improvements on an earlier analysis of these points.
11 To be clear, the chapter here considers only the coherence between these views. It does not evaluate how these views cohere with other facts or values (or the likelihood that an inadequate degree of such external coherence might be devastating for these views).
12 Of course, there are many permutations of the views engaged here. One need only look at earlier sections of the chapter to conclude that the Pro-RIF view might be supported by metaphysical claims instead of the social observations invoked in this example. Still, the example offered here is sufficiently representative of Pro-RIF views to establish their possible (but not necessary) coherence with other views. More detailed analyses of the permutations would be of interest but are beyond the chapter's scope.
13 Though there is normative content here, the view does not qualify as Pro-ARE as the project does not seek to *educate* students about race/racism. Instead, it sidesteps the educational process of endorsing students awareness of and subscription to engaging matters of race/racism, replacing this by seeking antiracist ends through non-educative methods.
14 Again, this is not impossible. An exclusively systemic view of racism could be endorsed such that individual identification with a racial identity is rather immaterial. This perspective is considered below.
15 See Haslanger (2019) for a distinct but related nuanced view.

References

Appiah, K. A. & Gutmann, A. (1996) *Color Conscious: The Political Morality of Race*. New Haven, CT: Princeton University Press.
Appiah, K. A. (2006) "How to Decide If Races Exist," *Proceedings of the Aristotelian Society* 106: 365–382.
Blum, L. (2012) *High Schools, Race, and America's Future: What Students Can Teach Us About Morality, Diversity, and Community*. Cambridge, MA: Harvard Education Press.
Blum, L. (2017) "Race and K-12 Education," in N. Zack (ed.) *Oxford Handbook of Philosophy and Race*. Oxford, UK: Oxford University Press, 436–448.
Bonilla-Silva, E. (2017) *Racism without Racists: Color-Blind Racism and the Persistence of Racial Inequality in the United States*. Oxford, UK: Rowman & Littlefield.
Coates, T. (2015) *Between the World and Me*. New York: One World Press.
Cross, W. E., Jr. (1991) *Shades of Black: Diversity in African-American Identity*. Philadelphia, PA: Temple University Press.
Darby, D. & Rury, J. (2018) *The Color of Mind: Why the Origins of the Achievement Gap Matter for Justice*. Chicago: University of Chicago Press.
Delpit, L. (1988) "The Silenced Dialogue: Power and Pedagogy in Educating Other People's Children," *Harvard Educational Review* 58(3): 280–298.
Dotson, K. (2018) "Accumulating Epistemic Harms," *Philosophical Topics* 46(1): 129–154.
Douthat, R. (2021) "The Excesses of Antiracist Education," *The New York Times* July 6. https://www.nytimes.com/2021/07/03/opinion/antiracist-education-history.html
Eddo-Lodge, R. (2017) *Why I'm No Longer Talking to White People about Race*. London: Bloomsbury Press.

Erickson, J. D. & Thompson, W. C. (2019) "Preschool as a Wellspring for Democracy: Endorsing Traits of Reasonableness in Early Childhood Education," *Democracy and Education* 2 (1): 1–22.

Erickson, J. D. & Thompson, W. C. (2021) "Engaging Particularly Vulnerable Students in Civic Education: An Argument for Avoiding unchecked Apprehension of Moral Indoctrination," *Journal of Curriculum Studies*, DOI: 10.1080/00220272.2021.1989049.

Fricker, M. (2007) *Epistemic Injustice: Power and the Ethics of Knowing*. Oxford: Oxford University Press.

Givens, J. (2019) "'There Would Be No Lynching If It Did Not Start in the Schoolroom': Carter G. Woodson and the Occasion of Negro History Week, 1926–1950," *American Educational Research Journal* 56(4): 1457–1494.

Gooding-Williams, R. (2001) "Race, Multiculturalism, and Democracy," in B. Boxill (ed.) *Race and Racism*. Oxford, UK: Oxford University Press, 422–447.

Gooding-Williams, R. (2006) *Look, A Negro!: Philosophical Essays on Race, Culture, and Politics*, New York City, NY: Routledge.

Hand, M. (2008) "What Should We Teach as Controversial? A Defence of the Epistemic Criterion," *Educational Theory* 58(2): 213–228.

Haslanger, S. (2000) "Gender and Race: (What) Are They? (What) Do We Want Them to Be?," *Noûs* 34: 31–55.

Haslanger, S. (2005) "You Mixed? Racial Identity Without Biology," in S. Haslanger & C. Witt (eds.) *Adoption Matters: Philosophical and Feminist Essays*, Ithaca, NY: Cornell University Press, 265–289.

Haslanger, S. (2019) "Tracing the Sociopolitical Reality of Race" in J. Glasgow, S. Haslanger, C. Jeffers, & Q. Spencer (eds.) *What is Race? Four Philosophical Views*. New York: Oxford University Press, 4–37.

Hill, J. (2017) "Is It Moral to Hold a Racial Identity? A Cosmopolitan Response," in N. Zack (ed.) *Oxford Handbook of Philosophy and Race*, Oxford: Oxford University Press, 402–410.

Jeffers, C. (2019) "Cultural Constructionism" in J. Glasgow, S. Haslanger, C. Jeffers, & Q. Spencer (ed.) *What is Race? Four Philosophical Views*. New York: Oxford University Press, 38–72.

Kendi, I. X. (2019) *How to Be an Antiracist*. New York City, NY: Random House.

Kim, J. (2001) "Asian American Racial Identity Theory," in C. L. Wijeyesinghe & B. W. Jackson III (eds.) *New Perspectives on Racial Identity Development: A Theoretical and Practical Anthology*. New York: New York University Press, 138–160.

Mallon, R. (2007) "A Field Guide to Social Construction," *Philosophy Compass* 2(1): 93–108.

Mallon, R. (2017) "Racial Identity, Racial Ontology, and Racial Norms," in N. Zack (ed.) *Oxford Handbook of Philosophy and Race*. Oxford: Oxford University Press.

McCarthy, T. (2009) *Race, Empire, and the Idea of Human Development*. Cambridge: Cambridge University Press.

Merriweather, T. (2018) *The Opportunity Gap at the Classroom Level: Validation of the Classroom Multicultural Competence Measure* [unpublished doctoral dissertation]. New York: Fordham University.

Mills, C. (1998) *Blackness Visible: Essays on Philosophy and Race*. Ithaca, NY: Cornell University Press.

Omi, M. & Winant H. (2014) *Racial Formation in the United States 3rd Edition*. New York: Routledge.

Outlaw, L. (1996) *On Race and Philosophy*. New York: Routledge.

Outlaw, L. (2005) *Critical Social Theory in the Interests of Black Folks*. Oxford: Rowman & Littlefield.

Patterson, O. (1997) *The Ordeal of Integration: Progress and Resentment in America's "Racial" Crisis*. Washington, D.C.: Civitas/Counterpoint.

Reddick, L. (1934) "Racial Attitudes in American History Textbooks of the South," *Journal of Negro History* 19: 225–265.

Shelby, T. (2002) "Foundations of Black Solidarity: Collective Identity or Common Oppression," *Ethics* 112: 231–266.

Shelby, T. (2007) *We Who are Dark: The Philosophical Foundations of Black Solidarity*. Cambridge, MA: Harvard University Press.

Skiba, R. J., Arredondo, M. I., Gray, C., & Rausch, M. K. (2016) "What Do We Know About Discipline Disparities? New and Emerging Research," in R. Skiba, K. Mediratta, & M. K. Rausch (eds.) *Inequality in School Discipline: Research and Practice to Reduce Disparities*. New York: Palgrave Macmillan, 21–38.

Spencer Q. (2015) "Philosophy of Race meets Population Genetics," *Studies in History and Philosophy of Biological and Biomedical Sciences* 52: 46–55.

Spencer, Q. (2019) "How to Be a Biological Racial Realist," in J. Glasgow, S. Haslanger, C. Jeffers, & Q. Spencer (eds.) *What is Race? Four Philosophical Views*. New York: Oxford University Press, 73–110.

Thompson, W. C. (2018) "Reconstructing a 'Dilemma' of Racial Identity Education," *Ethics and Education* 13(1): 55–72.

Tillson, J. (2020) "Knowledge, Moment, and Acceptability: How to Decide Public Educational Aims and Curricula," *Philosophy of Education* 76(3): 42–55.

West, C. (1994) *Race Matters*. New York: Vintage Books.

32

DISCIPLINE AND PUNISHMENT IN SCHOOLS

Bryan R. Warnick

At least since Saint Augustine recalled his prayer to "not be beaten at school," schools have often been remembered as places of strict discipline and harsh punishment (Augustine of Hippo 2002). Teachers have had the power to use force to impose school norms. Sometimes, that force has been manifest in corporal punishment, paddling, and whipping. At other times, the use of force has been employed to shame and humiliate students. More recently, the trend has been toward tactics of suspension and expulsion, meant to remove students from school altogether. While discussion of this or that form of punishment has been present throughout history, it is not as common to consider the more fundamental conceptual and ethical issues involved with school punishment: What does it mean to "punish," anyway, and how does it differ from "discipline"? Is punishment in schools ever justified? What would a view of punishment look like that coheres with educational aims and democratic school communities? This chapter will address these fundamental questions.

The Nature of Punishment

In philosophy, punishment has been defined as the imposition of a discomfort or other burden on an individual, by a social authority, because that individual has broken a community rule or norm (McPherson 1967). This is a helpful start in understanding the nature of punishment. Under this definition, students do not technically "punish" other students. They may inflict harm in direct response to violations of community norms, but they lack the authority to do so on behalf of a community. What this definition of punishment lacks, however, is the ability to help us to distinguish punishment from other sorts of social sanctions, like penalties. There is an important difference between the penalties assigned to manage complex social situations, like parking tickets, and the punitive burdens given in the face of moral wrongdoing. We usually do not morally condemn a person whose parking meter expires, but we do morally condemn perpetrators of serious crimes like assault, rape, theft, cheating, and so forth. A key feature of punishment, then, is that it *expresses moral disapproval of certain actions*, unlike penalties that manage social problems and conventions without moral judgment. This has been called the "expressive function" of punishment (Feinberg 1965). Punishment is meant to communicate something, perhaps a condemnation or perhaps an emotion such disgust, fear, or anger. This punitive expression is aimed at someone, perhaps the perpetrator or maybe the community, or both. There is much debate about the exact character of the expressive nature of punishment (Wringe 2016). For our purposes, it is enough to know that the expressive

DOI: 10.4324/9781003172246-37

function brings punishment squarely into the realm education. Punishment is meant to convey – or teach we might say – the moral norms of the community.

The difference between a "penalty" and a "punishment" in education relates to a distinction that can be made between "discipline" and "punishment." We can understand discipline as a type of educational penalty, which helps to organize a difficult social situation. A student leaving her chair in the middle of a lesson is not performing an immoral action, by itself, but it may violate the particular conventions meant to regulate the social situation. It might deserve a penalty, therefore, rather than a punishment. Other actions – school bullying, for example, which involves issues of basic respect and cruelty – are moral issues, and this would justify marshalling the expressive function. The expressive punishment conveys the community's moral concern for what has happened. This distinction between discipline, which is given to enforce school conventions, and punishment, which is given to enforce moral norms, has important implications for educators. It matters in making the appropriate responses to different student actions (more serious responses for moral failures perhaps), as well as for the tone and tenor of the teacher's response.

Clearly, this distinction between discipline and punishment is not always clear. Sometimes, violations of institutional conventions have moral implications. The school has important work to do and, if violating conventional rules disrupts this work, then other students might be harmed in some way. Their learning might be impaired, and their educational rights violated. This brings conventional rules into the moral universe. Moreover, the violation of conventions can be "weaponized" to express contempt for teachers or other students – willful tardiness, perhaps. Given these complexities, Joan Goodman (2006) helpfully divides the concept of discipline into three categories: moral infractions (that call for punishment), conventional infractions (that call for penalties), and the "derivatively moral." The derivatively moral action is a violation of a conventional school rule but performed with the purpose of showing contempt or insolence for another student or a teacher. Such actions might call for punishment, but they also demand careful interpretation: a student's tardiness may seem like insolence, but it may also reflect a personal issue. In such cases, the proper response would be caring discussion and problem solving, not punishment.

We have seen that the "expressive function" must be part of the concept of punishment. One of the central philosophical questions in an ethics of punishment is why hard treatment would be essential to the expression, communication, or teaching of moral norms. Almost everyone would agree that it is important that a community express its important moral ideals and condemn those who violate them. But couldn't such correction be done solely through discussion and teaching rather than through the intentional infliction of hard treatment?

In response, some contemporary theorists of punishment argue that words alone are often not enough to convey the gravity of what has occurred. A verbal reprimand, a call for dialogue, and so forth, cannot by themselves express how strongly the community condemns certain actions. Think about how inappropriate it would feel to respond to rape, say, with merely a strongly-worded letter aimed that the assailant. The symbolism is wrong, and words alone seem impotent. Some sort of action on the part of the community is required to focus the offender's attention on the seriousness of what has occurred. The hard treatment gives the community a communicative strategy: it allows the community to condemn in a way that words alone cannot. Just as important, the hard treatment also allows the perpetrators a chance to show remorse by *accepting that punishment.* Anthony Duff writes:

> Sometimes, however, a (mere) apology is not enough. If I have done a serious wrong to another person, I cannot expect to settle or resolve the matter merely by apologizing to him: something more than that is due to him and from me. This is not because a serious wrong is likely to involve some material harm for which compensation must also be paid. Some such wrongs (serious betrayals of a friendship or a marriage, for instance) involve no such harm, while some harms (the harm involved in a rape or in a fraud committed by a

> friend, for instance) cannot be made good by material compensation. The point is rather that the victim cannot reasonably be expected to forgive me, to treat the matter as closed, merely on receipt of a verbal apology, however sincere, and that the wrongdoer cannot reasonably expect to close the matter thus. The wrong goes too deep for that. It goes too deep for the victim ... It also goes too deep for the wrongdoer, whether or not she realizes it. To think that she could just apologize, and then return to her normal life, would be to portray the wrong as a relatively trivial matter that did not seriously damage the victim or their relationship.
>
> *(Duff 2001: 95)*

The hard treatment of punishment, then, allows for certain sorts of conversations to take place. The community is able to express the depth of its concern about what happened and, by accepting a punishment, offenders are able to offer a statement of remorse, showing that they are truly sorry for what has happened, an acceptance that gives heightened meaning to verbal apologies.

For these conversations to take place, it is necessary that the punishment be "symbolically adequate" to what has occurred. As Christopher Bennett says, a symbolically adequate punishment asks offenders "to undertake the sort of reparative action that they would be motivated to undertake were they genuinely sorry for what they have done" (2010: 31). An example of this sort of symbolically adequate punishment would be to replace an item that was stolen or clean up an area that was vandalized. The idea with a symbolically adequate punishment is not to replace moral dialogue with hard treatment, but to *add to* the moral dialogue by including actions that deepen and enhance a language of condemnation, apology, and restoration.

At this point, we should also distinguish between a more general expression of community disapproval that comes with punishment from what we might call "secondary expressions" attached to specific types of punishment. While the general expressive function may work to initiate students into moral norms, the secondary expressions may send unintended messages. These secondary messages may have undesirable consequences, as we will see in subsequent sections, or even work against the general expression. An ethic of school punishment needs to focus on making punishments symbolically adequate and ensuring that the secondary expressions of punishment are in line with educational ideals and the purposes of schools.

Is Punishment Justified in Schools?

At this point, some will question whether discipline and punishment are ever justified in schools. To be sure, there are powerful arguments against the very existence of school punishment. The first argument is simply that it is always wrong to intentionally impose a pain, hardship, or burden on another human being. The intention to harm is a vestige of violence that we should seek to eradicate from human communities rather than foster. This intention is particularly upsetting when it comes to vulnerable populations like children, who do not always understand the implications of their actions and do not possess full moral accountability. If punishment is justified, it is only justified in the case of full moral responsibility, which children in schools do not possess.

A second argument against discipline and punishment in education is that such things are, in fact, anti-educational. There is research in psychology, starting with behaviorists like B. F. Skinner (1972), suggesting that punishment does not actually work to change behaviors over the long run. More recently, researchers such as Elizabeth Gershoff have concluded that corporeal punishment decreases the internalization of moral principles (Gershoff 2002). More generally, critics might argue that education should be about discussion, dialogue, and cooperative action. It is about arriving at conclusions, not through brute force, but by the power of reasons. Punishment is the opposite of this sort of reasoning. Discipline and punishment send all the wrong messages about how human beings should live together.

A third argument has to do, not so much with punishment itself, but with what punishment allows teachers and schools to neglect. It is commonly noted that good teachers often have fewer disciplinary problems in their classrooms (Noguera 2003). One reason students misbehave is that classrooms are disordered and teaching is unimaginative and ineffective. The curriculum may be boring, irrelevant to the lives of students, and the teacher–student relationship may be distant and uncaring (Neill & Fromm 1960). In these circumstances, some students will either rebel or disconnect – nothing could be more natural or predictable. The problem with strict discipline and punishment is that is allows teachers, schools, and communities to skate by with poor teaching, poor leadership, and poorly resourced schools.

These criticisms all capture something important that an ethic of punishment must take seriously. Punishment is sometimes used to enforce order through force, and this sometimes stands in the way of improving teaching and educational institutions. And punishment can certainly be meted out in ways that run counter to reason and contrary to educational goals – particularly as the form of punishment ignores relevant "secondary expressions" pointing in this direction. In response to these criticisms, though, the defender of punishment also has several counterarguments.

In response to the criticism that schools can use punishment as a cover for poor teaching and ill-structured schools, the defender of punishment needs to concede a great deal of ground. There is much a skilled teacher can do to avoid the need for penalties and punishment, and there is much society can do to construct schools that children want to be a part of and participate in. A good teacher can do much to promote this discipline through pedagogy and curriculum, engaging students' interests. Schools can be well-resourced, which sends a message that students are important and education is valued. But the power of a teacher and school is not completely determinative. Students will spend most of their time outside of classrooms. Recesses, lunch times, and moments in between classes, will be left to students (to a certain degree) without the guidance of thoughtful teachers. In addition, some students will learn attitudes of cruelty and discrimination at home. Such attitudes may make expressive punishments necessary, even in the best schools. We also need to be realistic about the imperfections of schools from the teacher standpoint. A teacher may be skilled, but face unreasonably large classrooms, unsympathetic parents, aging facilities, and boring required textbooks. Under these conditions, schools are unlikely to be perfect pedagogical machines, capturing student interest and attention in every moment. Until resources are what they should be, discipline and punishment might be an imperfect alternative to difficult school situations.

In response to the criticism that punishment does not work and is anti-educational, the defender of punishment will want to talk about the expressive role of punishment and the types of conversations it makes possible, as described in the previous section. It is fair to say that much of the research on "punishment" comes from behavioral psychologists and often the research derives from animal studies or laboratory environments. Outside of such contexts, it is easy for many of us to think of times when threats of penalties or punishment changed our behavior (parking tickets are prominent in my mind, for example, when I decide where I park on my campus). Such things can clearly work to manage behavior, which is often simply what schools need in the case of penalties. Can punishment change attitudes or long-term behaviors? We need to question the psychological research saying it cannot. Corporal punishment, or giving electric shocks to rats, is very different from a symbolically-adequate punishment, given as part of a discursive moral context. If punishment can indeed promote certain sorts of moral conversations, if it can be invested with meaning as both a message from the community and as a pathway toward reintegration (as Duff argues), then it seems to have a power to change people that goes beyond behavioral experiments. And, if punishment allows for this sort of extra-linguistic communication, then it seems firmly planted within a realm of reasoned discourse that we should value in education.

Finally, is punishment itself a relic of barbarism? Is the intentional infliction of hardship on another human being something we should try to eradicate? This seems to depend on the sort of punishment that is being given. Certainly, some forms of punishment – whipping, beating, torturing, and so froth – seem to speak to something dark in the human psyche, something that seems to delight in the exercise of power and the infliction of pain. This is something we should try to move away from, and society's long move away from corporal punishment recognizes this. At the same time, requiring people to clean up a mess they made, to replace something that they stole or intentionally broke, or paying recompense for a harm they cause – all symbolically adequate punishments – do not seem barbarous at all. Rather, they seem required on the grounds of justice. This holds even in the case of children, who are being initiated into the moral universe.

The case against school punishment is strong, then, but it seems that the arguments are not fully decisive. The arguments against punishment in schools should work to give ethical refinement to punishment practices rather than ruling them out. They suggest that punishment (a) should only be implemented in schools that are also self-critical about their own pedagogical practices, (b) should be symbolically adequate to what has been done, and (c) should be implemented in conjunction with discursive practices of explanation, reason-giving, and listening.

Problematic Areas of Punishment

While punishment as a whole may be justified under these parameters, there are specific discipline and punishment practices within schools that need to be subject to serious scrutiny. This is because they violate certain principles of fair or equitable conduct, or because their "secondary expressions" are particularly problematic, or both. Two examples of problematic practices are corporal punishments and exclusionary punishments (i.e., expulsions and suspensions). In addition, educators need to be aware of how discipline and punishment practices are implemented differently across lines of race, gender, and special needs.

Corporal punishment is still legal in the public schools of nineteen US states (and legal, though rare, in private schools in 48 states). In those states that allow corporal punishment, 14% of public schools actually engage in the practice (Gershoff & Font 2016). Corporal punishment can sometimes cause non-trivial injuries to children, such as bruises and cuts, and its implementation can cause distress for students, distracting from the learning environment (Human Rights Watch/ACLU 2009). These things alone should be enough to cause us to be troubled by corporal punishments. Beyond that, though, the secondary expressions of corporal punishment seem to send messages of the appropriateness of violence as a means of human interaction. It validates the imposition of force through physical strength, expressing that this is how one deals with other human beings. There is research to suggest that this anti-social message is conveyed quite effectively to children: youth whose parents use corporal punishment are more likely to be violent themselves, that is, more likely to get into fights and exhibit tendencies toward bullying (Ohene et al. 2006). Corporal punishment harms students but can also disfigure teachers. Some teachers have reported getting caught up in the power of corporal punishment, relishing the suffering they cause, and realizing that this is a betrayal of their profession (see examples in Scribner & Warnick 2021).

Much more commonly practiced in American schools is the use of suspension and expulsion. Widespread use of this practice began in the 1990s in the wake of zero-tolerance laws passed after high-profile school shootings. Originally intended to cover bringing weapons to school, the scope of application expanded to include subjective offenses like "disrespect" or "disorderly conduct" (Insley 2001). The rates of expulsion have at least doubled since the 1970s (Skiba et al. 2002). There is mounting evidence of the harm the exclusionary punishments can cause across a range of measures (Council on School Health 2013). Suspension and expulsion violate many of the ethical guidelines on punishment discussed above. For example, is it hard to engage students in moral discourse when they are absent from the school and it is difficult to see how it is "symbolically adequate" to most offenses. Moreover, the secondary expressions of exclusionary punishment drive a wedge between student identities and the school community. Such punishments send the message that students are not wanted or welcome in the school.

The negative secondary expressions of both corporal punishment and exclusionary punishment are magnified when they occur in contexts of inequality. Punishment practices are applied unequally across categories of race, gender, and special education status. Boys are generally punished more frequently, and more harshly, than girls, blacks more than whites, and students in special education more than non-special education students (United States Government Accountability Office 2018). In the year 2013-14, for example, 13.7% of Black students were suspended, compared to only 3.4% of White students, 4.5% of Hispanic students, 1.1% of Asian students, 4.5% of Pacific Islander students, and 6.7% of all Native American students. The number of Black and Native American students that were expelled from school (0.4%) was nearly double the percentage of all other groups (0.2%) (de Brey et al. 2019). Black girls are suspended six times as often as white girls (Crenshaw et al. 2015). This gap has been called "the punishment gap," a companion in inequality to the "achievement gap" (Gregory et al. 2010).

Studies of the discipline gap reveal several important nuances. First, the punishment gap holds steady even when student class background is accounted for, suggesting that racial stereotypes are operative rather than being simply an issue of, say, poverty (Skiba et al. 2016). Second, it seems that students from different races are punished differently, even when their documented misbehavior is comparable, suggesting that the discipline gap is not explained by positing differences in student behavior across racial groups (Skiba et al. 2016). Third, there are an array of documented tendencies in teachers to interpret and surveil students differently according to race. For example, teachers tend to see behavior as more extreme when a student record of misbehavior is attached to a stereotypical African-American name than the same behavior attached to a stereotypical white name, and they tend to recommend harsher punishments for those students (Okonofua & Eberhardt 2015). Teachers also see black students as being older and more responsible for their behavior than are white students of the same age (Goff et al. 2014). Such biases are clearly part of what explains the punishment gap. The ramifications of these troubling disparities have been widely discussed, with many suggesting that unequal disciplinary practices in school are a major driver of the academic achievement gap (Morris & Perry 2016) and a contributor to a "school to prison pipeline" leading eventually to, say, the mass incarceration of black men. An analysis of the secondary expression of exclusionary punishment – particularly, its message of a lack of place and belonging – would further support these links.

Punishment and Educational Aims

When we consider an ethics of school punishment, we may think in terms of applying important ethical concepts of punishment from other domains of life. Outside of schools, we find some important standards governing the conduct of punishment in liberal-democratic societies. These standards are related to general justifications for punishment. The traditional justifications for punishment conceptualize punishment as retributive (giving people what they deserve for past offenses) or as a deterrence (trying to discourage future misbehavior). If punishment is justified because of deterrence, the key questions to ask are whether a particular penalty could indeed function as a deterrent and, if so, under what circumstances – questions that come up in, say, the debate about the death penalty. We will also want to know what unintended consequences there might be in the future if we implement particular punishments. These questions are inherently future looking, judging punishments through the future consequences that they produce. If punishment is instead justified on retributive grounds, the ethics of punishment will focus on other issues. We will want to make sure that, if punishment is about giving people what they deserve, then only the guilty are to be punished. Accordingly, there will be an emphasis on "due-process," ensuring that those who are accused of misbehavior are indeed at fault. Under this justification, there will also be an effort to make the punishment proportional to or "fitting" to the crime, paying homage to the ancient principle of *lex talionis*. An ethic of retributive punishment will look backwards, ensuring that those who are guilty of past behavior are punished proportionally to what has occurred.

These general principles are still useful in educational contexts. If discipline and punishment are meant to deter, then it is worth considering whether deterrence is actually produced and whether any unintended consequences are forthcoming. Due process must also be an important part of school punishment, when and if punishment is administered. Students must be able to defend themselves and speak to what has happened from their perspectives. Witnesses can be questioned and evidence examined, at least to the extent that school resources allow. Another parallel is that punishment of students should not be out of proportion to what has occurred. This principle of proportionality is widely violated in schools today – indeed, one of the key problems is that subjective accusations of "disrespect" have become punishable by suspension and expulsion. Violation of the principle that only the guilty should be punished also often occurs in schools. Educators sometimes employ group punishments, giving a hardship to an entire class after an incident rather than to the guilty few. If punishment is about giving students "what they deserve," group punishments that lump guilty along with innocent students violate the foundational justification for punishment in schools.

Still, we should be cautious in simply bringing general ethical principles governing punishment into school environments. The very idea of retribution rests on a shaky foundation in educational settings. The simple fact is that the population of schools is underage, either children or adolescents. The idea of getting "what you deserve" makes assumptions about moral responsibility that do not hold when it comes to this population – after all, moral responsibility demands emotional and mental competency. Children and adolescents lack the experience with the world – and of the cause-and-effect relationships – that allow someone to make responsible moral decisions. They also lack the appropriate brain development, which means they are more likely to act out of impulse, misinterpret social cues, and take greater risks. We should not underestimate the ability of students to think and act with wisdom, to be sure, but neither should they be treated as full moral agents, deserving of punishment fully proportional to misbehavior. Another fact about schools is that students and schools co-construct behavior. Students are put into environments explicitly constructed by school personnel and these environments create and make possible certain student behaviors. Therefore, schools are always at least partly complicit in what occurs in those environments. In short, moral responsibility, already a difficult concept, is an even more complex notion in schools.

In addition, schools have an explicit educational mission. They are charged with teaching academic subjects, and also developing democratic citizens, responsible moral agents, and thoughtful workers possessing both hard and soft vocational skills. Taken together, these goals all point to a need for students to develop an ability to communicate, to listen to the concerns of others, to talk through differences, to take responsibility for their behavior, to overcome disagreements and disappointments, to cooperate, to work toward mutually acceptable solutions, to apologize when appropriate, and to understand how their actions affect others. All of these skills are important parts of democratic citizenship, responsible moral agency, and even the "soft skills" valued by employers.

One problem with traditional paradigms of punishment is how little moral and civic reflection they ask of students. Students are beaten with paddles, humiliated with dunce caps, or expelled from schools, but they are not often asked to engage with others to fix the problems or restore relationships. On the flip side, traditional punishment practices demand little reflection on the part of schools or communities, something we have already seen to be important. They do not ask these parties to consider how school policies and practices might have contributed to a problematic situation. In any sort of reflective environment, the rules of the community and the behavior of those in authority should also be subject to scrutiny, not simply the behavior of students.

Exclusionary punishments like expulsion and suspension can be particularly weak on this front. If students are absent, obviously very little educational engagement is possible and the punishment will lack the discursive context that is so essential to the type of punishments that are justified in schools.

An alternative way of looking at punishment, a view better aligned with the educational mission of schools than traditional paradigms of punishment, is a paradigm called restorative justice. While restorative justice has older roots in indigenous communities, this view of crime and community reintegration was first used in criminal justice systems, with particular effectiveness in juvenile justice (Bergseth & Bouffard 2007). Implementation of restorative justice thinking in juvenile justice has seen noteworthy benefits, including reducing recidivism rates (Rodriguez 2007).

Restorative justice begins with a statement about the nature of crime – crime is what harms relationships. Crime is not (only) an abstract offense against the state; instead, it is a rupture of community ties. The goal of restorative justice is to restore the ties of relationship that have been broken when a crime has occurred, and it seeks to reintegrate offenders into the community. Restorative justice involves an exchange of experiences – the person who was harmed describes how they have been affected by a crime, how they have been hurt, and what it has cost them. They are also able to describe what, if anything, would help them to forgive and to co-exist with the perpetrator. Hearing the real effect on the victim has a number of consequences. For one thing, apologies can take on a new meaning in this context. After all, an apology that is given without full understanding of the harms that have been caused is shallow and meaningless to the victim. The restorative exchange allows the offender to take responsibility for what has occurred (contrast this with a traditional judicial proceeding, where the incentive is to deny and minimize what happened). The exchange can also create a better idea of what sort of action might be "symbolically adequate" to help heal the harm that has been caused. While the emphasis is on the victim, the perpetrators can also describe their own context, what they were thinking and what drove them to do what they did. Sometimes, this builds mutual understanding and may lead to a co-constructed solution moving forward. This can give a sense of control back to victims, and also to the offender, who now can do what needs to be done to reintegrate.

Schools should not be part of a criminal justice approach to punishment. Still, the principles of restorative justice lend themselves quite well to school discipline. In schools, restorative justice often takes the form of a restorative "circle," where students and teachers gather to talk about disagreements, problems, and challenges they are facing. Participants aim for mutual understanding, attempting to restore community where it has broken down. Where traditional punishment asks little of students, restorative justice asks students to do real moral work.

Notice how this restorative activity is deeply educational and how it connects with the aims of schooling. This work of listening, understanding, taking responsibility, problem solving, and co-operation, is precisely what we want students to learn in schools. It will help them as future citizens as they engage in cooperative and problem-solving dialogue in public life, and it will help them as workers, learning to work together and to repair relationships when things go amiss. Restorative justice asks students to take responsibility for their actions and for reestablishing relationships and therefore is quite suited to the development of moral autonomy. The secondary expressions of restorative justice point toward social inclusion and prosocial values, like cooperation and co-operative problem solving. This is in stark contrast to the secondary expression of corporal and exclusionary punishments. For these reasons, restorative justice seems to be uniquely educational, and, therefore, uniquely appropriate for school settings.

Recall that one criticism of punishment in schools is that punishment allows for the continuation of suboptimal educational conditions – bad teaching and poorly run schools. By giving students a voice in restorative dialogue, the restorative practices also become educational for the school. In a true restorative experience, blame and responsibility are not entirely assigned before the dialogue takes place. Through the dialogue, other school actors might discover that they share moral responsibility, or they might uncover mitigating factors within a particular classroom situation. Educators learn how they might have been partially complicit in a problematic situation and how they might improve in their pedagogical strategies.

What is the relationship between restorative justice and traditional punishment paradigms? In particular, how does it relate to the hard treatment and expressive function? For one thing, being asked to participate in restorative circles and to take responsibility for one's actions is itself an uncomfortable experience, an experience that might feel like hard treatment. This alone might be enough to express the moral sentiments of the community. Beyond that, though, it is possible that the victims in the school community might ask for an apology, compensation, or some sort of symbolic reparation. The desired compensatory action (cleaning up after an act of vandalism) or symbolic reparation (after-school detention, community service, and so forth) might sometimes look very much like a traditional punishment. Hard treatment still has a role to play here, in giving voice to the community, and in giving offenders a vehicle to show remorse. Restorative justice invigorates the hard treatment with greater meaning. In effect, it supplies the discursive context so essential in making punishment both ethical and educational.

There are critics of restorative justice who object on both philosophical and empirical grounds. Philosophically, they argue that restorative justice can lead to inconsistency in how people are treated. Some restorative conferences might result in hard symbolic compensations, while others might let offenders off easily. This is a feature, though, as much as it is a bug – individual relationships are all different, and will require different things for their restoration, and this is simply a fact of life. Besides, there is a process consistency to restorative justice: although the outcomes are not consistent (nor should they be), the process of getting to the outcome is consistent (Brooks 2016). Others criticize restorative justice in schools on empirical grounds: restorative justice programs simply do not work, they say, but instead breed chaos and disorder in schools (Eden 2019). To be sure, the best empirical studies to date on restorative justice programs are complex, with a mixed bag of results. Many of the results are positive, but some are also negative (Acosta et al. 2019; Augustine et al. 2018). There is reason to be careful about sweeping statements either for or against an abstract idea like "restorative justice." Restorative justice can be practiced in many different ways in many different contexts – very few of which have received any sort of research attention at all. Still, an overall view of the empirical data leaves room for optimism, I believe, that such an approach is both realistic and offers valuable outcomes.

Conclusion

Thinking deeply about punishment in education is valuable partly because it reveals so many assumptions about schools – assumptions about the nature of students, the nature of teaching, the purpose of education, and the role of power and authority in the educational enterprise. Students are not full moral actors, but rather moral agents in development. This does not mean that students avoid consequences of their actions; indeed, schools need to ask *more* from students than they currently do with traditional punishments. Students need to reflect, converse, explain, accept responsibility, and work to solve problems. They are not passive recipients for expressive messages; rather, they are in dialogue with those messages. At the same time, more also needs to be asked of schools. Educators need to examine both their pedagogical and disciplinary practices to ensure that everything points toward democratic educational ideals. Educators are given the authority to employ the expressive function of punishment, making sure the punishment is symbolically adequate, using punishment to open up conversations and to restore relationships, and working within ethical limits such as due process, proportionality, and the creation of appropriately discursive contexts. This authority assumes that teachers are not simply subject-matter specialists or pedagogues, but ushers, helping students find their seats within moral communities and initiating them into a realm of social cooperation and problem solving. Restorative justice helps move schools in this direction.

(Related Chapters: 3, 9, 14, 16, 22, 35.)

References

Acosta, J., Chinman, M., Ebener, P., Malone, P. S., Phillips, A., & Wilks, A. (2019) "Evaluation of a Whole-School Change Intervention: Findings from a Two-Year Cluster-Randomized Trial of the Restorative Practices Intervention," *Journal of Youth and Adolescence* 48(5): 876–890.

Augustine of Hippo (2002) *The Confessions of Saint Augustine*. Project Gutenberg. https://gutenberg.org/files/3296/3296-h/3296-h.htm

Augustine, C. H., Engberg, J., Grimm, G. E., Lee, E., Wang, E. L., Christianson, K., & Joseph, A. (2018) "Can Restorative Practices Improve School Climate and Curb Suspensions? An Evaluation of the Impact of Restorative Practices in A Mid-Sized Urban School District," RAND. https://www.rand.org/pubs/research_reports/RR2840.html

Bennett, C. (2008) *The Apology Ritual: A Philosophical Theory of Punishment*. Cambridge: Cambridge University Press.

Bergseth, K. J., & Bouffard, J. A. (2007) "The Long-Term Impact of Restorative Justice Programming for Juvenile Offenders," *Journal of Criminal Justice* 35(4): 433–451.

Brooks, T. (2016) *Punishment*. Abingdon, Oxon: Routledge.

Council on School Health (2013) "Out-of-School Suspension and Expulsion," *Pediatrics* 131(4): e1000–e1007.

Crenshaw, K., Nanda, J., & Ocen, P. (2015) *Black Girls Matter: Pushed Out, Overpoliced, and Underprotected*. New York: Center for Intersectionality and Policy Studies, Columbia University.

de Brey, C., Musu, L., McFarland, J., Wilkinson-Flicker, S., Diliberti, M., Zhang, A., Branstetter, C., & Wang, X. (2019) *Status and Trends in the Education of Racial and Ethnic Groups 2018* (NCES 2019-038). U.S. Department of Education. Washington, DC: National Center for Education Statistics. https://nces.ed.gov/pubs2019/2019038.pdf

Duff, A. (2001) *Punishment, Communication, and Community*. Oxford: Oxford University Press.

Eden, M. (2019, January 14) *Restorative Justice Isn't Working, But That's Not What the Media Is Reporting*. Fordham Institute. https://fordhaminstitute.org/national/commentary/restorative-justice-isnt-working-thats-not-what-media-reporting

Feinberg, J. (1965) "The Expressive Function of Punishment," *The Monist* 49(3): 397–423.

Gershoff, E. T. (2002) "Corporal Punishment by Parents and Associated Child Behaviors and Experiences: A Meta-Analytic and Theoretical Review," *Psychological Bulletin* 128(4): 539–579.

Gershoff, E. T., & Font, S. A. (2016) "Corporal Punishment in U.S. Public Schools: Prevalence, Disparities in Use, and Status in State and Federal Policy," *Social Policy Report* 30(1): 1–26.

Goff, P. A., Jackson, M. C., Di Leone, B. A., Culotta, C. M., & DiTomasso, N. A. (2014) "The Essence of Innocence: Consequences of Dehumanizing Black Children," *Journal of Personality and Social Psychology* 106(4): 526–545.

Goodman, J. (2006) "School Discipline in Moral Disarray," *Journal of Moral Education* 35(2): 213–230.

Gregory, A., Skiba, R. J., & Noguera, P. A. (2010) "The Achievement Gap and the Discipline Gap: Two Sides of the Same Coin?" *Educational Researcher* 39(1): 59–68.

Human Rights Watch/ACLU (2009) Impairing Education: Corporal Punishment for Students with Disabilities in US Public Schools. ACLU. https://www.aclu.org/report/impairing-education-corporal-punishment-students-disabilities-us-public-schools

Insley, A. C. (2001) "Suspending and Expelling Children from Educational Opportunity: Time to Reevaluate Zero Tolerance Policies," *American University Law Review* 50(4): 1039–1074.

McPherson, T. (1967) "Punishment: Definition and Justification," *Analysis* 28(1): 21–27.

Morris, E. W., & Perry, B. L. (2016) "The Punishment Gap: School Suspension and Racial Disparities in Achievement," *Social Problems* 63(1): 68–86.

Neill, A. S., & Fromm, E. (1960) *Summerhill: A Radical Approach to Child Rearing*. New York: Hart Publishing Company.

Noguera, P. (2003) "Schools, Prisons, and Social Implications of Punishment: Rethinking Disciplinary Practices," *Theory into Practice* 42(4): 341–350.

Ohene, S. A., Ireland, M., McNeely, C., & Borowsky, I. W. (2006) "Parental Expectations, Physical Punishment, and Violence Among Adolescents Who Score Positive on a Psychosocial Screening Test in Primary Care," *Pediatrics* 117(2): 441–447.

Okonofua, J. A., & Eberhardt, J. L. (2015) "Two Strikes: Race and the Disciplining of Young Students," *Psychological Science* 26(5): 617–624.

Rodriguez, N. (2007) "Restorative Justice at Work: Examining the Impact of Restorative Justice Resolutions on Juvenile Recidivism," *Crime & Delinquency* 53(3): 355–379.

Scribner, C. F., & Warnick, B. R. (2021) *Spare the Rod: Punishment and the Moral Community of Schools*. Chicago: University of Chicago Press.

Skiba, R. J., Arredondo, M. I., Gray, C., & Rausch, M. K. (2016) "What Do We Know About Discipline Disparities? New and Emerging Research," in R. Skiba, K. Mediratta, M. K. Rausch (eds.), *Inequality in School Discipline: Research and Practice to Reduce Disparities*. New York: Palgrave Macmillan, 21–38.

Skiba, R. J., Michael, R. S., Nardo, A. C., & Peterson, R. L. (2002) "The Color of Discipline: Sources of Racial and Gender Disproportionality in School Punishment," *Urban Review* 34(4): 317–342.

Skinner, B. F. (1972) *Beyond Freedom and Dignity*. New York: Bantam/Vintage Books.

United States Government Accountability Office. (2018) K-12 Education: Discipline Disparities for Black Students, Boys, and Students with Disabilities, Report to Congressional Requesters. United States Government Accountability Office. https://www.gao.gov/products/gao-18–258

Wringe, B. (2016) *An Expressive Theory of Punishment*. Houndmills, Basingstoke, Hampshire: Palgrave Macmillan.

33
ABILITY AND ABILITY GROUPING

Tammy Harel Ben Shahar

Introduction

The concept of ability is immensely important to educational theory and practice and permeates many of the fundamental philosophical discussions in the field. The definition of education (and learning), as well as the goals of education, almost always involve the development of certain abilities, and discussions of education policy and educational evaluation also build on the concept of ability and the ways in which ability can be developed. Ability is also an elementary concept in educational justice and plays a role in determining the allocation of resources and evaluation of education policy.

While ability is one of the key concepts of education, it also suffers from chronic ambiguity. For example, although people possess many kinds of learning-related abilities, the complexity of cognitive, behavioral, and social abilities that are instrumental in academic success are rarely appreciated. Discussions of student ability in the educational philosophy scholarship usually refer only to a narrow set of cognitive abilities.

Confusion regarding the concept of ability is caused also by the fact that "ability" is sometimes used interchangeably with other terms, including "intelligence," "IQ," "talent," "aptitude," "potential," "capabilities," "skills," "knowledge," "proficiency," and more. All of these terms have slightly different meanings in different contexts. Additionally, there are often discrepancies between the various meanings of "ability" we use when theorizing about education and the possibility of measuring (or affecting) them, creating discord between theoretical discourse and educational practice. A further source of confusion is that "student ability" is both a precondition for learning and the end product of education, and abilities acquired through education are themselves preconditions for developing still further abilities (Bailey & Bridges 1983; McGeer 2018; Ryle 1949).

When discussing ability, therefore, careful work is required to delineate the various meanings of "ability" and define the meaning of "ability" used in each specific context. This chapter offers a discussion of student ability through an examination of one, prevalent educational practice – ability grouping. In this chapter, I examine two ways to understand the term "ability" and question whether either of them is suitable as a criterion for student assignment, concluding that neither of them supports the robust forms of ability grouping common in contemporary education systems. The conceptual analysis of "ability" thereby contributes a novel perspective on the debate surrounding ability grouping.

The chapter proceeds as follows: first, I introduce the practice of ability grouping and rehearse the main arguments in the traditional debate surrounding it. I then move on to distinguish two

DOI: 10.4324/9781003172246-38

possible categories of ability: performative ability, and ability as a property of an agent. I argue that neither of these constitutes a suitable criterion for student assignment in most cases; they can support only limited cases of ability grouping.

The Debate Concerning Ability Grouping

Teaching students together inevitably raises the challenge of teaching children with diverse abilities, different levels of knowledge, areas of interest, propensities, needs, and motivation. Ignoring these differences and teaching all of them the same content, using the same pedagogies will, presumably, be ineffective. This is the axiom that underlies practices of differentiating between students according to their abilities; differential treatment is also indispensable for obtaining just educational outcomes (Anderson 2007; Brighouse 2011; Jencks 1988; Schouten 2012).

Differential treatment of children with different abilities, however, takes on more controversial forms that have been subject to extensive ethical and legal debate, including programs for gifted children (Merry 2008; Meyer 2014; Sapon-Shevin 1994), segregated special education (Norwich 2014), vocational education (Giesinger 2017), selective schools (Mason 2016; Mazie 2009), and ability grouping (Bailey & Bridges 1983; Brighouse et al. 2018; Cantu 2019; Hart 1998). While the relevance of considering children's ability in the educational setting is undisputed, it is much less clear which practices are morally permissible (or required), and under what circumstances.

Ability grouping involves sorting students to different schools, classes, tracks, courses, or groups according to their perceived ability. Understood widely, it includes all cases of such separation, including special education, gifted and talented programs, tracking in comprehensive schools, and even grouping students temporarily for specific tasks. It is practiced, in one form or another, in all education systems.

Despite commonalities shared by different cases of ability grouping, the practices may differ in important ways, including the age at which sorting occurs, the criterion used for it, and the differences in curriculum between the tracks. These differences affect the desirability of the practice.

Underlying all cases of ability grouping is the assumption that since teaching is more effective in homogeneous groups, all students will benefit from it – those with low abilities as well as those with high abilities. It is also argued that ability grouping is necessary for ensuring development of educational excellence, because learning in mixed ability groups slows down the pace and prevents teaching high-level material, thus denying high achievers the experience of a challenging and stimulating education (Merry 2008). But the educational benefits of ability grouping are subject to heated empirical debate that questions whether ability grouping constitutes optimal and effective education policy, and whether it conforms with the dictates of educational justice.

Critics of ability grouping argue that empirical evidence does not support the belief that ability grouping improves average educational attainment (Gorard & Siddiqui 2018; Slavin 1990). Students with low ability perform worse when separated than they do in mixed-ability classes (Werblow et al. 2013), and tracking (especially when children are young) reinforces the effect of family background on educational outcomes (Krause & Schuller 2014). Some studies show benefits for high ability students, but these benefits are obtained at the expense of low ability students.

Several factors may offer causal explanations of these findings. Lower ability tracks are allocated inferior resources, are taught by less qualified teachers, and teach less academically challenging material. It is hardly surprising, then, that students attending them are less academically successful.

Being assigned to low-ability tracks can have negative effects even absent these disadvantageous circumstances, since the labeling of students as "low ability" affects the expectations teachers have of them, their expectations of themselves, their self-esteem, and their motivation. Students in lower tracks are also denied the beneficial peer effects available in mixed ability classrooms (Zimmer & Toma 2000) and the non-academic gains of studying in mixed ability settings, including development of social and inter-personal skills needed for participation in the civic and professional spheres (but see Merry 2013).

These findings are especially worrying because many effects of ability grouping are quite irreversible (Gamoran 1992). Rejection from selective schools and gifted and talented programs is usually final, and assignment to special education or even tracking within comprehensive schools can be difficult to undo as students assigned to the less-demanding tracks study different curricula. The "failure to return" (Cartledge 2005) means that the stakes involved in ability grouping are very high (Mason 2016), and it discredits a stated aim of ability grouping, namely, to improve abilities of children with low abilities or disabilities so they can integrate easily in comprehensive schools.

Another source of criticism regarding ability grouping is consistent evidence that separating students according to their ability results in racial, ethnic, and class segregation. Gifted programs, selective schools, and high-ability tracks typically serve students from privileged backgrounds (Mickelson & Everett 2008; Mazie 2009; Solorzano & Ornelas 2002), and minority students and students from low-income families are overrepresented in low ability tracks and special education (Cipriano-Walter 2015), especially in restrictive educational environments (Graves & Ye 2017).

The correlation between academic performance and social categories can be explained by biases in educational evaluation (Ford 1998; Garda 2005), by unequal educational resources and opportunities (Erwin & Worrell 2012), and also by general social inequality and poverty that result in less nurturing environments for children from marginalized groups. Based on charges of indirect racial and ethnic discrimination, various jurisdictions have struck down policies involving ability grouping (Har-Carmel & Harel Ben Shahar 2017; Oakes 1995) and IQ testing (Wade 1980).

These problems are compounded by doubts concerning existing methods of measuring ability. In addition to the racial and ethnic biases already mentioned, measuring ability is, arguably, generally unreliable, resulting in arbitrary assignment of students to the wrong tracks. Thus, one-time, high stakes tests may misrepresent students' abilities if they are having a bad day, and tests conducted in unfamiliar settings can make it difficult for some children to express their abilities. When performed on young children, high stakes tests are especially problematic because small variations in age and developmental pace may be significant (Lohman 2005; Mason 2016).

In light of these concerns, opponents argue that ability grouping is an ineffective and unfair education policy. They also argue that it disrupts community and contributes to social divisiveness and relations of domination, thereby undermining the democratic goals of education (Mazie 2009, Sapon-Shevin 1994).

Any conclusive argument for or against ability grouping must consider further factors in addition to all the claims referred to so far, such as the various goals of education and the tradeoffs between them. For example, the democratic goals of education may preclude the practice of ability grouping altogether, whereas promoting excellence may lead us (given sufficient evidence) to favor gifted programs, all things considered. The theory of educational justice we favor would also affect our position regarding ability grouping. For example, as long as all students, including those directed to lower tracks obtain an adequate education, sufficientarians would be inclined to allow ability grouping on account of its possible advantages for high achievers. Egalitarians, on the other hand, would likely take issue with ability grouping even if all students reached the sufficientarian threshold.

A Conception of Ability for Student Assignment

So far, I have rehearsed the main claims in the ongoing debate concerning ability grouping. In the remainder of the chapter, I discuss ability grouping, by examining the possible conceptions of ability that might underlie the practice.

I distinguish between two main ways to understand the term "ability." The first involves the possibility of performing an action, and the second involves a property of an agent. I examine how these understandings of ability can be useful for theorizing about education in general and specifically whether they constitute suitable criteria for assigning students to classes or schools. The conclusion I draw is that neither of these concepts of ability can support the robust, institutional, and largely irreversible forms of ability grouping practiced today.

Current Performative Ability

One main way to understand the term "ability" is as a power of an agent. Ability is the current *possibility* of an agent performing a specified action. Various accounts of the nature of this possibility exist (e.g., ability could be understood as the lack of constraint on performing the action, or as the propensity to perform it (Scheffler 1985), the details of which are not crucial for our discussion. Following Thompson (2020), I call this conception of ability *performative ability*. Diverse human activities can be understood as performative abilities – riding a bicycle, baking a cake, or fishing – and in the educational context, it refers to a student's possibility of performing concrete actions (e.g., reading, writing, solving equations) at the present time. It can also apply to more abstract, or general abilities, such as the ability to perform critical evaluation, to engage in self-directed learning, and more.

Performative abilities are, at once, preconditions for some types of learning, but also the desired outcomes or goals of education. Performative abilities that students currently manifest also constitute an important measure of educational justice. Comparing the performative abilities of different groups of students (for example, low-income versus high-income students, or students identified as belonging to different racial groups) can tell us if equal educational outcomes obtain, or whether students have attained the standards of educational adequacy. Performative abilities can be useful in evaluating specific educational practices or policies, too. For example, reforms introducing online platforms for learning mathematics can be evaluated by, among other things, their effect on gender differences in performative abilities in mathematics.

Ability in this sense is, I argue, the currency of justice in the educational domain (or at least one of its components). It is what egalitarians think should be equalized, what sufficientarians think there should be an adequate amount of, and what prioritarians aim to maximize for the worst off. Performative ability is also the way to recognize the "worst-off" in the educational domain – who is the one with the lowest current ability.

Is performative ability a suitable conception of ability for the practice of ability grouping? Students' current performative abilities may seem, at first brush, an effective and fair criterion for assigning students. Certain performative abilities are preconditions for learning, so assigning students to a course who lack the necessary performative abilities for success in it would be wasteful, as would assigning students to it who already know what the course is meant to teach. Additionally, using performative abilities for assignment avoids essentializing students' abilities, or making assumptions about their future trajectories.

Yet, despite its initial attractiveness, performative current ability is not a suitable conception of ability for ability grouping, especially when separation is institutional and permanent.

To see why, think of the rationale behind admission to selective schools or gifted programs (or special education schools). The lack of a specific performative ability (or even several performative abilities) would usually not be considered a good enough reason to reject a candidate, and displaying certain performative abilities would not necessarily suffice as a basis for accepting students. Selective schools, gifted programs, and even high-ability tracks purport to see beyond the mastery of any specific ability and to recognize students' "raw" talent. Students who possess such ability, so it is thought, will be able to quickly pick up any missing performative abilities. Similarly, no reasonable educator would support assigning a student to special education or to a vocational track merely because she fails to demonstrate a specific performative ability.

Students may have unequal levels of performative abilities for the most mundane reasons – their teacher may have failed to complete all the required material in time, they may have been ill when the specific topic was taught, and so on. So, separating students according to their performative ability would not decrease heterogeneity in student ability in the long run, and it does not realize the goal of ability grouping. Indeed, differences in performative abilities might warrant differential treatment aimed at helping students develop those abilities, including temporary and local separation performed to that end.

It could be argued that even if performative ability is not what schools try to identify, it can serve as an indication of raw talent. Indeed, student achievement can indicate general ability, and I discuss this further below. For now suffice it to say that specific performative abilities are a coarse measure with limited predictive value, especially when comparing students from different environments and schools.

There is one case in which separation according to performative ability does seem reasonable, namely when the lack of a specific performative ability makes the student unable to benefit from participation in an educational activity. However, this does not justify complete separation of schools or tracks, in most cases. Students do not need to be able to benefit fully from every single activity or task for us to say that they are able to benefit from participation. Moreover, students also experience non-academic gains (social, civic, psychological) from attending schools (Meyer 2014), and they would have to obtain no academic or non-academic benefit for exclusion to be justified. Such cases would, likely, be limited to ability grouping such as advanced placement courses within comprehensive schools, rather than extensive separation. Generally speaking, all students who can benefit from learning in a school or class should be granted access, and when limited resources require it, prioritization should follow one's preferred principle of justice (Clayton 2012; Kotzee & Martin 2013).

Ability as a Property of an Agent

The second possible way to conceive of ability is as a property of an agent. To see what this signifies, think of physical ability. When we say that a person is physically able, we might mean that she has the ability to engage in various sports, such as swimming, even if she does not, as of yet, know how to swim. Ability as a property of an agent does not imply that the agent can currently perform any specific action (performative ability); it precedes performative ability and is a precondition for obtaining it. Further, ability as a property involves a relatively stable attribute of the individual. For example, fragility is an enduring property of glass. If glass were only likely to break in extraordinary occasions, we would not say that it is fragile.

Abilities in the educational domain are often understood as a property of students, meaning that students possess certain cognitive abilities that can be assessed, regardless of the specific tasks they are able perform at any given time (Curry 2021). Various forms of ability grouping, especially those that entail robust and extended separation, seem to be based on this conception of ability. Educators try to identify students' "native ability," assuming that this accurately predicts performance in more specific educational tasks.

Ability as a property of the agent is used not only in the context of student assignment; it is also implicitly assumed in other discussions in the philosophy of education, such as in the debate between meritocratic and luck egalitarian theories of justice. Unequal educational outcomes are just, according to meritocracy, if they are caused by differences in students "talent" and effort (Brighouse 2011; Brighouse & Swift 2014; Swift 2003). Luck egalitarian approaches, on the other hand, claim that talent cannot justify educational inequality because students have no control over it (Brighouse 2011). While the two theories offer different responses to unequal student ability, both use the term in this sense, namely as a property of students.

Figuring out what "native ability" might mean is tricky, however. Scientists dispute almost everything about cognitive abilities: how they develop and what affects them; how stable they are over time; whether different abilities are interrelated aspects of "general intelligence" ("g") or there are types of intelligences that derive from separate mechanisms; how ability should be measured. In discussing these matters I will try to rely on the things that scientists largely agree upon.

There is overwhelming evidence to the effect that our cognitive and other abilities are affected to some extent by genes. I am unaware of any theorist or scientist who argues that genes have no role *at all* in determining ability. On the other hand, even the most avid supporters of the thesis that genetic factors determine ability do not claim that genes account for 100% of people's ability, and all agree that environmental factors also affect ability (Carroll 1993). So while the disputes in the field are as fierce as ever, they lie elsewhere – for example, in describing the mechanisms through which ability is affected, the exact forms of interaction between genes and environment, and in the appropriate social and educational responses to the mechanisms that affect ability.

The fact that abilities are affected by both genes and the environment and are not biologically fixed, entails that any argument regarding natural talent or environmental circumstances of individuals apply only to the relevant component of ability. For example, theories of educational justice that require the neutralization of social influences on individual's educational trajectory need to be able to distinguish between the two components. This is more difficult than it may seem because nature and nurture are not only factors that shape ability; they also constantly affect one another, in a "dynamic interplay between genes and experience" (Sweatt 2013: 624). Environmental factors shape various physical dimensions of ability, such as the development of neural networks and the epigenetic alteration of gene functions (the process through which environmental circumstances affect the activation or deactivation of genes) (Bueno 2019; Payne 2021; Perry 2002; Sweatt 2013). In turn, the physical dimensions of an individual's ability shape the environment she is exposed to through her choices and through feedback loops (Jensen 1997). Figuring out the relative role of nature and nurture in people's ability therefore requires discerning and controlling for an endless set of variables, an endeavor fraught with severe methodological (and ethical) difficulties (Payne 2021). Practical difficulties in evaluating the relative role of each contributor does not make the theoretical discussion of its implications unimportant, however, and imprecise approximations may suffice for solving at least some of the practical problems.

Environmental influences on ability raise another challenge for ability as a property. Recall that for ability to be a property of agents it must be a relatively stable characteristic that can be depended upon to predict future performance better than current performative abilities do. Yet, if the environment constantly affects ability, ability is flexible and prone to constant change. Indeed, cognitive abilities are extremely flexible – they develop dramatically in childhood, and they continue to change (developing or stagnating) over the course of one's lifetime (Scheffler 1985; Walton 2013), depending on environment and education. If people's abilities change so dramatically over time, what is the stable property we are thinking of when we talk of people as possessing high ability?

The most plausible possibility is that what is relatively stable is comparative cognitive ability. Young children are, generally speaking, less cognitively able than adults, but we still often observe that a specific child is especially bright. What we mean by this is that the child has high ability compared to what we expect of children her age (Carroll 1993). Performance in school is measured relatively, and is a good predictor of future school performance, although its predictive power declines over time (Lohman 2005).

The stability of relative ability depends on stability of environmental conditions, however. Severe deterioration in education services, a sudden family crisis or accident, or conversely, exchanging a neglectful environment with a nurturing one, or receiving educational reinforcement, have dramatic influence on individuals' relative ability (Perry 2002). Importantly, educational decisions such as ability grouping are likely to significantly influence ability, since they create the environmental circumstances that contribute to the development (or stagnation) of cognitive abilities. Ability grouping is, therefore, not merely a response to preexisting differences in ability but rather a constitutive factor in recreating them. Relying on antecedent ability for assigning students is therefore problematic, in that it does not indicate a pre-existing, fixed trait.

It is worth noting at this point that the malleability of human ability has ramifications beyond the issue of ability grouping. For example, meritocratic theories of educational justice assume that students possess a constant "core" ability that can be discerned separately from the abilities demonstrated in school. Inequality that tracks students' core ability is not unfair, according to meritocracy. On the other hand, underachievement that cannot be explained by a low "core" ability (or by students' lack of effort) and is caused by environmental circumstances (lack of nurture by families, inadequate schools, etc.) constitutes an injustice. Underperformance in such cases gives rise to justice-based claims for additional resource allocation or other measures that can compensate students for their environmental disadvantage and improve their achievement so that it aligns with their "core" ability. Given the challenge described above, ability in this sense is not a useful yardstick for meritocratic educational justice (Harel Ben Shahar under review-b).

There are two further interpretations of ability as a property that might be suitable for ability grouping. The first involves intelligence, as measured by IQ tests. Intelligence, or g, is sometime referred to as the general ability to solve problems comparatively successfully. Abundant research demonstrates correlations between IQ test scores and various success measures in life including educational attainment, income, job security and others (Curry 2021). There are various objections to IQ tests, including that they may be culturally biased and that preparation improves scores (Steinberg 2003), but they are still considered a well verified measure of cognitive ability that measures a relatively stable and robust trait of individuals (Neisser et al. 1996).

IQ is sometimes used as a criterion for assignment to gifted programs and special education. Some experts argue, however, that IQ is not fine grained enough for the purpose of school assignment. Lohman, an educational psychologist, described the problem as follows: "selecting students for advanced instruction in science or literature using a measure of g is like selecting athletes for advanced training in gymnastics or basketball using a measure of general physical fitness" (Lohman 2005: 339; cf. Steinberg 2003). For selection to be effective and to avoid misclassifying students, schools must define the abilities they seek much more specifically. On the other hand, like physical ability, IQ might be an effective indication of people's general ability. General physical ability is needed to develop specific abilities such as swimming, and IQ might also be understood as a threshold needed for more specific cognitive abilities.

Ability as a property, therefore, seems to be useful for ability grouping mainly when understood as a threshold. I discuss this now through the concept of potential.

"Potential" signifies that an agent does not currently have a certain ability, but that she is likely to be able to develop it given the realization of certain conditions (Scheffler 1985). Ability, whichever way it is understood, is hypothetical in the sense that being able to x is not the same as actually doing x; but potential takes another step toward the hypothetical, since it involves the possibility of *developing an ability to x*.

Potential also signifies the limitations of agents' possible abilities by defining which abilities cannot be acquired under certain conditions. While people can and do develop their abilities, there are inescapable limitations to our abilities as a species. For example, humans do not have the ability to outrun an antelope or to calculate faster than a computer. More controversially, there are certain limitations on specific individuals' abilities. Although people's abilities can change and develop, often beyond expectations, each and every person has limitations – skills and abilities they will not be able to develop, although it may be impossible to know for sure what the limit is (as I discuss further below). Potential ability is a property of agents, because it is an enduring characteristic, however it is also a very limited descriptor of agents, because it stands at the very boundary of each individual's ability.

Students' potential is, like other types of ability, an intertwined product of both nature and nurture. It can also be altered, so that severe neglect or injury can impose new limitations on one's ability, and effective nurturing can expand what one is able to learn and do. If potential, like "talent" is also affected by nature and nurture and is also flexible, doesn't it encounter the same problems? Can it help us in our search for a conception of ability that can be useful for the practice of ability grouping?

I think that potential can indeed be a useful conception of ability for ability grouping. It cannot, however, tell us a whole lot about the agent. It indicates what abilities the agent is incapable of obtaining, at the present time, but because potential can be altered, what is currently impossible for a student may be possible in the future. Using potential as the conception of ability for ability grouping entails that instead of trying to find out students' (core) abilities, when assigning students to tracks or courses, we should ask "will this student be able to develop the relevant ability given suitable resources and effort?" Framed this way, the distinction between natural and environmental causes of ability is inconsequential (although causality and blame may retain moral significance in other contexts such as prevention or compensation). Additionally, asking whether students possess the potential to develop an ability does not give undue moral weight to measured ability at a specific point in time, and therefore is compatible with the malleability of ability – the fact that it can be altered. The evaluation of whether the student possesses the threshold ability applies only to the specific moment in which a resource is being distributed. If, at that time, limitations of the student's potential entail that she is unable to benefit from participating in a certain activity, withholding the resource is not unfair. Limitations of students' potential may similarly limit what we owe them in other contexts, excusing us from otherwise binding requirements of justice (Anderson 2007; Howe 2011; Mason 2016; Wilson 1991).

In the context of ability grouping, examining only present limitations on students' abilities implies that evaluations of ability should not result in long term, robust separation, as is the case in many of the forms of ability grouping practiced today. It also suggests that assignment policy should take the form of inclusion of all except those whose ability fall short of the threshold (assignment to special education typically follows this pattern), rather than choosing those with the highest abilities, as typically performed by selective schools (Clayton 2012; Terzi 2020). Remaining prioritization in assignment should follow one's preferred principle of justice (Clayton 2012; Kotzee & Martin 2013).

These conclusions align with the implications of the performative conception of ability described above. I argued that performative ability is an unsuitable criterion for ability grouping, but performative ability could serve as a threshold meant to prevent waste caused by assigning students to courses they cannot benefit from (either academically or non-academically). The conception of ability as potential leads to the same conclusion: separating students according to their abilities might be justified when students' abilities are limited so that they are unable to successfully participate in an academic activity (and if participation does not have other, non-academic benefits).

References to potential in any educational context, however, are cause for concern, given that evaluations of limitations of potential are self-fulfilling prophecies and may lead to denial of resources and opportunities (Books 1998; Hart 1998). The dangers are aggravated by the problems with current methods of evaluation. So, many of the traditional arguments against ability grouping described previously, would apply to evaluations of potential with equal force. Importantly for our discussion, however, the understanding of potential I outline above, and the limited role I suggest it can play in educational decision making, supports only short-term decisions of grouping that acknowledge the malleability of potential. It does not justify the kind of robust ability grouping accepted today. As a result, the dangers noted above are slightly less pressing.

Another important factor in easing some of these concerns is how educators would evaluate student potential. We might say that despite the inescapability of limitations on human ability, there is no reliable way to ascertain what these limitations are in individual cases, and therefore teachers are never allowed to act according to their assessments of potential. This argument, I think, is too strong. We may find ways to assess potential that do not have negative consequences. For example, after repeatedly trying, unsuccessfully, to teach a child how to read, using different methods, and along extended periods of time, it would be reasonable to say that the child is *currently* unable to learn how to read. Two things are crucial here. First, that the assessment was made retrospectively, rather than in advance, and second, that we regard it as valid only at that point in time, rather than describing the child's potential in general. As a result, resources are not denied children, and low expectations do not undermine her abilities. On the contrary, teachers are required, as a pedagogical strategy, to assume that a child's abilities are greater than their achievements suggest.

So one way to determine the limitations of potential is by repeatedly trying. The practical implications for practices of ability grouping would be that students can only be excluded after being included with suitable support, and that attempts at developing the required abilities must be conducted repeatedly and periodically.

This approach is very demanding in terms of the evidence needed for exclusion. I concede there may be cases in which a lower threshold may suffice for assessments of limited abilities. If we go back to the previous example, given the failed attempts to learn how to read, teachers may be allowed to assume the student is also unable to acquire other similar abilities. This would depend on various factors such as the type of ability, its importance, how difficult the ability is in relation to the student's existing performative abilities, and more. We might also concede that evidence concerning certain types of impairments can serve as an indication of limited potential, as well as exceptionally high or low IQ. This evidence, however, attributes abilities to an individual student on the basis of general statistical evidence concerning people similar to her, and it may underestimate her ability. Therefore, educators are required to take such evidence with a grain of salt, and to try to push students beyond what may be expected of them.

The conclusion is that potential can be used as a criterion for student assignment, however it can support only limited forms of separation, mostly temporary and only in extreme cases in which students are unable to gain academic and non-academic benefits from the course or class.

It should be noted, at this point, that the level of ability needed to perform in schools depends on the educational content that schools choose to teach. For example, some programs for extremely high achievers, such as college level science or accelerated math, are in fact beyond the abilities of most students. Although the conceptual discussion can support separation in this case, there may be convincing normative arguments against such separation, and moreover, against creating programs that require separating students. The fact that gifted programs or advanced courses are common practice does not mean we should take them as a given. It can be argued, for example, that schools are not the appropriate place for college level teaching (save that for college), or that enrichment for gifted children should be provided privately in the afternoon rather than in schools. The conceptual discussion performed here, therefore, does not exhaust all there is to say about ability grouping, but it sheds light on the nature of student ability and consequently examines which forms of ability grouping offer an appropriate reaction to it.

To conclude, the various available conceptions of ability do not offer a solid basis for robust and irreversible forms of ability grouping commonly practiced in schools today. They can, however, support temporary separation on the basis of student ability when a student cannot obtain any benefit (academic or non-academic) from participating in the educational program or activity. This conclusion, derived from a conceptual analysis of ability supports the various arguments against ability grouping presented earlier in the chapter.

None of the above entails that teachers are not allowed to treat children differently on account of their different abilities, for example by offering them additional support and resources. Such differential treatment does not raise any of the moral or conceptual objections that ability grouping creates and is indispensable for teaching inclusive classes.

Conclusion

This chapter examined the practice of ability grouping in light of various conceptions of student ability, concluding that although ability might seem a rational way to assign students to classes, none of these conceptions sit easily with most practices of ability grouping, especially when separation is robust and irreversible.

The analysis of the concept of ability offers a novel point of view in the debate concerning ability grouping. It invites all sides in the debate to engage in a meaningful discussion about human ability in all its variety, value and limits, and the consequences of these for educational theory and practice. The chapter also demonstrates that thinking about ability, and considering what science tells us about it, can offer new insights concerning some long-standing debates in the philosophy of education.[1]

(Related Chapters: 4, 5, 6, 15, 22, 34.)

Note

1 This work was supported by the Israel Science Foundation grant no. 848/19.

References

Anderson, E. (2007) "Fair Opportunity in Education: A Democratic Equality Perspective," *Ethics* 117(4): 595–622.

Bailey, C. & Bridges, D. (1983) *Mixed Ability Grouping: A Philosophical Perspective.* London: Routledge.

Books, S. (1998) "A Critique of the Discourse of Potential," *Journal of Thought* 33(1): 15–28.

Brighouse, H. (2011) "Educational Equality and School Reform," in G. Haydon (ed.) *Educational Equality.* London: Continuum, 15–70.

Brighouse, H. & Swift, A. (2014) "The Place of Educational Equality in Educational Justice," in K. Meyer (ed.) *Education, Justice, and the Human Good: Fairness and Equality in the Education System.* New York: Routledge, 14–33.

Brighouse, H., Ladd, H. F., Loeb, S., & Swift, A. (2018) *Educational Goods: Values, Evidence and Decision Making.* Chicago: University of Chicago Press.

Bueno, D. (2019) "Genetics and Learning: How the Genes influence Educational Attainment," *Frontiers in Psychology* 10, Article 1622. 10.3389/fpsyg.2019.01622

Cantu, G. C. (2019) "Tracking in Secondary Education: An Educational Injustice," *Theory and Research in Education* 17(2): 202–212.

Carroll, J. B. (1993) *Human Cognitive Abilities: A Survey of Factor Analytic Studies.* Cambridge: Cambridge University Press.

Carter, J. A. (2020) "Cognitive Goods, Open Futures and the Epistemology of Education," *Journal of Philosophy of Education* 54(2): 449–466.

Cartledge, G. (2005) "Restrictiveness and Race in Special Education: The Failure to Prevent or to Return," *Learning Disabilities: A Contemporary Journal* 3(1): 27–32.

Cipriano-Walter, M. (2015) "Falling Off the Track: How Ability Tracking Leads to Intra-School Segregation," *Thurgood Marshall Law Review* 41(1): 25–54.

Clayton, M. (2012) "On Widening Participation in Higher Education through Positive Discrimination," *Journal of Philosophy of Education* 46(3): 414–431.

Clayton, M. (2018) "Education," in S. Olsaretti (ed.) *The Oxford Handbook of Distributive Justice.* Oxford: Oxford University Press, 438–458.

Curry, D. S. (2021) "Street Smarts," *Synthese* 199(1–2): 161–180.

Erwin, J. O. & Worrell, F. C. (2012) "Assessment Practices and the Underrepresentation of Minority Students in Gifted and Talented Education," *Journal of Psychoeducational Assessment* 30(1): 74–87.

Ford, D. Y. (1998) "The Underrepresentation of Minority Students in Gifted Education: Problems and Promises in Recruitment and Retention," *Journal of Special Education* 32(1): 4–14.

Gamoran, A. (1992) "The Variable Effects of High School Tracking," *American Sociological Review* 57(6): 812–828.

Garda, R. A. (2005) "The New IDEA: Shifting Educational Paradigms to Achieve Racial Equality in Special Education," *Alabama Law Review* 56(4): 1071–1134.

Giesinger, J. (2017) "Educational Justice, Segregated Schooling and Vocational Education," *Theory and Research in Education* 15(1): 88–102.

Gorard, S. & Siddiqui, N. (2018) "Grammar Schools in England: A New Analysis of Social Segregation and Academic Outcomes," *British Journal of Sociology of Education* 39(7): 909–924.

Graves, Jr. S. L. & Ye, F. F. (2017) "Are Special Education Labels Accurate for Black Children? Racial Differences in Academic Trajectories of Youth Diagnosed With Specific Learning and Intellectual Disabilities," *Journal of Black Psychology* 43(2): 192–213.

Har-Carmel, Y., & Harel Ben Shahar, T. (2017) "Reshaping Ability Grouping Through Big Data," *Vanderbilt Journal of Entertainment and Technology Law* 20(1): 87–128.

Harel Ben Shahar, T. (under review-a) "Discriminating Underachievers."

Harel Ben Shahar, T. (under review-b) "Can Potential Save Meritocracy?"

Hart, S. (1998) "A Sorry Tail: Ability, Pedagogy and Educational Reform," *British Journal of Educational Studies* 46(2): 153–168.

Howe, K. R. (2011) "Educational Equality in the Shadow of the Reagan Era," in G. Haydon (ed.) *Educational Equality*. London: Continuum, 71–95.

Jencks, C. (1988) "Whom Must We Treat Equally for Educational Opportunity to be Equal," *Ethics* 98(3): 518–533.

Jensen, A. R. (1997) "The Puzzle of Nongenetic Variance," in R. J. Sternberg & E. L. Grigorenko (eds.) *Intelligence, Heredity, and Environment*. Cambridge University Press, 42–88.

Kotzee, B. & Martin, C. (2013) "Who Should Go to University? Justice in University Admissions," *Journal of Philosophy of Education* 47(4): 623–641.

Krause, A. & Schuller, S. "Evidence and Persistence of Educational Inequality in an Early-Tracking System: The German Case" (Discussion Paper IZA 2014).

Lohman, D. F. (2005) "An Aptitude Perspective on Talent: Implications for Identification of Academically Gifted Minority Students," *Journal for the Education of the Gifted* 28(3–4): 333–360.

Mason, A. (2016) "Fair Equality of Opportunity and Selective Secondary Schools," *Theory and Research in Education* 14(3): 295–312.

Mazie, S. (2009) "Equality, Race and Gifted Education: An Egalitarian Critique of Admission to NYC's Specialized High Schools," *Theory and Research in Education* 7(1): 5–25.

McGeer, V. (2018) "Intelligent Capacities," *Proceedings of the Aristotelian Society* 118(3): 347–376.

Merry, M. (2008) "Educational Justice and the Gifted," *Theory and Research in Education* 6(1): 47–70.

Merry, M. (2013) *Equality, Citizenship and Segregation: A Defense of Separation*. New York: Palgrave Macmillan.

Meyer, K. (2014) "Educational Justice and Talent Advancement," in K. Meyer (ed.) *Education, Justice, and the Human Good: Fairness and Equality in the Education System*. New York: Routledge, 133–150.

Mickelson, R. A. & Everett, B. J. (2008) "Neotracking in North Carolina: How High School Courses of Study Reproduce Race and Class-Based Stratification," *Teachers College Record* 110(3): 535–570.

Morgan, P. L., Farkas, G., Cook, M. & Strassfeld, N. M. (2017) "Are Black Children Disproportionately Overrepresented in Special Education? A Best-Evidence Synthesis," *Exceptional Children* 83(2): 181–198.

Neisser, U., Boodoo, G. Bouchard, T., Boykin, A. W., Brody, N., Ceci, S. (1996) "Intelligence: Knowns and Unknowns," *American Psychologist* 51(2): 77–101.

Norwich, B. (2014) "Recognizing Value Tensions that Underlie Problems in Inclusive Education," *Cambridge Journal of Education* 44(4): 495–510.

Oakes, J. (1995) "Two Cities' Tracking and Within-School Segregation," *Teachers College Record* 96(4): 681–690.

Payne, J. M. (2021) "Rethinking Nature and Nurture in Education," *Journal of Philosophy of Education* 55(1): 143–166.

Perry, B. D. (2002) "Childhood Experience and Expression of Genetic Potential: What Childhood Neglect Tells Us about Nature and Nurture," *Brain and Mind* 3(1): 79–100.

Ryle, G. (1949) *The Concept of Mind*. London: Hutchinson.

Sapon-Shevin, M. (1994) *Playing Favorites: Gifted Education and the Disruption of Community*. New York: SUNY Press.

Scheffler, I. (1985) *Of Human Potential: An Essay in the Philosophy of Education*. New York: Routledge.

Schouten, G. (2012) "Fair Educational Opportunity and the Distribution of Natural Ability: Toward a Prioritarian Principle of Educational Justice," *Journal of Philosophy of Education* 46(3): 472–491.

Slavin, R. E. (1990) "Achievement Effects of Ability Grouping in Secondary Schools: A Best Evidence Synthesis," *Review of Educational Research* 60(3): 471–499.

Solorzano, D. G., & Ornelas, A. (2002) "A Critical Race Analysis of Advanced Placement Classes: A Case of Educational Inequality," *Journal of Latinos and Education* 1(4): 215–229.

Steinberg, R. J. (2003) "'My House is a Very Very Very Fine House' But It is Not the Only House," in H. Nyborg (ed.) *The Scientific Study of General Intelligence: Tribute to Arthur R. Jensen*. Amsterdam: Pergamon, 373–395.

Sweatt, J. D. (2013) "The Emerging Field of Neuroepigenetics," *Neuron* 80(3): 624–632.

Swift, A. (2003) *How Not to be a Hypocrite: School Choice for the Morally Perplexed Parent*. London: Routledge.

Terzi, L. (2020) "On Educational Excellence," *Philosophical Inquiry in Education* 27(2): 92–105.

Thompson, W. C. (2020) "A Limited Defense of Talent as a Criterion for Access to Educational Opportunities," *Educational Philosophy and Theory* 53(8): 833–845.

Wade, D. L. (1980) "Racial Discrimination in IQ testing: Larry P. v. Riles," *Depaul University Law Review* 29(4): 1193–1214.

Walton, G. M. (2013) "The Myth of Intelligence: Smartness Isn't Like Height," in D. Allen & R. Reich (eds.) *Education, Justice, and Democracy*. Chicago: Chicago University Press, 155–172.

Werblow, J., Urick, A., & Duesbery, L. (2013) "On the Wrong Track: How Tracking Is Associated with Dropping Out of High School," *Equity & Excellence in Education* 46(2): 270–284.

Wilson, J. (1991) "Does Equality (of Opportunity) Make Sense in Education?" *Journal of Philosophy of Education* 25(1): 27–32.

Zimmer, W. & Toma E. F. (2000) "Peer Effects in Private and Public Schools Across Countries," *Journal of Policy Analysis and Management* 19(1): 75–92.

34

MALIGNANT ACCOUNTABILITY, FALSE PROMISES, AND THE FUTURE OF EDUCATION

Yael Yuli Tamir

IN COLLABORATION WITH ZVI ACKSTEIN AND ASSAF SARID

Preface

Every essay written these days must stand the test of relevance in the post-COVID era. The world is changing so fast that we are unable to assess the short- and long-term impact of the COVID pandemic on our world at large and on education systems in particular. The popular term VUCA (Volatility, Uncertainty, Complexity, and Ambiguity) describes the present state of affairs. Nevertheless, we must plan and operate large public systems. We need them more than ever: health services, geriatric support, education, innovation, ways of fighting global warming, and mitigating the climate crisis. Planning in times of uncertainty is a thorny business. One needs to be flexible enough to be able to take the unknown into account, yet at the same time, learn from past experiences. No wonder this is a time when many paradigms are broken.

The fact that we are going through a paradigm shift in macroeconomic policy was clear before the eruption of the pandemic. Since the "Great Recession," we have been witnessing the decline of the global neo-liberal model and the emergence of more national ways of thinking. This trend has motivated countries to look inwardly, putting their members first, and harnessing their inner abilities to cope with large-scale, complex social, medical, and economic issues (Tamir 2019). The growing importance of national markets and services raises doubts regarding the importance of international comparative tests of educational outcomes. When human capital is nurtured, not in order to be globally traded, but for the purpose of assisting a given economy to flourish, context is paramount. Different economies need to pave their way to success based on their special strengths and weaknesses. "One-size-fits-all" solutions have consequently lost their appeal.

Uncertainty has sparked an array of inquiries into new ways of understanding the world. This chapter examines one of the most influential doctrines in 20th-century education. It is grounded in a strong belief in a flat world that celebrates shared skills and capabilities that are best measured by success in international comparative tests. The tests measure skills in literacy, math, science, and other subjects, and are taken to assess the human capital needed for economic growth.

The Program for International Student Assessment (PISA) test marketed itself not only as a universal indicator for the level of education but also for growth. Its strength lies in the simplicity and universality of its model: contrary to VOCA it offers Linearity, Certainty, Simplicity, and Clarity. No wonder people find it comforting.

DOI: 10.4324/9781003172246-39

Yet the model is founded on four assumptions that I believe are misleading and false.

1 High-stake tests are the best way to evaluate and improve all school systems (Part I).
2 Measurable improvements in PISA will lead to measurable economic growth; namely there is a high correlation between PISA scores and the rate of real per capita growth (Part II).
3 One global strategy – improving PISA results – can equally boost all economies, irrespective of their stage of economic development (Part III).
4 Boosting an economy is best measured in terms of average growth rather than inclusive growth.

I am not very optimistic that challenging these assumptions will make a difference. The vast organizations surrounding PISA allow it to withstand criticism, but I hope that when the results of the next PISA come in, and social and political shockwaves rock the educational and political boat, some people will turn to this chapter and avoid rash responses.

PISA's power is not only a theoretical issue but a political one. I have experienced it myself during my term as Israel's Minister of Education (2006–2009). Being a policymaker and a theoretician allows me to move back and forth between these two spheres. My conclusion echoes the well-known saying that "in theory there is no difference between theory and practice, but in practice there is."

The Damage of High-Risk Tests

The publication of the results of the Trends in International Mathematics and Science Study (TIMSS) in 1999 was a defining moment in the history of Israeli education. Israel assumed it was doing well, very well. A single international math test conducted in 1968 using a selected sample, excluding Arabs, immigrants, and Ultra-Orthodox led to the happy conclusion – that resonated well in the post six-day war euphoria – that Israeli was an exceptional success. When the TIMSS results came in, they were disconcerting; Israel was placed 26th out of 38 countries. Its test scores fell short not only of those of the world's leading economies but also of those of countries such as Thailand, Moldova, Romania, Cyprus, Italy, and Lithuania. They surpassed only those of 10 countries: Tunisia, Macedonia, Turkey, Jordan, Iran, Indonesia, Chile, the Philippines, Morocco, and South Africa.

These poor results have repeated themselves time after time, and Israelis have become more frustrated and less confident in their education system. It has become a scapegoat on which all social ills are blamed. In the aftermath of the public storm that followed the publication of the 2009 PISA results, the Israeli economist Dan Ben-David handed policy makers a warning: "This is a socio-economic time bomb – an economy with a third world level education cannot have a first-world army, and in the neighborhood where Israel is located it is a privilege we cannot afford" (Led 2012). Military images are often used in educational crises, blaming the education system for its inability to protect their countries from social, economic, and military risks. In 2009, when the PISA results were published in the United States placing it in 25th out of 34 participating countries, Chester Finn, a senior education researcher and president of the Fordham Institute for Educational Research, wrote: "On Pearl Harbor Day 2010, the United States (and much of the rest of the world) was attacked by China. Too melodramatic? Maybe you'd prefer 'Sixty-three years after Sputnik caused an earthquake in American education by giving us reason to believe the Soviet Union had surpassed us, China delivered the aftershock'" (Strauss 2010).

Shock waves push education systems in conservative directions. Here is a short history of educational conservatism: The launching of the Sputnik lead to dramatic changes in the US curriculum, when in 1958 the US Congress passed the "National Defense Education Act" to ensure the security of the nation and sent US students Back to Basics. Similarly, PISA results in the 90s led to "No Child left Behind" and then, during Obama's presidency, to "The Race to the Top."

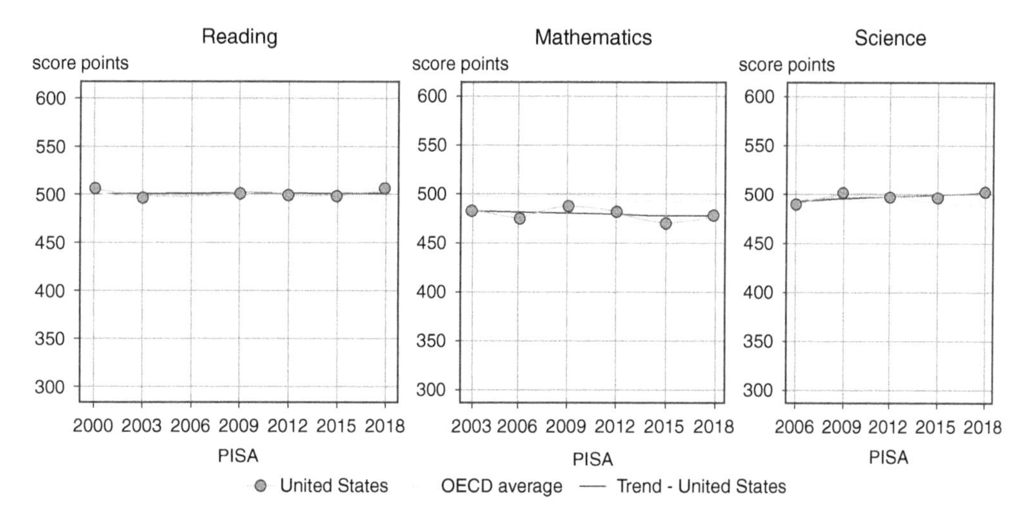

Note: *indicates statistically mean-performance estimates that are significantly above or below PISA 2018 estimates for the United States. The gray line indicates the average mean performance across OECD countries with valid data in all PISA assessments. The dotted line indiates mean performance in the United States. The black line represents a trend line for the United States (line of best fit).
The PISA 2006 reading literacy results are not reported for the United States because of an error in printing the test booklets.
Source: OECD, PISA 2018 Database, Tables I. B1.10, I. B1.11 and I. B1.12.

Figure 34.1 PISA scores in reading, mathematics, and science

These reforms have had little measurable impact on student achievement; the mean has not changed in reading since 2000, mathematics since 2003, and science since 2006, showing no significant improvement or decline (Figure 34.1). This straight line echoes the title of Charles Payne's book *So Much Reform, So Little Change* (Payne 2008). One conclusion to draw from this is that international test results have little to offer in the way of guidance for structuring educational policies. A second conclusion is that if post-test reactions are to have a positive and lasting impact they must coincide with social and economic change. Education alone cannot carry the burden.

When I took up my position as Israel's Minister of Education (2006), the latest test results were placed at the top of the education agenda. In my first meeting with the Prime Minister, he shared with me his intention to open the school year by making a public commitment that Israel would climb to the top of the test list. Politely, I asked him to refrain and pointed out there were far greater challenges than test results. Issues such as child poverty, malnutrition, social and economic gaps, and a shortage of skilled teachers, to name but a few. Making empty promises was the wrong way forward, I argued. The PM nodded and made the promise, nonetheless. Like other Prime Ministers around the world, he could not resist the temptation. But then, to his great credit, he supported a vast school reform effort that helped improve the education system but failed, as I had anticipated, to improve test results.

As the date of the 2006 PISA test approached, the education system became more stressed. Despite the obvious risk of concentrating on preparing 15-year olds for the test and putting students, teachers, and principals under duress, the lure of quick achievements or fear of failure was almost irresistible. My predecessor allowed special learning materials to be developed, resources to be allocated for teacher training, special study hours to be added for the relevant age group, as well as placing pressure on school-heads to prepare their schools for the coming exam (Zohar 2013: 36). Indeed, in the 2003 PISA test, Israel leaped to 19th place in mathematics and to 23rd place in science (out of the 45 countries that took the test). This seemed to be good news. Yet, a committee established to examine Israel's performance noted that the conduct of the Ministry of Education raised concerns. "Instead of thoroughly addressing basic problems, the system dealt with specific changes targeted at raising achievements in the forthcoming test" (Zohar 2013: 36–37). The committee found that schools received direct instructions from Ministry officials to train eighth graders and encourage those expected to achieve low results to stay at home. These policies caused considerable damage, slowed the assimilation of a new curriculum, stigmatized members of less well-performing groups, and fostered distrust among students and teachers alike.

To prepare or not to prepare? That was the question. I decided not to. I chose to initiate a comprehensive school reform, which was fully implemented ten years after it was launched (2007–2017), but in 2006 Israel's ranking dropped (again). Israel was ranked 25 out of the 49 participating countries. I was harshly criticized, the PM called me in for an angry conversation, and the Minister of Finance claimed that I was a burden on the economy. The Parliament assembled a special session to discuss my failure. I got first-hand experience and insights into the essence of "high-risk tests."

My successor overturned my decision, decided to prepare for the test, and sent a clear message to educators. A school principal in one of Israel's largest cities wrote to the education researcher Miri Yemini about an embarrassing phone call he received from the Ministry of Education. "You've entered the lottery," he was told, "your school will be included in the upcoming PISA test. The Ministry will fund preparation and training hours and deliver a list of students who are advised not to take the test" (Yemini 2012).[1] Once again, efforts bore fruits and in the next PISA tests Israel was ranked 7th in the world in mathematics and 13th in science. A 2012 report that examined the results of Israel, Qatar, Morocco, Turkey, and Saudi Arabia, suggested that they could not be compared to test scores of previous years. According to the report, Israel had altered the translation of the test in ways that intrinsically changed its nature and the ability to compare results across the years.

I have no first-hand knowledge of what happens behind the scenes in other countries. However, I have a hunch that things are rather similar. No one wants to carry the burden of failure especially when it is placed on the shoulders of the education system as a whole, filtering down from the Minister to teachers in the field. No wonder people try to game the results.

The more exposed assessment and measurement tools are, the greater the urge to adapt scores accordingly. Teachers, supervisors, administrators, and ministers are tempted to skew the results in order to protect their status. Sharon Nichols and David Berliner, who studied this phenomenon claim that

> Whenever you have a high stake attached to an indicator, such as test scores, you have a measurement system that has been corrupted, rendering the measurement less accurate … The higher the stakes, the more likely it is that the construct being measured has been changed.
>
> *(Nichols & Berliner 2007: 27)*

To describe this phenomenon, they introduced Campbell's Law: "The more any quantitative social indicator is used for social decision-making, the more subject it will be to corrupt pressures and the more apt it will be to distort and corrupt the social process it is supposed to measure" (26–27). George Mandus and Marguerita Clarke go even further, arguing that the probability of combining high stakes and high validity in one measure, such as a test, is low (Mandus & Clarke 2001).

In 2009, New York City's Education Commissioner Joel Klein and Mayor Bloomberg presented what they claimed was a historic achievement in narrowing gaps between white and racial minority students. This turned out to be an artifact of the way test results were reported (Ravitch 2010: 79). Systematic interventions in test results were also exposed in Washington, Atlanta, and in many other parts of the United States; teachers provided their students with the right answers, administrators organized "correction sessions" in which they reviewed and changed all students' exam forms, and supervisors were instructed to improve outcomes at all costs. Such actions are born out of an uncompromising demand to succeed.

In *The Death and Life of the American Education System: How Testing and Choice are Undermining Education*, Diane Ravitch, who served as an adviser to President Clinton and promoted the "No Child Left Behind" reform, writes in retrospect:

> Our schools will not improve if we rely exclusively on tests as the means of deciding the fate of students, teachers, principals and schools. When tests are the primary means of evaluation and accountability, everyone feels pressure to raise the scores, by hook and by crook. Some will cheat to get a reward or avoid humiliation. Schools may manipulate who takes the test and who does not; districts and state officials may fiddle with the scoring of the test … . Any test score gains that result solely from incentives are meaningless because gains that are purchased with cash are short-lived and have nothing to do with real education.
>
> *(Ravitch 2010: 226–227)*

On the 6th of May 2014, the *Guardian* published an open letter to Dr. Schleicher, signed by 874 leading educators from all over the world (Andrews et al. 2014). Their message was clear and unambiguous – educational policies enacted following PISA's "best-practice" recommendations influence the life of hundreds of millions of children all over the globe. Lack of progress on PISA rankings leads to a "PISA shock" followed by far-reaching reforms that educational experts see as damaging education worldwide:

> PISA results are anxiously awaited by governments, education ministers, and the editorial boards of newspapers, and are cited authoritatively in countless policy reports. They have begun to deeply influence educational practices in many countries. As a result of PISA, countries are overhauling their education systems in the hopes of improving their rankings. Lack of progress on PISA has led to declarations of crisis and 'PISA shock' in many countries, followed by calls for resignations, and far-reaching reforms according to PISA precepts. We are frankly concerned about the negative consequences of the PISA rankings. These are some of our concerns:
>
> - While standardized testing has been used in many nations for decades (despite serious reservations about its validity and reliability), PISA has contributed to an escalation in such testing and a dramatically increased reliance on quantitative measures … .
> - In education policy, PISA, with its three-year assessment cycle, has caused a shift of attention to short-term fixes designed to help a country quickly climb the rankings, despite research showing that enduring changes in education practice take decades, not a few years to come to fruition … .
> - By emphasizing a narrow range of measurable aspects of education, PISA takes attention away from the less measurable or immeasurable educational objectives like physical, moral, civic, and artistic development, thereby dangerously narrowing our collective imagination regarding what education is and ought to be about … .
> - Finally, and most importantly: the new PISA regime, with its continuous cycle of global testing, harms our children and impoverishes our classrooms, as it inevitably involves more and longer batteries of multiple-choice testing, more scripted "vendor"-made lessons, and less autonomy for our teachers. In this way PISA has further increased the already high stress-level in schools, which endangers the well-being of our students and teachers … . We assume that OECD's PISA experts are motivated by a sincere desire to improve education. But we fail to understand how

your organization has become the global arbiter of the means and ends of education around the world. OECD's narrow focus on standardized testing risks turning learning into drudgery and killing the joy of learning. As PISA has led many governments into an international competition for higher test scores, OECD has assumed the power to shape education policy around the world, with no debate about the necessity or limitations of OECD's goals. We are deeply concerned that measuring a great diversity of educational traditions and cultures using a single, narrow, biased yardstick could, in the end, do irreparable harm to our schools and our students.

Sincerely,
Paul Andrews et al. (2014)

The authors called for an end to the exam regime and for a democratic debate about international tests, their conduct, and the extent of their influence. Why was their advice ignored? Why has testing in general and comparative testing in particular persisted? How is it that testing has become a major component in the planning of educational reforms? The answer has to do with the difficulty of measuring the quality of education and the ambiguous causal correlation between test results, the quality of education and other variables. As PISA was ready to offer simple answers followed by a receipt, who could say no?

Tests (and other forms of measurements) turn malignant when they invade a system and change it in a way it fails to resist. They turn from a way to measure and improve a practice to a means of dictating the essence of the practice. The malignant potential of PISA is magnified by its national and international importance. High ranking on the PISA has become not only a matter of national pride, but also a way to assess future economic success. Once test scores are assumed to predict the economic future of a country, their power transcends the educational sphere. No one wants to trail behind at the bottom of the league.

In building its power PISA was supported by the World Bank. While tests are conducted, analyzed, and published by an OECD-related research body, the World Bank encourages countries to follow the rules. Francois Bourguignon, Senior Vice President and Chief Economist of the World Bank, writes that, "The Bank ... will contribute to ensuring that the measurement of learning achievements is undertaken in a more systematic way and is properly taken into account in the Bank's dialogue with partner countries" (Bourguignon 2007: vii). The clear implication is that the Bank's support for countries will be predicated on their positions in the international achievement rankings. This seems more of a unilateral threat than a piece of friendly advice.

PISA results made me uncomfortable. I looked at Israel's low ranking in the international tests and compared it to other factors: the country has grown more rapidly than most developed countries placed at the top of the PISA list, its young generations are creative and entrepreneurial, and many countries around the world look to recreate its success as a Start-up Nation. The reasons for this success are not entirely clear, presumably a cluster of variables that are characteristic of maturation processes including education for independence and entrepreneurship from an early age, the high rate of participation in youth movements and organizations, and service in the IDF.

Despite the low-test results Israel's growth rate between 2010 and 2019 is 4.2%, the highest among OECD countries. Between 2015 and 2019, when the children tested in 2003 and 2006 entered the work force, Israel's growth rate was 3.8%, almost double that of the OECD's average of 2.1% (Toker 2021: 3). Despite this rapid growth Israeli education has many faults, of which I am well aware: a high rate of poverty, growing social and economic gaps, reclusive sub-cultures, a shortage of high-quality teachers, military conflict that seems to be never-ending, and many others. All these must be addressed, but I cannot see how PISA could have helped. Swimming against the current you need to be sure you are right, so I started reading about PISA and that spawned an opportunity to learn more.

Meet the Minister of International Education

I was invited to attend the European Community Ministers of Education forum in Strasbourg. The key speaker was Dr. Andras Schleicher, director of the PISA exams. This was a fascinating opportunity to listen and ask some difficult questions, as Schleicher (Figure 34.2) presented a lecture with graphs showing how improvement in international tests could spur economic growth. The presentation was spectacular, and the graphs invited optimism. Follow the rules and you will be rewarded.

In a determined voice Schleicher announced that "One standard deviation on test performance relates to 1% difference in annual growth rates of GDP per capita" (Schleicher 2010). The ministers applauded enthusiastically and queued to receive guidance. I stood patiently. Reaching the top of the queue, I didn't take the booklet, I asked a simple question: "Looking at your presentation I wonder could there be such a close, unambiguous, direct, linear correlation between two variables such as test scores and economic growth, in all countries, regardless of their level of economic development, over the course of a hundred years?" There was no response. Admittedly, the question become close to an obsession.

PISA's linear curve provides a source of hope; an illusion that there is an easy way to generate constant growth. In a world plagued by repeated economic crises, PISA offers an irreplaceable assurance that we can outwit economic volatility and assure continuous progress. Here are some very concrete promises PISA analysts make: "A modest goal of having all OECD countries boost their average PISA score by 25 points over the next 20 years ... implies an aggregated gain of OECD GDP of 115 trillion dollars over the lifetime of the generation born in 2010," while "bringing all countries up to the average performance of Finland, OECD's best performing education system in PISA, would result in gains in the order of USD 260 trillion" (Hanushek 2010: 6).

Since tests are marketed as a means of promoting economic growth, it is interesting to analyze the correlation between high test results and the rates of real per capita GDP growth.[2] I created a very simple chart (Figure 34.3) with two variables: the top 10 countries in the international test rankings in 2000 and the average real GDP growth between 2006 and 2010 when the 15 years old who took the test in 2000 entered the market. The statistics were compiled from the International Monetary Fund World Economic Outlook Database.

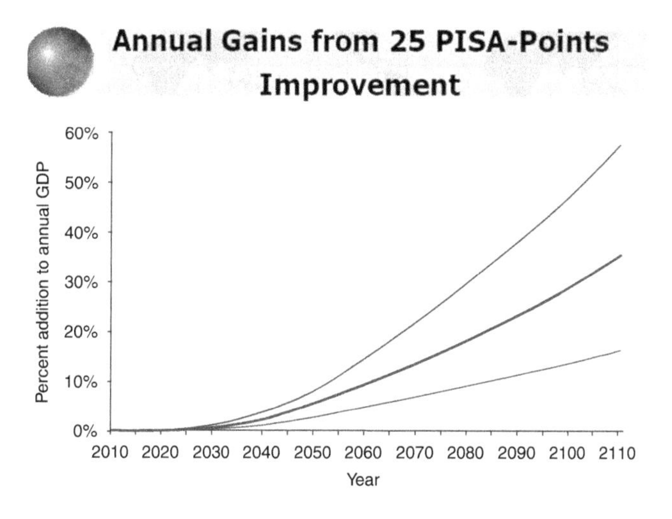

Figure 34.2 Schleicher's projection of test score impact on economic growth

Countries by average GDP (real) per capita growth rate between 2006-2010	Ranking according to the results of 2000s.	Country
0.67	1	Finland
3.5	2	South Korea
0.46	4	Japan
0.16	5	Estonia
2.93	6	Singapore
10.62	7	China
0.14	8	Canada
1.1	9	Australia
1.05	10	Netherlands
2.41	39 (40) [41]	Israel

Figure 34.3 Comparisons of GDP growth and PISA rankings by country

In these same years the fastest growing economies per capita were China 10.62%, Angola 8.72%, Belarus 8.53%, India 7.11%, and Papua New Guinea 6.5%. None of them are known for their high level of education. (Note that China tests only certain regions.) From a layperson's point of view, it seems that the correlation between rapid growth and illiteracy is stronger than that between growth and high PISA scores. This is no coincidence. More developed countries tend to grow at a slower rate.

The Research Department of the Swiss Bank HSBC published in 2011 a forecast for the next four decades (2010–2050) supporting the assumption that developed countries will grow at a slower rate than developing ones, a process that could lead to fluctuations in the global economic system (Ward 2011).

What are we to learn from this analysis? First there is no proven causal relationship between economic growth and levels of education. A decline in the impact of education on the level of economic activity occurred during the lifetime of the most educated generation in the history of the world, in both developing and developed countries. Second, rate of growth is not the best parameter to rely on. Developing economies have enormous growth potential due to their limited economic performance. Despite their rapid growth, there is still a considerable gap between them and developed countries. Third, the slowdown of economic growth in the developed world is caused by structural changes such as aging of the populations, low birth rate, a decline in the buying power of the middle classes, automation, and more.

HSBC also re-examined Robert Barrow's model that calculated the contribution of school years to economic growth. Barrow argued that each additional year of schooling would result in a 1.2% increase in GDP growth. As a result, he predicted that countries with a high level of education, such as Germany will grow faster than countries such as India. The report suggested that Barrow overestimated the impact of additional school years on economic growth. Re-calibrating the model and lowering the impact of education on growth "created incredibly accurate predictions …" (Ward 2011: 32).

Further evidence of the difference between the impact of education in developing and developed economies comes from the economist Christopher Tienken who analyzed the correlation between test scores and the Global Competitiveness Index (GCI), claiming that

> increases in the general population's education level may have a greater influence on the economy in nations with non-existent or lower-performing economies (e.g. Chad, Cameron, Ethiopia, Kyrgyz Republic) than in highly developed economies because

economically low performing countries lack the critical mass of human capital necessary to build a high-functioning economy. In fact, countries with already high levels of education attainment see no effect on GDP when the population's education level increases.

(Tienken 2008: 2)

Put together, these studies invite us to question the prevalent assumption that improvements in PISA ranking can assure economic growth in developed economies. A new study conducted by the Israeli economists Zvi Eckstein and Assaf Sarid reaffirms the difference between the influence of education on developing and developed economies.

OECD and Non-OECD 1960–2000 Results from the Eckstein, Sarid, Tamir Study

According to their findings, one should cautiously examine the relation between tests scores and economic growth as it is unclear whether improvements in education affect the long-term or its short-term pattern of growth. It turns out that there are differences between the impact of education on developed and developing economies. Education can impact growth in two ways: Long-term effect (also called a "growth effect") or the short-term (also called a "level effect"). A level effect implies that an increase in education contributes to the short-term growth rate (the *level* of the GDP per capita), whereas long-term effect means that education contributes to constant growth. Eckstein and Sarid demonstrate that in developed economies, improvements in education lead to level growth; namely they have a significant short-term effect but have little or no effect on long-term growth. Changes in variables such as the opening of new markets or innovative technologies can reignite the economy, while aging of the population, or a crisis like COVID can slow it down (Figure 34.4).

The distinction between growth effect vs. level effect is important for our understanding of the relationships between growth and education (Figure 34.5). Since 2008 many economies, including several OECD countries, have been experiencing lower growth rates. It is widely believed that their growth rates are about to decline to a level below that of the second half of the 20th century. When education produces more skillful workers than an economy can take advantage of, or nurtures different skills that the economy cannot use, we face a new phenomenon – the emergence of a class

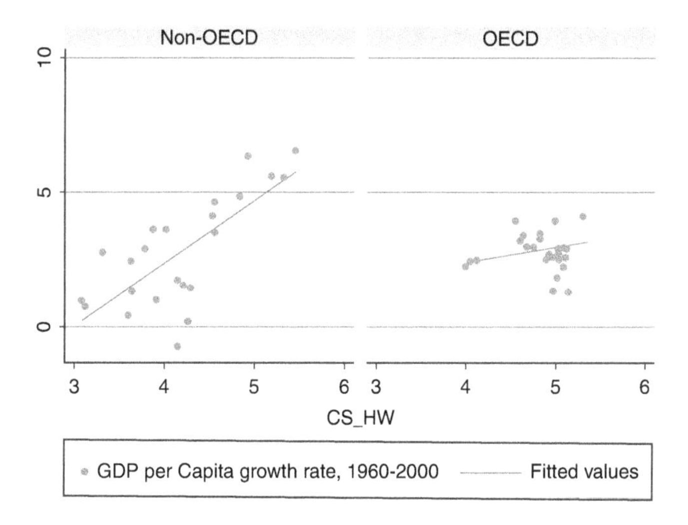

Figure 34.4 Relationships between education and economic growth rates in developing vs. developed (OECD) countries

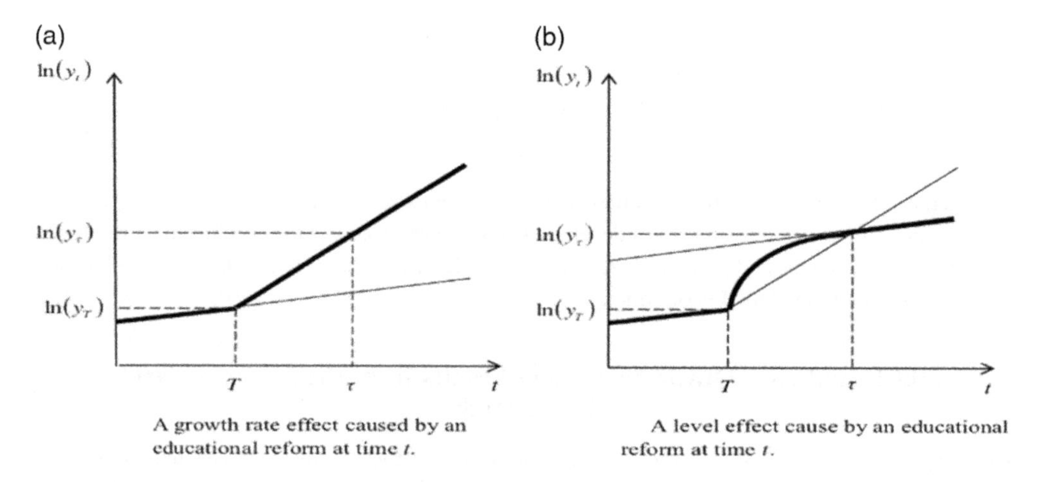

Figure 34.5 Growth vs. level effect of an educational reform

of educated poor. People who invested in education but for whom economic rewards are wanting. Governments and educators need to understand the conditions under which such a phenomenon develops, so that affected individuals may make informed decisions regarding their life-plans.[3]

Consequently, improvements in test results will have a far more modest influence on GDP growth per capita than what Hanushek and Woessmann have suggested. A new simulation of the evolution of GDP per capita following an educational reform that increases PISA results by one standard deviation was compared to that presented by Hanushek et al. (2013). As expected, it shows a much more modest correlation between the variables.

One thing is sure, the graph presented by Schleicher showing a linear correlation between improvements in PISA results and economic growth between the years 2010–2100 does not reflect what has happened so far, and what is likely to happen in the foreseeable future (Figure 34.6).

Inclusive Growth

PISA harms education twice. Once because it raises unrealistic expectations, and twice because it places the burden of unfulfilled expectations on the shoulders of educators. The "education industry" resists reform and fails to prepare children for the future, it is argued.

> In addition to teachers and their representatives, other organizations, and institutions in the education sector resist reform. School administrators rise from the ranks of the teaching profession, their salaries and pensions are connected to those of teachers, and they are expected to fight on behalf of the common interests of the sector. Other school personal – bus drivers, school guards, staff assistants, lunchroom aids, and many more – are often represented by unions and serve as valuable allies when school policy issues arise
>
> *(Hanushek et al. 2013: 100)*

Such claims make education a weak and undervalued profession. It is axiomatic that no education system can be better than its teachers. By making teachers and educators a scape goat, PISA cuts the branch upon which we are all perched.

Moreover, expectations that improvements in test results will generate growth convert education from a tool for nurturing "the educated person" or "the common good" into an economic tool. It is still true that "the more you learn, the more you earn," since education improves the human capital

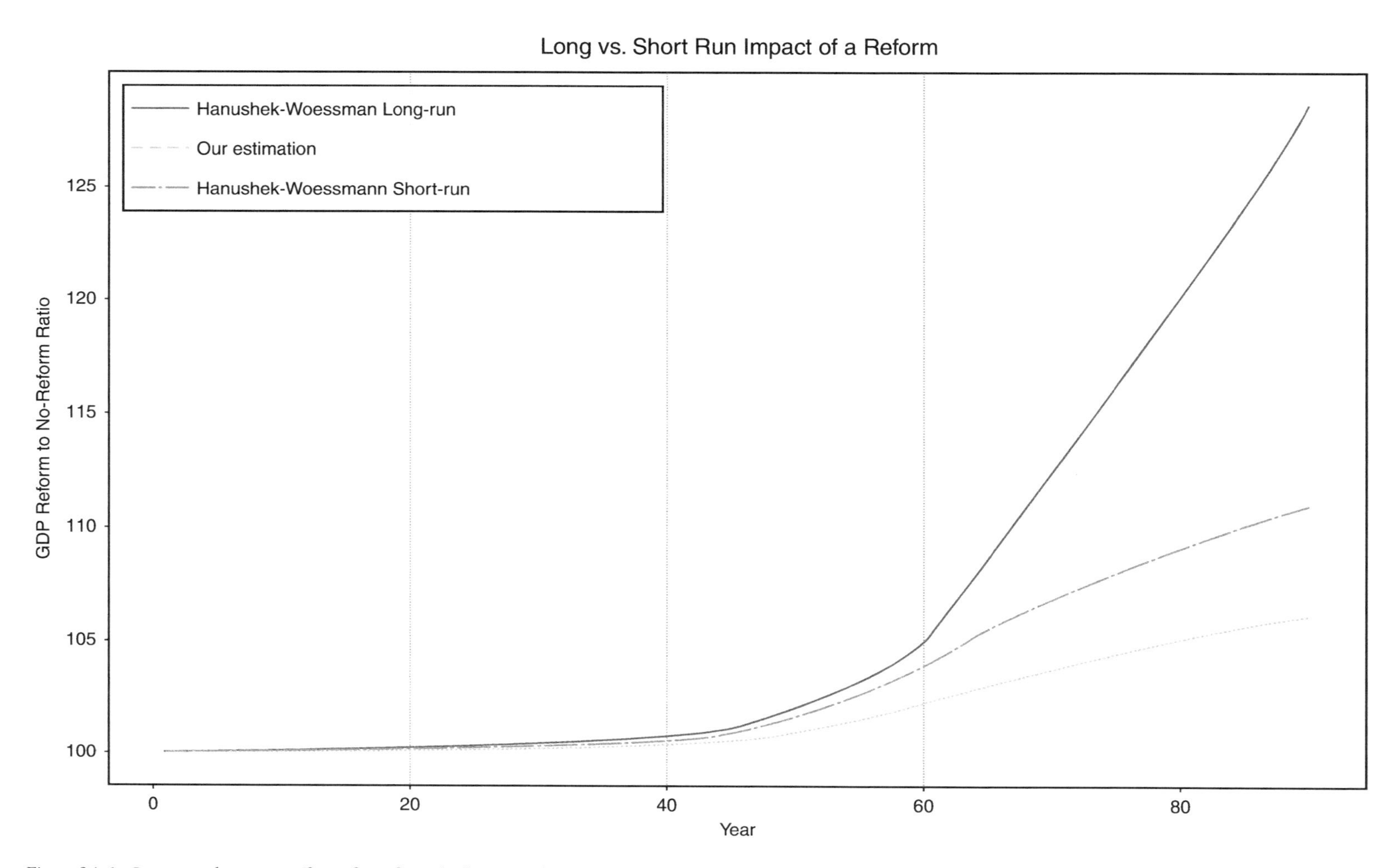

Figure 34.6 Long vs. short run effect of a reform (Eckstein and Sarid)

and life chances of individuals, even though economic returns for a wide range of degrees is in decline. When we move from the personal level to the national one, we find that in developed economies improvements in education have negligible effects. This important distinction between individual wellbeing and collective prosperity is absent from the PISA analysis.

Education, at least in the traditional sense of school years and degrees, is no longer a magic panacea. To prepare children for the future, we must re-assess the skills they will need and ways of developing these skills. A study analyzing the future of work predicts that new jobs will be created in leisure, recreation, and healthcare sectors and in technology-related fields. "New fields of work and professions are emerging in which basic human aptitudes like empathy and creativity are at a premium" (Daheim & Wintermann 2020: 7). Given this prospect, one can only mourn, as David Goodhart does, "the scandalously wrong-headed classification of social care as low-skilled work ... Helping an elderly person to eat and swallow, bathing someone with dignity, communicating with someone with early onset dementia; doing these things with intelligent kindness requires skill" (Coman 2020). Goodhart is right, there will certainly be a need for those who provide recreation, entertainment, art, and culture and related ancillary services. And if, as expected, automation and AI will lead people to work less, then one thing for them to learn is how to utilize free time.

This makes Howard Gardner's "Frames of Mind" the best guide for the future. Gardner sets out eight types of intelligence: linguistic, logical/mathematical, visual/spatial, bodily, musical, interpersonal, intrapersonal, and naturalist intelligence. Other candidates could be added such as spiritual, existential, and moral intelligence, which allow individuals to flourish in different ways. Some of these high achievers will score very low on PISA, and if they were removed from the classroom the day the PISA test was administrated, they may bare the scar for years to come. Giving room from a wider spectrum of intelligences is also important for closing social and economic gaps. Closing these gaps should be our first priority. In fact, there is only one linear universal graph I trust; it reflects the strong correlation between PISA results and results of other tests, with the social and economic background of the children tested (Figure 34.7).

PISA's decision to concentrate its recommendation for improvements of test scores on schooling while ignoring crucial issues such as class separatism, identity, alienation, violence, poverty, etc. turns it into a conservative force that fosters the illusion that education can be improved without major social change. In so doing PISA becomes one more tool of gap preserving strategies – strategies that perpetuate social and economic gaps and block a real and painful debate about social justice and the

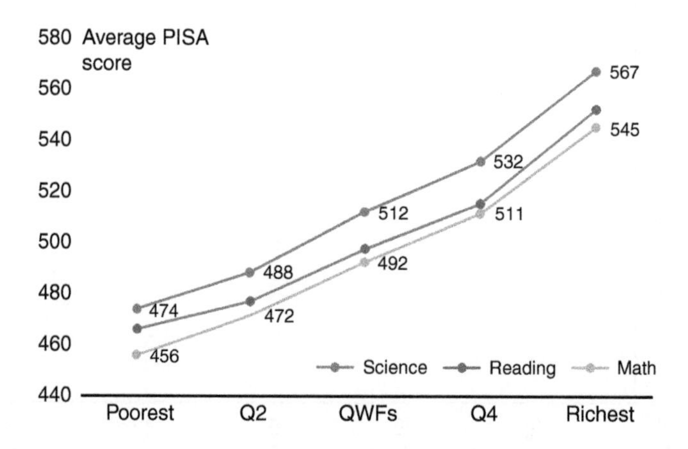

Figure 34.7 Correlation between PISA score and social and economic class

future of society (Tamir 2011). Since it is easier to raise the scores of stronger students, a desire to raise scores prioritizes investments in strong groups rather than weaker ones.

To change this reality, we need to set new goals. The American economist Dani Rodrik claims that rather than seeking average growth we should seek inclusive growth. This will shift our attention towards social justice instead of meritocracy. If PISA and the World Bank would rank and invest in societies according to their ability to reduce gaps and create equal opportunities, the international tests might become a progressive social tool. Were the World Bank to be more generous to countries that fight inequalities, perhaps societies would be motivated to adopt strategies directed towards increasing inclusiveness.

This is particularly important in the post-COVID era when governments will be tasked with addressing social, economic, and educational gaps that have widened considerably as a result of the world-wide pandemic. The most pressing task is the reduction of such gaps. As Rodrik writes:

> One of the biggest challenges countries face today is the very unequal distribution of opportunities, resources, income and wealth across people. ... Inclusive prosperity – whereby many people from different backgrounds can benefit from economic growth, new technologies, and the fruits of globalization – remains elusive. To address these issues, societies face choices among many different policies and institutional arrangements to try to ensure a proper supply of productive jobs and activities, as well as access to education, financial means, and other endowments that prepare individuals for their participation in the economy.
>
> *(Rodrik & Stantcheva 2021: 1)*

Tests, whether national or international, are a tool, a means to an end. Their purpose is not only to improve education but also the society we live in. For that purpose, we should reject the seductive optimism offered by PISA; improving performance in tests will not lead to social and economic improvements. Rather, we should think how to reform our society and make it more just and inclusive – better test results are likely to follow.

(Related Chapters: 1, 3, 6, 7, 8, 15, 16, 21, 23, 35.)

Notes

1 The Ministry of Education denied any involvement in the selection of students, but a large number of principals and teachers reported that pressure was exerted on them to contribute to the success of the test.

2 Real gross domestic product growth rate is the rate of growth of the value of all final goods and services produced within a state in a given year.

3 It is reasonable to ask whether understanding these conditions might have prevented or stunted the student loan crisis.

References

Andrews, Paul, et al. (2014) "OECD and Pisa Tests are Damaging Education Worldwide – Academics," *The Guardian* 6 May, https://www.theguardian.com/education/2014/may/06/oecd-pisa-tests-damaging-education-academics

Barrow, J. R. (1991) "Economic Growth in a Cross Section of Countries," *Quarterly Journal of Economics* 106(2): 407–443.

Bourguignon, F. (2007) "Forward," in E. A. Hanushek & L. Wössmann, *Education Quality and Economic Growth*. Washington, DC: World Bank, vii.

Coman, J. (2020) "Head, Hand, Heart by David Goodhart Review – Let's Think Practically," *The Guardian* 14 September, https://www.theguardian.com/books/2020/sep/14/head-hand-heart-by-david-goodhart-review-lets-think-practically

Daheim, C., & Wintermann, O. (2020) *The Future of Work. Findings of an International Delphi Study of The Millennium Project.* https://fsc-ccf.ca/references/2050-the-future-of-work-findings-of-an-international-delphi-study-of-the-millennium-project/

Hanushek, E. (2010) *The High Cost of Low Educational Performance.* OECD.

Hanushek, E., Peterson, P., & Woessmann, L. (2013) *Endangering Prosperity: A Global View of the American School.* Washington, DC: Brookings Press.

Led, M. (2012) "Dan Benn-David: An Existential Danger to the State," *Calcalist* 27 November (daily news opinion piece, in Hebrew).

Mandus, G., & Clarke, M. (2001) "The Adverse Impact of High-Stakes Testing on Minority Students: Evidence from One Hundred Years of Test Data," in G. Orfield, & M. L. Kornhaber (eds.) *Raising Standards or Raising Barriers? Inequality and High-Stakes Testing in Public Education.* New York: Century Foundation Press, 85–106.

Nichols, L. S., & Berliner, D. (2007) *Collateral Damage.* Cambridge, MA: Harvard University Press.

Payne, M. C. (2008) *So Much Reform, So Little Change: The Persistence of Failure in Urban Schools.* Cambridge, MA: Harvard Education Press.

Ravitch, D. (2010) *The Death and Life of the Great American School System; How Testing and Choice are Undermining Education.* New York: Basic Books.

Rodrik, D., & Stantcheva, S. (2021) "A Policy Matrix for Inclusive Prosperity," *National Bureau of Economic Research Working Paper 28736,* http://www.nber.org/papers/w28736

Schleicher, A. (2010) Keynote Lecture, European Community Ministers of Education Forum. Strasbourg.

Strauss, V. (2010) "Hysteria over PISA Misses the Point," *The Washington Post,* 7 December, https://web.archive.org/web/20121101151711/http:/voices.washingtonpost.com/answer-sheet/standardized-tests/hysteria-over-pisa.html

Tamir, Y. Y. (2011) "Staying in Control; Or, What Do We Really Want Public Education to Achieve," *Educational Theory* 61(4): 395–411.

Tamir, Y. Y. (2019) *Why Nationalism.* Princeton: Princeton University Press.

Tienken, C. (2008) "Rankings of International Achievements Test Performance and Economic Strength: Correlation or Conjunction?" *International Journal of Education Policy and Leadership* 3(4): 1–15.

Toker, N. (2021) "Israel Champions Growth Among OECD Economies," *De Marker,* 26 September (daily news opinion piece, in Hebrew).

Ward, K. (2011) *The World in 2050: Quantifying the Shift in the Global Economy.* London: HSBC Global Research.

Zohar, A. (2013) *It's Not All About Test Scores: Reviving Pedagogical Discourse.* Bnei Brak: Poalim – Hakibutz Hameuchad (in Hebrew).

Yemini, Miri (2012) "Does the Ministry of Education Maintain Fairness in the International Tests?" *De Marker,* 26 March (daily news opinion piece, in Hebrew).

35

BURNOUT, DEMORALIZATION, AND RACIALIZED FAILURES TO RECOGNIZE TEACHERS AS MORAL SUBJECTS

Doris A. Santoro

I have defined demoralization as "consistent and persistent frustrations in accessing the moral rewards of teaching" (Santoro 2011b: 3). The moral rewards, as I have described them, capture the moral (other- and craft-regarding) and ethical (personal flourishing) dimensions of the goods internal to a practice that teaching can offer (Higgins 2011; Green 1985; MacIntyre 1984). Demoralization occurs gradually and may become a chronic condition; it is rarely precipitated by a single event that presents as a discrete dilemma.

My development of the concept of demoralization emerged through a collaborative hermeneutic approach. I built, tested, and refined the concept in an iterative qualitative research process in collaboration with teachers (Santoro 2015). I saw a need to apply the concept of demoralization to teaching in order to provide an explanation for morally motivated teacher attrition (Santoro 2011a). Just as teaching enables some educators to find moral rewards through their work (Hansen 1995), I suspected moral and ethical concerns might motivate some teachers to leave their jobs. My first phase of this work studied experienced teachers who had left the profession (Santoro 2011a). Later, I extended the concept of demoralization to address persistent moral and ethical concerns for teachers who remained in their jobs, but who were seriously distressed (Santoro 2018).

For experienced teachers whose tenures exceed the five-year period of highest turnover, burnout is a common explanation for why they left. I have argued that applying the label of burnout to teachers when they are really experiencing demoralization is harmful because it is a misdiagnosis that fails to address the root cause of exhaustion, frustration, and sense of futility that stems from teachers' inability to do what Howard Gardner et al. have called "good work" (Gardner et al. 2001). I have also claimed that the diagnosis of burnout places the blame for these feelings on individual teachers because they are seen as having failed to conserve their personal resources (Santoro 2011b). Burnout suggests that teachers come with finite resources and their role is to appropriately pace themselves to mete those resources out over the long haul.

In addition to seeking a better description of morally motivated teacher attrition, my inquiry was a response to the primary data source on teacher attrition in the United States, the School and Staffing Survey and the Teacher Follow-Up Survey.[1] The data from these surveys show that the majority of teachers who leave the profession or who move to another school are "dissatisfied" (U.S. Department of Education 2016). This language has been taken up by researchers who study teaching

DOI: 10.4324/9781003172246-40

and who advocate for better working conditions for teachers, including myself (Carver-Thomas & Darling-Hammond 2017; Hodges et al. 2013; Moore 2012; Schutz & Zembylas 2009).

For instance, I have described the work I do as "philosophizing about teacher dissatisfaction" (Santoro 2015). I have argued that "[d]emoralization offers a more precise diagnosis of experienced teacher dissatisfaction" (Santoro 2018: 3). In numerous presentations to practitioners, I have sustained the discourse of teacher dissatisfaction by modifying it with the term "moral." My purpose was to engage with the largest data sources available about teachers' experiences and to intervene on a current conversation in the field of teacher research. I hoped, in part, to demonstrate how the constructs used in the surveys failed to ask normative questions and therefore limited the scope of understanding we might gain about educators' concerns about their work and teacher attrition.[2]

My characterization of demoralization as a *moral* form of dissatisfaction was a strategic move to import normative constructs into mainstream discussions of teachers' experiences of their work. The most recent phase of my research with educators of color has enabled me to recognize the shortcomings of characterizing demoralization as a moral form of teacher dissatisfaction for all teachers, but especially in the case of the teachers of color I have interviewed.

In my work, I am concerned with the everyday usage of terminology and how the philosophical concepts I build are taken up by those who are affected by them most directly. I believe that characterizing the normative concerns of teachers *merely* as a form of dissatisfaction, even if they are modified by the term "moral," could contribute to the trivialization of identity-conferring commitments (McFall 1987). Furthermore, I have come to believe that the language of dissatisfaction fails to capture the depth of experience that occurs when educators fail to be recognized as moral subjects. I will argue that the failure to recognize teachers' moral claims and, especially, to recognize teachers of color as moral subjects, is made worse when it is minimized as dissatisfaction. This unintentional minimization could activate what Cathy Park Hong (2020) calls "minor feelings" and further contribute to the effects of demoralization.

Dissatisfaction addresses a distinct dimension of wellbeing, and one that operates in a different realm from demoralization. Satisfaction entails the realization of pleasure through the actualization of one's desires. From one perspective in moral philosophy, we might argue that the good person would desire the good. However, in the parlance of the labor market, in which the majority of the teacher dissatisfaction discussion takes place, satisfaction entails the realization of preferences – a preference for autonomy, a preference for a lighter workload, a preference for a different kind of leadership, a preference for a different curriculum. This notion of dissatisfaction, framed in terms of preferences, perpetuates the consumer-oriented labor market notion of how to address teacher attrition. The discourse of job dissatisfaction can be demoralizing because it may perpetuate the misrecognition of teachers' moral motivations. The characterization of demoralization as a type of dissatisfaction misses the depth of harm that may occur when we fail to recognize teachers as moral subjects, especially when these failed recognitions are racialized – that is, impacted by perceptions of race.

As a White higher education-based researcher, I have partnered with K-12 educators and educators of color to explore the forms of demoralization encountered by experienced teachers of color.[3] Although I will be drawing on the interviews my team and I have conducted in a very limited way, what I have learned through our collaboration serves as the interpretive horizon of this chapter. Conducting research with educators of color has revealed the limitations of adopting the term "dissatisfaction." In doing so, I am not making empirical claims about educators of color but engaging in a conceptual refinement generated by new empirical evidence that demonstrated the weakness of characterizing demoralization as a form of dissatisfaction (Alcoff & Kittay 2007; Sullivan 2007).

The argument in this chapter represents my recognition that using the term "dissatisfaction" to describe demoralization might perpetuate demoralization by diminishing the moral significance of teachers' work. To make this argument, I will draw on Margaret Urban Walker's feminist moral framework to highlight the existential significance of moral recognition. Then, I will examine the violence of moral misrecognition and how the minimization of this experience as dissatisfaction could exacerbate what Hong calls "minor feelings." Using Lisa Delpit's early work, I will show how we require moral communities for moral recognition and may face moral burdens when trying to improve them from within.

Demoralization Is Not Simply Dissatisfaction

Teacher dissatisfaction is of major concern to policymakers, school leaders, and teacher educators in the United States. Teacher attrition has long been a challenge, but entry into the profession seems to be stalling as well. The United States has witnessed dramatic drops in enrollment in teacher education programs. Many states have set up commissions to recruit teachers, not just in traditionally hard-to-staff areas, and are considering lowering or removing licensure requirements. However, education labor economist Richard Ingersoll has argued that the United States cannot hire its way out of the teacher shortage. School leaders and policymakers must stem the tide of teacher attrition to meet present and future staffing needs (Papay et al. 2018).

In the last several years, many states and districts have made commitments to hire more educators of color (Philip & Brown 2020). Despite these efforts, the problem of attrition is even more pronounced for teachers of color. Although the percentage of educators of color hired across the United States has increased by 100% in the last 30 years, these gains have not resulted in coming closer to parity with the demographics of the student population. The rate of turnover for educators of color is 25% higher than that of their White peers (Ingersoll et al. 2017: 11).

I was curious if we could learn something new about teacher demoralization by focusing on educators of color. I also wondered if bringing a normative perspective might provide new avenues for addressing attrition in educators of color. I draw from Dorinda Carter Andrews et al. to explain the strategic value of studying teachers of color as a group, even though I recognize that this designation is an artificial grouping of diverse peoples and individuals. They explain

> While it would be inappropriate, and impossible, to make broad empirical claims about the moral life of all educators of color, there is strategic value in focusing on the experiences of teachers of color. Teachers of Color share sociopolitical histories of marginalization by education institutions, structures, policies, and practices, as well as transformative pedagogical and resistant community-based practices, in which positioning them from a group standpoint when theorizing and conducting research affords more comprehensive and complex understandings of their experiences.
>
> *(Carter Andrews et al. 2019: 10)*[4]

My research team and I began interviewing teachers of color with five or more years of experience in 2019. We continue to collect data and to broaden our perspectives on the moral and ethical concerns they encounter in their work.

Teaching for many educators can be an identity-conferring commitment (McFall 1987). That means that it is more than simply a job; it is one that is imbued with values that put one's sense of self at stake. Lynne McFall calls identity-conferring commitments those that "reflect what we take to be most important and so determine, to a large extent, our (moral) identities" (13). It is unsurprising, then, if teaching is a way to express the self and its moral commitments, that so many of the former teachers whom I've interviewed spoke of recovering, regrouping, and struggling to regain a sense of self after choosing to leave the profession. Teaching, for many practitioners, constitutes a moral identity as well as a professional identity. Identity-conferring commitments are "conditions of continuing as ourselves" (McFall 1987: 12). However, it is not simply the fact of being a teacher that is identity-conferring – it is the distinctiveness of the values that teachers bring to the work that confer their identities. So, it would not be the case that to be any kind of teacher would be identity-conferring, but that to embody particular values as a teacher is what confers the valued identity.

A number of studies focusing on attrition amongst educators of color highlight the significance of values that educators of color bring to their work. Their values are described as constitutive of who they are (i.e., identity-conferring) and serve as motivations for being in the classroom. For instance, in their study of Black and Latinx teachers, Dixon et al. (2019) reveal the close coupling of culture and values in their recommendations. They say, "Schools should be places that culturally affirm teachers of color, i.e., where the goals and values of the school match up with the goals and values of the teachers" (3). They found that "teachers of color stay in schools that have a commitment to equity, social justice, and the dismantling of racism" (Dixon et al. 2019: 14). The problem is not whether educators of color possess these values, but the struggles they encounter in trying to enact them in schools.

The Significance of Moral Recognition

Walker's (1998) "expressive-collaborative" model of morality shows the significance of teachers' value-laden commitments and helps us to understand how those commitments are identity-conferring. Feminist ethics aim to be both a correction to and an expansion of our moral epistemologies and are helpful in clarifying the nature of demoralization.

Walker explains that morality is expressed through "practices of responsibility" which include our actions and the narratives that we use to explain them. It is collaborative because we require others to recognize how we are expressing our responsibilities, and that recognition enables us to construct our sense of who we are.

> Morality allows and requires people to understand themselves as bearers of particular identities and actors in various relationships that are defined by certain values. People learn to understand each other this way and to express their understandings through *practices of responsibility* in which they assign, accept, or deflect responsibilities for different things.
> *(Walker 1998: 9, original emphasis)*

Describing morality as practices of responsibility will be intuitive to many teachers as will the need to have others recognize the circumstances and dilemmas that activate those practices. Teachers are responsible for the care and education of students. They are responsible to their communities, their schools, and their own families. Teachers are responsible for upholding civic virtues, the professional expectations of their field, and the standards of their content areas. This list could be extended – for responsibility is central to the work of teaching.

To what degree are these responsibilities, and the narratives teachers share about them, recognized? Walker's moral philosophy raises substantive questions about *how* and *when* and *for whom* moral claims are recognized as moral. In feminist moral theory, expressions and collaborations are situated in and impacted by contexts, particularities, identities, and their intersections with power hierarchies. This perspective is particularly useful for understanding the moral concerns of teachers who may be working in what I have called morally-constrained environments, where what one believes should be done cannot be done. Another form of moral constraint occurs when what counts as moral is limited to one perspective and there is no recognition for the possible plurality of moral positions (Santoro 2016). Walker's moral theory accounts for situations in which "responsibilities outrun control" (Walker 1997: 241) and the context-bound practices of responsibility that defy standardization.

Walker demands that those who engage in moral philosophy exercise more epistemological humility. It is only by seeking out the stories of differently-situated people that we can expand our notions of moral life; it is through narrative that we can begin to make sense of what differently situated people value. She explains, "Many situations cannot be reckoned with responsibly without seeing how people, relations, and even the values and obligations they recognize have gotten there" (Walker 1998: 110). Yet, it may also be the case that those values and obligations are less easily recognized for those who have not been in similar situations. There is always room to learn more through the narratives of others.

Practices of responsibility reveal who we are and what we value, but we depend on others to recognize us as engaging in practices of responsibility. Walker shows that there is vulnerability in expressing these narratives: "The very potential for intelligibility – for being understood as feeling what you are feeling and displaying what you are trying to express – may shift dramatically under the eyes of differently positioned viewers" (Walker 2007: 112). This interdependence also leads to the case that those who are similarly positioned may recognize our practices of responsibility more readily than others who are not.

This position does not need to be universalizing or essentializing, or even exclusionary, but it recognizes that social locations and identities seriously affect our interpretive frames.

> Both the environmental and interpersonal situations that confront people and provoke their [moral] feelings, and the ways people are apt to construe the nature and meaning of these situations, are affected by social experience conditioned by differences in social location, power, and opportunity. This leaves plenty of room for individual differences, but suggests at least that those who share many or particularly distinctive social experiences are equipped to find each other's emotional responses in certain situations more intelligible, apt, and more expressively legible than are others who do not share such experience.
>
> *(Walker 2007: 111)*

Walker explains that it could be more difficult to recognize moral claims when we occupy different social locations. It is an acknowledgement of our epistemological, and therefore moral, purview.

Walker's feminist ethics offers a corrective to traditional moral theory with its universalistic tendencies. Feminist ethics attends to contexts and subject positions. It calls upon us to listen more closely for moral concerns that do not align with our own, especially when engaged with people situated differently from ourselves. Teachers may more easily recognize the substantive moral content in their colleagues' narratives than non-educators do. Teachers of color may more easily recognize the values being challenged by simply *existing* as an educator of color than White teachers do. There is a built-in fallibility that requires we acknowledge the ways in which we could fail to hear the values expressed in others' narratives. This does not mean, however, that we are incapable of recognizing practices of responsibility across differences. It simply entails that we will need to have humility and do additional work to attend appropriately to the narratives that are shared across those differences.

To review, morality, according to Walker, is expressed through practices of responsibility and is collaborative because we rely on others to recognize our practices of responsibility. Through this process, our own understandings of morality and self may be modified. This recognition can fail in a few different ways, one of which is that others may not see our behaviors as forms of responsibility. For example, when Chicago teachers struck in 2019, in part to advocate for more nurses in schools, they saw themselves as exercising responsibility to the profession, to public schools, and to their students. However, some community members and pundits, and perhaps even some teachers, viewed the striking teachers as abdicating their responsibility to be present in their classrooms. This brief example reveals that practices of responsibility require an interpretive community to be recognized as moral, and that alternative moral interpretations are possible depending on how one is situated and how the value of responsibility is interpreted.

Demoralization and Moral Disqualification

One facet of the damage caused by misdiagnosing demoralization as burnout is moral disqualification. I already addressed how this form of misdiagnosis fails to recognize teachers' moral motivations by viewing the problem as the "burnt-out" teacher's lack of inner resources rather than their inability to access moral rewards of the work. The misdiagnosis of burnout also enacts moral disqualification *at the very moment teachers are making moral claims.* If we understand morality through practices of responsibility, then the labeling of teachers as burnt-out signals that they have failed to uphold their responsibilities. In failing to deliver on their responsibilities, they lose moral credibility. This can result in what I have termed the Cassandra-like syndrome of moral violence when moral claims are interpreted as madness (Santoro 2017). It occurs when teachers who make moral claims are not recognized as making moral claims.

Moral disqualification, experienced as a form of moral violence, can be one manifestation of teacher demoralization. This aspect of demoralization is a result of teachers failing to be recognized as making moral claims related to their professional roles. I have analyzed this situation for one woman teacher, Monica, when her moral claims were misrecognized by her district's paid consultants and her principal (Santoro 2017). My more recent interviews with educators of color have revealed a racialized dimension to moral violence. Several teachers of color have expressed the cognitive dissonance associated with failing to have their moral claims recognized in their professional roles, roles in which they are expected to be moral. To return to Walker's (1998) expressive-collaborative model – some teachers of color *expressed* moral concerns about their work, but within a workplace dominated by white norms, the collaborative piece of recognition was missing. The moral violence of failing to be recognized when making moral claims about their work, impeded their ability to reap the moral rewards of their work.

By virtue of their identities, some people will struggle to be heard as making moral claims; this phenomenon has shown up in interviews with teachers of many identities. However, it is only by focusing on the experiences of educators of color that the resounding theme of moral disqualification has emerged most significantly. It is for this reason that the characterization of demoralization as simply dissatisfaction seems most out of place. The serious and horrifying outcomes of a lack of moral recognition are evident in the dispossession of land and livelihood in settler-colonialism, the murders of Black Americans at the hands of police officers, the violence towards people of Asian descent in US streets, and the discourse of a sitting US president referring to Latinx peoples as criminals. To recapitulate Walker's argument: our moral lives are about our responsibility to others. These responsibilities are intelligible to ourselves and others because they are shared understandings. That is, we depend on others' regard to have our responsibilities and commitments recognized.

Educators of color may experience the minimization of moral misrecognition as simply dissatisfaction as another instance of minor feelings. Hong (2020) depicts minor feelings as one emotional response people of color may experience as a result of living in the conditions of interpersonal and institutionalized racism. They are the feelings that arise as the result of having one's interpretation of reality questioned, minimized, or misrecognized by those whose reality fails to take seriously their racialized lived experiences and the naming of those experiences. This imbalance of power attends directly to Walker's question that makes the expressive-collaborative nature of morality precarious: "Who sets the terms for moral judgment, and can all positions in a moral-social order find coherent expression in the moral terms that order provides?" (Walker 1998: 50).

Minor feelings are corrosive, explains Hong, because these felt, and racialized, experiences are difficult to convey because the dominant White American culture leaves no room for them to exist and be acknowledged. There is no room for them in the "moral-social order." Minor feelings are

> built from the sediments of everyday racial experience and the irritant of having one's perception of reality constantly questioned or dismissed. Minor feelings arise, for instance, upon hearing a slight, knowing it's racial, and being told, *oh, that's all in your head* ... When minor feelings are finally externalized, they are interpreted as hostile, ungrateful, jealous, depressing and belligerent, affects ascribed to racialized behavior that whites consider *out of line*. Our [BIPOC's] feelings are overreactions because our lived experiences of structural inequity are not commensurate with their [White Americans'] deluded reality.
>
> *(Hong 2020: 55, 57, original emphasis)*

Minor feelings can show up as "paranoia, shame, irritation, and melancholy" (Hong 2020: 55). The complicated mixture of these emotions renders them unlikely to be correctly characterized because of the dominance of tropes of individualistic catharsis and overcoming obstacles. Hong explains that minor feelings are not "overcome *personally*, after which the individual experiences some kind of self-affirmation and release. Minor feelings by contrast, are ongoing, stuck; they are more true to the trauma of living in a racist, capitalist society" (O'Rourke 2020, original emphasis).

Minor feelings are related to the demoralization of teachers (particularly teachers of color) in two ways: they evoke negative moral feelings (shame, regret) that implicate the one experiencing them in wrongdoing, even though the wrongdoing may reside outside of the educator (such as institutional or interpersonal racism). Minor feelings address the moral disqualification involved in demoralization – that is, the moral claims and concerns are potentially dismissed as individualized emotions and personality failures (paranoia, irritation, melancholy) rather than recognized as practices of responsibility. Finally, minimizing demoralization as a form of teacher dissatisfaction could exacerbate minor feelings that may arise in this form of demoralization.

The Need for Moral Communities

Hong's description of minor feelings provides some insight into the impact of the well documented and often publicized moral concerns of educators of color, which are misrecognized, misconstrued, and continue to go unaddressed: "Because minor feelings are ongoing, they lend themselves more readily to forms and genres that are themselves serial" (Hong 2020: 57). This is also why we need the narrative of interviews that enable us to see teacher demoralization is not just about a particular moment or discrete dilemma. There is not sufficient space to devote to an interview-length narrative here, but one teacher condensed his narrative so succinctly that we can use it as an example.

Black Chicago Public School teacher Dwayne Reed explained his substantive moral concerns in a *New York Times* article profiling teaching during the COVID-19 pandemic.[5] The article quotes him directly, "'Just the fact that I have to give grades to nine-year-olds right now doesn't seem morally right,' Mr. Reed said, noting that two of his students' grandparents recently died of COVID-19" (Singer 2020).

In this brief account, we can see the inadequacy of the term dissatisfaction, even when modified by "moral." If Reed's claim is reduced to "I don't want to give grades," it can be read as a personal preference. This preference could be understood as self-serving and a failure to fulfill his professional responsibilities. Perhaps Reed would rather develop his culinary skills instead of assessing students' work.

Instead, if we recognize Reed's claim as an expression of responsibility, we could imagine his statement emerging from the following questions: What are my responsibilities as a teacher? What are my responsibilities as a teacher of nine-year-olds? What are my responsibilities to nine-year-olds in a pandemic? What are my responsibilities to nine-year-olds in a pandemic whose grandparents recently died of COVID-19? What are my responsibilities in determining what is most important to my students and me within my professional role? These questions are relevant because of the context in which Reed is embedded. These questions of responsibility are raised against the backdrop of other responsibilities: What are my responsibilities as a teacher in Chicago Public Schools? What are my responsibilities to my colleagues? This community? This school? My profession? My family? Myself?

Even though Reed specifically uses moral language in highlighting his concern about assigning grades, the headline of the news story focuses solely on the material outcomes of what appears to be an assignment of blame to teachers. The subtitle reads, "Teacher burnout could erode instructional quality, stymie working parents and hinder the reopening of the economy." How might Reed's expression of his practices of responsibility be misrecognized? How could the application of the term burnout lead to Reed's moral disqualification? Might Reed experience the reframing of his moral concern as burnout as violence?

Elsewhere, I have suggested a two-pronged approach to remoralization: teachers identify and connect with an authentic professional community that affirms their values *and* policies, and practices and institutions need to change to enable teachers to enact their values (Santoro 2018). Walker's moral theory provides philosophical justification for the importance of these professional communities and reinforces the significance of shared values (Walker 1998: 66). What I mean by a "moral community" is not one in which no one ever transgresses shared expectations or everyone manages to live up to their responsibilities to self or others. Instead, a moral community is one in which one's narratives of responsibility are recognized by others, even when the narratives reveal that a person falls short of the shared values.

By being attuned to the moral content in these narratives there can be better recognition that individuals are making moral claims. Even within moral communities that share understandings of responsibilities and how to fulfill them, we will care about the credibility of the storyteller, and that may depend on their subject location (Walker 1998: 125). Read through the lens of dissatisfaction, a narrative might be dismissed as the failure to satisfy one's preferences. When narratives are recognized as conveying moral content, we can come to understand someone as being credible, reliable and having integrity. If we don't ever recognize the claim someone makes as moral, *how* we interpret that person and their behaviors will be dramatically different. For instance, the terms "burnout" and "dissatisfaction" each undermine the reliability of the educator as a moral narrator. "Burnout" suggests that the person recounting events failed to live up to their responsibilities or expended their energy trying to fulfill the wrong responsibilities. "Dissatisfaction" flattens the moral narrative to an expression of pleasure or displeasure and renders the speaker morally insignificant. The inability to be heard as making moral claims may also have significant implications for how the person views themselves (Carbonell 2019).

The significance of moral communities also provides some insight into why conscientious objection to teaching can be so contentious. Conscientious objection to teaching occurs when teachers refuse to continue to work as educators in a particular context on moral grounds (Santoro 2011a). Such acts rattle the agreed-upon values of a moral community. These moments of reckoning require teachers to ask: What is worth doing? On what grounds? When are the compromises too much to bear for the individual in service to the community? How does the refusal to teach by those whom you hold in high regard impact your conceptions of complicity and obligation?

In her public resignation from Goldsmiths, feminist scholar Sara Ahmed left her position in what could be interpreted as conscientious objection to the institution's failure to sufficiently address the concerns she and others had raised about sexual harassment at the university. In a blog post, she wrote, "I have resigned because the costs of doing this work have been too high" (Ahmed 2016). While Ahmed did not elaborate on what the precise costs were in this post, we can imagine that a commitment to truthfulness, integrity, and justice might have left her exhausted, weary, and embattled. Perhaps conditions rendered her incapable of engaging in what she viewed as the moral rewards of her work. Possibly, she had an experience similar to one recounted by a teacher of color my team and I interviewed who said, "In addition to whatever is problematic, it's more. You have the additional burden of having to convince people that it's actually a problem."

Feminist moral philosopher Lisa Tessman has explained that there are contexts in which the embodiment of virtues comes at a significant cost to the bearer. "Burdened virtues ... show that there are virtues whose exercise is, due to bad (including unjust or oppressive) conditions, not conducive to or constitutive of their bearers' flourishing" (Tessman 2005: 111). She describes how the outcomes of burdened virtues can actually change *who* one is: "[T]here is a certain sort of a self that one ought to be, but the unconducive conditions of oppression bar one from cultivating this self" (Tessman 2005: 4). The conditions of oppression cause the problem not the possession of virtues (or values). The latter would be a decidedly cynical view while the former allows for hope in transforming oppressive conditions.

Tessman's work focuses on public liberatory struggles. For many educators, teaching is a political act that entails resistance to oppressive cultural and institutional practices, both within and beyond one's teaching environment. Tessman explains that these costs may be difficult to bear.

> There is a heavy toll on the loyal critic, the political resister who remains situated; in many cases such a resister becomes a sort of outcast even among her/his own people, never fully supported or accepted. Furthermore, communities may be relatively impervious to change even when subjected to internal critique, and to the extent that the objections and protestations delivered by the loyal critic fail to result in significant change, the one who is loyal may still have to endure a community whose practices are oppressive to her/himself.
> *(Tessman 2005: 154–155)*

For the resister, like Ahmed, who identifies as a person of color within a predominantly White institution, the costs can be even more profound. While any resister faces the possibility of being rendered an outsider by their internal critique, those who are already considered "strangers" may encounter extraordinary challenges in the face of trying to exercise virtues, live with integrity or do good work. Ahmed argues that "to account for racism is to offer a different account of the world" (Ahmed 2012: 3). Ahmed's existential frustration in attempting to exercise her values might be understood as minor feelings, and these minor feelings could be exacerbated by minimizing their significance by characterizing them as a form of dissatisfaction.

Trying to improve one's community may come at a significant cost, especially when there is a lack of moral recognition. The conditions of implicit bias in a social world shaped by white supremacy make it difficult to determine whether we should call the failure to recognize the moral claims of educators of color moral disqualification (resulting from presumptions about the color of a person's skin and concomitant presumptions of capacity; Darby & Rury 2018) or misrecognition (resulting from the socialization of white supremacy, including the superiority regarding moral claims rooted in culturally-specific locations). An even more insidious form of white supremacy includes a failure to know much about the beliefs and commitments beyond one's own, a luxury not available to those with subordinated identities.

Teachers' values can also present a burden. Black teachers have "described their sense of obligation as a significant source of professional and personal stress, which is only intensified by their acute awareness of their own under-representation in teaching and administration" (Griffin & Tackie 2017). A familiar, and still relevant, example of moral misrecognition is Lisa Delpit's (1986) analysis of her experience as a Black woman teacher trying to convey the value of direct literacy instruction to her White colleagues. Her pedagogical concerns are not solely about the effectiveness or efficiency of pedagogical methods. Delpit raises clear moral concerns about what Black children deserve and indicts White teachers' limited knowledge of their students' cultures.

Yet, Delpit's moral claim cuts even deeper and is amplified by the resounding forms of recognition she received from her moral community, documented in "The Silenced Dialogue" (1988): White teachers are not giving Black teachers the moral recognition they deserve. Delpit's article demonstrates the burden carried by a Black teacher in trying to advocate for the wellbeing of students. We might describe this kind of advocacy as a virtue, perhaps as conscientiousness. Yet, the conditions of the work render engaging in this kind of advocacy potentially detrimental to Delpit. Nonetheless, we might laud Delpit for her steadfastness in speaking up for Black children, even as it comes with substantial costs – she is silenced by White colleagues, has her experience and expertise questioned, and must navigate "bitterness and resentment" in her chosen field (Delpit 1988: 282).

Tessman explains that it is conditions of oppression that render virtues burdened, not the simple fact of possessing virtues. "Normally, Aristotelian virtues are not (self)-sacrificial: quite the opposite, they are sources of well-being for their bearer" (Tessman 2005: 107). Delpit faces several challenges in her attempt to engage in good work. In her professional role, she attempts to do what is best for students and to provide them with the quality of education she believes they deserve. This is her moral commitment to the work. She also strives to be the best version of herself in her role that satisfies her intellectual and creative potential, among others. This is her ethical motivation for the work. In each of these normative aims, she is frustrated.

The more significant burden Delpit bears is attempting to offer an internal critique while her moral claims are misrecognized. A deracialized interpretation of Delpit's experience might portray her inability to transform reading instruction as one that is somewhat universal; teachers' voices and expertise are devalued and their concerns are regularly misrecognized by leaders and policymakers as crudely self-interested. Yet, Delpit's account demands that we address her racialized experience. The dominant paradigm of the good teacher and presumptions of who holds the knowledge of goodness and rightness are bound up with power and race. As a result, Delpit's attempted dialogue with her White colleagues is not only dismissed, but also results in moral misrecognition. Walker (1998) explains, "To fail to seek out and entertain many distinct moral understandings that supply a going social-moral order is to fail to honor people at those many different locations with the status of moral subject" (13–14). Delpit's burden manifests as familiar forms of additional labor: educating her White colleagues in the actual experience and in the writing of the subsequent articles. She likely also takes on the additional emotional labor of moral disqualification.

Delpit recommends White educators sustain pedagogical dialogues with their Black colleagues in order to better recognize their sound and moral reasoning. Her appeal resonates with the key features of Walker's moral theory. Delpit says,

> We must believe that people are rational beings, and therefore always act rationally. We may not understand their rationales, but that in no way militates against the existence of these rationales or reduces our responsibility to attempt to apprehend them … [W]e must learn to be vulnerable enough to allow our world to turn upside down in order to allow the realities of others to edge themselves into our consciousness.
>
> *(Delpit 1988: 297)*

Conditions of oppression place those with burdened virtues in a bind. Delpit demonstrates that advocating for Black students could be an "identity-conferring" commitment for a teacher (see also Labossiere 2019). In Delpit's case, as a Black woman educator, she encountered moral disregard when engaged in the virtue of conscientiousness. Her choice, at this point, is not to stop advocating for Black children in order to engage in self-preservation. Advocating for Black children is a part of what makes this work good and contributes to her moral self-understanding. Tessman shows the moral bind faced by individuals in situations such as this, "While the goal of liberatory struggle may be to make good lives possible, during the actual engagement in struggle one faces a steady stream of moral dilemmas in which there are no good choices" (Tessman 2005: 108).

Delpit's burden cannot be described merely as dissatisfaction, displeasure or the failure to realize preferences. Someone facing this kind of erasure experiences something much more profound and central to the narrative of self, as shown in Walker's account. The kind of advocacy Delpit describes is a practice of responsibility that reveals the person to themselves and others. Yet, when others do not recognize the practices of responsibility, the exercise of those virtues can be described as burdened. This burden is existential.

Conclusion

Moral misrecognition and disqualification are minimized if they are characterized as a form of teacher dissatisfaction. Chicago teacher Dwayne Reed's concerns are not likely the failure to realize pleasure; he is probably experiencing the anguish of someone who does not want to be complicit in inflicting harm on those to whom he is responsible. He may be experiencing the distress of his professional principles being at odds with the expectations of his job. And it is likely that he is experiencing the agony of being a Black man at a time when there are persistent and deadly reminders of the disregard for Black bodies. To label Reed's concerns as burnout is an utter negation of the moral claims he makes. To label Reed's concerns as burnout fails to accord him moral recognition. Similarly, to label Reed's moral concerns as a form of dissatisfaction is a minimization of the depth and reality of his distress.

My research with educators of color has enabled me to better see the prevalence and pain of moral misrecognition and disqualification as features of teacher demoralization. In the past, I had focused on the significance of gender in demoralization. Here, I addressed the racialized aspects of demoralization, especially in a numerically White-dominated profession within a society rooted in white supremacy. This research has led me to realize that demoralization needs to account for inequitable distributions of power in the moral-social order. I have defined demoralization as the "consistent and persistent frustrations in accessing the moral rewards of teaching" (Santoro 2011b: 3). In light of what I have learned, demoralization may also occur when teachers, and/or their students, are disregarded as moral subjects and persons accorded moral legitimacy as a result of social inequities that exist in schools and society.

The failure to experience moral recognition can be a primary source of demoralization. One remedy is to ensure that we cultivate communities with shared values that provide moral recognition. One reading of this recommendation is that it might appear to be advocating the kind of polarization and echo chambers that have characterized the worst of US politics. However, another reading, aligned with my intent, is to view these moral communities as sanctuaries that have the strength to engage in critique about the purposes, practices, and policies of education. What should not be challenged, however, is the moral subjectivity of educators, especially educators of color. By this, I do not mean that they are beyond moral examination, but that they must be taken to be subjects capable of and engaging in moral concerns.

By expanding my epistemological frame of reference, I was able to address the shortcomings of my original characterization of demoralization. This expansion is moral *and* epistemological, because it better captures the conditions faced by educators of color. In so doing, it also provides a simultaneously more precise and inclusive definition of demoralization that may more accurately name the experience of demoralization of educators of color and White educators. The better we become at identifying the challenges faced by teachers, the better we can become at devising responses that support teachers in fulfilling the values that sustain good work.[6]

(Related Chapters: 3, 16, 21, 22, 31, 34.)

Notes

1 The Schools and Staffing Survey, now called the National Teacher and Principal Survey, and the Teacher Follow-Up Survey are published by the National Center for Education Statistics. https://www.census.gov/programs-surveys/tfs.html
2 There have been positive outcomes from this strategy. Psychologists have built instruments to measure demoralization in individuals and I have participated in the development of large-scale teacher surveys that now include moral and ethical items.
3 My research collaborators are, in alphabetical order, Keith Eric Benson, Julia Hazel, Alberto Morales, Dave Stieber, and Darryl H. Yong. While I could not and would not have done this research without them, this chapter represents my own thinking. I am solely responsible for any errors or failures in the argument.
4 I will be using the terms "educators of color" and "teachers of color" interchangeably. Some of the research cited focuses on particular identities, and I will use the authors' language when that is the case.
5 Dwayne Reed was not interviewed by me or my team.
6 Thank you to Randy Curren, Sara Hardman, and Tomas Rocha for their helpful feedback and to Paloma Aguirre for editing and research assistance.

References

Ahmed, S. (2012) *On Being Included: Racism and Diversity in Institutional Life*. Durham, NC: Duke University Press.

Ahmed, S. (2016, May 30) "Resignation," *Feministkilljoys*. https://feministkilljoys.com/2016/05/30/resignation/

Alcoff, L. M. & Kittay, E. F. (2007) "Introduction: Defining Feminist Philosophy," in L. M. Alcoff & E. F. Kittay (eds.) *The Blackwell Guide to Feminist Philosophy*. Oxford: Blackwell Publishing, 1–13.

Carbonell, V. (2019) "Social Constraints on Moral Address," *Philosophy and Phenomenological Research* XCVIII (1): 167–189.

Carter Andrews, D. J., Castro, E., Cho, C. L., Petchauer, E., Richmond, G., & Floden, R. (2019) "Changing the Narrative on Diversifying the Teaching Workforce: A look at Historical and Contemporary Factors that Inform Recruitment and Retention of Teachers of Color," *Journal of Teacher Education* 70(1): 6–12.

Carver-Thomas, D. & Darling-Hammond, L. (2017) *Teacher Turnover: Why It Matters and What We Can do About It*. Virginia Beach, VA: Learning Policy Institute.

Darby, D. & Rury, J. L. (2018) *The Color of Mind: Why the Origins of the Achievement Gap Matter for Justice*. Chicago: University of Chicago Press.

Delpit, L. D. (1986) "Skills and Other Dilemmas of a Progressive Black Educator," *Harvard Educational Review* 56(4): 379–385.

Delpit, L. D. (1988) "The Silenced Dialogue: Power and Pedagogy in Educating Other People's Children," *Harvard Educational Review* 58(3): 280–298.

Dixon, R. D., Griffin, A. R., & Teoh, M. B. (2019) *If You Listen, We will Stay: Why Teachers of Color Leave and How to Disrupt Teacher Turnover*. Washington, D.C.: The Education Trust & Teach Plus.

Gardner, H., Csikszentmihalyi, M., & Damon, W. (2001) *Good Work: When Excellence and Ethics Meet*. New York: Basic Books.

Green, T. F. (1985) "The Formation of Conscience in an Age of Technology," *American Journal of Education* 94: 1–32.

Griffin, A. & Tackie, H. (2017) "Through Our Eyes: Perspectives from Black Teachers," *Phi Delta Kappan* 98(5): 37–40.

Hansen, D. T. (1995) *The Call to Teach*. New York: Teachers College Press.

Higgins, C. (2011) *The Good Life of Teaching: An Ethics of Professional Practice*. Oxford: Wiley-Blackwell.

Hodges, G. W., Tippins, D., & Oliver, J. S. (2013) "A Study of Highly Qualified Science Teachers' Career Trajectory in the Deep, Rural South: Examining a Link Between Deprofessionalization and Teacher Dissatisfaction," *School Science and Mathematics* 113(6): 263–274.

Hong, C. P. (2020) *Minor Feelings: An Asian American Reckoning*. New York: One World (Penguin Random House).

Ingersoll, R., May, H., & Collins, G. (2017) *Minority Teacher Recruitment, Employment, and Retention: 1987 to 2013*. Virginia Beach, VA: Learning Policy Institute.

Labossiere, N. (2019) "Who Do I Belong To?" in L. D. Delpit (ed.) *Teaching When the World Is on Fire*. New York: New Press, 128–132.

MacIntyre, A. (1984) *After Virtue*, 2nd ed. Notre Dame, IN: University of Notre Dame Press.

McFall, L. (1987) "Integrity," *Ethics* 98(1): 5–20.

Moore, C. M. (2012) "The Role of School Environment in Teacher Dissatisfaction among U.S. Public School Teachers," *SAGE Open,* 10.1177/2158244012438888
National Center for Education Statistics (2021) "National Teacher and Principal Survey," https://nces.ed.gov/surveys/ntps/
O'Rourke, M. (2020) "Cathy Park Hong on Minor Feelings: The Major Weight of Minor Feelings," *The Yale Review* 108(2), https://yalereview.org/article/cathy-park-hong-minor-feelings
Papay, J. P., Bacher-Hicks, A., Page, L. C., & Marinell, W. H. (2018) "America's Teacher Shortage Can't be Solved by Hiring More Unqualified Teachers," *The Washington Post* January 9, https://www.washingtonpost.com/news/posteverything/wp/2018/01/09/americas-teacher-shortage-cant-be-solved-by-hiring-more-unqualified-teachers/
Philip. T. M. & Brown, A. L. (2020) *We All Want More Teachers of Color, Right? Concerns About the Emergent Consensus.* Boulder, CO: National Education Policy Center.
Santoro, D. A. (2018) *Demoralized: Why Teachers Leave the Profession They Love and How They Can Stay.* Cambridge, MA: Harvard Education Press.
Santoro, D. A. (2017) "Cassandra in the Classroom: Teaching and Moral Violence," *Studies in Philosophy and Education* 36(1): 49–60.
Santoro, D. A. (2016) "'We're Not Going to Do That Because It's Not Right': Using Pedagogical Responsibility to Reframe the Doublespeak of Fidelity," *Educational Theory* 66(1–2): 263–277.
Santoro, D. A. (2015) "Philosophizing about Teacher Dissatisfaction: A Multidisciplinary Hermeneutic Approach," *Studies in Philosophy and Education* 34(2): 171–180.
Santoro, D. A., with Morehouse, L. (2011a) "Teaching's Conscientious Objectors: Principled Leavers of High-poverty Schools," *Teachers College Record* 113(12): 2671–2705.
Santoro, D. A. (2011b) "Good Teaching in Difficult Times: Demoralization in the Pursuit of Good Work," *American Journal of Education* 188(1): 1–23.
Schutz, P. A. & Zembylas, M. (2009) "Introduction to Advances in Teacher Emotion Research: The Impact on Teachers' Lives," in P. A. Schutz & M. Zembylas (eds.) *Advances in Teacher Emotion Research: The Impact on Teachers' Lives.* New York: Springer, 3–11.
Singer, N. (2020) "Teaching in the Pandemic: 'This is Not Sustainable.'" *The New York Times*, November 30, https://www.nytimes.com/2020/11/30/us/teachers-remote-learning-burnout.html
Sullivan, S. (2007) "Pragmatism," in L. M. Alcoff & E. F. Kittay (eds.) *The Blackwell Guide to Feminist Philosophy.* Oxford: Blackwell Publishing, 64–78.
Tessman, L. (2005) *Burdened Virtues: Virtue Ethics for Liberatory Struggles.* Oxford: Oxford University Press.
U.S. Department of Education (2016) "Teacher Job Satisfaction," *Data Point.* https://nces.ed.gov/pubs2016/2016131.pdf
Walker, M. U. (2007) "Moral Psychology," in L. Alcoff & E. Kittay (eds.) *The Blackwell Guide to Feminist Philosophy.* Oxford: Blackwell Publishers, 102–115.
Walker, M. U. (1998) *Moral Understandings: A Feminist Study in Ethics.* London: Routledge.
Walker, M. U. (1997) "Picking Up Pieces: Lives, Stories, and Integrity," in Diana T. Meyers (ed.) *Feminists Rethink the Self.* Boulder, Colorado: Westview Press, 62–84.

INDEX

Page numbers in *italics* refer to graphics; page numbers followed by "n" refer to notes

Printed in Australia
AUHW011035101222
372391AU00013B/63

9 781032 000039